Pro Visual Studio Team System with Team Edition for Database Professionals

Second Edition

■■■

Jeff Levinson and David Nelson

apress®

Pro Visual Studio Team System with Team Edition for Database Professionals, Second Edition

ISBN 978-1-4842-2012-2   ISBN 978-1-4302-0572-2   (eBook)

DOI 10.1007/978-1-4302-0572-2

Lead Editor: Ewan Buckingham

Technical Reviewer for Second Edition: Jason Clark

Technical Reviewers for First Edition: Gautam Goenka, Bata Chadraa, Anutthara Bharadwaj, Munjal Doshi, Winnie Ng, Joe Rhode, Siddharth Bhatia, Amy Hagstrom, Yogita Manghnani, Tom Patton, Alan Hebert, Bill Essary, Sam Jarawan, John Lawrence, Jimmy Li, Bryan MacFarlane, Erik Gunvaldson, Adam Singer, Chuck Russell, Kathryn Edens, Patrick Tseng, Ramesh Rajagopal, John Stallo, Jochen Seemann, Michael Fanning, Ed Glas, Eric Lee, Bindia Hallauer, Michael Leworthy, Jason Anderson, Michael Koltachev, Boris Vidolov, James Su, Thomas Lewis, Steven Houglum, Bill Gibson, Ali Pasha, Dmitriy Nikonov, Prashant Sridharan

Editorial Board: Steve Anglin, Ewan Buckingham, Gary Cornell, Jonathan Gennick, Jason Gilmore, Kevin Goff, Jonathan Hassell, Matthew Moodie, Jeffrey Pepper, Ben Renow-Clarke, Dominic Shakeshaft, Matt Wade, Tom Welsh

Production Director | Project Manager: Grace Wong

Associate Production Director | Production Editor: Kari Brooks-Copony

Copy Editors: Kim Wimpsett, Marilyn Smith, Jennifer Whipple

Compositor: Dina Quan

Proofreader: Broccoli Information Management

Indexer: Brenda Miller

Artist: April Milne

Cover Designer: Kurt Krames

Manufacturing Director: Tom Debolski

Distributed to the book trade worldwide by Springer-Verlag New York, Inc., 233 Spring Street, 6th Floor, New York, NY 10013. Phone 1-800-SPRINGER, fax 201-348-4505, e-mail orders-ny@springer-sbm.com, or visit http://www.springeronline.com.

For information on translations, please contact Apress directly at 2855 Telegraph Avenue, Suite 600, Berkeley, CA 94705. Phone 510-549-5930, fax 510-549-5939, e-mail info@apress.com, or visit http://www.apress.com.

The source code for this book is available to readers at http://www.apress.com in the Source Code/ Download section. You will need to answer questions pertaining to this book in order to successfully download the code.

For Tami, my wonderful new wife, who kept me going through everything. I love you.
and
For my cousin, Dr. Alicia Lindheim, who inspired me to go beyond myself with her courage, conviction, and strength. When the phrase "where there's a will, there's a way" was written, they were talking about her.

—Jeff Levinson

For Sammi, my love, my inspiration, and my beautiful bride of 20 years, and for our tribe, Jake, Josiah, Peter, Grace, and Lydia, my hope. I love you all with all my heart.
and
To my mom and dad, who gave me faith and belief in the Lord Jesus Christ, a marriage extending half a century, and a commitment to hard work, integrity, and family.

—David Nelson

Contents at a Glance

PART 4 ■ ■ ■ Team Edition for Software Testers

PART 5 ■ ■ ■ Team Edition for Database Professionals

v

Contents

PART 2 ■ ■ ■ Team Edition for Software Architects

PART 3 ■ ■ ■ Team Edition for Software Developers

PART 4 ■■■ Team Edition for Software Testers

PART 5 ■ ■ ■ Team Edition for Database Professionals

Foreword

Microsoft has always provided world-class development tools for developers. From the release of Visual Basic 1 to Visual Studio 2005, Microsoft has provided groundbreaking tools to make developers' lives easier. With the release of Visual Studio 2005, we've done a considerable amount of work to help the individual developer be even more productive—refactoring, My Namespace, edit-and-continue, and improvements in the .NET Framework are just a few examples.

But with Visual Studio 2005, we've expanded our focus beyond the developer to the entire development process. Visual Studio Team System takes a larger view of the developer's world. It acknowledges the project management aspects of development, the architecture, and the testing phase of the development life cycle; in other words, Visual Studio Team System takes into account the entire software development life cycle. This shift away from purely an individual's perspective is designed to ease the burden on development organizations by helping every member of the team gain more insight, and oversight, of the software development life cycle.

This larger view of the development process promotes communication and collaboration among groups that in the past almost never spoke with each other. It helps project managers communicate with architects, architects with developers, and developers with testers. And it helps everyone to communicate with stakeholders and to collaborate with other interested observers. By providing timely reporting of events, project status, development statistics, and other information, organizations can leverage Visual Studio Team System to streamline the development process.

Software development has shifted from groups of developers working in the same building to groups of developers working around the world. This shift crosses geographical boundaries and allows teams to collaborate with each other in real time. Visual Studio Team System enables the organization that owns the code to actually own the code! Nightly builds can be performed in the target environment instead of being built and tested in an environment that usually doesn't match the eventual deployment environment. It also helps organizations to keep better track of how their outsourced teams are progressing with the project.

There is an overwhelming industry trend toward a more agile approach to software development. At the same time, corporations are pushing for improved quality and reduced cost through repeatable processes. Out of the box, Visual Studio Team System provides two process templates aimed at meeting the vast majority of team project needs. The MSF for Agile template is great for teams that may not have used any "formal" methods in the past, while the MSF for CMMI process template complements the Capability Maturity Model Integration (CMMI) process improvement approach developed at Carnegie Mellon. These processes help developers to not only be productive but also to create a framework for repeatable development processes. These process improvements ultimately lead to higher-quality, lower-cost software development.

With all of this, Microsoft has absolutely not forgotten that it is developers who write the code and run the tests. One of the Visual Studio Team System development team's primary goals is to help developers to write high-quality code. We call this "helping teams drive better quality, early and often." With the new testing tools for developers and testers, code can be written with a higher quality (it follows standards, passes unit tests, and performs optimally), and that quality can be tested for at every step of the way. Visual Studio Team System makes continuous integration testing, build verification tests, and development standards easy to implement and follow. These processes, instead of being complicated and difficult to follow, are made exceptionally easy with Visual Studio Team System and will help developers write and release more stable code.

What's in store for the future then? At our core, the things we do at Microsoft are all about empowering people to drive business success. With Visual Studio Team System, we've taken the first steps toward helping individuals and teams be more productive in the development process. Our vision is to further expand our Visual Studio Team System offering to help all members of an IT team communicate and collaborate more effectively. Some of the areas that we're focusing on in the immediate future are better tools for working with databases, more advanced and complete testing tools, better integration with Microsoft Office, and better support for managing your organization-wide portfolio of projects. Though some of these new tools may not even be released under the "Visual Studio" brand, you can be assured that we will work diligently across all our product groups to deliver solutions that will help you and your organization be more successful.

We believe that Visual Studio 2005 Team System is a hallmark product for the software industry. To be sure, we're all extraordinarily proud of what we've released. But, even more than that, we're excited to see the overwhelming positive reaction to these first few steps in making our customers' lives easier. On behalf of the entire team in Redmond, North Carolina, India, Copenhagen, and elsewhere, thank you for your support, feedback, and encouragement.

Prashant Sridharan
prashant@microsoft.com
Director, Visual Studio
March 2006

About the Authors

 **JEFF LEVINSON** is a solution design and integration architect for the Boeing Company. He is the author of *Building Client/Server Applications with VB.NET: An Example-Driven Approach* (Apress 2003) and has written several articles for *Visual Studio Magazine*. He speaks at various Microsoft user groups and was a speaker at Microsoft's DevDays 2004. Jeff holds the following certifications: MCSD, MCAD, MCSD.NET, MCDBA, SCJP, and Security+. He is currently finishing his master's degree in software engineering at Carnegie Mellon University. He and his wife, Tami, live in Redmond, Washington. He enjoys golfing, reading, running, and spending time with his wife.

 **DAVID NELSON** is an enterprise solutions architect and associate technical fellow for the Boeing Company, where he has been employed for 20 years. His tenure at Boeing has allowed him to become expert at various technologies, including database solutions, grid computing, service orientation, and, most recently, Visual Studio Team System. David is currently responsible for architecture and design of computing solutions across Boeing, with primary focus on the application of emergent technologies. He has taught Windows Server System (SQL Server, SharePoint Server, and Windows Server) classes and is regularly invited to present at national industry conferences.

David resides in the state of Washington with his wife and five children, where he enjoys riding horses and motorcycles. He is building a tree fort with his sons, planting a garden with his daughters, and restoring a horse trailer for his wife.

About the Technical Reviewer (for Part 5)

JASON CLARK's software engineering career began in 1991. However, he picked up (and then had trouble putting down) his first book on programming nearly a decade earlier. His passion for all things software continues to the present. In 2000 he published his first book on software; today he continues to develop and write about software. Jason now works for Microsoft as a software architect. His software engineering credits include Microsoft Windows NT 4.0, Windows 2000, Windows XP and Windows 2003. Also in the lineup are the .NET Framework versions 1.0, 1.1, and 2.0. His recent projects include the Windows Communication Foundation and the "Data Dude" edition for Visual Studio .NET. Jason's only other passions are his wife and kids, with whom he happily lives in the Seattle area.

Acknowledgments

Writing a book—any book—is difficult at best. For a new product on which there really is no material to use to research on your own, it is even more difficult. The members of the Visual Studio Team System development team have been incredibly gracious and giving of their time to answer questions, go over features, and provide support in general while they were going through their development and release cycles. All of the information in this book comes from the authors fooling around with the product, trying to implement it in an enterprise environment, and from the developers and program managers at Microsoft. Having said that, the authors would like to thank the following people from Microsoft (in no particular order), keeping in mind that many, many more helped us bring this book to you: Gautam Goenka, Bata Chadraa, Anutthara Bharadwaj, Munjal Doshi, Winnie Ng, Joe Rhode, Siddharth Bhatia, Amy Hagstrom, Yogita Manghnani, Tom Patton, Alan Hebert, Bill Essary, Sam Jarawan, John Lawrence, Jimmy Li, Bryan MacFarlane, Erik Gunvaldson, Adam Singer, Chuck Russell, Kathryn Edens, Patrick Tseng, Ramesh Rajagopal, John Stallo, Jochen Seemann, Michael Fanning, Ed Glas, Eric Lee, Bindia Hallauer, Michael Leworthy, Jason Anderson, Michael Koltachev, Boris Vidolov, James Su, Thomas Lewis, Steven Houglum, Bill Gibson, Ali Pasha, Dmitriy Nikonov, and Prashant Sridharan.

We owe a special thanks to Gordon Hogenson. Neither of the authors is a C/C++ expert. Because of this, we turned to someone who is an expert for help with a section in Chapter 13 of this book. He wrote an excellent discussion of PREfast, clearly explaining what you can do with it to write better code. Thanks, Gordon!

For the first edition, the authors would like to also thank our editor, Ewan Buckingham, who stuck with us through this whole process, which took considerably longer than usual. Sofia Marchant, as the project manager for this book, kept us on track. She took care of getting the materials to the right people at the right time for reviews and pushing people to get information back to us. Thanks, Sofia! Without our copy editors, Marilyn Smith and Jennifer Whipple, this book would not flow nearly as well or be so readable. Thank you for all of your advice and rewording! Katie Stence kept everything on track for our production edits.

For the second edition, the authors would like to thank our editor Ewan Buckingham again for his efforts in getting this out; Grace Wong for managing the last-minute rush of, well, everything to get this book into your hands; and finally Kim Wimpsett, whom we were happy to be reunited with because she was responsible for the copy editing on *Building Client/Server Applications with VB.NET*. As with that book, the additions to this book would not be nearly as coherent without her help!

Without the hard work of everyone at Apress, this book would not be in your hands now.

Jeff Levinson and David Nelson

In addition to all of the great people at Microsoft and Apress, this book has had an effect on everyone around both David and myself. It has taken a lot of time and effort, more so because of the constantly shifting nature of working with a new product. As usual, I would like to thank my family for their support and shoulders to lean on.

Finally, I would like to thank my coauthor, David. When I first envisioned the idea for this book, I knew there were two issues: there was just too much to write about on my own, and I knew this was going to be a very long road. So I convinced David that we should write the book together. He hung in there with me, even when it seemed like we were getting new builds every month (which we were most of the time), Microsoft kept changing the name of portions of the product, and they kept changing the feature set. His wife was ready to cause me serious harm for monopolizing David's time, and he got to see his kids for only an hour a day or so. Sammi, I'm sorry! But we're done, and in the end, it was a great experience. Thanks, David!

Jeff Levinson

I would like to thank everyone who has been excited and encouraging regarding this project. It has been a long road, and we have learned much. Thanks to those who have listened, guided, and supported this effort: the Guys (Brad Carpenter, Tim Pearson, John Rivard, Sam Jarawan, Jeff Whitmore, Gerd Strom, and Johnny Couture) are my rock. Thanks also to Dr. Karl Payne, my mentor, teacher, and friend. The Cassandra Team (Roger Parker, Richard Lonsdale, Gary Westcott, Fred Ervin, and John Zhang) is an early adopter of ideas and technology. The ValSim Team (Mike Maple, Kaaren Cramer, Jacques Rousseau, Phil Trautman, and others) pushes the edge of technology and thought. Team Canada (Steven Guo, Rob Hickling, Stig Westerlund, and others) takes beta tools and makes products that work. The Architects (Todd Mickelson, Mick Pegg, Dick Navarro, Brad Belmondo, David Rice, Marty Kitna, and others) have vision, trust, and work to "get'r" done.

And lastly, thanks to Jeff Levinson, my partner in this endeavor. I have learned a great deal over the past 22 months (yeah, it really has been that long; I found the first e-mail). I would never have taken on a project like this book without Jeff's encouragement, expertise, and drive. Since this was his second book, he patiently guided me through some of the finer points of authorship. He would often say, "This isn't a blog; you need to write it like a book." Jeff did the greater portion of work, and I appreciate him letting me join him on this journey. I also want to thank his new bride, Tami, for letting us work at the house and take time away from the more important wedding plans. He's all yours now! Thanks, Jeff, it was a great adventure.

David Nelson

Introduction

Software development is undergoing a huge revolution right now. That is not to say that this is different from any other time in the history of software development—it is always undergoing a revolution of one type or another. This "new" revolution is a shift in development methodologies from teams working in tightly knit groups in geographical proximity to a global development strategy. Software development teams are now faced with communicating with each other from half a world away.

This book talks about how to perform this work *effectively* using the new Microsoft Visual Studio Team System (VSTS) product. This book covers all areas of VSTS, from the basics to tips and tricks to make it easier to use. Because of our work with the development team at Microsoft, we have been able to include several undocumented features and describe some of the thought processes involved in developing various portions of VSTS. In addition, as architects in a Fortune 500 company, we have a unique experience in starting to implement VSTS in an enterprise environment.

This book begins with a chapter that introduces VSTS. Chapter 1 provides a general overview of VSTS, its various components and editions, and who should use it and why. This chapter also introduces the sample application that we use throughout the book. Following the first chapter, the book is organized into five parts.

Part 1, Team Foundation: The Team Foundation Server is the mechanism (set of integrated services and stores) that enables the communication and collaboration aspect of VSTS. The web services provide a loosely coupled interface between the various artifacts (work item tracking, version control, build, and test). The operational stores provide a real-time repository of team activity that feeds the aggregated data warehouse for team reporting and analysis. Part 1 of the book covers this crucial component of VSTS.

- *Chapter 2, Team Project:* This is your first hands-on introduction to VSTS. Chapter 2 walks you through creating a new team project, introduces you to the Project Portal, and explains how VSTS leverages various software development life cycles and provides integrated process guidance. Chapter 2 also discusses Team Foundation Server security, from both the user's and administrator's perspective.

- *Chapter 3, Team Foundation Version Control:* One of the much anticipated new features of VSTS is Team Foundation Version Control, a new, enterprise-class source code control system. This chapter covers all of the aspects of the VSTS source code control system. It also gives an in-depth look at the new check-in policies and touches on how these policies integrate with the work item tracking system.

- *Chapter 4, Project Management*: Microsoft has expended considerable effort to bring project managers into the software development life cycle. VSTS provides integration between Microsoft Project, Excel, and the work item tracking store. Project managers can extend the default mappings to any field available in Microsoft Project. Team Explorer provides rapid triage of work items. The Project Portal and reporting site provide a wealth of information about the status of the team project. This chapter describes all of these features.

- *Chapter 5, Team Work Item Tracking*: Work item tracking is one of the hottest new features in VSTS. This feature allows a project manager to create a work item (a task, a bug, an issue, and so on), assign it to a team member, and track the status of it from beginning to end. Stakeholders can see how a certain item is progressing as well. Work item tracking is a fully extensible system, so project teams can create their own work item types. Work item attachments can include documents, links to other work items, code, or URLs. This chapter covers work item tracking in detail.

- *Chapter 6, Team Reporting*: SQL Server Reporting Services (SSRS) was introduced as an add-on to SQL Server 2000 several years ago. With the new SQL Server 2005 and the new SSRS, Microsoft has made this tool the core of the VSTS reporting infrastructure. This chapter covers the details—from the out-of-the-box reports (associated with each process template) to the specific features on which the VSTS data warehouse allows you to report.

- *Chapter 7, Team Foundation Build*: In the past, performing automated builds required a great deal of extra work using Microsoft tools. This chapter covers the new Team Foundation Build functionality and shows how you can use it to increase the quality of the final software product.

Part 2, Team Edition for Software Architects: This part of the book is dedicated to the new distributed designers in VSTS. These designers allow you to architect an entire application and then implement portions of the application: projects, configurations, and settings.

- *Chapter 8, Application Designer*: In this chapter, an overview of model-driven development, Software Factories, and Domain-Specific Languages leads into a discussion of the Application Designer. The Application Designer allows you to take the first step in a "contract-first" development process, in which you design the interface before writing the application. Having defined the operations for your services, you can implement real code that stays in sync with the models.

- *Chapter 9, System and Logical Datacenter Designers*: Systems are defined as deployable units of the overall application. The level of abstraction provided by the System Designer allows multiple designs to facilitate deployment onto varying datacenters, customer sites, or geographic locations. The Logical Datacenter Designer allows the creation of models depicting interconnected hosts and provides invaluable implementation details to both the application architect and the developer at design time. Chapter 9 describes how to use both of these designers.

- *Chapter 10, Deployment Designer*: As you will learn in this chapter, the Deployment Designer allows architects and developers to deploy systems into the target logical datacenters. The result is instant validation on configuration, setting, or hosting constraint conflicts.

Part 3, Team Edition for Software Developers: Software developers now get the benefits of a concrete modeling language and strong unit testing tools to help them visualize and implement code with higher quality. To augment this capability, developers can analyze their code for common errors and ensure their code meets organizational coding standards. They can also analyze their code for performance impacts and ways to improve the application's performance. This part of the book describes the VSTS tools for modeling code, unit testing, and code analyses.

- *Chapter 11, Class Designer*: UML can be confusing and complicated. It can take a long time to write and even longer to implement. The implementation is often poorly done because UML is an abstract modeling language. As you'll learn in this chapter, the Class Designer is a concrete modeling language for .NET. The Class Designer can both forward- and reverse-engineer code in a way that makes sense with .NET.

- *Chapter 12, Unit Testing and Code Coverage*: Developers now have the ability to test their own code directly from within Visual Studio. You can perform detailed tests and gather code coverage statistics to ensure your code is of high quality and is thoroughly tested. This chapter explains how these VSTS features work.

- *Chapter 13, Static Code Analysis*: Static code analysis deals with examining code in order to ensure that standards were followed and that any known defects are caught ahead of time. This includes managed *and* unmanaged code (C/C++). In this chapter, you will learn about how the FxCop and PREfast utilities can reduce coding errors and increase maintainability.

- *Chapter 14, Performance Analysis*: Is your application not performing as you expected? Does it need more speed? Analyze your application and improve your users' experience with the new VSTS performance analysis tools. You can either instrument your application for detailed analysis or sample it for long-term performance monitoring. Use these techniques for code under development or production code. Chapter 14 describes how.

Part 4, Team Edition for Software Testers: Testing is becoming an increasing critical area of software development. Customers expect fewer bugs out of the box, and that means development teams need to provide more testing resources. This part of the book discusses the new VSTS testing tools and how to use them to create more reliable applications.

- *Chapter 15, Web Testing*: Many companies are switching to web applications as a way to decrease maintenance costs and allow users to access applications from anywhere. Testing can often be difficult and time-consuming. With the new web testing tools, you can now easily create scripts to test your web application *or* web services. This chapter covers web testing in detail.

- *Chapter 16, Load Testing*: Do you want to know how your application will stand up under high load? Are you wondering when it will fail and what you need to do to prevent it from failing? As you will learn in this final chapter, using the new load testing tools, you can identify points of failure and determine strategies for dealing with high-load situations.

Part 5, Team Edition for Database Professionals: Database Professionals is the latest addition to the Visual Studio Team System family of products. It is designed to substantially reduce the amount of time you spend working on database development, deployment, and traceability. Now you can determine the truth of the database schema at a point in time.

- *Chapter 17, Database Projects*: Get the details on how to work with database projects in the Visual Studio IDE. Learn how the projects work with Team Foundation Server and best practices for using many of the tools. In addition learn about the new features in the newly released Power Tools!

- *Chapter 18, Unit Testing and Data Generation*: Is one group building the database and another building the user interface? How do you know the database code you write and deploy is free from defects? Are you using production data in your development environment, including possibly using sensitive data? Learn how to generate your own data and create unit tests against your SQL Server objects.

- *Chapter 19, Building and Deploying Databases*: Now that you can version control your database, in this chapter you'll learn how to perform builds, run unit tests, and deploy changes to your environments. Responsibilities are explained as well as best practices for promoting your code.

- *Chapter 20, Extending the Database Professionals Edition*: As with the rest of VSTS, you can extend Database Professionals! This chapter walks you through the details of creating your own data generators and unit test conditions to meet your specific needs.

At the end of the book, you will find an appendix that lists all the command-line tools available for use with VSTS (client and server).

So, now that you know what this book contains, let's get started.

■ ■ ■

CHAPTER 1

Introduction to Visual Studio Team System

In the modern world of development, developers no longer work alone or in groups of three or four people in a set of side-by-side cubicles. Today's developers typically work in larger teams scattered across the globe. Developers have become a global commodity. Many companies in the United States perform some type of outsourcing in which they hire developers who work in India, China, Canada, Russia, or other parts of the United States. This presents a unique challenge to software project teams.

Development teams may include project managers, developers, architects, testers, support staff, and others. How do the team members communicate? What information should be shared, and whom should it be shared with? Should some people have access to some code but not other code? These questions apply not only to developers located in different parts of the world, but also to teams that work in the same building or the same city.

The number of issues that face development teams today is huge. The preceding questions cover only the communication of information. This list can be expanded to include (but not limited to) the following:

- What is the application architecture?

- What is our methodology and what are the deliverables?

- How is the application going to be deployed?

- How will the various components communicate with each other?

- What am I responsible for and when do I have to have this work done by?

- Has anyone tested this code yet? Did it pass the tests?

- What are the object dependencies?

- How are we doing change management?

The list of relevant questions grows very quickly. Up until now, there was no easy way to answer these questions except with regular status meetings, a large amount of e-mail, or a lot of expensive phone calls. The information is not always up-to-the-minute accurate, and it takes a lot of time to sift through all of it. These are some of the issues that Microsoft set out to solve with the introduction of Visual Studio Team System (VSTS).

What Is Visual Studio Team System?

VSTS is a suite of tools designed to allow members of a development team to communicate not only with one another, but also with stakeholders, in real time. It also contains a set of tools for developing architectural views of a system, generating code from certain views, testing code at all stages (during and after development), and integrating the development experience with project management.

At a high-level view, VSTS is divided into four areas: integration, architecture, development, and testing. Each of these areas contains tools that cater to a different facet of the development team. Some of the tools are available to all groups of users, and some are targeted at a specific group because they pertain to a responsibility associated with only one role.

But this is a superficial view of VSTS. It is also designed, from the ground up, to help an organization implement an effective development methodology, whether it is the Microsoft Solutions Framework (MSF), the Rational Unified Process (RUP), Extreme Programming (XP), or any of a dozen other types of methodologies. The purpose in implementing a structured methodology is the same as the goals of the rest of the VSTS suite of tools: to build better applications for a lower cost, both in the short term and the long term. This concept of integrating methodology into the development process is ingrained in all aspects of VSTS.

What Are the Benefits of Using Visual Studio Team System?

Who would benefit from using VSTS for their projects? In short, the answer is everyone. Specifically, it benefits project managers, architects, developers, testers, infrastructure architects, users, and stakeholders. Here's how:

- *Project managers* can get up-to-date information on which items on the project schedule are being worked and when they are completed through familiar tools like Microsoft Project and Excel.

- *System architects* can design an application as it applies to the network infrastructure and communicate that to the deployment and development team.

- *Infrastructure support* gets a solid understanding of the deployment needs of the application.

- *Technical architects* can design classes, relationships, and hierarchies that automatically generate skeleton code.

- *Developers* can look at the class diagrams to understand what is occurring. Any changes they make to the code will be reflected in the diagrams—no reverse-engineering of the model is necessary. Code can be effectively unit tested.

- *Testers* can use integrated testing tools, which allow for more thorough testing. Tests can also be run automatically via automated build tools.

- *Application stakeholders* can view reports on the progress of the application through Microsoft SharePoint Services.

As you can see, many individuals can benefit from the use of VSTS. These benefits translate directly in a higher return on investment because everything becomes easier and faster for everyone.

Aside from individuals who benefit from using VSTS, organizations and departments will also find tremendous advantages in using this tool. The first and most obvious benefit is that it promotes communication between team members, which is crucial to the success of a project. It allows for problems to be caught early and solved quickly before they become serious issues that affect the schedule. These problems can range from developers not completing work on time to bugs in the code.

VSTS also allows for the analysis of work across multiple projects. It becomes simple for organizations to track their project history and use that information to predict future project schedules. Projects can be reported on by category, developer, deliverable, milestone, and so on. You literally have the power of an online analytical processing (OLAP) database at your fingertips, filled with all of your project information down to the code level and bug-tracking level. To achieve this type of reporting, you've needed to use several different, costly systems. With VSTS, it is all rolled into one integrated system.

All of these benefits come down to one thing: a higher return on investment with one tool than you would get with combinations of tools. When you use one tool for each area of development—such as Borland JBuilder for development, CVS for source control, Rational ClearQuest for issue tracking, Cognos ReportNet for reporting, Ant for building, and JUnit for testing—it becomes exceedingly difficult to keep things simple. On the other hand, you have the following benefits with VSTS:

- VSTS allows all developers to use one tool with which they are familiar. It does not require a developer to learn how to use six different tools to perform the task.

- VSTS integrates all of the needed functionality, including a project management tool and reporting tool, directly into one interface—something that no other integrated development environment (IDE) can do in its out-of-the-box version.

But let's say that you have an in-house testing tool that you would rather use than the tool that comes with VSTS. Because VSTS is an extensible environment, integrating other tools into it requires a minimal amount of work (depending on what you want to integrate). Many tool vendors have been working with Microsoft to create integration points with their tools so that you can swap them with ones that come with VSTS. You are not locked into a wholly Microsoft solution.

All of these points lead to only one conclusion: there is no downside to using VSTS.

Visual Studio Team System Editions

VSTS comes in three different editions and a core component called Team Foundation. This section describes each of these (which correspond to the sections in this book), their tools, and their goals. While this is the out-of-the box functionality available with VSTS, as noted in the previous section, is also highly extensible. Figure 1-1 shows an overview of the VSTS suite.

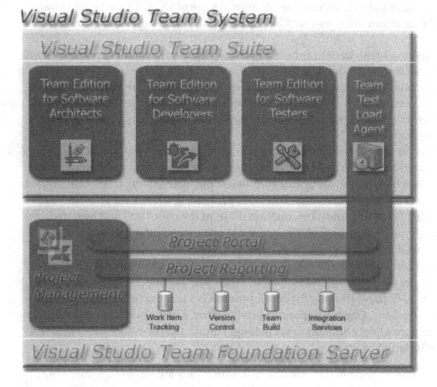

Figure 1-1. *Visual Studio Team System editions and main components*

Team Foundation

Team Foundation is the server-based component of VSTS. It is the *Team* in Team System. Without Team Foundation, all of the other components of VSTS are essentially stand-alone components that run on the client. Once Team Foundation becomes part of the picture, the various client pieces work together as a cohesive unit. Chapters 2 through 7 cover Team Foundation.

As we mentioned previously, VSTS is designed to provide a framework in which applications can be built. Many companies are working to improve their processes by using the Capability Maturity Model Integrated (CMMI) from Carnegie Mellon's Software Engineering Institute (SEI). With VSTS, Microsoft is releasing the only methodology recognized by SEI as being CMMI level 3 compliant. This methodology is the MSF for CMMI Process Improvement, Version 4.0. The template and instructions on how to use the methodology are all included with VTST. So, what is so significant about this? The U.S. Government uses CMMI levels in determining source selections for contract awards.

Team Foundation Version Control

Team Foundation contains a brand-new version control tool, which is designed for large-scale teams and is backed by SQL Server 2005. For developers, it will be a welcome addition to their toolbox and offer an easy alternative to Visual SourceSafe. Also, unlike Visual SourceSafe, Team

Foundation version control supports document (or code module) security. In addition to supporting developers, it also supports project managers and overall application reporting to the stakeholders.

The final touch for the new version control tool is that it allows you to implement policies to make sure that code meets certain requirements before it is checked in. This helps to ensure that the code goes through a consistent, repeatable process check before check-in.

Project Portal

Another key piece of Team Foundation is the Project Portal. This is a Windows SharePoint Services (WSS) site that serves as a central communication tool for the entire team. Stakeholders can go to this website to review the current status of various tasks on the project, view nightly build and test reports, and communicate with team members.

SharePoint also serves as a project documentation repository (with versioning). This is in contrast to how teams typically set up repositories today—in the file system.

Team Foundation Build

Team Foundation Build is a component that allows a server or workstation to become a build machine. Team Foundation Build automatically gets the latest version from the version control tool, compiles it, deploys it, and runs any automated tests (unit or web tests) against the build. The results of the compilation and testing are stored in the VSTS data warehouse.

Work Item Tracking

Work item tracking is another feature of Team Foundation. Work items can be created in Microsoft Project (directly from the work breakdown structure) or Excel and loaded into Team Foundation as a work item. These work items can be assigned to developers. When team members check their items into the version control, they can associate changes with specific work items. The status of these work items is then reflected on the Project Portal. Work item association can be enforced via policies as well.

Reporting

The final feature of Team Foundation is the reporting component, backed by the new version of SQL Server Reporting Services (SSRS). Out of the box, the reports cover areas such as the number of open bugs, closed bugs, and in-work bugs; work item status; build results; and other information.

As an added bonus, the SSRS features an end-user ad-hoc report builder, so users can create their own reports or customize existing reports. This, combined with the VSTS data warehouse, allows an organization to mine the data for trends in the overall software development life cycle.

Team Edition for Software Architects

Various types of architects may be assigned to a project, and each has different responsibilities. The one thing that all architects have in common is that they must communicate aspects of the architecture to stakeholders in various ways. To facilitate building and then communicating an architecture, Team Edition for Software Architects provides a set of design-ers, as well as other tools to ease the job of the architect. Chapters 8 through 10 cover the Team Edition for Software Architects.

Designers

The four VSTS designers are Application Designer, System Designer, Logical Datacenter Designer, and Deployment Designer. These designers are a core tenant of Microsoft's focus on Model Driven Architecture (MDA). However, VSTS moves models out of the cumbersome, documentation-only realm and into the practical realm.

The problem with modeling with other tools is that the models are abstract representa-tions of the architecture. They do not mean anything from a tangible perspective. The designers in VSTS have a concrete implementation. When you create a model with VSTS, you also generate the configuration for that model, which is based on physical properties of the object to which you are deploying your application. This allows VSTS to check for inconsisten-cies in your architecture against the actual physical machines with which you will be working.

Domain-Specific Language

On top of this approach, VSTS leverages the concept of Domain-Specific Languages (DSL). DSL is the language in which the concrete implementation of hardware or software is written. This allows the end users of VSTS to build model objects against which specific implementa-tions can be validated.

Tip Microsoft has released a set of tools specifically for creating domain-specific frameworks. These tools can be found at http://lab.msdn.microsoft.com/teamsystem/workshop/dsltools/default.aspx.

The language is a set of metadata that describes the physical implementation of a given configuration. Microsoft has introduced the System Definition Model (SDM) to provide a schema definition for distributed systems. Because these designers are built in concrete terms, they are easily understandable by their intended audience—data architects, infrastruc-ture architects, or other application architects.

Visio

Team Edition for Software Architects also includes everyone's favorite modeling tool: Visio. This tool is available in all editions of VSTS, but will probably be most used by architects.

Visio for Visual Studio allows for the creation of Unified Modeling Language (UML) diagrams and provides the ability to model different views for different audiences of the application. Visio allows you to create those abstract, notional views, which are helpful in trying to figure out and pinpoint what the architecture will be and then communicate it to everyone else.

Team Edition for Software Developers

Team Edition for Software Developers provides tools that allow developers to quickly understand code structure, generate code from models, write unit tests, and analyze code for errors. The goal of these tools is to reduce the amount of time developers need to actually write code and to ensure that the code that is produced is of a higher quality. Chapters 11 through 14 cover the Team Edition for Software Developers.

Class Designer

To understand and generate code, VSTS provides the Class Designer. This is one of the tools available in all editions of VSTS because it is useful to a wide range of people. Architects can use the tool to create high-level class designs. Developers can generate skeleton classes, for which they can then fill in the details. Testers can use the Class Designer to understand the relationship between classes in order to help them analyze errors. We have included the Class Designer in the Team Edition for Software Developers section of the book because, for the most part, the primary audience is the developer.

The Class Designer also dynamically generates code based on the model, reads changes in code, and incorporates those changes into the model. The key point here is that the model and the code *are never out of sync.* This solves the problem of documentation becoming stale.

Unit Testing

Once the general outline of code is produced, tests can be written for the code. They can also be written after the code is finished. It is entirely up to you, but one thing is certain—with the VSTS unit testing tools, testing will be a lot easier, faster, and more streamlined.

Creating a unit test is as easy as right-clicking a class or a method, selecting Create Unit Tests, and filling in a couple of variables. It could also be more complicated, since unit testing supports data-driven testing, which allows for more complex scenarios without having to continually rewrite the unit tests or write many tests for one method. The unit testing functionality is also part of the Team Edition for Software Testers.

As part of the unit testing functionality, VSTS provides a very cool code coverage tool. This tool not only tells you what percentage of your code was covered versus not covered, but it can also highlight code to show you fully covered lines of code, partially covered lines of code, and code that was not covered at all. We'll elaborate on this in Chapter 12, but to give you an idea of how important this tool is, let's consider an example. Suppose you write a method 100 lines long and you run the unit tests against the code. The results all come back as passing, which is good, but the code covered comes back as 60%, which is bad, because 40 lines of code were never touched. This indicates that while all your tests passed, either you did not test something you should have or there is no way to test that code, and so it is dead code that should be removed.

Code Analysis

Since the inception of .NET 1.0, Microsoft has offered a relatively unsupported tool called FxCop (available for free from http://www.gotdotnet.com). VSTS incorporates this tool into the IDE so that static code analysis on managed code can be performed as part of a compilation, and policies can be written against the results of the analysis. This tool was originally created to ensure that Microsoft developers were following the correct standards when writing the .NET Framework. So, if you follow the coding recommendations of this tool, you will be writing to the same standards as Microsoft (in terms of format, completeness, and the standards of the .NET Framework).

VSTS also incorporates a tool to help developers of unmanaged code. This tool, called PREfast, has been in use within Microsoft for several years as a means for developers to check their C/C++ code for common errors such as buffer overruns. This analysis tool is run simply by checking a box in the project properties. It is customizable to an extent that allows you to implement checks not included in the out-of-the-box product.

Performance Analysis

VSTS also incorporates performance analysis tools, which allow developers to test their code for bottlenecks. In the past, performance testing around a .NET application typically involved monitoring a lot of Windows Performance Monitor logs, which provided less-than-helpful information.

The new performance analysis tools allow you to either instrument or sample your code, depending on the situation, so you can gather details at the individual method level or at the application level. Best of all, you can institute performance monitoring on a production application to pinpoint specific problems that may not have been apparent during development.

Team Edition for Software Testers

Team Edition for Software Testers is devoted to testing all aspects of your code. It includes the unit testing functionality (described in the preceding section about the Team Edition for Software Developers), load testing, manual testing, and web testing, as well as the Test Manager tool. Chapters 15 and 16 cover the Team Edition for Software Testers.

■**Note** While VSTS does not include a Windows Forms testing capability, forms can be tested via the manual tests. In addition, the test facilities are highly extensible, and many third-party tools will probably be available to fill this niche!

Test Manager

Test management is a key component of the testing infrastructure because it allows you to organize your tests. You can run these tests in a noninteractive fashion from the command line or from the Team Foundation Build process. You can organize your tests into lists in order to run tests on like processes. Dependencies can be created between tests via an ordered test list and individual tests, or lists of tests can be slated to run at any given time. The Team Edition for Software Developers includes a subset of the Test Manager tool.

Web Testing

More and more applications are moving to the Web in today's Internet- and intranet-based world. Because of this, Microsoft rewrote the Application Center Test (ACT) web testing tool and included it with VSTS. And when we say they rewrote it, we mean it. It is a completely different tool and far, far more powerful than ACT was. You can interactively record tests and play back tests (which are displayed visually for you as the test is running). The tests can be changed in the IDE, and they can be converted to coded tests, which allow you the freedom to do virtually anything in a test you want via managed code instead of scripting, which had to be done with ACT.

All of the information about a test is recorded. If there is something additional you want to record, a custom extraction rule can be coded to do it. If you want to validate a result in the page and take an action based on the result, you can. The tests can also be run with values supplied from a database. That means that the testing can include dynamic navigation of a website. Think times can be added to each step of the test to simulate real-world browsing of a website.

Manual Testing

Another Team Edition for Software Testers feature is manual testing. This allows you to run tests that are based on a list of steps. The pass/fail status of these tests is recorded, just as any additional test is. Code coverage (if enabled) is captured for these tests as well. The steps for these tests can be written in Microsoft Word or in a plain text file in any format your organization may use.

Load Testing

Finally, the Team Edition for Software Testers provides for load testing. Load testing is designed to see how your application (hardware and software) performs under a real-world load. The options available allow for the testing of almost any situation imaginable. You can set the type of browser that is accessing the site, the type of network connection the browser is using to access the site, the way in which the think times are simulated (set times or a normal distribution, if at all), which tests are actually run as load tests, and their distribution. Ramp up times can also be set, or the tests can be run at a constant user load.

You can run the load tests from the local machine, which will simulate all of the connections. Alternatively, you can test via agents and a controller from many different machines. The controller directs the agents to run the test(s) and records the result in one location. A typical setup for this is a lab where you may have 20 test machines hitting one box with a website. This saves you the time and effort of starting the tests on all of the machines individually. The data that is collected is detailed and useful, and there is a lot of it. Every aspect of the test is recorded from both the software and the hardware perspective, and errors are stored for later analysis. The entire test result is saved to the VSTS data warehouse (if you are working with the Team Foundation piece).

Visual Studio Integration Partners Program

Visual Studio Integration Partners (VSIP) is a Microsoft program that gives developers and companies access to the application program interface (API) documentation, extensibility toolkit, and samples for Visual Studio and VSTS. With the toolkit, VSTS supports extensibility in all areas. This extensibility ranges from customizing the designers to incorporating new types of tests (such as Windows Forms tests). Many of these aspects of VSTS are touched upon briefly in upcoming chapters, and some examples are shown. However, Microsoft prefers that developers and companies who wish to provide extensibility for VSTS join the VSIP program. It is free, so there is no reason not to join it.

■**Note** There are various "levels" of the VSIP program. Free access to the extensibility toolkit is the basic level. Additional levels provide partnerships with Microsoft and access to various groups within Microsoft. It is well worth joining for commercial software development companies.

You can access the VSIP website (and join the program) at http://msdn.microsoft.com/vstudio/partners/default.aspx. There is a wealth of extensibility information located here.

The Effort Tracking Application

Throughout this book, we'll use a simple application as an example. This is a web-based application that records work engagements and stores them in a SQL Server database. The web application connects to a web service, which connects to the database. The deployment of this application is shown in Figure 1-2.

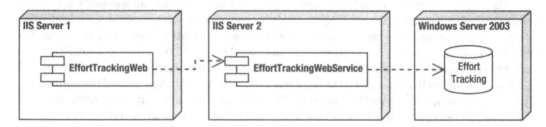

Figure 1-2. *Effort Tracking application logical deployment*

■**Note** The actual physical deployment is such that the website and web service are on the same machine but completely separated so they can be deployed in either configuration. The database itself can be located on the same machine or another machine.

The security is controlled via standard Forms security, where the username and password are stored in the database (obviously not a best practice, but for demonstration purposes only). The database contains four tables, as shown in Figure 1-3.

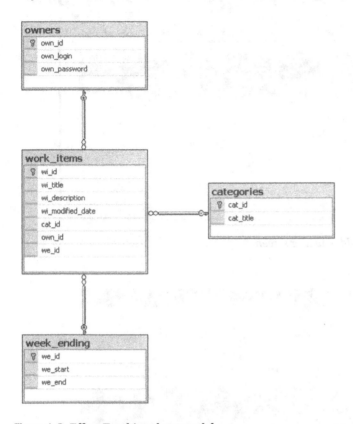

Figure 1-3. *Effort Tracking data model*

The application works as follows:

- User logs on to the system (or registers).

- User is redirected to the Effort Tracking page.

- User selects the week he wants to view.

- User adds a new engagement by clicking Add and entering the title, description, division, and the week ending date, and then clicks OK.

- User can edit or delete a record by clicking the appropriate link. The detail window is displayed, and the user can either confirm the deletion or change and save the record.

The various screens of the application are shown in Figures 1-4, 1-5, and 1-6.

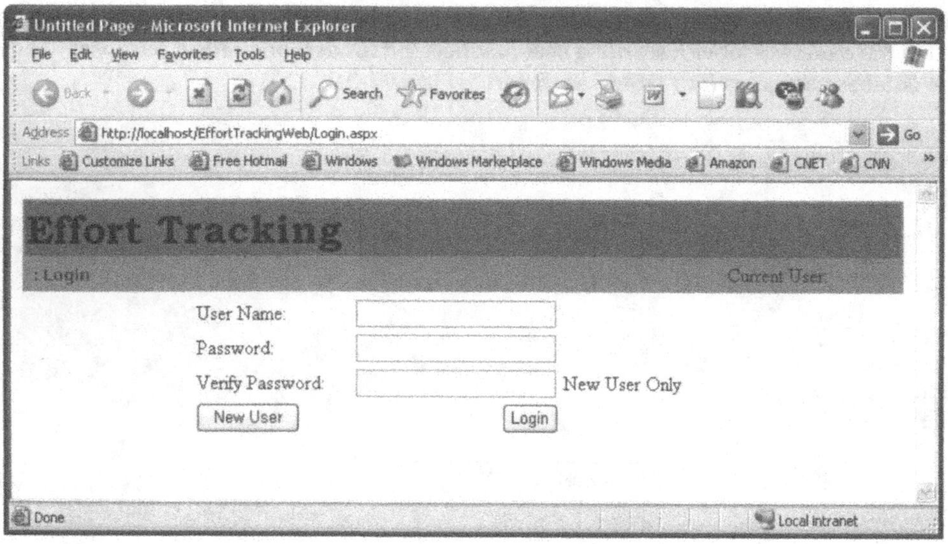

Figure 1-4. *Effort Tracking login/add new user screen*

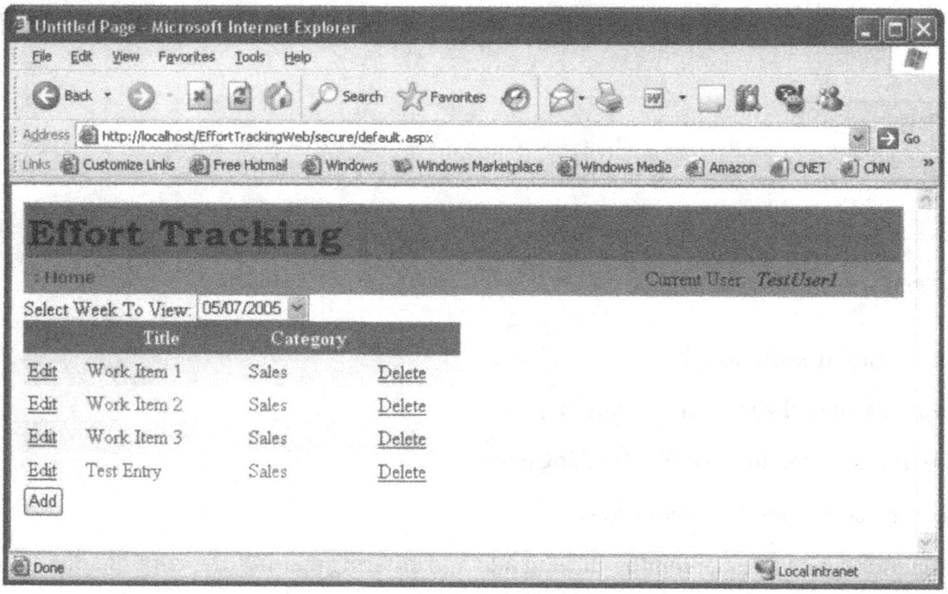

Figure 1-5. *Effort Tracking homepage*

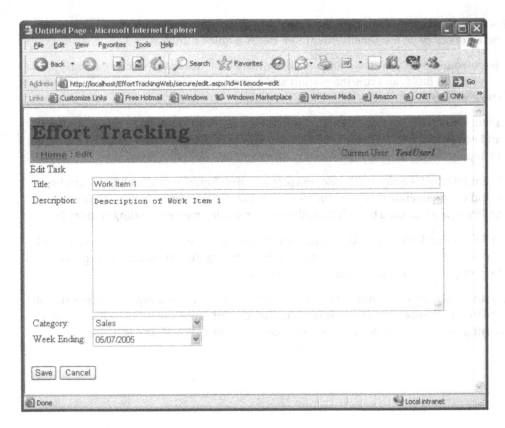

Figure 1-6. *Effort Tracking add/edit/delete page*

The web service comprises the bulk of the code for this application. There are eight methods in the web service, which handle all of the functions of the user interface.

■**Caution** The sample application is designed to be used with the examples included in the various chapters. In many cases, it does not conform to proper development guidelines, especially with regard to security. While we do point out some best practices in this regard, this application should not be used as a model for building any type of secure applications.

Summary

Various problems face development teams today, and these can cause a project to fail. You have seen how VSTS can help organizations and individual projects solve these problems and provide a positive return on investment for everyone.

This chapter has provided a high-level view of VSTS. It described each of the editions of VSTS and an overview of the benefits they offer. Here's a quick summary:

- Team Foundation provides a new version control tool, work item tracking, Team Foundation Build, and core integration and communication features available to all stakeholders in a project.

- Team Edition for Software Architects provides architects the ability to design a system and communicate that design effectively to the stakeholders. It also provides the ability to deploy the design into logical data centers and autogenerate real code.

- Team Edition for Software Developers provides developers with the ability to understand code, generate code, and unit test code quickly and easily. It also provides the ability to analyze code for defects and to ensure conformance to coding standards.

- Team Edition for Software Testers provides testers with the ability to test all aspects of the code. Testing covers web, manual, and load testing. Test management is provided to help organize and describe the testing process.

Chapter 2 introduces the process of creating a team project. You'll explore the methodology templates and process guidance, along with how to customize them. You will also learn how to configure the security for Team Foundation, the Project Portal, and SQL Server.

PART 1

■■■

Team Foundation

CHAPTER 2

■ ■ ■

Team Projects

In our current positions (our "day jobs," when we're not authoring books), Jeff and I spend a great deal of time performing independent reviews of projects in some form of peril. We are brought in for technical expertise and insight, but the vast majority of time, the key finding is a lack of communication. The classic line from *Cool Hand Luke* (1967) is fitting: "What we have here is a failure to communicate."

The *team project* is all about communication. The resounding message throughout VSTS is that of the team, and this concept comes to life by the instantiation of a team project.

The notion of a team project appears at several levels. The conceptual level is that of the business view or customer view. It is the reason the project exists. What problem are you trying to solve, how is the project being funded, how large is the team, and most important, what will the code name and logo be for the project? The logical level includes the technical view of the team project. What is the underlying architecture, which set of technologies are being used, what process is being followed, and will it fit with our existing infrastructure? Finally, there is the VSTS view of a team project. A VSTS team project is a physical thing.

This chapter will explore all of the features of the team project, how it integrates with VSTS, and how it makes the exchange of information easier for everyone on the team.

Starting Your Team Project

Before you dive into creating a team project, you should take the time to plan what template it will use, its roles and security, and other aspects. We'll begin with some guidance on planning your project, and then get started with a new team project.

Planning a New Team Project

You might have heard of the carpenter's expression "measure twice, cut once." It is meant to remind the novice that acting without planning can be very expensive. Consider also the account of a groundskeeper who lays intricate pathways through his meticulous lawns. After a few months of use, dirt pathways are etched in the grass, because the planned pathways were inconvenient. This second tale is intended to highlight that if your plan is impractical, it will be bypassed for convenience at the expense of elegance. Therefore, the realistic conclusion is that planning is both necessary and dangerous. That statement will send most project managers running for their Gantt charts. But we have seen far too many overplanned projects that never see the light of day. Fortunately, the Team Foundation Server bridges the gap between acting without planning and overplanning the unknown.

Both the Agile and Formal methodologies provide prescriptive guidance with the goal of delivering quality solutions, not just pretty documents. Best of all, you can tailor your process at any stage of the project to provide the ultimate in flexibility. In planning a team project, you need to address seven high-level areas:

Determine the process template to be used: If you are part of a large enterprise, you may already have a process methodology that is prescribed for you. If you are supporting specific industry or government contracts, you may be required to support the Capability Maturity Model Integration (CMMI) process improvement approach. If you use a third-party process that is supported by a template such as Scrum, Rational Unified Process (RUP), or Fujitsu, you should use the third party's provided template. If you have a relatively small project with a short life cycle, the Agile process would be a good place to start. Even after you have chosen your process template, you have a lot of freedom to add or change components, such as work item types, reporting, areas, and iterations.

Define roles and security: Roles and security for a project can be either fine- or coarse-grained, depending on your needs. You may find that only a few security groups cover all the roles on your project, or you may need to build a multilayered structure to meet all your needs. This chapter covers server-level security. Source code security will be discussed in Chapter 3.

Gather team work products: If you have existing artifacts that you want to reuse in other projects, such as best practices, coding standards, or templates, you can include these in the document libraries of the Windows SharePoint Services (WSS) portal. You can also design a standard structure for your work products, leveraging the portal document libraries that can be reused by subsequent projects.

Plan for version control: When you create a new team project, you are prompted either to create an empty source code control repository or to branch off an existing one. If you have unique check-in policies, you will want to create a new source code control repository. You will need to determine which fields you want to capture at check-in time and what type of check-in policies you want to enforce. If your organization already has mandatory policies, you can extend the predefined policies by creating a custom policy plugin. Version control will be covered in detail in Chapter 3.

Determine project work item types: Your team will need to agree on the set of work items to include in the project template. It is best to review the work item types that ship with the existing templates and choose the ones that work best for your project. It is easy to export, modify, and import work item types for a project or to create your own from scratch. Work item customization is covered in Chapter 5.

Determine the project structure: To properly categorize and report on your project, you will need to determine the organizational areas and the project iterations you want to include. This classification structure is made up of parent and child nodes. The project areas may be organizational, feature areas, or technical tiers (such as database, application layer, and client layer). The iterations have to do with the repeating cycles your project will go through. You can also apply security to areas of your project.

Determine project reporting needs: Your organization may already have a discrete set of metrics that each project is measured against. If not, there are a number of predefined reports provided in each of the default process templates. Project reporting is built off of SQL Server Reporting Services (SSRS) and an integrated data warehouse. SSRS provides complete report customization for your project to leverage. Team reporting is discussed in Chapter 6.

Connecting to the Team Foundation Server

Before you can create a new team project, you need to connect to the Team Foundation Server.

■**Note** You must install the Team Explorer add-in to Visual Studio in order to connect to a Team Foundation Server and launch the New Team Project Wizard. There is no command-line tool for creating a new team project.

Follow these steps to connect to the Team Foundation Server:

1. Select View ➤ Team Explorer from the main menu bar, if the Team Explorer is not already visible.

2. Select Tools ➤ Connect to Team Foundation Server from the main menu bar.

3. Click the Servers button, and then click the Add button.

4. Enter the name of the server where the Team Foundation application tier is located, as shown in Figure 2-1, and then click OK.

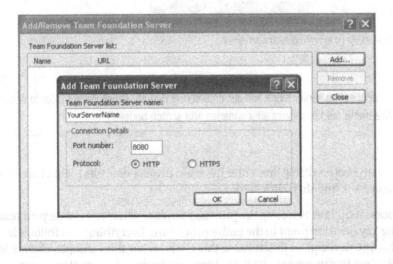

Figure 2-1. *The Add Team Foundation Server dialog box*

5. Select the Server you just added, and then click OK.

6. Click OK in the Connect to Team Foundation Server dialog box.

Any team projects that have previously been created on the Team Foundation Server are listed here. The Team Explorer will now list your server, along with a My Favorites node (discussed in the "Working with the Team Explorer" section later in this chapter).

Creating a New Team Project

If you are a project lead or administrator, you can create a team project using the New Team Project Wizard and an existing process template.

To create a team project, follow these steps:

1. Right-click the Team Foundation Server node in the Team Explorer and select New Team Project, as shown in Figure 2-2. This will launch the New Team Project Wizard. Optionally, you can select File ➤ New ➤ Team Project.

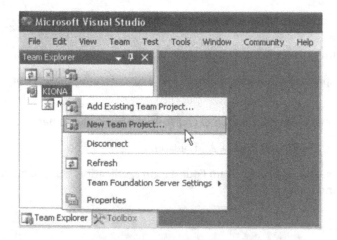

Figure 2-2. *Selecting to create a team project*

Note We named our application server Kiona and our data server Januik. These names refer to wineries in Washington State. (We name our lab servers after wineries and scotch houses.)

---

2. In the New Team Project dialog box, enter the team project name as EffortTracking, as shown in Figure 2-3, and then click Next.

3. Select a process template. Selecting the process template when you create your team project is the key decision point in the entire procedure. Everything that follows is based on this one decision, as described in this chapter. For this example, choose MSF for CMMI Process Improvement – v4.0, as shown in Figure 2-4. Click Next to continue.

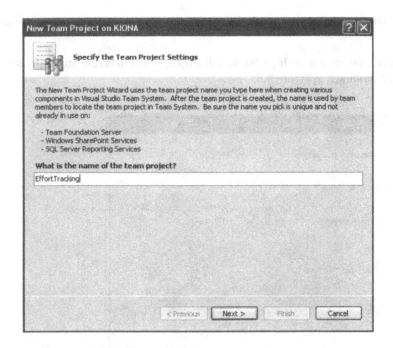

Figure 2-3. *Naming your team project*

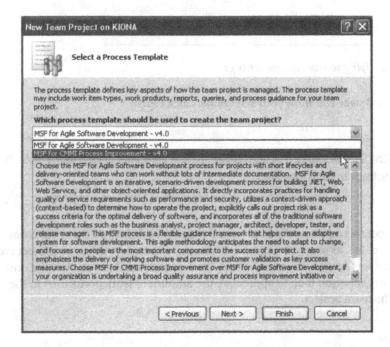

Figure 2-4. *Selecting a process template*

4. On the next wizard page, provide a title for the team project portal site and an optional description.

5. Specify your source control settings. For this example, select to create an empty source control folder, as shown in Figure 2-5.

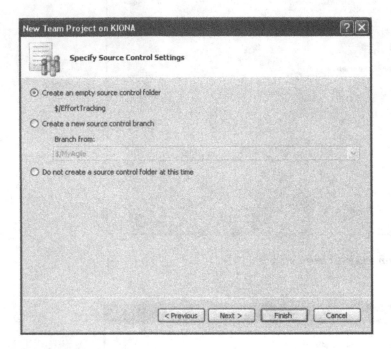

Figure 2-5. *Specifying source control settings*

6. The next wizard page will show your selections. Click Finish.

Note It can take a long time to create a new team project. Behind the scenes, a lot is taking place. You can follow along by watching the status messages.

---

7. After the process is complete, the final wizard page will inform you that your team project was created, as shown in Figure 2-6. You can either view the team project creation log or select Close to finish the wizard. We recommend that you view the creation log, if for no other reason than to appreciate the amount of work performed in the creation of the team project.

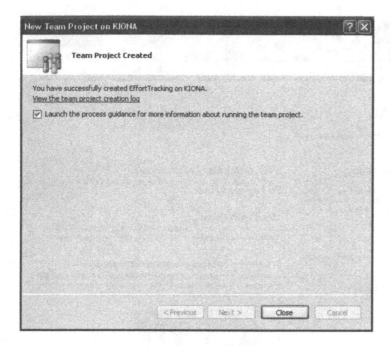

Figure 2-6. *Team project completion message*

If you left the "Launch the process guidance . . ." check box selected at the end of the New Team Project Wizard, the process guidance page will automatically be displayed, as described next.

Viewing Process Guidance

The *process guidance* documents the roles, activities, work products, and reports tailored to a specific software engineering method. The process guidance provided in Team Foundation is a collection of XML, XSL, and HTML files. Essentially, you get an out-of-the-box website describing the work streams, roles, activities, and work products for your chosen process template, as shown in Figure 2-7.

The process guidance is distinctive for each process template and is intended to remain intricately tied to the template. Therefore, if a new component is added to the process template, then the corresponding process guidance will need to be created, as described in the "Customizing the Process Guidance" section later in this chapter.

Spend some time reviewing the seven overview topics provided down the left side of the site. This will give you a good foundation for the Microsoft Solution Framework (MSF) approach, principles, and paradigms. You should then move though the top-level navigation into roles, work items, views, and the Capability Maturity Model Integration (CMMI) in general.

Figure 2-7. *Process guidance for the MSF CMMI Process Improvement – v4 process template*

Working with the Team Explorer

Now that you have created your first team project, EffortTracking is the only project listed in the Team Explorer, with no other information, as shown in Figure 2-8.

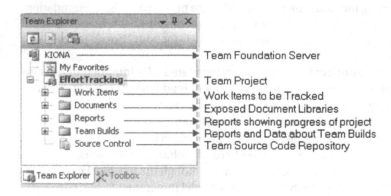

Figure 2-8. *Team Explorer components*

The Team Explorer has a My Favorites node located just under the Team Foundation Server name and above the Team Project name. It functions similarly to the Internet Explorer Favorites and has the familiar star symbol. Most of the items contained in the nodes below the

Team Project are eligible to be favorites. To add an item to the My Favorites node, just right-click an item (a report, for example) and select Add to My Favorites, as shown in Figure 2-9.

Figure 2-9. *Adding to the Team Explorer My Favorites node*

Introducing VSTS Components

All of the capabilities of the Team Foundation Server are instantiated by the creation of a new team project. The project instantiation is determined by the process template you select. The preconfigured work items, reports, classifications, version control, portal structure, groups, and permissions available to the project are all determined from the process template. Let's begin with the process template choices.

Process Templates

The two collections being offered in this first release of the Team Foundation Server are MSF for Agile Software Development – v4.0 and MSF for CMMI Process Improvement – v4.0. Third parties are working to incorporate various other methodologies into VSTS process templates. The templates being developed at the time of this writing are RUP (www.osellus.com/solutions/microsoft/rup-vsts_solutions.html), Macroscope (www.fujitsu.com/us/services/consulting/method/macroscope/index_p2.html), and Scrum (www.scrum-master.com/ScrumVSTS).

Both the Agile and CMMI methods are based on the MSF. MSF 4.0 is a full-grown process framework recognized as being compliant with CMMI level 3.

■**Note** The Capability Maturity Model Integration (CMMI) is a method for evaluating and measuring the maturity of the software development process of organizations on a scale of 1 to 5. The CMMI was developed by the Software Engineering Institute (SEI) at Carnegie Mellon University in Pittsburgh (www.sei.cmu.edu) in the mid-1980s as CMM and revised in 2000 as CMMI.

SOFTWARE ENGINEERING METHODOLOGIES

Software engineering methodologies are the frameworks that tell us how we should go about developing our software systems. Also known as the Software Development Life Cycle (SDLC), the most common frameworks or paradigms include the following:

- *Waterfall:* The classic method, which breaks the project into phases for comprehending and constructing information systems. Some of the more popular phases include opportunity, analysis, design, code, test, and implementation. The key understanding is that each prior phase must be completed before moving to the next phase. The Waterfall method has been criticized for being heavy, bureaucratic, and slow.

- *Evolutionary Prototyping:* This method's goal is to build a very robust prototype of the target system and then constantly refine it. The mantra of this process is to refine and rebuild. Evolutionary Prototyping led to Evolutionary Rapid Development.

- *Spiral:* This method includes the phases of the Waterfall approach with the agility of the prototyping model. The larger "big bang" of a complex project is broken into iterations that can be rapidly moved through the phases of the traditional Waterfall type approach and built one upon the other. Boehm's Spiral Model was first postulated in 1986.

- *Agile:* This method had its four values solidified in the spring of 2001. These four values include the value of individuals and interactions over processes and tools, the value of working software over documentation, the value of customer collaboration over contract negotiation, and the value of responding to change over following a plan.

Project Portal

You can access the Project Portal by right-clicking the team project and then choosing Show Project Portal, as shown in Figure 2-10, or by selecting Team ➤ Show Project Portal from the Team menu.

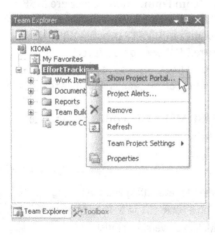

Figure 2-10. *Choosing to show the Project Portal*

The out-of-the-box Project Portal contains a single column of content showing announcements, links, and a single report named Remaining Work, as shown in Figure 2-11. The quick launch bar on the left is arranged by documents, process guidance, and reports. This default layout is highly customizable, as described in the "Customizing the Project Portal" section later in this chapter.

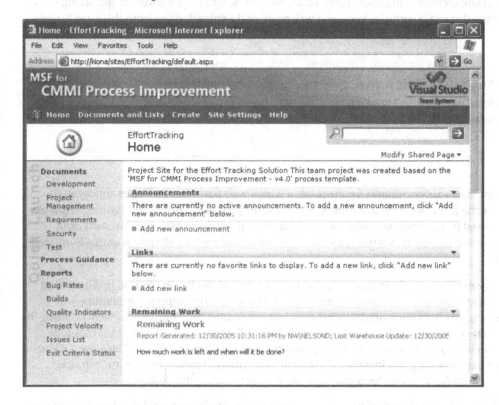

Figure 2-11. *The Project Portal default site*

The Project Portal is a Windows SharePoint Services (WSS) team site based on a custom site definition. Out-of-the-box, VSTS provides two SharePoint custom template files: MSFAgile.stp and MSFFormal.stp. Custom site definitions provide a complete layout for all the items to be housed inside a team Project Portal.

Note Many companies already have an enterprise SharePoint installation. It is possible to use a remote WSS server (the enterprise service), though it isn't a currently supported configuration. A whitepaper is being written to describe the steps that need to be taken for this to function properly with the Team Foundation Server. Once the Team Foundation Server is pointed at the enterprise WSS server, it is recommended that all future team project portal sites are located on the enterprise server.

The Project Portal includes the following:

Web parts: These are predefined web components designed to address a specific task. Basically, they are nothing more than ASP.NET custom server controls. Visually, they are composed of a frame, title bar, and content. Common web parts on the default Project Portal site include Announcements, Links, Members, and Page Viewer for rendering reports. You can customize your own web parts or download many from third-party sites.

■**Note** Other files associated with web parts are .dwp files, which are XML files containing details of the web part (title, description, link to assembly); . dll, which are web part assemblies; .htm and .gif, which are class resource files; and manifest.xml, which is a configuration file that describes the structure and contents.

Zones: These are containers on the page in which web parts reside. Zones allow you to create the framework for a common layout within your site. The default Project Portal site is created from a template with only a single zone titled loc:Left. You can easily add, delete, and modify zones using a web page design tool such as Microsoft Office FrontPage 2003.

Document libraries: These are the most-used feature of the Project Portal. It is here that documents are stored, managed, and shared. These libraries support versioning—or creating a backup copy of a file whenever you save a file to the library—as well as check-in and check-out, subfolders, and alerts. The Project Portal includes viewers for files that enable you to view documents from programs such as Microsoft Office 2003, even if you don't have the program installed. By default, document libraries include an "explorer view," in which files can be copied, moved, or deleted from the desktop.

Lists: Issue lists, calendar views, group-by views, personal views, and rich text expand the possibilities of the Project Portal lists. You can use formulas and functions in lists to create calculated columns and views. Creating a list is even easier from the one-stop Create page. Lists can be set up to require the list owner's approval before new items appear.

■**Note** For managed lists such as Requirements, Bugs, and Tasks that require state and transition behavior, you will want to use the work item tracking feature of VSTS. This feature is covered in Chapter 5.

Picture libraries: You can store photos and graphics in the picture libraries. View pictures as thumbnails, filmstrips, or in standard file lists. You may want to create a site image library (SIL) to store site-related logos, images, and graphics.

Notification (alerts): the Project Portal uses alerts to notify you through e-mail about additions, deletions, and changes to lists, list items, libraries, and other parts of sites. You can receive alert results immediately, or request daily or weekly alert results summaries.

Work Item Tracking

Work items are the currency of Team Foundation. A work item is a database record used to track the assignment and state of work. Work item types are definitions of specific work items including fields, forms, states, and transitions. Work item queries are predefined views into the work item database.

By default, the MSF for Agile Software Development - v4.0 process template comes with five predefined work item types: Bug, Task, Risk, Scenario, and Quality of Service Requirement. The MSF for CMMI Process Improvement - v4.0 process template includes Scenario and Quality of Service as types of the Requirement work item and an additional three: Review, Change Request, and Issue, as shown in Figure 2-12. Chapter 5 covers work item tracking in detail.

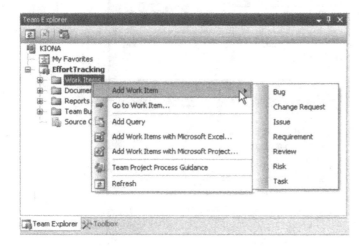

Figure 2-12. *Work item types*

Documents

Documents in the Project Portal are simply links to the underlying document libraries and the items they contain. These are predetermined by the process template selected. However, you can easily add or remove document libraries.

Click Documents and Lists on the Project Portal menu bar to see a list of all your document libraries. From the Team Explorer, you can right-click the Documents node and choose to add a document library. This will display the dialog box shown in Figure 2-13.

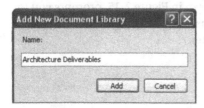

Figure 2-13. *The Add New Document Library dialog box*

Reports

Each process template includes a predefined set of SSRS-based reports. For the MSF for CMMI Process Improvement - v4.0 process template, there are more than 20. The MSF for Agile Software Development - v4.0 process template focuses on around 10 core reports in the process guidance. These reports are a mix of tabular, graphical, and subreport types.

SSRS reports query data from a centralized data warehouse based on SQL Server Analysis Services (SSAS) cubes. You can view these reports directly in the Project Portal or by browsing the Report Manager window, as shown in Figure 2-14. Reports are discussed in detail in Chapter 6.

Figure 2-14. *The Report Manager window*

Team Builds

The goal of Team Foundation Build was to provide a "build lab out of the box." Team Foundation Build provides a very simple way to kick-start this build process. You go through a simple wizard that generates a build script for you. The wizard, shown in Figure 2-15, prompts you to select a solution to build from source control, configurations, locations, and options to run tests. Team Foundation Build is discussed in detail in Chapter 7.

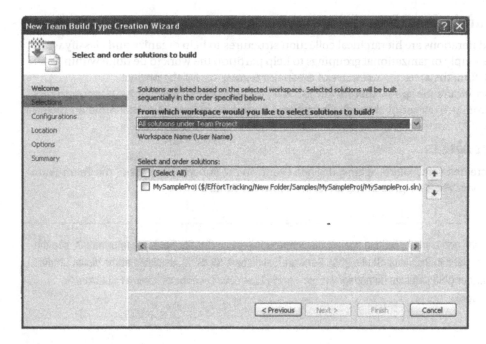

Figure 2-15. *Using the New Team Build Type Creation Wizard*

Version Control

Version Control is the enterprise source code control tool in the Team Foundation Server. Key features include changesets, branching and merging, shelving, and integrated check-in and check-out. Check-in policy provides a mechanism for validating source changes on the client, including things like a Bad Word check-in policy, which won't allow a developer to check in code containing bad words without a warning.

The Source Control Explorer, shown in Figure 2-16, is activated when you double-click the Source Control node in the team project. Chapter 3 covers the Version Control tool in detail.

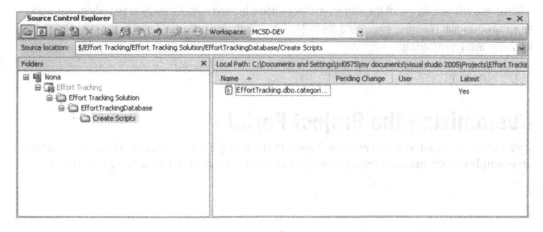

Figure 2-16. *The Source Control Explorer*

Areas and Iterations

Areas and iterations are hierarchical collection structures to help organize and classify work. *Areas* are simply organizational groupings to help partition the work to be done within a project. Often, the areas are reflective of the major feature set for the project.

Iterations are the spirals that the project has predetermined. MSF for Agile recommends moving from project setup, through a number of feature iterations, to a final build and release.

Project Alerts

You can create project alerts against defined events in the subcomponents of the Team Foundation Server. The four predefined alerts are shown in Table 2-1.

Tip You can add alerts by writing against the notification service directly. For more information, see the guidance provided in the Visual Studio 2005 Software Developers Kit (SDK), available at the Visual Studio Industry Partner (VSIP) Affiliate homepage (`http://affiliate.vsipmembers.com/affiliate/default.aspx`).

Table 2-1. *Project Alerts*

Alert	Description
My work items are changed by others	Alert sent when your work items are changed by others
Anything is checked in	Alert sent when anything is checked in to the project source control
A build status is changed	Alert sent when the status of a project build is changed
A build completes	Alert sent when any build is completed for the project

---

Note You will probably want the alert on your work items to send e-mail directly to you when your work items are changed. The other three alerts are project-level alerts and are usually sent to an alias made up of the entire team membership.

Customizing the Project Portal

If you are so inclined, you can edit the Project Portal using a website editor. Figure 2-17 shows an example of a customized Project Portal we created for one of our labs using FrontPage.

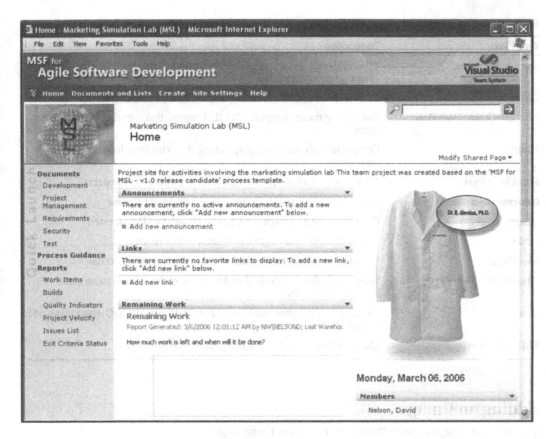

Figure 2-17. *A Project Portal customized in FrontPage*

Note For a high level of customization, you can create your own site template to be used in the creation of the team project site.

The easiest way to customize the Project Portal is to modify its web parts. You can add web parts to the Project Portal by clicking the Modify Shared Page link at the top-left side of the Project Portal. Table 2-2 lists the built-in web parts that are available in WSS. Additionally, there is one web part for viewing each document library in the team project.

Table 2-2. *Default Project Portal Web Parts*

Web Part	Description
Announcements	Typically contains news of interest; allows attachments; can be set to expire
Contacts	Contact list important to the project; can be imported from Outlook
Content Editor Web Part	For adding more complex HTML, images, links, and code within a zone
Events	Complete with start and stop times, descriptions, locations, and recurrence
Form Web Part	Used to connect simple form controls to other web parts
General Discussion	Used to allow newsgroup type discussions of interest
Image Web Part	Container for an image; link to the image by URL or path
Links	List of links to web pages of interest to the team
Members	List of team project site members and their online status
Page Viewer Web Part	Used to display a specified page within a zone; used to render reports from SSRS
Task	General task list that can be assigned and prioritized, with start and stop dates and percentage complete
XML Web Part	Used for XML and XSL transformation of the XML

Adding an Image

To add a new image to your Project Portal, follow these steps:

1. Click Modify Shared Page at the top-left side of the Project Portal, select Add Web Parts, and then click Browse.

2. Select the Image Web Part from the EffortTracking Gallery list, as shown in Figure 2-18, and then click Add.

3. Click the down arrow on the title bar of the new web part and select Modify Shared Web Part.

4. In the Image Web Part Editor, enter the URL of the image you would like rendered, adjust the alignment, and set the border style. Click OK when you are finished.

Figure 2-18. *Adding a web part*

Adding Reports

Reports on the Project Portal are accessed using the Page Viewer web part. The easiest way to add a new report is to copy the link in the existing Remaining Work report, as shown in Figure 2-19.

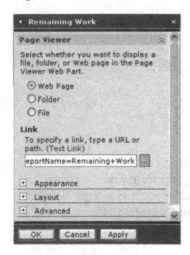

Figure 2-19. *The Page Viewer web part*

To get to the web part, click the arrow on the Remaining Work title bar in the Project Portal and select Modify Shared Web Part. Copy the path in the Link text box. Add a new Page Viewer web part to the page and modify the report name to match one of the existing reports listed in the Report Manager window. Paste the previously copied path into the Link text box and modify the report name. Use the Test Link link to verify that the report name is correct before clicking Apply.

Working with Lists

Each list on the Project Portal has a corresponding web part for displaying and managing content. You can view the available lists by clicking the Documents and Lists link at the top of the Project Portal.

You can edit lists in a datasheet, which provides an easier mechanism for adding multiple items to the list at one time. For example, to work with the Links list, click the Links title at the top of the Links web part. When the empty Links list appears, select Edit in Datasheet to allow multiple-line entry, as shown in Figure 2-20.

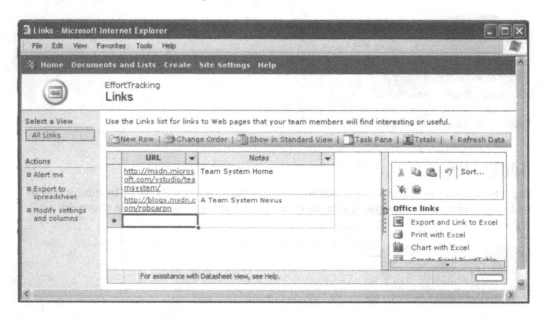

Figure 2-20. *Editing lists in a datasheet*

Customizing a Process Template

The process template is the blueprint for a team project. When you create your own team project, you may find that you need to add or change items, such as security groups, policies, and work item types. Here, we will describe how to modify the process template.

Understanding the Process Template Architecture

A process template includes descriptions of the following components:

- *Portal:* The portal is based on WSS. The portal site is just a predefined SharePoint Team Site. The portal definition includes a custom site template, document libraries, files, and folders.

- *Process Guidance:* Process Guidance is a subsite on the Project Portal. This section describes the website pages, images, and script to support the integration of the process guidance with the rest of VSTS.

- *Work Items:* This section includes work item type definitions (WITD), work item queries (WIQ), and the initial set of prepopulated tasks.

- *Areas and Iterations:* This section describes the hierarchical structures enumerating the phases (iterations), organizational units (areas), and the mappings to Microsoft Project.

- *Reporting:* This section includes the predefined reports for the template against the underlying VSTS data warehouse.

- *Security Groups and Permissions:* This section defines a team project's initial security groups and their permissions. Security is covered in detail in the "Managing Team Foundation Security" section later in this chapter.

- *Source Control:* This section includes Checkin Notes, Checkout Settings, and Security.

The best way to understand the process template architecture is to download one of the two existing templates shipped with the product. To accomplish this, right-click the Team Foundation Server in the Team Explorer and select Team Foundation Server Settings ➤ Process Template Manager. This opens the Process Template Manager window, as shown in Figure 2-21.

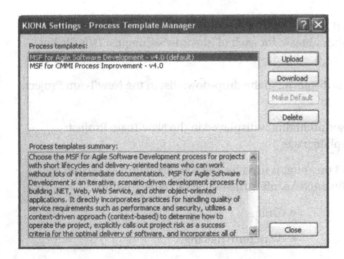

Figure 2-21. *Process Template Manager window*

Select one of the process templates (MSF for CMMI Process Improvement - v4.0 for this example) and click Download. Select an appropriate location on your local machine and click Save. After several minutes, you will receive a confirmation that the process template has been downloaded, as shown in Figure 2-22.

Figure 2-22. *Process template download verification*

Navigate to the folder in which you just saved the process template, and you will see the structure shown in Figure 2-23.

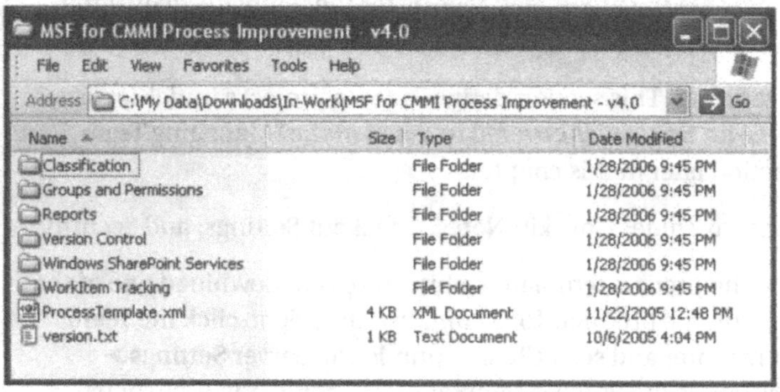

Figure 2-23. *Process template download folder structure*

The ProcessTemplate.xml file is the root XML file that describes the entire assemblage for the prescribed template, including the subtasks for each of the process plugins. This file has four main segments:

- <name>: This is the name that is displayed in the drop-down list in the New Team Project Wizard.

- <description>: This is the description that is displayed in the New Team Project Wizard's Select a Process Template page.

- <plugins>: This section lists all the plugins used by the New Team Project Wizard to create the team project. The first release offers the following plugin options:

  - Classification
  - Reporting
  - Portal (wizard page)

  - Groups
  - WorkItemTracking
  - VersionControl (wizard page)

- <groups>: This section describes the actions to be performed within the plugin. It has the following nodes:

  - <group id> contains the name of the plugin group.

  - <description> provides a meaningful narrative.

  - <completionMessage> provides a message that is displayed at task completion.

  - <dependencies> includes a list of dependent group IDs (names) to identify any other plugin's tasks that must complete prior to launching this plugin's tasks.

  - <taskList> points to an XML file of tasks for plugin actions to be performed for the plugin.

Listing 2-1 shows a snippet of the ProcessTemplate.xml file containing three of the four key sections.

Listing 2-1. *Portion of ProcessTemplate.xml*

```
<?xml version="1.0" encoding="utf-8" ?>
<ProcessTemplate>
 <metadata>
  <name>MSF for CMMI Process Improvement - v4.0</name>
<description>Choose the MSF for CMMI Process Improvement process for
  projects with longer life cycles and that require a record of
  decisions made. Choose MSF for CMMI Process Improvement over MSF
  for Agile Software Development, if your organization is undertaking
  a broad quality assurance and process improvement initiative or
  your team needs the assistance of explicit process guidance rather
  than relying on tacit knowledge and experience.</description>
<plugins>
<plugin name="Microsoft.ProjectCreationWizard.Classification"
    wizardPage="false"/>
    <plugin name="Microsoft.ProjectCreationWizard.Reporting"
    wizardPage="false"/>
    <plugin name="Microsoft.ProjectCreationWizard.Portal"
    wizardPage="true"/>
    <plugin name="Microsoft.ProjectCreationWizard.Groups"
    wizardPage="false"/>
<plugin name="Microsoft.ProjectCreationWizard.WorkItemTracking"
    wizardPage="false"/>
    <plugin name="Microsoft.ProjectCreationWizard.VersionControl"
    wizardPage="true"/>
  </plugins>
 </metadata>
```

Listing 2-2 shows the <groups> section. Notice that each of the six plugins has its own <group> section.

Listing 2-2. *ProcessTemplate.xml Groups Section*

```
<groups>
 <group id="Classification"
   description="Structure definition for the project."
   completionMessage="Project Structure uploaded.">
  <dependencies>
  </dependencies>
  <taskList filename="Classification\classification.xml"/>
 </group>
 <group id="Groups"
   description="Create Groups and assign Permissions."
   completionMessage="Groups created and Permissions assigned.">
  <dependencies>
   <dependency groupId="Classification" />
  </dependencies>
  <taskList filename="Groups and
  Permissions\GroupsandPermissions.xml" />
 </group>
 <group id="Portal"
   description="Creating project Site"
   completionMessage="Project site created.">
  <dependencies>
   <dependency groupId="Classification"/>
   <dependency groupId="WorkItemTracking"/>
   <dependency groupId="VersionControl" />
  </dependencies>
  <taskList filename="Windows SharePoint Services\WssTasks.xml"/>
 </group>
 <group id="Reporting"
   description="Project reports uploading."
   completionMessage="Project reports uploaded.">
  <dependencies>
   <dependency groupId="Classification"/>
   <dependency groupId="Portal"/>
  </dependencies>
  <taskList filename="Reports\ReportsTasks.xml"/>
 </group>
 <group id="WorkItemTracking"
   description="Workitem definitions uploading."
   completionMessage="Workitem definitions uploaded.">
  <dependencies>
```

```
  <dependency groupId="Classification"/>
  <dependency groupId="Groups"/>
 </dependencies>
 <taskList filename="WorkItem Tracking\WorkItems.xml"/>
</group>
<group id="VersionControl"
  description="Creating Version control."
  completionMessage="Version control task completed.">
 <dependencies>
  <dependency groupId="Classification"/>
  <dependency groupId="Groups"/>
  <dependency groupId="WorkItemTracking" />
    <!-- This is just to serialize execution with WIT -->
 </dependencies>
 <taskList filename="Version Control\VersionControl.xml"/>
</group>
</groups>
</ProcessTemplate>
```

Modifying a Process Template

Customizing the process template is an incremental, iterative, and often irritating endeavor. To help you, we have composed a ten-step guide, as illustrated in Figure 2-24.

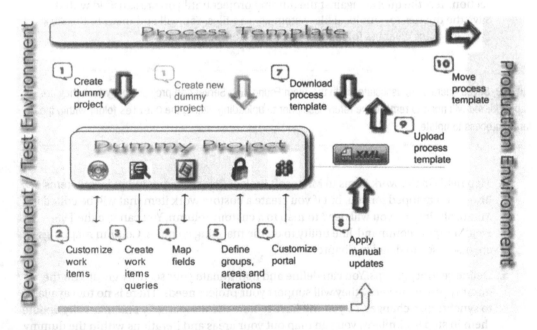

Figure 2-24. *Process template customization steps*

■**Caution** We strongly recommend that you do not attempt to modify the process template against a production Team Foundation Server. Since the process is both incremental and iterative, you will find the procedure a lot smoother if you practice on a test system. A virtual build of the Team Foundation Server using a differencing disk is preferred for manipulating and testing a process template.

Here are the steps:

1. Select one of the two predefined process templates (MSF for Agile Software Development - v4.0 or MSF for CMMI Process Improvement - v4.0). Choose the one that best resembles your target process. Create a dummy project based on the selected template. This will give you an environment in which to validate your changes as they are being applied.

2. Customize the work items to reflect your process. You most likely will need to create custom work items to support your unique development process. Two utilities exist to enable you to manipulate work item structure: the witimport and witexport command-line utilities (discussed in Chapter 5). Other tools, such as the Process Template Editor and Work Item Type Designer, allow you to modify work items in a graphical user interface and are available from the GotDotNet community.

3. Create and save custom work item queries. The simplest way to create work item queries is in the Team Explorer. In the dummy project, add queries in the work item section. Test the queries against the dummy project until you are satisfied with them. Save the queries to your local file system as .wiq files. You will add these to the Work Item Tracking\Queries folder of your process template in step 8.

■**Note** Saved queries are associated with the Team Foundation Server and project from which they are captured. You will need to remove the references prior to uploading files to the Queries folder within the target process template.

4. Map fields in the work items to Microsoft Project fields. The predefined work items have been mapped for you, but if you create a custom work item that will be edited in Microsoft Project, you will need to map to a custom column. You can use the TFS-FieldMapping command-line utility to do the mapping changes. Column mappings are discussed in detail in Chapter 4.

5. Define security groups. You can define and manipulate your security groups on the dummy project to verify they will support your project needs. There is no tool available to synchronize changes, so you will have to note them separately and manually update them in step 8. Similarly, you can map out your areas and iterations within the dummy project to verify the correct organizational groupings and project cycles are captured. Last, define security groups and check-in notes for version control.

6. Customize the WSS portal. You can use the dummy project to test the structure for your WSS portal sites. Create document libraries and compose process template artifacts within the libraries. However, the final modification to the WSS XML template will need to be manual.

7. Download the process template. Now that you are comfortable with the changes to be made to the base process template, you can set the baseline for the modifications. This downloaded template is unchanged from when the dummy project was created; however, you now know explicitly the changes to make. Furthermore, many of the changes have been tested against an instantiated project.

8. This is where all your prior work gets implemented. Change the name and description of your process template in the root ProcessTemplate.xml file. Move your custom work item definitions from step 2 into the TypeDefinitions folder and modify the workitemtypes section of workitems.xml to recognize them. Move your custom work item queries from step 3 into the Queries folder under the WorkItem Tracking folder and modify the queries section of workitems.xml to recognize them. If needed, duplicate any custom Microsoft Project mappings from step 4 in the Classification folder to the FileMapping.xml. Reapply any custom security groups defined in step 5 to the GroupsandPermissions.xml file in the folder of the same name. Manually describe the document libraries, folders, and individual files from step 6 in the WssTasks.xml file under WSS. Make any changes to the version control security or check-in policies in the VersionControl.xml file in the Version Control folder.

9. Test the work from step 8. Upload the new template (refer to Figure 2-21) within the development environment. If the upload fails, you will need to review the log file and fix the XML. Once the template is successfully uploaded, you will want to start the process again and create a new dummy project to verify your template changes.

10. Once you have tested your new process template and fully exercised the modified components within the new dummy project, you are ready to move the template into the production environment.

Customizing the Process Guidance

The MSF process guidance consists of XML, XSL, and HTML files. You will need the following tools to customize the process guidance files:

- Microsoft Office InfoPath 2003 with Service Pack 1

- An XML or XSL editor

- The MSFWinBuild tool (available from www.gotdotnet.com/workspaces/ workspace.aspx?id=c0ce8992-2955-4371-904b-1f93a9efffe6)

Customizing the process guidance consists of four general steps, as illustrated in Figure 2-25.

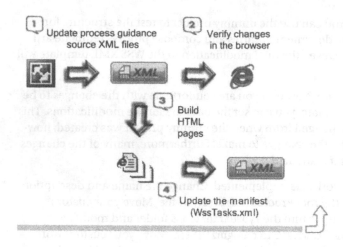

Figure 2-25. *Process guidance customization steps*

1. Update the process guidance source XML files. The easiest way to start updating the process guidance files is by using Microsoft InfoPath and the supplied template. When you bring up a source XML file in InfoPath, you are presented with a standard framework for the page content, as shown in Figure 2-26. Click the buttons across the top of the form to access the different views: Content, Bullet Menu, Glossary, Help Map, Image, Index, and Menu. Each view allows you to work with various types of content.

■Note There are two modes for the process guidance files: edit and run. The editable files are XML and stored in the Process Guidance\Source\XML folder. The run files are prerendered HTML and stored in the Process Guidance\Supporting folder.

---

2. Verify your changes in the browser. Working within the Source folder, you can open ProcessGuidance.htm, and your changes within the XML documents will be rendered.

3. Build pregenerated HTML content. To build the prerendered HTML files, you will need to run the MSFWinBuild tool.

4. Update the XML manifest. Any files that were added or deleted in the modification process need to be noted in the WssTasks.xml manifest file. Note that the MSFWinBuild tool will automatically update the WssTasks.xml file.

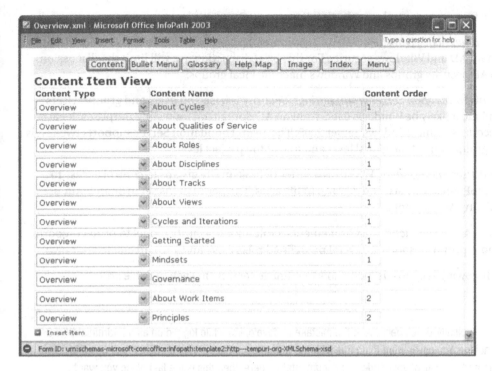

Figure 2-26. *InfoPath view of process guidance overview.xml*

Managing Team Foundation Security

In this section, we'll cover security from the Team Foundation Server perspective; that is, how it relates to server operations. (See Chapter 3 for a discussion of item-level permissions from within the source code system.)

Security for the Team Foundation Server is not fully integrated in this release. You will need to manage at least four areas, as shown in Figure 2-27.

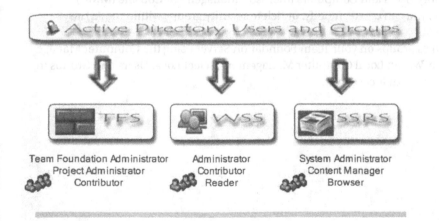

Figure 2-27. *Team Foundation security areas*

These four areas control security as follows:

- *Windows Active Directory (AD) and computer management:* Entire books are written about AD and Windows security. For this brief discussion, we will limit the discussion to AD security groups and Windows machine local groups.

- *Team Foundation Server group settings:* Security is based on users and groups. Users will most likely be Windows users from an AD domain or, for testing purposes, local accounts within Windows Server 2003. The Team Foundation Server supports two levels of groups: one at the global level and one at the project level.

- *WSS user management:* WSS uses a series of built-in site groups to control access to SharePoint sites, lists, and document libraries. The permissions set in SharePoint use existing AD accounts.

- *SSRS role assignment:* SSRS implements a role-based security model to protect reports and reporting resources. Several predefined roles exist, and you can create your own.

The following sections describe how to manage security in each of these areas.

Caution Typically, developers make the mistake of developing while logged on as an Administrator user on their machine. You never want to do this with the Team Foundation Server though. If you use this server as intended and store all of your code and documentation here, then this is the last place you want an intruder to be able to access or unauthorized users to be allowed to make changes. Because of this, it is important that you take some time to think about who gets access to what when you create a new team project.

Managing Windows AD Security

Windows Server 2003 provides a client-based set of remote administration tools in the Windows Server 2003 Administration Tools Pack (adminpak.msi). Included in this set is the Active Directory Users and Computers Microsoft Management Console (MMC) snap-in. From here, you can create, modify, or delete security groups within the AD, as shown in Figure 2-28.

You manage local groups on your Team Foundation Server using the Computer Management MMC snap-in. Within Local Computer Management, select Local Users and Groups to add users or groups to your local server.

Figure 2-28. *Active Directory Security Groups*

Managing Global Team Foundation Security

All security for the Team Foundation Server (not a specific project) is accessed by right-clicking the name of the server in the Team Explorer. Only one server can be displayed in Team Explorer at a time, so this will always be the root node of the Team Explorer.

By default, the Team Foundation Server comes with three preinstalled global groups, which are described in Table 2-3.

Table 2-3. *Team Foundation Server Default Global Groups*

Group	Description
Service Accounts	Any service accounts that are used to run various portions of the Team Foundation Server. If you set up the Team Foundation Server by following the installation instructions, the Windows account TFS Service is the only account in this group.
Team Foundation Administrators	Users in this group can perform any operation on the server.
Team Foundation Valid Users	Users in this group can access the server. All users are a part of this group; they do not need to be assigned specifically. When a new project is created, each group in that project is added to this group during project creation.

> **Note** Team Foundation Server Workgroup Edition includes a fourth security group, named Team
> Foundation Licensed Users. In order to use the Team Foundation Server Workgroup Edition, a user must be
> added to this group.

Group Permissions

To set group permissions, right-click the server name (Kiona in this example) and select Team
Foundation Server Settings, as shown in Figure 2-29. From the submenu, choose Security.

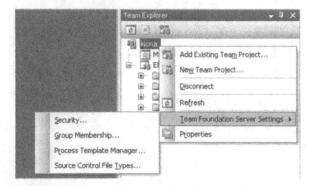

Figure 2-29. *Team Foundation Server security options*

The Global Security dialog box appears, as shown in Figure 2-30. Note that you cannot
create new global Team Foundation Server groups through this dialog box. You create new
groups via the Global Groups dialog box, as described in the next section.

You can add Windows users and groups to the Global Security dialog box list by selecting
the Windows User or Group option and clicking the Add button. You will be taken to the standard Windows Select User or Group dialog box to add users or groups.

You can allow or deny permissions by checking the corresponding check box. The available permissions—all the permissions available at the server level—are described in Table 2-4.
Item permissions work the same from Team Foundation Server as they do for Windows. If a
user belongs to multiple groups, and one group gives a user permission to perform an action,
and the group does not give the permission but does not specifically deny it, then the user has
permission to perform the action. If one group gives a permission but another group explicitly
denies a permission, the user cannot perform that action. By default, none of the permissions
are set to Deny.

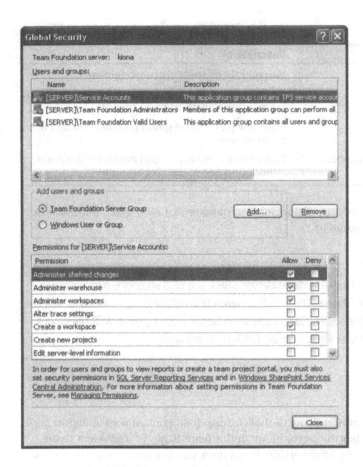

Figure 2-30. *The Global Security dialog box*

Table 2-4. *Team Foundation Server Permissions*

Permission	Description
Administer shelved changes	Can delete shelvesets created by other users
Administer warehouse	Can change warehouse settings (see Chapter 6 for more information)
Administer workspaces	Can create/delete workspaces for other users
Alter trace settings	Can change trace settings for detailed diagnostic information regarding Team Foundation Server Web Services
Create a workspace	Can create a version control workspace
Create new projects	Can create new projects in the Team Foundation Server (must be an Administrator user for SharePoint and SQL reporting)
Edit server-level information	Can edit server-level groups and permissions (create, delete, and rename)

Continued

Table 2-4. *Continued*

Permission	Description
Manage process template	Can modify or add a process template
Trigger events	Can trigger project events (alerts) within the Team Foundation Server (service account)
View server-level information	Can view server-level group membership and user permissions
View system synchronization information	Can trigger synchronization events for the Team Foundation Server (service account)

At the bottom of the Global Security dialog box is a message explaining that permissions for SSRS and WSS must be set separately.

> **Note** Obviously, having to manage Team Foundation Server, SSRS, and WSS security separately is not ideal. The Developer Division Customer Product Lifecycle Experience Team (DDCPX) has released an administration tool to help manage permissions across Team Foundation Server project groups, WSS site groups, and SSRS role assignments. This tool is available from the GotDotNet community.

Group Management

You can manage group membership from the Global Groups dialog box, shown in Figure 2-31. To access this dialog box, right-click the server name in the Team Explorer and select Team Foundation Server Settings ➤ Group Membership. From here, you can add new groups, view group properties, and edit some group properties.

Figure 2-31. *The Global Groups dialog box*

Click the New button to add a new global group. You'll be prompted for the group name and a description, as shown in Figure 2-32.

Figure 2-32. *The Create New Team Foundation Server Group dialog box*

■**Note** You cannot remove the three default security groups. The Remove option is available only for groups that you added.

To view and, in certain cases, edit group properties, select the group in the Global Groups dialog box and click the Properties button. Figure 2-33 shows the Properties box for the Team Foundation Valid Users group.

Figure 2-33. *The Team Foundation Server Group Properties dialog box*

You can see in Figure 2-33 that all of the default groups for the EffortTracking project and subsequent projects have been added to the Team Foundation Valid Users group (this occurs during project creation). Selecting Properties for any selected member will display the Team Foundation Server Group Properties dialog box for that member. The Member Of tab lists all of the groups to which the current group or user belongs.

There are several items to note with regard to the Team Foundation Valid Users group:

- The Team Foundation Valid Users group and Service Accounts group cannot be edited through the Global Groups dialog box.

- Team Foundation Valid Users group members are added when new projects are created or new groups are created within those projects.

- Team Foundation Valid Users is the base group for all users and has the lowest level of permissions. This group is not a member of any other group.

- Users are never directly added to the Team Foundation Valid Users group. Only groups are added.

For custom groups, any Team Foundation Server group, Windows group, or Windows user can be added or removed.

Managing Project Security

The security settings for a team project are identical in structure to the security settings for the server. Along with setting group permissions and managing groups, you can also set security for Area Nodes within Areas and Iterations.

Project Group Permissions and Management

To access the group settings for a project, right-click the project name in the Team Explorer and select Team Project Settings ➤ Security or Team Project Settings ➤ Group Membership. The dialog boxes are identical to those you saw for the Team Foundation Server in the previous section. However, the project security settings have different default groups and permissions. At a project level, the groups and permissions are more granular in order to control access to certain functions/items within the project. When a new project is created, four new groups are created by default, as described in Table 2-5.

Table 2-5. *Default Project Groups*

Group	Description
Build Services	Can perform actions related to building and publishing build results. A build manager or developer in charge of running nightly builds would be in this group.
Contributors	Can add, modify, and delete items. All developers need to be members of this group.
Project Administrators	Can perform any action within a specific project. A project manager would most likely be in this group.

Group	Description
Readers	Can view all information about a project, but cannot add, modify, or delete items. Stakeholders would typically belong to this group.
Team Foundation Administrators	Can perform all tasks for the project. This group is added by default to all new projects.
Team Foundation Valid Users	Can view information in a project (by default, members are assigned the same permissions as the Readers group). This group is added by default to all new projects.

■Tip In order to deny access to users of other projects who should not be able to view project information, just uncheck the View Project Level Information permission for the Team Foundation Valid Users account. The change is specific to the project only.

The project permissions are at a fairly high level, even for a project, as shown in Table 2-6. The reason for this is that the majority of security for project items is controlled at the source code control level and is not needed at this higher level of permissions. The project permissions cover project security as it relates to performing operations on the server and publishing information to the server. The documentation control (requirements, scope, and so on) is handled through the WSS security, and access to reports is managed through the SSRS security. Both of these types of security are covered in upcoming sections of this chapter.

Table 2-6. *Project Permissions*

Permission	Description
Administer a build	Can delete a completed build or stop a build in progress
Delete this project	Can delete the project for which the user has this permission
Edit build quality	Can change the quality of a build from one value to another (see Chapter 7 for more information about builds)
Edit project-level information	Can edit project-level permissions for users and groups; this includes work item queries and source control write access
Publish test results	Can publish test results to the server and associate the test results with a particular build
Start a build	Can start a new build
View project-level information	Can view project-level permissions for users and groups
Write to build operational store	Can write to the build store (build service account permission)

Areas

Areas are used to categorize items within a project—to segregate items for clarity and security. Because areas allow you to categorize information, you can also control the security of work items in specific areas. (Work items are covered in Chapter 5.) This functionality allows you to set permissions for work items, which is different from setting permissions for accessing documents in WSS or accessing code (or a changeset) associated with a specific work item.

To access the security for areas, right-click the project name in Team Explorer and select Team Project Settings ➤ Areas and Iterations. This will display the Areas and Iterations dialog box, as shown in Figure 2-34. On the Area tab, click the Security button in the lower-right corner. This displays the Area Node Security dialog box (which looks like the Global Security dialog box, shown earlier in Figure 2-30), which lists the permissions described in Table 2-7.

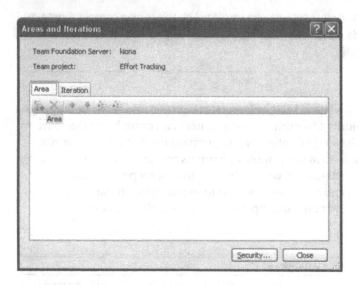

Figure 2-34. *The Areas and Iterations dialog box*

Table 2-7. *Area Permissions*

Permission	Description
Create and order child nodes	Can add new areas and order the areas
Delete this node	Can delete the selected node
Edit this node	Can edit the name of the selected node
Edit work items in this node	Can modify work items that are characterized as a member of the selected node
View this node	Can see the selected node
View work items in this node	Can see the work items associated with the selected node

Managing WSS Security

One of the key tenets of the Project Portal is that it should be a "lightweight access point for casual stakeholders." This means that it should have the ability to communicate project information to anyone with a browser. Your organization may choose to allow access to any authenticated user within your corporation. In order to do that, you will need to be able to manage user access to your project site. If you have the Administrator privileges, you can manage WSS users.

To add a member to the WSS site, open the Project Portal and select the Site Settings link at the top of the page. Within the Administration section, select Manage Users to bring up the Manage Users form. Click Add Users to start the Add Users process, as shown in Figure 2-35.

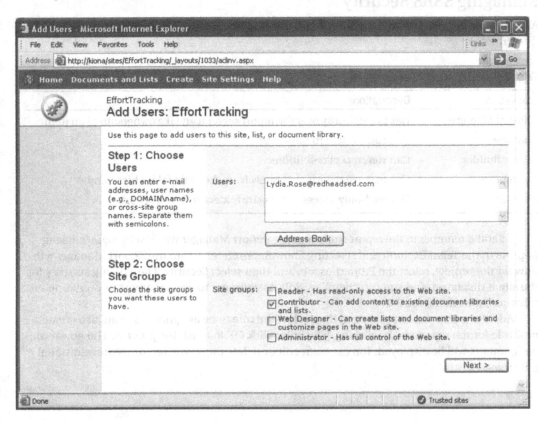

Figure 2-35. *The Add Users page for WSS*

Table 2-8 shows the default groups for WSS.

Table 2-8. *WSS Default Groups*

Site Group	Description
Administrator	Has full authority over the website
Web Designer	Can create document libraries and lists, and customize website pages
Contributor	Can add content to document libraries and lists
Readers	Has read-only access to the website

Managing SSRS Security

As noted earlier, you can manage SSRS security by assigning roles. Table 2-9 shows the predefined roles.

Table 2-9. *SSRS Default Groups*

Site Group	Description
Content Manager	Has full authority over the report server (can take ownership of an item)
Publisher	Can add content to the server
Report Builder	Can view report definitions
My Reports	Can manage reports separately from the main folder hierarchy
Browser	Has read-only access to navigate folders and view reports

To add a member to the report site, open the Report Manager window by right-clicking Reports in the Team Explorer and selecting Show Report Site. Within the Report Manager window for the project, select the Properties tab, and then select Security. The existing security for the site is displayed, and you can click New Role Assignment to add members to predefined roles, as shown in Figure 2-36.

Add the group or username, and then select the role to be assigned. You can also create a new role for the report site by clicking New Role. Click OK to finish the process. The new role assignments will be displayed. You can then edit or delete the new roles, or create additional new roles.

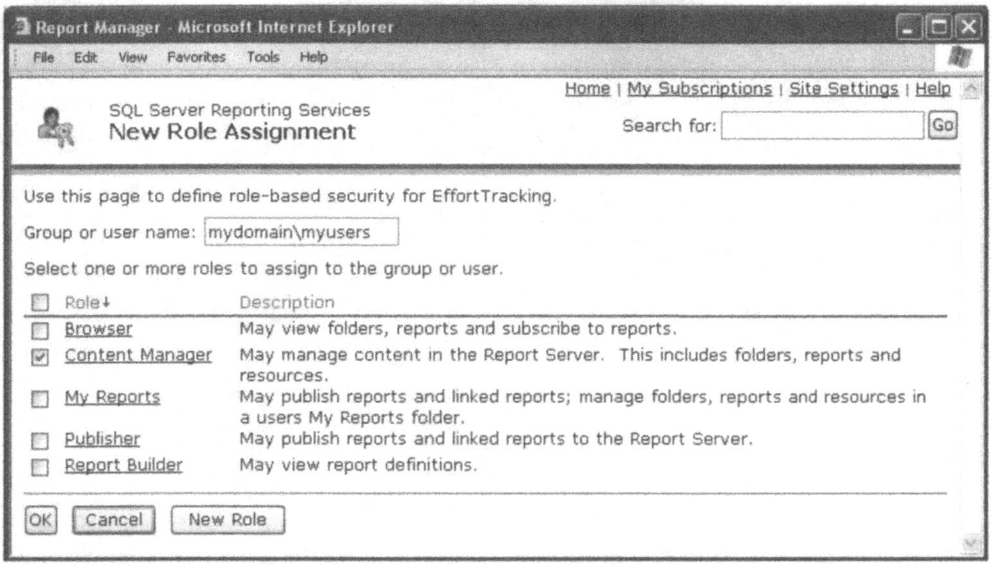

Figure 2-36. *The Report Manager's New Role Assignment window*

Summary

In VSTS, a team project is an instantiation of a development project. Within VSTS, there are templates, guidance, best practices, source control, work items, build machines, a portal for the project, reporting, and more. This chapter has introduced you to the various components of VTST by way of the team project. Many of these components will be covered in more detail in later chapters.

First, we talked about creating a new team project, including the prerequisites. Then we presented an overview of the various components that come with your chosen project process template, which is the blueprint for a team project.

Then we described how to customize your Project Portal, project template, and process guidance. Finally, we took a look at security across three major platforms: Team Foundation Server, WSS, and SRSS.

CHAPTER 3

■■■

Team Foundation Version Control

Raise your hand if you worked on a large-scale project and were absolutely frustrated by the limitations in Visual SourceSafe (VSS). Okay, you can put your hand down now. Welcome to the new wave of source code control from Microsoft. The Team Foundation Version Control (TFVC) system takes the best features of various enterprise-class source code control systems, incorporates them, and makes them better and easier to use in the classic Microsoft style. This chapter explores all the facets of the TFVC and how it integrates with Visual Studio and makes developing on large-scale teams easier for you.

Note TFVC is definitely an enterprise-class repository. It is much more powerful than needed for small-scale development teams (three to five people). For small teams, it is still perfectly acceptable to use Visual SourceSafe. The new features add some ease and a little more flexibility for teams, making VSS a perfectly acceptable source code control system.

TFVC is an extensible source code control system that underpins the project management aspects of Visual Studio Team System (VSTS). You will see how it fits in with work-item tracking and policies and makes VSTS a truly integrated solution. Finally, VSTS includes a utility to migrate your code stored in Visual SourceSafe to TFVC.

Starting with Version Control

When you created your first team project (in the example in the previous chapter), you had the option to create a new source control folder, branch from an existing source control folder, or not create a folder at all.

If you elected to create a new source control folder, then a brand new root-level folder was added to the version control repository as shown in Figure 3-1 (the Source Control Explorer is covered in the next section).

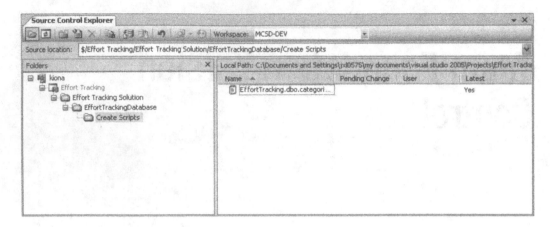

Figure 3-1. *Source Control Explorer*

If you elected to branch from an existing source control folder (at least one folder in version control must exist for you to do then) then the existing data in the branch you selected was copied into a new folder in version control (Figure 3-2). You will note that everything in the new project (Demo Project in Figure 3-2) is grayed out. This is because there is no default workspace (discussed later in the "Workspaces" section) for the files, and the latest version has not been retrieved.

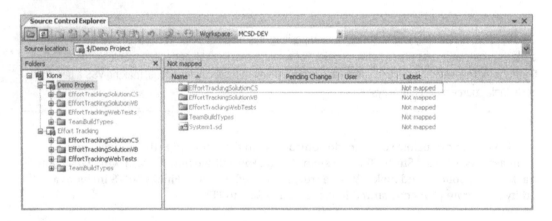

Figure 3-2. *A new project starting with branched source code*

If you did not create a new source control folder, you can do so at a later date.

These three options are your first introduction to Team Foundation Version Control. Welcome.

■**Note** As of this writing, Microsoft has released tools that allow previous versions of Visual Studio .NET and Visual Studio 6 to integrate with Team Foundation Version Control. In addition, various tools are being released to incorporate TFVC and work item tracking with Eclipse.

Source Control Explorer

The Source Control Explorer (SCE) is your view into the TFVC. From it you can control all aspects of files under version control. You can add files, delete files, check files out, check files in, branch files, compare files, examine file history, and the list goes on. Figures 3-1 and 3-2 show the SCE. To get to it, you have two options: expand the Team Project node in Team Explorer and double-click the Source Control node or, from the main menu, select View ➤ Other Windows ➤ Source Control Explorer.

As with the Windows Explorer, the folder structure is contained on the left and the files within those folders are shown on the right. Additionally, any information about pending changes is noted along with the files.

The root node in the SCE is the server. The nodes below the server level are the team project nodes. All of the solutions for a team project are located below the Team Project node. Right-clicking any item within the SCE (either in the tree view or the details view) will bring up the options menu described in Table 3-1.

■**Note** Some of the terminology at this point may not be familiar to you. Each of these terms is discussed in detail later in the chapter.

Table 3-1. *Source Control Explorer Options*

Option	Description
View	Opens TFVC's version of the file for viewing. This will use the application registered for use with the file extension to view the file.
Get Latest Version	Retrieves the latest version of the file to your workspace.
Get Specific Version	Allows you to retrieve any particular version of the file.
Check Out For Edit	Allows you to check out a file. Gives you the option to perform a shared check-out, lock the file so only you can edit it, or allow other users to check out the file but not check it in.
Lock	Either locks the file so no one can check it out, or allows people to check it out, but not check it in.
Delete	Deletes a file. When you select a file for deleting directly from the SCE you must also commit that change in order for the file to be deleted.
Rename	Renames a file.
Undo Pending Changes	Cancels any pending changes to the item and any subitems.
Check In Pending Changes	Checks in the pending changes to the item and any subitems.
Shelve Pending Changes	Shelves pending changes.
View History	Displays the history window.

Continued

Table 3-1. *Continued*

Option	Description
Compare	Allows you to compare the TFVC version to the local version of a file, the version in a particular changeset, the version on a specific date, or a labeled version.
Branch	Allows you to create a separate tree of changes to a file independent of the original code base.
Merge	Allows you to merge two files from separate branches.
Move	Allows you to move the file from the current location in the TFVC to another location in the TFVC.
Apply Label	Allows you to label an entire project, a selected folder, or a single file within a project or folder with a specific label.
New Folder*	Creates a new folder in the TFVC project.
Properties	Views the TFVC properties of the file or folder.
Refresh	Refreshes the contents of a folder or the status of a single file.

* *New Folder only appears in the menu when you click on a blank area in the details pane (right window), although you can add a new folder from the SCE's toolbar while you are in the tree view pane.*

File/Folder Properties

To view the File or Folder properties, right-click the item and select Properties. This displays the Properties dialog box shown in Figure 3-3. This dialog box is the same for all items under version control.

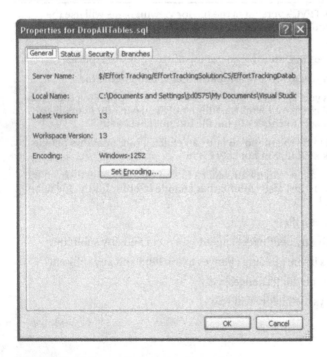

Figure 3-3. *The Item Properties dialog box*

General

The Server Name is the name of the file under version control. The Local Name is the name of the file currently on your hard drive. The same is true for the version numbers. The Latest Version is the version on the server, and the Workspace Version is the version on your hard drive. The Encoding is the file system encoding. VSTS automatically detects this so you should never have to change it. If you do have to change it, there are about 100 different encodings to choose from.

Status

The Status tab shows any pending changes to the item as shown in Figure 3-4.

Figure 3-4. *Status tab*

Figure 3-4 shows that users jxl0575 and alicew are both making changes to the file. It also shows which workspace the items are checked out to. Because both are checked out to the same workspace it indicates that both users are using the same machine (which is true!).

Security

Let us talk about security for a moment. Do you remember how security works (or does not work as the case may be) in Visual SourceSafe? You can set security for the file share and you can allow or not allow a user access to a repository. You can even set whether they had read-only or read-write privileges—but you cannot do anything else.

The VSTS team took this into account when designing TFVC. You can now control security at all levels and to a very granular degree (Figure 3-5).

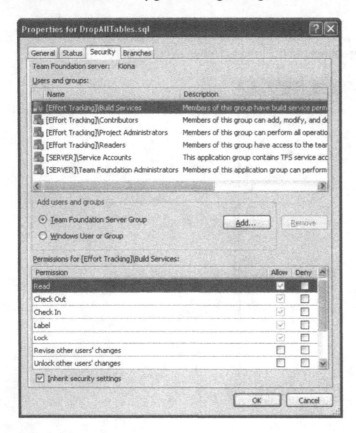

Figure 3-5. *Security tab*

The users and groups list contains all the users (or groups) that have access to the given folder or file in the folder. By default, all project members have some type of access to the items in version control. The server accounts shown in Figure 3-5 (Service Accounts and Team Foundation Administrators) have administrator rights to the items in version control which cannot be removed. You can add additional users or groups to this list.

■**Note** If you add a user or a group that is not at least already a part of the Readers account for the project, they will be unable to access the file (or folder). Aside from this one restriction, adding users and groups and setting permissions is done as normal.

The available permissions for a given file or folder are listed in Table 3-2.

Table 3-2. *Item Permissions*

Permission	Description
Read	Can read an item.
Check out	Can check out an item.
Check in	Can check in an item.
Label	Can label the item
Lock	Can lock an item.
Revise other users' changes	Allows user to change the comments, work item associations, or check-in notes associated with a changeset they did not create.
Unlock other users' changes	Allows a user to unlock another user's locked item.
Undo other users' changes	Lets pending changes be cancelled on an item that another user has checked out.
Administer labels	Allows users to label changes and alter labels.
Manipulate security settings	Indicates the user has permissions to change the security of the item.
Check in other users' changes	Causes items checked out by another user to be checked in.

The four default groups associated with every project have certain permissions by default which cannot be removed, only revoked (in other words, the group either has the right or it is specifically denied). These permissions are listed below:

- *Build Services*: Read, Check out, Check in, Label, Lock

- *Contributors*: Read, Check out, Check in, Label, Lock

- *Project Administrators*: All permissions

- *Readers*: Read

Additional permissions may be assigned to these groups. All in all, security has been greatly improved over VSS and this is a welcome change.

Branches

The Branches tab shows the branches that exist for the selected item as shown in Figure 3-6.

Figure 3-6. *Branches tab*

This dialog box shows that a branch exists for DropAllTables.sql at version 3. It also shows that the branched file is part of the Demo Project. This allows you to trace back to where a branch came from. This dialog box does not show shelved items, as they are not part of any code base (see the "Shelvesets" section later in this chapter for more information).

Workspaces

One of the key things to note is the Workspace setting. A workspace (similar to a collection of working folders as in Visual SourceSafe) is a local "sandbox" where the project code is stored and where you work with it. Any changes you make to the code are made in the local workspace, and when you sync your code with the repository, the changes you made are uploaded to the repository.

■**Tip** You can maintain multiple workspaces on a single system for a single project. One reason to do this is to handle working on multiple branches at once, where you want to avoid shelving items (discussed later in this chapter).

To create additional workspaces (or to set up a new workspace on a system that does not have one) select the Workspace drop-down in the SCE and click Workspaces (or select File ➤ Source Control ➤ Workspaces). This will bring up the Manage Workspaces dialog box shown in Figure 3-7.

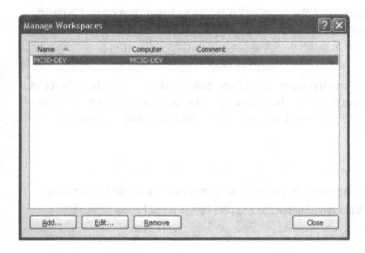

Figure 3-7. *Manage Workspaces dialog box*

This dialog box will list all of the workspace names and the systems on which those workspaces are located. Selecting the Edit or Add button will bring up the Add/Edit Workspace dialog box shown in Figure 3-8.

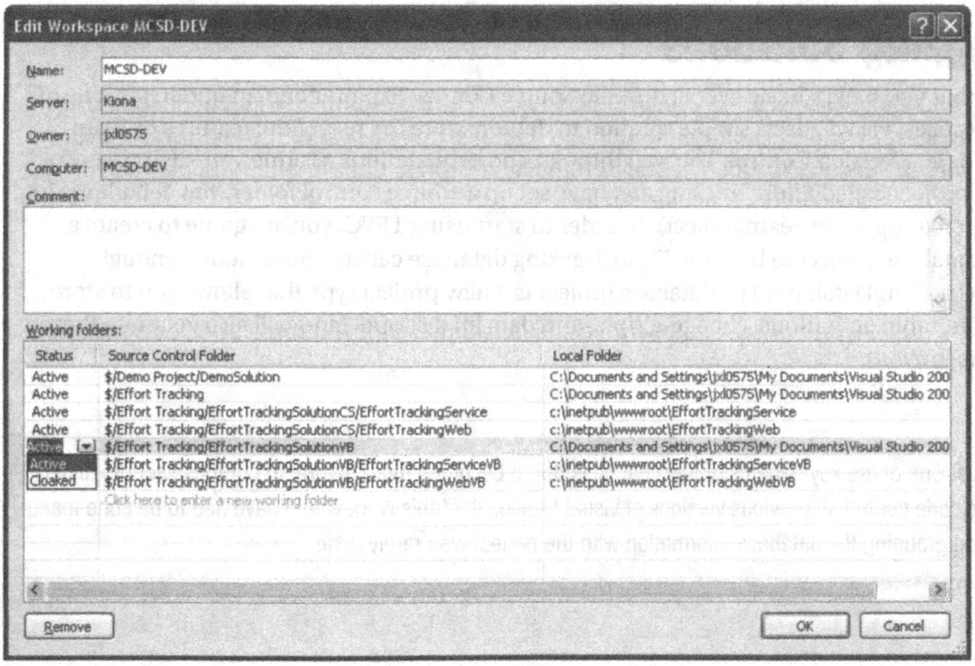

Figure 3-8. *Add/Edit Workspace dialog box*

Here you can add a comment or create additional working folders and map them to repository folders.

Tip As a best practice, the workspace layout should match the repository layout upon which it is based. This makes it easier to navigate both of them.

To set up the working folders, you have a couple of options. The first option is to do a Get Latest on a folder. SCE will prompt you for the local folder, and a working folder entry is automatically made for the workspace. The second option is to do the task manually in the Edit Workspace dialog box.

Tip Another best practice is to map the root team project folder (in this example the $/Effort Tracking folder) to a folder on your hard drive and keep all of the other folders for the project under this directory.

One other thing you can do in the Edit Workspace dialog box is to cloak a folder. Cloaking a folder sets the folder to be "invisible" to the local workspace. For example, if you were to cloak the $/Effort Tracking/EffortTrackingSolutionVB folder, when you did a Get Latest on the root folder, the cloaked folder would not be retrieved. To cloak a folder, select the Status column and select Cloaked.

Creating Solutions

Now that you have a basic overview of the Source Control Explorer and an understanding of workspaces, we will use a simple solution to demonstrate the rest of the features of Team Foundation Version Control. The walkthrough and explanations assume you have created a team project called Effort Tracking and have set up a source control folder (the default setting when creating a new team project). In order to start using TFVC, you are going to create a new database project to hold the Effort Tracking database called, conveniently enough, EffortTrackingDatabase. The database project is a new project type that allows you to store queries, table definitions, change scripts, and data load scripts (and will also generate these scripts for you).

Note One of the key benefits of this change is that it becomes more natural to put these scripts under source code control. In previous versions of Visual Studio, all of this work would have had to be done manually, and grouping the database information with the project was rarely done.

To create the new solution (remember that at this point you have only created a team project not an actual solution) and project, do the following:

1. Select File ➤ New ➤ Project.

2. Select Other Project Types ➤ Visual Studio Solutions ➤ Blank Solution.

3. Call the solution "Effort Tracking Solution," select Add to Source Code Control and click OK. This will display the Add Solution dialog box shown in Figure 3-9.

4. Leave the default settings as they are and select OK.

5. Right-click the created solution and select Add ➤ New Project.

6. Select Other Project Types ➤ Database Project.

7. Enter the name as "EffortTrackingDatabase" and select OK.

Figure 3-9. *Add Solution dialog box*

Tip The Advanced button allows you to override the default workspace mappings.

At this point you will have a Solution Explorer structure that looks like the one in Figure 3-10.

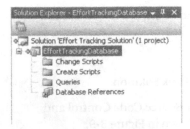

Figure 3-10. *Solution Explorer*

The pluses next to the solution and the project indicate that these items have pending adds but have not yet been stored in the source code repository.

Pending Changes Window

Right-click either node and select View Pending Changes. This will display the Pending Changes dialog box shown in Figure 3-11 where you have a number of options for handling items in your workspace.

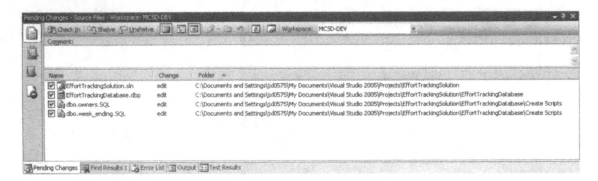

Figure 3-11. *Pending Changes dialog box*

The Pending Changes window is where you see the work you have done in preparation for your next check-in. Here you can associate work items with code, check that your changes comply with the check-in policy, add comments, and have reviewers sign off on your code.

The tab buttons down the left side of the window change the view displayed in the Pending Changes window. The selected tab in Figure 3-11 is the Source Files tab which displays this window.

Source Files

The Source Files section allows you to work with the files from your project and provide status on those files. Every file with a check next to it is a change that will be committed. The type of change is noted here and can be one of the following: Add, Edit, Rename, Merge, Branch, Delete, or Undelete (if a file is locked for editing, "locked" will appear in this column in addition to the type of change). In this example, all of the changes are additions. The folder list displays where that item is in the workspace on your local drive. Holding your cursor over the item will show the version number of the item to be added. The Comments field at the top of the pane allows you to add a comment that will be applied to all changes that are committed at the same time.

Tip It is a good practice to work on only one change at a time or one piece of functionality at a time. That way it is easy to add comments to the files you are committing. However, if you work on multiple changes at once, it is worthwhile to do your changes in batches so that you apply a uniform comment to groups of related work.

To check in the files, you simply click the Check In button on the toolbar. For right now, check in the pending changes. Once the changes are successfully checked in, the files will no longer be displayed in the Pending Changes dialog box, and the plus icon next to each file will become a lock (in the Solution Explorer).

Note Before checking the changes in, review the information on the other tabs, because some of the information will not be displayed after all pending changes are checked in.

Later in this chapter the section "Shelvesets" explains the shelving and unshelving options available via the Source Files tab.

You can work with individual files by right-clicking the file in the Solution Explorer and selecting the appropriate option.

Work Items

Work items are essentially assignments tracked by the system. Chapter 4 deals entirely with work items and work item tracking. The work items that show up in the Pending Changes dialog box allow you to associate a given task with the given changeset. Changesets are discussed later in this chapter in the "Changesets" section.

Check-in Notes

For now you will notice that the check-in notes consist of three fields: Code Reviewer, Security Reviewer, and Performance Reviewer. These are configurable fields that can be made mandatory prior to a check-in or left as optional. Right now they are optional but you will see how to change this later in this chapter in the "Configuring Version Control" section.

Policy Warnings

The policy warnings page, at this point, contains no policies. Any policies that have been violated are listed here. You will see how to create and enforce policies later in this chapter in the "Configuring Version Control" and "Creating Custom Check-in Policies" sections.

Changesets

A changeset is a grouping of all metadata related to changes checked in at the same time from the same workspace. The metadata includes files, work items, comments, check-in notes, policy violation overrides, the user, and the date. Changesets are persisted for the life of the source control repository.

Note Visual SourceSafe has no equivalent to a changeset. In VSS, every check-in you make is an independent check-in and there is no way to track which other files are checked in at the same time (although you can run a report on the date and time checked in but this is difficult at best).

Changeset numbers start at one and are incremented by one for each new changeset. The Get Latest Version option (available from various places such as right-clicking on a node in the Solution Explorer) will retrieve the latest version from the latest changeset. To retrieve a specific changeset version the Get option can be used and the appropriate version chosen. The Get option will be described in more detail in the section "Retrieving Versions" later in this chapter.

To see how changesets work, create a new table in the EffortTrackingDatabase project by right-clicking the Create Scripts folder and selecting Add New Item. Then select the Table Script and call it dbo.Categories.sql.

Note While this is certainly not a book on database projects, it should be noted that all objects in a database can be reverse-engineered into a database project. This is one of the great new features of Visual Studio 2005.

Add the SQL statements in Listing 3-1 to the categories script (replacing what is autogenerated in the file).

Listing 3-1. *Create Categories Script v1*

```
CREATE TABLE [dbo].[categories]
(
    [cat_id] [int] IDENTITY(1,1) NOT NULL,
    [cat_title] [varchar](100) NOT NULL,
    CONSTRAINT [PK_categories] PRIMARY KEY CLUSTERED
    (
        [cat_id] ASC
    ) ON [PRIMARY]
) ON [PRIMARY]
```

In the Pending Changes window, add the comment "Added the categories table create script" and check in the pending changes. Now you discover that you have a problem—you did not check to see if the table existed before you tried to create it. A common component of a create script is a check to see if the table is there, so you want to add the check for the table. Add the SQL statement in Listing 3-2 above the create table statement.

Listing 3-2. *Create Categories Script v2*

```
IF  EXISTS (SELECT * FROM dbo.sysobjects
WHERE id = OBJECT_ID(N'[dbo].[categories]')
AND OBJECTPROPERTY(id, N'IsUserTable') = 1)
DROP TABLE [dbo].[categories]
GO
```

Notice that when you make the additions, the file is automatically checked out for you, but not the database project, because the project structure did not change, only a single file within the project. Again, check in the changes but make a comment to the effect that you added a drop existing categories table section.

History

To view the history of changes for a given file, right-click the file in the Solution Explorer and select View History. Alternatively, you can select the file in the Solution Explorer and select File ➤ Source Control ➤ View History from the main menu (you can also view the history from with the SCE). This will show the History window seen in Figure 3-12.

Note There is a 99% chance that the changeset numbers you see on your system will be different than those shown here. Not to worry, though; just remember that the lower the number, the earlier the version.

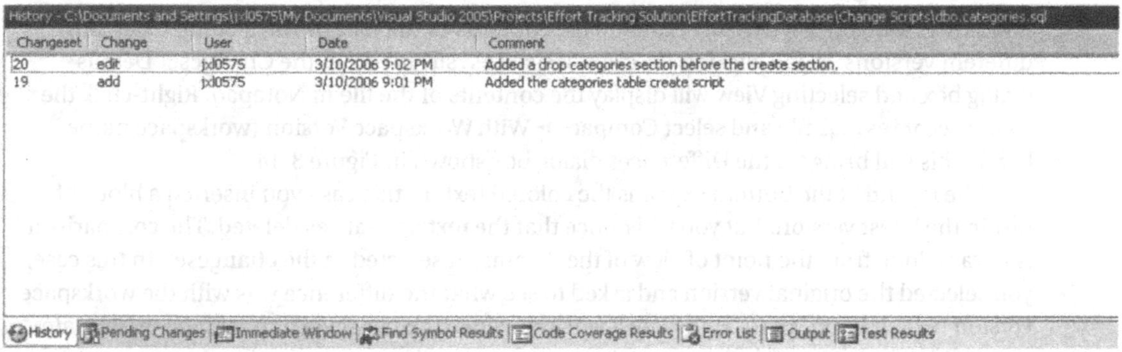

History - C:\Documents and Settings\jxl0575\My Documents\Visual Studio 2005\Projects\Effort Tracking Solution\EffortTrackingDatabase\Change Scripts\dbo.categories.sql

Changeset	Change	User	Date	Comment
20	edit	jxl0575	3/10/2006 9:02 PM	Added a drop categories section before the create section.
19	add	jxl0575	3/10/2006 9:01 PM	Added the categories table create script

History | Pending Changes | Immediate Window | Find Symbol Results | Code Coverage Results | Error List | Output | Test Results

Figure 3-12. *History window*

The initial version is version 19, and the change is noted as an add. Version 20 contains the addition of the drop categories section. To view the changeset information for a given entry, double-click the version in the list. This will bring up the Changeset Details dialog box shown in Figure 3-13.

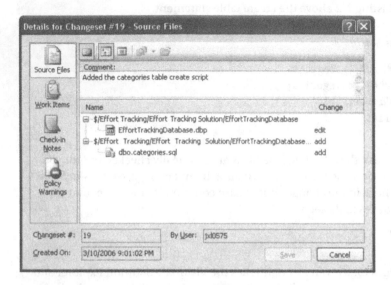

Figure 3-13. *Changeset Details dialog box*

This shows the changes that were made when each of the files was checked in. Here it notes that the categories script was added (along with the Change Scripts folder) and the database project itself was edited. The view of the files shown in Figure 3-13 is the folder view as opposed to the flat view that is displayed by default (this can be changed by selecting the appropriate icon above the Comment field).

Comparing Versions

From this view you can actually examine the contents of the files or run a compare against different versions. Right-clicking the dbo.categories.sql file from the Changeset Details dialog box and selecting View will display the contents of the file in Notepad. Right-click the dbo.categories.sql file and select Compare ➤ With Workspace Version (workspace name here). This will bring up the Differences dialog box shown in Figure 3-14.

The legend at the bottom explains the colored text. In this case you inserted a block of text in the latest version. But you will notice that the text appears as deleted. The comparison is always done from the point of view of the document selected in the changeset. In this case, you selected the original version and asked to see what the difference was with the workspace version (which happens to be the latest version). Since the latest version had the exists statement and the earlier version does not, it appears to the differencing engine that the text was deleted. All other comparisons work from the latest version to the previous version (which is the best way to do comparisons).

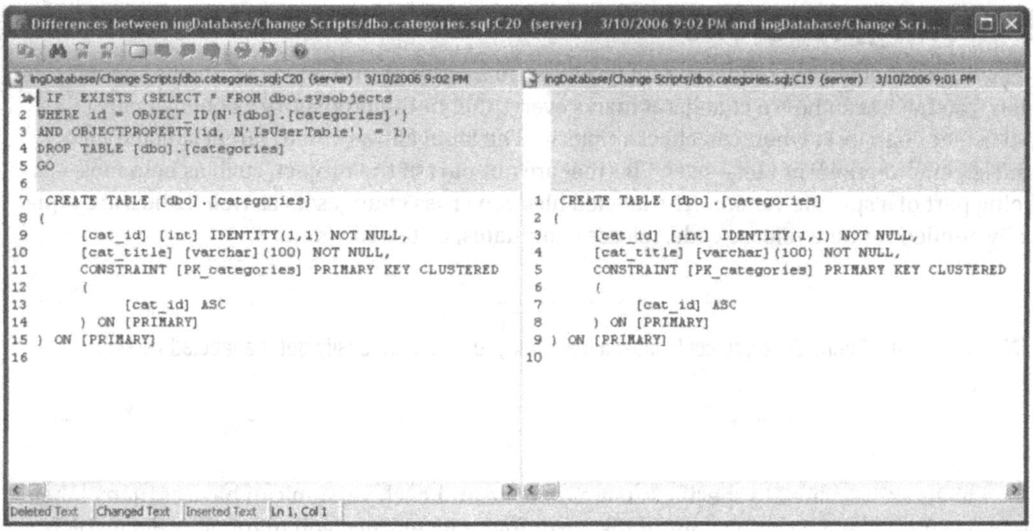

Figure 3-14. *Differences dialog box*

Tip To see how this works, close this window and close the changeset window. In the History window, select both changesets, right-click, and select Compare. You will see the exists clause as green text in the latest version.

The various options going across the top are Copy, Find, Find Next, Find Previous, Toggle Bookmark, Next Bookmark, Previous Bookmark, Clear All Bookmarks, Next Change, and Previous Change.

Note Bookmarks are not persisted between comparisons. Once you close the Differences dialog box, all of your bookmarks are cleared.

You may also compare different versions by selecting both of the versions to compare in the History window, or you can compare any version to the latest version by right-clicking the file in the History window and selecting Compare.

In the "Configuring Version Control" section you will see how to change the tools used to do comparisons and merges in case you want to use your own tools.

Labeling Versions

Applying a label to a set of files or folders gives you a more granular way to mark a specific version. You have seen how a changeset marks everything in the repository as being a part of a particular changeset when you check things in. The label allows you to target specific files and specific versions of files—even files that are not part of the project, such as help files—as being part of a specific version. The labeled files can cross changesets as well. Labels are typically applied for beta release code, release candidates, or tested versions.

Note In Visual SourceSafe you could label a build but you could not easily get the labeled version afterward.

Labels are attached to specific versions of a file and each version can have as many labels as you want. Labeling can be done at the file or folder level since you manually select which files and folders, from which changesets, you would like to add. To label a version, do the following:

1. Right-click the Effort Tracking Solution in the Source Control Explorer and select Apply Label. The Choose Item Version dialog box is displayed (Figure 3-15).

Figure 3-15. *The Choose Item Version dialog box*

2. Click OK and the Apply Label dialog is displayed (Figure 3-16).

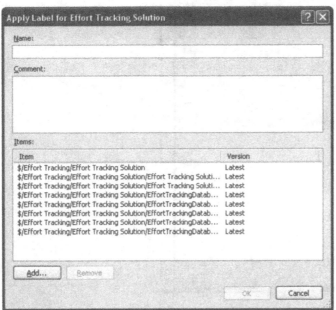

Figure 3-16. *Apply Label dialog box*

3. Enter the label "First Label" in the Name box.

4. Click OK and the label is applied.

A label can also be applied via the File ➤ Source Control ➤ Label ➤ Apply Label menu item (Source Control Explorer must be open and a node or item selected).

Now that the version is labeled you can retrieve it at a later date, delete the label, or add additional files to the label. The easiest way to work with labels is via the File ➤ Source Control ➤ Label ➤ Find Label menu item (SCE must be open and active in the IDE). Selecting this brings up the Find Label dialog box (Figure 3-17).

From this dialog box you can search for a specific label by name, project, or owner. Clicking Find displays all of the labels that match your criteria. Once you select a label you can either edit it (which allows you to add or remove items from the label) or delete it. You may also create new labels from this dialog box.

■**Note** When you delete a label, only the label is deleted, not the versions attached to it.

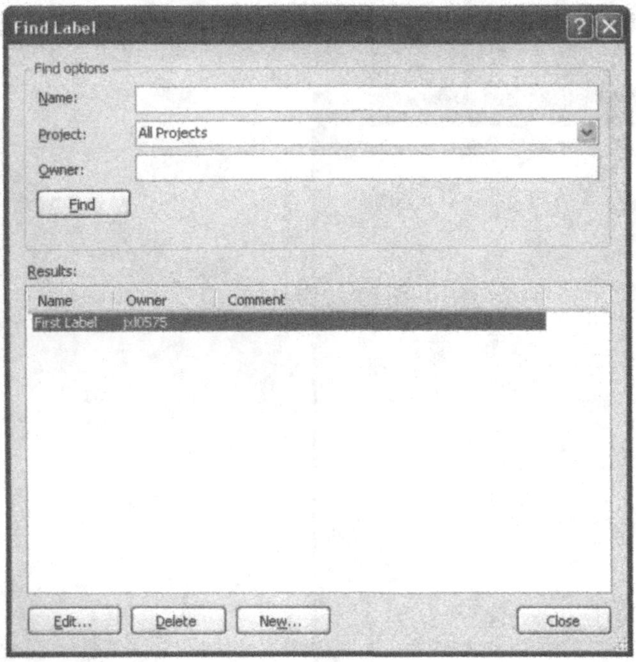

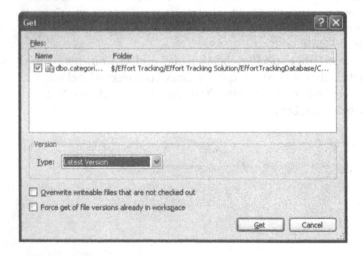

Figure 3-17. *Find Label dialog box*

Retrieving Versions

There are many ways to retrieve versions in TFVC. The Get Latest Version option (available in several locations—SCE, Solution Explorer, File ➤ Source Control, the History window, or the Changeset dialog box) always retrieves the latest checked-in version from the server. The Get Specific version displays the dialog box shown in Figure 3-18.

Figure 3-18. *Get dialog box*

The item(s) selected when you click Get Latest Version are displayed in this dialog box. If a folder is selected, the Get operation is a recursive operation—all files within the folder that match the specified version will be retrieved. The Version Type drop-down lets you choose the version based on the following items:

- *Changeset*: Specifies a specific changeset (see Figure 3-19).

- *Date*: Specifies a date/time.

- *Label*: Specifies a specific label.

- *Latest Version*: Nothing to specify.

- *Workspace Version*: Specifies files that match a user's workspace. This is useful if you need to duplicate another user's workspace.

To locate a specific changeset (or the files in a specific changeset) you can use the Find Changesets dialog box (Figure 3-19).

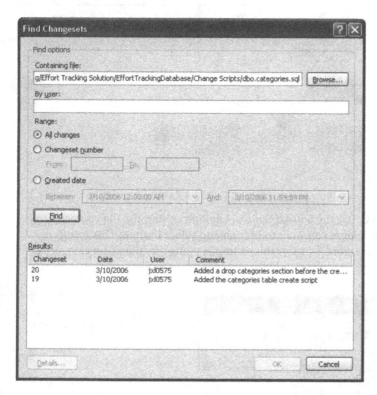

Figure 3-19. *Find Changesets dialog box*

For this dialog box you can specify two options: the file contained in the changeset, and who created the changeset. You can search all of the changesets or just a specific range—either by number or by the date they were created.

Branching

Now that you have seen the basics of working with the version control tool, it is time to move on to cover more complex scenarios.

Branching is the act of splitting files into separate development paths—it is also known as *forking*. Typically code is branched for one of two reasons: there has been a software release (usually on a commercial product) and it needs to be supported while updated versions are developed; or a developer needs to experiment with a different way of writing code or with new techniques but does not want to contaminate the base code, which may cause production problems. In the latter case, assuming the experimentation works out, the branched code is almost always merged back in with the main code and with any changes made up to that point by the maintenance team. See Figure 3-20.

Note Shelving can be used to accomplish the same thing. Shelving is covered later in this chapter.

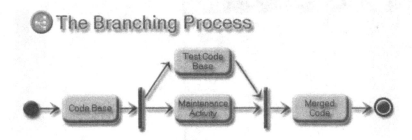

Figure 3-20. *Branched code flow*

To branch code using TFVC, use the Source Control Explorer to find the file you want to branch. Right-click the files or folders you want to branch and select Branch. This brings up the Branch dialog box shown in Figure 3-21 (for this example, continue to use the categories sql file).

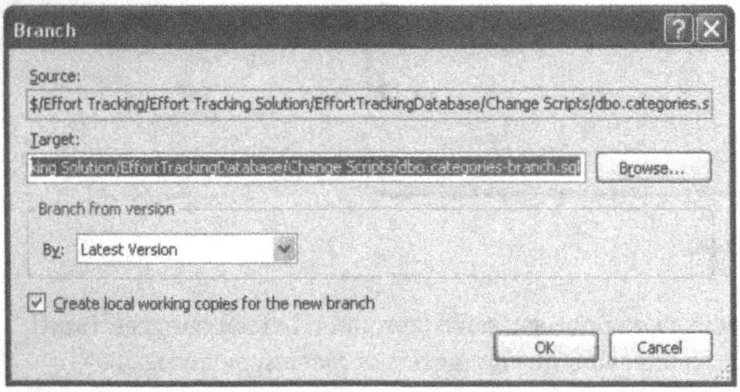

Figure 3-21. *Branch dialog box*

This dialog box indicates that a single file was selected to be branched. The branched file, by default, has a target name of the filename + "-branch." This will become the name of the file in your local workspace so it does not conflict with the original file. The branch-from version can be based on the changeset, the date, the latest version, the workspace version, or a specific label. The result of a branch is shown in Figure 3-22.

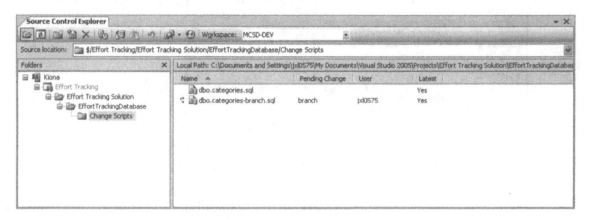

Figure 3-22. *Branch results*

A new file (the branched file) is created and added to the source code control. At this point you can add the branched file to another project and work on it as normal (or add it to the same project if you want).

■**Tip** If you are branching a file or a project but not editing it, you can uncheck the "Create local working copies for the new branch" option (see Figure 3-21). This creates a new branch on the server but does not retrieve the branched version, which can save a lot of time, depending on the number of files involved.

To see how this works, right-click the Change Scripts folder in the Solution Explorer and select Add Existing Item. Select the dbo.categories-branch.sql file and click OK. Add a comment to the top of the branched file (any comment will do—a double dash (--) followed by any text). Check in the change. When you have reached the point that the branched file (or folder) and main file (or folder) are ready to be merged back into each other, right-click the main or the branched file (or folder) in TFVC and select Merge.

VSTS knows the original file that you branched from (this can be seen by right-clicking either file and selecting Properties and then selecting the Branches tab) and displays the Source Control Merge Wizard dialog box (shown in Figure 3-23).

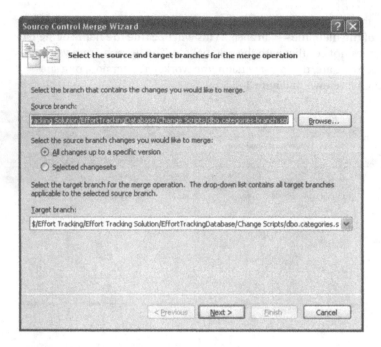

Figure 3-23. *Source Control Merge Wizard*

The source branch is the code that has been changed that you want to merge with the original code. Selecting "All changes up to a specific version" gives you the option of selecting a version in the main version control path to merge with. Selecting "Selected changesets" allows you to select a specific changeset. By default, the merge process tries to perform an automated merge that merges the two versions if the areas of change do not cause any conflict. If a conflict is detected (this scenario is covered in the "Merging Files" section later in this chapter), you will have to resolve the conflicts manually.

At this point you can delete the branched file (note that it will still be a part of that particular changeset so you can always get back to it).

Shelvesets

Frequently, when developers are working on changes, another change will be required that has a higher priority. Usually a developer stops work on the changes he or she is working on and begins working on the new change. The problem with this is that it leaves the code in an unstable state. The shelveset solves that problem for you. The process of shelving a change, or a set of changes, allows you to store pending changes under source control without creating a branch and to revert your workspace to a known, stable version of the code base. The high-priority change can then be performed, and after it is checked in, the editing on the shelved changes can continue. Figure 3-24 shows a typical process flow for how this might work.

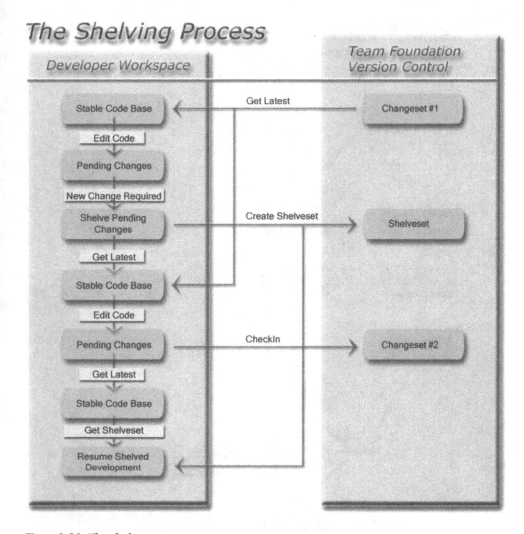

Figure 3-24. *The shelveset process*

Shelvesets exist in TFVC but are unversioned. They can also be deleted, whereas a changeset cannot be deleted. Another common scenario is that you can share your code with other developers without contaminating the code base (for example, if you are experimenting and want to get help with code from another developer).

Merging Files

Merging is the process of taking multiple changes in a file and combining them into the original file. You saw a small example of this in the "Branching" section of this chapter. This situation can arise in branching, shelveset, or multiple check-out scenarios. Figure 3-25 depicts a multiple check-out scenario.

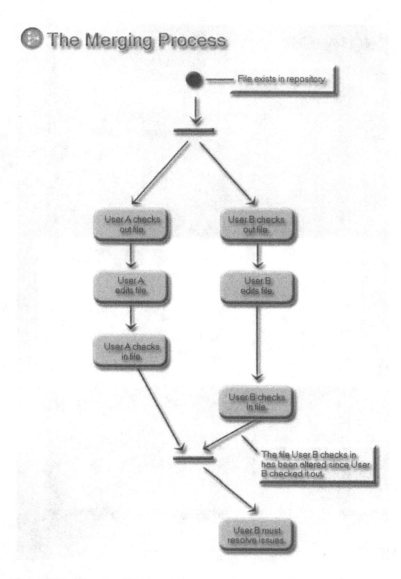

Figure 3-25. *Merging files scenario*

This behavior can typically be avoided on small development teams by just not allowing multiple check-outs (see the "Configuring Version Control" section). It also does not usually occur when code is structured very tightly (i.e., it is highly object-oriented and only one person is working on one particular piece of functionality).

In the scenario in Figure 3-25, the first thing User B would see during check-in is the dialog box shown in Figure 3-26.

Note If User B looks in the Source Control Explorer, he or she would notice that the latest version (the root-level folder would be grayed out and No would be listed under Latest next to the file) is no longer there.

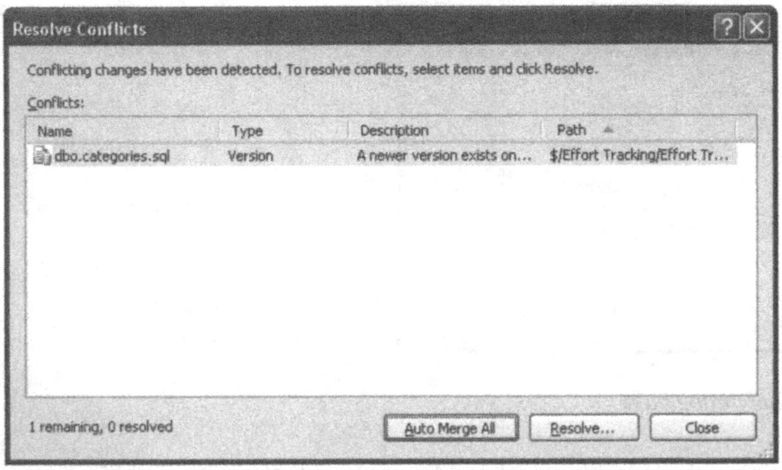

Figure 3-26. *Resolve Conflicts dialog box*

Note To see this dialog box, so you can see how it works for you, you can do the following: Have two users set up for a project. Log on as one user and make a change to the file. Log off and then log on as the other user, make a change, and check in the file. Then log off and log on as the original user. Try to check in the changes.

This dialog box describes any conflicts that exist with a given file. It can be shown for several reasons, which include problems with invalid mappings between the repository and the working folder of the workspace. In that case, the dialog box is telling User B that a newer version of the file exists on the server.

Tip The Auto Merge All option attempts to figure out what to keep from each file without user intervention. In general, it works very well if edits have not been made to the same section of code. If such edits have been made, using the Resolve option to perform a manual merge is the only way to merge files.

Selecting the Resolve option brings up the Resolve Conflict dialog box shown in Figure 3-27.

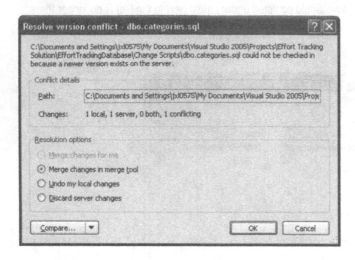

Figure 3-27. *Resolve Conflict dialog box*

Path shows the location of the local file, which is different from that on the server. Changes indicates how many changes are different in each file and how many are conflicting. Resolution options are described in Table 3-3.

Table 3-3. *Resolution Options*

Option	Description
Merge changes for me	Attempts to merge the files automatically. Same as the Auto Merge option.
Merge changes in merge tool	Allows the developer to manually work through the files to choose the correct lines to merge.
Undo my local changes	Discards the local changes, does not check in the file, retrieves the server version to the local workspace.
Discard server changes	Overwrites the changes on the server with the changes from the local file.

The Compare option allows you to view the differences between the local version and the server version or the original version of the file that was checked out. When you select OK, the Merge Tool shown in Figure 3-28 is displayed.

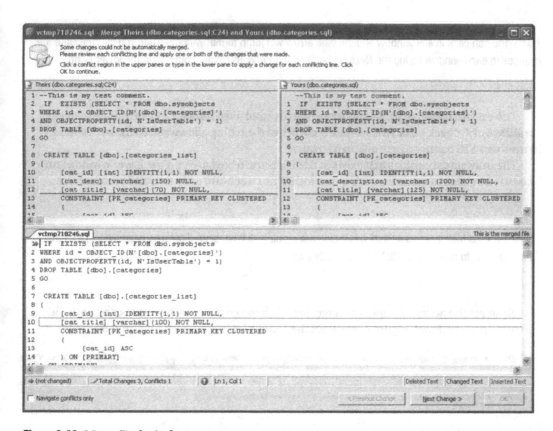

Figure 3-28. *Merge Tool window*

There are a number of important pieces of information available to you in this window. The first piece of information is in the title bar. Theirs (dbo.categories.sql;C24) indicates the file on the server that the local file is attempting to be merged with and the changeset that the file exists in. The two windows at the top of the dialog box are the two different versions of the file. The server version of the file is located on the left and the local version on the right. Changes are noted by the lines in colors (the legend is in the lower right of the window). In Figure 3-28, three lines were changed in the server version, two lines were changed on the local version, and one line was deleted from the local version. The lower window shows you what the final merged file will look like.

So, what is the merge tool telling you? First, looking at the bottom left of the window you can see that there are three changes in total, and one conflict. The blue arrow in the lower window is pointing at the first change in the file.

■**Tip** You can click in any window and the blue arrow will jump to that window. Then you can navigate the changes in each window (using the Next Change and the Previous Change buttons in the lower right).

The exclamation mark tells you there is an unresolved conflict. Checking the "Navigate conflicts only" check box in the lower left corner of the dialog allows you to move between items that VSTS cannot figure out on its own.

The only actual conflict that exists in the file is the boxed area (in the lower window) on line 10. The changes made in one file or another, but not both, are resolved automatically.

■**Note** If Auto Merge was selected, this dialog box would still have been displayed because VSTS cannot figure out how to merge a conflict like this on its own.

To select the actual changes to merge, just click the correct row from either or both files (in the upper windows). Figure 3-29 shows the result of selecting each line from each file.

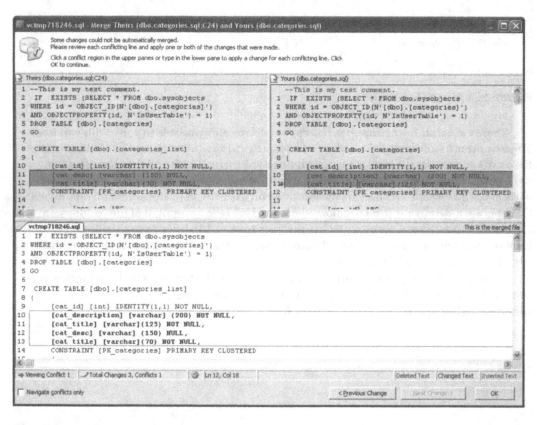

Figure 3-29. *Merge Tool with code lines selected*

The lines of code are added bottom to top. So if the conflict on line 11 from the server file is selected (as shown in Figure 3-29) and then the conflict on line 11 from the local file is selected, the resulting merge file would be as shown, at the bottom of the merge dialog box. Obviously, this is not the desired solution. You can unselect a change from one of the files and click OK. After OK is selected the files are merged and saved in the repository.

Configuring Version Control

Now that you have seen how to use Team Foundation Version Control, you will see how to configure it and what your options are. TFVC is configured on a per-team-project basis (although there are some options that are specific to the IDE and not a team project).

There is one option that is specific to the server and spans all team projects—file types. To see the file types supported by the server, right-click the server name in the Team Explorer and select Team Foundation Server Settings ➤ Source Control File Types. This displays the dialog box in Figure 3-30.

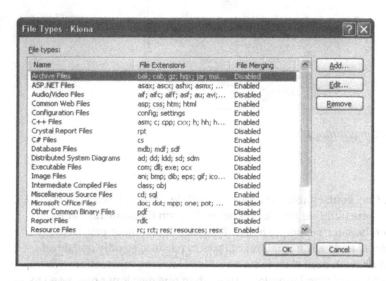

Figure 3-30. *File Types dialog box*

This dialog box allows you to specify a couple of options related to how specific types are supported on a global basis. You can edit any of the values or add new file types. The purpose of this dialog box is to configure file merging and check-out options. If File Merging is enabled, then the file type is supported by multiple check-outs as well. The other information is just classification information and has no effect on the file.

Configuring Project Settings

To configure a team project, right-click the project in Team Explorer and select Team Project Settings ➤ Source Control. There are three different categories of options you can set: Checkout Settings, Checkin Policy, and Checkin Notes (Figure 3-31).

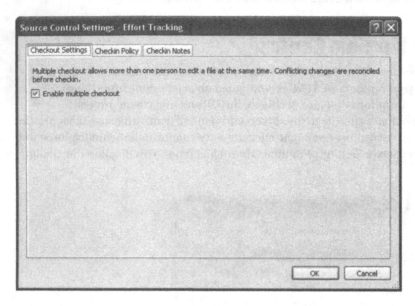

Figure 3-31. *Source Control Settings dialog box*

Checkout Settings

There is only one option for Checkout: enable (or disable) multiple checkout. Multiple checkout is designed for projects where multiple people will be working on the same files at the same time (but hopefully not the same section of a file). Typically, in an object-oriented design, objects are encapsulated and have a small set of tasks to perform so only one developer is working on a given class (with each class in its own file). However, in situations where there are very large classes with specialized functions, more than one developer may need to work on the code at the same time. To facilitate this you can enable multiple checkout. When multiple checkout is disabled, only one person at a time can check the file out. Other developers can perform a Get on the file, but they cannot check it out for editing.

Checkin Policy

Policies allow you to control when a file can get checked in by ensuring that the file, or the build in the developers' workspace, meets certain criteria.

■**Tip** Policies are good if everyone follows them. But there are always ways to get around checks like this, so a rigorous process on top of this is a good idea.

To create a new policy, switch to the Checkin Policy tab and select Add. This brings up the Add Check-in Policy dialog box shown in Figure 3-32.

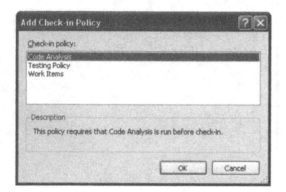

Figure 3-32. *Add Check-in Policy dialog box*

There are three basic policies which you can customize based on the needs of the project. You can also create custom policies.

■**Caution** It is critical to note that any policy can be overridden, but it is a bad practice and should not be done. However, if you do override a policy to check in code, everyone will know about it and you will have to provide an explanation.

Creating custom check-in policies is covered toward the end of the chapter.

Code Analysis

Selecting the code analysis policy brings up the Code Analysis Policy Editor shown in Figure 3-33.

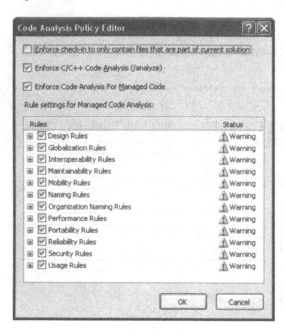

Figure 3-33. *Code Analysis Policy Editor*

Code analysis is discussed in detail in Chapter 13. For now, you should understand that you can enforce conformance to a set of design standards. The standards that come with VSTS out of the box are the standards Microsoft uses in .NET Framework and Visual Studio. You can select all or just a subset of code analysis warnings to enforce.

Note C/C++ code analysis engages a separate code analysis tool for unmanaged code. This is covered in Chapter 13.

Testing Policy

This policy ensures that the code to be checked in has passed a given set of tests. These tests are not tests created on the local machine. They are loaded from a test meta data file (.vsmdi) located in TFVC. This prevents a developer from writing any test that will work in order to get the code checked in. It also ensures that the checked-in code will work as advertised before it is checked in.

When you select this option, you will be able to browse to a specific .vsmdi file and will be given a list of tests that exist for the current project. You can then select the specific lists you want to ensure are run before code is checked in.

Tip You cannot specify individual tests, only specific lists of tests. This is a best practice because it allows a project to ensure that certain basic standards are met (for example, can whatever code you write integrate with the security system, or something along those lines?).

You can also add additional tests to the list(s) without having to change the policy. Keeping a base set of mandatory test lists is a good idea.

Work Items Policy

The work items policy says you must associate a work item with the code you are checking in. Work items are discussed in detail in Chapter 4. For the moment it is enough to understand that you can associate specific pieces of work with specific tasks. For example, if a project manager assigns you a bug to work on, you will check out the code necessary to fix the bug. When the bug is fixed you will check the code back in. By requiring that you associate checked-in items with a work item, the status of bugs and other assignments can be reported and tracked at the project-management level.

Check-in Notes

This setting allows you to specify who must review the changes before they are checked in. The default values are Code Reviewer, Security Reviewer, and Performance Reviewer. These are user-defined values and you can enter your own titles, such as Developer Lead or some other value. None of these reviews are required by default but checking the Required check box will make them required.

Caution As mentioned earlier, there are ways around the check-in settings. In the case of the reviewers, all a developer has to do is type anything into the entry field when they go to check in a file and it will be accepted. This is one of those areas to watch out for.

IDE Version Control Configuration

Certain settings are available in the IDE and support a specific developer's needs when working with version control. To access the IDE configuration, select Tools ➤ Options, and select Source Control from the tree view (Figure 3-34).

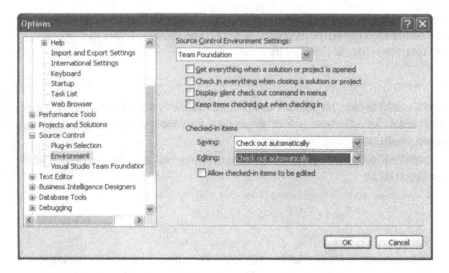

Figure 3-34. *Environment Options*

Plugin Selection

This displays the list of available source control providers. For example, a typical installation of VSTS might have Visual Studio Team Foundation Server, Microsoft Visual SourceSafe, and Microsoft Visual SourceSafe (Internet). There are also other plugins available from other vendors. If you have any problems with TFVC (for example, everything is grayed out and you have no menu options for dealing with version control), then it is a good bet that the wrong source control provider has been selected.

Environment

This allows you to specify how the IDE will react to given situations. Figure 3-34 shows the various options you can set.

For dealing with checked-in items, you have the following options when performing a save: check out the file automatically; prompt for check-out; or perform a Save As. For files you are editing: check out automatically (when you start editing); prompt for check-out; prompt for exclusive check-out; or do nothing. If you choose the last option you will not be able to edit the file at all unless you check "Allow checked-in items to be edited."

Visual Studio Team Foundation

These options deal with how your local system will interact with the Team Foundation Server. The first option is whether to use the Team Foundation Proxy Server (TFPS). TFPS was built to facilitate remote access to the Team Foundation Version Control. Often the Internet is less than reliable—there are outages or there are a large number of files involved. TFPS is installed on a server in a remote location. When you use TFPS, the first check for a file is made on the proxy server. If the file is found, it is downloaded from the cache. If it is not found it is downloaded from the central repository. The proxy server ensures that files are kept in a consistent state (i.e., you cannot do a Get Latest, and it retrieves the latest version of the proxy server, which is actually two versions behind the central server). This can help ease the burden of slow connections on remote teams.

Tip For more information on setting up a Team Foundation Proxy Server, see the Team Foundation Installation Guide.

You also have the option to show deleted items in SCE. This will show the item grayed out and noted as deleted. By default this is off.

Finally, there is a Configure User Tools section. This allows you to specify your own tools (as opposed to the default tools provided for you by VSTS). It allows you to specify your own Merge or Compare tools. For example, Diff Doc is a popular (and free) tool for comparing Microsoft Word documents. Figure 3-35 shows the settings for DiffDoc.exe.

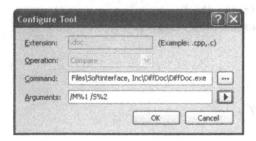

Figure 3-35. *Diff Doc tool settings*

The arguments for various tools can be somewhat confusing and difficult to configure. James Manning at Microsoft has an excellent blog describing how to configure different tools at http://blogs.msdn.com/jmanning/articles/535573.aspx.

Creating Custom Check-in Policies

Custom check-in policies allow you to specify your own constraints, which must be met before items can be checked in. Creating a check-in policy is fairly straightforward. The example presented here was originally written by Jeff Atwood of Vertigo Software (you can check out his blog at http://blogs.vertigosoftware.com/jatwood/default.aspx) and was helped along by James Manning.

Creating the Policy

This example requires that a user enter a comment before checking code in. All in all this is probably the most useful check-in policy ever, as we are notorious for *not* entering comments! Listing 3-3 shows the code for the empty comment check-in policy.

Listing 3-3. *Required Comment Check-in Policy*

```csharp
[C#]
using System;
using System.Windows.Forms;
using Microsoft.TeamFoundation.VersionControl.Client;
[Serializable]
public class CheckForCommentsPolicy : PolicyBase
{
    public override string Description
    {
        get { return "Remind users to add meaningful comments "
                    + "to their checkins"; }
    }

    public override string InstallationInstructions
    {
        get { return "To install this policy, follow the "
                    + "instructions in CheckForCommentsPolicy.cs."; }
    }

    public override string Type
    {
        get { return "Check for Comments Policy"; }
    }

    public override string TypeDescription
    {
        get { return "This policy will prompt the user to decide whether or not "
                    + "they should be allowed to check in."; }
    }

    public override bool Edit(IPolicyEditArgs args)
    {
        // no configuration to save
        return true;
    }

    public override PolicyFailure[] Evaluate()
    {
        string proposedComment = PendingCheckin.PendingChanges.Comment;
        if (String.IsNullOrEmpty(proposedComment))
        {
            return new PolicyFailure[] {
                new PolicyFailure("Please provide some comments "
                        + "about your checkin", this) };
```

```
        }
        else
        {
            return new PolicyFailure[0];
        }
    }

    public override void Activate(PolicyFailure failure)
    {
        MessageBox.Show("Please provide comments for your checkin.",
                        "How to fix your policy failure");
    }

    public override void DisplayHelp(PolicyFailure failure)
    {
        MessageBox.Show("This policy helps you to remember to "
          + "add comments to your checkins.", "Prompt Policy Help");
    }
}
[VB]
Imports System
Imports System.Windows.Forms
Imports Microsoft.TeamFoundation.VersionControl.Client

<Serializable()> _
Public Class CheckForCommentsPolicy
    Inherits PolicyBase

    Public Overrides ReadOnly Property Description() As String
        Get
            Return "Remind users to add meaningful comments " _
                    & "to their checkins"
        End Get
    End Property

    Public Overrides Property InstallationInstructions() As String
        Get
            Return "To install this policy, follow the " _
                & "instructions in CheckForCommentsPolicyVB.vb."
        End Get
        Set(ByVal value As String)
            MyBase.InstallationInstructions = value
        End Set
    End Property
```

```vb
    Public Overrides ReadOnly Property Type() As String
        Get
            Return "Check for Comments Policy"
        End Get
    End Property

    Public Overrides ReadOnly Property TypeDescription() As String
        Get
            Return "This policy will prompt the user to " _
                & "decide whether or not they should be " _
                & "allowed to check in."
        End Get
    End Property

    Public Overrides Function Edit(ByVal args As IPolicyEditArgs) As Boolean
        ' no configuration to save
        Return True
    End Function

    Public Overrides Function Evaluate() As _
Microsoft.TeamFoundation.VersionControl.Client.PolicyFailure()
        Dim proposedComment As String = PendingCheckin.PendingChanges.Comment
        If String.IsNullOrEmpty(proposedComment) Then
            Dim msg As String = "Please provide some comments " _
                & "about your checkin"
            Dim p As PolicyFailure() = New PolicyFailure(1) {}
            p(0) = New PolicyFailure(msg, Me)
            Return p
        Else
            Return New PolicyFailure(0) {}
        End If
    End Function

    Public Overrides Sub Activate(ByVal failure As PolicyFailure)
        MessageBox.Show("Please provide comments for your checkin.", _
                        "How to fix your policy failure")
    End Sub

    Public Overrides Sub DisplayHelp(ByVal failure As PolicyFailure)
        MessageBox.Show("This policy helps you to remember to " _
            & "add comments to your checkins.", "Prompt Policy Help")
    End Sub

End Class
```

Now, what does all of this mean? Table 3-4 describes each custom policy method.

Table 3-4. *Custom Policy Methods Described*

Method	Description
Description	This provides a description of the policy.
InstallationInstruction	The return value of this method is stored on the Team Foundation Server and is displayed when a user does not have the policy installed. As a best practice, a policy should be installed on the local machine that needs the policy. In version 1 of VSTS, partially trusted code is not allowed to be executed. That means that to install the policy in a remote location requires that full trust is enabled for code running on a remote system, which is not recommended.
Type	This describes the type of policy.
TypeDescription	This gives a more detailed identification of the type.
Edit	This method displays a UI and saves the configuration of your type if your custom check-in policy contains configuration options (such as the Testing Policy).
Evaluate	This validates that what you are checking in passes the policy check.
Activate	This method displays information to the user when they double-click an item on the Policy Failure page to explain why a policy failed (or whatever other information you want to present to the user).
DisplayHelp	This can be used to display a custom help file or link to a web page or to just display a simple message. It is invoked when the user presses the F1 key and the policy is selected on the Policy Failure page.

Registering the Policy

Creating the policy is the first part of the process. Once you create it, you have to install it.

■**Caution** Microsoft recommends that policies be installed on the local machine. If this is not done, you will have to allow full trust of assemblies residing on remote machines, which, in general, is not a secure practice.

To install the policy, copy the assembly to your local machine (preferably, all assemblies that need to be downloaded to a developer's machine should be stored on a secure network share). Make the following entries in the registry:

Key: HKLM\Software\Microsoft\VisualStudio\8.0\TeamFoundation\SourceControl\ Checkin Policies or HKCU\Software\Microsoft\VisualStudio\8.0\TeamFoundation\ SourceControl\Checkin Policies

Type: Reg_sz

Name: Policy Class (in this example, Check for Comments Policy)

Data: Absolute path to the assembly

Alternatively, you can (and probably should) configure a .reg file, the contents of which are shown in Listing 3-4.

Listing 3-4. *Registration File*

```
Windows Registry Editor Version 5.00

[HKEY_LOCAL_MACHINE\SOFTWARE\Microsoft\VisualStudio\8.0\
    TeamFoundation\SourceControl\Checkin Policies]
"CheckForCommentsPolicy"="[Full Path to File]\\CheckForCommentsPolicy.dll"
```

After you run this file (simply double-click on it and you will be prompted to make the change to the registry), the Check for Comments Policy will be displayed in the list of available policies (Figure 3-36).

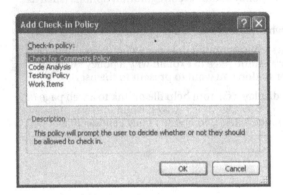

Figure 3-36. *Custom check-in policy*

With this example in hand, you should be able to create any type of policies you or your organization feel are necessary.

Converting from Visual SourceSafe to Team Foundation Version Control

Needless to say, this is a welcome conversion tool. In addition to this, you can migrate from Rational ClearQuest. The process of migration is an extensive process that needs to be carefully planned. We have not included this process here, since Microsoft has done a very thorough job of explaining it in the MSDN documentation. We just wanted to let you know that you could do it!

Command-Line Access

Team Foundation Version Control allows you to perform all of the operations you normally would through Visual Studio via the command line. This powerful feature means you can easily incorporate version control actions within batch files.

■**Tip** Microsoft provides excellent documentation on the version control command-line tool (tf.exe) in its MSDN documentation. The broad overview of topics covered will give you a solid introduction to using the tool.

The command-line application is tf.exe. It resides in the C:\Program Files\Microsoft Visual Studio 8\Common 7\IDE folder. You can use this tool to perform individual commands at the command prompt or to process scripted files that contain version control commands. The best use of the command-line tool is with scripted files. When used with a scripted file, the command-line tool can accept any number of arguments that can be referenced in the scripted file by using %1, %2, …, %n where the number refers to the argument number on the command line. To invoke a script file, use the following syntax:

```
tf.exe @filename.tfc arguments
```

You can also change directories and include comments in the script files. The available commands are grouped into two categories: informational and action. Each of these commands has various options that allow you to control which objects they are applied to. They are fairly self-explanatory and are described in detail in the MSDN documentation.

Informational commands allow data concerning various items under version control to be retrieved.

- *Branches*: Lists the branch history of a file or a folder.

- *Changeset*: Lists information regarding changesets.

- *Difference*: Compares and displays (depending on the mode used) differences between two files or folders.

- *Dir*: Lists files and folders in a given directory.

- *Labels*: Lists all labels in the repository.

- *Permission*: Lists users and groups along with their permissions.

- *Properties*: Lists information about a given file or folder.

- *Shelvesets*: Lists information about shelved changes.

- *Status*: Lists information concerning pending changes.

- *WorkFold*: Creates, modifies, or lists mappings between repository folders and the corresponding work folders.

- *Workspaces*: Lists information about workspaces in the repository.

Action commands, listed below, allow you to perform various actions on those items under source code control.

- Add
- Branch
- Branches
- Checkin
- Checkout
- Configure
- Delete
- Dir
- Get
- History
- Label
- Lock
- Merge

- Merges
- Permission
- Properties
- Rename
- Resolve
- Shelve
- Status
- Undelete
- Undo
- Unlabel
- Unshelve
- View
- Workspace

Summary

At this point you now have extensive knowledge about using the new Team Foundation Version Control. You know how to create repositories, check items in, check them out, alter them, resolve conflicts, and merge them. You have been introduced to the concepts of shelving and branching, which ensure that you never have to worry about a hard-drive crash causing you to lose work (but it is not our fault if you forget to actually add the code to the repository!).

You can also configure check-in policies, which in our opinion is one of the best features of TFVC. And you have the ability to create your own check-in policies that fit your organization's specific needs. The ability to supply your own merge and compare tools to replace the out-of-the-box versions that come with Team Foundation will no doubt be a welcome option to many developers. And you have seen how the Team Foundation Proxy Server helps support distributed teams by caching versions of files on a local network; this should ease the burden when projects are outsourced around the globe.

Chapter 4 gives you the ins and outs of project management and VSTS integration. You will learn how to use Microsoft Project and Excel to create schedules, assign work, and track issues without using Visual Studio or Team Explorer.

CHAPTER 4

■■■

Project Management

Neither of the authors has ever been a project manager. We have had the luxury of leading teams from a technical perspective and have left the high-profile leadership to others. Project management is, to say the least, a thankless job at times. We have worked with numerous project managers and have seen the problems they face. These problems range from getting developers to track their time against work items, to explaining to the customer why the project is not going as smoothly as the customer imagines it will go. There are many more problems in between that the project manager has to deal with.

At the base of the project manager's job is creating schedules, recording data, and reporting data. This is where Visual Studio Team System plays a role in simplifying the project manager's role. The tools in VSTS that relate to project management help bring together tasks performed by Microsoft Project (or Excel), work item tracking, and the Project Portal. VSTS allows the project manager to create schedules in Microsoft Project (these schedules include the work items for the team members), add work items from Microsoft Excel (or Project), track changes to work items via the project schedule, and publish updates to the Project Portal. No longer do team members have to report status to the project manager—the project manager can just pull the data.

■Note Okay, let us face facts. Team members (and you know who you are) do not report anything to the project manager. It's like pulling teeth. So, in this case, project managers no longer have to pester team members to report what they are working on.

The heart of this system is the work item tracking system and the version control system. They work together to supply the information the project manager needs to provide accurate information in a timely fashion to the appropriate people—the people who ultimately continue to fund the development of a project.

In this chapter you will see how the integration with MS Project works, and how to add work items, update work items, and refresh work items using both Microsoft Project and Microsoft Excel. We discuss work items in great detail in Chapter 5.

A Week in the Life of a Project Manager (without VSTS)

Before showing you how to use VSTS to manage projects, let's take a look at what project managers actually do by looking at the starting week of a new project.

Day 1, Monday

The project manager, whom we'll call John, sets up Microsoft Project with all of the resources available at the time (typically, the system architect and/or the application architect, and possibly a lead developer and tester). John creates the basic outline of the project (system development life cycle phases and high-level deliverables) and assigns some deliverables to the available resources. In real life this usually takes more than a day but in this case John is very fast.

Day 2, Tuesday

John creates Excel spreadsheets for each member of the project team. He transfers the tasks they are responsible for from Microsoft Project to each of the spreadsheets (if John is really technical, he has written or has used a previously created macro to do this automatically). John has to do this at the beginning or end of every week for the following week for each member of the team. This becomes more tedious as more resources are added.

Day 3, Wednesday

Now the project manager has to set up a communication plan with the stakeholders. John has to find out what the stakeholders want to know and when they want to know it. He needs to figure out how to configure a change management system (i.e., create the process for the system and integrate it with the tools—usually Excel spreadsheets and e-mails). This is sometimes exceedingly difficult because different classes of stakeholders want to know different things.

Day 4, Thursday

On the fourth day of the week, the project manager has to set up shares, folders, etc., for the project team to store their files (user requirements, owner specifications, architecture documents, etc.). He then has to publicize and document the structure so the location of all of the deliverables and related documents is known.

Day 5, Friday

The end of the first week. Whew. John is almost done. Now he just needs to find out what everyone did for the week so he can report their status to the stakeholders and find out what is left to do for each deliverable assigned to the various project team members. The only problem is that no one filled in the Excel time sheets and mailed them to John. Now he has to send e-mails and hound team members for their status. Once they send him the Excel spreadsheets (because everyone on the team is really good at doing that) he has to extract all of the numbers and update Microsoft Project with the number of hours left to complete a deliverable, or mark the deliverable as complete.

Two Days in the Life of a Project Manager (with VSTS)

Now, let's see that scenario with Visual Studio Team System's project management integration capabilities.

Day 1, Monday

The project manager creates a new team project using Visual Studio Team System (selecting the appropriate methodology template). He adds all of the resources that he knows about to the new team project. John opens Microsoft Project and adds all of the project resources to the new project file. John creates the basic outline of the project (SDLC phases and high-level deliverables) and assigns some deliverables to the available resources. In real life this usually takes more than a day, but in this case John is very fast. John updates the changes he made in Microsoft Project with the Team Foundation Server.

Day 2, Tuesday

John sends out an e-mail to the stakeholders detailing where the team project portal is and how to access the available reports. John sets the policy that changesets must be associated with work items, and then John spends the rest of the week fishing.

Okay, it is not quite that cushy for a project manager, but you get the idea. Much of the tedious work simply does not need to be done. In the rest of this chapter, you will see how this is actually accomplished.

■**Note** There is a lot more that goes into creating a project schedule than is described here. For the purposes of this chapter, only those items that are directly related to Visual Studio Team System will be discussed. The "schedule" will only consist of the items assigned when the project was created.

Using Microsoft Project

The first thing a project manager will do (after the team project is created) is create a project schedule. The project schedule consists of a series of tasks, which may also include other tasks—in other words, a hierarchical structure of tasks. They consist of start times, due dates, descriptions, and to whom the tasks are assigned.

Note Tasks are a type of work item. These terms are used interchangeably in this chapter.

To begin with, launch Microsoft Project from the Start menu (Start ➤ Programs ➤ Microsoft Office ➤ Microsoft Project). If everything is installed correctly, you will see an additional toolbar in Project (shown in Figure 4-1).

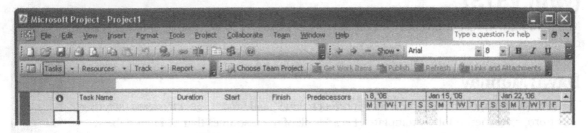

Figure 4-1. *VSTS toolbar in Microsoft Project*

As you can see, before you can create a schedule, you need to select the team project this schedule will be associated with. To do this, select Choose Team Project (also available from the Team menu on the main menu). This brings up the Connect to Team Foundation Server dialog box shown in Figure 4-2.

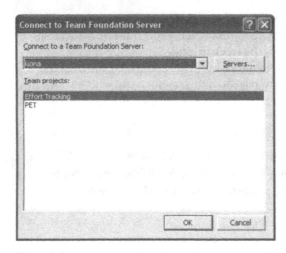

Figure 4-2. *Connect to Team Foundation Server dialog box*

Select the server where your project resides, then select the Effort Tracking project and click OK.

Tip You can also open a project from Team Explorer by selecting Server ➤ [Project Name] ➤ Project Management ➤ Development Project Plan.mpp which is associated with the project by default.

Once you have done this, the Get Work Items, Publish, and Refresh options become available to you. At this point though you still do not have any work items visible.

Retrieving, Adding, and Updating Work Items

To get the work items from the server, select Get Work Items from the toolbar. This will display the Get Work Items dialog box shown in Figure 4-3.

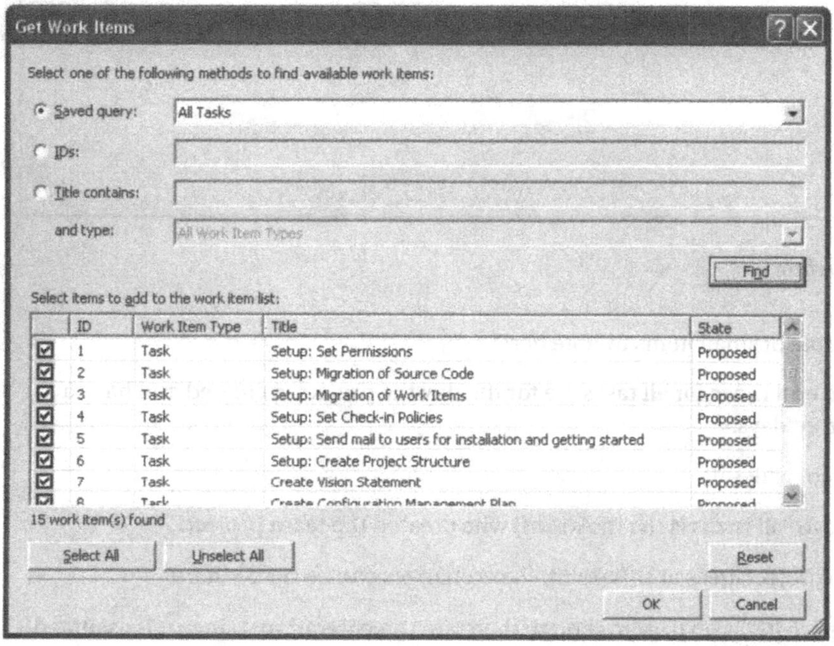

Figure 4-3. *Get Work Items dialog box*

For this exercise, select the All Tasks saved query and click Find. Note though that you can search on various items depending on what your needs are. At the beginning of a project, the All Tasks query is a good place to start, as these are the only tasks that are currently part of the project. By default, everything returned by the lookup is selected for inclusion in the project schedule. Click OK to import the items into Microsoft Project (Figure 4-4).

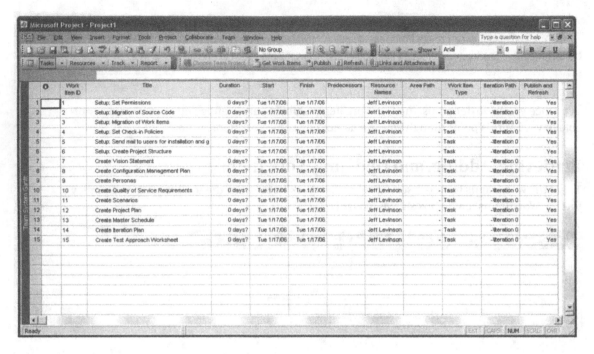

Figure 4-4. *Initial project schedule*

There are a couple of small items to note here:

- The start and end times for all tasks are for the day the project is created and have a duration of zero days.

- No predecessors are set.

- The resource for all items is the individual who created the team project.

- There are no project areas at this point, so no changes can be made there.

- All iterations are iteration 0, even though there are three iterations, since it is assumed these tasks occur at the start of the project.

At this point you can change whatever you want to change as needed. To begin with, you would probably remove any items that were not needed on your project. To delete an item, select it (item 15 is a good choice here) and press the Delete key (or right-click the item and select Delete. After you have completed making changes, you must publish the changes to the server. To publish the changes, just select the Publish button from the toolbar.

■**Tip** You can elect *not* to publish an item by selecting either No or Refresh Only from the Publish and Refresh column. Selecting No indicates that the item will never be published, and selecting Refresh Only indicates that the item will be refreshed, but no changes you make to the item will ever be published.

This updates Team Foundation Server and if you added any items will return the Work Item ID to populate the project schedule.

■**Caution** In version 1 of VSTS you cannot assign multiple resources to a single task. You have to duplicate the task and set one resource per task. The VSTS development team is actively looking at this issue. If
you try to assign multiple resources to a single task, an error message will be displayed when you publish
the changes.

The ability to publish only certain items is important. A project manager would probably *not* want to publish the roll-up tasks because those are not tasks that can be "worked," per se.

■**Tip** To assign work items to multiple resources, you must create the work item several times and assign
only one resource to each work item.

Adding Attachments and Links

In addition to adding, retrieving, and updating items, you can also attach files and links to specific work items. To attach files and links, an item must already be published. Select a published item in the list and then select Links & Attachments. This will bring up the View/Edit Work Item Links and Attachments dialog box (Figure 4-5).

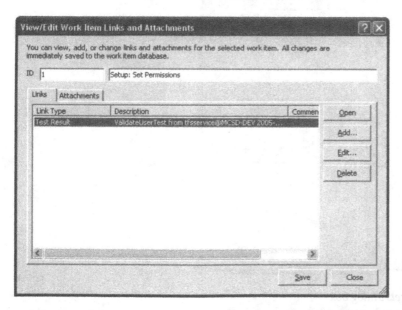

Figure 4-5. *View/Edit Work Item Links and Attachments dialog box*

A link can be one of the following: Changeset, Work Item, Versioned Item, Test Result, or a regular hyperlink. Depending on the type of link you are adding, the options are different. The Add Link dialog box is shown in Figure 4-6.

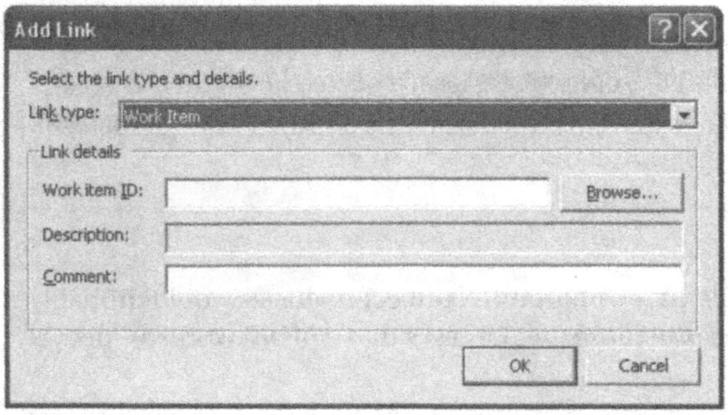

Figure 4-6. *Add Link dialog box*

The dialog in Figure 4-6 shows the options for a Work Item link type. Clicking the Browse button will display the Get Work Items dialog box shown in Figure 4-3. The Find Changesets dialog box will be displayed if you elect to link to a changeset (Figure 4-7).

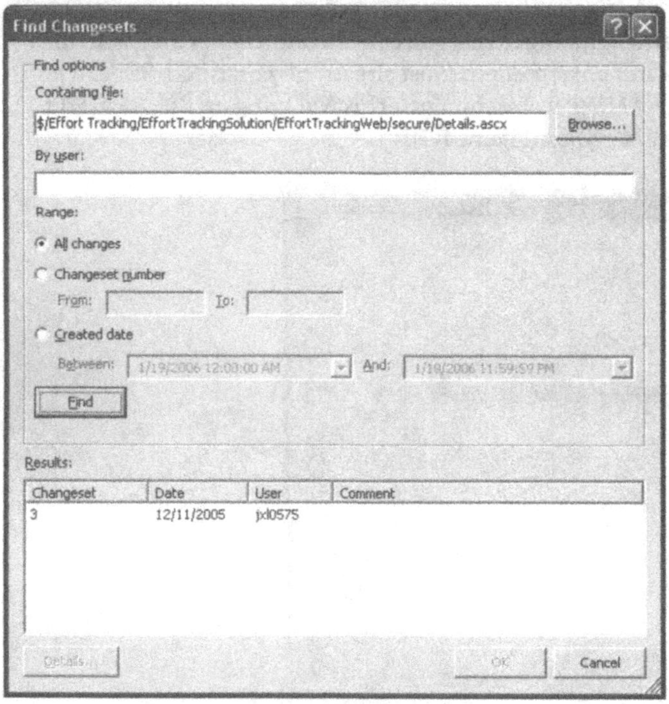

Figure 4-7. *Find Changesets dialog box*

For the Find Changesets dialog, you browse to a specific file (contained in the source code control system) or enter a specific user's name and click Find. This will return all of the changesets for either that file or that user. The Range options let you filter the result set more granularly. From there you may either view the details of the changeset or select a result to link to.

The Versioned Item option provides the same dialog, only it lets you link to the item in a specific changeset (which you can browse for) or to the latest version of the item.

Selecting the Test Result option lets you browse for a specific test result (Figure 4-8).

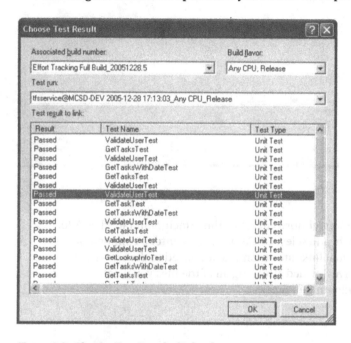

Figure 4-8. *Choose Test Result dialog box*

In this dialog box you can select the build number, the type, and a specific test run. From there you can select the specific test to link an item to. In this case, select any test that appears in the list and click OK.

All link types allow you to enter a comment against the link.

Once you have selected your links, they will be displayed in the list view in Figure 4-5. Selecting an item in the list and then clicking Open will cause various windows to open, depending on the type of link you select. With the previous example, using a test result link, clicking the Open button displays the result shown in Figure 4-9.

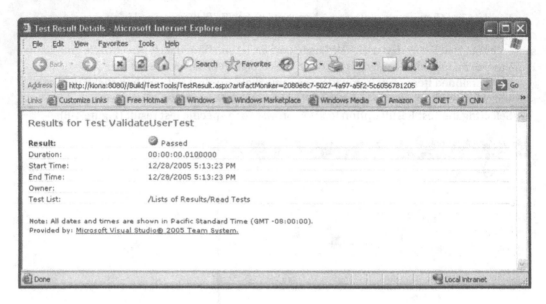

Figure 4-9. *Test Result Details link*

Adding an attachment is fairly straightforward. Click the Attachment tab, click Add, browse to the file you want to attach, and select OK. You can also enter a comment against the file. The one difference here is that links are automatically saved to the server as they are entered; files are not. When you have finished attaching all of the files you want, click the Save button. This will upload the files to the server.

Areas and Iterations

Areas and iterations can be added, deleted, and configured from within Microsoft Project, which displays the same dialogs as described in detail in Chapter 2.

Column Mapping

Finally, a project manager can view column mappings in Microsoft Project. Figure 4-10 shows a column displayed in Microsoft Project and the equivalent column in the VSTS database. You cannot actually make changes to the mapping through this dialog box. In order to make changes you will need to use the TFSFieldMapping command-line tool described next.

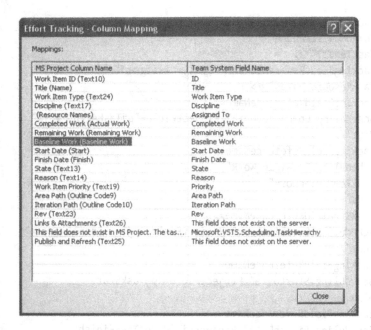

Figure 4-10. *Column Mapping dialog box*

■**Note** The work item tracking command-line tools provide the ability to add and remove columns from the TFS database in order to support custom fields. These tools are discussed in Chapter 5.

To use the TFSFieldMapping tool, open the Visual Studio Command Prompt. Before changing mappings, you need to have a copy of the mapping file. To download the mapping file, run the following at the command prompt (or replace the items with appropriate values):

```
Tfsfieldmapping download kiona "Effort Tracking" "c:\mapping.xml"
```

This will download the mapping file for your project. The file is in, as with almost every other file in VSTS, an XML format. This file is shown in Listing 4-1.

Listing 4-1. *TFS Field Mapping File*

```
<?xml version="1.0" encoding="utf-8"?>
<MSProject>
  <Mappings>
    <Mapping WorkItemTrackingFieldReferenceName="System.Id"
      ProjectField="pjTaskText10" ProjectName="Work Item ID"/>
        <Mapping WorkItemTrackingFieldReferenceName="System.Title"
          ProjectField="pjTaskName" />
      <Mapping WorkItemTrackingFieldReferenceName="System.WorkItemType"
        ProjectField="pjTaskText24" />
```

```
      <Mapping WorkItemTrackingFieldReferenceName=
        "Microsoft.VSTS.Common.Discipline"
        ProjectField="pjTaskText17" />
      <Mapping WorkItemTrackingFieldReferenceName="System.AssignedTo"
        ProjectField="pjTaskResourceNames" />
      <Mapping WorkItemTrackingFieldReferenceName=
        "Microsoft.VSTS.Scheduling.CompletedWork" ProjectField="pjTaskActualWork"
        ProjectUnits="pjHour"/>
      <Mapping WorkItemTrackingFieldReferenceName=
        "Microsoft.VSTS.Scheduling.RemainingWork"
        ProjectField="pjTaskRemainingWork"
        ProjectUnits="pjHour"/>
      <Mapping WorkItemTrackingFieldReferenceName=
        "Microsoft.VSTS.Scheduling.BaselineWork" ProjectField="pjTaskBaselineWork"
        ProjectUnits="pjHour"/>
      <Mapping WorkItemTrackingFieldReferenceName=
        "Microsoft.VSTS.Scheduling.StartDate" ProjectField="pjTaskStart"
        PublishOnly="true"/>
      <Mapping WorkItemTrackingFieldReferenceName=
        "Microsoft.VSTS.Scheduling.FinishDate" ProjectField="pjTaskFinish"
        PublishOnly="true"/>
      <Mapping WorkItemTrackingFieldReferenceName="System.State"
        ProjectField="pjTaskText13" />
      <Mapping WorkItemTrackingFieldReferenceName="System.Reason"
        ProjectField="pjTaskText14" />
      <Mapping WorkItemTrackingFieldReferenceName="Microsoft.VSTS.Common.Priority"
        ProjectField="pjTaskText19" ProjectName="Work Item Priority" />
      <Mapping WorkItemTrackingFieldReferenceName="System.AreaPath"
        ProjectField="pjTaskOutlineCode9" />
      <Mapping WorkItemTrackingFieldReferenceName="System.IterationPath"
        ProjectField="pjTaskOutlineCode10" />
      <Mapping WorkItemTrackingFieldReferenceName="System.Rev"
        ProjectField="pjTaskText23" />
      <ContextField WorkItemTrackingFieldReferenceName=
        "Microsoft.VSTS.Scheduling.TaskHierarchy"/>
      <LinksField   ProjectField="pjTaskText26" />
      <SyncField    ProjectField="pjTaskText25" />
    </Mappings>
  </MSProject>
```

In order to change the mappings, simply update the WorkItemTrackingFieldReference-Name values or the ProjectField values. When you have finished making changes, upload this file back to TFS to complete the mapping update. To do that, use the same command as you did to download the file—just use the word "upload" instead of "download" and you are done.

■Tip The PublishOnly setting is an incredibly useful field. As a project manager, you may not want people to be able to change start and end dates of work items via Microsoft Project or Excel. You may not want them to change other items that you consider important. Adding this attribute allows people to retrieve the value, but not update it.

Using Microsoft Excel

Microsoft Excel is everyone's favorite friend. If some major problem caused Excel to go down all over the world, virtually every business on the planet would grind to a halt rather suddenly. Knowing how useful Excel is to everyone, the VSTS team used the capabilities of Excel to allow team members to enter items into TFS through the Excel interface.

■Note Excel is a part of Microsoft Office; Microsoft Project requires a separate license. In general, only the project manager needs to be using Project, and everyone else can use Excel to make entries if they need to (all entries by the development team can be made from within Visual Studio though).

If you are a project manager reading this, how often have you had to create macros to pull data from MS Project into Excel so developers can log their hours against specific items? If you are a developer reading this, how many times have you gone from project to project, where everyone has a different way of recording hours? The beauty of this solution is that it is all automatic. You can get your work items (if you need to fill this sheet in); you can get everyone's work items (if you are a project manager); you can customize the query to see if work was completed (or just filter this list); or you can perform a hundred other operations to slice and dice the data any way you see fit to gather useful information.

■Tip Another key benefit of Excel, and one of the reasons Microsoft chose to use it as the interface, is its easy ability to create charts from any type of data in VSTS. Even though you have the benefits of SQL Server Reporting Services, using Excel is often much faster—especially if the reports are for the project manager only.

The Excel interface is slightly different from the Project interface. When you first launch a new Excel file, the toolbar shown in Figure 4-11 is displayed.

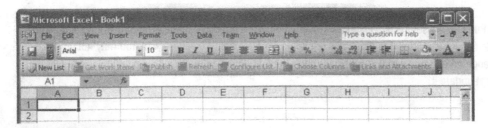

Figure 4-11. *The Excel Team System toolbar*

Creating Lists in Excel

Before you can do anything with Excel and VSTS, you need to create a new list by selecting
New List from the toolbar. This displays the Connect to a Team Foundation Server dialog box
(Figure 4-2). Once you connect to a Team Foundation Server you have the option of retrieving
the results of a query or inputting new items (Figure 4-12).

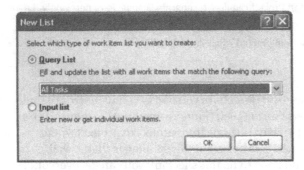

Figure 4-12. *The Excel New List dialog box*

For this first example, assume that you select the All Tasks query and click OK. This
creates the list in Excel as shown in Figure 4-13.

This list should immediately validate why this is a popular tool for both project managers
and other team members alike.

Note Some fields in this list are read-only. For instance, you cannot change the work item type once it
has been created.

Publishing items from Excel works the same way as it does in Project—you just click the
Publish button. However, you can also configure a list in Excel and choose which columns you
want to view as part of the list.

Selecting the Input List option (Figure 4-12) creates a blank list with several default
columns. This allows you to enter items without having to first retrieve items from the server.

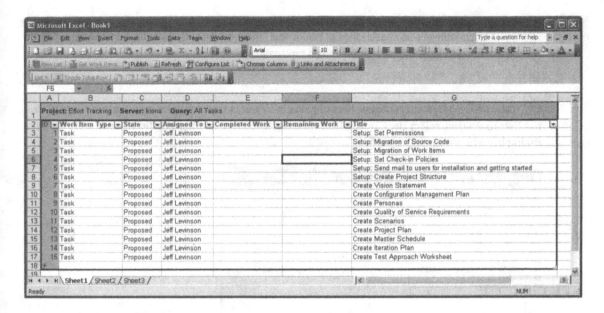

Figure 4-13. *Query results in Microsoft Excel*

Configuring Lists in Excel

To configure the list, select Configure List from the toolbar. This will display the Configure List Properties dialog box shown in Figure 4-14.

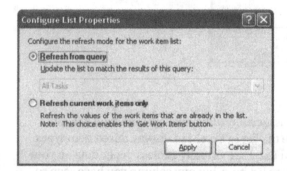

Figure 4-14. *Configure List Properties*

This dialog box in itself does not do anything; however, it affects how the list is updated from the server. The default is to Refresh from query. This means that whenever you click Refresh on the toolbar, the same query will be run over again and any new or updated items will be shown in the list. Selecting the "Refresh current work items only" option means that when you click Refresh, only items that are currently in the list will be updated.

Note Clicking Refresh also enables the Get Work Items button, which allows you to add other items not in the current list (see Figure 4-3 and the associated explanation).

The other option to configure lists in Excel is to select the columns you want to display in the list. To do this, select the Choose Columns button. This will display the Choose Columns dialog box shown in Figure 4-15.

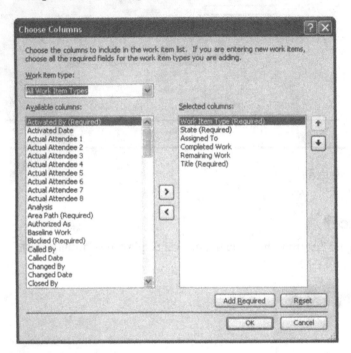

Figure 4-15. *Choose Columns dialog box*

This dialog box lets you choose columns associated with any work item type (via the drop-down list at the top of the form) because the list in Excel can display mixed item types. This means that the possible configurations in Excel are virtually endless depending on your need. The available columns are too extensive to list here, but any column you have seen so far, and in the next chapter, is available through this dialog box. To add a column, just select the column on the right and click the right arrow button. Click the left arrow button to remove an item from the selected columns list.

Clicking reset will reset the columns to the default for the given list. Selecting Add Required will add all required items from the Available Columns list (those identified with a "Required" after the column name) to the Selected Columns column.

Links and attachments work the same way as described in the "Adding Attachments and Links" section.

Using Visual Studio

You can of course use Visual Studio to perform project management duties. You can add tasks, assign tasks, and set start and end dates all from within Visual Studio (see Figure 4-16).

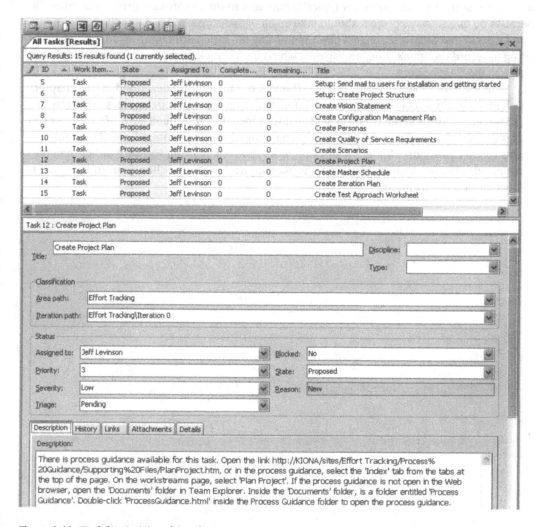

Figure 4-16. *Task list in Visual Studio*

The details tab contains the schedule information. Virtually everything else on this work item form (bottom portion of Figure 4-16) maps to a field in Excel or Microsoft Project. In general, this is not a very friendly view for project managers, which Microsoft realizes. This is the reason for the Excel and Microsoft Project integration. However, when a project manager finds himself or herself looking at a task list in Visual Studio (come to think of it, this applies to anyone who works with VSTS), the team member can view everything in the task list in Excel or Microsoft Project. To do this, simply select all of the items you want to export, and select the appropriate icon on the task list toolbar. Enough said about project management from within Visual Studio.

Summary

In this chapter you saw how the integration between Visual Studio Team System and Microsoft Project and Excel will save you countless hours of work and allow you to manage a project's data more easily. A project manager typically manages multiple software projects at once, because no one software project should take up all of their time. At least, that is the theory. The reality is that project managers often spend way too much time figuring out how they are going to record the team's time, and against which items, track the status of items, and report status to the stakeholders.

With the simple but powerful and well thought out integration described in this chapter, much of the grunt work is simply removed. Teams will now have a repeatable, simple way to track their activities and the hours logged against items, the amount of work left, whether estimates are accurate, and so on. It all leads to one thing: through continued use of the tool, teams will become more efficient and spend more time engineering software rather than performing administrative tasks (which no one likes anyway). The next chapter introduces you to the details of the work items.

CHAPTER 5

■■■

Team Work Item Tracking

When you're working on a project of any size, you need to manage a number of lists. Even building a tree fort for your kids may involve several lists: the list of local building projects where you could acquire spare lumber, the list of priority features (like trapdoors, escape ropes, and an electronic drawbridge), and the list of friends who actually know how to build things.

At the startup of a software project, there are the customer requirements, startup tasks, and many other lists to manage. As the project evolves, the team begins to compile lists of bugs, issues, and change requests. Team Foundation addresses the concept of list management in a feature area called work item tracking (WIT). WIT originated from the Microsoft internal bug-tracking systems. Per Kevin Kelly's weblog on MSDN (http://blogs.msdn.com/kkellyatms/archive/2004/05/28/144108.aspx):

> We knew we had to settle on something . . . ideally somewhat unique, and something folks would just get. The essence of our system helps teams manage discrete units of work, assigned to individuals and, when taken as a whole, it represents all activities (another famous term! and taken) managed in a software development project. They're all the work items of a project . . . work item tracking. Teams define the types of work items they want to track . . . and I'll leave details of this for later posts.

This chapter introduces WIT, which is arguably the core component of Team Foundation. In a sense, work items are the glue that holds Team Foundation together. If we were discussing a banking scenario, the work items would be analogous to account entries. The common definition for VSTS work items is that they are assigned to an individual for someone to act upon.

Working with Work Items

Work Items is the first node in the Team Explorer window under the project name. Right-click the Work Items node to see the options for working with work items, as shown in Figure 5-1. Table 5-1 describes each of these options.

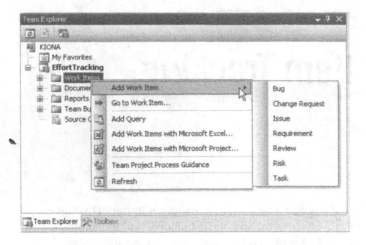

Figure 5-1. *The Work Items context menu*

■Note The Work Items context menu will show the four most recent selections made. For example, if you selected Add Work Item ➤ Bug, then Add Bug would appear above Add Work Item the next time you right-clicked the Work Items node.

Table 5-1. *Work Items Explorer Options*

Option	Description
Add Work Item	Opens a form for the work item type selected
Go to Work Item	Opens a form for the work item based on the ID entered
Add Query	Opens the New Query window
Add Work Items with Microsoft Excel	Allows you to populate a Microsoft Excel spreadsheet with work items and publish them to the Team Foundation Server (as described in Chapter 4)
Add Work Items with Microsoft Project	Allows you to populate a Microsoft Project task list with work items and publish them to the Team Foundation Server (as described in Chapter 4)
Team Project Process Guidance	Opens the Process Guidance Work Items section within the Project Portal (as described in Chapter 2)

Optionally, you can create and manage work items from the Team menu, as shown in Figure 5-2.

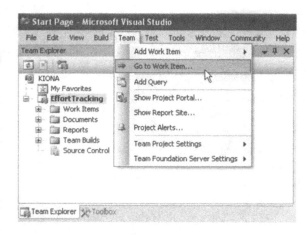

Figure 5-2. *Team menu options*

Team Foundation provides three views for creating and managing work items:

- The *form view*, as its name suggests, presents each field of the work items in a standard-ized form layout.

- The *query view* allows you to query the work item database based on selection criteria and provides a list of results.

- The *results* (or *triage*) *view* displays the results of saved queries in a combination of form and list view, which makes it easy to route and assign work items.

The following sections describe these views in more detail.

Using the Form View

The first view most people encounter is the form view of the work item. When you select Add Work Item from the Work Items context menu, you will be presented with this view. Figure 5-3 shows the first task work item in the EffortTracking project.

The standard layout for the work item form is to have the summary information at the top of the form and detail items presented at the bottom on separate tabs. The middle section contains status fields, including State and Reason, which represent basic elements of workflow in this first release of Team Foundation Server.

Two of the key features for work items are the ability to link to other items and to include attachments.

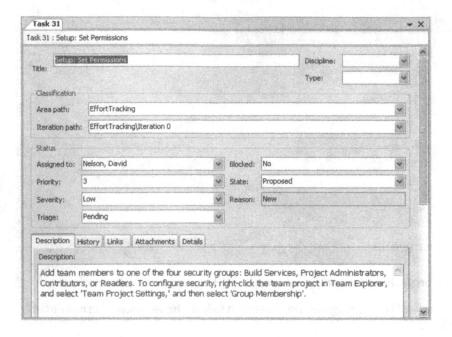

Figure 5-3. *Form view of a work item*

Adding Links

Click the Links tab at the bottom of the form to view the Links pane, which shows the link type, description, and comments. Click the Add button on the right side of the pane to open the Add Link dialog box, shown in Figure 5-4.

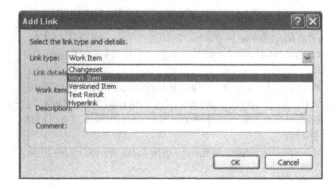

Figure 5-4. *The Add Link dialog box*

Here, you can select from four Team Foundation Server elements (Changeset, Work Item, Versioned Item, or Test Result) and the hyperlink to any URL (Web) or UNC (server) location. After you've added the link, you can open the linked item by double-clicking the item in the Links pane or by selecting the Open button for a highlighted link.

Adding Attachments

Click the Attachments tab at the bottom of the form to view the Attachments pane, which shows the name, size, and comments for any attached items. Click the Add button on the right to open the Add Attachment dialog box, as shown in Figure 5-5.

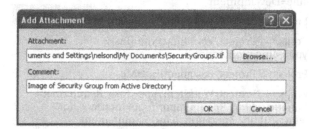

Figure 5-5. *The Add Attachment dialog box*

In this example, we added a picture of the security groups from Active Directory for the Set Permissions task.

Using the Query View

The query view is very similar to the query builder for SQL Server. In fact, the project team refers to the query builder as "sick SQL" and the query language as Work Item Query Language (WIQL).

Using Predefined Queries

A number of predefined project queries are provided, depending on the selected process template. In the MSF for CMMI Process Improvement - v4.0 process template, 16 predefined project queries are available, as shown in Table 5-2. The MSF for Agile Software Development - v4.0 process template has 11 predefined project queries.

Table 5-2. *Predefined Project Queries (MSF for CMMI Process Improvement - v4.0 Template)*

Query Name	Query Parameters
Active Bugs	Team Project=@Project, WorkItemType=Bug, State=Active
All My Team Project Work Items	Assigned To=@Me
All Tasks	Team Project=@Project, WorkItemType=Task
All Work Items	Team Project=@Project

Continued

Table 5-2. *Continued*

Query Name	Query Parameters
Blocked Work Items	Team Project=@Project, Blocked=Yes
Change Requests	Team Project=@Project, WorkItemType=Change Request
Corrective Actions	Team Project=@Project, WorkItemType=Task, Task Type=Corrective Action
Customer Requirements	Team Project=@Project, WorkItemType=Task, Requirement Type=Scenario (or) Requirement Type=Quality of Service
Development Tasks	Team Project=@Project, WorkItemType=Task, Discipline=Development
Issues	Team Project=@Project, WorkItemType=Issue
Mitigation Action Status	Team Project=@Project, WorkItemType=Task, Task Type=Mitigation Action
My Work Items	Team Project=@Project, Assigned To=@Me
Product Requirements	Team Project=@Project, WorkItemType=Task, Requirement Type=Functional (or) Requirement Type=Interface, (or) Requirement Type=Operational, (or) Requirement Type=Security, (or) Requirement Type=Safety
Resolved Bugs	Team Project=@Project, WorkItemType=Bug, State=Resolved
Reviews	Team Project=@Project, WorkItemType=Review
Risks	Team Project=@Project, WorkItemType=Risk

Creating Queries

You can create your own queries and save them in the My Queries folder under Work Items. To create a new query, right-click Work Items and select Add Query, as shown in Figure 5-6.

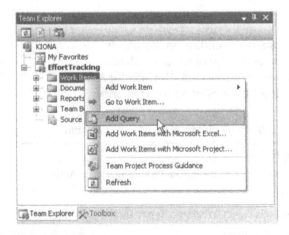

Figure 5-6. *Choosing to add a query*

■**Note** If you have the appropriate permissions, you can edit and modify the project queries themselves.

You'll see the New Query window, as shown in Figure 5-7. Create your query, and then right-click in the New Query window and select Run Query to see the query results.

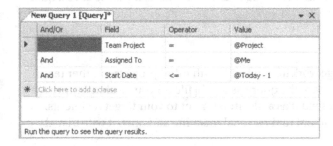

Figure 5-7. *The New Query window*

Saving Queries

Another nice feature is the ability to save a private or team query to a file. This allows you to send queries via e-mail and port them between installations of Team Server. To save your new query, select File ➤ Save New Query1 [Query] As to open the Save Query As dialog box, as shown in Figure 5-8.

Figure 5-8. *The Save Query As dialog box*

Here, you can give your query a unique name and then choose from three options:

- Allow your query to be used as a team query by everyone.

- Save it as a private query visible only to you.

- Save it to a local file for e-mail distribution as a `.wiq`.

You can also select the team project in this dialog box, which makes it easy to save a query from one project to another project.

Sending Queries in E-Mail

Occasionally, you will want to exchange work item queries with other projects or other team members via e-mail. To do this, simply save the query as a `.wiq` file on you local machine, as described in the previous section, and send it as a file attachment to your target recipients. The recipients can then save the attachment to their local machine and open it with Visual Studio to run it.

Tip If you have e-mail access on the same computer as Team Foundation, you can right-click the query you want to send and select Send to Mail Recipient.

Using Query Macros

WIQL provides some convenient macros to make the query process more convenient and portable. In the example in Figure 5-7, we used three of the most popular: @Me, @Project, and @Today. The prebuilt query macros are described in Table 5-3.

Table 5-3. *Prebuilt Query Macros*

Query	Description
@Project	Inserts the current project context into the query
@Me	Inserts the Windows integrated account name into the query
@Today	Inserts midnight of the current date of the local machine running the query
@Today-1	Inserts the date of yesterday (@Today minus 24 hours)
@Today-7	Inserts the date of last week (@Today minus 7 days)
@Today-30	Insert the date of the last month (@Today minus 30 days)

You can execute the query and view the results in a list by pressing F5. To adjust the result display, right-click the Results pane and select Column Options, as shown in Figure 5-9. These options allow you to add columns, sort, and adjust the column width.

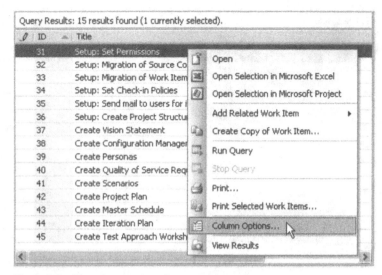

Figure 5-9. *Choosing to set column options*

Finally, you can click the View Results icon in the task pane of the query window as shown in Figure 5-10, to display the third type of view.

Figure 5-10. *Choosing to view results*

Using the Results (Triage) View

The other view for working with work items is the results view. You can display this view by either running a previously saved query or clicking the View Results icon in the query window (see Figure 5-10). The results view shows the list in the upper half of the window and the full form for the selected work item in the bottom section, as shown in Figure 5-11.

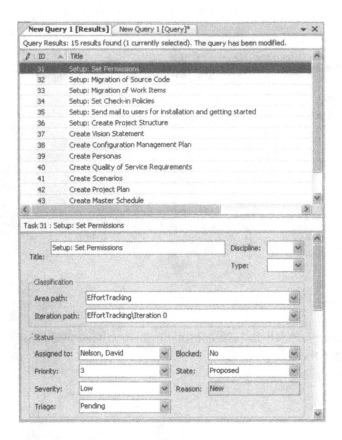

Figure 5-11. *Results (triage) view*

The project manager can use the results view to quickly review the work items that come in over a period of time, assign them to the appropriate resources, and manage the state and transition for each. The developers can use this view to review items assigned to them and rapidly prioritize, transition, or transfer items to other team members.

Understanding Work Item Types

Each work item type consists of fields, forms, rules, and states (work item life cycle), which are defined in Table 5-4.

Table 5-4. *Work Item Type Information*

Item	Description
Fields	Global across an installation of Team Foundation Server. Fields include a name, reference name, type, help text, and applicable constraints.
Forms	Controls the layout of the form that is displayed. The goal is to provide a single form definition (fields, groups, and tabs) that can be used in VSTS and with Share-Point web parts.
Workflow	Describe the valid states, transitions, and reasons for the transitions.

The specific work item types differ depending on the process template used for the team project. The MSF for CMMI Process Improvement - v4.0 process template defines seven work items to assign and track work. The MSF for Agile Software Development - v4.0 process template defines five work items. (We'll refer to these as the CMMI template and the Agile template.) The specific work item types and associated process templates are shown in Table 5-5.

Table 5-5. *Work Items by Process Template*

Work Item	Agile	CMMI
Task	X	X
Bug	X	X
Risk	X	X
Requirement*	--	X
Quality of Service	X	--
Scenario	X	--
Change Request	--	X
Issue*	--	X
Review	--	X

* Both Quality of Service and Scenario are subtypes of Requirement in the CMMI template. Additional requirement subtypes include Function, Interface, Operation, Safety, and Security. Issue is a unique work item type for the CMMI template and an attribute of work items under the Agile template.

The following sections describe each of the work item types.

Task Work Items

A Task work item type is the most generic type and communicates the need to do some work. All of the predefined work items in the provided process templates are of type Task.

Within the team of peers on a project, each member has his own share of tasks. For instance, a project manager uses the Task work item to assign defining personas to the business analyst, assign defining a test approach to the test manager, and assign fixing a bug to a developer. A Task can also be used generally to assign work within the project.

The required Task work item type fields are described in Table 5-6.

Table 5-6. *Required Task Work Item Fields*

Field Name	Description	Default
Title	Brief explanation of task	None; must be supplied
State	Proposed, Active, Resolved, Closed	Proposed
Reason	Basis for existing state	New
Priority	Subjective importance of task (1–3)	3
Triage	Info Recv, More Info, Pending, Triaged	Pending

Note For the Agile template, the default state is Active and the initial priority (rank) is blank.

Figure 5-12 shows the states, transitions, and reasons for the Task work item type. In the normal path for a Task work item, the Task is initiated when there is work to be done. A Task starts in the Proposed state pending agreement, with a reason of New. It is then triaged and placed into the Active state as Accepted (if it is to be implemented in the current iteration) or as Investigate (if analysis of impact is needed). An investigated Task should go back to the Proposed state at the conclusion of the impact analysis. The Task can move to the Resolved state with the Complete or Requires Review/Tests transition reason. Once the Task passes the review or testing, it can be moved from the Resolved state to the Closed state.

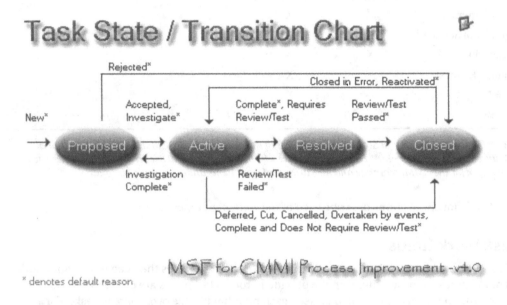

Figure 5-12. *States, transitions, and reasons for the Task work item type*

Alternate paths exists for moving Tasks directly to the Closed state if they are Rejected, Deferred, Cut, Cancelled, Overtaken by Events, or simply have no review or test criteria. A task may also revert from the Resolved state to the Active state with a reason of Review/Test Failed.

Note It is important to understand that when a work item is Closed, the Assigned To field is cleared. This is the default transition for a work item, so that you don't see all your completed work items in queries for items assigned to you. This is described in the work item definition XML file. Some teams assign the Closed work item to a fictitious user named Closed, which gets it off the developers' radar but allows for some optional reporting capabilities.

Bug Work Items

The original bug-tracking system, Product Studio, used within Microsoft was the code base for the WIT feature. Therefore, the tracking of bugs is at the core of the WIT system.

The motivation of opening a Bug work item should be to clearly describe the problem in a way that allows the developer to fully understand the weight of the problem. The teams at Microsoft are very familiar with the bug rates and the concept of zero bug bounce (ZBB). ZBB is the point in the project where you have eliminated your bug backlog, and the development team is handling bugs that are coming in real time. This is a major milestone for any project on the way to beta or final release.

Table 5-7 shows the required Bug work item type fields.

Table 5-7. *Required Bug Work Item Fields*

Field Name	Description	Default
Title	Brief explanation of bug	None; must be supplied
State	Proposed, Active, Resolved, Closed	Proposed
Reason	Basis for existing state	New
Priority	Subjective importance of bug (1–3)	3
Severity	Critical, High, Medium, Low	Low
Triage	Info Recv, More Info, Pending, Triaged	Pending
Symptom	Description of the problem	None; must be supplied
Steps to Reproduce	Detail on how to reproduce the bug	None; must be supplied

Note For the Agile template, the default state for a Bug work item is Active and the initial priority is 2.

Figure 5-13 shows the states, transitions, and reasons for the Bug work item. In the normal path, the Bug work item is initiated when someone identifies a potential problem in the product or a build error exists. This Proposed state can require Investigate, or as the bug is triaged, the work item is assigned directly to a developer (as Approved). Both reasons move the Bug into the Active state. The Bug work item is moved to the Resolved state once the problem is Fixed and the bug is linked to the changeset at check-in. Once the Fixed bug is part of the build, it is moved to the Closed state.

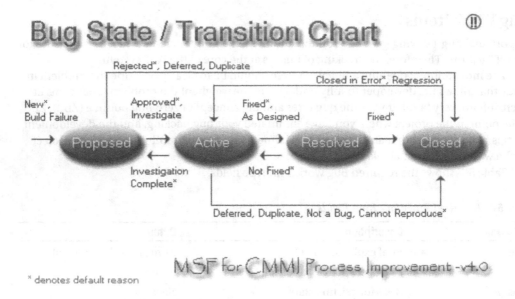

Figure 5-13. *States, transitions, and reasons for the Bug work item type*

Alternate paths exist for moving Bug work items to the Closed state if they are Rejected, Deferred, Not a Bug, Determined a Duplicate, or Cannot Reproduce. A Bug work item may also revert from the Resolved to Active state if testing finds the problem was Not Fixed.

Risk Work Items

Risk is defined as the expectation of loss. It is a function of the probability and the consequences of harm. A Risk work item is used to track potential risk impacts to the project. A successful risk management practice is one in which risks are continuously identified and analyzed for relative importance. Risks are mitigated, tracked, and controlled to effectively use program resources.

Risk work items differ from Issue work items in that a risk is a look into the future and requires a continuous review of the probability of its occurrence. An issue has a more immediate, in-the-trenches team dynamic that is addressed in the daily standup meeting or late-night Xbox lounge.

Table 5-8 shows the required Risk work item type fields.

■**Note** For the Agile template, the default state for a Risk work item is Active, the initial Severity is blank, and the initial priority (rank) is blank. It does not include Probability and Blocked fields.

Table 5-8. *Required Risk Work Item Fields*

Field Name	Description	Default
Title	Brief explanation of risk	None; must be supplied
Probability	Chance the risk will occur (1–99)	None; must be supplied
State	Proposed, Active, Resolved, Closed	Proposed
Reason	Basis for existing state	New
Priority	Subjective importance of risk (1–3)	3
Severity	Critical, High, Medium, Low	Low
Blocked	Indicates progress in mitigating the risk is blocked	No

Figure 5-14 shows the states, transitions, and reasons for the Risk work item. In the normal path, risks are potential events or conditions in the future that may have negative impact on the project. A Risk work item is initiated when this potential is identified. In the Proposed state, a risk is analyzed for likelihood and cost of occurrence, mitigation options, triggers, and proposed contingency plan. A Risk work item is moved to the Active state when the conditions warrant, for the Mitigation Triggered reason. Active Risk work items require tasks to perform the mitigation options. Once these tasks have been executed (the Mitigate Action Complete reason), a Risk work item is moved to the Resolved state. Once the mitigation tasks are verified as sufficiently Mitigated, the Risk work item is moved to the Closed state.

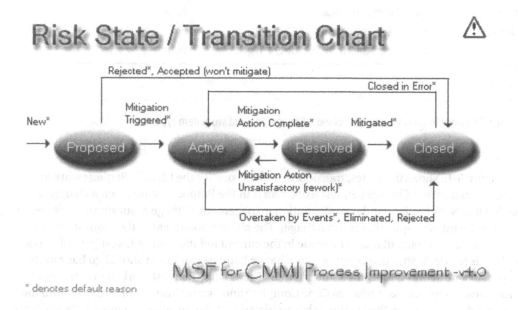

Figure 5-14. *States, transitions, and reasons for the Risk work item type*

Alternate paths exists for moving Risk work items to the Closed state if they are Accepted (assume the risk), Rejected (not a risk), Eliminated, or Overtaken by Events (the risk no longer exists). A Risk work item may revert from the Resolved state to the Active state due to the Mitigation Action Unsatisfactory (Rework) reason.

Change Request Work Items

A change request (CR) is a formal request for modifying the behavior of a system due to normal business changes or because there is a bug in the system. A change request expresses a change in the project baseline, including a previously approved project component. A change request can be introduced during any iteration of the project.

Change requests are governed by a thorough control process intended to reduce the impacts of changes on the work of the delivery team, while still allowing modifications after user specifications have been approved. Once a Change Request work item has been approved, it will initiate other work items to carry out the change.

Table 5-9 describes the required fields for a Change Request work item type.

Table 5-9. *Change Request Work Item Required Fields*

Field Name	Description	Default
Title	Brief explanation of CR	None; must be supplied
State	Proposed, Active, Resolved, Closed	Proposed
Reason	Basis for existing state	New
Priority	Subjective importance of CR (1–3)	3
Triage	Info Recv, More Info, Pending, Triaged	Pending

■**Note** The Agile template does not include a Change Request work item type.

Figure 5-15 shows the states, transitions, and reasons for the Change Request work item. In the normal path, a Change Request work item is in the Proposed state when a change is needed to a work product under configuration management. Change requests are reviewed by a change board for disposition (formal triage). The change board places the request into the Active state as Accepted (if it is to be made in the current iteration) or as Investigate (if impact analysis is needed). After investigation, the Change Request work item should go back to the Proposed state at the conclusion of the analysis. The Change Request work item can move to the Resolved state only as it reaches Code Complete and System Tested and is placed into the daily build process. Once the customer has validated that the proposed changes have successfully been implemented with Validation Test Passed, the Change Request work item can be moved from the Resolved state to the Closed state.

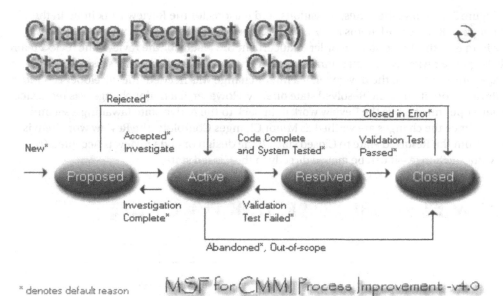

Figure 5-15. *States, transitions, and reasons for the Change Request work item type*

Alternate paths exist for moving Change Request work items to the Closed state if they are Rejected, Abandoned, or determined Out of Scope. A Change Request work item may also revert from the Resolved state to the Active state due to the customer Validation Test Failed reason.

Review Work Items

A program management best practice is to perform periodic reviews during the software development life cycle. The Review work item type provides a mechanism to initiate and track these sessions. Many types of reviews are performed during the life of a project, including code, critical-design, architecture, best practice, security, and deployment reviews.

Table 5-10 shows the required fields for the Review work item type.

Table 5-10. *Review Work Item Required Fields*

Field Name	Description	Default
Title	Brief explanation of review	None; must be supplied
State	Active, Resolved, Closed	Active
Reason	Basis for existing state	New
Purpose	Focus area of the review	None; must be supplied

Note The Agile template does not include a Review work item type.

Figure 5-16 shows the states, transitions, and reasons for the Review work item. In the normal path, Review work items record the outcome of a design or code reviews. A Review work item is in the Active state in order to document the results of the review. The review team will accept the review with either minor or major changes at the end of the session. These changes are assigned to the developer. If a minor change was needed, the developer can move the Review work item to the Resolved state directly. However, if a major change was requested, the developer must move the Review work item back to the Active state (awaiting a second review). Once the changes are verified as Minor Changes Complete, the Review work item is moved from the Resolved state to Closed state. If the design or code review is Accepted (As Is)—without change—it can be moved directly to the Closed state.

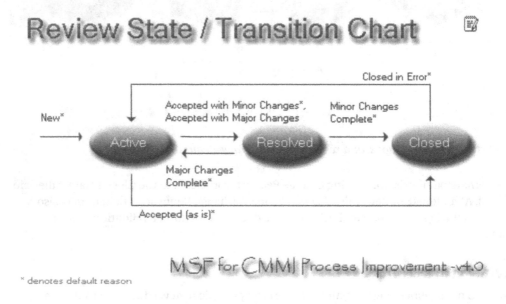

Figure 5-16. *States, transitions, and reasons for the Review work item type*

Requirement Work Items

A requirement is a stated or implied expression of a business need. Requirements orient and constrain the products or services to be delivered.

The Requirement work item type captures and tracks what the solution needs to provide to meet the customer's desires. Requirement work items within the CMMI template are divided into Customer and Product requirements. Customer types of requirements include scenario and quality of service (QoS). Product requirements include safety, security, functional, operational, and interface.

Table 5-11 shows the required fields for the Requirement work item type.

Note For the Agile template, the customer-focused requirements of Scenario and Quality of Service (QoS) are separate work item types.

Table 5-11. *Requirement Work Item Required Fields*

Field Name	Description	Default
Title	Brief explanation of requirement	None; must be supplied
Type	Functional, Interface, Operational, QoS, Safety, Scenario, Security	None; must be supplied
Blocked	Progress blocked (Yes, No)	No
State	Proposed, Active, Resolved, Closed	Proposed
Reason	Basis for existing state	New
Priority	Subjective importance of requirement (1–3)	3
Triage	Info Recv, More Info, Pending, Triaged	Pending
Committed	Committed project requirement	No

Figure 5-17 shows the states, transitions, and reasons for the Requirement work item. In the normal path, the Requirement work item tracks "what" the product needs to perform to solve the customer's problem. A Requirement work item starts in the Proposed state at the time it is identified. It is then triaged and placed into the Active state as Accepted (if it is to be implemented in the current iteration) or as Investigate (if impact analysis is needed). After investigation, a Requirement work item should go back to the Proposed state at the conclusion of the study. The requirement can move to the Resolved state only as it reaches Code Complete and System Tests Passed. Once the customer has validated that the requirement has successfully met expectations, it can be moved from the Resolved state to the Closed state.

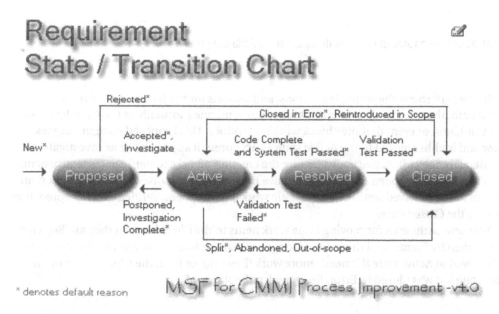

Figure 5-17. *States, transitions, and reasons for the Requirement work item type*

Alternate paths exist for moving Requirement work items to the Closed state if they are Rejected, Abandoned, Split, or determined Out of Scope. A Requirement work item may also revert from the Resolved to Active state if the customer Validation Test Failed.

Issue Work Items

An issue is an actual event, condition, point of discussion, debate, or dispute that needs to be proactively managed. Unlike a risk, which will not harm the project unless it materializes, an issue is currently harming it or will definitely harm it unless the project is changed.

The Issue work item provides the user with a way to report an issue, track progress toward its resolution, and know who is responsible for resolving the issue.

Table 5-12 shows the required fields for the Issue work item type.

Table 5-12. *Issue Work Item Required Fields*

Field Name	Description	Default
Title	Brief explanation of issue	None; must be supplied
State	Proposed, Active, Resolved, Closed	Proposed
Reason	Basis for existing state	New
Escalate	Raise the criticality of the issue	No
Priority	Subjective importance of the issue (1–3)	3
Triage	Info Recv, More Info, Pending, Triaged	Pending

■**Note** Issues are an attribute of work items under the Agile template.

Figure 5-18 shows the states, transitions, and reasons for the Issue work item. In the normal path, the Issue work item is initiated when someone (normally at the team level) identifies a situation or event that may block work on product. This Proposed state undergoes review and is either moved to the Active state as Accepted (if approved) or as Investigate (if more detail is needed). Active issues require the creation of tasks to perform corrective action. Once these tasks have been executed to remove the blockage (Resolved), an Issue work item is moved to the Resolved state. Once the Issue work item has been Verified and Accepted, it is moved to the Closed state.

Alternate paths exist for moving Issue work items to the Closed state if they are Rejected or Overtaken by Events (and the issue no longer exists). An Issue work item may revert from the Resolved to Active state if it needs more work (Rework), or from the Closed state to the Active state if it was Closed in Error, Reopened, or Reoccurred.

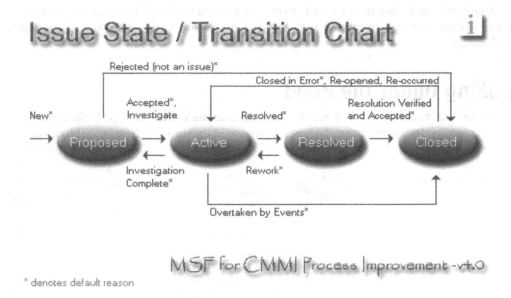

Figure 5-18. *States, transitions, and reasons for the Issue work item type*

Configuring Project Alerts for Work Item Tracking

In VSTS, you can configure project alerts to send e-mail messages based on specific events. This feature leverages the underlying notification service and is customizable and expandable for more granular event notification. For work item tracking, only one project alert is predefined. This alert is to receive notification when your work items are changed by someone else.

To set up this alert, right-click the EffortTracking project and select Project Alerts. A dialog box with several alert options appears. Check the "My work items are changed by others" alert and enter your e-mail address in the Send To column, as shown in Figure 5-19. Optionally, you can have the message sent in either HTML or plain text.

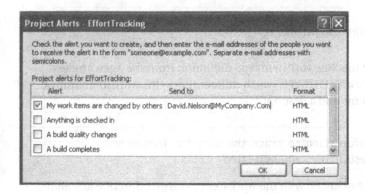

Figure 5-19. *The Project Alerts dialog box*

Once configured, each time a work item assigned to you is changed by another project member, a detailed e-mail message is sent, showing the core work item fields and the changed fields' history.

Looking Under the Hood

Work items must conform to a XML schema referred to as the Work Item Type Definition (WITD) language using a few basic elements. A portion of the WorkItemTypeDefinition.xsd is shown in Figure 5-20.

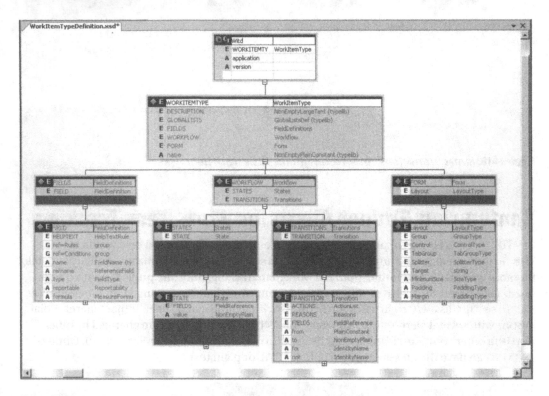

Figure 5-20. *WorkItemTypeDefinition.xsd fragment*

As an example, we'll look at the Bug work item type definition from the Agile process template. The first element is the WORKITEMTYPE, which differentiates this work item from all others. It includes the unique name and a description.

```
<WORKITEMTYPE name='Bug'>
    <DESCRIPTION>Includes information to track the work to resolve the
    Bug and to verify its resolution.</DESCRIPTION>
```

Next, it identifies the fields associated with the work item to further describe any additional information about the work item. This snippet shows the Id and Title field definitions.

```
<FIELDS>
    <FIELD name="Id" refname="System.Id" type="Integer" />
    <FIELD name="Title" refname="System.Title" type="String" >
        <REQUIRED/>
    </Field>
```

In addition, field rules define the constraints on fields and field values as they move through the transition states defined for the work item. Here is an example of the Issue field:

```
<FIELD name="Issue" refname="Microsoft.VSTS.Common.Issue"
    type="String" reportable="dimension">
        <REQUIRED/>
        <ALLOWEDVALUES>
            <LISTITEM value="Yes"/>
            <LISTITEM value="No"/>
        </ALLOWEDVALUES>
        <DEFAULT from="value" value="No"/>
</FIELD>
```

Note The reportable attribute dictates how the field is used in the data warehouse and reporting cubes. Valid values are measure, dimension, and detail. Reporting is discussed in Chapter 6.

Next is the definition of the workflow and state transitions for the Bug work item type. First is the STATES section, which defines the state valid values and the associated fields for the state with the values they are to receive. The workflow is found in the TRANSITION section, as in this example for the Active to Resolved state of a Bug work item:

```
<TRANSITION from="Active" to="Resolved">
    <ACTIONS>
            <ACTION value="Microsoft.VSTS.Actions.Checkin"/>
    </ACTIONS>
    <REASONS>
            <DEFAULTREASON value="Fixed"/>
            <REASON value="Deferred"/>
            <REASON value="Duplicate"/>
            <REASON value="As Designed"/>
            <REASON value="Unable to Reproduce"/>
            <REASON value="Obsolete"/>
    </REASONS>
    <FIELDS>
            <FIELD refname="System.AssignedTo">
                <COPY from="field"
                    field="System.CreatedBy"/>
            </FIELD>
            <FIELD refname="Microsoft.VSTS.Common.ActivatedDate">
                <READONLY/></FIELD>
```

```
        <FIELD refname="Microsoft.VSTS.Common.ActivatedBy">
        <READONLY/></FIELD>
        <FIELD refname="Microsoft.VSTS.Common.ResolvedBy">
            <COPY from="currentuser"/>
            <VALIDUSER/>
             <REQUIRED/>
        </FIELD>
        <FIELD refname="Microsoft.VSTS.Common.ResolvedDate">
        <SERVERDEFAULT from="clock"/></FIELD>
    </FIELDS>
</TRANSITION> >
```

The final element defines the display of the Bug work item in a form.

```
<FORM>
<LAYOUT>
<GROUP>
```

And that is about it. Business rules and behavior for a work item type are also defined in the WITD language as rules associated with fields and scoped by state and transition.

Note For work item tracking, two database tables and two views are of particular interest. The WorkItemsAre table contains the current version of the work item, and the WorkItemsWere table contains all the old versions, one entry per client update. The WorkItemsAreUsed view brings in the namespace column names used in queries, and the WorkItemsWereUsed view brings in the namespace column names used in queries. The VSTS team highly recommends that you do not modify any of the underlying tables. The database is discussed in more detail in Chapter 6.

Customizing Work Item Types

You can customize work item types in a variety of ways. Here, we will look at examples of modifying the list displayed by a field, adding a new field that references a global list, and creating a brand-new work item type.

In these examples, you'll use several of the following command-line tools:

- witimport: Imports an XML work item type definition to a team project or validates a definition before import.

- witexport: Exports an existing work item type from a team project as XML.

- witfields: Allows you to view, rename, report, or delete a work item field or reset the Rebuildcache flag for all clients.

- glimport: Imports an XML global list definition to a team project or validates a definition before import.

- glexport: Exports an existing work global list from a team project as XML.

Note In the current version of Team Foundation Server, there is no official way to delete individual work items from a project. You can use the `DeleteTeamProject`, but that will obliterate all work items and the project itself. The reason is that Team Foundation provides a robust auditing function and preserves links between items. There are several discussions in the newsgroups on how to delete from the underlying database tables, but they are all with the caveat "use at own risk" because there are invariably links you will have missed. We hope that the product team will provide a tool or power toy to delete individual work items cleanly.

Modifying the Assign To List

One of the first modifications you may want to make in the work item type definitions is the list of team members who are represented in the Assigned To field. By default, the Assigned To field uses <VALIDUSER> as the source of the display names. <VALIDUSER> corresponds to the Everyone group for Team Foundation Server. In a large enterprise, this list includes Team Foundation Server service accounts, system administrator accounts, and a host of others that may never be assigned to work items.

To customize the list of allowed values in the Assigned To field list, you perform the following steps:

1. Create the global groups for AssignTo using Team Explorer.

2. Export the Task work item type using `witexport.exe`.

3. Rename the work item type `name` field using the XML editor.

4. Modify the XML file for the new type using the XML editor.

5. Import the new Task work item type using `wiimport.exe`.

6. Test the form in Visual Studio using Team Explorer.

The following sections describe each of these steps in detail.

Creating Groups

As mentioned in Chapter 2, you have several options for creating groups with Team Foundation Server. If you maintain your own security groups in Active Directory, you can add those groups to predefined or custom groups in the Team Foundation Server. Optionally, you can add members directly to Team Foundation Server groups at both the server and project level. For this example, you will create a new project group called AssignTo and add members directly to that group.

1. Open Visual Studio. Right-click your team project and select Team Project Settings ➤ Group Membership to open the Project Groups dialog box.

2. Select New to open the Create New Team Foundation Server Group dialog box. Enter **AssignTo** in the Group Name field and a short description, as shown in Figure 5-21. Then click OK.

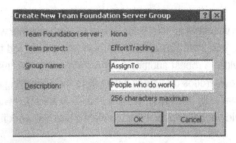

Figure 5-21. *The Create New Team Foundation Server Group dialog box*

3. Double-click the new AssignTo group to add members. You can select members from Team Foundation Server groups or Windows Users or Groups. Select one of more groups containing a few different members to make this exercise useful.

Exporting a Work Item Type

To export the Task work item type, open a Visual Studio command prompt and enter witexport /? to see the list of parameter definitions. To export the Task work item definition from your server, enter the following:

```
witexport /f mytask.xml /t [Team Foundation Server Name] /p [Team Project Name]
/n Task
```

After a few seconds, you will receive the message "work item type export complete." This will verify that a file called mytask.xml has been placed into the current directory.

Renaming the Work Item Type

It is a good idea to rename the work item type so you don't destroy the original copy of the work item while you are making your changes. In a sense, you are doing development on the production server, so you need to be careful. A best practice is to have a separate sandbox server to test your modifications.

To rename the work item type, open the newly created file in Visual Studio (or your favorite XML editor) and change the name field from this:

```
<WORKITEMTYPE name="Task">
```

to this:

```
<WORKITEMTYPE name="MyTask">
```

The change is shown in Figure 5-22. Then save the file.

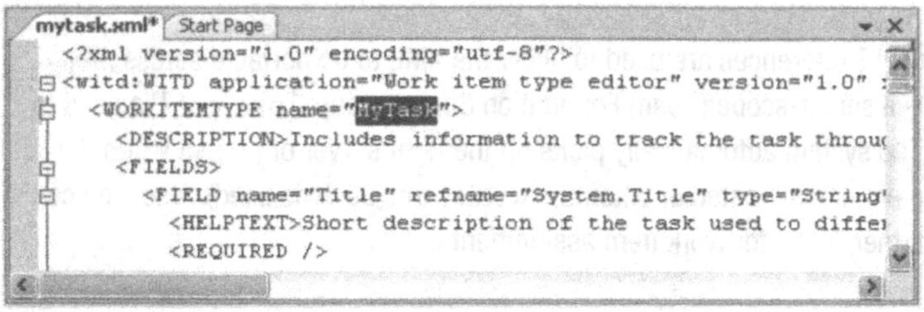

Figure 5-22. *Renaming the work item type*

Modifying the Assigned To Field

Next, you need to find the Assigned To field in the mytask.xml file. Do a quick search on Assigned To and you will be taken to the field description section.

```
<FIELD name="Assigned To"
    refname="System.AssignedTo" type="String"
    <VALIDUSER />
</FIELD>
```

Remove the <VALIDUSER /> tag, which, as noted earlier, corresponds to the Everyone group, and add field list items. Field lists define permissible values for a field and provide list items for users to choose. Field lists can be used for String field types only. There are three types of field lists:

- ALLOWEDVALUES provide an exclusive list from which the users must select.

- SUGGESTEDVALUES provide an optional list from which the users may select or they may provide their own value.

- PROHIBITEDVALUES provide a restricted list from which the users may not provide a matching value.

Two optional attributes related to field lists are expanditems and filteritems. These are used to manage items that represent a group of discrete values such as a security group. The expanditems attribute, if set to true, will recursively unpack the individual values from a group. Setting the filteritems attribute to excludegroups will remove the group names from the expanded list.

In this example, you want to set the field list type to ALLOWEDVALUES and provide a list of the project's AssignTo group, and expand the items, as follows:

```
<FIELD name="Assigned To"
    refname="System.AssignedTo" type="String"
    <HELPTEXT>The person assigned to do the work</HELPTEXT>
    <ALLOWEDVALUES expanditems="true" filteritems="excludegroups">
        <LISTITEM value="[project]\AssignTo" />
        <LISTITEM value="PartnerTeam" />
    </ALLOWEDVALUES>
</FIELD>
```

■**Note** The [global] and [project] references are used to allow the XML to be portable across projects. [global] is used to reference a server-scoped Team Foundation Server group. [project] is used to reference a project-scoped group. The system automatically picks up the right server or project when the work item type is uploaded (when a project is created or when the witimport utility is used). Also, you can add placeholder groups, such as Partner Team, for work item assignments.

Finally, to exclude a value from the list, add the following XML for the prohibited values list item:

```
<PROHIBITEDVALUES expanditems="false">
    <LISTITEM value="Bob" />
</PROHIBITEDVALUES>
```

Save the file.

Importing a Work Item Type

Reopen the Visual Studio command prompt (if it's not still open from the export operation). Enter witimport /? to see the list of parameter definitions. To import the new MyTask work item definition to your server, enter the following:

```
witimport /f mytask.xml /t [Team Foundation Server Name] /p [Team Project Name]
```

After a few seconds, you should receive the message "work item type import complete." This will signify the MyTask work item has been uploaded to your server within the specified team project.

Validating a New Work Item Type

For this example, the validation consists of verifying that the expected values show up in the Assigned To list in the form and that the prohibited values are not allowed. To test the form, follow these steps:

1. Open Visual Studio, and the Team Explorer will connect to your Team Foundation Server.

2. Expand your team project, right-click the Work Items node, and Select Add Work Item.

3. Select the new work item type: MyTask. You should see the form view of the MyTask work item with the modified Assigned To field, as shown in Figure 5-23.

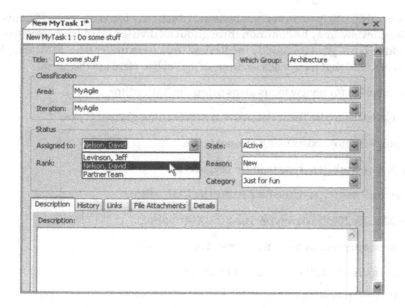

Figure 5-23. *Modified MyTask work item type*

4. Enter **Bob** in the Assigned To field and attempted to save the form. You should see the error message shown in Figure 5-24.

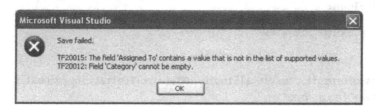

Figure 5-24. *The error message when you enter an invalid value for the modified work item type*

That's it. You have successfully modified your first work item type definition. Now let's see how to customize a work item type by adding a field.

Creating a New Field That References a Global List

Global lists are used to store common lists that will be used throughout the Team Foundation Server. They are server-scoped lists that can be referenced by any team project. Global lists can be used for many purposes.

■Tip You can see an example of populating your global lists from an external source on the Team Foundation weblog at `Populating Lists on Work Items from an External Source`.

Architects frequently participate in various reviews, which may focus on a specific customer concern. These reviews may be common throughout all divisions and projects within the company. To address this, you can modify the Review work item under the CMMI template to include a Focus Area field that references a common global list. Here are the steps:

1. Create the global list for review focus areas using the XML editor.

2. Import the global list to the Team Foundation Server using `glimport.exe`.

3. Verify the global list now exists using `glexport.exe`.

4. Export the review work item type using `witexport.exe`.

5. Rename the work item type name field using the XML editor.

6. Modify the XML file for the new type using the XML editor.

7. Import the new work item type using `witmport.exe`.

8. Test the form in Visual Studio using Team Explorer.

Now we'll go through the process.

Setting Up the Global List

The global list is just an XML file. Open Visual Studio, select File ➤ New File, and then select the XML file template. Insert the following XML, which defines a new global list called Focus Area with six distinct list items.

```xml
<?xml version="1.0" encoding="utf-8"?>
<gl:GLOBALLISTS
    xmlns:gl=
        "http://schemas.microsoft.com/VisualStudio/2005/workitemtracking/globallists">
        <GLOBALLIST name="Focus Area">
            <LISTITEM value="Architecture" />
            <LISTITEM value="Critical Design" />
            <LISTITEM value="Best Practice" />
            <LISTITEM value="Code" />
            <LISTITEM value="Security" />
            <LISTITEM value="Deployment" />
        </GLOBALLIST>
</gl:GLOBALLISTS>
```

Select File menu ➤ Save As and save your global list under the name `MyGL.xml` to your local directory `C:\Temp`.

To import the global list, open a Visual Studio command prompt and type the following:

```
glimport /f c:\temp\mygl.xml /t [Team Foundation Server Name]
```

After a few seconds, the prompt will return.

Since there is no confirmation that the global list has been loaded, run the glexport command with the display set to the screen to verify that it exists. Type the following:

```
glexport /t [Team Foundation Server Name]
```

After a few seconds, you will see the XML representing the global list displayed in the command window.

Adding a Field to the Work Item Type

First, follow the same process as in the previous example to export the work item type. This time, export the Review work item type from the CMMI process template by entering the following at the command prompt:

```
witexport /f myreview.xml /t [Team Foundation Server Name] /p [Team Project Name]
/n Review
```

Next, open the newly created file in Visual Studio and change the name field from WORKITEMTYPE name="Review"> to <WORKITEMTYPE name="MyReview">.

Now you need to define the Focus Area field and specify where to place the item on the form. The easiest way to create a new field is to copy and paste an existing one. Scroll down until you find the name Meeting Type. Copy the field definition, insert a line, and paste the definition back into the XML file. Make the following changes to the field definition:

```
<FIELD name="Focus Area" refname="MyCompany.VSTS.Common.FocusArea" type="String">
<HELPTEXT>The Focus Area of the review meeting</HELPTEXT>
        <ALLOWEDVALUES>
                    <GLOBALLIST name="Focus Area" />
        </ALLOWEDVALUES>
</FIELD>
```

The field reference name, refname, refers to a namespace constructed according to the recommended guidelines, as explained in the "Assigning Field Reference Names" section later in this chapter.

You will place the new field item below the Reason field on the form. Scroll down farther in the XML file and find the Reason field in the Form Layout section. It is the last field in the Status section. Copy the following Control line for the Reason field definition:

```
<Control Type="FieldControl" FieldName="System.Reason"
    Label="&amp;Reason:" LabelPosition="Left" />
```

Paste it as a new field below the Reason field. Make the following changes for the Focus Area definition:

```
<Control Type="FieldControl" FieldName="MyCompany.VSTS.Common.FocusArea"
    Label="Focus &amp;Area:" LabelPosition="Left" />
```

Then save the file.

With the command prompt still open, enter the following:

```
witimport /f myreview.xml /t [Team Foundation Server Name] /p [Team Project Name]
```

After a few seconds, you will receive the message "work item type import complete." This indicates that the MyReview work item has been uploaded to your server within the specified team project.

Open Visual Studio, and Team Explorer will connect to your Team Foundation Server. Expand your team project, right-click the Work Items node, and select Add Work Item. Select the new MyReview work item type.

Select the new Focus Area field, and in the drop-down list, you should see the six review areas listed, as shown in Figure 5-25.

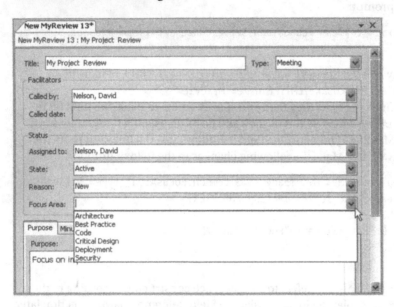

Figure 5-25. *MyReview modified work item type*

Creating a New Work Item Type

You may find that you need a completely custom work item type for your organization, such as one to track engagements—short duration activities in support of a variety of projects, teams, and initiatives. Here is the process for adding a new work item type:

1. Determine a base template type.

2. Design the states and transitions.

3. Export the base template type.

4. Rename the work item type.

5. Modify the work item type definition to add the fields and set the workflow.

6. Import the new work item type.

7. Test the form.

Let's go through the steps to add an Engagement Request type.

Setting Up the Base Template Type

The simplest way to create a brand-new work item type definition is to find an existing one close to what you want to track and modify the definition. For this example, you can use the Issue work item type and a few fields from the Requirement type. The Requirement type is designed for tracking a business need, and the Issue type is designed to investigate and resolve intermittent problems. That fairly completely describes the engagement process.

After you've determined the base work item type, it is best to diagram your states and transitions. You can capture the states and transitions in a specific tool like Visio or just graphically in a tool like Photoshop. Figure 5-26 shows the transition chart for the Engagement Request work item.

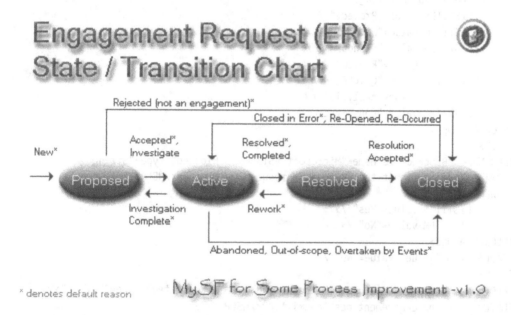

Figure 5-26. *State and transition chart for the custom Engagement Request work item type*

Adding the New Work Item Type

Follow the same process as in the previous examples to export the base work item type. If you have a combination, you need to pick just one for the base. You can export both, and then cut and paste items into the base type. For the Engagement Request, export the Issue work item type from the CMMI process template by entering the following from the command prompt:

```
witexport /f engagement.xml /t [Team Foundation Server Name] /p [Team Project Name]
/n Issue
```

Also use witexport to export the Requirement work item type for reference.

Open the newly created file in Visual Studio and change <WORKITEMTYPE name="Issue"> to <WORKITEMTYPE name="Engagement Request">.

When you are creating a new work item type, several items need to be addressed. As stated previously, the basic components of the work item type definition are the field, form, and workflow. Each of these must be addressed for the new Engagement Request type.

You need a new field to capture the type of engagement requested. Copy the XML for the Engagement Type field and paste it into your Engagement Request work item type between two existing fields. Bring over the Blocked field and the Committed field from the Requirement type. Also, do a quick search and replace to change the help text from issue to engagement request. (Be careful not change the field named Issue.)

```
<FIELD name="Engagement Type" refname="MyCompany.VSTS.Common.EngagementType"
 type="String" reportable="dimension">
<HELPTEXT>Indicates the type of engagement request</HELPTEXT>
<REQUIRED />
<ALLOWEDVALUES expanditems="true">
        <LISTITEM value="Project" />
        <LISTITEM value="Direction" />
        <LISTITEM value="Standards" />
        <LISTITEM value="Review" />
        <LISTITEM value="QuickFix" />
        <LISTITEM value="Analysis" />
        <LISTITEM value="Consultation" />
</ALLOWEDVALUES>
</FIELD>
<FIELD name="Blocked" refname="Microsoft.VSTS.CMMI.Blocked" type="String">
<HELPTEXT>Indicates that the engagement request is blocked</HELPTEXT>
<ALLOWEDVALUES>
        <LISTITEM value="Yes" />
        <LISTITEM value="No" />
</ALLOWEDVALUES>
<DEFAULT from="value" value="No" />
</FIELD>
<FIELD name="Committed" refname="Microsoft.VSTS.CMMI.Committed" type="String">
<HELPTEXT>Has the engagement been committed?</HELPTEXT>
<REQUIRED />
<ALLOWEDVALUES expanditems="true">
        <LISTITEM value="Yes" />
        <LISTITEM value="No" />
</ALLOWEDVALUES>
<DEFAULT from="value" value="No" />
</FIELD>
```

Next, you need to include the new fields on the form in the desired locations. Scroll down to the Form section and below the Title field on the top line, add the Type field. Change the Column PercentWidth for Title from 100 to 70 and add a Column PercentWidth tag above your Type field with a value of 30. The label should read Type:, and the FieldName must match the reference name above "MyCompany.VSTS.Common.EngagementType". Add the Committed and Blocked fields to the end of each column in the Status section. Place Committed under the Triage FieldName and Blocked under the Escalate FieldName.

Finally, set the DEFAULTREASON and additional reasons on each TRANSITION from one state to another. The following example is the default transition from Proposed to Active for the base Issue work item type. You can modify the workflow to be whatever fits your needs.

```
<TRANSITION from="Proposed" to="Active">
    <REASONS>
        <DEFAULTREASON value="Accepted" />
        <REASON value="Investigate" />
    </REASONS>
```

Save the file.

Now return to the command prompt and enter the following to import the new work item type:

```
witimport /f engagement.xml /t [Team Foundation Server Name] /p [Team Project Name]
```

After a few seconds, you will receive the message "work item type import complete."

You're ready to check that the new work item type works. Open Visual Studio and wait for the Team Explorer to connect to your Team Foundation Server. Expand your team project, right-click the Work Items node, and select Add Work Item. Select the new Engagement Request work item type to view the form, as shown in Figure 5-27.

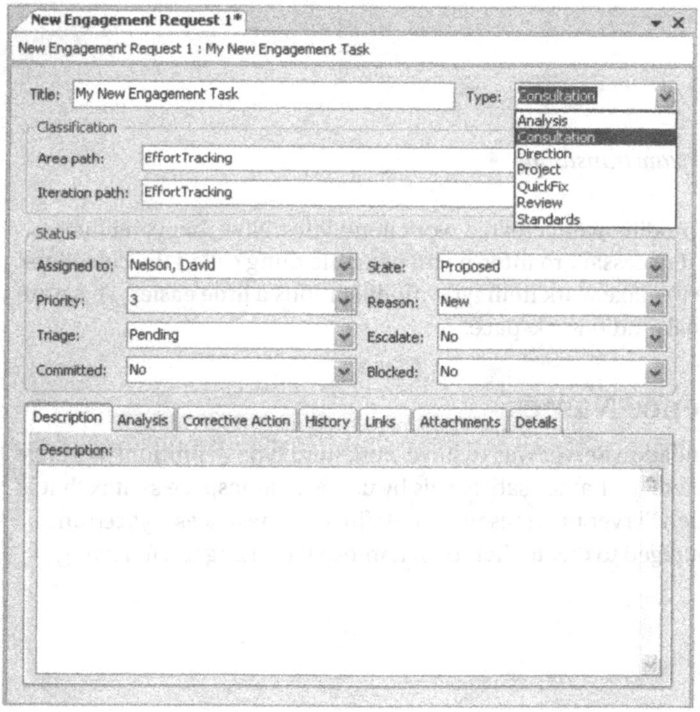

Figure 5-27. *Engagement Request work item type*

Check that the expected values show up in the Type, Committed, and Blocked fields. Also test any new transitions for your Engagement Request type. Fill out the required fields, and then save the work item in the proposed state. You can now move the work item from state to state and verify that the correct reason codes appear, as shown in Figure 5-28.

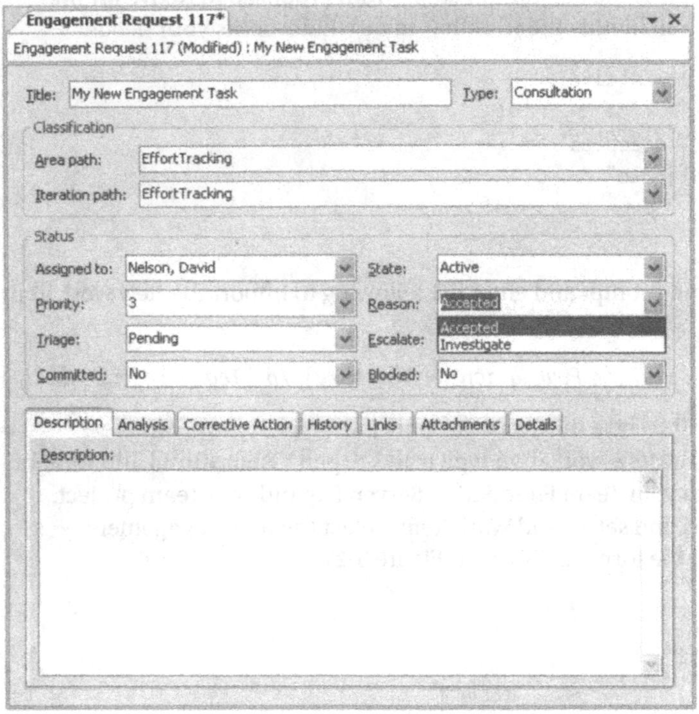

Figure 5-28. *Engagement Request state transitions*

Congratulations, you have modified and created work item types. Now that you have mastered long division, we feel it necessary to inform you of a little thing called the calculator. Graphic tools are now available to make work item type modifications a little easier. These are available on the GotDotNet Visual Studio workspace.

Assigning Field Reference Names

A key design goal for Team Foundation Server was to have work item type definitions portable between instantiations. Field reference names satisfy this by using a namespace syntax that is globally unique. Team Foundation Server provides two predefined namespaces: System and Microsoft. Customers are encouraged to create their own namespaces using the following guidelines:

- The reference name may be up to 70 characters long.

- The reference name must consist of two or more words separated by period. Each word may include English alphanumeric characters, digits, and underscores. The first word can begin only with an English letter (*a–z*) or an underscore.

- The custom reference name must not belong to System namespace (cannot begin with System).

Note The System namespace includes all system fields that are mandatory for Team Foundation system functions. These mandatory system fields are also referred to as *core fields*. Core fields like System.ID, System.AssignedTo, System.State, and System.Reason have their own rules that are hard-coded and cannot be changed. These fields are critical to the workflow, and it is extremely important that they behave in the same manner across the Team Foundation Server.

A common naming convention is to follow the Microsoft namespace and replace Microsoft with your company name, as in the following examples:

- MyCompany.VSTS.Agile.FieldName

- MyCompany.VSTS.Common.FieldName

- MyCompany.VSTS.MyProcess.FieldName

Summary

This chapter covered VSTS's work item tracking feature. We discussed the three different views for managing and creating work items: form, query, and result views. Then we looked at each default work item type provided with the MSF for CMMI Process Improvement - v4.0 process template.

We then took a quick peek under the hood and began to customize a default work item type. You learned how to create your own global lists, and also how to author a unique work item type using several base types. You should now have a good feel for the structure of the work item type. Feel free to explore your own modifications and creations.

CHAPTER 6

■■■

Team Reporting

The Team Foundation Server includes a data warehouse based on SQL Server 2005 Relational Database and Analysis Services. In this data warehouse, operational data from work item tracking, version control, team builds, and test results is gathered and rendered into multidimensional cubes. This data warehouse is used by Team Foundation and SQL Server 2005 Reporting Services (SSRS) for out-of-the-box reporting functionality. The schema for these databases is tailored to the methodologies used on the Team Foundation Server. SSRS is integrated with Team Foundation to provide easy access to reports and to offer a convenient mechanism for custom extensions.

In this chapter, you will learn how to produce project reports, including predefined reports, customized reports, and entirely new reports. But first, we'll start with an introduction to the SQL Server 2005 Business Intelligence platform.

Introducing the Business Intelligence Platform

Business Intelligence (BI) is a broad term for the services and process that turn a repository of obscure data into valuable business information. Business Intelligence is predicated on the notion of a central data warehouse that pulls disparate data from a wide variety of sources. Customarily, these extract, transform, and loads (ETL) of data are scheduled to occur on a regular basis and process the data into the online analytical processing (OLAP) cubes for reporting.

SQL Server 2005 has been termed "The BI Release." Included in this latest release are vastly upgraded versions of SQL Server Integration Services, SQL Server Analysis Services, and SQL Server Reporting Services, as illustrated in Figure 6-1.

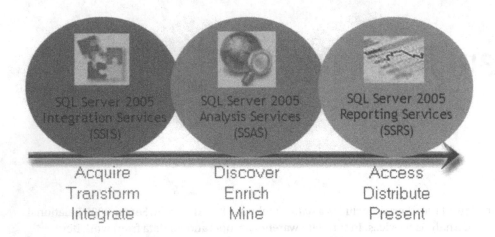

Figure 6-1. *SQL Server Business Intelligence platform*

These services perform the following functions:

SQL Server Integration Services (SSIS): This is the ETL tool provided with SQL Server 2005. SSIS is a rewrite of the Data Transformation Service (DTS) that shipped with SQL Server 2000. SSIS is a very powerful tool that provides many discrete events exposed at all levels of the transforms, as well as a complete workflow engine.

Note The Team Foundation Server does not use SSIS to migrate data between data stores. The Team Foundation Server uses custom adapters on the application tier to facilitate the data movement. SSIS will most likely be used by administrators to perform backup and maintenance functions.

SQL Server Analysis Services (SSAS): This is all about providing real-time business intelligence to the knowledge worker. The ability to combine the most recent information with historical information has been a difficult problem. Customarily, the most current data resides in the OLTP systems, while the historical data is normally stored in the enterprise data warehouse. This release of SSAS introduces the Unified Dimensional Model (UDM), which brings a balance in strength between the relational and OLAP constructs.

SQL Server Reporting Services (SSRS): This is positioned as an enterprise reporting platform and is provided as a core service of the SQL Server 2005 Business Intelligence suite. SSRS has a web services infrastructure and is easy to embed into other applications. SSRS is integrated with existing Microsoft Office applications, from SharePoint to Excel.

As we've mentioned earlier VSTS reporting is based on SSRS. Before we dive into the specifics of generating reports, let's take a look at the reporting life cycle.

Understanding the Reporting Life Cycle

The SSRS reporting life cycle includes authoring, management, and delivery, as illustrated in Figure 6-2.

Figure 6-2. *The reporting life cycle*

Reports can be authored in Visual Studio 2005 or by end users with the Report Builder graphical user interface. Table 6-1 shows a comparison of the features of these authoring tools. Creating reports is discussed in detail in the "Customizing Team Reports" and "Creating New Reports" sections later in this chapter. The report is an XML file based on the Report Definition Language, which has an .rdl filename extension.

Table 6-1. *Report Authoring Tools Feature Comparison*

Report Designer	Report Builder
Targeted at developers	Targeted at business users
Integrated into Visual Studio	Click-once application
Managed reports	Ad hoc reports
Native queries	Autogenerates queries
Free-form reports	Reports built on templates
Works with reports built in Report Builder	Cannot import Report Designer reports

■**Note** All of the reports shipped with the Team Foundation Server are built with Report Designer. Since Report Builder cannot import Report Designer reports, modifications must be done using Report Designer. Additionally, there are some difficulties using Report Builder against the Team Foundation Server cube structure.

Managing reports involves administering the reports, data sources, and permissions on the report server. Authored reports can be published to the report server from within Visual Studio, Report Builder, or by using the rs command-line utility (you must have appropriate permission granted on the server). You can also upload reports from within Report Manager on the server itself. Report Manager also provides the ability to organize content, define permissions, and manage properties for reports and data sources.

Delivering reports consists of publishing and managing them on the report server. The publication model can be either a pull or push to the consumer. To pull a report, you can browse to the Report Manager website and navigate to the desired report. If the My Reports feature is enabled, the server users can manage a My Reports page and create custom linked reports tailored for them. SSRS supports rendering of reports into various formats, including HTML, XML, PDF, TIFF, CSV, and Microsoft Excel. Finally, SSRS supports a subscription model in which consumers can subscribe to reports and receive e-mail notification on a scheduled basis.

Using Predefined Team Reports

The predefined reports supplied with your selected process template are listed on the SQL Server Reporting Services site. To access this site, open the Team Explorer window within Visual Studio 2005, right-click the Reports node and select Show Report Site, as shown in Figure 6-3.

Figure 6-3. *Choosing to go to the report site*

Figure 6-4 shows the SQL Server Reporting Services site for the EffortTracking project, which uses the MSF for CMMI Process Improvement - v4.0 process template. The predefined reports available with this process template are listed in Table 6-2.

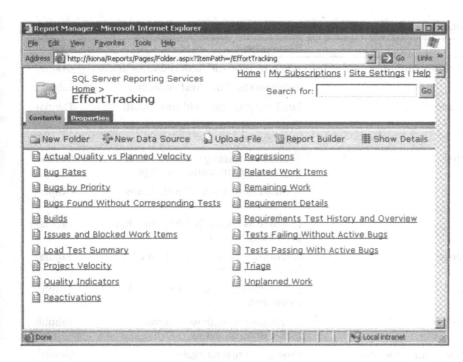

Figure 6-4. *EffortTracking Report Manager*

■Note In the current version of Team Foundation Server, the number of default reports provided is a bit confusing. Currently, the MSF for CMMI Process Improvement - v4.0 process template contains 19 reports in the default list view on the report server, 23 reports in the detail view, and 25 reports in total as .rdl files included with the process template. The MSF for Agile Software Development - v4.0 process template includes 16 reports in the default list view on the report server, 20 reports in the detail view, and 22 .rdl files.

Table 6-2. *MSF for CMMI Process Improvement*

Report	Description	Type
Actual Quality vs. Planned Velocity[1]	Bugs found per requirements resolved	Graph
Bug Rates[1]	Progress in finding, fixing, and closing bugs	Graph
Bugs by Priority[1]	Number of bugs active, found, and fixed by priority	Graph
Bugs Found Without Corresponding Tests	List of bugs found that have no associated tests	Tabular
Builds[1]	Build summary with test result details	Tabular

Continued

Table 6-2. *Continued*

Report	Description	Type
Issues and Blocked Work Items[1]	Issues by type with blocked work items	Graph
Load Test Detail	Subreport for Load Test Summary	Tabular
Load Test Summary	Load tests run by Build with Detail	Tabular
Project Velocity[1]	Direct comparison of resolve and close rates	Graph
Quality Indicators[1]	Number of tests by result vs. active bugs, code churn, and coverage	Graph
Reactivations[1]	Number of reactivated work items related to total work items	Graph
Regressions[1]	List of tests currently failing that had previously passed	Tabular
Related Work Items[1]	List of work items by iteration with linked work items	Tabular
Remaining Work[1]	Active, Resolved, and Closed work items by day	Graph
Requirements Detail[2]	Requirements with work item task/test result detail	Tabular
Requirements Test History and Overview[1]	Progress of testing against requirements over the duration of the project iteration	Graph
Tests Failing Without Active Bugs[1]	List of failing tests without active bugs to fix	Tabular
Tests Passing with Active Bugs[1]	List of passing tests with active bugs still against them	Tabular
Triage[1]	Proposed work items by type over time	Graph
Unplanned Work[1]	Amount of work added since start of iteration vs. planned	Graph
Work Items with Tasks	Subreport for Requirements Detail	Tabular
Work Items with Test Results	Subreport for Requirements Detail	Tabular
Work Items[3]	List of work items by iteration	Tabular

[1] *The report is detailed in the CMMI process guidance.*
[2] *The report is detailed in the process guidance, where it is called Scenario Detail.*
[3] *Work Items by Owner and Work Item by State are listed in the process guidance, but there is but no* `.rdl` *for them in the template.*

Table 6-3 lists the predefined reports that are available with MSF for Agile Software Development - v4.0 process template.

Table 6-3. *MSF for Agile Software Development - v4.0 Process Template Default Reports*

Report	Description	Type
Actual Quality vs. Planned Velocity[1]	Average number bugs per scenario for each iteration	Graph
Bug Rates[1]	Progress on finding, fixing, and closing bugs	Graph
Bugs by Priority[1]	Number of bugs active, found, and fixed by priority	Graph
Bugs Found without Corresponding Tests	List of bugs found that have no tests associated	Tabular
Builds	Build summary with test result details	Tabular
Load Test Detail	Subreport for Load Test Summary	Tabular
Load Test Summary	Load tests run by Build with Detail	Tabular
Project Velocity[1]	Direct comparison of resolve and close rates	Graph
Quality Indicators[1]	Number of tests by result vs. active bugs, code churn, and coverage	Graph
Reactivations[1]	Number of reactivated work items related to total work items	Graph
Regressions	List of tests currently failing that had previously passed	Tabular
Related Work Items	List of work items by iteration with linked work items	Tabular
Remaining Work[1]	Progress on scenario, including work item subreports	Graph
Scenario Detail	Scenario with work item task/test result detail	Tabular
Tests Failing Without Active Bugs	List of failing tests without active bugs to fix	Tabular
Tests Failing with Active Bugs	List of failing tests with active bugs still against them	Tabular
Unplanned Work[1]	Amount of work added since start of iteration vs. planned	Graph
Work Items with Tasks	Subreport list of work items for the Scenario Detail report	Tabular
Work Items with Test Results	Subreport test cases showing outcome, category, and machine for Scenario Detail report	Tabular
Work Items	List of work items by iteration	Tabular

[1] *The report is detailed in the Agile process guidance.*

Customizing Team Reports

Reports contained within the Team Foundation default process templates are simply SSRS custom reports. You can modify these reports to suit your needs using the Report Designer.

To use the Report Designer, you need to install Business Intelligence Development Studio (BIDS), which ships as a client component with SQL Server 2005, as shown in Figure 6-5.

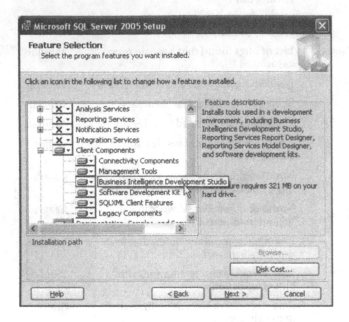

Figure 6-5. *Business Intelligence Development Studio is a SQL Server Setup option.*

BIDS is simply the Visual Studio shell with additional packages for SSAS, SSIS, and SSRS. If you already have VSTS, installing BIDS adds those project types to your suite in the same manner as adding the Team Explorer, as shown in Figure 6-6.

Once you have BIDS installed, you are ready to customize a report. Figure 6-7 illustrates the basic process for customizing a project report.

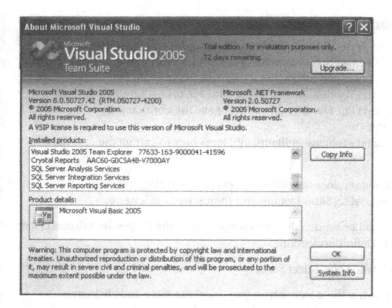

Figure 6-6. *Visual Studio installed products*

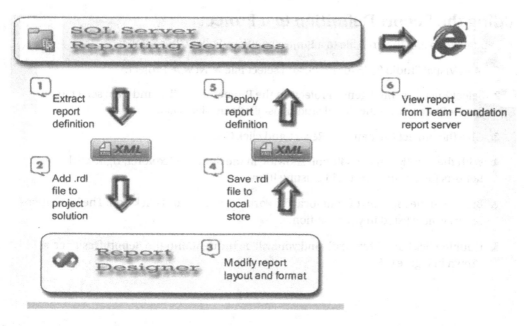

Figure 6-7. *Team report customization steps*

Here, we will work through a simple example of customizing the Work Items report. We will change the layout of the fields and modify the display elements on the report.

Extracting the Report Definition

To get started, you need access to the .rdl file for the existing report you want to customize. If you downloaded the MSF for CMMI Process Improvement - v4.0 process template through the Process Template Manager, as described in Chapter 2 (right-click the Team Foundation Server in the Team Explorer, select Team Foundation Server Settings ➤ Process Template Manager, select the process template, and click Download), you will have the entire report definition set resident on your local machine.

Alternatively, you can extract each one individually. Here's how to extract the .rdl file for the Work Items report:

1. Browse to your reporting services site (http://[*server*]/reports), select the EffortTracking project, select Show Details, and then select Work Items.

2. The Work Item report will be rendered in view mode. Select the Properties tab and click Edit under the Report Definition section.

3. In the File Download dialog box, select Save.

4. In the Save As dialog box, select a location on your local machine and click Save. An XML version of the report (.rdl) has now been saved.

Adding the Report Definition to a Project

Next, you need to add the .rdl file to a Project solution. Follow these steps:

1. Start Visual Studio 2005 (or BIDS) and select File ➤ New ➤ Project.

2. Select Business Intelligence Projects in the Project Types list, and then select Report Server Project from the Visual Studio installed templates list.

3. Give the project the name My Report and click OK.

4. With the new My Report solution showing in the Solution Explorer, right-click the Reports folder and select Add Existing Item.

5. Browse to the location of your local file Work Items.rdl and click Add. The Work Items report is now listed in your solution.

6. Double-click Work Items.rdl, and you will be brought into the Report Designer, as shown in Figure 6-8.

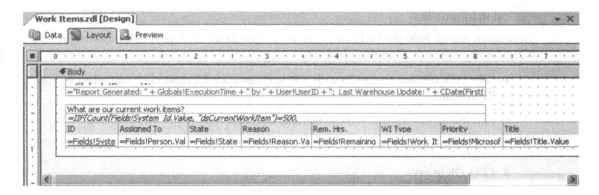

Figure 6-8. *Report Designer Layout tab*

The Report Designer includes three tabbed surfaces for working with reports:

- The Data tab is where you generate the queries for the report.

- The Layout tab is where you lay out and format the report.

- The Preview tab shows a rendered view of the report.

Note Reports in the Team Foundation Server use two predefined data sources stored on the report server at the root level: TfsOlapReportDs for the OLAP database and TfsReportDS for the relational database. You will want to create both of these data source references in your project to allow the process template-based reports to function properly.

Modifying the Report

For this example, we will make three changes to the report: move a field to another position, remove some information that is displayed, and add an image.

Moving a Field

Currently, the Title field is in the last column in the row. We will move it to appear next to the ID field.

1. Click inside the table near the word *Title*. This will expose the underlying table.

2. Click the blank header bar directly above the word *Title* to select the entire column.

3. Select Edit Cut to remove the Title field from the end of the row.

4. Press the left arrow key to move the cursor until the Assigned To field is highlighted, and then select Edit Paste. The Title field is now in the second position of the report row.

Removing Information

The default report includes the ID of the user who generated the report in the status text box. We will now remove that bit of information.

1. Select the text box that starts with =*"Report Generated:"*, right-click and select fx Expression.

2. Edit the expression and remove the following text:

   ```
   " by " + User!UserID +
   ```

3. Click OK to save.

Adding an Image

Finally, we will add an image to give the report some color.

1. Click the open space above the Priority column and then drag the Image object from the Report Items list.

2. The Image Wizard will start. Select Next.

3. Keep the default embedded for the image source and click Next.

4. Choose New Image and navigate to a small image you have stored locally. Click Next, and then click Finish. Your image is now embedded in the report definition.

Your layout should look something like that shown in Figure 6-9.

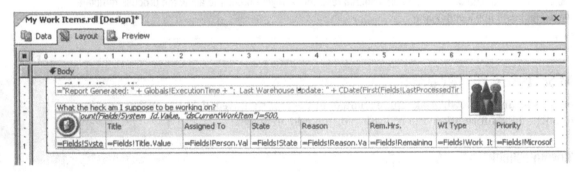

Figure 6-9. *Report Designer custom layout*

Saving the Modified Report Definition

After you've made your changes, you need to save your modified .rdl file.

1. Select File ➤ Save Work Items.rdl As. Click the Create New Folder icon.

2. Type Version One for the folder name, and then click OK.

3. In the Save File As dialog box, change the filename to My Work Items.rdl, and then click Save.

Tip Sometimes it takes several iterations before your report functions as intended. By saving the modified file in a separate folder each time, you can always go back to the previous versions.

Deploying and Viewing Your Report

You can deploy your new report to the Team Foundation report server directly from within Visual Studio. First, you must set the deployment properties for your My Report project.

1. Right-click My Report in the Solution Explorer and select Properties. The My Report Property Pages dialog box will be displayed, as shown in Figure 6-10.

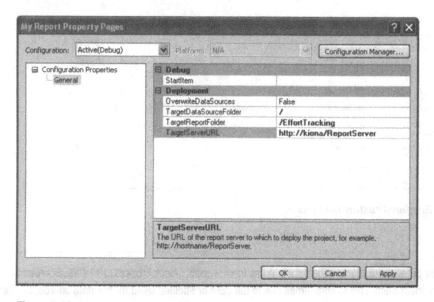

Figure 6-10. *My Report Property Page*

2. Verify that OverwriteDataSources is set to False. Enter / for the Target DataSourceFolder. Enter /EffortTracking for the TargetReportFolder. For TargetServerURL, enter your report server's URL. Click Apply to save the changes, and then click OK to close the dialog box.

3. On the main menu, select Build ➤ Deploy My Report.

4. Watch the output window for messages. You should see the message "Deploy: 1 succeeded."

5. Save and close the My Report project.

> **Note** Alternatively, you can browse to your reporting services site (http://[server]/reports), select the EffortTracking project, and then select Upload File from the Contents menu bar. Click the Browse button next to the File to Upload text box, locate your saved My Work Items.rdl file, and then click OK.

6. Open your browser and navigate to your report server site (http://[server]/reports).

7. Select the EffortTracking project, and then choose My Work Items from the Contents list. Your custom report will be rendered, as shown in Figure 6-11.

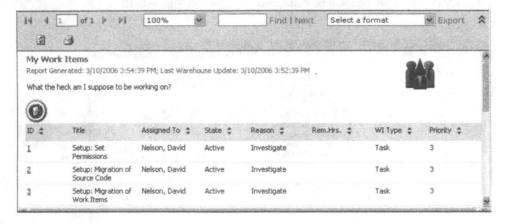

Figure 6-11. *Rendered customized report*

> **Note** If you get an error binding the data sources to the report, select Properties ➤ Data Sources and manually reconnect them. This is sometimes due to the case or spelling used for the data source; the data source names need to be exact.

Introducing the Team Foundation Data Warehouse

The Team Foundation Server contains a relational data warehouse and an OLAP database, both named TFSWarehouse in their respective environments. Relational databases are by definition two-dimensional, based on rows and columns, and rooted in mathematical set theory. OLAP databases introduce the concept of dimensions, which provide multidimensional views of the data.

Understanding the Data Warehouse Architecture

The relational data warehouse is populated from the main operational data stores within Team Foundation. This architecture is shown in Figure 6-12.

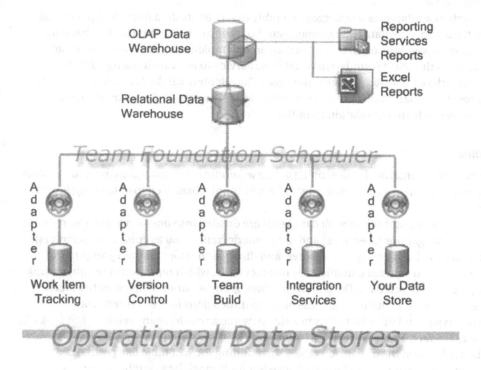

Figure 6-12. *Data warehouse architecture*

Operational Data Stores

Four operational data stores are provided with the Team Foundation Server:

- Work Item Tracking includes both the work item tracking store (TfsWorkItemTracking) and the work item tracking attachments store (TfsWorkItemTrackingAttachments).

- Version Control holds a single data store (TfsVersionControl) containing all the tables to operate the versioning subsystem.

- Team Build contains one data store (TfsBuild), which combines the build and test data stores.

- Integration services include both the activity logging data store (TfsActivityLogging) and the integration store (TfsIntegration).

Warehouse Adapters

Each operational data store has its own version of the warehouse adapter. Because each data store is customizable, it must be able to convey underlying changes to be incorporated into the data warehouse.

The warehouse adapter is a managed assembly that extracts data from the operational data store, transforms the data to a common warehouse format, and then writes that data into the relational warehouse. Each managed assembly implements the IWarehouseAdapter interface to allow the Team Foundation Warehouse Service to activate it, along with the IDataStore interface for writing to the warehouse. The adapters can be found in C:\Program Files\Microsoft Visual Studio 2005 Team Foundation Server\Web Services\Warehouse\ bin\Plugins on the Team Foundation Data Tier server.

Star Schema

The most common construct for describing a data warehouse is the star schema. This schema portrays the multidimensional arrangements for relational tables used in data analysis and reporting.

When designing a star schema, all data items are divided into one of two groups: numeric items used in aggregations (measures) and nonnumeric items used as context (descriptors). Fact tables contain the grouping of measures, and dimension tables contain groupings of descriptors. Each star schema contains only one fact table, which represents the subject area to be analyzed and reported on. Descriptors are then grouped around logical entity areas, such as person, date, and builds, and these become dimensions in the star schema.

Only one type of relationship exists in a star schema: a one-to-many relationship from the dimension to the fact. The star schema gets its name by the common arrangement of the fact table in the middle and the dimension tables surrounding the fact table like points on a star.

The Team Foundation reporting warehouse is a traditional data warehouse consisting of a relational database roughly organized around a star schema and an OLAP database built over the top. Figure 6-13 shows one of the subject areas, Code Churn, from TFSWarehouse.

Exploring the Data Warehouse Schema

The data warehouse schema is the template for the layout of the tables in TFSWarehouse. The initial schema can be found at \Program Files\Microsoft Visual Studio 2005 Team Foundation Server\Tools\warehouseschema.xml on the Team Foundation Data Tier Server. An updated copy is stored in the ConfigXML setting in the _WarehouseConfig table of TFSWarehouse. The three main areas in the template are Facts, Dimensions, and FactLinks. Each represents a significant component in the data warehouse and OLAP cube, as described in the previous section.

■**Note** Setupwarehouse.exe uses the version of warehouseschema.xml under the Tools folder during setup to build the warehouse. It is copied to the _WarehouseConfig table during the setup process. Ongoing schema changes update the version in the _WarehouseConfig table.

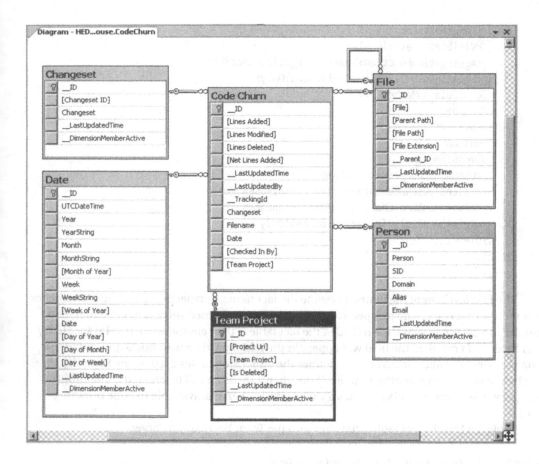

Figure 6-13. *Code Churn star schema*

Data Warehouse Facts

The fact table holds the primary (measurable) data for analysis. Facts are represented by `Fact`, `Fields`, and `DimensionUses`, as shown in Listing 6-1.

Listing 6-1. *Warehouse Template Facts Section*

```
<Facts>
  <Fact>
    <Name>Code Churn</Name>
    <FriendlyName>Code Churn</FriendlyName>
    <PerspectiveName>Code Churn</PerspectiveName>
    <IncludeCountMeasure>true</IncludeCountMeasure>
    <Fields>
      <Field>
        <Name>Lines Added</Name>
        <FriendlyName>Lines Added</FriendlyName>
        <Type>int</Type>
```

```
      <Length>0</Length>
      <Visible>true</Visible>
      <AggregationFunction>Sum</AggregationFunction>
      <RelationalOnly>false</RelationalOnly>
      <CalculatedMembers />
    </Field>
  <Measures />
  <DimensionUses>
    <DimensionUse>
      <UseName>Changeset</UseName>
      <FriendlyUseName>Changeset</FriendlyUseName>
      <DimensionName>Changeset</DimensionName>
      <RelationalOnly>false</RelationalOnly>
    </DimensionUse>
  </DimensionUses>
  </Fact>
</Facts>
```

The first few lines of the template define the fact name, perspective name, and whether or not to include a count. The perspective name refers to predefined subsets of cube metadata, similar to SQL Server views. Each field of the fact table is then enumerated. If `RelationalOnly` has a value of `true`, then the field will appear in the relational data warehouse but not in the analysis services cube. `DimensionUses` defines the dimension tables used by the `Fact`. If `IncludeCountMeasure` contains a value of `true`, then a measure will be created containing an integer value for `count`. If `Visible` has a value of `true`, then it is available to cube browsing tools.

Table 6-4 lists the fact tables that ship with the Team Foundation Server.

Table 6-4. *Fact Tables for the Team Foundation Server*

Number	Fact Table	Fields
1	Code Churn	Lines Added, Lines Modified, Lines Deleted, Net Lines Added
2	Work Item Changeset	Work Item, Changeset
3	Work Item History	Logical Tracking ID, Record Count, Revision Count, State Change Count
4	Current Work Item	Logical Tracking ID
5	Build Changeset	No fields are specified
6	Build Project	Compile Errors, Compile Warnings, Static Analysis Errors, Static Analysis Warnings
7	Build Details	Logical Tracking ID, Build Duration
8	Load Test Counter	Value
9	Build Coverage	Lines Covered, Lines Not Covered, Lines Partially Covered, Blocks Covered, Blocks Not Covered

Number	Fact Table	Fields
10	Run Coverage	Lines Covered, Lines Not Covered, Lines Partially Covered, Blocks Covered, Blocks Not Covered
11	Load Test Page Summary	Sequence, Test, Response Time, Page Count
12	Test Result	Result Record Count, Result Count, Result Transition Count
13	Load Test summary	Start Time, Actual Duration, Load Test Duration, Load Test Warmup Time
14	Load Test Details	Sequence, Test, Total Tests, Failed Tests, Average Duration
15	Load Test Transaction	Sequence, Test, Transactions, Response Time, Elapsed Time

Data Warehouse Dimensions

Dimensions are the descriptive data or categorical variables. The primary key of the dimension will be stored with the associated fact table. Dimensions are represented by Dimension, Fields, KeyFieldName, and OrderByField, as shown in Listing 6-2.

Listing 6-2. *Warehouse Template Dimensions Section*

```
<Dimensions>
  <Dimension>
    <Name>Changeset</Name>
    <FriendlyName>Changeset</FriendlyName>
    <Fields>
      <Field>
        <Name>Changeset ID</Name>
        <FriendlyName>Changeset ID</FriendlyName>
        <Type>int</Type>
        <Length>0</Length>
        <Visible>true</Visible>
        <RelationalOnly>false</RelationalOnly>
        <CalculatedMembers />
      </Field>
    <KeyFieldName>Changeset ID</KeyFieldName>
    <OrderByField>Changeset ID</OrderByField>
    <Levels />
  </Dimension>
```

Table 6-5 lists the dimension tables that ship with the Team Foundation Server.

Table 6-5. *Dimension Tables for the Team Foundation Server*

Number	Dimension Table	Fields
1	Area	Area, Area Uri, Parent Area Uri, Area Path, Forwarding ID, Project Uri
2	Assembly	Assembly
3	Build	Build Artifact Moniker, Build, Build Type, Drop Location, Build Start Time
4	Build Flavor	Build Flavor
5	Build Quality	Build Quality
6	Build Status	Build Status
7	Changeset	Changeset ID, Changeset
8	Date	UTCDateTime, Year, YearString, Month, MonthString, Month of Year, Week, WeekString, Week of Year, Date, Day of Year, Day of Month, Day of Week
9	File	File, Parent Path, File Path, File Extension
10	Iteration	Iteration, Iteration Uri, Parent Iteration Uri, Iteration Path, Forwarding ID, Project Uri
11	Load Test Counter Dimension	Counter ID, Counter Object, Counter, Counter Instance, Counter Result, Higher Is Better
12	Load Test Page Summary Dimension	URL
13	Load Test Scenario	Load Test Scenario
14	Load Test Transaction Dimension	Transaction
15	Machine	Machine
16	Outcome	Outcome, Outcome Passing
17	Person	Person, SID, Domain, Alias, Email
18	Platform	Platform
19	Result	Result ID, Result, Test, Test Type, Test Description, Parent Result, Result Root, Error Message, Load Test Agent List, End Time
20	Run	Run ID, Run, Run Description, Remote Run
21	Run Result	Run Result, Run Result Message
22	Team Project	Project Uri, Team Project
23	Test Category	Category ID, Test Category, Category Full Name, Parent Category
24	Today	Index, UTCDateTime, Year, YearString, Month, MonthString, Month of Year, Week, WeekString, Week of Year, Date, Day of Year, Day of Month, Day of Week
25	Tool Artifact Display URL	Tool Type, Tool Artifact, Display URL
26	WorkItem	Work Item, Previous State

Figure 6-14 shows the dimension tables used by facts for the Team Foundation Server data warehouse.

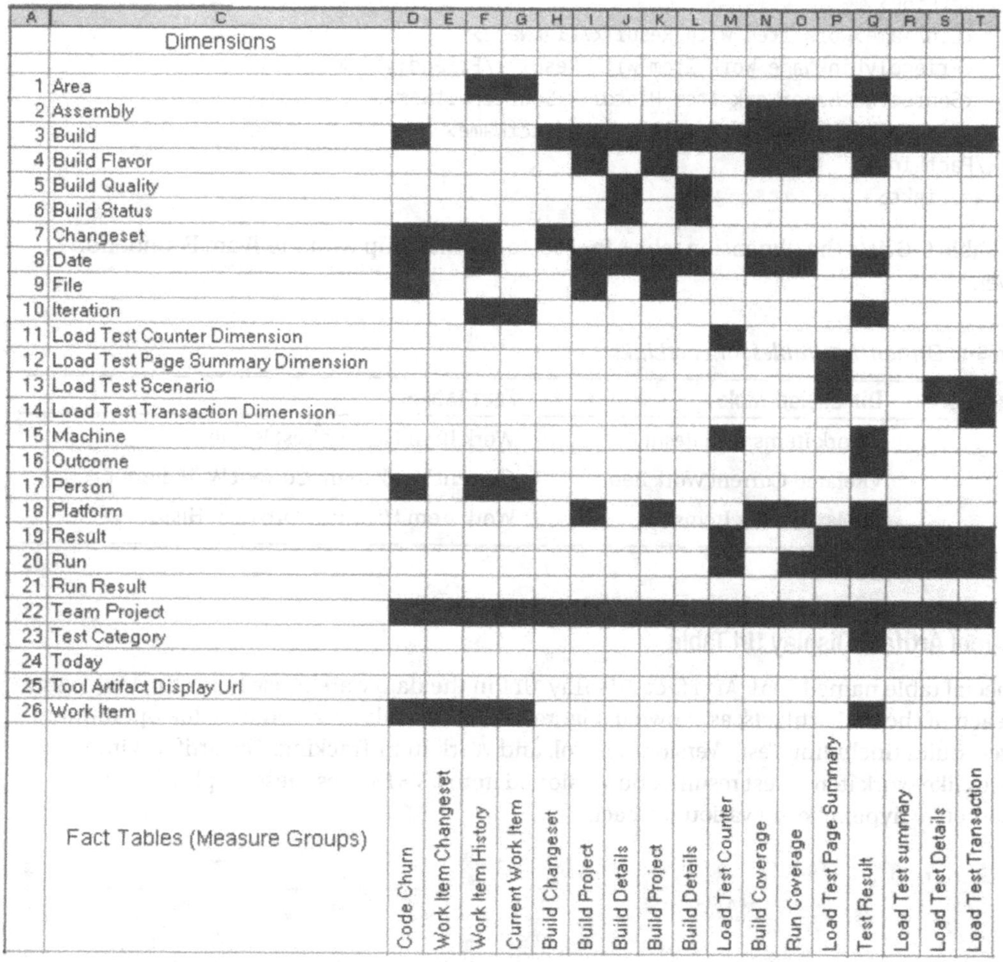

Dimensions

1. Area
2. Assembly
3. Build
4. Build Flavor
5. Build Quality
6. Build Status
7. Changeset
8. Date
9. File
10. Iteration
11. Load Test Counter Dimension
12. Load Test Page Summary Dimension
13. Load Test Scenario
14. Load Test Transaction Dimension
15. Machine
16. Outcome
17. Person
18. Platform
19. Result
20. Run
21. Run Result
22. Team Project
23. Test Category
24. Today
25. Tool Artifact Display Url
26. Work Item

Fact Tables (Measure Groups): Code Churn, Work Item Changeset, Work Item History, Current Work Item, Build Changeset, Build Project, Build Details, Build Project, Build Details, Load Test Counter, Build Coverage, Run Coverage, Load Test Page Summary, Test Result, Load Test summary, Load Test Details, Load Test Transaction

Figure 6-14. *Dimension tables used by facts*

■**Note** Every fact in the data warehouse contains a dimensional relationship with the team project dimension. This ensures that all fact data in the warehouse can be sliced by project.

Data Warehouse FactLinks

FactLinks are a view joining two related fact tables in the data warehouse. The result is that all fields from both fact tables are available for reporting. FactLinks are represented by the LinkName, SourceFactName, and LinkedFactName, as shown in Listing 6-3.

Listing 6-3. *Warehouse Template FactLinks Section*

```
<FactLinks>
  <FactLink>
    <LinkName>Work Item with Result</LinkName>
    <FriendlyLinkName>Work Item with Result</FriendlyLinkName>
    <SourceFactName>Work Item History</SourceFactName>
    <LinkedFactName>Test Result</LinkedFactName>
  </FactLink>
</FactLinks>
```

Table 6-6 lists the dimension tables for FactLinks that ship with the Team Foundation Server.

Table 6-6. *Dimension Tables for FactLinks*

Number	Dimension Table	Fact Tables
1	vWork Items with Result	Work Item History, Test Result
2	vRelated Current Work Items	Current Work Item, Current Work Item
3	vRelated Work Items	Work Item History, Work Item History

The Tool Artifact Display Url Table

A special table named Tool Artifact Display Url in the data warehouse holds the URL paths for each of the tool artifacts, as shown in Figure 6-15. The tools correspond to the operational stores: Build (including Test), Version Control, and Work Item Tracking. The artifacts include entries like work items, test results, and versioned items. VSTS uses these display URLs to allow active hyperlinks on various artifacts.

ID	Tool Type	Tool Artifact Display Url	LastUpdat...	Dimensi...
1	Build/Build	http://kiona:8080/Build/Build.aspx?artifactMoniker=	12/27/2005 ...	True
2	WorkItemTracking/HyperLink	http://kiona:8080/WorkItemTracking/HyperLink.aspx?artifactMoniker=	12/27/2005 ...	True
3	WorkItemTracking/Workitem	http://kiona:8080/WorkItemTracking/Workitem.aspx?artifactMoniker=	12/27/2005 ...	True
4	VersionControl/Changeset	http://kiona:8080/VersionControl/Changeset.aspx?artifactMoniker=	12/27/2005 ...	True
5	VersionControl/Label	http://kiona:8080/VersionControl/Label.aspx?artifactMoniker=	12/27/2005 ...	True
6	VersionControl/LatestItemVersion	http://kiona:8080/VersionControl/LatestItemVersion.aspx?artifactMoniker=	12/27/2005 ...	True
7	VersionControl/VersionedItem	http://kiona:8080/VersionControl/VersionedItem.aspx?artifactMoniker=	12/27/2005 ...	True
8	TestTools/TestResult	http://kiona:8080//Build/TestTools/TestResult.aspx?artifactMoniker=	12/27/2005 ...	True
NULL	NULL	NULL	NULL	NULL

Figure 6-15. *The Tool Artifact Display Url table*

Managing the Data Warehouse

The Controller web service exposes eight operations to help manage the TFSWarehouse, as shown in Figure 6-16. To access this service, log on to the application tier and browse to http://localhost:8080/Warehouse/v1.0/warehousecontroller.asmx.

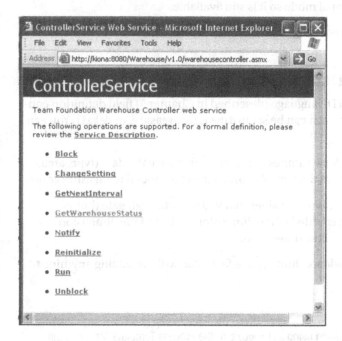

Figure 6-16. *Team Foundation Warehouse Controller web service*

These operations work as follows:

- *Block:* Turns off warehouse processing until Unblock is called.

- *ChangeSetting:* Allows you to change settings stored in the warehouse database table _WarehouseConfig via the web service (settings include RunIntervalSeconds and DailyFullProcessingHour).

- *GetNextInterval:* Returns RunIntervalSeconds from the _WarehouseConfig table.

- *GetWarehouseStatus:* Gets the current status from the warehouse. The service will respond with ProcessingAdapters (schema modifications), ProcessingOlap (schema modifications), ProcessingAdapters (pulling data), ProcessingOlap (processing the cube), or Idle (waiting).

- *Notify:* Makes a Run call. Used by the Project Creation Wizard to bring the warehouse online quicker after project creation.

- *Reinitialize*: Reinitializes the warehouse by reloading the adapters and initializing state. The warehouse must be in a blocked and idle state.

- *Run:* Sets two distinct activities in motion. Each of the operational store plugins will gather data from its associated data store and write to the data warehouse. Next, it will process the cube in transactional mode so it is still available.

- *Unblock:* Turns warehouse processing back on after a Block call.

Adding Elements to the Data Warehouse

The Work Item Type Definition (WITD) language (described in Chapter 5) field definition contains an option named reportable, which can be set to dimension, measure, or detail. You can use these as follows:

- Use reportable="dimension" for attributes that you want to slice the data (type, area, and so on). A column is added to the fact table and a measure added to measure group.

- Use reportable="measure" for numeric values that you want to aggregate (hours, counts, and so on). A column is added to the dimension table and the dimension ATTRIBUTE is added to the Work Item dimension.

- Use reportable="detail" to add a column to the fact table without adding anything to the cube.

Note After the process template is updated using witimport or the Process Template Manager, the new reportable fields will be put in the data warehouse the next time the adapters are executed.

Data Mining with Microsoft Excel

Microsoft Excel is an excellent client to manipulate data stored in the Team Foundation Server data warehouse. As an example, we'll go through the steps for bringing some data into Excel and then creating a simple report.

Note This functionally is fully support in Microsoft Excel 2003 and enhanced in Microsoft Excel 2007 (currently in beta).

Bringing Team Foundation Data into Excel

Follow these steps to bring Team Foundation data into an Excel pivot table:

1. Open Microsoft Office Excel 2003.

2. From the main menu, select Data ➤ Pivot Table and Pivot Chart Report.

3. On the first page of the wizard, select External Data Source, as shown in Figure 6-17, and click Next

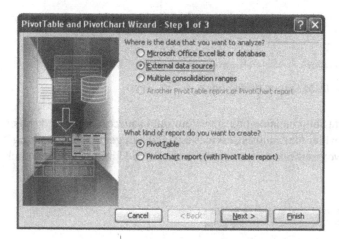

Figure 6-17. *Excel PivotTable and PivotChart Wizard Step 1*

4. On the second page of the wizard, shown in Figure 6-18, click Get Data.

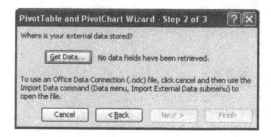

Figure 6-18. *Excel PivotTable and PivotChart Wizard Step 2*

Note If Microsoft Query is not installed, you will be prompted to install it.

---

5. In the Choose Data Source dialog box, select the OLAP Cubes tab, and then select <New Data Source>, as shown in Figure 6-19. Click OK.

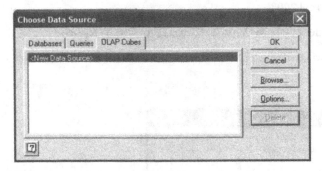

Figure 6-19. *The Choose Data Source dialog box*

6. In the Create New Data Source dialog box, give your data source a name and select Microsoft OLE DB Provider for Analysis Services 9.0 (you can get this by installing the SQL Server 2005 workstation components), as shown in Figure 6-20. Then click Connect.

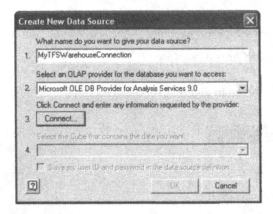

Figure 6-20. *The Create New Data Source dialog box*

7. In the Multidimensional Connection 9.0 dialog box, make sure Analysis Server is selected. Provide the name of your data tier server and your login credentials, as shown in Figure 6-21. Then click Next.

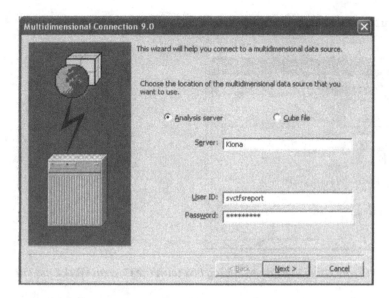

Figure 6-21. *The Multidimensional Connection dialog box*

8. Select the OLAP database (TfsWarehouse), as shown in Figure 6-22, and then click Finish.

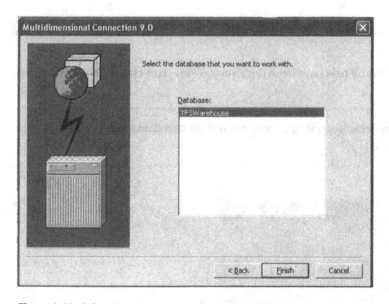

Figure 6-22. *Selecting the TFSWarehouse database*

9. Select the Current Work Item cube, as shown in Figure 6-23, and then click OK.

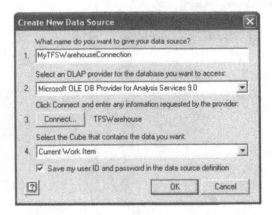

Figure 6-23. *The Create New Data Source dialog box with the Current Work Item cube selected*

■**Note** With SQL Standard Edition, only one perspective (cube), called Team System, is used.

---

10. Make sure your new data source is selected in the Choose Data Source dialog box, and then click OK.

11. The data fields will now have been retrieved, as shown in Figure 6-24. Click Next.

■**Note** If you get an error messages stating "Initialization of the data source failed," you will need to register the msolap90 dll.

Figure 6-24. *Excel PivotTable and PivotChart Wizard Step 2 after retrieving data*

12. Select the default location on the existing worksheet, as shown in Figure 6-25, and then click Finish.

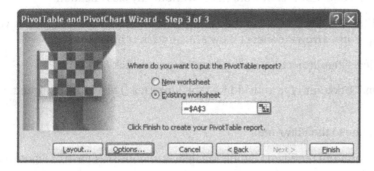

Figure 6-25. *Excel PivotTable and PivotChart Wizard Step 3*

At this point, you have an empty pivot table bound to the Current Work Item Fact cube, as shown in Figure 6-26.

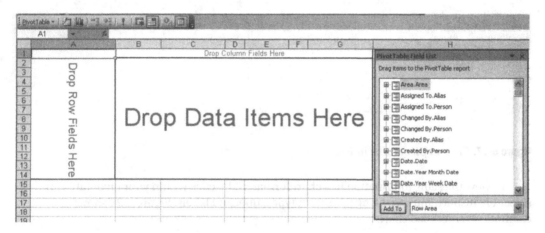

Figure 6-26. *Empty pivot table in Excel*

Creating a Report

There are four measures at the end of the Pivot Table Field List: Current Work Item Count, Remaining Work, Completed Work, and Baseline Work. You'll use Current Work Item Count, which gives you the total counts for any slice, for most queries.

For example, if you want to create a list of your Work Items by Type report, use the Current Work Item Count measure, filter to Team.Project=EffortTracking, and slice by Type. TransitionCount is used to show the state transition activity.

To see how this works, follow these steps:

1. Select the Current Work Item Count measure and add it to the data area. This will now show a count of the total number of work items without any classification.

2. Select Assigned To.Person and add it to the Row Area. If there are multiple people, you can use the drop-down arrow, deselect (Show All), and select only yourself.

3. Select TeamProject.TeamProject, select the Page Area, and click Add To.

4. Select Work Item.Work Item Type and add it to the Row Area. The Work Items are now sliced by Type.

5. Add Work Item.State to the Row Area.

The simple Excel report from the Team Foundation data warehouse is shown in Figure 6-27.

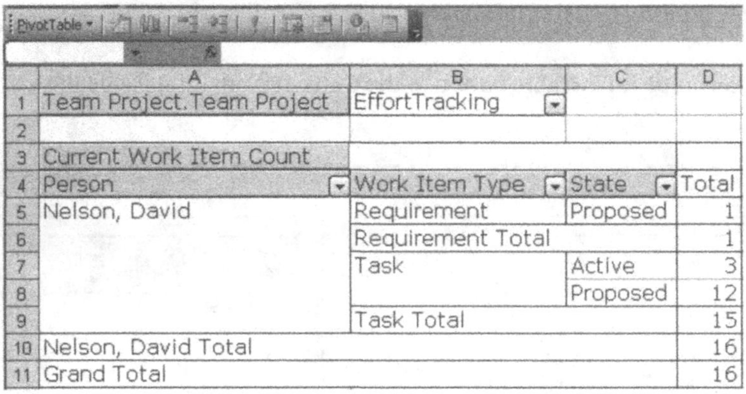

	A	B	C	D
1	Team Project.Team Project	EffortTracking		
2				
3	Current Work Item Count			
4	Person	Work Item Type	State	Total
5	Nelson, David	Requirement	Proposed	1
6		Requirement Total		1
7		Task	Active	3
8			Proposed	12
9		Task Total		15
10	Nelson, David Total			16
11	Grand Total			16

Figure 6-27. *Custom pivot table in Excel*

To view the same information in a chart format, right-click within your pivot table and select PivotChart. You can change the chart types, title, and labels. Figure 6-28 shows an example of a modified chart.

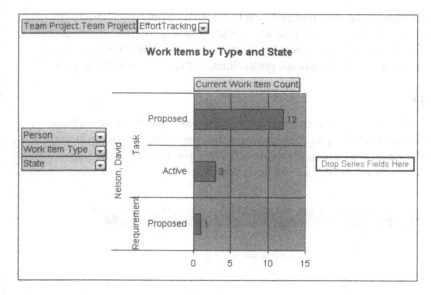

Figure 6-28. *Custom pivot table chart in Excel*

Creating a New Report

Creating a new report from scratch is not difficult using a Visual Studio Business Intelligence Project template, which was introduced earlier in the section about customizing reports. Although you do not have a base report to use as a starting point, you do have the help of the Report Server Project Wizard. An overview of the process is shown in Figure 6-29.

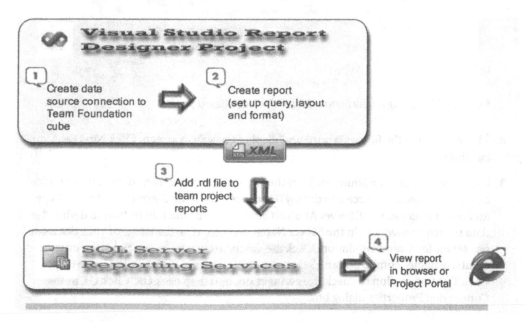

Figure 6-29. *Creating a new report*

As an example, we'll create a simple report. It will be based on a query that shows the distinction between the cumulative count and transition (State Change) count. The cumulative count (sliced by state and date) will show totals for the period (week). The transition count (sliced by state and date) will reveal activations, resolutions, and closures within the period (week).

Follow these steps:

1. Start Visual Studio 2005 (or BIDS) and select File ➤ New ➤ Project. Select Business Intelligence Projects in the Project Types list, and then select Report Server Project Wizard from the Visual Studio installed templates list. Give the project the name MyNewTFSReport, as shown in Figure 6-30, and then click OK.

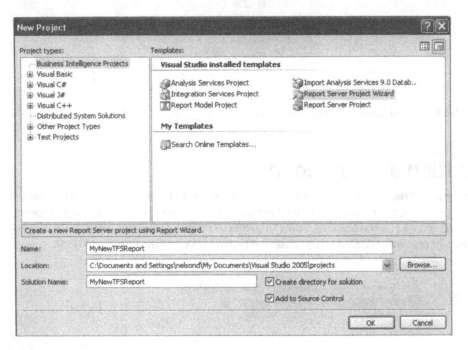

Figure 6-30. *Starting a new Report Server Project Wizard project*

2. This will launch the Report Wizard and display the splash screen. Click Next to continue.

3. On the Select the Data Source page of the wizard, select the "New data source" radio button and give the source a name (myTFSsource). Click the down arrow for the Type and select Microsoft SQL Server Analysis Services. Click the Edit button to define the data source connection. In the Server Name text box, type the name of your database tier server for Team Foundation. Click the down arrow next to the "Select or enter a database name" combo box and select the TFSWarehouse, as shown in Figure 6-31. Click Test Connection to check the connection, and then click OK. Click OK in the Connection Properties dialog box.

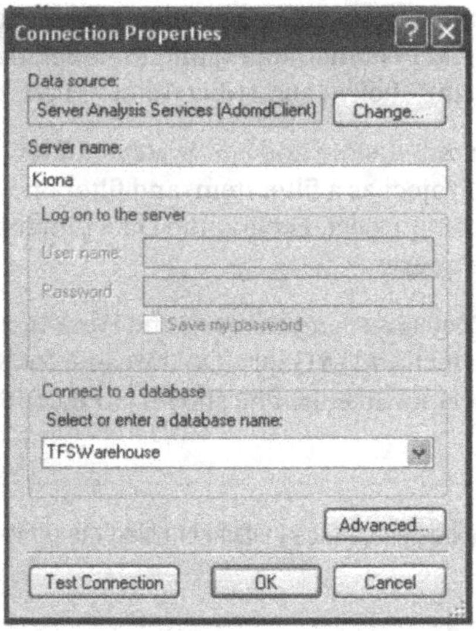

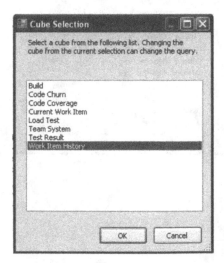

Figure 6-31. *The Connection Properties dialog box*

4. You will now see the connection string populated in the Select the Data Source page. Click Next.

5. On the Design the Query page, click Query Builder to launch the Multidimensional Expressions (MDX) query builder. (MDX allows you to query multidimensional sources such as TFSWarehouse cubes and return cell sets of the cube's data.)

6. Now you need to select the cube for the query. Click the ellipsis button in the top-left pane to open the Cube Selection window. For this example, select Work Item History, as shown in Figure 6-32, and then click OK.

Figure 6-32. *The Cube Selection window*

7. Within the Work Item History cube, expand the Assigned To dimension. Right-click Person and select Add to Query. Click to expand Person, then expand Member, then expand All. Scroll down to find your name, right-click it, and select Add to Filter.

8. Repeat this process to expand the Work Item dimension, and add System_State and System_Reason to the query. Add Team Project as a filter item, and filter on EffortTracking if you have more than one team project. Expand the Date dimension, expand Year Week Date, and add Week to the query.

9. To add the measures to your query, expand Measures, and then expand Work Item History. Right-click Cumulative Count and select Add to Query. Do the same for State Change Count. Your query design should now look like the one shown in Figure 6-33.

■**Note** If you prefer, you can drag-and-drop items onto the design surface instead of using the right-click and add method.

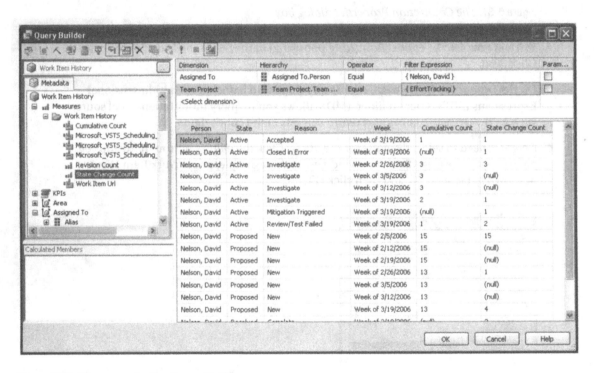

Figure 6-33. *The query in the Query Builder*

10. Click OK in the Query Builder, and you will see your MDX query displayed in the Design the Query page of the wizard, as shown in Figure 6-34. Click Next to continue.

Tip If you would like to see the MDX query while using the designer, you can click the design mode icon in the Query Builder to toggle back and forth between the design and the MDX query.

Figure 6-34. *The query built with the Query Builder*

11. You will be prompted for the report type. Select the default Tabular report type and click Next.

12. The Design the Table page shows the six available fields. Select Person in the Available fields and click the Page button to move it to the Page level fields. Select Week and click the Group button to move it to the Group level. Move the remaining four fields to the Details level. Your page should look like the one shown in Figure 6-35. Click Next.

Select the Stepped layout and check both Include Subtotals and Enable Drilldown, as shown in Figure 6-36. This will allow you to expand the rows for more detail and provide subtotals on the rows when the detail is collapsed. Click Next.

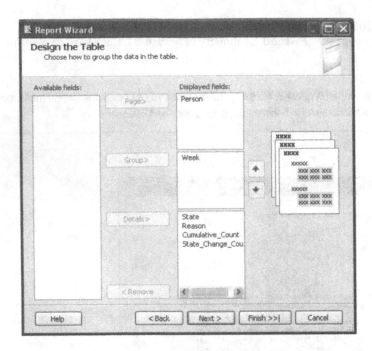

Figure 6-35. *Designing the tabular report*

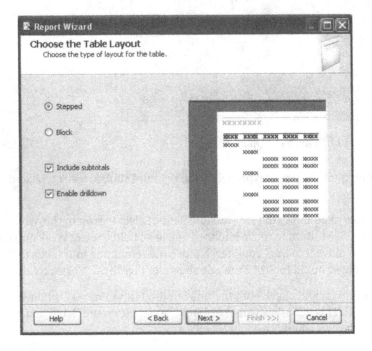

Figure 6-36. *Designing the tabular layout*

14. Select the Forest style sheet on the Choose the Table Style page, and then click Next.

15. Select the deployment location for your report: the Team Foundation report server and the team project name for the Deployment folder.

16. Name the report **MyTFSReport**. Then review the summary information, select Preview report, and click Finish.

17. Once the report is rendered in a preview, you can toggle to the layout view and change the title or other layout features. Your final report is shown in Figure 6-37.

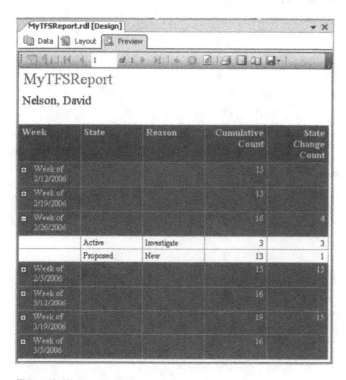

Figure 6-37. *Preview of a custom report*

18. To deploy your custom report, right-click MyTFSReport.rdl in the Solution Explorer and select Deploy.

Summary

This chapter opened with a brief introduction to the SQL Server 2005 Business Intelligence platform and an overview of SSRS and the reporting life cycle. Then we covered the predefined reports shipped with both the MSF for Agile Software Development - v4.0 and MSF for CMMI Process Improvement - v4.0 process templates. We walked through the process of customizing a report from the CMMI template using the Report Designer integrated within Visual Studio.

We then took a look at the Team Foundation data warehouse and how it works. Next, we worked through an example of data mining with Microsoft Excel against the data warehouse. Finally, we created a report from scratch.

CHAPTER 7

■ ■ ■

Team Foundation Build

This chapter describes how to perform automated builds using VSTS. Automated builds are a key part of ensuring a high-quality, low-cost system. That is not to say that using nightly, automated builds will result in a low-cost system, but that it will result in a lower cost when compared to an equivalent system that does not perform these builds. That statement in itself should be highly suspect to you right now, because performing builds in and of itself does nothing to reduce cost. With that in mind, it might be a good idea to understand what occurs with these types of builds. So, first we'll explain the automated build process and its benefits, and then we'll look at using Team Foundation Build.

Benefits of Automated Builds

The process of nightly builds typically follows this path:

- Get the latest version of code from the source code repository.

- Perform a build.

- Deploy the build (this may or may not be necessary depending on the type of application).

- Run *all* of the unit tests associated with the code.

- Publish the test results to the Team Foundation Server.

This type of test is called a build verification test (BVT). Believe it or not, this is a concept that has been adopted very slowly. Tools such as Ant, NAnt, JUnit, and NUnit have made this process much easier to implement. There were always barriers for developers though. These revolved around the source code repository itself. Have you ever tried to write code that would automatically pull the latest version of code or a specific version of code from Visual Source-Safe (or CVS for that matter)? If you have, you know that that is a software development project in and of itself.

So how does this help reduce cost and increase quality? First, by performing nightly builds, you know exactly when the code breaks. Compare this to running builds once a week. When did the code break? Who broke it? Where is it broken? By doing this nightly, you avoid these issues.

Second, running the unit testing provides a measure of the quality of the build. It allows for regression testing to be performed every night. Breaks are discovered immediately and corrected immediately. This means that as you work closer toward release, you can be confident that your code works. The other advantage of this approach is that the software can always be demonstrated to the stakeholders because it always works.

This is not to say that you should not worry about the testing using this process, because you still need to perform function and system testing. However, performing BVTs adds a level of confidence in working with your code. It also increases the confidence that your stakeholders have in you and your team because they can see that things are working. And finally, it decreases the number of bugs and the amount of work to fix those bugs that are found as you approach the release date.

Tip If you are using a test-driven development methodology, or even just good coding change management practices, developers should be performing builds and running tests *before* checking their code in anyway. If this process is followed, it is unlikely that the BVTs will report errors, but they may help find errors that were overlooked because of a break in the processes. And any errors found before functional or system testing are that much easier and cheaper to correct.

Using Team Foundation Build

You can use Team Foundation Build simply to perform regular builds to make sure that the project can be built. However, to truly take advantage of Team Foundation Build's capabilities, you should establish procedures that promote using it. This means that there should be rules that say that developers will *not* check in code that a) does not build, b) does not have unit tests, and c) does not pass its unit tests. Following these three, sometimes not-so-simple rules, will increase the quality of your code greatly and allow you to gain more benefit from performing these nightly tests.

Note Chapter 3 discusses setting up check-in policies. One of the available policies is the Testing Policy, which ensures that code passes certain tests before it is checked in. There are no policies to enforce code passing a BVT.

Creating a Build Type

To set up Team Foundation Build, you configure a Team Foundation build type. A *build type* is a set of instructions, or steps, that guide the process of creating and testing an application. These instructions are stored as a build type on the Team Foundation Server.

Caution Even though you can create build types without having Team Foundation Build installed, you do need Team Foundation Build (a separate installation) in order to be able to run the builds. For this demonstration, Team Foundation Build is installed on the same machine as the development machine (mcsd-dev).

To create a build type, follow these steps:

1. Select the Team Explorer pane and expand the Team Foundation Builds node.

2. Right-click the Team Foundation Builds node and select New Team Foundation Build Type. This starts the New Team Build Type Creation Wizard.

3. On the wizard's Welcome page, enter a title and optionally a description, as shown in Figure 7-1. The description should describe in detail what this particular build does, as there may be many different build types for various parts of the system, especially when you're working on a large system with many different projects or solutions. After you've entered the information, click Next to continue.

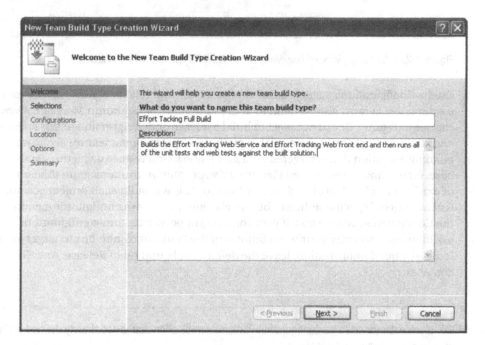

Figure 7-1. *Starting the New Team Build Type Creation Wizard*

4. On the Selections page, select which solutions you want to build. The workspace options allow you to select workspaces defined in version control. Once you have made this selection, the solutions listed are those located within the selected workspace. For this example, select the EffortTrackingSolution, as shown in Figure 7-2, and then click Next.

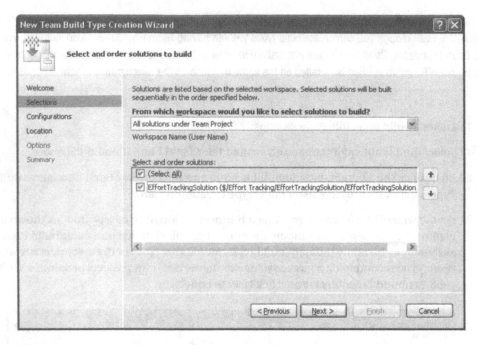

Figure 7-2. *Selections page of the New Team Build Type Creation Wizard*

5. On the Configurations page, you can choose to test your release against various configurations, which must also be defined in the solution's Configuration Manager. As you can see in Figure 7-3, you can elect to build a release or debug version of the solution, and you can target any of the available platforms. This is a great feature if you are building a solution that is targeted for a 32-bit and 64-bit release using the same code base, for example. Select Mixed Platforms if your solution contains more than one type of platform (such as Web, Windows, and so on). This will build each project according to that projects' specific settings. You can also enter your own configuration name in the Configuration combo box, if your solution supports a custom configuration. In addition, you can enter your own platform in the Platform combo box to target in the build. For this demonstration, leave the default configuration of Release/Any CPU and click Next.

■**Caution** If you enter (or select) a Configuration/Platform combination that is not already defined in the solution, that particular build will be skipped.

---

6. On the Location page, select where the build and tests will be performed and where the completed build will be placed after everything has been done, as shown in Figure 7-4. For this example, select the local machine on which you are running VSTS, which must have Team Foundation Build installed on it, and specify a local directory (if it does not exist, it will be created). The drop location can be anywhere.

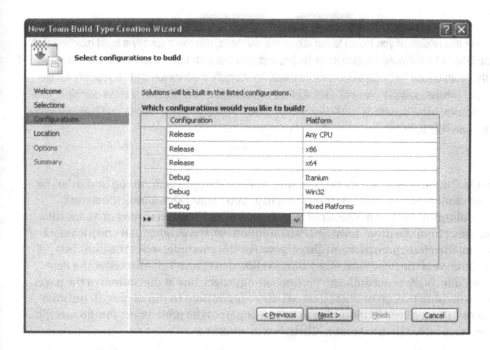

Figure 7-3. *Configurations page of the New Team Build Type Creation Wizard*

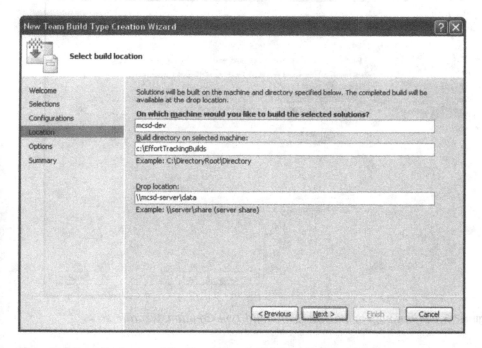

Figure 7-4. *Location page of the New Team Build Type Creation Wizard*

■**Caution** For this release, if you intend to run any of the unit tests, you must specify a build machine that has the Team Edition for Software Developers or Testers installed. For web tests to run, the build machine must have the Team Edition for Software Testers installed. Additionally, the location that you specify for the build must have enough available space to hold all of the source files for the solution and the compiled solution. This is because Team Foundation Build does a "Get Latest" from the version control, and then builds the solution in the specified location.

7. On the Options page, specify the tests and analysis that you want to run as part of the build. Notice that you can select only test lists; you cannot select individual tests (including ordered tests). The list of tests is controlled by which testing metadata file you select from the drop-down list. Each solution can have more than one metadata file and therefore more than one list of tests. For this example, select the Run Test check box and the Read Tests check box, as shown in Figure 7-5. Also select the Perform Code Analysis According to Project Settings check box at the bottom of the page. This will cause FxCop (or PREfast for a C/C++ application) to run as part of the build process, *if* you selected this option to be run as part of the preferences for the specific projects involved in the solution. Click Next to continue.

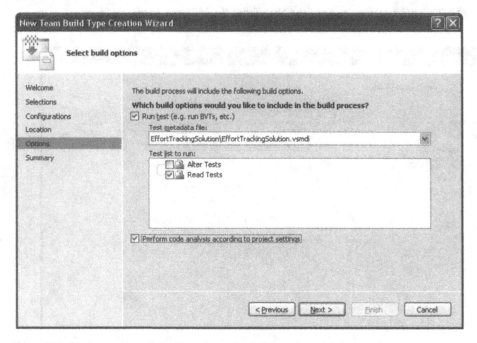

Figure 7-5. *Options page of the New Team Build Type Creation Wizard*

8. The Summary page provides a list of all of the choices you have made in the wizard, as shown in Figure 7-6. Click Finish to complete the wizard.

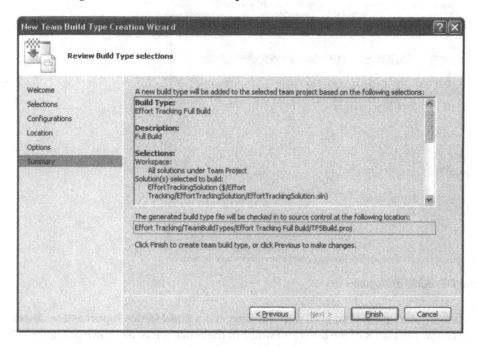

Figure 7-6. *Summary page of the New Team Build Type Creation Wizard*

Team Foundation Build will then display the XML configuration file used to store the settings, which can be edited by hand at any time, as described in the "Customizing the Build Process" section later in this chapter. In addition, the build type that you just created will appear under the Team Foundation Builds node in the Team Explorer.

If you need to delete a build type, open the Source Control Explorer and drill down to the build type folder ((*Server*)\(*Solution*)\TeamBuildTypes\(*BuildType*)). Right-click the build type that you want to delete (the folder) and select Get Latest. Then right-click the build type folder and select Delete. Finally, commit the deletion in the Pending Changes dialog box.

Running the Build and Viewing Build Results

Once you've set up the build type, running the build is simple. Right-click the build type under the Team Foundation Builds node and select Build Team Project Effort Tracking. This displays the Build dialog box, which allows you to make any last-minute changes to the build machine or directory, as shown in Figure 7-7. Click the Build button to run the build.

Figure 7-7. *Build dialog box*

At this point, the solution will start building, and a Build Detail Report will be displayed to let you know the status of the build and where in the process it is, as shown in Figure 7-8.

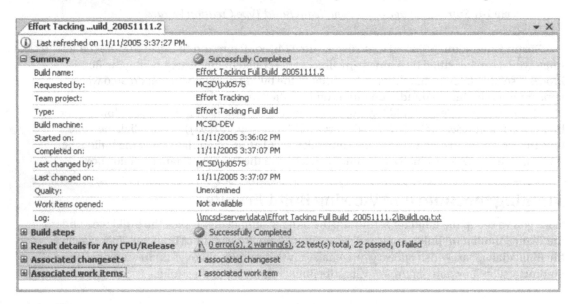

Figure 7-8. *Summary section of the Build Detail Report*

Tip You can be alerted when a build is performed. To set this up, refer to discussion of project alerts in Chapter 2.

The same report that shows the status of the build progress also shows the results when the build is completed. The results are broken into five areas:

- Summary
- Build steps
- Result details (for each configuration type)
- Associated changesets
- Associated work items

Build Summary

The summary lists basic information about the build (see Figure 7-7). Clicking the build name link will open the folder where the build was output to (specified in the build configuration location section). Opening the build log will provide you with detailed information of everything that occurred as part of the build.

Build Steps

The build steps section shows all the steps that Team Foundation Build took as it was performing the build test and copying the file to the drop location, as shown in Figure 7-9. The details for each of these steps can be found in the build log.

Effort Tacking ...uild_20051111.2		▾ ×
ⓘ Last refreshed on 11/11/2005 3:37:27 PM.		
⊞ **Summary**	✅ Successfully Completed	
⊟ **Build steps**	✅ Successfully Completed	
Build Step	Completed On	
Initializing build	11/11/2005 3:36:18 PM	
Getting sources	11/11/2005 3:36:24 PM	
Compiling sources	11/11/2005 3:36:29 PM	
Compiling EffortTrackingSolution.sln for Any CPU/Release	11/11/2005 3:36:29 PM	
Compiling EffortTrackingServiceTests.csproj	11/11/2005 3:36:25 PM	
Compiling EffortTrackingWebTests.csproj	11/11/2005 3:36:28 PM	
Getting changesets and updating work items	11/11/2005 3:36:42 PM	
Running tests	11/11/2005 3:37:05 PM	
Running tests for Any CPU/Release	11/11/2005 3:37:05 PM	
Copying binaries to drop location	11/11/2005 3:37:06 PM	
Copying log files to drop location	11/11/2005 3:37:06 PM	
Successfully Completed	11/11/2005 3:37:06 PM	
⊞ **Result details for Any CPU/Release**	⚠ 0 error(s), 2 warning(s), 22 test(s) total, 22 passed, 0 failed	
⊞ **Associated changesets**	1 associated changeset	
⊞ **Associated work items**	1 associated work item	

Figure 7-9. *Build steps section of the Build Detail Report*

Result Details

If there were any errors or warnings, they will be summarized in the result details section, as shown in Figure 7-10.

Effort Trackin...uild_20051228.4					▾ ✕
ⓘ Last refreshed on 12/28/2005 5:06:31 PM.					
⊞ **Summary**	✅ Successfully Completed				
⊞ **Build steps**	✅ Successfully Completed				
⊟ **Result details for Any CPU/Release**	⚠ 0 error(s), 2 warning(s), 22 test(s) total, 22 passed, 0 failed				
Errors and warnings:	⚠ 0 error(s), 2 warning(s) (Release.txt)				
Test results:	1 test run(s) completed, 22 test(s) total, 22 passed, 0 failed				
Test Run	Run By	Total	Passed	Failed	Other Re...
tfsservice@MCSD-DEV 2005-12-28 17:05:15 Any CPU Release	MCSD\tfsservice	22	22	0	0
Code coverage results:	55 % blocks covered, 45 % blocks not covered				
Assembly		Covered (Blocks)	Not Covered (Blocks)	Covered (% Blocks)	
App_Code.gvwp83db.dll		102	85	54.55 %	
⊞ **Associated changesets**	2 associated changesets				
Associated work items	No associated work item				

Figure 7-10. *Result details section of the Build Detail Report*

Clicking the Release.txt link will open the release.txt file and display the details of the errors and warnings. In the case of this particular test, the database projects caused the warnings, because the .dbp file could not be built by the build engine, as it is not a supported type. So these warnings are perfectly acceptable.

■**Note** Because database projects cannot be built, you may want to store them in another solution. Of course, then you will need to have multiple instances of Visual Studio open in order to work with your database information and project information at the same time. Alternatively, you could just keep in mind that you will always have as many warnings as you have database projects in your solution. If you see more warnings, it is time to investigate.

The next line details the test results. In this case, all of the tests passed. Under Test Run, the test results link is displayed. Clicking this link allows you to download the test results to your workstation in order to examine the details. These details are presented in the same way that a test run on your local machine is presented.

Finally, the code coverage results are listed here in total and by each assembly. In this case, only the web service assembly was tested. The blocks that were not covered are those that deal with altering data that you did not include in the tests run during the build.

Associated Changesets

All changesets which contribute to a build are showcased in the form of associated changesets. Hence, it becomes easy to figure out which changesets were checked in for each build.

Figure 7-11 shows the associated changesets for the first build that was run against the Effort Tracking solution.

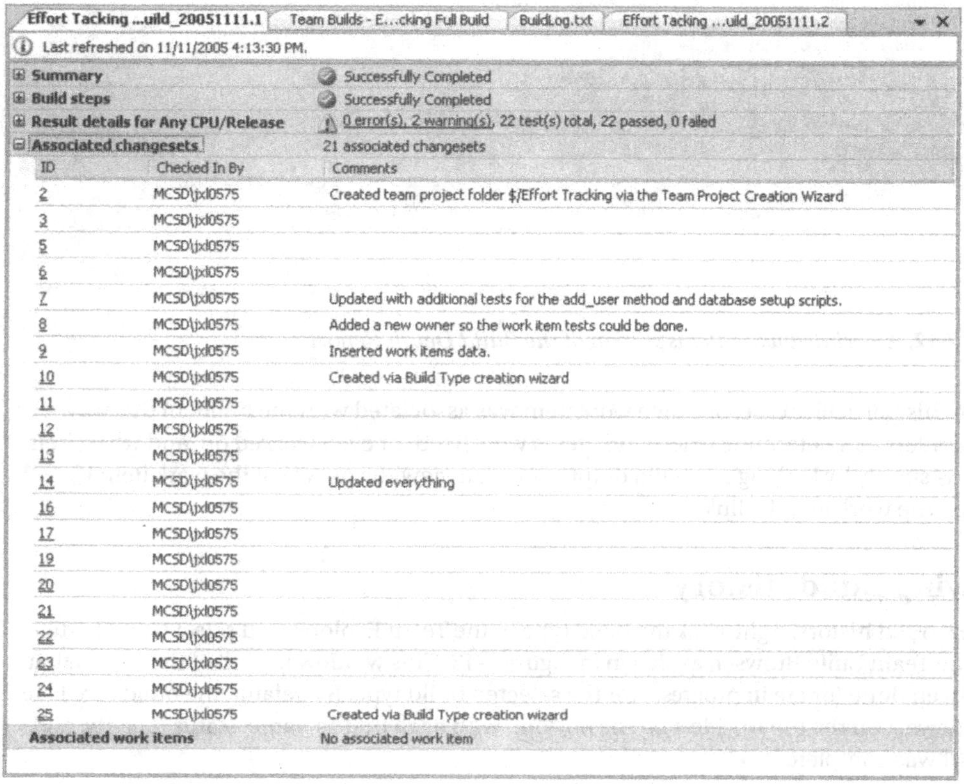

ID	Checked In By	Comments
2	MCSD\jxd0575	Created team project folder $/Effort Tracking via the Team Project Creation Wizard
3	MCSD\jxd0575	
5	MCSD\jxd0575	
6	MCSD\jxd0575	
7	MCSD\jxd0575	Updated with additional tests for the add_user method and database setup scripts.
8	MCSD\jxd0575	Added a new owner so the work item tests could be done.
9	MCSD\jxd0575	Inserted work items data.
10	MCSD\jxd0575	Created via Build Type creation wizard
11	MCSD\jxd0575	
12	MCSD\jxd0575	
13	MCSD\jxd0575	
14	MCSD\jxd0575	Updated everything
16	MCSD\jxd0575	
17	MCSD\jxd0575	
19	MCSD\jxd0575	
20	MCSD\jxd0575	
21	MCSD\jxd0575	
22	MCSD\jxd0575	
23	MCSD\jxd0575	
24	MCSD\jxd0575	
25	MCSD\jxd0575	Created via Build Type creation wizard

Summary — Successfully Completed
Build steps — Successfully Completed
Result details for Any CPU/Release — 0 error(s), 2 warning(s), 22 test(s) total, 22 passed, 0 failed
Associated changesets — 21 associated changesets
Associated work items — No associated work item

Figure 7-11. *Associated changesets section of the Build Detail Report*

Clicking the changeset ID will display a dialog box indicating what changes were made in the changeset (files that were changed). This is the same dialog box displayed when viewing a changeset from the Source Control Explorer.

Tip Obviously, based on Figure 7-11, you want to make sure that you provide comments describing each changeset (when you check in code), so that you know what changes the changeset covered. (It is also obvious that the authors do not do follow that advice regularly enough.)

Associated Work Items

The associated work items section contains a list of all work items that are associated with the build. For instance, developers fixing work items will associate that work item with the changeset in which the issue is fixed. All of the work items that were associated with the changesets that were included in the build are displayed here, as shown in Figure 7-12.

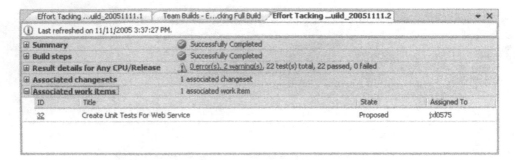

Figure 7-12. *Associated work items section of the Build Detail Report*

In this particular case, only one work item was associated with the build. In this way, stakeholders can determine when work items were fixed, or even worked on, and what their status is simply by looking at a build output. You can view the details of the work item by clicking the work item ID link.

Viewing Build History

To view build history, right-click the build type in the Team Explorer and select Open to display the Team Build Browser, as shown in Figure 7-13. This window lists all of the builds that have been done (or are in progress) for the selected build type. By default, the builds are listed from newest on the top to oldest on the bottom, with each build's name, status, quality, and when it was completed.

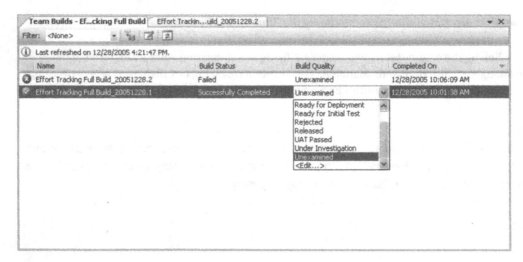

Figure 7-13. *Team Build Browser*

To see the details of a specific build, right-click it and select Open or double-click the build. This also gives you the option to edit its build quality.

Build Quality

The *build quality* is a value that describes the general condition of the build and what stage of quality checks it has passed. Build quality is determined by whoever is reviewing the build and is not set automatically.

■Note A person must have Edit Build Quality permissions in order to change the build quality. See Chapter 2 for details about permissions.

As you can see in Figure 7-13, the options for the build quality are as follows:

- Initial Test Passed

- Lab Test Passed

- Ready for Deployment

- Ready for Initial Test

- Ready for Release

- Rejected

- Released

- UAT Passed (Unit Acceptance Test)

- Under Investigation

- Unexamined (default)

You can edit this list by selecting the final option in the drop-down list, <Edit>. This allows you to add your own statuses to the build quality, which can help you to keep track of the purpose of that build.

Build Details

Every completed build has its results published to the Team Foundation Server. The results on the server provide slightly different information than the results reported on the client. A build report is shown in Figure 7-14.

Builds
Report Generated: 11/11/2005 6:03:53 PM by MCSD\jxi0575; Last Warehouse Update: 11/11/2005 5:16:34 PM

What are the details for each build?

Build Name	Build Quality	% Tests Passed	% Code Coverage	% Code Churn
⊟ Effort Tacking Full Build 20051111.1	Unexamined	100 %	0%	65.7501 %

⊟ Test Run Results: 1 test run(s) completed, 5/ 5 test(s) passed.

Test Run Name	Total Tests	Passed	Failed	Other Result
⊞ tfsservice@MCSD-DEV 2005-11-11 15:28:36_Any CPU_Release	5	5	0	0

⊞ Code Coverage Results: 0 % lines covered, 0 % lines not covered, 0 % lines partially covered.

⊟ Code Churn Details: 7492 Total Line of Code, 69 Line(s) Churned, 4908 Line(s) Added, 18 Line(s) Deleted

Relative Code Churn Measure	Value
Line(s) Churned/Total Line of Code	0.00921
Line(s) Added/Total Line of Code	0.6551
Line(s) Deleted/Total Line of Code	0.0024

⊟ Effort Tacking Full Build 20051111.2	Unexamined	100 %	0%	0 %

⊞ Test Run Results: 1 test run(s) completed, 5/ 5 test(s) passed.

⊞ Code Coverage Results: 0 % lines covered, 0 % lines not covered, 0 % lines partially covered.

⊟ Code Churn Details: 7492 Total Line of Code, 1 Line(s) Churned, 0 Line(s) Added, 0 Line(s) Deleted

Relative Code Churn Measure	Value
Line(s) Churned/Total Line of Code	0.00013
Line(s) Added/Total Line of Code	0
Line(s) Deleted/Total Line of Code	0

Figure 7-14. *Published build results*

All of the builds are listed on the report, and you can drill down into the results. The results shown in Figure 7-14 map to the results shown earlier in Figures 7-8 through 7-12. Note that in addition to the information shown on the client, the published results show the code churn as well. These results are generated by an analysis performed by the Team Foundation Server. The information here can provide your team with a good idea of how much work the team is doing and if that is translating into more passed tests, more failed tests, and so on.

■**Note** Team Foundation Build outputs all of the resulting binaries, the test results, and the build type information. This information is stored in the location on the machine on which Team Foundation Build ran (specified in the build configuration). On the build machine, the binaries are in (*configured location*)\ *teamprojectname*\(*buildTypeName*)\Binaries, the source code is in *BuildTypeName*\Sources, and the test results are in *BuildTypeName*\TestResults. In the drop location, the folder structure is (*build name*)\Release(*GeneralConfigurationName*)\TestResults. Included in the root of this structure are the BuildLog.txt, ErrorsWarningLog.txt, and Release.txt files. All of this information is available by clicking various links in the build results report.

Customizing the Build Process

Team Foundation Build is fully customizable using a number of different features. To change the build process, you can either create your own TFSBuild project (.proj) file or edit the generated project file. As with all of the tools in Visual Studio 2005, when you edit the XML in the file, you'll have the benefit of almost full IntelliSense (although Team Foundation Build properties are not listed in the IntelliSense drop-down list).

Reviewing the Build Type Configuration File

Because there are so many options, it is almost always easier to start off with a generated build type template. Listing 7-1 shows the build configuration file generated by the New Team Build Type Creation Wizard (minus the XML comments and with line numbers for reference only).

Listing 7-1. *Build Type Configuration File*

```
1 <?xml version="1.0" encoding="utf-8"?>
2 <Project DefaultTargets=
     "DesktopBuild" xmlns="http://schemas.microsoft.com/developer/msbuild/2003">
3 <!-- Do not edit this -->
4 <Import Project=
     "$(MSBuildExtensionsPath)\Microsoft\VisualStudio\v8.0\
     TeamBuild\Microsoft.TeamFoundation.Build.targets" />
5 <ProjectExtensions>
6 <Description>Builds the Effort Tracking Web Service and Effort Tracking
     Web front end and then runs all of the unit tests and web tests against the
     built solution.</Description>
7 <BuildMachine>mcsd-dev</BuildMachine>
8 </ProjectExtensions>
9 <PropertyGroup>
10    <TeamProject>Effort Tracking</TeamProject>
11    <BuildDirectoryPath>c:\EffortTrackingBuilds</BuildDirectoryPath>
12    <DropLocation>\\mcsd-server\data</DropLocation>
13    <RunTest>true</RunTest>
14    <WorkItemFieldValues>Priority=1;Severity=1</WorkItemFieldValues>
15    <RunCodeAnalysis>Default</RunCodeAnalysis>
16    <UpdateAssociatedWorkItems>true</UpdateAssociatedWorkItems>
17 </PropertyGroup>
18 <ItemGroup>
19    <SolutionToBuild  Include=
     "$(SolutionRoot)\EffortTrackingSolution\EffortTrackingSolution.sln" />
20 </ItemGroup>
21 <ItemGroup>
22    <ConfigurationToBuild Include="Release|Any CPU">
23        <FlavorToBuild>Release</FlavorToBuild>
24        <PlatformToBuild>Any CPU</PlatformToBuild>
25    </ConfigurationToBuild>
26 </ItemGroup>
```

```
27 <ItemGroup>
28    <MetaDataFile Include=
      "$(SolutionRoot)\EffortTrackingSolution\EffortTrackingSolution.vsmdi">
29       <TestList>Read Tests</TestList>
30    </MetaDataFile>
31 </ItemGroup>
32 </Project>
```

As you can see, the format is very straightforward. Updating it may seem a little complicated at first, but as soon as you understand the procedure, you'll be able to do almost anything you want to (in terms of a build) with this tool. Here are the basics:

- You can reference any node as a variable that you create (or that already exists) in the PropertyGroup node by using the $(*variableName*) convention.

- A Target is the node that runs when TFSBuild builds the project.

- You can incorporate custom code that performs some operation in a custom task. This compiled assembly can then be used during the build process by including the assembly in a UsingTask node.

Keeping these three concepts in mind will allow you to customize a lot of tasks for use with TFSBuild.

Retrieving the Build Type

In order to actually edit this file manually, you need to do the following:

1. Open Source Control Explorer, expand your team project (in this case, the Effort Tracking solution), and then expand the TeamBuildTypes node.

2. Select TFSBuild.proj, right-click the file, and select Get Latest.

3. Choose the location to download the file to, and then click OK.

4. Right-click the TFSBuild.proj file and select Check Out for Edit.

At this point, you can edit the build file.

Editing the Build File

The build file will be located in the output folder (selected in step 3 in the previous section): (*Location*)\TeamBuildTypes\(*BuildType Name*)\TFSBuild.proj. It is best to edit this in Visual Studio, as you will get the benefit of IntelliSense support.

You can do a lot of customization by editing the project file or creating custom tasks. Microsoft is releasing several labs that describe all of the steps you can take during a project build. Look for this information on the MSDN site or search for Team Foundation Build in the Visual Studio Help.

Tip Implementing your own custom task is fairly straightforward. To do that, create a project and reference `Microsoft.Build.Utilities.dll` and `Microsoft.Build.Framework.dll`. Create a class that inherits from the `Task` class (located in the `Microsoft.Build.Utilities` namespace) and override the `Execute` method.

Using the Build Command-Line Tool

Team Foundation Build comes with a command-line tool, which can be used in conjunction with the Windows Scheduler to schedule nightly builds and publish the results. The command-line tool is called `tfsbuild.exe` and is located in the `C:\Program Files\Microsoft Visual Studio 8\Common7\IDE` folder. With `tfsbuild.exe` you can start a build, delete a build, or stop a build that is in progress. The abilities to delete and stop builds are available only from the command line.

To start a build, use the following syntax:

```
tfsbuild.exe start <Team Foundation Server> <Team Project Name> <Build Type Name>
 [/m:<Build Machine>] [/d:<Build Directory>]
```

If no build machine is specified, the build machine in the build type will be used. Similarly, if no build directory is specified, the build directory in the build type will be used. Here is an example of starting a build from the command line:

```
tfsbuild.exe start kiona "Effort Tracking" "Effort Tracking Full Build"
```

Notice that all entries with a space in them must be enclosed in quotation marks.

`tfsbuild.exe` will supply you with the current build number when it begins the build process. The output from a `tfsbuild.exe` operation is shown in Figure 7-15.

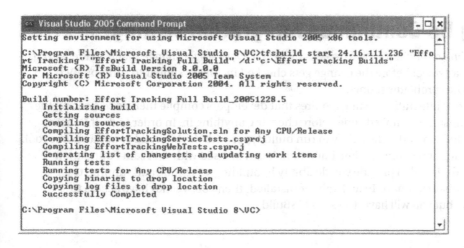

Figure 7-15. *Using the tfsbuild.exe command-line tool*

> ■**Caution** The server name must be a name from the list of servers known by the local machine. In this case, kiona was the specified server name. However, there are numerous occasions when you may not be working on your local network and instead need to enter an IP address to reach the server. If you do this, you must supply the IP address as the server name.

To stop a build, use this syntax:

```
tfsbuild.exe stop <Team Foundation Server> <Team Project Name> <Build Number>
[/noprompt]
```

As just mentioned, tfsbuild.exe indicates the build number when it starts a build. You can specify multiple build numbers by separating each number with a comma (but no spaces) between the build numbers. The /noprompt option suppresses the confirmation question for the stop and delete options. You must specify noprompt when doing any type of automated process using either the stop or delete command. Here is an example of stopping a build:

```
tfsbuild.exe stop kiona "Effort Tracking" "Effort Tracking Full Build_20051228.3"
/noprompt
```

To delete a build, use this syntax:

```
tfsbuild.exe delete <Team Foundation Server> <Team Project Name> <Build Number(s)>
[/noprompt]
```

Here's an example of deleting a build:

```
tfsbuild.exe delete kiona "Effort Tracking" "Effort Tracking Full Build_20051228.1"
/noprompt
```

Setting Up Continuous Integration Testing

Continuous integration testing is a process by which every single change that is made is compiled against a project before the change gets checked in. This is similar to running BVTs, except it catches problems sooner.

Continuous integration testing requires that developers compile their code and run the unit tests against the compiled code before checking anything in. In order to do this, Team Foundation Build includes the ability to run build types with the MSBuild command-line tool. MSBuild is a desktop command line build tool. It can be used without Team Foundation Server and is designed to provide you flexibility in building your code and running tests against it. If you do not have Team Explorer installed, then you will not have access to tfsbuild.exe, but you will have access to MSBuild.

MSBuild also has the ability to process a build type in order to perform a build. Before you can run MSBuild against a build type, you need to retrieve the build type from the server. To do this, follow the steps outlined in the "Retrieving the Build Type" section earlier in this chapter. Once you have the file loaded to the local machine, you can run MSBuild simply by passing in the name of the type and setting the solution root. Open a Visual Studio command prompt, navigate to the folder containing the TFSBuild.proj file ((*Location*)\TeamBuildTypes\ (*BuildType Name*)), and enter the following:

```
msbuild /p:SolutionRoot="(path to solution root)" tfsbuild.proj
```

Summary

In this chapter, you have learned how to create build types, which can be used to build a project, run specified tests against a project, and publish those results to a project SharePoint site. You have also seen how to view the results of the build and learned what the results indicate in terms of code churn, what was tested, code coverage, and whether any errors occurred. Finally, you learned how the build process can be customized and how to run nightly builds using the command-line tools to build a project and schedule a project.

The bottom line is that using the built-in build tools provides a project team immediate feedback as to whether anything is broken and how much code has been tested from one build to another. This provides customers with good feedback as to the progress of the development team and will give them confidence in the development team.

PART 2

Team Edition for Software Architects

CHAPTER 8

■■■

Application Designer

The Application Designer is one of four distributed system designers supplied with Team Edition for Software Architects. In this chapter, we will look at how to use the Application Designer to model the services of your system and the applications that consume these services. We are focusing on services here because they are fundamental in the current application model Microsoft promotes as *connected systems*.

The connected systems approach moves to interface-based service contracts, or *contract-first*, as opposed to the traditional code-first approach. Contract-first focuses first on the interface leveraging the Web Service Definition Language (WSDL). This first release of the Application Designer focuses on the contracts from a remote procedure call (RPC) perspective, supporting methods (operations) and parameters, as opposed to a message-centric approach of schema types and elements. Furthermore, you will be defining .NET Framework types, not XML Schema Definition (XSD) types. This full contract-first experience will be provided in a following release of the product.

In this chapter, we will approach service design from two different perspectives. First, we will build a sample application design from scratch. The Application Designer provides a clean design surface for "whiteboarding" your application. The Visual Studio Toolbox comes preconfigured with application building blocks, including Windows applications, web services, web applications, and Office applications. Once you've described your web service endpoints and modeled the application, the Application Designer allows you to generate the skeleton projects for all or part of the system. This includes all of the code needed to implement and consume the defined service contracts. Second, we will generate an application design from our sample book application. When an application diagram is added to an existing solution, it is reverse-engineered, and the application diagram is created for you.

But before we get started using the Application Designer, let's take a broad look at the distributed system designers.

Overview of the Distributed System Designers

Team Edition for Software Architects ships with four distributed system designers:

- *Application Designer (AD):* Represents applications that expose services and communicate through endpoints.

- *Logical Datacenter Designer (LDD):* Represents the logical structure of some portion of the datacenter.

- *System Designer (SD):* Represents the composition of applications defined in the Application Designer for the purpose of composing connected systems.

- *Deployment Designer (DD):* Used to create a deployment configuration for a system.

The design goal for the distributed system design suite is that third parties will document and model aspects of their distributed system for a more complete definition of an application. These extended application or logical server prototypes could then be incorporated in defining connected systems. Figure 8-1 illustrates the artifacts associated with each designer.

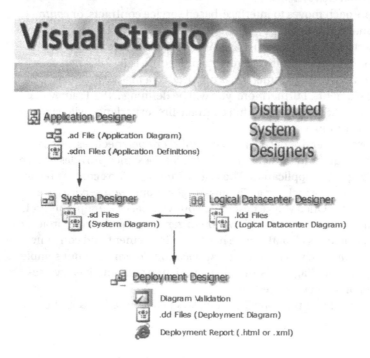

Figure 8-1. *Visual Studio 2005 designers*

System Definition Model

The System Definition Model (SDM) is simply a schema definition for describing distributed systems. SDM views the world as being composed of systems. It is important to distinguish between the notion of atomic and composite systems. Atomic systems are made up of resources such as configuration files, assemblies, and dynamic link libraries (DLLs), and are referred to as *applications*. Composite systems are made up of other systems or applications and referred to as *application systems*. The schema being shipped with VSTS is located at http://schemas.microsoft.com/SystemDefinitionModel/2005/1/DesignData/VisualStudio.

Table 8-1 shows the file extension within the solution and the type of SDM information stored.

Table 8-1. *SDM File Types and Data*

Extension	File	Description
.ad	Application Designer	Presentation and preimplementation endpoint information
.sdm	Project	Information about the project implemented
.sdm	External Components	Information about external entities (databases)
.ldd	Logical Datacenter Designer	Presentation, endpoint, zone, and host information
.sd	System Designer	Presentation and system information
.dd	Deployment Designer	Presentation and system deployment information

As you build your sample designs and deployments in the next few chapters, make sure you take the time to open the generated files in the XML editor and review the structure and information contained in each.

Benefits of the Distributed Designers

The distributed designers were conceived to support both the infrastructure architect (in charge of the network and datacenter designs) and the solution architect (in charge of designing and deploying connected systems). In a small shop, one person may perform both roles, but in more complex enterprise scenarios, many architects may need to communicate their designs and deployments to a host of project constituents.

The distributed system designers provide benefits in three ways:

- They are a rich set of domain-specific designers that target the service-orientation space. If you are building connected systems, the distributed designers are a first step at making Model Driven Architecture (MDA) a reality.

- They are an example of what can be done by targeting the Domain-Specific Language (DSL) framework toward a specific domain (service-oriented architecture in this specific instance). If you want to dive deeper, you can build your own DSL using the same modeling framework on which the distributed system designers are built.

- They begin to address the life cycle issues plaguing software development. Providing a common framework for distinct viewpoints (the application and datacenter) and the ability to deploy one viewpoint onto another is a positive step in reducing ambiguity and reducing cost.

MODEL-DRIVEN DEVELOPMENT

Rick LaPlante, General Manager for VSTS, explains that the design goals of VSTS are two-fold: integration and ease of use. The value proposition for the tools suite is predictable collaboration. Rick stated, "The distributed system designers allow you to enable validation of system configurations against models of target environments to increase the predictability of deployment." It really is a shift of focus from the developer to the entire breadth of development. Modeling will no longer be relegated to the "ivory tower," but will be a normal part of the development life cycle. To facilitate this, VSTS has adopted four main ideas:

- Models are to be "first-class" citizens. They should be thought of not as documentation, but as source code with their own set of implementers (compilers).

- Models are to represent a set of abstractions in a well-defined domain.

- Models are to abstract and aggregate information from a number of artifacts, thereby providing analyses such as consistency and validation checks.

- Models are to be implemented by a process similar to compilation. The generated output is not intended to be edited by hand.

During Jochen Seemann's "Future Directions in Modeling Tools" presentation at the 2005 Professional Developer Conference (PDC), he remarked that for the model-driven development approach, "Don't think about round-trips; think trip-less," and said that it was "bringing modeling to the masses."

Visual languages are a common tool we use in our everyday lives. Maps may be the most common visual language to help get us from point A to point B. Blueprints are useful for putting together a piece of furniture or your million-dollar dream home. A common saying goes, "A picture is worth a thousand words." Unfortunately, one of the biggest problems in the software industry is that we cannot agree on what the thousand words are saying. This is where model-driven development takes center stage.

Back in the 1980s, computer-aided software engineering (CASE) offered the promise of modeling applications at an abstract level, and then "automagically" generating the code to be used to operate the system. While this code generation was the promise of CASE tools, it was also the greatest drawback. These early modeling tools could not be easily kept in sync with the development tools. New revisions to the underlying tools were late to be integrated into the CASE engine. This lag caused the development to get out of sync with the models, and there was no going back. VSTS takes on this challenge by making models first-class development artifacts and an intricate part of the development process. By "making modeling mainstream," Microsoft hopes to change the economics of software development and ensure software systems meet the needs of the business. This approach to model-driven development is part of an initiative called Software Factories.

Software Factories

The 1990s ushered in the world of object-oriented programming to the mainstream and the first work on the Unified Modeling Language (UML). UML comes out of the effort to unify the object modeling world headed by Grady Booch, Ivar Jacobson, and James Rumbaugh. This work was taken industry-wide through the Object Management Group (OMG), and in 1997, the first proposal, UML 1.0, was published. Somewhere in the trudge from UML 1.0 to UML 2.0, a division arose around the appropriateness of applying UML to "all" domains. This led to a spirited debate between Grady Booch (IBM) and the Software Factories team at

Microsoft. The debate centers around the goal of UML. It was developed to provide a common notation for the practice of object-oriented analysis and design. Should it then be the de facto standard beyond its original scope into the realm of model-driven development and Software Factories?

Some of the same people who were driving CASE tools and early UML a decade ago are leading the work being done on Software Factories and Domain-Specific Languages (DSLs) at Microsoft and other corporations.

The concept of Software Factories lives at two levels today. First it is a vision for the future. So a few years out, the Software Factories concept is an ideal for bringing significant automation to the software development process. Today, building software is still very much a craft. We tend to design applications as if they were the first of their kind. We need to automate the parts that are the same every time and concentrate on the key differentials. Steve Cook, an architect for Microsoft's DSL Toolkit team and coauthor of Software Factories, made some interesting observations in one of his talks related to Software Factories: "There is no generic software factory (think about this!)," and "A generic factory that produces bicycles one day and laptop computers the next?"

Second, Software Factories are an initiative grounded in VSTS to provide the framework (tools, SDKs, APIs, and so on) to enable Visual Studio to be purposed into a tool for a specific type of development. One of the key components in this initiative is the concept of DSLs.

Domain-Specific Languages

DSLs are small, highly focused languages for solving some discrete problem space within a specific domain. The DSL framework is Microsoft's modeling platform.

DSLs enable the mapping of the business processes (capabilities) to the technology services (interfaces and implementation). Models are the preferred way of communicating complex ideas and constructs between groups holding diverse viewpoints. An example is a blueprint (architecture model) to map the homeowner's needs and the builder's implementation. Consider how it would affect the construction of your new home if you did away with the blueprint and handed the builder a 1,000-page document describing the home of your dreams.

The distributed designers provided with Team Edition for Software Architects are simply an implementation of a DSL language targeted at visual design and validation of connected systems.

Using the Application Designer

As an example of using the Application Designer, you will create a simple application design consisting of a web application, a web service, and a sample SQL database. The final implemented design is shown in Figure 8-2.

■**Note** The application diagram shows the applications defined within a single Visual Studio solution; therefore, you can have only one .ad file per solution. If you attempt to add a second .ad file to your solution, you will get an error.

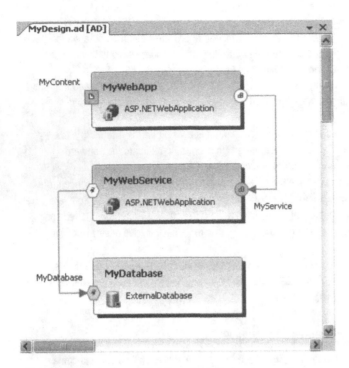

Figure 8-2. *Sample application design*

Getting Started with the Application Designer

To start the diagram, follow these steps:

1. Start a new project. A separate project type has been added to the New Project dialog box to make it easier to find the distributed system designers. They are now located under Distributed System Solutions. There, you will find the Distributed System and Logical Datacenter templates. For this example, select Distributed System, as shown in Figure 8-3.

2. Enter the name MyDesign.

3. Click OK. You will be brought into the Application Designer.

You now have a blank work surface, a default application diagram (.ad), and the Application Designer Toolbox. You are reminded from the blank design surface to "Drag from the Toolbox to define applications." This message is like the sign at the end of the ski lift warning, "Keep your tips up." Although such signs may be safely ignored by experts, more than a few novice skiers have learned the hard way.

The Application Designer Toolbox contains eleven predefined prototypes (.adprototype) to be used while designing your application model. These include eight application prototypes and three endpoint prototypes. We will look at each in detail in the following sections. Table 8-2 describes the Toolbox objects.

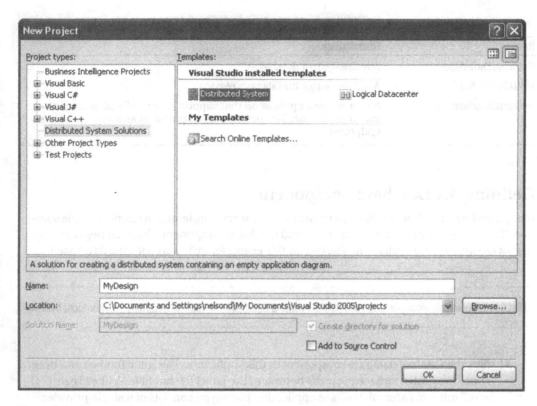

Figure 8-3. *The New Project dialog box with Distributed System Solutions templates*

Table 8-2. *The Application Designer Toolbox Objects*

Item	Description
Pointer	Pointer tool used for selection (one available in each category)
Connection	Connection tool to link two application prototype endpoints
Comment	A comment text box
WebServiceEndpoint	Represents a connection point for a web service (provider)
WebContentEndpoint	Represents a connection point to web content (provider)
GenericEndpoint	Represents a connection point to services of an unspecified type (provider)
WindowsApplication	A Windows application
ASP.NETWebService	An ASP.NET web service application that includes a web service endpoint
ASP.NETWebApplication	An ASP.NET web application that includes a web content endpoint
OfficeApplication	Represents a Microsoft Office application supporting Excel, Word, and Outlook templates
ExternalWebService	A reference to a single web service defined by a single Web Services Description Language (.wsdl) file

Continued

Table 8-2. *Continued*

Item	Description
ExternalDatabase	A reference to a database
BizTalkWebService	A reference to a BizTalk web service
GenericApplication	A user-defined application that supports user-defined settings and constraints; exists for documentation purposes and supports generic endpoints

Defining the Database Component

Using the drag-and-drop method, you will now design and implement a simple sample solution. To start with, you will define the back-end database component. (You can begin on any part of the application design you like, but for this example, we'll start with the database.)

■**Note** To follow this example, you will need to create a database named MyDatabase on your local system.

---

1. Click the ExternalDatabase component in the Application Designer Toolbox and drag it onto the design surface (near the bottom of the page). It should look like Figure 8-4. By default, the ExternalDatabase application prototype consists of a single provider endpoint. Notice that the database prototype has a shadow effect on the border, which designates an implementation has occurred. Also notice that the solution now has a new file named Database1.sdm.

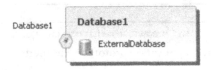

Figure 8-4. *ExternalDatabase component on the diagram*

2. To examine the generated XML for your new database, right-click the Database1.sdm file and choose to open it with the XML editor. You cannot have the XML editor and the Application Designer open at the same time. You will be prompted to close and save the diagram prior to opening the .sdm file. Listing 8-1 shows a snippet of the .sdm file verifying that Database1 has a state of "Implemented" but still "NeedsGeneration".

Listing 8-1. *Generated Database1.sdm File Portion*

```
<Endpoint Name="Database1" Definition="Database1.DatabaseProviderEndpoint1"
        MinOccurs="1" MaxOccurs="1" Reference="false">
    <DesignData>
        <VisualStudio xmlns=
```

```
             "http://schemas.microsoft.com/SystemDefinitionModel/2005/1/
             DesignData/VisualStudio">
                   <ModelElement Type=
                   "Microsoft.VisualStudio.EnterpriseTools.Application.
                    Modeling.PlugIns.DeployedDBProviderPort">
                         <Property Name="State" Value="Implemented" />
                         <Property Name="NeedsGeneration" Value="true" />
                   </ModelElement>
             </VisualStudio>
         </DesignData>
      </Endpoint>
```

3. Close the XML editor and reopen MyDesign.ad. On your diagram, click the Database1
   provider endpoint, which is represented by the plug abstract type icon:

4. Press F4 to open the Properties window. Change the name element from Database1 to
   MyDatabase. Notice that the name for the external database changes as well, as shown
   in Figure 8-5.

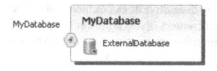

Figure 8-5. *External database renamed to MyDatabase*

Adding a Web Service Component

Now that the back-end database has been defined, it is time to add a web service to perform
the data access function for the application.

1. Click the ASP.NETWebService application prototype in the Application Designer Toolbox and drag it onto the design surface (just above the database component).

2. Double-click the default name (WebApplication1) to open the name property box.
   Change the name to MyWebService. Optionally, you can select the web service, press F4
   to open the Properties window, and change the name under the Design section.

3. On the MyWebService application type, click the web service provider endpoint, represented by this icon:

4. Change the name to MyService. Your diagram now has two application types, as shown in Figure 8-6.

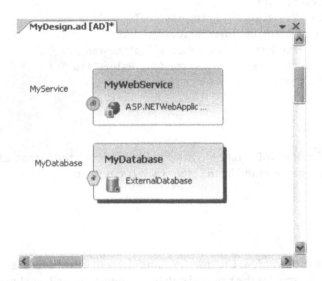

Figure 8-6. *Web service added to the application diagram*

Notice that MyWebService is not implemented by default. It does not have a shadow effect on its border, and no MyWebService.sdm file has been created. If you right-click the MyWebService application type, you will see an option to implement the application. You will do this after you complete the initial design.

Connecting the Application Types

You now need to connect the web service to the database. When you begin a connection directly from an application, the application that starts the connection must be the consumer application. To begin from the provider application, just start the connection from the provider endpoint instead of the application itself. If you begin a connection from the wrong component, you'll see the universal "No" sign, as shown in Figure 8-7.

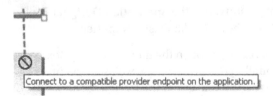

Figure 8-7. *Incompatible endpoints*

1. Right-click MyWebService on the design surface and select Connect.

2. In the Create Connection dialog box, click the down arrow of the Application box in the Connect To section and select the name of your back-end database component, MyDatabase, as shown in Figure 8-8. Click the down arrow in the Endpoint selection box and select the name of the endpoint associated with the database you selected. This will be the same name as the database, by default. Click OK.

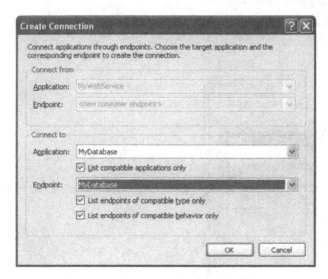

Figure 8-8. *The Create Connection dialog box*

■**Note** When using the Create Connection dialog box, by default, you are presented with only endpoints that are compatible with the component with which you are working. In this simple example, we have only two components so far. In a complex solution with many components, this feature helps aid in maintaining the overall integrity of the design.

---

3. In the Choose Data Source dialog box, enter the data source and data provider. For this example, select Microsoft SQL Server and the .NET Data Provider for SQL Server, respectively.

4. In the Connection Properties dialog box, enter the database server name, the security context, and the database name. (You can simply enter a period for the server name to indicate your local SQL Server installation, or enter `.\sqlexpress` for default installations of SQL Express edition.) Click Test Connection to verify that the configuration information for the data source is correct, as shown in Figure 8-9.

Figure 8-9. *Testing your connection from the Connection Properties dialog box*

Note Optionally, if you are just whiteboarding an application design, you can cancel out of the Connection Properties dialog box, and then complete the details for the connection later.

---

5. Click OK. Your diagram should now look similar to Figure 8-10.

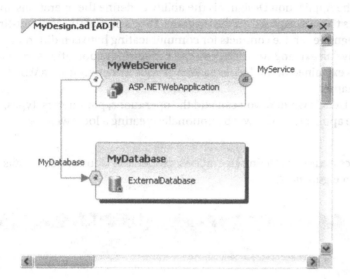

Figure 8-10. *Adding the connection*

6. To verify the connection properties, right-click the database consumer endpoint of
   MyWebService and select Properties. You will see that the connection information has
   been captured, as shown in Figure 8-11. This Connection String property will be generated in the Web.config file of the MyDatabase application when it is implemented.

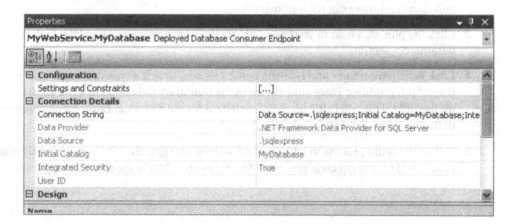

Figure 8-11. *MyDatabase properties with connection information*

Defining Operations for ASP.NET Web Service Prototypes

One of the key features of the Application Designer is the ability to define the operations and parameters for web services that are exposed on the diagram. This is part of the contract-first design, where you first design the service contracts for communicating between different application types. If you have an existing .wsdl file, you can consume the operations from the existing exposed service, as explained in the "Adding a Web Service Endpoint from a WSDL File" section later in this chapter.

Using the Web Service Details window, you can add the operations, parameters, types, and details. For this sample application, you will be notionally creating a local weather-reporting web service.

1. Right-click MyService and select Define Operations to open the Web Service Details window, as shown in Figure 8-12.

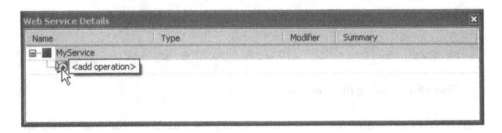

Figure 8-12. *The Web Service Details window*

2. Click <add operation> and type the name GetLocalWeather. Give it a type of string and add some comments in the Summary field.

3. Click the plus sign next to your new GetLocalWeather service to reveal the <add parameter> section.

4. Click <add parameter> and type the name ZipCode. Give it a type of integer and accept the default modifier. Place your cursor in the Summary field and click the ellipsis (. . .) on the right. This will bring up detail metadata for your service. Enter some comments in the Summary field and click OK.

5. Follow the same process to add a second service that gets the city name from the database based on the zip code provided. The MyService details are shown in Figure 8-13.

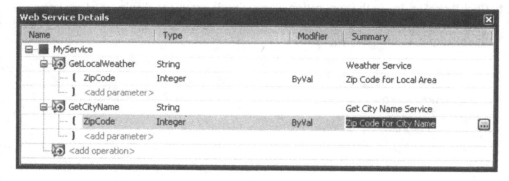

Figure 8-13. *The Web Service Details window with two services*

Implementing the Application

At this point in the design process, you can generate actual framework code for the application. First-time generation of code is referred to as *implementation*. Application definitions can be implemented incrementally or all at once. When an application is implemented, the Application Designer automatically generates the corresponding project, code files, and configuration files. Because the application diagram is synchronized with the code and configuration files, the diagram is immediately updated if the files are modified. Similarly, changes to the diagram are reflected in the code and configuration files. Upon implementation, the application prototypes will be identified by the presence of the shadow effect around the object shape.

■**Tip** Deferred implementation allows you to create what-if designs of your application without the overhead of actual implementation. The Application Designer supports a deferred implementation approach, allowing an architect to create and validate a design before committing the design to code. This whiteboarding approach allows the architect to brainstorm on the design surface and choose the point of generation.

Selecting the Language

First, you will want to select the implementation language to generate. Visual Basic is the default, but you can choose from multiple languages.

A common feature request of the VSTS team early on was the ability to have a global setting where you could change the language choice and have it stick for all prototypes. While this feature does not exist in version 1, if you do not want select a different default language, you can create a custom prototype. To demonstrate this, you will use MyWebService as an example.

1. Click MyWebService in the application diagram and press F4 to display the Properties window. In the Implementation section, select the language to generate—Visual C# in this example, as shown in Figure 8-14.

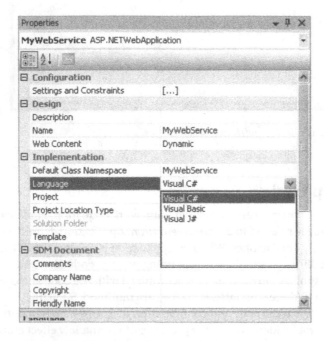

Figure 8-14. *Choosing a language for implementation*

2. In the Application Designer, right-click MyWebService and select Add to Toolbox. In the Name field, type in a descriptive name, such as MyWebServiceC#, as shown in Figure 8-15. Then click OK.

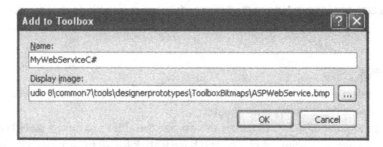

Figure 8-15. *The Add to Toolbox dialog box*

3. The Save File dialog box shows the existing designer prototypes on your system and allows you to save your custom C# version of the AspNetWebService. Click Save, and MyWebServiceC# is added to your Toolbox.

4. Add a new tab to the Toolbox called **My Prototypes** and drag all custom prototypes in there, as shown in Figure 8-16. This allows you to keep custom items separate from Visual Studio's built-in items.

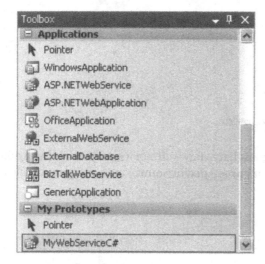

Figure 8-16. *Adding a new tab to the Toolbox for your custom items*

Generating Framework Code

Now that your language of choice has been selected, you can implement the application.

1. Right-click the MyWebService application and choose Implement Application. Alternatively, you can select Diagram ➤ Implement Application from the main menu. This will launch the Confirm Application Implementation dialog box, where you will be notified of the projects about to be generated, as shown in Figure 8-17.

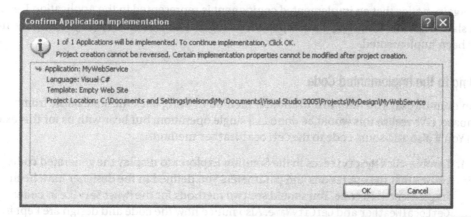

Figure 8-17. *The Confirm Application Implementation dialog box*

2. Select OK and wait for your application framework code to be propagated inside the solution. You may receive a warning that the connection string is being written into the configuration files unencrypted, as shown in Figure 8-18.

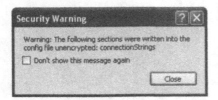

Figure 8-18. *The Security Warning dialog box*

The result of implementing your design is that a new web service project has been added to the solution. This new project includes language-specific source and configuration files, as shown in Figure 8-19.

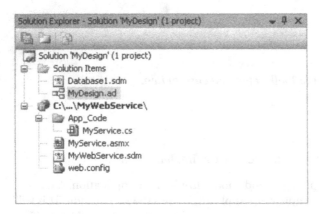

Figure 8-19. *The Solution Explorer window for MyDesign*

Again, notice that an implemented component is represented in the Application Designer by a shadow border outlining the component on the diagram surface. Your MyWebService has now been implemented.

Adding to the Implemented Code

As an example, say you want to add another method to bring back the state name from the database. (We realize this would be done in a single operation, but bear with us for this example.) You'll also add some code to the GetLocalWeather method.

1. Double-click MyService.cs in the Solution Explorer to display the generated code. Notice that the operations and parameters you defined in the designer have been implemented in code. You should see two methods for the MyWebService in code: GetLocalWeather and GetCityName. Also notice how the code and design are kept in sync. Remember that models in Visual Studio are "first-class" citizens and not just documentation.

2. Copy the code for the GetCityName method and paste it below as GetStateName. Change the method name and descriptive metadata, as shown in Listing 8-2.

Listing 8-2. *Added GetStateName Method*

```
/// <summary>
/// Get State Name Service
/// </summary>
/// <param name="ZipCode">Zip Code for State Name</param>
[System.Web.Services.WebMethod(Description = ""),
 System.Web.Services.Protocols.SoapDocumentMethod(Binding = "MyService")]
public string GetStateName(int ZipCode)
{
   throw new System.NotImplementedException();
}
```

3. Save the code file.

4. Switch back to the Application Designer by selecting MyDesign.ad from the Window menu.

5. Right-click the MyService endpoint and select Define Operations. The Web Service Details window now reflects the additional GetStateName method, as shown in Figure 8-20.

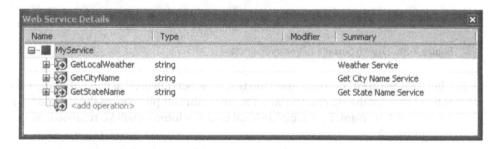

Figure 8-20. *The Web Service Details window with updates*

6. Switch back to MyService.cs. Since it is still winter in the greater Seattle metropolitan area, replace the throw new System.NotImplementedException() template code for the GetLocalWeather operation so that it looks like Listing 8-3.

Listing 8-3. *Additional Code for the GetLocalWeather Method*

```
[System.Web.Services.WebMethod(Description = ""),
 System.Web.Services.Protocols.SoapDocumentMethod(Binding = "MyService")]
public string GetLocalWeather(int ZipCode)
{
     return "Rain Today, Rain Tomorrow - always damp and dreary";
}
```

Testing the Web Service

Now you're ready to test the web service.

1. Press Ctrl+F5 and start the application without debugging. The directory listing will display for MyWebService.

2. Click MyService.asmx to open the web service .asmx page, as shown in Figure 8-21.

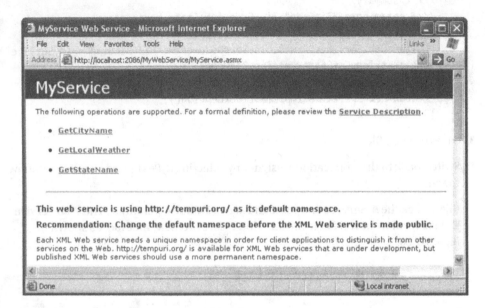

Figure 8-21. *The MyService web service page*

3. Click GetLocalWeather to bring up the test parameter page. You can enter any valid integer here for the zip code parameter, since our sample ignores the zip code. Click Invoke, and the dismal yet accurate local weather forecast will be returned, as shown in Figure 8-22.

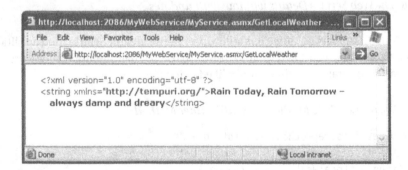

Figure 8-22. *MyWebService response for GetLocalWeather*

Hooking Up the Database

For a more realistic example, we will hook up the database portion to return the city name when you pass in the zip code.

1. Create a table in your MyDatabase database named CityZip. The CREATE TABLE statement is shown in Listing 8-4.

Listing 8-4. *CityZip CREATE TABLE Statement*

```
USE [MyDatabase]
GO
/****** Object: Table [dbo].[CityZip] ******/
SET ANSI_NULLS ON
GO
SET QUOTED_IDENTIFIER ON
GO
CREATE TABLE [dbo].[CityZip](
        [zipcode] [int] NULL,
        [city] [nvarchar](50) COLLATE SQL_Latin1_General_CP1_CI_AS NULL
) ON [PRIMARY]
```

2. With this simple two-column table, you need to insert only one row to get things started. You can add any others for your local town.

```
Insert into CityZip (zipcode, city) Values (98024, 'Seattle')
```

3. Replace the throw new System.NotImplementedException() template code for the GetCityName service with the code for accessing the database from the web service, as shown in Listing 8-5.

Listing 8-5. *Get City Database Lookup*

```
{
    SqlConnection cn = new  SqlConnection(
        ConfigurationManager.ConnectionStrings["MyDatabase"].ToString());
    SqlCommand cmd = new SqlCommand("SELECT city FROM cityzip "
        + "WHERE zipcode = @zipcode", cn);
    SqlDataReader dr;
    string mystring = "";

    cmd.CommandType = CommandType.Text;
    cmd.Parameters.AddWithValue("@zipcode", ZipCode);

    cn.Open();
    dr = cmd.ExecuteReader(CommandBehavior.CloseConnection);
    while (dr.Read())
        {
            mystring = dr["city"].ToString();
        }
    return mystring;
}
```

Note You must add *using* System.Data, *using* System.Data.SqlClient, and *using* System.Configuration in the using section. Also, you need to make sure the connection string name matches the one in your Web.config file.

4. Press F5 and start the application (you may need to do some debugging). The directory listing will display for MyWebService.

5. Click MyService.asmx. This time, select GetCityName for the test parameter page. Enter a valid database value for the zip code parameter and click Invoke. The simple database result is returned, as shown in Figure 8-23.

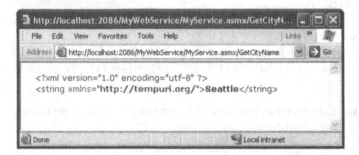

Figure 8-23. *MyService response for GetCityName*

Adding a Web Application Component

Now that your web service is working with the database, you still need to add a front-end to the application. For simplicity, let's add a web application to the application diagram.

Adding and Implementing the Web Application

You'll add the web application, and then follow the same pattern for the web application implementation as you did for the web service implementation.

1. Return to your MyDesign application diagram.

Note If your application diagram is grayed out, you may still be running in debug mode. Select Debug ➤ Stop Debugging.

2. Click the ASP.NETWebApplication prototype in the Toolbox and drag it just above `MyWebService`.

3. Rename `WebApplication1` to `MyWebApp` and the provider `WebContent1` endpoint to `MyContent`.

4. To connect the web application to the web service, right-click `MyWebApp` and select Connect. In the Connect To section, select `MyWebService` for the application and `MyService` for the endpoint and click OK. The completed diagram is shown in Figure 8-24.

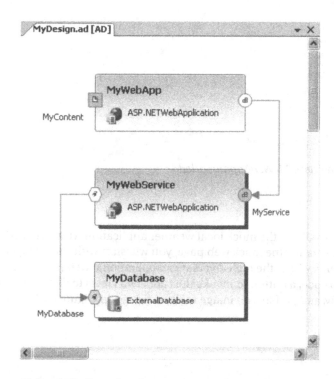

Figure 8-24. *Completed MyDesign application diagram*

5. Select Visual C# as the language for implementation by using the Properties window for `MyWebApp`.

6. Implement the application (by right-clicking `MyWebApp` and selecting Implement Application or choosing that option from the Diagram menu). The result of implementing your design is that a new web application project has been added to the solution, as shown in Figure 8-25.

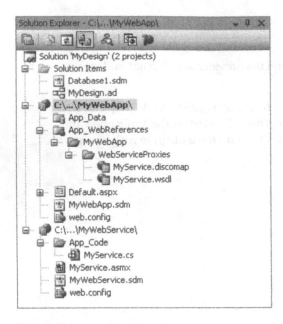

Figure 8-25. *The Solution Explorer with MyWebApp included*

Creating a User Interface

To create a simple user interface (UI) for the mock local weather application, you will need to edit Default.aspx. To facilitate creating the mock web page, you will start with a table layout. You will drop various UI elements within the table to create an operational web page. You will need a text box to enter the zip code, a button to invoke the code, two labels to display the city name and weather, respectively, and perhaps an image to dress things up. Figure 8-26 shows the mock UI.

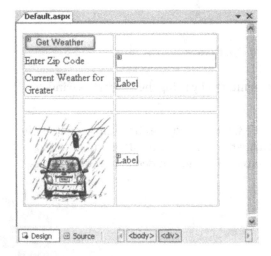

Figure 8-26. *Table layout for mock UI*

1. Double-click Default.aspx to view the source code.

2. Click the Design tab to create the UI.

3. Click Layout ➤ Insert Table. Enter **5** in the Rows field and **2** in the Columns field. Click OK to view your table.

4. Drag a standard button to row 1, column 1 and change the text from Button to **Get Weather** (this will call the service).

5. Drag a standard text box to row 2, column 2 and add the text **Enter Zip Code** to row 2, column 1 (this will accept the user-supplied zip code).

6. Drag a standard label to row 3, column 2 and add the text **Current Weather for Greater** to row 3, column 1 (this will hold the lookup city name).

7. Drag a second standard label to row 5, column 2 (this will hold the local weather forecast).

8. You need to add a few lines of code to finish a working UI. Double-click the Get Weather button to open the Default.aspx.cs code-behind. Copy the code in Listing 8-6 and paste it as the Button1_Click event.

Listing 8-6. *Sample Button Code-Behind*

```
{
//Get the zip code requested
    int myzip = Convert.ToInt32(TextBox1.Text);
//Get the Local Data
MyWebApp.WebServiceProxies.MyService s = new
    MyWebApp.WebServiceProxies.MyService();
        Label1.Text= s.GetCityName(myzip);
        Label2.Text = s.GetLocalWeather(myzip);
}
```

9. You can tweak the layout and add an image or two.

10. Press F5 to build the application.

11. Enter a valid zip code and click the button. Your solution should look something like the web page shown in Figure 8-27.

Figure 8-27. *Sample Default.aspx web page invoked*

Adding Comments to Application Diagrams

In addition to creating items with semantic meaning, you can also add comments to your design by dragging the comment shape onto the design surface and adding text. Figure 8-28 shows an example of a comment added to an application diagram.

■**Tip** As a good practice, comment your diagrams heavily where the design purpose is not obvious.

Hello Dad :)

Figure 8-28. *A comment added to a diagram*

Understanding Connections and Endpoints

In the Application Designer, endpoints on applications define services they provide or specify the requirement to use services.

Endpoint Notation

Figure 8-29 shows some examples of endpoints. A provider endpoint (shaded circle attached to the CommonService in Figure 8-29) is used to represent services provided by the application. A consumer endpoint (open circle attached to SampleApp1 and SampleApp2 in Figure 8-29) is used to represent the use of services offered by other applications. Put simply, a provider endpoint is represented by a shaded object, and a consumer endpoint is represented by an unshaded object.

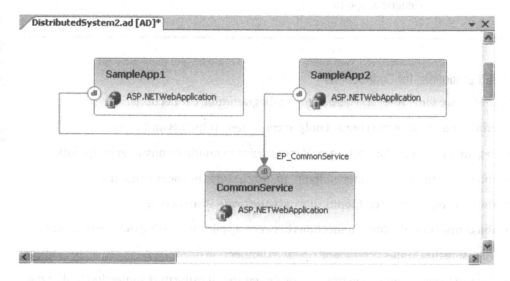

Figure 8-29. *Connection endpoints*

Figure 8-29 illustrates a simple connection between two separate web applications (the consumer of the data services) and the common service (the provider of data services). The connection shown is an ASP.NETWebService provider endpoint connecting to two distinct ASP.NETWebService consumer endpoints.

As a rule, you can connect a provider endpoint to multiple consumer endpoints, but you can connect a consumer endpoint to only a single provider endpoint. (Additional rules and guidelines are covered in the next section).

Table 8-3 shows the notations and the abstract types they represent.

Table 8-3. *Abstract Types and Graphical Representations*

Representation	Abstract Type
	Web service endpoint
	Web content endpoint
	Database endpoint
	Generic endpoint

Rules and Guidelines for Connections

The following are some rules and guidelines for diagramming connections:

- Provider endpoints can connect only to consumer endpoints and vice versa.

- In general, you can connect a provider endpoint to multiple consumer endpoints.

- You can connect a consumer endpoint to only a single provider endpoint.

- You can connect only endpoints that have the same abstract type.

- You cannot directly draw connections between applications using the Connection tool.

- Choosing the Connect command opens a Connection dialog box.

- You can begin a connection from a provider endpoint using the Connection tool or the Connect command.

- If compatible provider and consumer endpoints exist, you can begin connections from either endpoint using the Connection tool or Connect command.

Adding a Web Service Endpoint from a WSDL File

You can add a web service endpoint to your web service from an existing WSDL. To demonstrate, you'll add one to your MyDesign.ad application diagram.

1. Right-click the MyWebService and select Create Web Service Endpoints from WSDL.

2. In the Add Web Reference dialog box, select Web Services on the local machine. You should find the book's sample application Service, as shown in Figure 8-30.

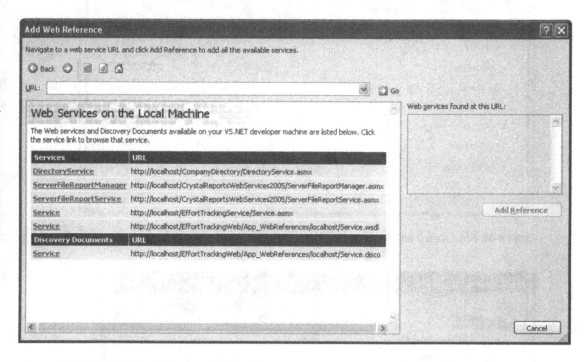

Figure 8-30. *The Add Web Reference dialog box*

3. Select the Service link in the Add Web Reference dialog box. You will see "1 Service Found" in the right side display area, as shown in Figure 8-31.

4. Click Add Reference to add this Service endpoint to your application diagram.

5. Select the new Service endpoint, and then open the Web Service Detail window by selecting Diagram ➤ Define Operations. Here, you can review the operations associated with your imported service, as shown in Figure 8-32.

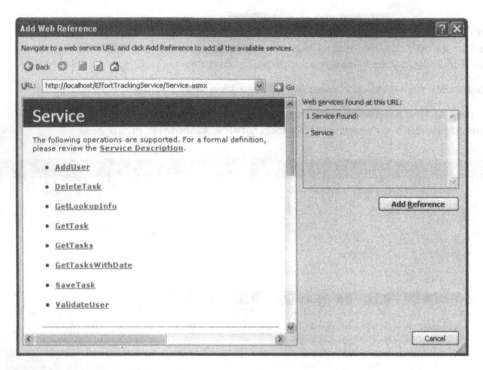

Figure 8-31. *Finding a web service*

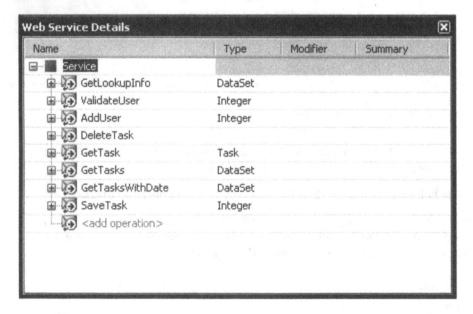

Figure 8-32. *The Web Service Details window showing the added service from the WSDL file*

Understanding Constraints and Settings

The distributed system designers allow you to set constraints and settings for your designs. To view the Settings and Constraints window, shown in Figure 8-33, right-click any application type in the Application Designer and select Settings and Constraints.

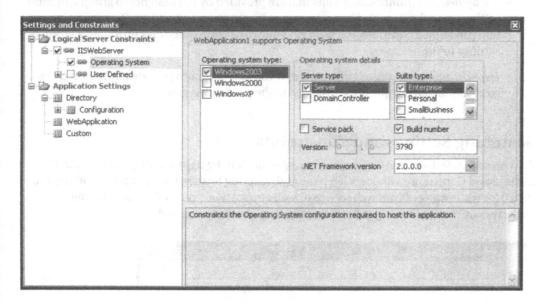

Figure 8-33. *The Settings and Constraints window*

A *constraint* is a requirement that a configuration value be set in a certain way. Constraints can be created in one layer against settings in another layer. For example, constraints can be set from the application layer against settings on the application hosting layer and vice versa. The application layer is modeled in the Application Designer. The application hosting layer is modeled in the Logical Datacenter Designer. However, constraints can also be created in the same layer. For example, in the Logical Datacenter Designer, zone constraints can be authored against the logical servers the zones contain, as well as the applications hosted on the logical servers within the zones. Zones and zone constraints are discussed in detail in Chapter 9.

Settings are configurable elements of your application environment that control the way your application behaves. For example, for an IIS web server under the SmtpSection, you can set the specific delivery methods allowable for inbound SMTP messages.

Setting Constraints

Constraints are requirements targeted at configuration values. For example, several of the application prototypes allow you to set the constraint on the operating system type, service pack, and build number on which to run. Constraints fall into three categories:

- *Implicit constraints:* Constraints that are nonnegotiable and well defined, authored by the application prototype providers themselves. For example, a Windows Forms application cannot be hosted on a client operating system without the .NET Framework installed.

- *Predefined constraints:* Constraints that are provided by the designer to group common settings to make it more efficient for you to locate groups of settings. The operating system predefined constraint is a good example of a group of settings providing a group of settings to the designers.

- *User-defined constraints:* Constraints that you can author to provide any required constraints that fall outside those provided in the predefined groups.

Searching Settings and Constraints

You can search settings and constraints for a specific item by right-clicking anywhere in the Settings and Constraints window's left pane and selecting Search. For example, if you required IIS 6.0 for the hosting of your web service or web application, you could search for the MajorVersionNumber setting and select Find All, as shown in Figure 8-34.

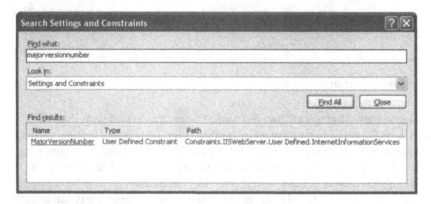

Figure 8-34. *The Search Settings and Constraints dialog box*

Selecting the highlighted constraint in the Find Results list takes you to the constraint. For this example, you would go to the MajorVersionNumber constraint for the InternetInformationService, as shown in Figure 8-35. Here, you could change the Value setting to 6, to require IIS 6.0.

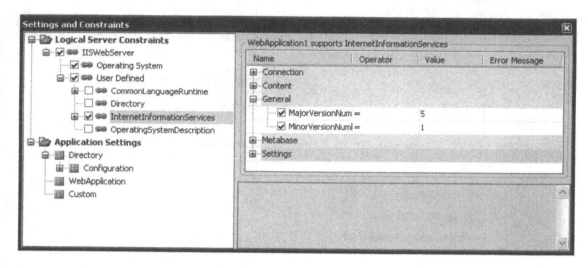

Figure 8-35. *Settings and Constraints detail*

You will explore more details of settings and constraints in the following two chapters.

Reverse-Engineering Existing Solutions

You can also reverse-engineer your Application Designer diagram from an existing solution. In this section, you will reverse-engineer an application diagram from the book's sample Effort Tracking application.

1. Open Visual Studio 2005. Select File ➤ Open Project/Solution, and open the sample solution, `EffortTrackingSolution.sln`.

2. Right-click the `EffortTracking` solution and select Add ➤ New Distributed System Diagram.

3. The Add New Item window displays the solution items available for the distributed system diagrams. Highlight Application Diagram, change the name to `EffortTracking`, and click Add. The result is the implemented application design, as shown in Figure 8-36. You need to make only a few modifications to the default diagram to make it useful.

4. Move `EffortTrackingWeb` directly above `EffortTrackingService`. Right-Click `EffortTrackingWeb` and select Add ➤ New WebContentEndpoint and rename to `ETWebContent`. Now drag an ExternalDatabase application prototype just under `EffortTrackingService`. Rename `Database1` to `EffortTracking`.

5. You now need to connect the database to the web service. Starting with the `EffortTrackingService` database consumer endpoint, use the Connection tool to drag the consumer endpoint of the service to the provider endpoint of the `EffortTracking` database, as shown in Figure 8-37. The final version of the `EffortTracking` application diagram is now complete.

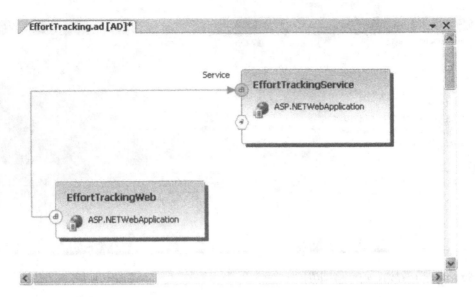

Figure 8-36. *Default application diagram from the EffortTracking solution*

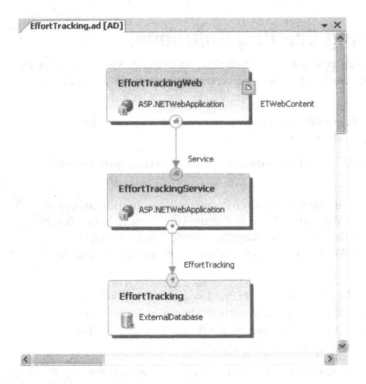

Figure 8-37. *Revised EffortTracking application diagram*

With the sample application for the book now reverse-engineered in the Application Designer, take some time to explore the properties, settings, and constraints.

Troubleshooting Application Diagrams

When working in distributed system designers, performing certain actions often affect the current diagram as well as other distributed system diagrams. The following are three types of errors related to diagrams:

- *Alert states:* A red dashed outline, red error (X), or yellow warning (!) on the diagram indicates an anomaly.

- *Locking:* A shaded diagram (read-only) indicates a check-out, compile, parse, or missing file issue.

- *Synchronization:* Once implemented, a diagram must be kept in sync with the .sdm document. Out-of-sync diagrams will trigger an alert state.

For more information about troubleshooting application diagrams, see the MSDN online help.

Summary

In this chapter, you learned how to design and implement a simple connected system from scratch using the Application Designer. This included defining the application prototypes, connecting them via exposed endpoints, and defining the operations on the web service. You then implemented your design, creating both a web application and web service connected to your local database. Finally, you imported an existing WSDL endpoint. This chapter also introduced constraints and settings. Finally, you learned how to reverse-engineer an entire application in the Application Designer.

In the following chapter, you will use the Logical Datacenter Designer to create an environment in which to deploy your sample application.

■■■

CHAPTER 9

System and Logical Datacenter Designers

The System Designer is used to arrange and configure systems from the applications defined in the Application Designer. In the context of the System Designer, a *system* is defined as a single unit of deployment. Since systems can be composed of other systems, very large and complex designs can be accommodated. This should satisfy the "wall-chart" architects (those who spend their time creating application diagrams that fill an entire wall or more). The level of abstraction provided by the System Designer allows multiple designs to facilitate deployment onto varying datacenters, customer sites, or geographic locations.

The Logical Datacenter Designer allows you to "create" a logical structure of interrelated servers describing your physical environment. These designs are used in the Deployment Designer to validate the deployment of systems into the logical infrastructure. A future goal of this designer is to allow the physical instantiation of the logical design into physical and/or virtual datacenters.

In this chapter, you will learn how to use both of these designers.

Using the System Designer

The system diagram depends on the application diagram to provide the basis for a deployable system. (See Figure 8-1 in the previous chapter for an overview of the distributed system designers and how they are related.) So, before you get started with the System Designer, it is best to have a repository of applications (at least one existing application diagram created with the Application Designer) from which to work. One advantage of selecting your applications from the Application Designer as the basis for your system design is that your connections between applications are carried forward. However, as you will discover in the first example in this chapter, you can start from scratch.

SYSTEMS, APPLICATIONS, AND THE SYSTEM DEFINITION MODEL

From a System Designer perspective, the terms *system* and *application* can be a bit confusing. In the industry, these words are often interchangeable. We talk about a sales application or a marketing system. Often, the deciding factor in choosing the term *system* or *application* is how it sounds with the three-letter acronym (TLA). However, there are some differences in how these terms are actually defined.

Whatls.com defines application as "A shorter form of application program. An application program is a program designed to perform a *specific* function directly for the user or, in some cases, for another application program. Applications use the services of the computer's operating system and other supporting applications."

Whatls.com defines system as "A *collection* of elements or components that are organized for a common purpose. The word sometimes describes the organization or plan itself (and is similar in meaning to *method*, as in 'I have my own little system') and sometimes describes the parts in the system (as in 'computer system')."

From these definitions, we get a general idea that the application is the specific thing and the system is the collection of those specific things.

At the heart of the System Definition Model (SDM) is the notion of a system. Fundamentally, the system is an independently deployable configuration of resources. Two types of systems are supported within the SDM: atomic and composite. Atomic systems are composed of the specific things, such as assemblies, configuration files, and SQL scripts. Composite systems are composed of applications and/or other systems.

With this fundamental understanding, we see that the Application Designer supports application prototypes (encapsulations of the underlying resources for the base type). These *specific* types can be implemented and synchronized with the actual code. The System Designer provides for the *collection* of applications and other systems for the purpose of deployment validation. This supports repurposing for different environments and nesting for complex scenarios.

Creating a New System Diagram

Most likely, you will create the system diagram directly from the application diagram, which is covered in the "Building a System Diagram from an Application Diagram" section later in the chapter. In this example, you will start with a new project and use copy and paste to get the application information into the new design. You might do this when you want to copy in a section of a larger application to start your system diagram. This example will demonstrate the issues involved with adding an implemented application directly from another diagram. For this example, you will copy the MyDesign application diagram you created in Chapter 8.

1. Start a new project. In the New Project dialog box, select Distributed System Solutions, and then select Distributed System. Enter the name MySystem, as shown in Figure 9-1, and click OK. At this point, you have an empty solution, as shown in Figure 9-2.

Note If you create a new Distributed System Solutions project type, there is no option to start with a system design. The default selection is Distributed System, which provides you with a blank application diagram from which to construct your system diagram.

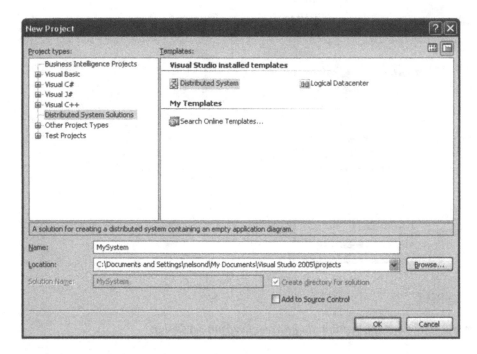

Figure 9-1. *Creating a new Distributed System project*

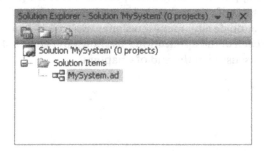

Figure 9-2. *The empty MySystem solution*

2. Open the MyDesign solution you created in the previous chapter and double-click MyDesign.ad to display the application diagram. Right-click the design surface and choose Select All. From the main menu, select Edit ➤ Copy (or press Ctrl+C).

3. Close the MyDesign solution and reopen the MySystem solution. Double-click MySystem.ad, and then paste the copied application diagram using Edit ➤ Paste (or press Ctrl+V). Your resulting diagram should look like Figure 9-3.

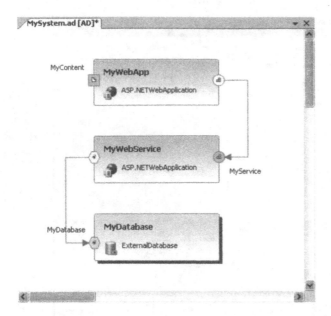

Figure 9-3. *MySystem application diagram copied from MyDesign*

Notice that even though MyDesign was an implemented application in the MyDesign solution, an unimplemented version of the application diagram is provided. This is a great advantage of using the copy-and-paste method. If you had added MyDesign.ad to this solution instead of using copy and paste, the application design operation signatures would be incorrect, and you would see red boxes around each of the applications, as shown in Figure 9-4. This indicates a .synchronization alert, as discussed at the end of Chapter 8.

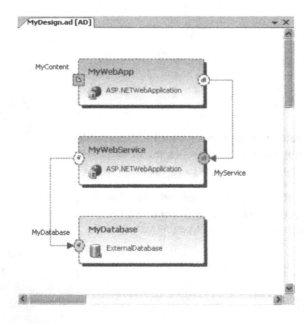

Figure 9-4. *Application Designer synchronization error alert*

> **Note** An application diagram always needs to exist for a system diagram to be present. If you delete the default application diagram, and then try to add a new system diagram, another application diagram will be created for you. Also, if you delete the application diagram from which a system is built, when you reopen the system diagram, Visual Studio will try to re-create the application diagram.

Starting a System Design Diagram

Now that you have a copy of an application design, you can start to create your system diagram. There are several methods for creating a system diagram:

- From within the Solution Explorer, right-click Solution Items and select Add ➤ New Distributed System Diagram. In the Add New Item dialog box, select System Diagram.

- Select Diagram ➤ Design Application System from the main menu.

- Select any or all of the applications on the design surface, right-click, and select Design Application System.

For this example, you will start with a blank system diagram and create a deployable system, exposing the web service with the associated database.

1. In the Solution Explorer, right-click Solution Items and select Add ➤ New Distributed System Diagram. In the Add New Item dialog box, select System Diagram. Provide the name MySystem, and then click Add. The System View window now contains the applications that were copied into the MySystem application designer, as shown in Figure 9-5.

Figure 9-5. *The System View window*

2. You can now just drag-and-drop applications from the System View window onto the designer to create your deployable systems. For this example, drag MyWebService and MyDatabase into the system diagram.

3. Using the Connection tool in the System Designer Toolbox, connect the database endpoints and add a comment that says **MySystem for the Northwest Region**. Your diagram should look like Figure 9-6.

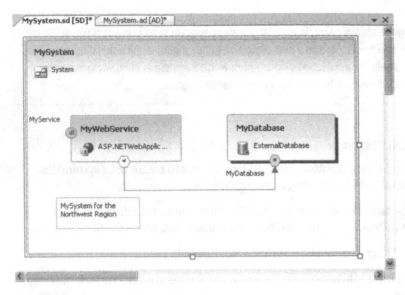

Figure 9-6. *MySystem system diagram*

The System Designer Toolbox contains only three predefined objects to be used while designing your system model. The reason that there are so few tools is that the system diagram is really a container for deployment scenarios of an application diagram. The Toolbox objects are described in Table 9-1.

Table 9-1. *The System Designer Toolbox Objects*

Item	Description
Pointer	Pointer tool used for selection (drag-and-drop)
Connection	Connection tool to link two system endpoints
Comment	A comment text box

Creating a Proxy Endpoint for Applications

Your new system will ultimately need to be connected with other systems or might be nested within a larger system context. To keep the database endpoints properly encapsulated, you need to expose only the web service endpoint. This exposure of an application endpoint to a system boundary is termed *delegation*. Once the endpoint has been delegated, a proxy endpoint is created within the system diagram.

1. Right-click the MyService provider endpoint and select Add Proxy Endpoint.

2. Rename the proxy endpoint to distinguish it from the application endpoint. Name it MyServiceProxy, as shown in Figure 9-7.

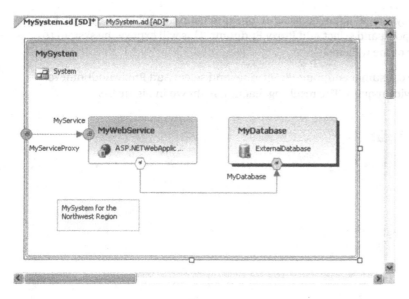

Figure 9-7. *MySystem diagram proxy endpoint*

■**Tip** The Application Designer is always sitting right behind the System Designer. To quickly view the detail in the Application Designer, right-click the application you are interested in and select Go to Definition.

Building a System Diagram from an Application Diagram

In this section, you will create a second system directly from an application diagram, and then connect the two systems via the proxy endpoints.

1. In the MySystem solution, double-click MySystem.ad. Click the Pointer in the Toolbox and drag a selection box around the MyWebApp application.

2. Right-click the MyWebApp application and select Design Application System. This will bring up the Design Application System dialog box, where you can enter a name for your new system diagram. For this diagram, enter MyExposed, as shown in Figure 9-8, and then click OK.

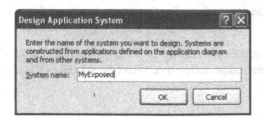

Figure 9-8. *The Design Application System dialog box*

3. The MyExposed system diagram consists of one application, MyWebApp. Right-click the MyContent endpoint and select Add Proxy Endpoint. This will expose the system to HTTP requests of the website.

4. Right-click the consumer endpoint (MyService) and select Add Proxy Endpoint to expose the service request. The resulting diagram is shown in Figure 9-9.

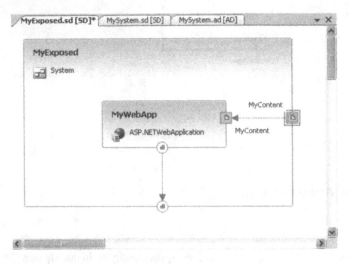

Figure 9-9. *MyExposed system diagram*

Nesting Systems

For a large or complex enterprise scenario, you may need to combine or nest systems. With several systems identified and proxy endpoints exposed, you can create a more complex system diagram. As a simple example, you will create a new complex system that is composed of both the MySystem and the MyExposed systems.

1. In the Solution Explorer, right-click Solution Items and select Add ➤ New Distributed System Diagram. In the Add New Item dialog box, select System Diagram, name it MyComplex, and click Add. The System View window now includes the systems you have defined in the previous exercises, as well as the application you defined in Chapter 8, as shown in Figure 9-10.

2. With a blank system design template open, you can drag-and-drop any combination of applications and systems on the design surface. For this example, drag MySystem and MyExposed onto the design surface.

3. Connect the systems by right-clicking the MyServiceProxy endpoint of MySystem and selecting Connect. In the Create Connection dialog box, select MyExposed as the system and MyService as the endpoint in the Connect To section.

Figure 9-10. *The MyComplex system*

4. Extend the MyContent endpoint (by adding a proxy endpoint) to expose the endpoint to other systems. Your complex system design should look like Figure 9-11.

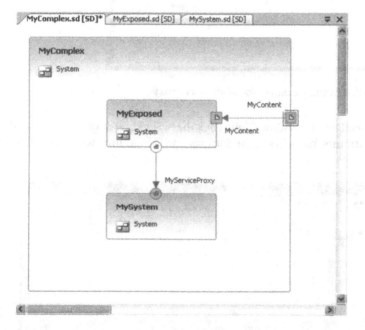

Figure 9-11. *Sample nested systems diagram*

Tip With a multilevel system diagram, you can easily traverse the hierarchy by right-clicking a subsystem and selecting Open in System Designer. You can continue to open subsystems until you get down to the actual application. Once at the application level, you can still select Go to Definition to view the actual application diagram.

Viewing Web Service Details, Settings, and Constraints

The System Designer allows you to view the operation, settings, and constraints of the endpoints and applications exposed on the system design surface. A key item to note is that you can only view these elements. Unlike with the Application Designer, where you can define operations and configure settings and constraints, this is primarily a view into the underlying metadata. We say "primarily" because you do have the option to override certain settings, as described in the next section.

For example, right-click the MyServiceProxy endpoint within the MyComplex system diagram and select View Operations. You will see a list of operations defined in the Application Designer, as shown in Figure 9-12.

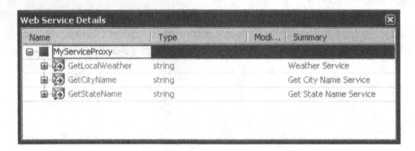

Figure 9-12. *The Web Service Details window for MyServiceProxy*

Close the Web Service Details window. Right-click the MyServiceProxy endpoint again and select Settings and Constraints. You will see the Settings and Constraints window, as shown in Figure 9-13.

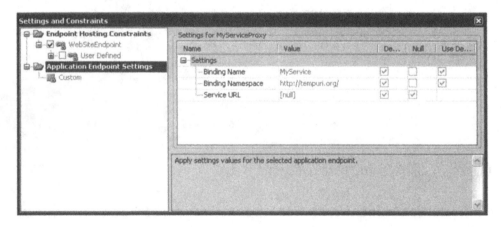

Figure 9-13. *The Setting and Constraints window for MyServiceProxy*

Overriding Settings and Constraints

A key feature of the distributed designers is the ability to override the settings in a system design that have been provided by an underlying application design. This provides for reusable configurations and tailored deployments of systems. However, before you can override settings in the System Designer, they must first be specified as overridable within the Application Designer. Let's try this out.

1. In the MySystem solution, double-click MySystem.ad. Within the Application Designer, right-click the MyService endpoint and select Settings and Constraints.

2. Choose Application Endpoint Settings and verify that they are set to overridable, as shown in Figure 9-14.

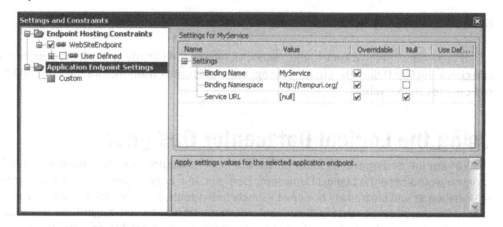

Figure 9-14. *Setting and constraints can be set as Overridable.*

3. Open MySystem.sd and view the settings and constraints for the MyService web service provider endpoint. Notice that the Binding Namespace is set to the template-coded http://tempuri.org. As a best practice, you should change the binding namespace from this default value on web service endpoints.

4. To comply with the best practice suggestion, change the Value field for the Binding Namespace to http://mysystem.org, as shown in Figure 9-15.

5. Close the Settings and Constraints window and save your MySystem solution. You will use it when you work with the Deployment Designer in the next chapter.

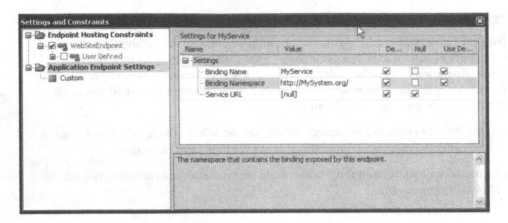

Figure 9-15. *Overriding the Binding Namespace setting*

If you ever want to go back to the original value provided by the application design, you can check the Use Default box in the Settings and Constraints window, and the value will be reset to the original value.

Using the Logical Datacenter Designer

Unless your job description includes infrastructure architecture, you are probably wondering why you would need the Logical Datacenter Designer. In a large organization, the design of the datacenter will most likely be done by lonely individuals, in locked rooms, with high levels of security clearance. For the smaller organizations, this might be you. Regardless, the design of the application and the design of the supporting infrastructure need to be worked in tandem.

A disconnection between the development teams and infrastructure support has been all too apparent in our experience of designing and deploying enterprise systems. For many years now, customer organizations have been forced to build and maintain separate lab environments of production-quality hardware to test applications prior to deploying them in the enterprise datacenter.

Five years ago, we presented the diagram shown in Figure 9-16 to the vice president of information systems of a large corporation to graphically depict the need for architects, developers, and infrastructure groups to work together to provide integrated solutions.

During the presentation, we stressed, "Our key motivation is getting the solution to the customers before the opportunity for benefit has slipped away." Today, as then, we work to engage the architecture, infrastructure, and development communities to advance this framework. Fortunately, a key design goal for VSTS addressed what we already knew needed to be accomplished: "Facilitate collaboration among all members of a software team (including architects, developers, testers, and operations managers)." This focus on bringing the full team together was the key reason we jumped in so early in the release cycle of VSTS.

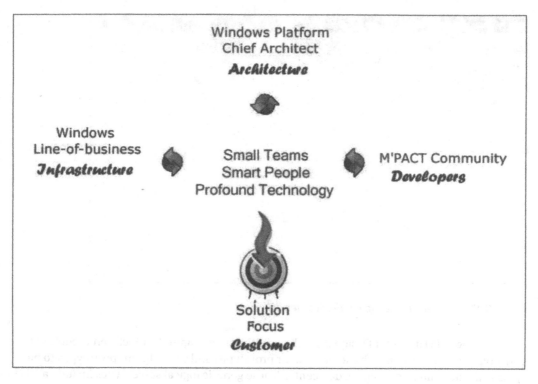

Figure 9-16. *Collaborative team environment*

In this section, you will look at how to use the Logical Datacenter Designer to define and configure logical servers that will be part of the logical datacenter structure. From the overuse of "logical" in the previous sentence, you can see one of the shortcomings of the Logical Datacenter Designer. There is no physical implementation in this release. This fact gave rise to a blogging stream titled "Why the VSTS Logical Datacenter Designer (er, Deployment Designer) Sucks." A reply is posted at http://blogs.msdn.com/a_pasha/articles/409396.aspx.

Creating a Logical Datacenter Diagram

Your logical datacenter design can be created from scratch or may be provided to you by an infrastructure architect in your organization. For this example, you will use Visual Studio 2005 to add a new logical datacenter diagram to the solution you created in Chapter 8.

1. Right-click your MyDesign solution and select Add ➤ New Distributed System Diagram.

2. Select Logical Datacenter Diagram and provide the name MyDesign.ldd, as shown in Figure 9-17, and then click Add. You will be brought in to the Logical Datacenter Designer with a blank work surface and a default logical datacenter diagram (.ldd).

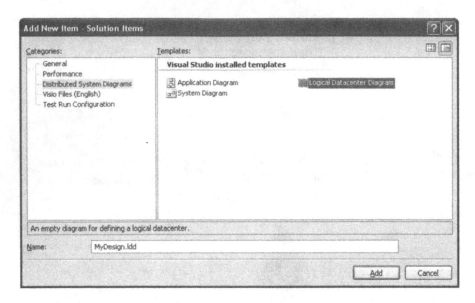

Figure 9-17. *Creating a new logical datacenter diagram*

The Logical Datacenter Designer Toolbox comes preconfigured with eleven predefined prototypes (.lddprototype): five logical server prototypes and six endpoint prototypes to be used while designing your logical datacenter. These generic logical server types include a Windows client, Internet Information Server (IIS) web server, database server, generic server, and zone. The Toolbox objects are described in Table 9-2.

Table 9-2. *The Logical Datacenter Designer Toolbox Objects*

Item	Description
Pointer	Pointer tool used for selection
WebSiteEndpoint	Manages server-side communication with a logical IIS web server
HTTPClientEndpoint	Manages client-side communication with a logical IIS web server
DatabaseClientEndpoint	Manages client-side communication with a logical database server
GenericServerEndpoint	Describes server-side communication with a logical generic server
GenericClientEndpoint	Describes client-side communication with a logical generic server
ZoneEndpoint	Manages communication on the edge of a zone
WindowsClient	Corresponds to a Windows client or server that hosts a Windows application
IISWebServer	Corresponds to an IIS server that hosts web services or ASP.NET web applications
DatabaseServer	Corresponds to a database server
GenericServer	Corresponds to a user-defined server or component
Zone	Logical boundary, such as a firewall, that is separated from other portions of the datacenter; zones can be nested

Item	Description
Pointer	Pointer tool used for selection (again!)
Connection	Connection tool to link two endpoints
Comment	A comment text box

You can extend the Logical Datacenter Designer prototypes, just as you can extend the Application Designer prototypes (as explained in Chapter 8). For example, if you have a hardening policy on your IIS servers, you might want to configure those settings on an IIS server prototype and then save it as Corporate Hardened IIS Server. Similarly, if you have created a certain zone definition that you plan to reuse or share, it would be a good idea to create a prototype of that zone.

To extend a prototype, select the design element (logical server or endpoint) and choose Diagram ➤ Add to Toolbox. To share your prototype with others, you can provide them with a copy of your .lddprototype file, which they can add to their default prototype folder. In the future, Microsoft will be providing additional datacenter prototypes (such as SQL Server), which you can add to your designer.

Adding Zones

To create a logical datacenter diagram, you should begin by adding zones. Zones are an important concept within the Logical Datacenter Designer. They are used to define communication boundaries, physical boundaries (different sites), or security boundaries (internal servers or perimeter servers).

To understand zones, you just need to think about games you played as kid. Games such as capture the flag and dodge ball have the notion of zones. Most of them involve lines that cannot be crossed or policies such as "safety zones," where you cannot be hit or tagged. This is the most secure area during the game and is similar to a datacenter zone. The wide-open spaces are the risky areas, where you might be taken out at any time. In our analogy, this is like the public Internet. In the network world, these zone boundaries are defined by firewalls, routers, ports, and virtual local area networks.

Let's get started by adding some zones to the new diagram.

1. Click the Zone prototype in the Logical Datacenter Designer Toolbox and drag it onto the design surface. Optionally, you can right-click the design surface and select Add New ➤ Zone.

2. By default, the zone is named zone 1. Double-click the name and change it to DMZ (for demilitarized zone). Change ZoneEndpoint1 to something a bit shorter, like DMZ_ZEP.

■Note The term *demilitarized zone* (DMZ) is taken from the military meaning: "An area from which military forces, operations, and installations are prohibited." Corporations have adopted the DMZ concept of "the area between two enemies" and applied it to networking to mean "A middle ground between an organization's trusted internal network and an untrusted, external network such as the Internet. This is also referred to as a *perimeter network*.

---

3. Add a second zone and rename it to CIZ (for corporate intranet zone), as shown in Figure 9-18. You can simply copy your DMZ zone and paste it back onto the design surface. Change the zone and endpoint names to CIZ and CIZ_ZEP, respectively.

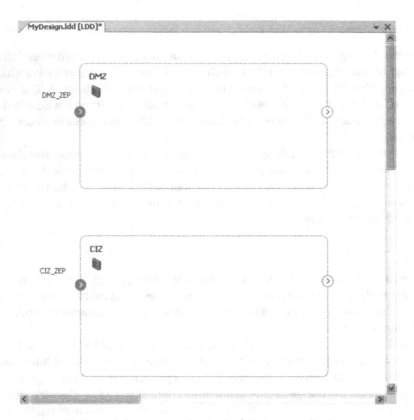

Figure 9-18. *Zone definitions in the Logical Datacenter Designer*

Setting Zone Constraints

As you've learned, constraints are used to enforce requirements in one layer of the distributed systems model (such as the Application Designer) against those in another layer (such as the Logical Datacenter Designer). You can think of these constraints as house rules. Some households have a rule that requires you to take your shoes off at the door, and there is even a little sign posted in the entryway:

If you forget or ignore the sign, "agents" of the house will remind you of your error. In a similar way, the constraints defined in the distributed designers are enforced across the platform to ensure that corporate policy is integrated into the design tools.

Settings are configuration elements in the environment that control the behavior of the application or server. If you think of constraints as the allow or disallow rules, settings would be the conditions. If we allow you go to the high school dance (constraint), you must be home by 11:00 p.m. (setting).

For example, a common networking practice is to restrict the type of servers allowed within the DMZ. Let's set a zone constraint to do this.

1. Right-click within the DMZ zone and select Settings and Constraints.

2. Under Zone Containment Constraints, deselect the WindowsClient and Zone check boxes, as shown in Figure 9-19. This will restrict Windows clients to within the protected CIZ zone, as well as other zones hosted within this zone (nested zones).

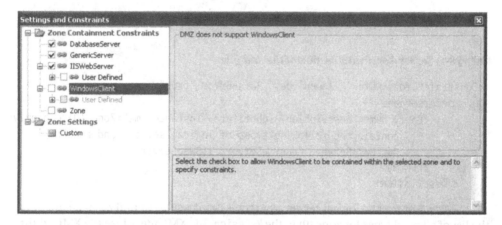

Figure 9-19. *Settings and Constraints for zones*

■**Note** The settings and constraints information that is entered via the Settings and Constraints window maps to data that is generated in the corresponding .sdm file. Editing a setting or a constraint directly affects the generated SDM.

---

3. Verify the constraint by trying to drag a WindowsClient or Zone object from the Toolbox into the DMZ zone on the design surface. Notice also that you can still drag both of these within the CIZ zone.

4. Verify the changes were written into the SDM (.ldd file) for the logical datacenter design. You need to save and close any open designers. Then right-click MyDesign.ldd and select Open With. In the Open With dialog box, select the XML editor. This will open the .ldd file in the XML editor within Visual Studio.

5. Press Ctrl+F to bring up the Find and Replace dialog box. Type **logical servers and zones** in the Find What text box, as shown in Figure 9-20. Click the Find Next button, and you should see the XML fragment shown in Listing 9-1, which is part of the SDM for the DMZ.

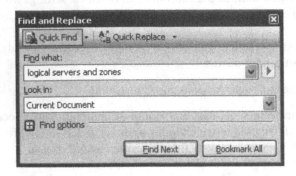

Figure 9-20. *Finding the server constraint*

Listing 9-1. *Server Constraint Section of the .ldd File*

```
<ConstraintGroup Name="AllowedTypes" RaiseError="true">
    <Description>
        <Entry Name="Description" Substitute="InstanceName">Zone {0} can only
            contain the following types of logical servers and zones:
            DatabaseServer, GenericServer, IISWebServer.
        </Entry>
    </Description>
```

Notice that the two logical server prototypes (WindowsClient and Zone) are missing from the list of allowed types for zone (0) in the MyDesign.ldd XML file. Close the XML editor.

Placing Servers Inside Zones

Now that the zones have been defined on your design surface, you can start adding servers within the zones. The first server you will add is an IIS server in the DMZ to provide an access point to external clients. Next, you will add another IIS server and database server to host the web service and back-end database, respectively, in the CIZ.

1. Double-click MyDesign.ldd to open. Right-click within the DMZ zone and select Add ➤ IISWebServer. Rename the web server by double-clicking the name and changing it to Exposed_IIS.

2. Add a second IISWebServer to the CIZ zone and name it Safe_IIS.

3. Add a DatabaseServer to the CIZ zone and name it Safe_DB.

■**Tip** If you place a server in the wrong zone or outside a zone on the design surface, you can easily relocate it by right-clicking the lost server and selecting Move to Zone.

---

4. The incoming zone endpoint within the DMZ zone should already be labeled DMZ_ZEP, and the CIZ zone's endpoint should labeled CIZ_ZEP. If the endpoint label is not showing on the diagram, right-click the endpoint and select Show Label. Rename the endpoints on the logical servers themselves to give them meaningful names. In this case, the chosen convention is to use the server name with the suffix of _EP, as shown in Figure 9-21.

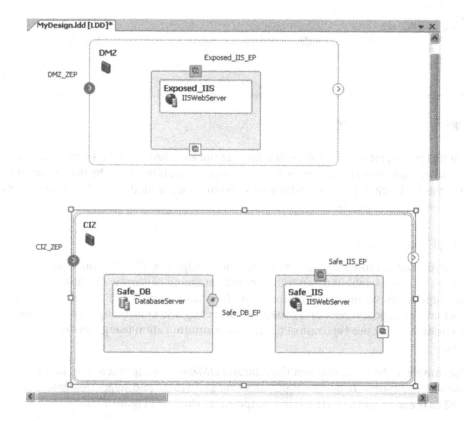

Figure 9-21. *Logical Datacenter Designer with zones and servers identified*

Setting Specific Zone Constraints

You can define a policy for a zone that applies to all the items within that zone. Let's say that you want to make sure that all IIS servers in the CIZ are running the current production version of the Common Language Runtime (CLR), and no beta versions of the CLR are allowed to be present in that zone.

1. Select the CIZ zone. Right-click and select Settings and Constraints to open the Settings and Constraints window.

2. Select User Defined and CommonLanguageRuntime from the list on the left.

3. On the right, select Version and enter the correct version number in the Value field. You can also enter descriptive error text in the Error Message field, as shown in Figure 9-22.

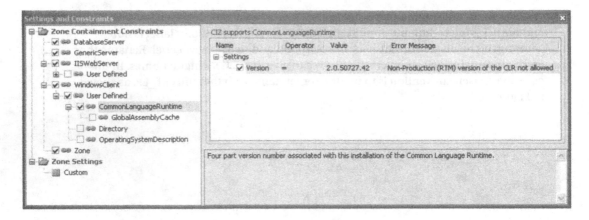

Figure 9-22. *Setting constraints on a zone*

Since this constraint on the CLR version is set at the zone level, any IIS server added to the zone will be required to meet the version-level restriction. If you take the time to open the .ldd file in the XML editor, you will notice a version constraint added to the CIZ zone regarding the CommonLanguageRuntime.

Connecting Servers to Zones

Communication across zones is managed by the zone endpoints. The communication through the zone can be inbound, outbound, or bidirectional. The arrow displayed within the zone endpoint represents the communication flow. You can then define communication pathways between logical servers and zones by connecting and controlling these pathways via their endpoints. You also can control the type of communication using constraints on endpoints.

1. Beginning in the DMZ, connect the inbound DMZ zone endpoint to the IIS server provider endpoint. To do this, right-click Exposed_IIS_EP and select Delegate. Select DMZ as the zone and DMZ_ZEP for the endpoint, as shown in Figure 9-23.

2. Connect the exposed IIS server client endpoint to the outbound DMZ zone endpoint. This time, try using the Connection tool from the Toolbox. Select the Connection tool, click the Exposed_IIS client endpoint, and drag the connection to the outbound DMZ zone endpoint.

3. Continue with the Connection tool and connect that same outbound DMZ zone endpoint to the inbound zone endpoint on the CIZ zone.

4. Connect that inbound zone endpoint on the CIZ zone to the provider endpoint on the Safe_IIS. Your diagram now shows a compete flow from the outside to your safe IIS server.

5. To finish the diagram, right-click Safe_IIS and select Connect. Choose the Safe_DB as the zone and Safe_DB_EP as the endpoint, and then click OK. Your diagram should look like Figure 9-24.

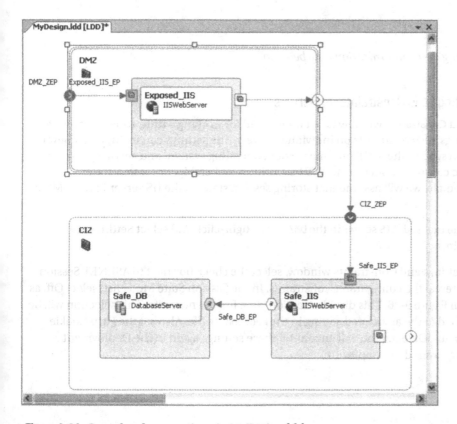

Figure 9-23. *The Delegate to Endpoint dialog box*

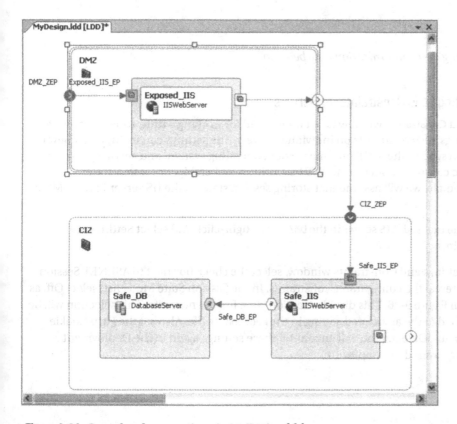

Figure 9-24. *Completed connections in MyDesign.ldd*

You can set the flow behavior on a zone endpoint through its Properties window, as shown in Figure 9-25. Select the zone endpoint you want to configure and press F4 to display the Properties window. In the Behavior section, set the Communication Flow property to Inbound, Outbound, or Bidirectional, based on your scenario.

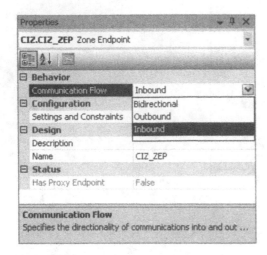

Figure 9-25. *Setting the communication flow behavior*

Specifying Settings and Constraints for Servers

The Settings and Constraints window is not only useful for working within zones, but also for specifying settings and constraints on individual servers. The settings can include configuration information such as the .NET runtime version, operating system, and service packs. They can also include constraints such as ASP.NET security, membership, or session state.

For this example, we will assume that storing session state on the IIS server in the DMZ is not allowed.

1. Select the Exposed_IIS server in the DMZ zone. Right-click and select Settings and Constraints.

2. In the Settings and Constraints window, select the check box next to ASP.NET Session State to reveal the configurable constraints. In the Session State Mode list, select Off, as shown in Figure 9-26. This disables session state for an entire site. This selection will be propagated to the associated setting in the Web.config file. Also set the Http Cookie Mode to AutoDetect. (You will encounter these settings again in the Deployment Designer, covered in Chapter 10.)

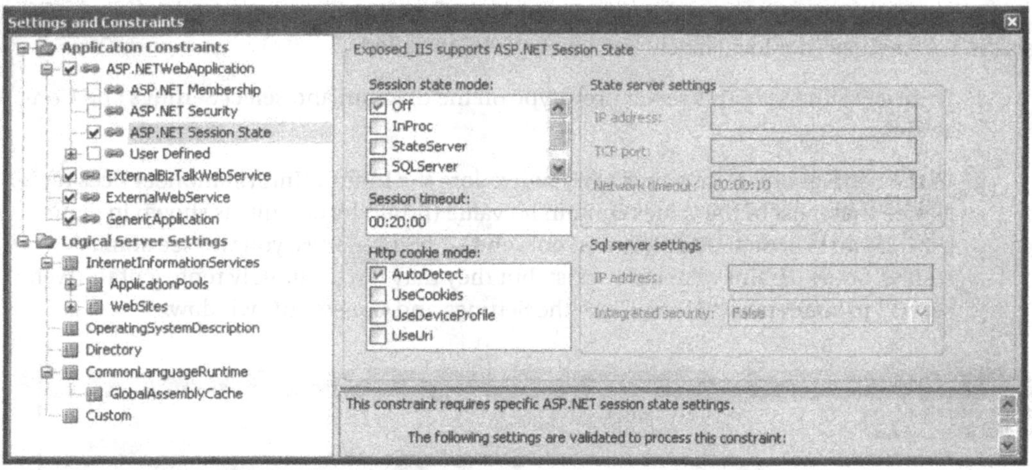

Figure 9-26. *Disabling session state on the IIS web server*

As explained in Chapter 8, three types of constraints are supported in the distributed designers. Here is how each type might be used with your logical datacenter design:

- Implicit constraints are "baked" into the SDM. An example of an implicit constraint is the available endpoints for a database server prototype. These constraints cannot be edited by users, but they can be authored using the SDM SDK.

- Predefined constraints logically group together settings of a particular type, such as ASP.NET membership or website configuration. These dialog boxes have editing rules built into them to allow specific combinations of settings to define the constraint.

- User-defined constraints allow a user to have full control over desired values and ranges for any setting available on the logical server. These constraints are created by manually defining one or more settings.

Constraints placed on endpoints restrict the type of communication allowed to be carried through the endpoint. For example, a zone endpoint can be constrained to permit only HTTP traffic over a specific port. Establishing such a constraint will affect connections within the Logical Datacenter Designer, as well as restrictions on implementations in the Deployment Designer.

Importing Settings from IIS

You can manage many settings and constraints within the Logical Datacenter Designer, but it can be a daunting task to manually configure all of these for each logical server. Fortunately, there is a wizard that allows you to import your settings from an existing IIS web server.

To demonstrate how this works, you will import the settings and constraints from an IIS server. You can use your local machine if you have IIS installed.

1. Right-click the Safe_IIS server prototype on the diagram and select Settings and Constraints.

2. In the Settings and Constraints window, explore the InternetInformationServices node. Notice that most of the values contain no value ([null]) by default, as shown in Figure 9-27. If you browse the ApplicationPools and WebSites nodes, you will see similar results. Some default values may exist, but they may not accurately represent the web servers in your environment. Close the Settings and Constraints window.

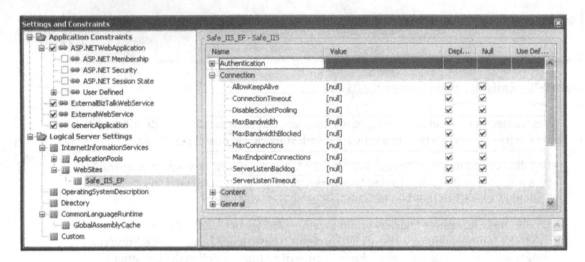

Figure 9-27. *The Setting and Constraints window for the default IIS web server*

3. Right-click the Safe_IIS server prototype on the diagram and select Import Settings to start the Import IIS Settings Wizard. Click Next.

4. As shown in Figure 9-28, the Import IIS Settings Wizard presents three check boxes on the next page:

   • The first option imports all of the websites that reside on the server and creates a new endpoint representing each site on the IIS web server prototype. If you don't select this option, the proceeding page will provide the option to import individual sites to either new or existing endpoints.

   • If the second box is checked, the global configuration settings for the web server will be imported. These settings map to the InternetInformationServices node in the Settings and Configuration window.

   • The third check box determines if application pools will be imported.

   For this example, enter your server name and administrator credentials (administrator credentials are required in order to access certain metabase keys and values), accept the defaults for the check boxes, and click Next.

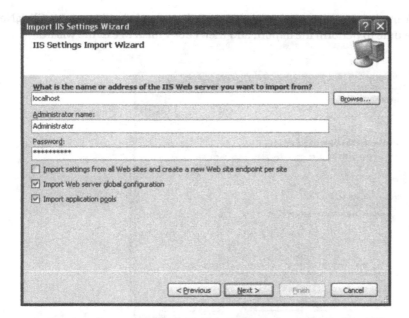

Figure 9-28. *Import IIS Settings Wizard set to import from the local machine*

5. The wizard prompts you to select the websites and endpoint bindings. Click the down arrow in the Endpoint section and select Safe_ISS_EP, as shown in Figure 9-29. Then click Next.

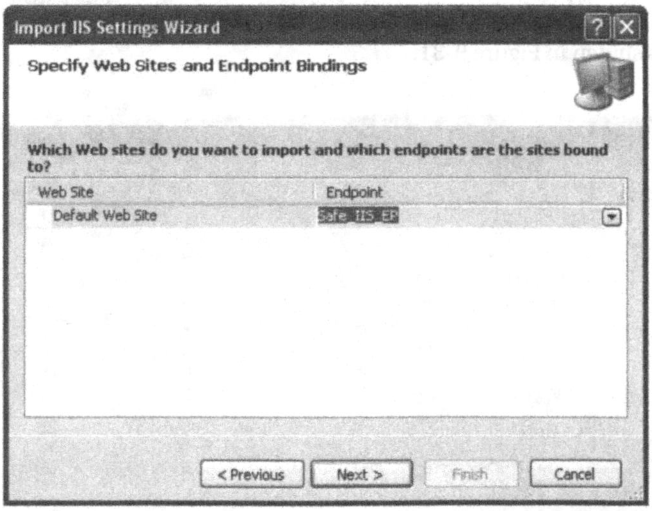

Figure 9-29. *Import IIS Settings Wizard websites and bindings*

6. The confirmation page lists what will be imported, as shown in Figure 9-30. Click Next one more time to perform the import, and then click Finish to exit the wizard.

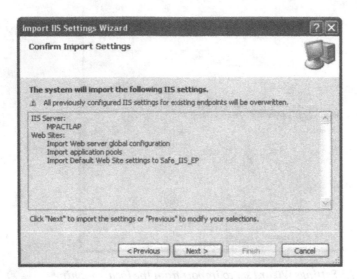

Figure 9-30. *Import IIS Settings Wizard confirmation*

7. Open the Settings and Constraints window again for the Safe_IIS server prototype. Notice that the InternetInformationServices node has been renamed to the server name from which the settings were imported. Select this node, and you will see that the global configuration settings for the web server have been populated with the IIS metabase settings. You can also see that the Connection properties now reflect the imported settings, as shown in Figure 9-31.

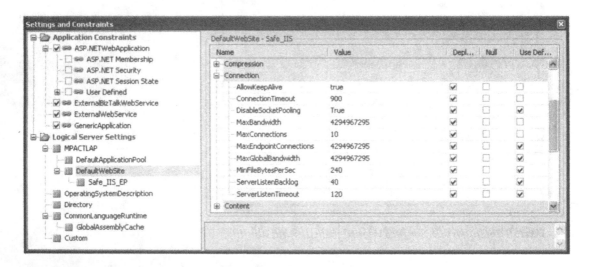

Figure 9-31. *Settings and constraints imported from the local IIS server*

Building a Logical Datacenter Diagram for the Sample Application

In this section, you will build a simple logical datacenter diagram to support the sample application you reverse-engineered using the Application Designer in Chapter 8.

1. Open Visual Studio 2005. Select File ➤ Open Project ➤ Solution and open the sample solution, EffortTrackingSolution.sln.

2. Right-click the EffortTracking solution and select Add ➤ New Distributed System Diagram. Select Logical Datacenter Diagram and change the default name from LogicalDatacenter1.ldd to EffortTracking.ldd. Click the Add button to open the Logical Datacenter Designer.

3. You need a web server to host the web application and the web service. Drag an IISWebServer logical server from the Toolbox onto the design surface, as shown in Figure 9-32. Rename the default provider WebSiteEndpoint1 to ET_Site_EP.

Note With Visual Studio 2005, you can run a virtual web server, which means that you do not need to have IIS. However, throughout the book, IIS is used to host the sample application in order to illustrate certain points and eliminate some of the confusion.

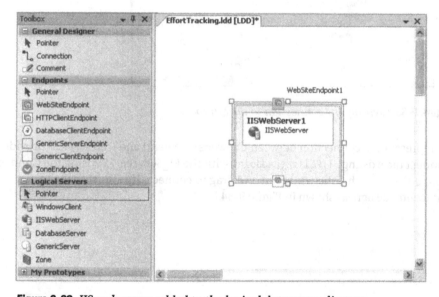

Figure 9-32. *IIS web server added to the logical datacenter diagram*

4. Add a second website endpoint by right-clicking IISWebServer1 and selecting Add New ➤ WebSiteEndpoint. Rename it ET_Service_EP.

5. Rename the server itself to EffortTrackingWebServer.

6. You need a back-end database server to host EffortTracking. Drag the DatabaseServer logical server from the Toolbox onto the design surface below the IISWebServer server. Rename the database provider endpoint from DatabaseServerEndpoint1 to ET_DB_EP. Rename DatabaseServer1 to EffortTrackingDatabase.

7. Since the web service connects to the database using ADO.NET, you need to provide the connection. Right-click inside EffortTrackingWebServer and select Connect. In the Connect To section, select EffortTrackingDatabase for the logical server and ET_DB_EP for the endpoint, as shown in Figure 9-33. Click OK. Notice that the connection appears between the IIS server and the database.

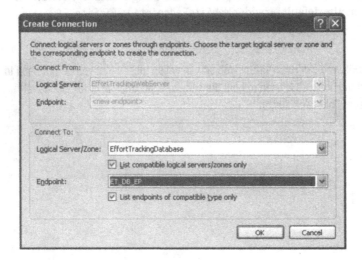

Figure 9-33. *Creating the connection to the database*

8. To represent the connection between the website (client) and web service (provider), connect the existing HTTPClientEndpoint with the ET_Service_EP. Using the Connection tool, start with either endpoint and drag to connect. This finishes the logical datacenter design, as shown in Figure 9-34.

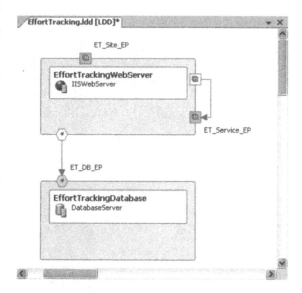

Figure 9-34. *Logical datacenter design for the Effort Tracking application infrastructure*

Summary

In this chapter, you looked at the System Designer and Logical Datacenter Designer. The System Designer is the critical link between your application design and the logical datacenter. You learned how to design and build system diagrams and how to nest systems. You also learned how to view and override settings provided by the Application Designer.

Next, you explored the Logical Datacenter Designer. You saw how to separate your logical datacenter into zones and how to interconnect servers, zones, and endpoints. You worked with settings and constraints on both zones and servers to provide configuration information or constrain the scope within the zone or server. You then learned how to import settings from existing servers. Finally, you built a logical datacenter diagram to support the sample application. In a future version of Visual Studio, you will be able to deploy your logical datacenter onto physical devices or into virtual datacenters.

The final step in the process is to "bind" the applications you created in the Application Designer and grouped in the System Designer to the Logical Datacenter Designer diagram you just completed. This binding process is performed by the Deployment Designer, as explained in the following chapter.

CHAPTER 10

■■■

Deployment Designer

The final member of the distributed designer suite is the Deployment Designer. Once you have your applications defined and grouped into deployable systems, and have defined one or more logical datacenters, you are ready to validate the deployment into a target datacenter.

The Deployment Designer allows the architect/developer to evaluate the appropriateness of a particular system for a specified logical datacenter. This evaluation occurs between the system diagram (.sd) and the logical datacenter diagram (.ldd), which were discussed in Chapter 9.

VSTS provides two methods for arriving at your deployment diagram: explicit and implicit. The explicit, or formal, method is to first define a system diagram from which to invoke the deployment. The implicit, or quick-and-dirty, method is to invoke the deployment directly from the application diagram and force a default system diagram to be generated.

In this chapter, we will cover the formal method first with our sample design from Chapters 8 and 9. Then we will use the implicit method to start the deployment design from the application diagram of the book's sample Effort Tracking application.

Using the Explicit Deployment Method

Using the explicit deployment method, you start from an existing system diagram that you have defined. Let's begin by reviewing the MyComplex system diagram that you created in Chapter 9.

Open the MySystem solution within Visual Studio 2005 and double-click MyComplex.sd. This complex system is composed of two subsystems and one application diagram, and they are all opened in the System Designer, as shown in Figure 10-1. Notice that the application diagram is sitting in the background and cannot be closed separately from the System Designer.

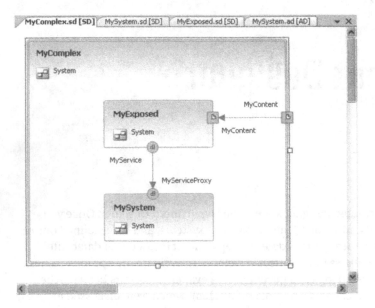

Figure 10-1. *MyComplex in the System Designer*

All the information (metadata) in this diagram is expressed in the underlying System Definition Model (SDM) file. Take some time to review the XML in the MyComplex.sd file, as shown
in Figure 10-2. You will need to close the open diagrams and open the MyComplex.sd file using
the XML editor. Within the file, you will recognize the association with your other diagrams,
the detailed properties for each model element, and the incorporation of versioning.

```
MyComplex.sd                                                                    ▼ ×
 1  <?xml version="1.0" encoding="utf-8"?>
 2  <!--System Definition Model (SDM) based file generated by Visual Studio.-->
 3  <!--Manual editing of this file is not recommended and can result in errors.-->
 4  <SystemDefinitionModel xmlns:xsi="http://www.w3.org/2001/XMLSchema-instance" xmlns:xsd="http://www.w3.org/2001/XMLSchema"
 5    <Import Alias="System" Name="System" Version="1.0.50729.0" />
 6    <Import Alias="MicrosoftDistributedApplication" Name="Microsoft.DistributedApplication" Version="1.0.50729.0" />
 7    <Import Alias="MyExposed" Name="MyExposed" Version="1.0.0.0" Culture="en-US" />
 8    <Import Alias="MySystem" Name="MySystem" Version="1.0.0.0" Culture="en-US" />
 9    <Import Alias="MicrosoftWeb" Name="Microsoft.Web" Version="1.0.50729.0" />
10    <Import Alias="MyWebApp" Name="MyWebApp" Version="1.0.0.0" Culture="en-US" />
11    <Import Alias="MicrosoftWebApplication" Name="Microsoft.WebApplication" Version="1.0.50729.0" />
12    <DesignData>
13      <VisualStudio xmlns="http://schemas.microsoft.com/SystemDefinitionModel/2005/1/DesignData/VisualStudio">
14        <ModelElement Id="dd1c9a8b92bf4a7f90ec3ff0007f3e3b" Type="Microsoft.VisualStudio.EnterpriseTools.Application.Modeli
15          <Property Name="DocumentType" Value="ApplicationCompoundComponent" />
16          <Property Name="Version" Value="1" />
```

Figure 10-2. *MyComplex.sd in the XML editor*

Note SDM files are identified based on five key attributes: the name, version, culture, platform, and public
key token. Only the name attribute is required.

Creating a Deployment Diagram

In this example, you will create a deployment diagram using MyComplex.sd. When you choose to define your deployment, you also need to supply a logical datacenter design for deployment validation. You will use the MyDesign.ldd file from the MyDesign solution you created in Chapter 8.

Starting a Deployment Diagram

Follow these steps to begin your deployment diagram:

1. Open the MyComplex system diagram by double-clicking the MyComplex.sd file in the Solution Explorer.

2. In the System Designer, right-click the design surface and select Define Deployment, as shown in Figure 10-3.

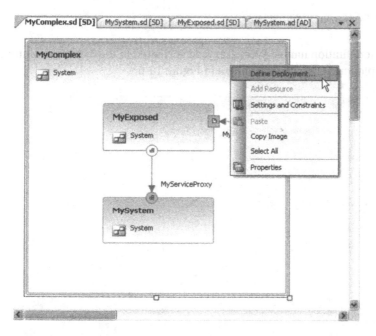

Figure 10-3. *Choosing to start a deployment diagram*

3. In the Define Deployment dialog box, choose MyDesign.ldd, as shown in Figure 10-4. (Since you do not have the logical datacenter diagram already attached to your solution, browse to the MyDesign solution and select MyDesign.ldd from there.) Then click OK.

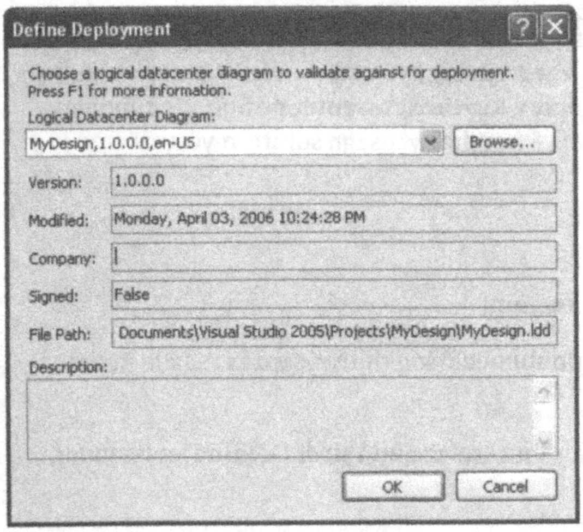

Figure 10-4. *The Define Deployment dialog box*

A new deployment definition named MyComplex1.dd is created in the MySystem solution and opened in the Deployment Designer, as shown in Figure 10-5.

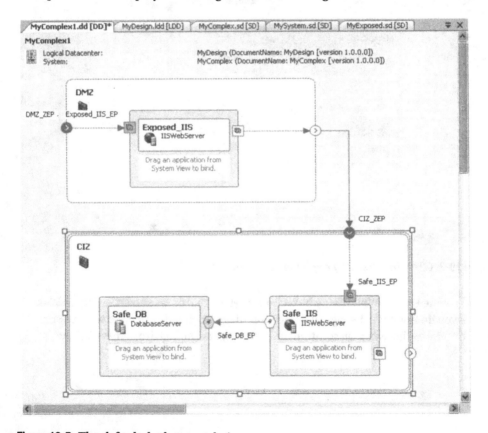

Figure 10-5. *The default deployment design*

Also, the logical datacenter diagram, MyDesign.ldd, has been added to your solution, as shown in Figure 10-6.

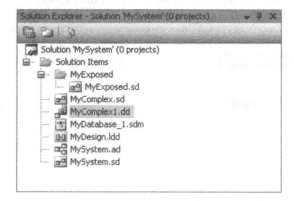

Figure 10-6. *The Solution Explorer window showing the new MyComplex1.dd and MyDesign.ldd files*

The Toolbox for the Deployment Designer contains only two items: a Pointer tool for making selections and Comment tool for adding comments.

A more interesting aspect of the Deployment Designer is the System View window. It contains the application artifacts from the Application Designer inside your MyComplex system, as shown in Figure 10-7.

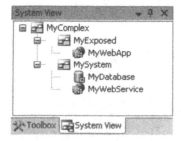

Figure 10-7. *The System View window*

Binding the Applications to Logical Servers

Using the System View window, you can drag the applications onto the reproduced logical datacenter diagram. Alternatively, you can right-click an application in the System View window and select Bind Application. This will bring up a dialog box that shows the suitable hosts in your target datacenter. Using either method, the Deployment Designer will not allow you to bind applications to unsuitable hosts. However, you can choose to override this default behavior.

1. In the System View window, right-click the MyDatabase application and select Bind Application. (If the System View window isn't visible, select View ➤ Other Windows ➤ System View). In the Bind MyDatabase to Logical Server dialog box, your only choice will be Safe_DB, as shown in Figure 10-8. Select it and click OK.

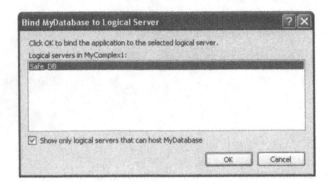

Figure 10-8. *The Bind MyDatabase to Logical Server dialog box*

2. Drag MyWebApp onto the Exposed_IIS server.

3. Drag MyWebService over to the design surface. Notice that the only acceptable location is the Safe_IIS server.

The System View window will indicate the binding of the application to the host by placing an arrow to the left of the application and showing <Bound> after the application name, as shown in Figure 10-9.

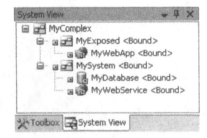

Figure 10-9. *The System View window with bound application prototypes*

At this point, all your applications are bound to the target datacenter hosts, as shown in Figure 10-10.

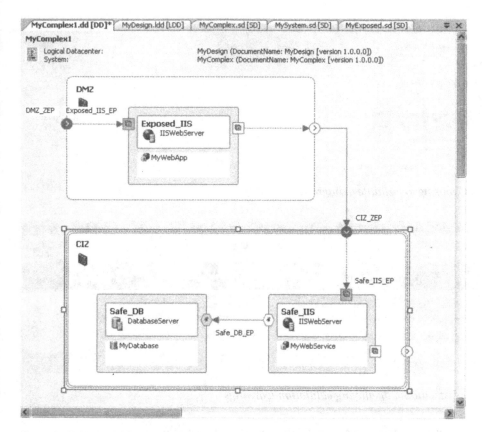

Figure 10-10. *The deployment diagram with applications bound to logical servers*

Validating a Deployment Implementation

After you've created your deployment diagram, it's time to validate the proposed deployment definition. When you choose to validate the diagram, the Deployment Designer validates the settings and constraints specified in the .sd file for the system against those specified in the .ldd file for the target datacenter. The Error List window will display any errors, warnings, or messages associated with the validation of the system against the logical datacenter, along with a little white x in a red circle (error mark) inside each offending application, server, or zone. Let's see this in action.

1. Right-click the deployment diagram and select Validate Diagram, as shown in Figure 10-11. Alternatively, you can select Diagram ➤ Validate Diagram from the main menu or click the Validate Diagram icon in the toolbar.

2. The Error List window, shown in Figure 10-12, indicates that four validation warnings occurred. You should see error marks next to the MyWebService application, the MyWebApp application, and the Exposed_IIS logical server. Look over the descriptions of each warning. You will address each one of these in order. Your Errors List may differ depending on settings imported from your IIS Server.

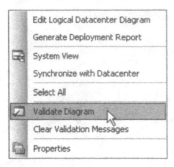

Figure 10-11. *Choosing to validate a diagram*

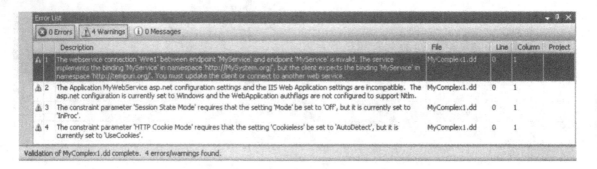

Figure 10-12. *The Error List window displaying validation warnings*

3. Double-click the first warning in the Error List window. The Settings and Constraints window will open to the configuration setting causing the conflict, as shown in Figure 10-13. Also, the underlying application, system, or logical datacenter diagram will be brought into focus. Here, the MyExposed system diagram is brought forward.

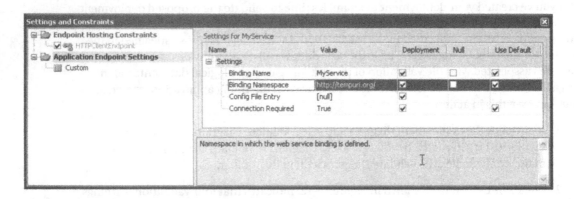

Figure 10-13. *Settings and Constraints window for the MyService endpoint*

4. You overrode the default Binding Namespace setting on the MyService endpoint in the creation of the MySystem system diagram (in Chapter 9); however, the client (consuming endpoint) within the MyExposed system still expects the default. Select the MyComplex.sd system diagram, and you'll see that the mismatch is clearly depicted, as shown in Figure 10-14. Right-click the MyServiceProxy endpoint and select Settings and Constraints. Notice the Binding Namespace setting of http://MySystem.org. With the Settings and Constraints window still open, click the MyService endpoint. You'll see that the Binding Namespace setting is http://tempuri.org. Now you can override the client (MyService) setting within the MyExposed system to match.

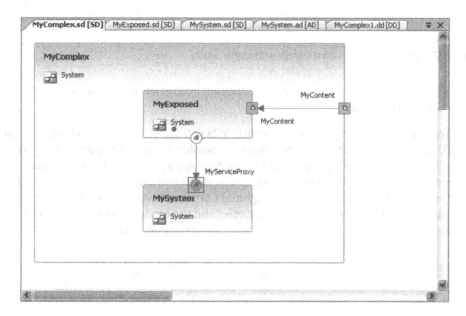

Figure 10-14. *MyComplex system diagram showing error marks*

5. Click the first validation error in the Error List window again to bring up the Settings and Constraints window within the MyExposed system context. Change tempuri to MySystem for the Binding Namespace setting, and then close the Settings and Constraints window.

6. Select the MyComplex1.dd deployment diagram and revalidate it. Notice that the first error has now been resolved, and three warnings remain.

7. Select the next warning in the Error List window to bring up the Settings and Constraints window within the MySystem system design. In this case, the authentication setting for the MyWebService application does not match the configuration settings for the IIS web server. (Your particular IIS setting may not cause this error.) In this simple example, address this issue by setting the mode from Windows to Forms, as shown in Figure 10-15. Then close the Settings and Constraints window.

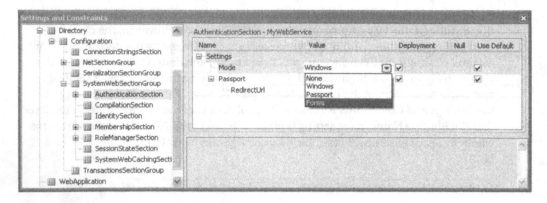

Figure 10-15. *Setting the web service authentication mode*

8. Select the MyComplex1.dd deployment diagram and revalidate it. The second error has now been resolved.

9. The final two warnings regard the constraints you set within the demilitarized zone (DMZ) for the Exposed_IIS server regarding session state (in Chapter 9). You turned off session state for the logical server, but the MyWebApp application has the session state set to InProc. To fix the problem, double-click either of the last two warnings in the Error List window to open the Settings and Constraints window for the MyExposed system. Set the Cookieless value to AutoDetect and the Mode value to Off, as shown in Figure 10-16. Then close the Settings and Constraints window.

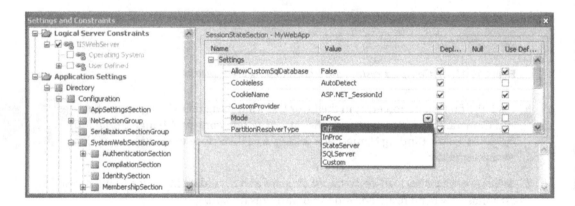

Figure 10-16. *Session state settings for MyWebApp*

10. Select the MyComplex1.dd deployment diagram and revalidate. You'll see that all of the warnings have been resolved, as shown in Figure 10-17.

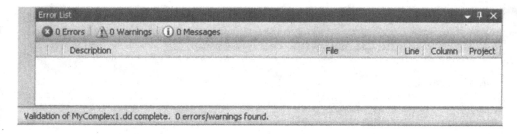

Validation of MyComplex1.dd complete. 0 errors/warnings found.

Figure 10-17. *All errors and warnings resolved*

Generating the Deployment Report

After you've created and validated your deployment design, you will want to generate a
Deployment Report, which can help you to create installation scripts. Before you generate the
report, you should set the deployment properties in the Deployment Designer. We'll discuss
this in more detail in the "Setting Deployment Properties" section later in this chapter. For this
example, you will leave the default properties and simply generate the Deployment Report.

1. Right-click the design surface for the MyComplex1 deployment diagram and select
   Generate Deployment Report, as shown in Figure 10-18.

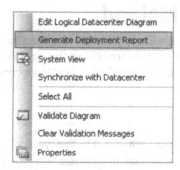

Figure 10-18. *Choosing to generate a Deployment Report*

2. The MyComplex1.html report appears within your solution. Right-click the report and
   select View in Browser.

3. Notice the wealth of information provided for you in the Deployment Report. Take
   some time to browse the content and search on some of the areas we have just
   resolved. For example, search for MySystem.org, and you will see details on the settings
   for the MyService endpoint, as shown in Figure 10-19. You can also click the "back to
   parent" link to navigate up to the application to which that endpoint belongs
   (MyWebApp).

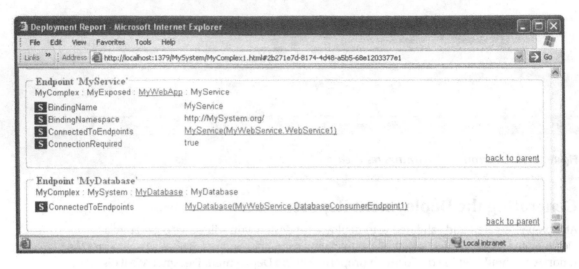

Figure 10-19. *Deployment Report sample section*

We will explore the Deployment Report in more detail after we define the deployment for the book's sample application in the next section.

Using the Implicit Deployment Method

Another way to start a deployment definition is directly from the application diagram, rather than from a system diagram, as in the previous example. This is referred to as the implicit method of deployment. In this section, we'll demonstrate this method and also take a closer look at the Deployment Report.

Note The early builds of the distributed designers called the implicit method a "trial deployment." This early terminology has been dropped, but there are still cautionary notes about running your final deployments from the generated default system. The main issue is that a default system is a direct image of the application diagram, and as such, the configuration cannot be modified independently. For additional information about using the default system, see the TechNote at http://msdn.microsoft.com/vstudio/teamsystem/reference/technotes/apps_designer/default_sys.aspx.

Building the Deployment Diagram

In this section, you will build a deployment diagram for our book's sample Effort Tracking application. You will begin from the EffortTracking.ad application diagram you created in Chapter 8.

Starting the Deployment Diagram

Follow these steps to start the deployment diagram from the Application Designer:

1. Open Visual Studio 2005. Select File ➤ Open Project/Solution and open the sample solution, EffortTrackingSolution.sln.

2. Double-click the application diagram (EffortTracking.ad) to open it in the Application tion Designer, as shown in Figure 10-20.

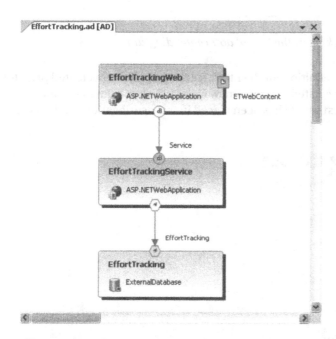

Figure 10-20. *The application diagram for the Effort Tracking application*

3. Select Diagram ➤ Define Deployment from the main menu. In the Define Deployment dialog box, select to use EffortTracking as the logical datacenter diagram (created in Chapter 9), as shown in Figure 10-21. Then click OK.

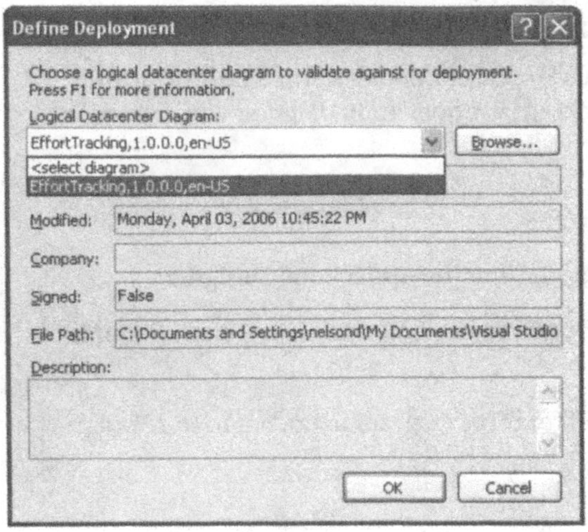

Figure 10-21. *Choosing EffortTracking as the logical datacenter diagram*

Since there was no system definition for the Effort Tracking application created prior to deployment, a default system is created for you. A new Default System folder is added to you solution, and the DefaultSystem1.dd has been placed in this new location, as shown in Figure 10-22.

Figure 10-22. *The Solution Explorer for the EffortTracking sample*

On the design surface, you have a fresh deployment design, which employs the selected logical datacenter diagram, as shown in Figure 10-23.

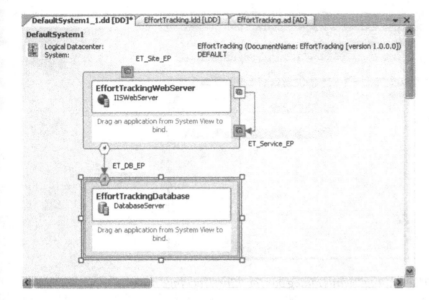

Figure 10-23. *Default EffortTracking deployment diagram*

The System View window contains the Default System and three components of your application design, as shown in Figure 10-24.

Figure 10-24. *The System View window for the EffortTracking sample*

Binding the Applications to Logical Servers

For our sample book application, both the web service and web application will be hosted on a single logical IIS server (EffortTrackingWebServer), and the database will be hosted on the database server (EffortTrackingDatabase).

1. Drag EffortTrackingService from the System View window onto EffortTrackingWeb➥ Server, and the Bindings Detail dialog box will open. The database endpoint should have been resolved to DatabaseClientEndpoint1. However, since you have exposed two provider endpoints on the IIS server, you need to select ET_Service_EP to bind to the Service endpoint of the EffortTrackingService, as shown in Figure 10-25. Select OK, and you will see the EffortTrackingService bound in the System View window.

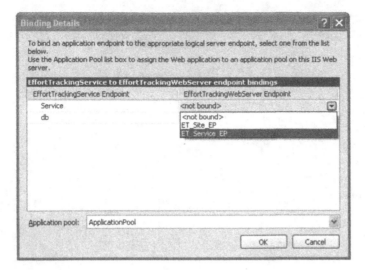

Figure 10-25. *The Binding Details dialog box for EffortTrackingService*

2. Drag EffortTrackingWeb onto the same IIS server (EffortTrackingWebServer). Set the binding for the Service to the HTTPClientEndpoint1 and the ETWebContent endpoint to ET_Site_EP, as shown in Figure 10-26.

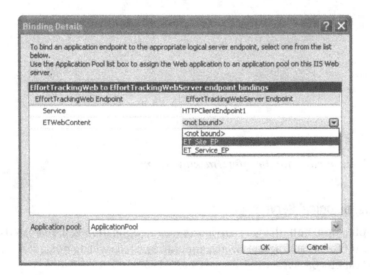

Figure 10-26. *The Binding Details dialog box for EffortTrackingWeb*

3. Drag EffortTracking onto EffortTrackingDatabase. Since there is only one exposed endpoint, no binding details are requested. You can right-click EffortTracking and select Binding Details to verify that the mapping is correct. You should see the EffortTrackingDatabase endpoint from the application design bound to the ET_DB_EP of the logical datacenter design.

Your sample application is now bound to your target datacenter, as shown in Figure 10-27.

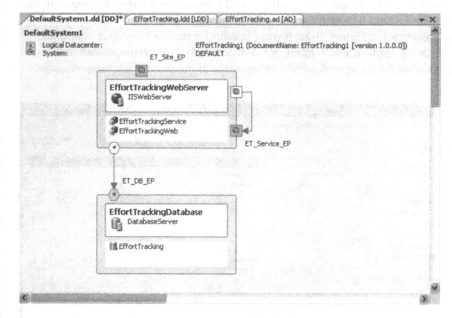

Figure 10-27. *Deployment diagram with application bindings*

Validating the Diagram

Now that you've completed all the bindings between the application components and the logical datacenter, it is time to validate the diagram.

1. Select Diagram ➤ Validate Diagram. The Error List window shows two warnings, indicating that there is a mismatch between the EffortTrackingService, EffortTrackingWeb, and the IIS server in which they are being deployed, as shown in Figure 10-28.

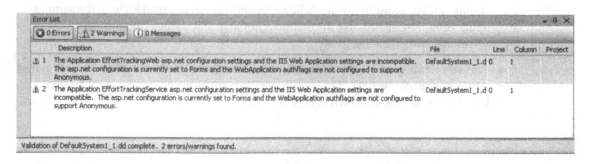

Figure 10-28. *The Error List window for the EffortTracking validation*

2. Double-click the first warning in the Error List window to go to the Application Designer for EffortTrackingWeb. The Settings and Constraints window is opened to the AuthenticationSection, where the mode is set to Forms (which is inconsistent with the IIS server), as shown in Figure 10-29. If you click the EffortTrackingService application profile in the application diagram, you will notice that the web application has the Mode value set to Forms as well, which corresponds to the second warning message.

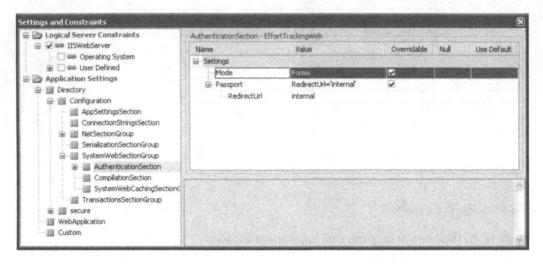

Figure 10-29. *The Settings and Constraints window for EffortTrackingWeb*

3. Switch to EffortTracking.ldd and open the Settings and Constraints window for EffortTrackingWebServer. Within the Logical Server Settings ➤ WebSites ➤ Authentication, notice that AuthFlags is set to Ntlm. Therefore, the Forms authentication in the application needs to support Anonymous, and the IIS server is configured to support only Integrated Windows via Ntlm. You can solve this conflict in two ways: you could change both the web and service applications to use Windows authentication, or you could add Anonymous to the Authentication AuthFlags on the IIS server to allow the support for Forms authentication. Since we want to use our own login in the sample application, you should take the second approach, and change the settings on the IIS server as shown in Figure 10-30.

4. Close the Settings and Constraints window. Select DefaultSystem1.dd from the Window menu, and then select Diagram ➤ Validate Diagram. You will see that the warnings have been resolved, as shown in Figure 10-31.

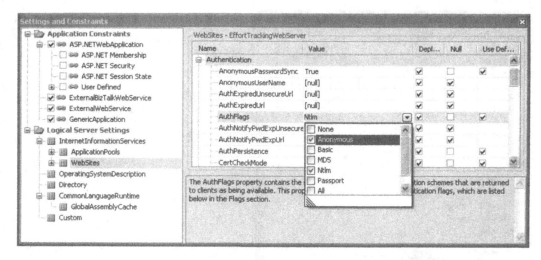

Figure 10-30. *The Settings and Constraints window for EffortTrackingWebServer*

Figure 10-31. *The Error List window with prior warnings resolved*

Setting Deployment Properties

As noted earlier in the chapter, the goal of the Deployment Report is to assist you in creating installation scripts from the XML-based information in the report. A key prerequisite is to set the deployment properties in the Deployment Designer, which you'll do now.

1. Right-click the design surface and select Properties, or press F4, to open the Properties window.

2. Set the Destination Path property to C:\MyDeployments, as shown in Figure 10-32. Set all the Include properties to True. Leave the remaining properties set to their defaults.

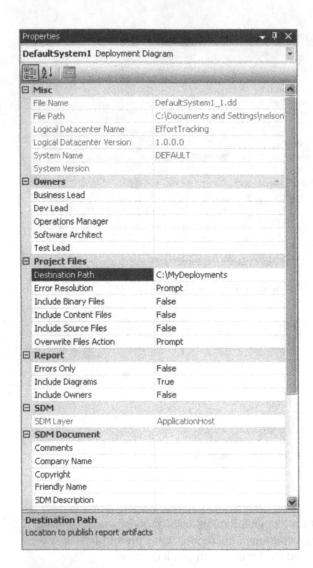

Figure 10-32. *The Deployment Designer Properties window*

Table 10-1 describes the key properties for the Deployment Designer.

Table 10-1. *Key Properties for the Deployment Designer*

Property	Description
Destination Path	This property specifies a path (on disk or a UNC path) to copy source, content, or binary files associated with your applications. By default, this property is blank. If you do not set this property, no files will be copied.
Include Binary Files, Include Content Files, Include Diagrams, Include Owners, and Include Source Files	By default, only diagrams will be included in the Deployment Report. To copy source, content, and binary files to the destination path location, set the corresponding properties to True.
Overwrite Files Action	By default, this property will display a prompt when overwriting files. This can be set to Yes to automatically overwrite files.
Error Resolution	By default, this property will display a prompt when an error occurs. It can be set to Ignore to facilitate automation, or you can also choose to abort Deployment Report creation if an error occurs.
Errors Only	By default, this property is set to False. If set to True, the Deployment Report will contain only the list of validation errors and warnings.

Generating the Deployment Report

Now you're ready to generate the Effort Tracking application Deployment Report. Just right-click the design surface and select Generate Deployment Report. Alternatively, you can select Diagram ➤ Generate Deployment Report. In the status bar at the bottom of the Visual Studio IDE, you will see the Deployment Report generation in progress:

```
Publishing EffortTrackingService: Copying Files…(EffortTrackingService.sdm)
Publishing compiled SDM files: Copying Files…EffortTracking.sdmDocument)
Publishing deployment report: Copying Files…(DefaultSystem1.html)
Deployment report generated.
```

The final report contains detailed information about the bindings, deployment diagram, logical servers, logical datacenter diagram, systems, system diagram, resource settings by type, and endpoints. The Deployment Report for your simple application will be well over 1,000 lines of source HTML. Sample output is shown in Figure 10-33.

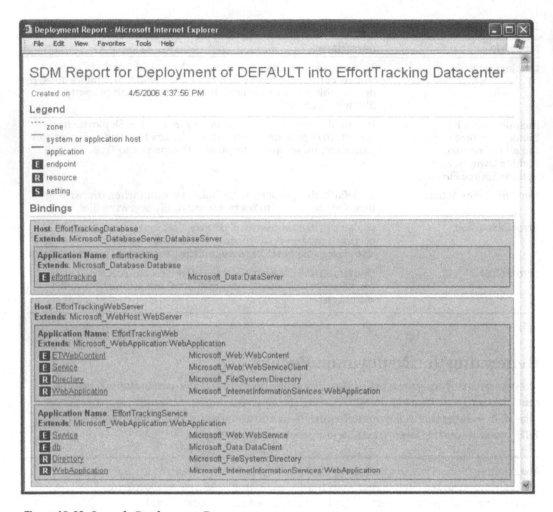

Figure 10-33. *Sample Deployment Report output*

Browse the Deployment Report and search for some of the items we worked on throughout the chapter. Search the document for your favorite endpoint, application, or that elusive AuthFlags setting. Open the File Explorer and see what was deposited in the destination path at C:\MyDeployments, as shown in Figure 10-34.

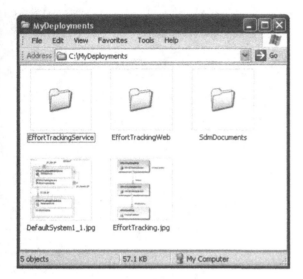

Figure 10-34. *Sample deployment project files*

Summary

In this chapter, you learned how to take your application diagrams or, preferably, your predefined systems and deploy them into target logical datacenters. You've had a wonderful time dropping applications onto the Deployment Designer surface, validating the deployment as you go. Finally, you created a Deployment Report (HTML), including deployable files copied to your selected deployment path.

PART 3

Team Edition for Software Developers

CHAPTER 11

■■■

Class Designer

The Class Designer is both an architect's tool and a developer's tool. Architects can use it to communicate ideas about an application's structure to the development team. Developers can use it to build a skeleton of the classes before they dive in to the coding of those types.

In this chapter, you will learn how to use the Class Designer, and then see what happens under the hood. We'll begin by looking at what the Class Designer was designed to do.

Design Goals

The VSTS team set out to accomplish four specific goals when they created the Class Designer:

- Help the developer understand existing code.

- Provide a jump-start on creating the initial class design.

- Review and refactor application structure and code easily.

- Provide diagrams and documentation that are relevant throughout the life of the application and aid in its maintenance.

The VSTS team wanted the class diagrams to be relevant when looking at the code. The code generation and synchronization is first-class and seamless in the IDE.

Let's take a look at each of these goals and see how they benefit you.

Understanding Existing Code

Oftentimes you, as a developer, architect, or tester, are called on to review the code of applications that you have not worked on directly. But where do you start when you perform a code review of another application? Typically, this might involve reviewing the UML diagrams, user requirements, and functional specifications, and then diving into the code. But frequently, the UML diagram turns out to be out-of-date, and the requirements have changed, so these are not very helpful.

Being able to generate an entire class diagram directly from the code means that it is accurate and up-to-date. This functionality will save you hours and hours of headaches. On top of this, you have the ability to reverse-engineer any class from any assembly, including .NET Framework classes.

Initial Class Design

Designing classes and their relationships is the first thing that architects or development leads do once the overall requirements and high-level architecture are understood. Many times during this process, the views on how objects relate to each other, what objects should be created, and what properties and methods they should have change. The Class Designer is meant to be a simple tool to quickly and easily generate and change class and application structure. On this front, it succeeds admirably. Creating classes is as simple as drag-and-drop, and relating classes is as simple as three clicks of a mouse button. This will most likely become your primary class design tool because of its simplicity and power.

Reviewing and Refactoring

One of the key things that architects and developers do is to create an object model and examine it. During that examination, they are likely to discover changes that need to be implemented. In some cases, these changes are discovered after the code is implemented. Typically, this is a problem, since you need to rework the diagram, and then rework the code. Many diagramming tools do not give you the ability to refactor models directly from the user interface.

The VSTS team went the extra length to allow you review and change your application structure directly from the design surface of the Class Designer. These steps can range from creating interfaces based on already existing methods to encapsulating a private field as a public property without having to write any additional code.

■**Note** VB and C# support many of the same operations on the Class Designer, but some of the operations are available only when using a particular language. These will be pointed out throughout the chapter.

Relevant Diagrams and Documentation

How many projects have you been involved with that started out by creating a class diagram, only to discover about two weeks into the actual coding that the classes no longer looked like the diagram? Even tools like Rational, which let you forward-engineer your diagrams and synchronize the diagram and code later, have some problems. They require you to manually start a sync process and fix any issues that come up. The VSTS team devised the Class Designer so that there is an instant update between a change in the class diagram and the code and vice versa. Yes, you read that right. If you change the code, the diagram is immediately updated to reflect the change.

■**Caution** If you have a method with code in it, and you delete the method from the class diagram, your code is lost. Anything contained within the method body is deleted along with the method. However, you also have the option to hide a class member, which will cause that member to not be displayed in the Class Designer but to remain in the code.

The advantage to this is that your code and diagrams are always synchronized. The developers and architects can really see the class structure. Additionally, it makes maintenance far easier because the documentation will always be accurate.

■**Note** Almost all code generators/reverse-engineering tools put GUIDs and other identifiers in the code. Microsoft's implementation does not do that, so you get the added benefit of clean code.

Microsoft, UML, and Visio

Microsoft has begun shifting from a purely UML view of the world. The introduction of the domain-specific designers and Class Designer are a first step in that direction. The Class Designer departs from a standard UML model in numerous small ways, but overall, it maintains the type of structure you would find in a typical UML static model. Microsoft has taken this step away from UML for several reasons.

The first is that UML is outdated, especially in terms of .NET. Have you seen how UML represents a read-write property in .NET? It creates two methods: get*MethodName* and set*MethodName*. But if you ever try to forward-engineer a .NET class from this UML notation, it literally creates two different methods to match the diagram. UML also does not understand events. This is a critical point because application development is now (for the most part) *event-driven*.

Another reason for the move away from UML is that it makes diagramming too difficult when dealing with certain types of relationships. A perfect example is object aggregation. What is the difference between an open diamond, closed diamond, and an arrow in a UML diagram? An open diamond is a loose aggregation, a closed diamond is a strong aggregation, and an arrow indicates a dependency. But what is the difference between these three options? What's the point of fooling around with these subtleties? They are so close in actual practice that spending time on the theory is wasteful, and in many cases, their use is incorrect anyway.

Finally, Microsoft wanted to bring the power of structured application development to people who are not experts in UML. The Object Technology Series of books published by Addison-Wesley is the gold standard in explaining UML. The core set of books were written by Ivar Jacobson, Grady Booch, and James Rumbaugh—the fathers of UML. These books cover several thousand pages in total! To use UML effectively, you need a trained team of experts. To read the UML diagrams in such a way that they are of effective use to you as a developer requires a lot of training (and how the UML diagrams are implemented in code is always language-specific). Most people cannot afford the time or effort it takes to go into this type of detail.

The Class Designer addresses these issues. Microsoft has strived to make this tool simple yet powerful. Rather than an abstract diagram that has general relevancy across all languages, it produces a concrete diagram that has specific relevancy for the language you are using. It ignores the nuances of certain types of relationships because the implementation cannot really be determined by the diagram. And the Class Designer allows anyone to provide a simple and straightforward view of object relationships.

Microsoft will continue to ship Visio with the UML stencils, so that developers and architects can leverage their existing skill set in their current environment.

UNIFIED MODELING LANGUAGE TODAY

Of course, UML still has its place in modern development. We are not advocating that you do not learn UML. However, we are questioning the need for such a rigorous standard that provides only abstract definitions of objects and applications. In addition, UML has nine different types of diagrams. Most applications typically use only a few of these types of diagrams: the use case, class (static), sequence, activity, and deployment diagrams. You have already seen in the previous chapters how Microsoft has created concrete instances of the deployment diagram with the logical designers and that these logical designers do a much better job in terms of documenting the correct deployment of an application (as well as allowing you to configure the deployment nodes).

At many of the meetings we attended at Microsoft, the Microsoft developers said that they were going to include some more of the UML model types in later version of VSTS, but that they could not specify which types (we would argue that the only other model types that are very important are the use case and sequence diagrams). However, they also pointed out that Microsoft will continue to distribute Visio and the UML modeling tools included with Visio. This will allow developers and architects to continue to choose how they model their applications.

You will have to make your own choice in terms of the benefit of an investment in learning UML to the degree needed to create robust diagrams. To learn more about UML, read *UML Distilled (Third Edition)* by Martin Fowler (Addison-Wesley, 2003). This is an excellent introduction to the main diagrams in UML and the correct usage of those diagrams.

Using the Class Designer

As an example of using the Class Designer, we will go through the steps of building the EffortTracking web service diagram. Your completed diagram will look like the one shown in Figure 11-1.

Note The VB version will not have the ITaskService interface since it does not support interface refactoring.

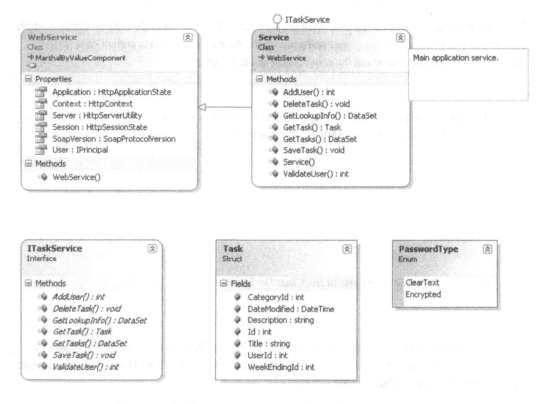

Figure 11-1. *The completed EffortTracking web service*

Note You can create this as a file-based solution or an HTTP-based solution. The sample code distributed with this book is HTTP-based.

To start the diagram, follow these steps:

1. Create a blank solution called EffortTracking.

2. Right-click the EffortTracking solution and select Add ➤ New Website.

3. Select ASP.NET Web Service. Select HTTP (or File) for the location and either C# or VB (whichever you are comfortable with) for the language. Enter the name as http://localhost/EffortTrackingService (or the file location if you selected File). Then click OK. This creates a new web service with a single class called Service.

4. Delete the HelloWorld example from the Service class.

5. Right-click the project, select Add New Item, and then select the Class Designer from the New Item dialog box. Click OK.

Tip Alternatively, you can click the View Class Diagram button from the top of the Solution Explorer, which will also add a class diagram to the project and generate the diagram based on the current code in the application. This makes it easy to see the entire project laid out at once.

---

6. Drag the Service.cs file from the Solution Explorer to the Class Designer surface. This creates the Service class, as shown in Figure 11-2.

Figure 11-2. *The Service class in the Class Designer*

Tip You can add existing classes to the diagram by dragging and dropping classes from the Class View window (or right-clicking a class and selecting View Class Diagram) and from the Object Browser, in addition to adding them from the Solution Explorer.

Now, let's look at this single class and some of the options you have for manipulating it.

Exploring a Class

The class name (Service) is shown in bold at the top of the class representation. You can edit the name simply by clicking it in the class and changing it. The chevron button in the upper-right corner expands or collapses the class.

Caution Changing the name of the class once you have created it will *not* change the name of the file in which the class is contained. Microsoft is aware of this and hopefully will have this functionality in the next release of VSTS.

Below the object name is the type of object. In this case, Service is a class (as opposed to a struct, enum, interface or delegate). This is not editable. Below the object type is the base class from which the current class derives—in this case, the WebService class. (If the base class type is Object, then no base class type will be displayed.)

When building an object model, you often want to know what the properties of the base classes are or what classes derive from a given class. To see this, right-click the Service class and select Show Base Class. This will result in the WebService class being added to the diagram, as shown in Figure 11-3.

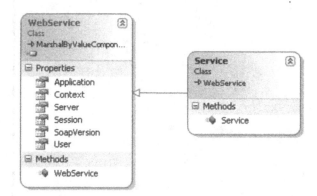

Figure 11-3. *The Service class and WebService class relationship*

If you remove the Service class from the diagram (right-click the Service class and select Remove from Diagram), and then select Show Derived Classes from the WebService class, the Service class would be readded to the diagram. This makes it easy to adjust the depth of information you want to display on the class diagram.

Viewing Properties

The Properties window shows specific property information for the object (or method) that is selected in the Class Designer window, as shown in Figure 11-4.

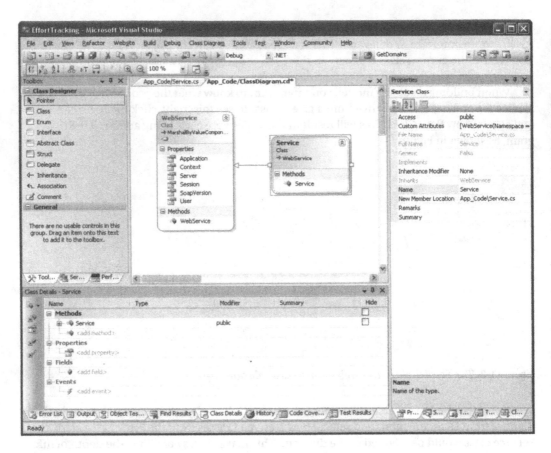

Figure 11-4. *The Class Designer portion of the IDE*

Table 11-1 describes the class and structure properties that are available. We'll introduce the properties for the other objects in the upcoming sections about those object types.

Table 11-1. *Class/Structure Properties*

Property	Description
Access	Access modifier (public, private, etc.)
Custom Attributes	Any custom attributes that are applied to the class
File Name	Read-only property containing the name of the file in which the class is located
Full Name	Read-only property that gives the full, namespace-qualified name of the class
Generic	Read-only property that indicates if the class is a generic class (for more information, see Generics in the MSDN documentation)
Implements	Read-only property that lists all of the interfaces implemented by this class

Property	Description
Inheritance Modifier	Indicates how (if) this class can be inherited: None, Abstract (MustInherit in VB), Sealed (NotInheritable in VB), or Static (no equivalent in VB) (does not apply to structures)
Inherits	Read-only property indicating the base class of this class (does not apply to structures)
Name	The name of this class
New Member Location	The name of the class file in which new members are added, for use with partial classes (for more information, see Partial Classes in the MSDN documentation)
Remarks	General comments about the class
Summary	A summary of the class's purpose/functionality

■**Note** All of the read-only attributes can be modified by choices made in code. They are just not modifiable via the Properties window.

Working with Class Designer Tools and Options

The Class Designer Toolbox (on the left side of Figure 11-4) shows a list of all of the items that can be added to your applications. Table 11-2 describes the available tools.

Table 11-2. *Class Diagram Toolbox Options*

Shape	Description
Class	Represents a concrete class (i.e., a class that can be instantiated directly)
Enum	Represents an enumeration
Interface	Represents an interface
Abstract Class	Represents a class that cannot be instantiated
Struct (Structure in VB)	Represents a structure
Delegate	Represents a delegate
Inheritance	Represents an inheritance relationship between two classes
Association	Represents an association relationship (aggregation or dependency between two classes)
Comment	A comment regarding the class diagram
Module	A VB code module (not available in C#)

Table 11-3 lists other Class Designer options. These options are accessed either by right-clicking the designer surface or via the Class Diagram menu.

Table 11-3. *Class Designer Menu Options*

Option	Description
Zoom	Allows you to zoom in and out on the diagram
Layout Diagram	Arranges the shapes in a "logical" way (fortunately, this can be undone)
Display Member Types	Displays the field types and the method return types
Adjust Shape Widths	Resizes all shapes on the drawing surface to be as wide as the widest entry in each shape
Group Members ➤ By Kind	Groups each shape by fields, properties, methods, events, etc.
Group Members ➤ By Access	Groups members by access type (public, private, protected, etc.)
Group Members ➤ Sort Alphabetically	Groups all members together alphabetically
Add	Allows you to create types from the design surface without dragging and dropping type shapes from the Toolbox
Export Diagram As Image	Allows you to export any or all of the diagrams in a project to a graphics file (.gif, .jpg, .tif, .png, .emf, and .bmp)

Adding Items to the Class Diagram

When you add items to your diagram, you use the Class Details window, shown in Figure 11-5, to set its attributes. To see this window, right-click an object and select Class Details. It appears at the bottom of the IDE (as shown earlier in Figure 11-4).

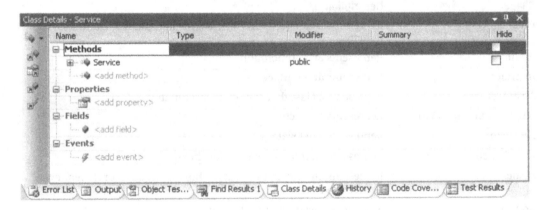

Figure 11-5. *The Class Details window*

The title of this window indicates which class you're viewing. All of the methods, properties, fields, and events of a class are listed in this window. The top icon on the left side of this window gives you the option of entering any new item for the class. The four icons below that are used to navigate to different sections of the Class Details window.

The layout will vary depending on the type of object selected on the design surface. The Class Details window for a class includes the Type column, which provides IntelliSense functionality as you enter the member types; the Modifier column, which is a drop-down list of scope options; and the Summary column. To add a summary, click the ellipsis in the Summary column to open the Description dialog box, as shown in Figure 11-6.

Tip By placing a `using` statement (or an `Imports` statement in VB) at the top of the code module, you can avoid having to enter the complete namespace of the type you are trying to add.

Figure 11-6. *The Description dialog box*

Adding Enumerations

You will start the class diagramming process by creating the basic building blocks of the service. The first task is to add a simple enumeration, which will allow the consumer of the service to specify whether the password that is being passed in the `ValidateUser` method (which you will create shortly) is encrypted or in plain text.

Caution Obviously, you would never send a password in clear text in a real application, but this provides a simple example for adding enumerations in the Class Designer.

---

1. Drag an Enum from the Toolbox onto the design surface. This will bring up the New Enum dialog box.

2. For this enumeration, set the name to PasswordType. Notice that a code file named PasswordType.cs (or PasswordType.vb, depending on the language) is also added to the solution, as shown in Figure 11-7. Click OK to add the enumeration.

Figure 11-7. *The New Enum dialog box*

3. The Class Details window switches to have only four columns: Name, Value, Summary, and Hide. Enter the information in Table 11-4 into the Class Details window.

Table 11-4. *PasswordType Enumeration Details*

Name	Value	Summary
ClearText	0	Indicates the password is unencrypted
Encrypted	1	Indicates the password is encrypted

Tip It is not necessary to enter a value for an enumeration, because the default is to have them sequentially numbered. In many cases, however, it is desirable to be able to perform bitwise operations on an enumeration, so you will want to add specific values.

Now that the information has been entered, you can look at the Properties window for both the enumeration and each class. (The properties are different for almost every item that you can select in the Class Designer.) Table 11-5 describes all of the enumeration properties.

Table 11-5. *Enumeration Properties*

Property	Description
Access	The scope of the enumeration
Base Type	The type of values used for the enumeration (a valid numeric type)
Custom Attributes	Any custom attributes that apply to the enumeration
File Name	Read-only attribute containing the name of the file in which the class is located
Full Name	Read-only attribute that gives the full, namespace-qualified name of the class
Name	The name of this enumeration
Remarks	General comments about the enumeration
Summary	A summary of the enumeration's purpose

Adding Structures

Next, you need to add a Task structure to the class diagram. This structure holds a single task item that is used to pass the task from the web service to the web application for use in editing, viewing, and adding information.

1. Drag a Struct (Structure in VB) from the Toolbox to the designer surface.

2. In the New Struct dialog box, enter the name as Task and click OK.

3. In the Class Details window, enter each of the items shown in Table 11-6 for the Task structure under the Fields node.

Table 11-6. *Task Structure Details*

Name	Type	Modifier	Summary
Id	int (Integer in VB)	public	ID of the task
Title	string	public	Brief description of the task
Description	string	public	Complete description of the task
DateModified	DateTime (Date in VB)	public	Date the task was last updated
WeekEndingId	int (Integer in VB)	public	ID of the week in which the task was performed
CategoryId	int (Integer in VB)	public	ID of the category under which the task falls
UserId	int (Integer in VB)	public	ID of the user who created and owns the task

Note that because a structure is almost identical to a class, all of the options available to you for a regular class are available to you for a structure, except for base classes and derived classes, since structures don't have these. Table 11-1 earlier in the chapter describes the structure properties.

Adding Methods

Now that you have the underlying enumeration and structure, you can start creating methods in the Service class. Since the Service class is already on the class diagram, you can just start adding methods to it.

1. Select the Service class on the design surface. If the Class Details window is not already open, right-click the Service class and select Class Details.

2. Click the <add method> entry under the Methods node in the Class Details window and enter ValidateUser.

3. Enter int (Integer in VB) for the Type.

4. Click the ellipsis in the Summary column.

5. Enter **Validates that the user is in the system** for the Summary.

6. Enter **0 if the user is not found, otherwise the ID of the user** for the Returns value.

7. Expand the ValidateUser node to expose the method's parameters.

8. Click the <add parameter> entry under the ValidateUser method (or press the (key on the keyboard) and enter userName. The type defaults to string.

9. Enter **The user's name** for the Summary.

10. Click the <add parameter> entry under the userName parameter and enter password.

11. Enter **The user's password**.

12. Enter a last parameter called PassType with a type of PasswordType.

13. Enter **Indicates if the user's password is in clear text or plain text** for the Summary.

14. Repeat steps 2–13 for each of the other six methods listed in Table 11-7.

Table 11-7. *Service Class Methods*

Method	Return Type	Parameters	Description
GetLookupInfo	DataSet	N/A	Returns a dataset containing week and category information for use as lookups
ValidateUser	int	string userName, string password, PasswordType type	Validates that the user is in the system

Method	Return Type	Parameters	Description
AddUser	int	string userName, string password	Adds a new user to the system
DeleteTask	void*	int taskID	Deletes a single task item
GetTask	Task	int taskID	Returns a single task
GetTasks	DataSet	int weekID, int userID	Returns an array of Task objects for the given week and user
SaveTask	void*	Task taskToSave	Saves or updates a task in the database

* *Void indicates a Sub rather than a Function in VB. When entering these methods in VB, leave the return type blank.*

Now that you have all of the methods and descriptions added, switch to the code view for the Service class by double-clicking the class in the diagram (or by right-clicking the class and selecting View Code). Listing 11-1 shows the ValidateUser method.

■**Note** To switch back to the class diagram from the code view, double-click the diagram in the Solution Explorer or select the Class Diagram tab in the main window.

Listing 11-1. *The ValidateUser Method*

C#
```
/// <summary>
/// Validates that the user is in the system.
/// </summary>
/// <param name="userName">The user's name</param>
/// <param name="password">The user's password</param>
/// <param name="passType">Indicates if the user's password is in
/// clear text or plain text.</param>
/// <returns>0 if the user is not found, otherwise the ID of the user</returns>
public int ValidateUser(string userName, string password, PasswordType passType)
    {
        throw new System.NotImplementedException();
    }
```

VB
```
''' <summary>
''' Validates that the user is in the system.
''' </summary>
''' <param name="userName">The user's name.</param>
''' <param name="password">The user's password</param>
```

```
'''  <param name="passType">Indicates if the user's password is in clear text or
'''  plain text.</param>
'''  <returns>0 if the user is not found, otherwise the ID of the user</returns>
Public Function ValidateUser(ByVal userName As String, ByVal password As String, _
ByVal passType As PasswordType) As Integer

End Function
```

All of the information you entered via the Class Details window shows up here in XML comments or in the method signature. All methods created via the Class Details window are created with NotImplementedException thrown as the single line of code in the method. Any changes made to either the XML comments or the method signature are automatically updated in the Class Designer. Similarly, if you delete a method from the class in code, it is removed from the designer.

■**Caution** It is critical that you understand that deleting a method in the Class Designer causes the method and *all* of the code in that method to be deleted—nothing will be saved. It is a good idea to ensure that everything is under source code control before you start deleting items from the Class Designer if you have already started writing code. The good news is that you can undo a change to the class diagram.

You also have the option to reorder the parameters of a method. This is available only in C# (in VB you need to do it manually). To do this, right-click the GetTasks method in the Service class in the diagram and select Refactor ➤ Reorder Parameters. This will bring up the Reorder Parameters dialog box, as shown in Figure 11-8.

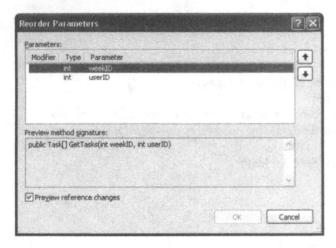

Figure 11-8. *The Reorder Parameters dialog box*

Using this dialog box, you can shift the parameters and view the signature of the method while you are shifting them. This is also the same dialog box that is displayed if you choose to delete a parameter, except that a large warning is displayed at the bottom.

Table 11-8 lists all the method properties, as well as the property, field, and event properties.

Table 11-8. *Method/Property/Event/Field Properties*

Property	Description
Access	The scope of the item (does not apply to destructors)
Accessors	Indicates if the property is read, write, or read-write (applies only to properties)
Constant Kind	Allows you to specify that a field is a constant or read-only field (applies only to fields)
Custom Attributes	Any custom attributes that apply to the item
File Name	Read-only attribute containing the name of the file in which the item is located
Inheritance Modifier	Indicates how (if) this class can be inherited: None, Abstract (MustInherit in VB), Sealed (NotInheritable in VB), and Static (no equivalent in VB) (does not apply to constructors)
Name	The name of this item
New	Indicates if this item overrides or shadows an item with the same name or signature in the base class (applies only to C#) (applies only to properties or methods)
Property Signature	Read-only attribute showing the signature of the property (applies only to properties)
Remarks	General comments about the item
Returns	Description of the value returned (applies only to methods)
Static (Shared in VB)	Indicates if the item is static
Summary	A summary of the item's purpose/functionality
Type	The type the item deals with—the type of the value or the returned value type
Value	The definition of the value supplied to the property (applies only to properties)

Working with Interfaces

While an interface supports essentially all of the same things that a class supports, there are a couple of differences. First, interface methods can only be public—otherwise, why have an interface? And second, there is no implementation in an interface—it is just a set of method signatures. Aside from these two differences, interfaces behave the same as classes in the Class Designer.

Refactoring Interfaces

Refactoring is a fancy term for reorganizing code to make improvements in the architecture of an application. In some cases, it refers to going back and altering code to make it more efficient, but for the purposes of the Class Designer, the first definition applies. (Refactoring is available from a variety of locations, not just the Class Designer.)

▪**Note** Refactoring is available only in C#. However, a VB Powertoy is available from www.gotdotnet.com, which provides roughly the same functionality.

---

demonstrate how this works, you will extract all of the methods in the Service class in order to create an interface (the interface will not affect the application in any way; it is for demonstration purposes only). To refactor the Service class and create an interface, switch to the designer view (double-click the diagram in the Solution Explorer) and follow these steps:

1. Right-click the Service class, and select Refactor ➤ Extract Interface. This will bring up the Extract Interface dialog box, shown in Figure 11-9.

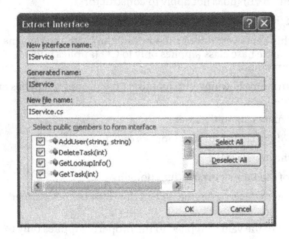

Figure 11-9. *The Extract Interface dialog box*

2. Name the interface ITaskService and click Select All to include all of the methods as part of the interface. Then click OK.

Extracting the interface does several things:

- Copies the methods to a new interface called ITaskService

- Adds a new code file to the project with the same name as the interface

- Implements the interface on the Service class (represented as a lollipop attached to the Service class)

It will *not* do the following:

- Copy over the XML comments.
- Enclose the ITaskService methods in the Service class in a region.
- Add the ITaskService interface to the Class Designer.

Displaying Interfaces

On the designer, an interface can be represented in a couple of different ways. As you saw when you refactored the ITaskService methods, an interface can be represented as a lollipop attached to the class that implements the interface. When the interface is displayed as a lollipop, you can drag it around the outside the class that implements it to any position you want.

You can display an interface on the design surface just as you would any other type of object. To see the refactored ITaskService interface, right-click the ITaskService lollipop attached to the Service class and select Show Interface, or double-click the ITaskService text. You can then expand the interface implemented by the class by right-clicking the interface icon and selecting Expand. Figure 11-10 shows the expanded ITaskService interface. To collapse the interface display to just the lollipop, right-click and select Collapse.

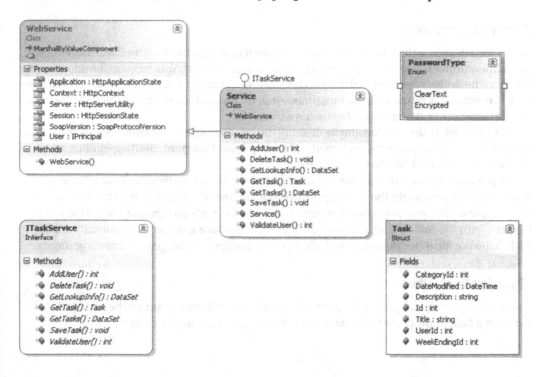

Figure 11-10. *The ITaskService interface*

Deleting Interfaces

You can delete an interface from a class by selecting the interface name and pressing Delete. While the class will no longer implement the interface, the methods are *not* deleted; they are just no longer accessible via the interface definition. To demonstrate how this works, delete the ITaskService interface from the Service class. You'll see that nothing else is deleted. To reimplement an interface, undo the deletion.

Implementing the Interface

Right-clicking the ITaskService lollipop attached to the Service class gives you two different options: implement the ITaskService interface implicitly or explicitly. Selecting Implicitly (the default) will not make any change to the methods of the implemented interface. Electing to implement the interface explicitly will cause the fully qualified name of the method to be used (while this is an option, it is not recommended).

Showing Object Relationships

With the Class Designer, you can show inheritance and association relationships. Typically, you would do this to identify relationships between classes so that they are explicitly understood.

Displaying Inheritance

Object inheritance is the "classic" relationship shown in diagrams, and the Class Designer will show this automatically between a base class and a derived class. You can see this relationship between the WebService class and the Service class you created. You can create an inheritance structure manually by clicking the Inheritance tool in the toolbox, selecting the class that you want to subclass, and then selecting the superclass.

You can delete the relationship by deleting the connecting line, or you can hide the inheritance line to help improve the readability of a complicated diagram. Both operations are available by right-clicking the inheritance line.

If you have a generic base class and a superclass of this class, the inheritance Properties window allows you to edit the type arguments that are then displayed in the subclass. To see an example of this, you can create a generic class with the method signature of public class Class1<T> (in VB, Public Class Class1(of T)), and then have another class inherit from it. Right-clicking the inheritance line will allow you to manipulate the generic type arguments.

Displaying Associations

You can show fields and properties as *associations*. Associations can simply be connections between a field or property and a class or a collection association for an array.

For this section, you will add a field to the Service class for demonstration purposes only. You can delete it at the end of the chapter (again, it does not affect the application in any way).

1. In the Service class, add a field with the name _task of type Task with a private modifier.

2. Right-click the _task field in the Service class (in the class diagram) and select Show As Association. The results are shown in Figure 11-11. This is an alternate way to represent the _task field on the class diagram; it does not alter your class in any way.

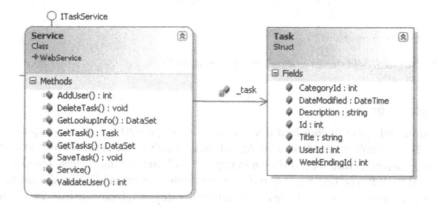

Figure 11-11. *The _task field shown as an association*

Note Typically, you will have many connections between items in your diagram and it is impractical to show all of them with an association line. It is best to limit how many of the fields and properties you show like this.

---

3. To convert _task back to the standard type of design, right-click the connection line and select Show As Field.

4. In either the Class Details window or the code, change the _task field to an array of tasks:

    ```
    private Task[] _tasks;
    ```

5. In the diagram, right-click the _task field again. This time, select the Show As Collection Association option. The results are shown in Figure 11-12. The _task field is now shown as an array with a double arrow. This is yet another way of representing a relationship between two types.

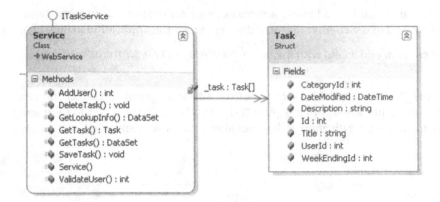

Figure 11-12. *The _task field shown as a collection association*

Using the Association Tool

The Association tool in the Toolbox facilitates the creation of properties that are properties of a given type. For example, if you clicked the Association tool, then the Service class, and then the Task class, the results would be as shown in Figure 11-13. Behind the scenes, a read-write property called Task of type Task was created, with no implementation in either the get or set method (in the next section, you will see how to automate this by refactoring the _task field). This relationship can be converted into a property of the Service class (on the diagram) by right-clicking the association and selecting Show As Property. (Delete the Task property if you added it to experiment.)

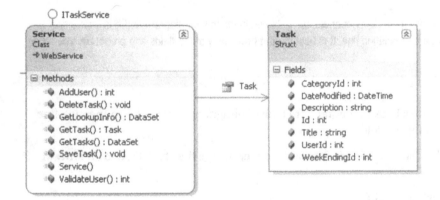

Figure 11-13. *The Task property*

> ■**Note** Unfortunately, in the first release of VSTS, you cannot draw association lines from one type to another that do not have a semantic meaning. Microsoft knows that this is a feature developers and architects want, and realizes that the purpose of the designer is to visualize object relationships, so it is a good bet that you can look forward to this feature in the next release.

Adding Fields and Properties

Properties and fields share similar functionality in the Class Designer. The main difference is that properties have a read-write property. One other difference is the refactoring options. Take a common example: You add a bunch of private fields for which you need to create properties. It is something that we all have to do and we all hate. Microsoft has reduced this effort to zero by allowing you to refactor fields into properties (this is available only in C#).

Tip Many free add-ons duplicate the refactoring options in VB. The VSTS team has noted that this is one of the single most requested features for VB, so it will probably show up in the next version. Until then, any of the add-ons that are available will provide good refactoring support. A web search will return a list of available products (both free and commercial).

Let's see how this works.

1. Select the _task field in the Service class, right-click it, and select Refactor ➤ Encapsulate Field. This will display the Encapsulate Field dialog box, shown in Figure 11-14. Table 11-9 describes all of the fields in the Encapsulate Field dialog box.

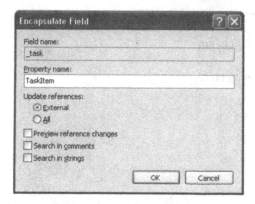

Figure 11-14. *The Encapsulate Field dialog box*

2. Select the Preview Reference Changes check box and click OK. This displays the dialog box shown in Figure 11-15.

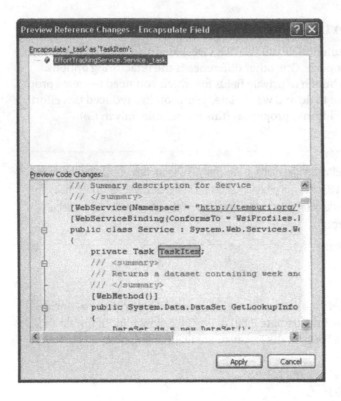

Figure 11-15. *The Preview Reference Changes dialog box*

3. Select Apply. This generates the following code.

```
C# (Only)
public Task TaskItem
{
    get { return _task; }
    set { _task = value; }
}
```

As you can see, this will be a tremendous time-saver for developers in that they need to code only the fields that persist the data.

Note The preview screen displays the signature of the new item as it will be seen by other objects and does not necessarily represent the actual format of the final generated code.

Table 11-9. *Encapsulate Field Dialog Box Options*

Option	Definition
Field name	The name of the field to be encapsulated as a property
Property name	The name of the property that will encapsulate the field
Update references	Updates code external to the class that references the field and switches it to use the property
Preview reference changes	Shows a dialog box that previews the code changes (see Figure 11-15)
Search in comments	Performs a search and replace for the field name in comments as well (useful for fixing comments in external classes where the references will be updated)
Search in strings	Performs a search and replace in strings used in code for the field name

Adding Comments

The Class Designer also allows you to add comments. To insert a comment, simply drag-and-drop it from the Toolbox to the designer and enter a note, as shown in Figure 11-16.

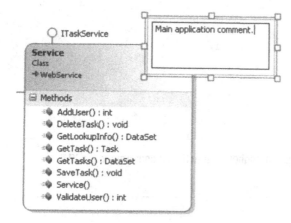

Figure 11-16. *A Class Designer comment*

You can add comments anywhere on the diagram, but unfortunately, you cannot link a note to a particular object.

Looking Under the Hood

This section explains how the Class Designer works behind the scenes. To see how the Class Designer generated your diagram, close the Class Designer window, right-click ClassDiagram1.cd, select Open With, and then select the XML Editor. Figure 11-17 shows the XML for the class diagram you created in this chapter. The header information is the standard XML header. Each node of the XML schema is described in Table 11-10.

```
1   <?xml version="1.0" encoding="utf-8"?>
2   <ClassDiagram MajorVersion="1" MinorVersion="1" DisplayMemberTypes="true">
3     <Font Name="Tahoma" Size="8.25" />
4     <Comment CommentText="Main application service.">
5       <Position X="5.177" Y="1.302" Height="0.75" Width="1.7" />
6     </Comment>
7     <Class Name="Service">
8       <Position X="3.75" Y="1.75" Width="2.25" />
9       <TypeIdentifier>
10        <FileName>App_Code\Service.cs</FileName>
11        <HashCode>AAAAQAAAAAAAAAAgAAAAAAAgBAAAAAgiAAAAAAAAAA=</HashCode>
12      </TypeIdentifier>
13      <Lollipop Position="0.302" />
14    </Class>
15    <Class Name="System.Web.Services.WebService">
16      <Position X="0.5" Y="0.5" Width="2.5" />
17      <TypeIdentifier />
18    </Class>
19    <Struct Name="Task">
20      <Position X="7" Y="1.75" Width="2" />
21      <TypeIdentifier>
22        <FileName>App_Code\Task.cs</FileName>
23        <HashCode>AAAAAAACAAAggEAAAAAAAwAAAAATAAAAAAAAAAAAAA=</HashCode>
24      </TypeIdentifier>
25    </Struct>
```

Figure   *XML view of the Class Designer*

Note All of the XML generated by Microsoft for use throughout Visual Studio conforms to the XML standard.

Table 11-10. *Class Designer Schema Description*

Node	Description
Font	The font family and size used on the Class Designer
Class	The fully qualified name of the class (this node will be the object type—note Struct for the Task object)
Position	The X and Y position and the width of the class
TypeIdentifier	Contains the specification for the class type
FileName	The name of the file in which the type is contained
HashCode	A hash of all of the properties, methods, fields, and events of the type

Microsoft is not, at this time, publishing an "official" XML schema for the Class Designer. Any code that you create to work directly against the schema (there is no good reason for doing this) is created at your own risk because it may not be compatible with the next version.

When we first looked at this, we had only two questions: How does the designer know what is contained within the class if it is not held in the XML, and what the heck is the HashCode for? It turns out that both are excellent questions, although the answer to the first question was obvious after it was explained to us.

All of the information displayed on the design surface is gathered from the class itself. It is not stored as metadata specifically for the Class Designer. This is how Microsoft ensures that the data displayed on the designer is identical to the information in the code.

The HashCode's purpose turns out to be a lot more complicated. As noted in Table 11-10, the HashCode is a hash of everything found in the type. But what is it used for? It is used to match the object on the designer to the type in the code. It allows the Class Designer to know what object to find and interrogate in order to populate the class details. The explanation makes sense, but then you may have yet another question: What if you change the name of the file that your type is stored in, change the name of the type, change the method names, add or a delete a few methods or properties, and so on? Another good question. The Class Designer uses a fuzzy logic search algorithm to try to match up the type of the Class Designer with the type in your solution. If it cannot do this, the type shape will still appear in the designer, though it will be red. You will need to manually attach it to the correct type in the solution or delete it and readd it. To readd the type, just drag-and-drop it from the Solution Explorer or Class View window.

Note It is unfortunate to note that for this release of VSTS, the Class Designer is not designed to be extensible. We hope this will be a feature added in the next version.

Summary

This chapter has presented an in-depth view of the Class Designer. Throughout the chapter, you have seen how each of the features of the Class Designer supports the four user scenarios that were the guiding factors in the design of the Class Designer. The Class Designer gives you the opportunity to reverse-engineer existing code and visualize existing code in order to better understand it. It allows you to refactor code through the designer without diving into the code itself. The key feature of the Class Designer is that it ensures that your object model and documentation remain accurate and helpful from the first day of the application to the last day of an application, and into the maintenance cycle.

CHAPTER 12

■■■

Unit Testing and Code Coverage

Unit testing is a repeatable, automated process of testing specific methods in code to make sure that they do what they are supposed to do. By testing the smallest unit of code for defects, you can be sure that when you are finished, you have a stable base on which to build. The automated nature of unit tests also allows for *regression testing*, which is the process of retesting previously tested units of code after a modification is made.

Unit testing is an area of testing that for many years was performed in a nonrepeatable and haphazard way. Typically, developers would, in addition to having to write the application, also need to write a test harness to run tests. With the introduction of tools such as JUnit for Java and NUnit for .NET, unit testing has become much easier.

This chapter explains how to perform unit tests with VSTS, ranging from simple one-method tests to data-driven tests based on data stored in a testing database. In addition, we will look at code coverage results from the unit tests. *Code coverage* describes the amount of code covered by the unit tests (including manual unit tests).

We've included this chapter in the Developers section of this book because developers are responsible for their code. While testers also may create unit tests, they generally test larger pieces of functionality. However, some items covered in this chapter relate to all types of testing, so it is worthwhile for testers to read through this chapter as well.

Planning Unit Tests

Before you can start performing unit tests, you need a plan. It is not enough to just sit down and write some unit tests without having thought through all of the possible scenarios (or at least all of the common scenarios). You need to start by drawing up a set of unit testing rules that can be used by everyone on your team.

Take a look at this sample method:

C#

```
//Method returns true if the person is over age 18, otherwise false
public bool AgeCheck(DateTime dayOfBirth)
{
//Some processing code here…
}
```

VB

```
'Method returns true if the person is over age 18, otherwise false
Public Function AgeCheck(dob as Date) as Boolean
     'Some processing code here…
End Function
```

The premise of this code is fairly straightforward. It accepts a date of birth and validates the age. At first glance, you may think that you simply need to run a test that provides a date of birth prior to 18 years ago and a date of birth later than 18 years ago. And that works great for 80% of the dates that someone is likely to provide, but that only scratches the surface of what needs to be tested here. The following are some of the tests you may need to run for the AgeCheck method:

- Check a date from exactly 18 years ago to the day.

- Check a date from further back in time than 18 years.

- Check a date from fewer than 18 years ago.

- Check for a null value.

- Check for the results based on the very minimum date that can be entered.

- Check for the results based on the very maximum date that can be entered.

- Check for an invalid date format being passed to the method.

- Check two year dates (such as 05/05/49) to determine what century the two-year format is being treated as.

- Check the time (if that matters) of the date.

- Check for graceful failure.

- If the age to check against is provided via a configuration file, check that the correct age to check against is being set/read.

As you can see, based on just a simple method declaration, you can determine at least 5 and maybe as many as 11 valid unit tests (not all tests may be required). Dates are, in general, one of the most difficult things to handle in development (right behind strings). Therefore, you will almost always have more rules for date testing than any other type of tests.

Here are the basic unit testing areas:

Boundary values: Test the minimum and maximum values allowed for a given parameter. An example here is when dealing with strings. What happens if you are passed an empty string? Is it valid? On the other hand, what if someone passes a string value of 100,000 characters and you try to convert the length of the string to a short?

Equality: Test a value that you are looking for. In the case of the age check example used here, what if the date passed also includes the time? An equality check will always fail in that case, but in every other case, the results would come out correctly.

Format: Never trust data passed to your application. This is particularly applicable to any boundary methods, where you can get malicious hackers looking to crack your system. But poorly formatted data from any source can cause problems if you do not check it.

Culture: Various tests need to be performed to ensure that cultural information is taken into account. In general, you can skip these tests if the application is written for a single culture only (although, even this is not a good indicator, because you can write a test for a U.S. English system but have it installed by someone in the U.K.). Otherwise, string, date, currency, and other types of values that can be localized should always be checked (for example, if you are expecting a date in the U.S. format but get it in the European format, then some values will work, but some will not). An example is the date 02/01/2000. In the U.S. format, this is February 1, 2000; in the European format, it is January 2, 2000. While this test would pass (most of the time), changing the U.S. format to 01/23/2000 would fail in the European format.

Exception paths: Make sure that the application handles exceptions—both expected and unexpected—in the correct manner and in a secure fashion. Frequently, developers test the normal path and forget to test the exception path. VSTS includes a special process for testing the exception paths. Additionally, this will test how data is logged during a failure.

Tip Not *everything* needs to be tested. In most cases, you want to test the most used paths of the application for the most common scenarios. An example of wasted time would be writing tests for simple property assignments. While this may be needed in specific situations, you cannot possibly write every test for every scenario—it takes too long even with VSTS!

These five areas cover the majority of the situations you will run into when performing unit tests. Any plan should take into account tests that cover these areas of potential failure. Of course, this is by no means a comprehensive set of rules for unit testing. You will undoubtedly discover others related to your specific applications.

Note The unit testing areas listed here apply to the .NET platform. We have not included basic testing rules regarding languages such as C and unmanaged C++. Tools like PREfast are designed to catch those areas of potential failure that are outside the realm of unit testing. PREfast (discussed in Chapter 13) catches typical unmanaged code errors, such as buffer overflow errors.

TEST-DRIVEN DEVELOPMENT

In the past several years, Agile Development methodologies have risen in popularity. Extreme Programming (XP) is probably the best known Agile Development methodology, and a core tenet of XP is that unit tests are written before the code is written. One of the key benefits of writing unit tests first is that you know, without a doubt, when a piece of functionality has been completed, because that's when the test succeeds. Because XP is a short-release cycle methodology, coding must often be done as quickly and as accurately as possible. The practice of writing unit tests first supports this goal.

The process of creating tests first (at the construction stage) to validate your application is called *test-driven development*. The methodology of test-driven development follows this path: Write the unit test, write enough code for the test to succeed, and then refactor the code to make it more efficient. Another way of saying this in the test-driven development terminology is "red/green/refactor." Red is the test fail stage, green is the test pass stage, and refactoring is altering the code to make it more efficient. While VSTS does not, per se, support this specific process, since it is a process and not a technology, you can use VSTS to support the test-driven development methodology.

The problem with test-driven development is that it still relies on developers to plan the unit tests, write them, and execute them. While tools like JUnit, NUnit, and VSTS make this process a lot easier, it is still a process that needs to be followed by all. Most developers (and we are speaking from experience here) cannot stand to do testing. VSTS helps eliminate that problem by providing policies, which you can enable to say that unit tests must have been performed before code can be checked in (refer to Chapter 3).

Then there is the problem of how to come up with a comprehensive set of criteria on which the individual unit tests should be based. The list of tests must be developed by the developer in conjunction with a functional or business analyst. The analyst alone will not supply you with all of the possible combinations of issues that could arise, simply because analysts do not think like developers. Likewise, a developer cannot necessarily come up with all of the valid tests because some of those tests may be predicated on business situations. In the list of unit tests shown earlier for the sample AgeCheck method, an analyst might supply you with the first three items in the list. All of the other tests in the list are generally language-specific tests and input validation tests, so they are not tests that a business user would consider.

You can find a lot more information about test-driven development on the Web. An excellent book on unit testing is *Test Driven Development: By Example* by Kent Beck (Addison-Wesley, 2002).

Creating Unit Tests

Now that you have seen some of the thought that goes into planning for unit testing, it is time to look at how to create unit tests. In this section, you will learn how to generate unit tests.

▪Note For the examples in this chapter, use the downloadable code available from the Source Code section of the Apress website (www.apress.com).

To create your first test, follow these steps:

1. Open the Service class.

2. Right-click within the Service class (but not within a specific method) and select Create Tests.

3. In the Generate Unit Tests dialog box, ensure that the AddUser method is checked and that the output project is set as Create a New Visual [*Language Choice*] Test Project, as shown in Figure 12-1.

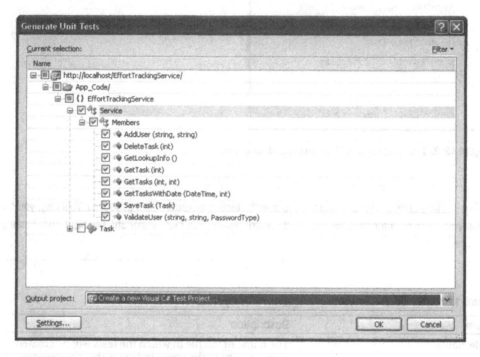

Figure 12-1. *The Generate Unit Tests dialog box*

4. Optionally, click the Settings button to configure how the tests are generated. This displays the dialog box shown in Figure 12-2. Table 12-1 describes the settings available in this dialog box. For this example, we will use the defaults, so you don't need to change any of these settings. Click Cancel to close the dialog box.

5. Click OK in the Generate Unit Tests dialog box.

6. Enter the project name as EffortTrackingServiceTests, and then click OK. A new project called EffortTrackingServiceTests will be added to the EffortTracking solution.

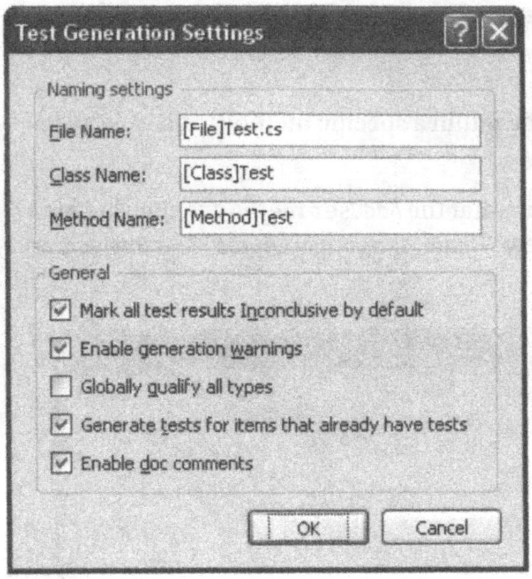

Figure 12-2. *The Test Generation Settings dialog box*

Tip While you do not have to add tests to specific testing projects, it is a good idea. This way, you can keep your tests separate from the code that you are testing, and more important, separate from those you are releasing.

Table 12-1. *Test Code Generation Configuration Options*

Item	Description
File Name	The name of the file in which the tests will be created. The [File] in front of the name indicates that the generated test file will be prefixed with the name of the file in which the class you are testing resides.
Class Name	The name of the class given to the test class. The [Class] in front of the name indicates that the generated class will be prefixed with the name of the class being tested.
Method Name	The name of the generated test method. The [Method] in front of the name indicates that the generated method will be prefixed with the name of the method that you are testing.
Mark all test results Inconclusive by default	The Assert statement will identify this method as being inconclusive. Checking this adds the following line to the end of each test method: Assert.Inconclusive("Verify the correctness of this test method.").
Enable generation warnings	Reports any warnings during the test code generation process.

Item	Description
Globally qualify all types	Adds the root namespace to all type declarations. This is important if you have classes with the same names in multiple namespaces. If you do not select this, the compiler makes a best guess, which frequently can be wrong.
Generate tests for items that already have tests	Creates additional tests for the same method by appending an incremented number to the end of the test method name. If you don't select it, a test method will not be generated.
Enable doc comments	Generates XML comments with each test. Turning this off simply removes the comments.

You can also start the Unit Test Wizard from the main menu. Just select Test ➤ New Test to open the dialog box shown in Figure 12-3. Select Unit Test Wizard and click OK. This will take you to the dialog box shown in Figure 12-1.

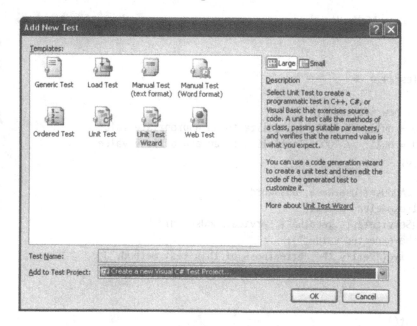

Figure 12-3. *The Add New Test dialog box*

As you can see, the Add New Text dialog box offers several other test types. Selecting the Unit Test icon from the Add New Test dialog box will create a blank testing class in the test project of your choice. The Manual Test and Ordered Test types are covered later in this chapter. The other test types are covered in Chapters 15 and 16.

Note Generic Tests are not covered in this book. The reason for this is that the Generic test is a wrapper for use with simple, existing test tools. More information on this "test type" can be found in the MSDN documentation.

Understanding Unit Tests

VSTS creates several files in your testing solution. In reality, VSTS can only do so much work for you. It generates the skeleton, which you will need to complete. Here, we'll look at the key parts of the unit test. In the "Completing the Test Methods" section later in this chapter, you'll see how to add the other necessary pieces.

The primary file in the testing solution is the ServiceTest file. (The naming convention for this file is customizable, but in general it is best to leave it in the *ClassName*Test form.) First, we'll look at a method in this file, and then we'll look at the test class.

Exploring a Test Method

Open the ServiceTest file and scroll down to the AddUserTest method, which is shown in Listing 12-1.

Listing 12-1. *The AddUserTest Method*

```csharp
C#
 [TestMethod()]
public void AddUserTest()
{
    Service target = new Service();
    string userName = null; // TODO: Initialize to an appropriate value
    string password = null; // TODO: Initialize to an appropriate value
    int expected = 0;
    int actual;
    actual = target.AddUser(userName, password);
    Assert.AreEqual(expected, actual,
    "EffortTrackingServiceTests.localhost.Service.AddUser did "
    + "not return the expected value.");
    Assert.Inconclusive("Verify the correctness of this test method.");
}
```

```vbnet
VB
<TestMethod()>
Public Sub AddUserTest()
    Dim target As Service = new Service()
    Dim userName As String = nothing ' TODO: Initialize to an appropriate value
    Dim password As String = nothing ' TODO: Initialize to an appropriate value
    Dim expected As Integer
    Dim actual as Integer
     Actual = target.AddUser(userName, password)
    Assert.AreEqual(expected, actual, _
    "EffortTrackingServiceTests.localhost.Service.AddUser did " _
    & "not return the expected value.")
    Assert.Inconclusive("Verify the correctness of this test method.")
End Sub
```

The first line is the TestMethod attribute, which denotes that this is a test method. This allows this method to be displayed in the various test management dialog boxes. The TestMethod attribute takes no arguments; it is simply an identifier.

Each test method is created based on the settings in the Test Generation Settings dialog box (Figure 12-2). The default setting creates the test method in the format of the name of the method being tested followed by Test.

■**Tip** Because you can have more than one test method that targets a given application method, you want to make sure you develop a standard naming convention. A good naming convention is the method being tested, plus the type of test, followed by Test. For example, if you were testing a null username value in the AddUser tests, you might name the test AddUserNullUsernameTest.

Each test method that is set up for you will provide a variable for each of the parameters requested by the method being tested and an instantiated reference to the object being tested—in this case, a web service. The call to the method being tested is created for you. All you need to do is initialize the variables for the call to work (unless you are testing null values).

Notice the last two lines of the method, which contain the Assert statements. These are the most important statements in the method because they report the status to the testing infrastructure to enable the infrastructure to mark the test as a success or failure. If the Assert statement is true, then no exceptions are thrown and the method is marked as "passed." If the Assert statement is false, an exception is thrown and the test is marked as "failed."

In the case of a generated test where the method being tested returns a value, two calls to Assert are made. The first one is the standard comparison statement, which will throw an exception if the values are not equal. The second statement is placed in all generated tests to indicate that no one has yet looked at the method and initialized the values used in the method call or the expected value.

■**Caution** Never catch an AssertFailedException, as this exception is used by the testing infrastructure to mark a test as failed.

When generating a unit test for a method that does not return a value, the Assert statement reads, "A method that does not return a value cannot be verified." For these types of methods, a different process must be followed in order to verify the outcome of a test, depending on the purpose of the method being tested. For methods that write to a database, for example, you could write a statement that reads from the database to verify that the method succeeded.

Exploring a Test Class

The ServiceTest class is a test class because it is tagged with the TestClass attribute, which makes the ServiceTest class visible in the various test management windows. The TestClass attribute takes no arguments. Several attributes are provided for you automatically upon the creation of a test class.

The method tagged with the TestInitialize attribute will be called before each and every run of a test in the given test class. This is important to note because it limits when and how you should use this method. The TestCleanup attribute is used to denote the method that will be called after each and every test is run in a given class. For example, suppose you are running a test that changes or adds data, but you need to run the test several times to test various aspects of a change. You could use a method tagged with the TestInitialize attribute to start a transaction that can be rolled back in the TestCleanup method, or you might perform some other action to reset test conditions for the next run.

■**Caution** If more than one method is tagged with the TestInitialize attribute, an exception will be thrown.

The TestContext class is used in data-driven tests and to gather information for a *specific* test that is currently running. You will see how this works in the "Data-Driven Testing" section later in this chapter.

Other attributes are listed in Table 12-2. Several of these attributes will be demonstrated later in this chapter.

Table 12-2. *Additional Testing Attributes*

Attribute	Description
AssemblyInitialize	Runs before any other classes in an assembly are run.
AssemblyCleanup	Runs after all other classes in an assembly are run.
ClassInitialize	Runs before any tests in a class are run. See the "Preparing the Production Database" section later in this chapter.
ClassCleanup	Runs after all tests in a class are run. See the "Preparing the Production Database" section later in this chapter.
DataSourceAttribute	Specifies the data source for a data-driven test. See the "Data-Driven Testing" section later in the chapter.
DeploymentItemAttribute	Specifies specific items (typically files), which must be deployed to the test directory (which is different from the debug folder) before a test is run.
DescriptionAttribute	Describes the test in the test management screens.
PriorityAttribute	Sets the priority of the test. This is more of a notational attribute as it has no actual effect on the order in which tests are run.

Attribute	Description
OwnerAttribute	Indicates who owns the test.
TestPropertyAttribute	Allows you to specify custom properties for a test. See the "Adding Test Properties" section later in this chapter.
AspNetDevelopmentServerAttribute	Specifies that the given test is hosted by either the ASP.NET Development Server or IIS if this is an ASP.NET test.
UrlToTestAttribute	The URL that contains the website that will be tested.
AspNetDevelopmentServerHostAttribute	Provides various settings to point the test to the correct web server host.

Managing Unit Tests

VSTS gives developers and testers the ability to manage tests in many different ways. It provides ways to view both high-level and detailed information. You can view test results or code coverage results from within the IDE, and test management is intuitive, so you do not need to learn how to use a new and complex tool.

The two main starting places for test management are the Test View window and the Test Manager window.

Using the Test View Window

To open the Test View window, select Test ➤ View and Author Tests from the main menu.

Figure 12-4. *The Test View window*

As shown in Figure 12-4, the Test View window displays the list of tests and the type of test. The options at the top of the window allow you to run the tests, edit the test configuration, and apply a filter in order to be able to find specific tests. You can start a test run in debug mode. This allows you to run the test and debug the unit test code and the code in the method being tested.

Double-clicking the test will open the code module where the test is contained. Right-clicking a test will allow you to perform various actions such as running a specific test, creating a new test, and viewing the properties of a test. The properties of the tests are described in Table 12-3.

Note Manual tests, such as `manualtest1` in Figure 12-4, are treated somewhat differently in the IDE. When you double-click a manual test, VSTS will open the manual test in a Word or another text editor, so it can be edited. Manual tests are covered in the "Manual Testing" section later in this chapter.

Table 12-3. *Test Properties*

Property	Description
Associated Work Items	Work items associated with the specific test in the Team Foundation work item database (applicable only if Team Explorer is installed)
Class Name	The name of the class in which the test method resides
Data Access Method	For use by data-driven testing; specifies sequential or random access
Data Connection String	The connection string to the database providing the data to drive tests
Data Provider	The database connection provider
Data Table Name	The table from which the data to drive the test is pulled
Deployment Items	List of all items to be deployed (see the `DeploymentItemAttribute` in Table 12-2)
Description	A description of the purpose of the test
Full Class Name	The fully qualified name of the class
ID	Unique test name
Iteration	The iteration in the life cycle with which this test is associated
Namespace	The namespace in which the test resides
Non-runnable	Error
Owner	The name of the individual who owns the test
Priority	Indicates the importance of the test but has no effect on the order in which the test is run
Project	The project in which the test resides
Project Area	The area (in the Team System methodology being used) where the test resides (active only when using Team Explorer and when the test is associated with a team project)
Project Relative Path	The path to the file in which the test class resides relative to the project

Property	Description
Solution	The solution in which the test resides
Test Enabled	Indicates if the test will be executed during a test run
Test Name	The name of the test
Test Storage	The assembly that contains the compiled test
Test Type	Unit or manual test

With the Test View window, you can look at, categorize, and view test properties. The Test Manager window offers other options for managing your tests.

Using the Test Manager Window

The main window for managing tests is the Test Manager window, shown in Figure 12-5.

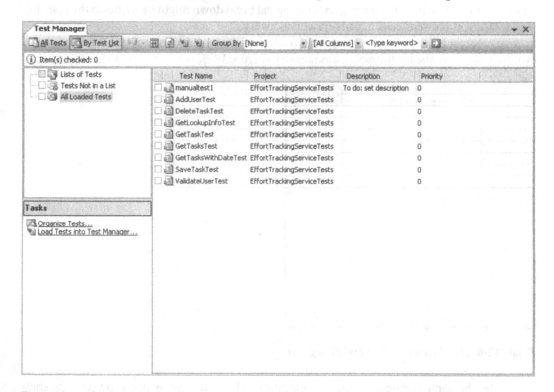

Figure 12-5. *The Test Manager window*

■**Note** The Test Manager window is available only in the Team Edition for Software Testers edition, not the Developers edition. To manage tests in the Developers edition, you must use the Test View window.

As you can see, there are a few more options for managing and categorizing your tests in this window than in the Test View window. You can view lists of tests, tests that are not in a list, and all loaded tests. In addition, you can load additional tests that are not part of the current solution by selecting the Load Tests into Test Manager option from the list of available tasks in the lower-left side of the Test Manager window.

Note To view the different tests in each grouping, just select the text in the tree view. Do not check the box next to the test. Checking the box will mark the test as enabled for the next test run.

Creating Test Lists

Test lists allow you to organize tests into distinct groupings to make them easier to manage. In the example you have been using so far, a logical breakdown might be to group the tests in Tasks, Users, Build Verification, and Miscellaneous lists.

To create a new test list, click Organize Tests in the lower-left corner of the Test Manager window. This will display the dialog box shown in Figure 12-6.

Figure 12-6. *The Create New Test List dialog box*

Enter the name and description for your new test list and select where you want it to show up in the list of existing test lists (note that there is no existing hierarchy when you create your first list).

Note You can nest the lists as deep as you like, but in general, they should not be listed too deep. As a best practice, do not nest tests any more than two deep to keep the test order and dependencies understandable and maintainable.

To organize the tests into the test lists, simply drag tests from the Tests Not in a List view to the appropriate lists. A test can also be associated with more than one list. To do this, hold down the Ctrl key and drag the test to the additional list. This will cause the test to be displayed twice in the full list of tests—once for each list it is in.

As you add items to the lists, they will disappear from the Tests Not in a List view. You can select to view all the loaded tests to see all of your tests at once, or you can view a specific list to see only the tests associated with that list.

Tip In the Test Manager window, you can select the Add/Remove columns option and add the Test List column, which will allow you to see which list each test is associated with when you have all of the loaded tests displayed.

Adding Test Properties

The TestProperty attribute is a special attribute that allows you to define one or more additional properties for any specific test. The TestProperty attribute accepts a property name and a description. This is useful as a way to further describe tests with information that is displayed in the Properties window.

To see how this works, switch to the code view for the ServiceTest class and select the ValidateUserTest method. Add the following attribute to the method:

```
C#
[TestProperty("My Property", "A new attribute")]
VB
<TestProperty("My Property", "A new attribute")>
```

Next, switch to the Test Manager window and select the ValidateUserTest. Right-click it and select Properties. In the Properties window, you will see a new property called My Property with the accompanying description. These properties are accessible from within the tests through the use of reflection. See the MSDN TestPropertyAttribute topic for more information.

Creating Ordered Tests

Another step you can take to manage your tests is to specify the order in which they run. For example, you might be testing that a user can be added to the system, and then that this new user can log on to the system successfully. This means that you need to execute the AddUser method and then the ValidateUser method. If you execute the second test first, then both methods will fail. To make sure the methods are executed in the correct order, you can create an *ordered test*.

■**Note** It is considered a best practice to write tests that are independent of one another (again, the goal of a unit test is to test the smallest unit of code available and not a whole chain of events if possible). To do this, you can run scripts that set the database up before each test run. However, in real-world practice, circumstances may prevent this. In those cases, an ordered test run is the best solution to the problem.

To create an ordered test, follow these steps:

1. Select Test ➤ New Test from the main menu.

2. Select Ordered Test. Name it NewUserLogonTest, and make sure it is set to be added to the EffortTrackingServiceTest project. Then click OK

3. In the Ordered Test window, shown in Figure 12-7, select AddUserTest and then ValidateUserTest.

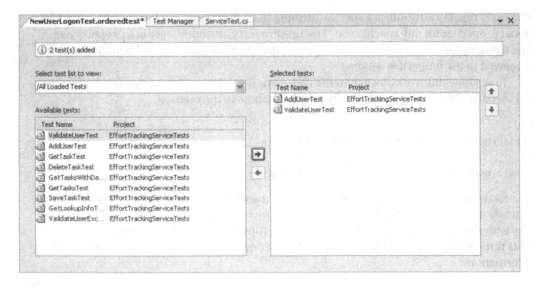

Figure 12-7. *The Ordered Test window*

4. Save your changes.

In the Test Manager window, you will now see an additional test called NewUserLogonTest. Double-clicking this test will reopen the Ordered Test window. When you run this test, both the AddUserTest and the ValidateUserTest will run in the correct order.

■**Note** While you can nest ordered tests inside each other (that is, create one ordered test and then a second ordered test that contains one or more other ordered tests), a best practice is not to nest them any more than two tests deep. This will help make it easier to determine which tests you are going to run and will keep the interdependencies to a minimum.

Setting Up Tests

Up to now, you have seen how to create and manage tests. But you're still not ready to run your tests. Before you run a test, you should configure it so that it runs the way you want it to run. You also need to complete the test methods so the tests run correctly. You need to go through the setup process for each group of tests only once.

Configuring Test Runs

Under the Solution Items folder in your solution is a file called `localtestrun.testrunconfig`. This file contains all of the test configuration information for your solution. Double-click this file to open the dialog box shown in Figure 12-8.

■**Tip** Your solution can have multiple test run configuration files associated with it and you can specify, for each test run, which configuration file will be used.

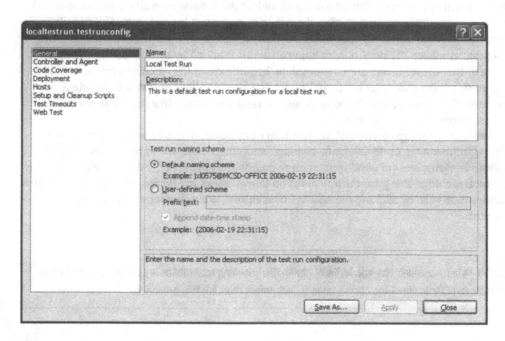

Figure 12-8. *The Test Run Configuration dialog box*

The Test Run Configuration dialog box allows you to configure properties that apply to any tests associated with this test configuration. To associate a configuration file with a test run, select Test ➤ Select Active Test Run Configuration from the main menu and choose the appropriate configuration file.

The Test Run Configuration dialog box includes eight sections, which are described in the following sections.

General

The General section allows you to specify a configuration name and optionally a configuration description. The naming scheme section is used for the report of results for the given test run. The default naming scheme uses the currently logged-on user logon name and the name of the machine on which the tests are run, followed by the date and time of the test run. You can also create a user-defined naming scheme and choose whether to append the date and time.

Controller and Agent

In the Controller and Agent section, you can specify whether to run the tests locally or on a remote machine. Change this setting with care, however, because you cannot debug the test code or the code being tested if you choose to run the test on a remote machine. Controllers and agents are discussed in more detail in Chapter 16.

Code Coverage

Code coverage is an important companion to unit testing. For example, suppose you have an application that is 1,000 lines long scattered in several classes, and it seems to work fine. Now say that you run unit tests (which all pass) and look at the coverage results, and find that only 790 lines of code were actually run (also described as *exercised*) by your tests. This would indicate that even though all of your unit tests passed, you are not testing everything! It may indicate that you have 210 lines of code that cannot be reached by the current application structure or that the unit tests are not complete. In some cases (especially in reference to regression tests), the code may be "dead," which is a situation that occurs when code is no longer needed. In these cases, the code should be removed. Issues like these cannot be discovered simply by unit testing alone.

In the Code Coverage section of the Test Run Configuration dialog box, you can specify that you want to enable or disable code coverage statistics during a test run by selecting the assemblies or web pages for which you want to enable the coverage. By default, all of the web pages and assemblies that your current solution knows about are displayed. You can add other assemblies to this list by clicking the Add Artifacts button and selecting the assemblies to instrument.

■**Caution** When you select the Add Artifacts option, the resulting assemblies are copied and altered by Visual Studio in order to insert the correct code to instrument them for this procedure.

When you select the option to use code coverage, you have two additional options:

- Instrument the Assembly in Place, which specifies that the assemblies are altered and placed in the same deployment area as your project would normally place them. If the assemblies are not instrumented in place, they are placed in a separate test directory, which contains all of the binaries for the given test.

- Re-sign the Assembly, which allows Visual Studio to re-sign the assemblies after they have been altered.

■**Caution** Code coverage and performance testing do not play well together. In general, if you have code coverage enabled, your performance sessions will not run correctly.

Deployment

In order to isolate tests from any other environment, Visual Studio runs the test in a location different from the one where the code is compiled. The Deployment section of the Test Run Configuration dialog box allows you to specify where that code is copied (a local folder or a remote folder). In addition, you can specify other files (such as database files, configuration files, or graphics files that are not directly part of your project) or folders to be deployed to the temporary testing folder.

Hosts

The Hosts section allows you to specify the host for your code. There are two options: Default and ASP.NET. The Default setting is used for non-ASP.NET unit tests. There are no configuration options for the Default setting.

Selecting ASP.NET allows you to specify some additional settings. You will need to supply the URL to test, and then specify if the tests will be run in a virtual web server or an IIS web server. If you specify a virtual web server (ASP.NET Development Server), you will need to provide the path to the website (the physical location of the files, not a URL) and the application root name. For ASP.NET applications, if you select Default, everything will be configured according to the project settings.

■**Note** The Hosts section properties correspond directly with the attributes listed in Table 12-2 earlier in this chapter. Entering these properties causes the information to be added in the form of attributes to the test class.

Setup and Cleanup Scripts

The Setup and Cleanup Scripts section allows you to specify a script that will run at the beginning of an entire test run and another script that runs at the end. This is different from the initialize and cleanup methods in an actual test class, because those are run at the beginning and end of tests that reside in the given test class. The scripts themselves can be batch files, executables, or virtually any other type of script that can be executed. Additionally, these scripts are independent of the test itself so they will run before and after any test associated with the configuration file.

Test Timeouts

The Test Timeouts section allows you to specify that a test will be either aborted after a given period of time or marked as failed after a given period of time.

Web Test

The Web Test section allows you to specify properties specific to web applications, including the following:

- The number of times a test is run

- Whether that run count is specified by you or by the data available in a database

- The type of web browser that the test requests will come from

- The connection speed of those requests

- Specify think times (delays between actions) for the requests to provide a more realistic simulation of how your website will be used

---

Caution The Web Test settings do not take the place of true load tests. See Chapter 16 for details about performing load tests.

Completing the Test Methods

For your test to run correctly, you need to complete the test methods. Listing 12-2 shows the changes necessary for the `ValidateUserTest` method. The database included with the code for this chapter has two entries in the `Owners` table, `TestUser1` and `TestUser2`, both with a password of `password`.

Listing 12-2. *The Finished ValidateUserTest Method*

C#

```
    [TestMethod()]
    public void ValidateUserTest()
    {
        Service target = new Service();
        target.Credentials = System.Net.CredentialCache.DefaultCredentials;
        string userName = "TestUser";
        string password = "password";
        PasswordType type = PasswordType.ClearText;

        int expected = 1;
        int actual;

        actual = target.ValidateUser(userName, password, type);

        Assert.AreEqual(expected, actual,
            EffortTrackingServiceTests.localhost.Service.ValidateUser did not " +
                "return the expected value.");
    }
```

VB
```vb
    <TestMethod()>
  Public Sub ValidateUserTest()
      Dim target As Service = New Service()
      target.Credentials = System.Net.CredentialCache.DefaultCredentials
      Dim userName  As String = "TestUser"
      Dim password  As String = "password"
      Dim type As PasswordType = PasswordType.ClearText

      Dim expected  As Integer = 1
      Dim actual  As Integer

      actual = target.ValidateUser(userName, password, type)

      Assert.AreEqual(expected, actual, _
          EffortTrackingServiceTests.localhost.Service.ValidateUser did not " _
          & "return the expected value.")
    End Sub
```

These changes must be made for each of the tests in your solution.

Setting Other Configuration Options

Visual Studio provides some default options for testing that you can change via the IDE. To edit these values, select Tools ➤ Options from the main menu and expand the Test Tools node. You'll see three sections of options:

- The Default Dialog Box Action section allows you to specify the prompt settings that Visual Studio will display to you based on certain actions.

- The Test Execution section allows you to specify the defaults for code coverage coloring, in-place instrumentation, and the web root for all web-based tests.

- The Test Project section allows you to specify the default type of test project created (the language that it is created will appear as the default in the Add New Test dialog box, shown earlier in Figure 12-3) and the files that are automatically added to the new test project.

Running Tests

You are finally ready to run a test. Go to the Test Manager window and check the ValidateUserTest method and the DeleteTaskTest (without making any changes to the DeleteTaskTest code). Make sure that you have selected the Code Coverage option in your configuration file.

■**Caution** Because selecting the Code Coverage option modifies your assemblies, make sure that if the class files are under configuration control, they are checked out. Otherwise, the debugging and instrumentation will not work!

From the Test Manager window, click the Run icon and select the Run Checked Tests option. Alternatively, you can select the Debug Checked Tests option, which allows you to add breakpoints in the test class. With breakpoints, you can trace through setup and teardown and into the actual code being tested.

After you select to run a test, you will see the Test Results window, as shown in Figure 12-9. While the test is running, you can pause or cancel the test run as a whole by clicking the Pause or Stop button in the Test Results window.

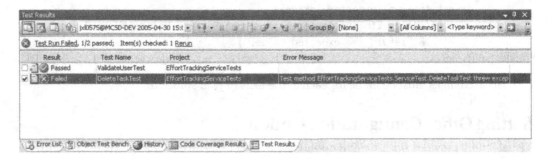

Figure 12-9. *The Test Results window*

During the test run, the status of the test is shown on the yellow status bar of the Test Results window, and each test is shown in the list below with its status (Pending, Running, Passed, Aborted or Failed). If a test fails, the error message for the failure is also shown, as you can see for the DeleteTaskTest in Figure 12-9. Also notice the Rerun link in the Test Results window, which allows you to rerun tests that failed (note that the one failed test was left checked).

■**Note** To delete a specific run (or all of the runs), right-click in the Test Results window and selecting Delete Test Run.

Viewing the Test Run Information

Through the Test Results window, you can get more information about specific tests as well as the test run as a whole. Let's begin with the Test Run Failed link in the yellow bar of the Test Results window. Clicking this link displays the window shown in Figure 12-10.

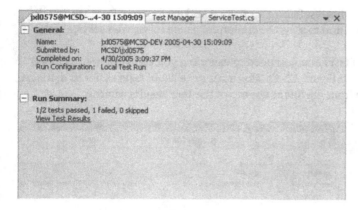

Figure 12-10. *The test run details window*

The test run details window contains general information about the test run, such as the name of the test run, who submitted it, when it was completed (notice that the run took 28 seconds, which is derived by subtracting the timestamp at the end of the test run name by the timestamp on the Completed On line), and which configuration was used for it. The run summary contains either details of the test run (as shown in Figure 12-10) or exception information (a complete stack trace) if there was a catastrophic failure with the tests and none of the tests were able to run. Clicking the View Test Results link returns you to the Test Results window.

Double-clicking any of the tests in the Test Results window displays the detailed test results window, as shown in Figure 12-11.

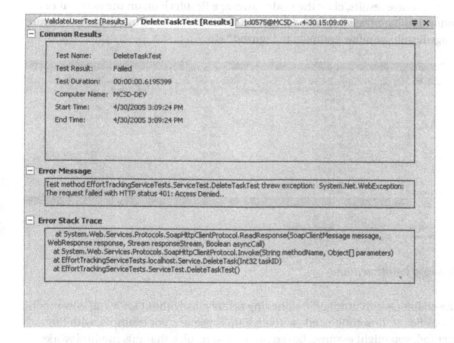

Figure 12-11. *Detailed test results window*

As you can see, the reason for this test failure is obvious and easily fixed. Because you did not modify the DeleteTaskTest method to pass the credential cache to the web service, your access was denied.

If you have a large number of tests that you need to examine, you can view the list based on your task list entries, as shown in Figure 12-12. This makes the list of tests easier to manage. To do this, select the second icon from the left at the top of the Test Results window.

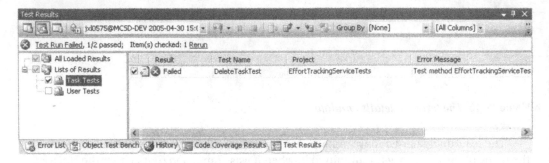

Figure 12-12. *Test Results displayed by result list*

From the Test Results window, you can also export the test results to a test results file (with a .trx extension) for later review. Another option is to import previously saved test results for a nicely formatted view in the Test Results window.

Viewing Code Coverage Results

To view your code coverage results, click the Code Coverage Results icon on the far right of the Test Results window toolbar or select Test ➤ Measure Test Effectiveness from the main menu. The Code Coverage Results window is shown in Figure 12-13.

Hierarchy	Not Covered (Blocks)	Not Covered (% Blocks)	Covered (Blocks)	Covered (% Blocks)	Not Covered (Lines)	Not Covered (% Lines)
⊟ jxd0575@MCSD-DEV 2005-04-30 15:34:29	163	90.06 %	18	9.94 %	121	88.97 %
⊟ App_Code.gdqhkb87.dll	163	90.06 %	18	9.94 %	121	88.97 %
⊟ { } EffortTrackingService	163	90.06 %	18	9.94 %	121	88.97 %
⊟ Service	163	90.06 %	18	9.94 %	121	88.97 %
AddUser(string,string)	28	100.00 %	0	0.00 %	15	100.00 %
DeleteTask(int32)	12	100.00 %	0	0.00 %	10	100.00 %
GetLookupInfo()	21	100.00 %	0	0.00 %	13	100.00 %
GetTask(int32)	28	100.00 %	0	0.00 %	21	100.00 %
GetTasks(int32,int32)	25	100.00 %	0	0.00 %	20	100.00 %
GetTasksWithDate(valuetype System.DateTi	17	100.00 %	0	0.00 %	12	100.00 %
SaveTask(valuetype EffortTrackingService.T	29	100.00 %	0	0.00 %	28	100.00 %
ValidateUser(string,string,valuetype EffortTr	3	14.29 %	18	85.71 %	2	11.76 %

Figure 12-13. *The Code Coverage Results window*

Earlier in the chapter, we mentioned that having test results without knowing how much code was exercised (that is, how much code actually ran) is useless. For example, with the ValidateUser method, you might assume, based on the test results, that this method works fine and that there is nothing more to test. But looking at the code coverage, you can see that this is not true at all. Table 12-4 contains a complete list of the code coverage statistics for the ValidateUser method.

Table 12-4. *Code Coverage Statistics for the ValidateUser Method*

Item	Value
Not Covered (Blocks)	3
Not Covered (% Blocks)	14.29%
Covered (Blocks)	18
Covered (% Blocks)	85.71%
Not Covered (Lines)	2
Not Covered (% Lines)	11.76%
Covered (Lines)	14
Covered (% Lines)	82.35%
Partially Covered (Lines)	1
Partially Covered (% Lines)	5.88%

The numbers themselves may be somewhat confusing, because they indicate how many lines of code were covered but not which lines of code were covered. But the VSTS testing tools allow you to put it in perspective by graphically showing the code coverage directly over the code, as shown in Figure 12-14. To see this display, in the Code Coverage Results window, double-click the ValidateUser method line or right-click the ValidateUser result and select Go to Source Code.

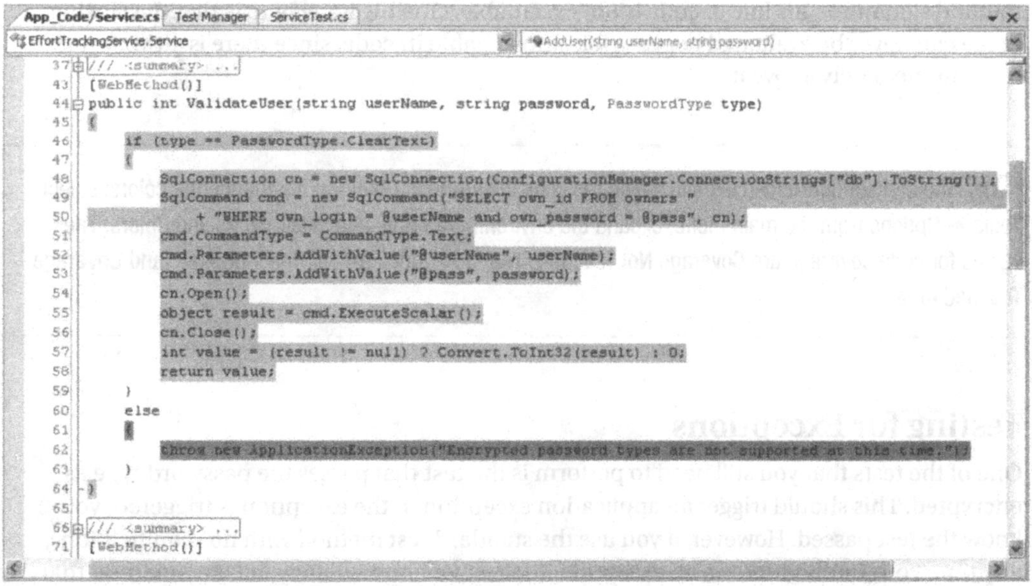

Figure 12-14. *The ValidateUser method code coverage display*

In the graphic display, the green lines were executed, the blue lines were partially executed, and the red lines were not executed at all. The method signature is not covered because it is not an executable line of code and so is not included in the code coverage statistics.

Note For VB developers, the partially executed line is a conditional if statement, which is almost identical to the iif statement. In this case, the result was not null, so only the first part of the conditional statement ran. The last part (0) did not run.

Now the numbers in Table 12-4 should make more sense. The lines indicated by the Not Covered (Blocks) number refer to the closing brace of the if block, the else line, and the closing brace of the else block. You might think that because the first part of the if block executed that the closing bracket was executed, but you will notice that the return statement occurs above this brace. Also note that the method's closing brace was executed because the return statement caused a jump to the end of the method (in VB, the End Function would be highlighted).

Note Another item you might notice is that in VB there are no braces in an if block. Therefore, the percentage of code coverage, and indeed even the number of lines executed, would be different.

Because the password type was Clear, the else statement was never evaluated. You might be wondering why it was not marked as a line not tested. The reason is that, as with the method signature, this line of code is not executable. One big issue here is that the closing brace can never be evaluated because it is unreachable in code, since there is a throw statement immediately above it.

Tip You can configure the colors in which the code coverage is rendered. To change the colors, select Tools ➤ Options from the main menu, expand the Environment node, and select Fonts and Colors. The values for code coverage are Coverage Not Touched Area, Coverage Partially Touched Area, and Coverage Touched Area.

Testing for Exceptions

One of the tests that you still need to perform is the test that passes the password type as encrypted. This should trigger an application exception. If the exception is triggered, you know the test passed. However, if you use the standard test method with no modifications, any time your method throws an exception, the test will immediately fail. Any method that throws an exception that you need to test for *must* be tested with a separate method.

Tip While testing for the success path is always a good idea, because you want to know if your code actually works, an exception path is just as valid a path. Too often, the issues that cause exceptions are not tested for at all and when they do occur, the code cannot handle them.

To demonstrate how this works, add the method shown in Listing 12-3 to the ServiceTest class.

Listing 12-3. *The Exception Test for ValidateUser*

C#

```
/// <summary>
///An exception test case for ValidateUser (string, string, PasswordType)
///</summary>
 [TestMethod()]
 [ExpectedException(typeof(System.Web.Services.Protocols.SoapException),
      + "An encrypted password type was allowed which is not supported.")]
public void ValidateUserExceptionTest()
{
      Service target = new Service();
      target.Credentials = System.Net.CredentialCache.DefaultCredentials;
      string userName = "TestUser";
      string password = "password";
      PasswordType type = PasswordType.Encrypted;
      int actual;

      actual = target.ValidateUser(userName, password, type);
}
```

VB

```
''' <summary>
'''An exception test case for ValidateUser (string, string, PasswordType)
'''</summary>
 <TestMethod()> _
 <ExpectedException(GetType(System.Web.Services.Protocols.SoapException), _
      "An encrypted password type was allowed which is not supported.")> _
Public Sub ValidateUserExceptionTest()
      Dim target As Service = new Service()
      target.Credentials = System.Net.CredentialCache.DefaultCredentials
      Dim userName As string = "TestUser"
      Dim password  As string = "password"
      Dim type As PasswordType = PasswordType.Encrypted
      Dim actual As integer

      actual = target.ValidateUser(userName, password, type)
End Sub
```

The key to this type of test is the ExpectedException attribute. Notice that the Assert method is not even called here because it is not needed. The ExpectedException attribute ensures that .NET will wait for a SoapException to be thrown, and if it is, the test will be marked as successful. If it is not thrown, the message included with the ExpectedException attribute will be displayed as the failure message.

Caution You will notice that something appears to be wrong with what you are testing here. Your application throws an ApplicationException, yet you are testing for a SoapException. The reason is that when an exception is thrown during the invocation of a web service, the service throws its own exception and includes the message from any other exceptions as part of its message.

Once you have made this change, run this test plus the original ValidateUser test. Your test results will show that both tests pass. Your code coverage results will be 100% because the two lines in the else statement have been reached.

Now, the problem with this is that you still do not know if the right exception was thrown, but there is a way to solve this. Modify the code in the ValidateUserExceptionTest method to match that shown in Listing 12-4 (note that this is a partial listing only) and *remove* the ExpectedException attribute.

Listing 12-4. *Modified ValidateUserTestException Method*
C#

```csharp
    int actual;

    try
    {
        actual = target.ValidateUser(userName, password, type);
    }
    catch (Exception ex)
    {
        if (ex.Message.IndexOf("ApplicationException") > 0)
            Assert.Equals(1, 1);
        else
            Assert.Fail();
    }
```

VB

```vb
    Dim actual As integer

    Try
        actual = target.ValidateUser(userName, password, type)
    Catch (Exception ex)
        If (ex.Message.IndexOf("ApplicationException") > 0)
            Assert.Equals(1, 1)
        Else
            Assert.Fail()
    End Try
```

This simple modification allows you to check to see if a specific exception was thrown when throwing an exception from a web service.

Data-Driven Testing

As you've seen in this chapter, you might need to create an enormous number of tests in order to test your entire application. As you saw earlier, if a parameter is a date or there is an intensive amount of processing occurring in a method, you might have to create in the vicinity of 20 tests for just one method, just to test different method arguments. This not only does not make a lot of sense, but it is extremely time-consuming. This is where *data-driven testing* comes in.

Data-driven testing is not only helpful in keeping down the number of tests that you need to write, but it also makes it easier to change tests later on without having to change the test code itself. Data-driven testing is the process of feeding data to test your methods from a database instead of coding values directly into the test code. The TestContext object, which you looked at briefly earlier in the chapter, makes this task extremely easy. The basic principle is that you create a separate test database with one table per test method, which will supply the values for that test to use.

■**Note** The SQL Express components make data-driven testing incredibly easy, as they can handle a fairly high volume of data and the test data can remain with the testing solution. However, if you are performing load testing or other very high-volume tests, you will probably want to create a separate SQL Server 2005 database to store the test data.

Building a Test Database

Before you start constructing the test table, you need to determine what it should contain. Each test will have a different number of columns because the columns will always relate to the number and type of parameters that need to be passed to the method. However, you should always have a primary key, which is an identifier column, and you will always need a column that holds the expected value.

For this demonstration, you will build the table shown in Table 12-5 to hold the information to test the ValidateUser method.

Table 12-5. *ValidateUser Test Table*

Column	Type	Nullable	Purpose
vu_id	int (Identity)	No	Primary Key
vu_username	varchar(50)	No	Holds the username
vu_password	varchar(50)	No	Holds the password
vu_pw_type	int	No	Indicates clear text or encrypted
vu_expected	int	No	Indicates the value that should be returned

Now that you know what the test table is going to contain, you need to build the database and create the table, as follows:

1. In the Solution Explorer, right-click the EffortTrackingServiceTests project and select Add New Item.

2. Select the SQL Database and name it ServiceTestDB.mdf.

3. In the Server Explorer, select Add a New Data Connection, and then browse to the ServiceTestDB.mdf file and select it.

4. Expand the ServiceTestDB.mdf file, right-click the Tables node, and select Add New Table.

5. Enter the information shown in Table 12-5.

6. Name the table ValidateUserTest.

7. In the ValidateUserTest table, enter the information shown in Table 12-6. These values will be used by the test method to pass values to the ValidateUser method in the service.

Table 12-6. *The ValidateUserTest Table Values*

vu_id	vu_username	vu_password	vu_pw_type*	vu_expected
1	TestUser1	password	1	1
2	TestUser1	pass	1	0
3	TestUser5	password	1	0

* *The* vu_pw_type *value corresponds with the* PasswordType *enumeration.*

This is everything you will need to perform the tests for this method. Note that we are *not* testing for the exception condition by passing a password type of 2. Exception tests must be carried out as separate tests. Theoretically, you could create exception handling as you did in the previous section on testing for exceptions and handle it appropriately, but it is usually easier to keep those tests separate.

Preparing the Production Database

The tests that we have come up with so far are perfectly acceptable (although you could quite easily come up with some tests that are not listed in Table 12-6), but they will not work every time. This is because the Owners table in the EffortTracking database uses an Identity column and you are looking for very explicit values to be returned (listed in the vu_expected column). In order for these tests to work correctly every time, the data you are testing against must be the same every time. To do this, you need to load the production database with the correct information before a test run. This is where the Initialize method is very helpful.

Table 12-2 earlier in the chapter includes the ClassInitialize and ClassCleanup attributes. Whereas the TestInitialize and TestCleanup methods are executed at the beginning and end of each and every test, the ClassInitialize and ClassCleanup methods are executed before any test in a class is run and after all of the tests in a class are run. This means that each method is guaranteed to execute only once during the course of a test run, regardless of how many tests are in the class. In this example, you will use the ClassInitialize attribute to tag a method, which will set up the production database for testing. No cleanup will be necessary for this set of tests.

Based on the information in Table 12-6, only one row of data needs to be created in the Owners table of the production database. The information is listed in Table 12-7.

Table 12-7. *The Owers Table Entry*

Column	Value
own_id	1
own_login	TestUser1
own_password	password

Before doing anything else, add a reference to the System.Configuration assembly in the EffortTrackingTests project and import the System.Data.SqlClient and System.Configuration namespaces. In order to set up the database, add the code shown in Listing 12-5 to the ServiceTests class.

Listing 12-5. *The TestClassInitialize Method*

C#

```csharp
[ClassInitialize()]
public static void TestClassInitialize(TestContext context)
{
    SqlConnection cn = new SqlConnection(
        ConfigurationManager.AppSettings["db"].ToString);
    SqlCommand cmd1 = new SqlCommand("SET IDENTITY_INSERT owners ON", cn);
    SqlCommand cmd2 = new SqlCommand("DELETE FROM work_items", cn);
    SqlCommand cmd3 = new SqlCommand("DELETE FROM owners", cn);
    SqlCommand cmd4 = new SqlCommand("INSERT INTO owners (own_id, "
        + "own_login, own_password) VALUES (1, 'TestUser1', 'password')",
        cn);
    SqlCommand cmd5 = new SqlCommand("SET IDENTITY_INSERT owners OFF",
        cn);

    cmd1.CommandType = CommandType.Text;
    cmd2.CommandType = CommandType.Text;
    cmd3.CommandType = CommandType.Text;
    cmd4.CommandType = CommandType.Text;
    cmd5.CommandType = CommandType.Text;

    cn.Open();
    cmd1.ExecuteNonQuery();
    cmd2.ExecuteNonQuery();
    cmd3.ExecuteNonQuery();
    cmd4.ExecuteNonQuery();
    cmd5.ExecuteNonQuery();
```

```
            cn.Close();
    }
```

VB

```vb
    <ClassInitialize()>
    Public Shard Sub TestClassInitialize(TestContext context)
        Dim cn As SqlConnection = new SqlConnection( _
            ConfigurationManager.AppSettings("db").ToString)
        Dim cmd1 As SqlCommand = new SqlCommand( _
            "SET IDENTITY_INSERT owners ON", cn)
        Dim cmd2 As SqlCommand = new SqlCommand("DELETE FROM work_items", cn)
        Dim cmd3 As SqlCommand = new SqlCommand("DELETE FROM owners", cn)
        Dim cmd4 As SqlCommand = new SqlCommand("INSERT INTO owners (own_id, " _
            & "own_login, own_password) VALUES (1, 'TestUser1', 'password')", cn)
        Dim cmd5 As SqlCommand = new SqlCommand( _
            "SET IDENTITY_INSERT owners OFF", cn)

        cmd1.CommandType = CommandType.Text
        cmd2.CommandType = CommandType.Text
        cmd3.CommandType = CommandType.Text
        cmd4.CommandType = CommandType.Text
        cmd5.CommandType = CommandType.Text

        cn.Open()
        cmd1.ExecuteNonQuery()
        cmd2.ExecuteNonQuery()
        cmd3.ExecuteNonQuery()
        cmd4.ExecuteNonQuery()
        cmd5.ExecuteNonQuery()
        cn.Close()
    End Sub
```

Now that the ClassInitialize method is set up to re-create the database for each of the tests necessary for the data-driven tests, you can move on to actually setting up the test to use data from the database.

Setting Up the Test

In the Test Manager window, select the ValidateUserTest and view its properties. Select the ellipsis for the Data Connection String property, and then browse to the ServiceTestDB.mdf file and select it. Leave the Data Access property as Sequential. Next, select the ValidateUserTest table from the Data Table Name property. This will add the DataSource attribute to the ValidateUserTest method in the ServiceTests class (it is much easier to do it this way than typing the attribute in manually).

Now that everything is hooked up, you need to be able to read the information from the ValidateUserTest table. To access the information in the row, you use the TestContext.DataRow property and access the data as you normally would from a database, as shown in Listing 12-6.

Listing 12-6. *Data-Driven Test Method*

C#
```
/// <summary>
///A test case for AddUser (string, string)
///</summary>
 [TestMethod()]
 [DataSource("System.Data.SqlClient", "Data Source=.\\SQLEXPRESS;
AttachDbFilename=\"C:\\ServiceTestDB.mdf\";Integrated Security=True;
User Instance=True",
"AddUserTest", DataAccessMethod.Sequential)]
public void AddUserTest()
{
    Service target = new Service();
    string userName = testContextInstance.DataRow["au_username"].ToString();
    string password = testContextInstance.DataRow["au_password"].ToString();
    PasswordType type =
    (PasswordType)testContextInstance.DataRow["au_password_type"];

    int expected = Convert.ToInt32(testContextInstance.DataRow["au_expected"]);
    int actual;

    actual = target.AddUser(userName, password);

    if (userName == "Test User 2")
        _newUserId = actual;

    Assert.AreEqual(expected, actual,
    "EffortTrackingServiceTests.localhost.Service.AddUser did "
        + "not return the expected value.");
}
```

VB
```
''' <summary>
'''A test case for AddUser (string, string)
'''</summary>
 <TestMethod()> _
 <DataSource("System.Data.SqlClient", "Data Source=.\\SQLEXPRESS; " & _
"AttachDbFilename=\"C:\\ServiceTestDB.mdf\";Integrated Security=True; _
    User Instance=True", _
"AddUserTest", DataAccessMethod.Sequential)>
Public Sub AddUserTest()
    Dim target As Service = New Service()
    Dim userName As String = testContextInstance.DataRow("au_username").ToString()
    Dim password As String = testContextInstance.DataRow("au_password").ToString()
    Dim type As PasswordType = _
        CType(PasswordType, testContextInstance.DataRow("au_password_type"))
```

```
        Dim expected As Integer = _
        Convert.ToInt32(testContextInstance.DataRow("au_expected"))
        Dim actual As Integer

        actual = target.AddUser(userName, password)

        If userName = "Test User 2" Then
            _newUserId = actual
        End If

        Assert.AreEqual(expected, actual, _
        "EffortTrackingServiceTests.localhost.Service.AddUser did " _
            & "not return the expected value.")
End Sub
```

The DataSource attribute indicates to VSTS that an external data source is being used to drive this particular test method. The syntax for the DataSource constructor is *Connection String, Table, Access Method*. The connection string is a standard database connection string. The table is the table in the database that contains your test data, and the access method is how the test should access the data.

■**Note** The access method has no effect on a unit test. The test will always be run using the sequential access method. This setting has an effect for load testing, which is covered in Chapter 16.

The test will be run once for every row of data in the table. The DataRow property of the testContextInstance changes for every method according to the DataSource attribute for the method.

■**Note** You cannot artificially change the row that is currently being used in the test.

The test results from a data-driven test look slightly different than those you've seen so far, as shown in Figure 12-15.

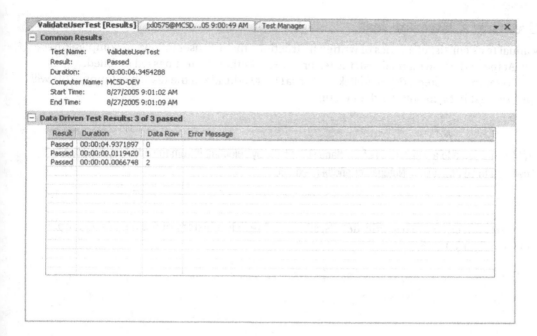

Figure 12-15. *Data-driven test results*

For each row in the test, the result and the amount of time the test took are displayed. If there were any errors, those messages will be displayed here as well.

Tip As a best practice, and to make the results of this test more valuable, the error message should also come from the test database. This allows you to more easily tie a failure to a specific entry, since it is difficult to do that with the data displayed. You could also provide the supplied values in the error message. To do this, simply add a description column to each test table and use it to supply the exception message. Now your tests will be self-documenting.

Manual Testing

Some tests just cannot be run in an automated fashion. These tests may require some external actions to prepare certain aspects of a server. An example of this may be testing an IIS failure in which the manual step of stopping the World Wide Web service may be required. Or if you are using VSTS, which does not currently support Windows Forms testing, and you want to test the user interface, then manual testing would be the way to go.

Creating a Manual Test

Manual tests consist of a series of written instructions that the user follows to complete the test. At the end of the manual test, the tester marks whether the test passed or failed.

To set the test steps, double-click the ManualTest1.mht file in the testing solution. This will open the test in Microsoft Word for editing.

■**Note** You can add a text version of the ManualTest file by selecting it from the Add Test Wizard, which allows you to edit the test in Notepad or another text editor.

Here, you enter the test title, details, steps, and revision history of the test. An example is shown in Figure 12-16.

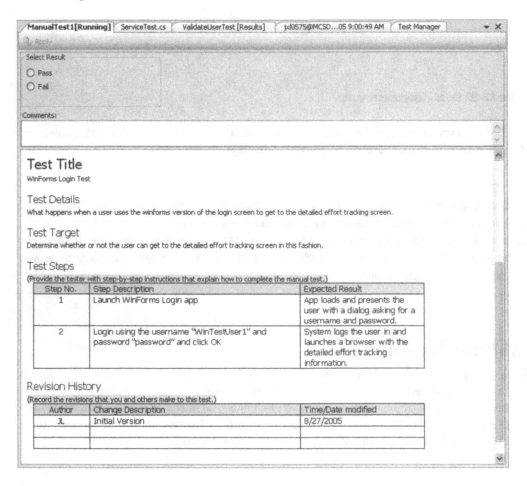

Figure 12-16. *Manual test run*

Note Figure 12-16 shows the file during an actual manual test run so it is not displayed in the Word environment here. This test is not a test you will be running, but is for example purposes only.

The test steps are the key to this test. The tester simply walks through the steps of the test performing the actions noted in the step description. The result of each step should be documented in the far-right column. If the expected result is not the actual result at any point in the set of steps, the test should be marked as failed and a comment explaining which step failed and the actual result that was displayed. The version history should also be maintained so you know who made changes, if any, to the test script.

Running a Manual Test

When a test run reaches a manual test, it will pause and wait for you to complete the manual test. When you have finished with the manual test, you mark it as Pass or Fail using the options at the top of the manual test window, and then click Apply. Once the test is marked as Pass or Fail, the rest of the tests in the test run will continue.

Caution Do not include manual tests in automated test runs as a rule. If, for example, you set up a series of tests for the nightly build and you include a manual test, the nightly set of tests will *not* run. The test will be paused at the first manual test in the list of tests.

Manual testing gives you the ability to perform virtually any test in Visual Studio and have those tests recorded just as it would with any automated tests.

Tip One added benefit of running manual tests this way is that code coverage results are recorded for these tests.

Testing Using MSTest

VSTS includes a command-line tool called MSTest. The executable is located in the C:\Program Files\Microsoft Visual Studio 8\Common7\IDE folder. This tool provides a simple way to automate the tests. Team Foundation Build invokes this tool when performing automated builds, but you can include it in batch files or invoke it manually for whatever purposes you may need.

For example, to invoke MSTest in order to run the tests included with the sample Effort Tracking application, open a Visual Studio command-line prompt and navigate to the folder that contains the EffortTrackingServiceTests.dll. Then enter the following at the command prompt:

```
Mstest /testcontainer:efforttrackingservicetests.dll /test:orderedTest1
```

The results will be displayed in the command window. There are numerous options for customizing the output, choosing the configuration file, columns to display, and so on. You can also publish tests to Team Foundation Server using this tool. See the MSDN documentation for more information.

Summary

As you've seen in this chapter, unit testing is an integral part of any development process. Without unit tests, you cannot be assured that the code works as planned at the method level.

In this chapter, you learned how to plan the unit tests and create them. This includes being able to prepare the development database so that tests are repeatable using the various methods of the test class. You learned how to manage and group test runs, as well as how to order test runs so that dependent tests run in the correct order. You have seen how to configure a test run to accomplish specific goals and the benefits of using code coverage and understanding what that coverage means. Then you learned how to run data-driven tests, which allow you to create a test database to supply values to your tests without having to create a myriad of different test methods for each method to be tested. Next, you learned about manual testing. Finally, we briefly covered the MSTest command-line tool.

In short, this chapter has provided you with a new set of tools that you can use to make your code more stable than it has ever been before. This leads to fewer bugs, a shorter time to fix discovered bugs, and fewer regression bugs.

CHAPTER 13

■ ■ ■

Static Code Analysis

S*tatic code analysis* is the process of examining your code, while it is not in a running state, for defects. These defects can range from naming conventions not being followed to potential security holes, which can lead to buffer overrun attacks and many other problems. (Performance analysis, which occurs while the code is running, is covered in the next chapter.)

VSTS provides two tools for static code analysis: PREfast and FxCop. PREfast is a tool for checking for potential issues when dealing with C/C++ code bases. It was originally developed as an internal tool for use by Microsoft developers to check their own code. FxCop is a tool developed for .NET in order to check code for proper formatting, correct usage of the language, potential security holes, and other issues.

In this chapter, you will examine both of these tools. You will see how to use them and where they fit into an automated build process (particularly the FxCop tool). You will also learn how to extend and customize the FxCop tool so that you can check that the code meets your organization's standards as well as the predefined rules.

Note that pointer issues are only a problem in C++; they do not occur in C# or VB .NET code. If you do not program in C or C++, you may want to skip the section on PREfast. If you are a development manager, you will probably want to at least be aware of what PREfast does.

Static Code Analysis vs. Code Reviews

You may have never performed a static code analysis before except via code reviews. Code reviews are great tools, and you should in no way discount them because VSTS has provided tools to help with the analysis. But what's the first thing to go when you hit crunch time on a project? It's the meetings—*all* of the meetings, including code reviews.

The static code analysis tools are another example of VSTS working to help ensure that you produce the highest quality code base with the fewest number of defects. The static code analysis tools provide a way to automate some of the process of code reviews. The tools can be run manually or via an automated build process using Team Foundation Build. At the very least, they provide a backup in case your code review process gets cut because of project deadlines (which, of course, causes more problems than it solves). At best, they provide a more robust set of checks for you and your development team.

THE VALUE OF CODE REVIEWS

Code reviews are often the first things to get the axe when push comes to shove and deadlines start looming over a development team. When this happens, bugs are not spotted during development time when they are easier to fix. Typically, the product is just about ready for shipping when a tester discovers a bug while performing functional tests, or worse yet, during user tests. The code goes back for review, where it takes a team of people some work to find and fix it, and then the product goes through the testing process all over again. At this point, the release date has slipped, and the entire development team is in trouble. Instead, a fraction of the time could have been spent on code reviews, and the problem could have been captured and fixed in about five minutes.

Have you had this experience? We have seen many projects start off with lofty goals regarding code reviews, only to have those plans sacrificed because of budget and time constraints. VSTS, by integrating these analysis tools, has given developers a huge hand in exposing potential problems. But the results of these tools should always be checked by others in code reviews.

There is a common misconception that a developer with his head down coding is more effective than one who takes the time to review his code with others. This has given rise to many of the Agile Development methodologies, which have the advantage of code reviews during coding.

Steve McConnell, in his book *Code Complete, Second Edition* (Microsoft Press, 2004) takes a great deal of time to examine the cost of fixing bugs at various points in the development process. It has been proven that the costs of fixing bugs found during testing or after release are orders of magnitude higher than catching and fixing them during development. We recommend that developers read this book.

Using PREfast

PREfast was originally developed by Microsoft Research and has been employed for several years within the company to check for coding defects in Microsoft products. At this time, running these checks is seen as an essential part of getting a product ready for shipping. If you are shipping a product written in C or C++, you will certainly want to make sure that these checks are run on your code. PREfast is designed to detect some of the most serious coding errors that a normal compilation alone will not detect, including buffer overruns, dereferencing null pointers, using uninitialized variables, and so on.

Enabling PREfast Checking

PREfast was integrated into the VSTS version of the Visual C++ 2005 compiler, so it is available to you when using any release of the Visual C++ 2005 C/C++ compiler, cl.exe. Unlike FxCop, PREfast does all its checking at compile time, so it makes sense as an add-on to the compiler. In fact, all you need to do to enable the PREfast code analysis is to set the /analyze compiler option, which you can also do from a Visual Studio project. In the Project Properties dialog box, under C/C++, look under Advanced and set the Enable Code Analysis for C/C++ option to Yes.

You can enable the PREfast checking when compiling C or C++ code. Regardless of whether C or C++ code is being checked, the effect of setting the option is to enable specific diagnostics (compiler warnings) that are not generated in a compilation without the /analyze option.

The PREfast diagnostics are normally issued as warnings. Often, code projects have the /WX compiler option set, which changes warnings to errors. However, you probably won't want all the PREfast warnings to be issued as errors, since you may not be able to fix these immediately. To tell the compiler to report PREfast diagnostics as warnings even when the /WX option is set, use the /analyze:WX- version of the /analyze option.

Reviewing PREfast Results

The PREfast diagnostics can be distinguished from other compiler warnings by the range of the codes. PREfast warnings have codes between 6000 and 6999. Table 13-1 lists the PREfast checks and their associated warning codes.

Table 13-1. *PREfast Checks*

Category	Warning Codes	Items Checked
Bad memory use	C6001, C6011, C6200, C6278, C6279, C6280, C6283	Use of uninitialized memory, dereferencing a null pointer, using out-of-range array indices, new and delete mismatches
Buffer overruns	C6029, C6057, C6201, C6202, C6203, C6204, C6327, C6383, C6385, C6386	Code that could allow writing past the end of a buffer, which is a serious security vulnerability
Unchecked return values	C6031	Failure to check for error codes returned from functions
Null termination	C6053, C6054	Strings that are not null-terminated passed to functions that expect it
Incorrect arguments	C6059, C6066, C6067, C6270, C6271, C6272, C6273, C6274, C6284, C6298, C6306, C6309, C6328, C6331, C6332, C6333, C6381, C6387, C6388	Various invalid or incorrect arguments
Format string errors	C6063, C6064	Using the incorrect or wrong number of conversion characters in a formatting string
Wide/narrow character and character vs. byte count issues	C6209, C6260, C6303	Using sizeof with a wide character string as the length, passing a wide character string to a function that requires a narrow character string, using sizeof * sizeof

Continued

Table 13-1. *Continued*

Category	Warning Codes	Items Checked
Memory leaks	C6211, C6308	Leaking memory due to an exception
Questionable casts	C6214, C6215, C6216, C6217, C6218, C6219, C6220, C6221, C6225, C6226, C6230, C6276	Various dangerous casts and conversions
Questionable expressions	C6235, C6236, C6237, C6239, C6240, C6268, C6269, C6281, C6282, C6285, C6286, C6287, C6288, C6289, C6290, C6291, C6299, C6302, C6313, C6314, C6315, C6316, C6317, C6323, C6326, C6336	Operator precedence errors, Boolean expressions that are always true or always false, confusion between bitwise operators and relational operators, incorrect use of bit fields, confusion between equality and assignment operators, and so on
Questionable Case statements	C6259	Case statements that have values that are not reachable
Questionable looping constructs	C6292, C6293, C6294, C6295, C6296	Loops that count down from the minimum or up from the maximum, loops that never execute, loops that execute only once
Variable hiding	C6244, C6246	Hiding a variable at a larger scope with one at a smaller scope
Incorrect use of sizeof or countof	C6305, C6334, C6384	Potential mismatch between sizeof and countof quantities, sizeof applied to an expression with an operator, dividing sizeof a pointer by another value
Exception handling problems	C6242, C6310, C6312, C6318, C6319, C6320, C6322	Actions that trigger a local unwind, improper use of __try/__except blocks and exception filters, and so on
Stack corruption	C6255, C6262, C6263	Using _alloca instead of _alloca_s, calling _alloca in a loop, using a stack greater than specified stack size set with /analyze:stacksize*nnnn* (where *nnnn* is the stack size above which the warning will be issued)
Security risks	C6248, C6277	Improper use of access control lists (ACLs)
Resource leaks	C6250, C6335	Failing to release various Windows resources

Category	Warning Codes	Items Checked
Thread termination	C6258	Terminating a thread without proper cleanup
Case-insensitive comparisons	C6400, C6401	Comparison functions used in a way that doesn't work on non-English locales
Integer overflow error	C6297	32-bit value shifted and cast to a 64-bit value
Possible wrong function call	C6324	Using a string copy function (such as strcpy) where a string comparison function (such as strcmp) should have been used

To see PREfast in action, try compiling the code in Listing 13-1 with the /analyze option. Also specify _CRT_SECURE_NO_DEPRECATE so that you can use strcpy without getting a warning that it is deprecated in favor of the more secure strcpy_s version, new with Visual C++ 2005. If you used the strcpy_s version, you won't get the warning we are demonstrating in this example: a potential buffer overrun.

Listing 13-1. *Buffer Overrun Example*

```cpp
// buffer_overrun.cpp
// compile with /D_CRT_SECURE_NO_DEPRECATE /analyze
#include <string.h>
#include <malloc.h>
#include <stdio.h>

void f(char* str)
{
   char* x = (char*) malloc(10 * sizeof(char));

   if (x != NULL)
   {
      strcpy(x, str);
   }
}

int main()
{
  f("A random string of arbitrary length");
}
```

The output is as follows:

```
Microsoft (R) 32-bit C/C++ Optimizing Compiler Version 14.00.50727.42 for 80x86
Copyright (C) Microsoft Corporation.  All rights reserved.

buffer_overrun.cpp
c:\nutshell\PREfast_code\buffer_overrun.cpp(12) : warning C6204:
Possible buffer overrun in call to 'strcpy': use of unchecked parameter 'str'
```

As you can see, warning 6204 is generated, letting you know of a potentially serious error. To address this, you might modify the code as shown in Listing 13-2.

Listing 13-2. *Buffer Overrun Correction*

```cpp
// buffer_overrun.cpp
// compile with /D_CRT_SECURE_NO_DEPRECATE /analyze
#include <string.h>
#include <malloc.h>
#include <stdio.h>

void f(char* str)
{
    char* x = (char*) malloc(10 * sizeof(char));

    if (x != NULL)
    {
        if (strlen(str) < sizeof x)
        {
            strcpy(x, str);
        }
        else
        {
            printf("The string passed in was too long.");
        }
    }
}

int main()
{
  f("A random string of arbitrary length");
}
```

You, the developer, may already be certain that there cannot be any input that would actually cause an overrun. PREfast does not look beyond the individual function scope to try to analyze what input might be passed to a function. However, you can extend PREfast's reach by using attributes to annotate your code. This lets you specify in metadata which constraints PREfast should check. You'll learn how to use such annotations shortly, after we explain how to turn off the undesired warnings, since there are often quite a few of them.

Enabling, Disabling, and Suppressing PREfast Warnings

Some PREfast warnings are more serious than others, and you will probably want to enable some of them and disable others, depending on the goals for a particular project and the risks associated with the particular type of error. For example, if you are shipping consumer software, you may have more stringent requirements than if you are working on a research project.

For a large body of existing code that has not been checked with PREfast or a similar source analysis tool before, the number of warnings generated may be quite large. You will need to make a business decision that balances the risks of not detecting certain types of errors versus the risks of changing code that has been stable and tested, as well as taking into account the time it will take to make the code changes to eliminate the warnings.

Another factor to consider is who will be addressing the errors with the code. Are these developers familiar with that code? If you have a stable code base, you certainly don't want to allow code changes that eliminate the warnings but introduce semantic errors that might be hard to detect.

Another issue you are likely to encounter is PREfast warnings in header files from third parties or from libraries that you have no direct control over. You may want to disable some of these warnings.

Development teams may want to agree on the set of warnings that will be enforced and those that will be disabled, with an understanding of the risks and costs associated with each warning. Once these are agreed upon, it is a simple matter to set up an include file with the appropriate pragma directives to disable or enable the desired warnings.

The easiest way to add a consistent level of checking to your existing build process is to add an include file to the compilation using the /FI (Force Include) compiler option. Listing 13-3 shows an example of an include file with pragma directives.

Listing 13-3. *PREfast pragma File*

```
// PREfast.h -- add /FIPREfast.h to your compilation command line
#pragma once

#pragma warning(disable: \
        6001 6002 6003 6004 6005 6006 6007 6008 6009 \
    6010 6011 6012 6013 6014 6015 6016 6017 6018 6019 \
    6020 6021 6022 6023 6024 6025 6026 6027 6028 6030 \
    6031 6032 6033 6034 6035 6036 6037 6038 6039 6040 \
    // etc...
    )
```

```
/* It's a good idea to explicitly list those PREfast warnings
 * you do enable.  This is a list of PREfast
 * warnings that are considered a minimum bar for a shipping
 * product.
 *
 * 6029;6053;6056;6057;6059;6063;6067;6200;6201;6202;6203;6204;
 * 6205;6207;6241;6243;6248;6252;6259;6260;6268;6276;6277;6281;
 * 6282;6287;6288;6289;6290;6291;6296;6298;6299;6305;6306;6308;
 * 6334;6383
 */
```

You may also want to disable specific occurrences of a given warning on a case-by-case basis. To do this, surround the code with #pragma warning (suppress: C6xxx) with the specific warning number. You could also use #pragma warning (disable: Cxxxx), as with any other warning, but this has the effect of suppressing the warning throughout the remainder of that file. The suppress version of this pragma affects only the line of code immediately following the pragma, so it is preferable since it avoids the risk of missing other errors in the file. An example of suppressing a warning is shown in Listing 13-4.

Listing 13-4. *PREfast Warning Suppression Example*

```
// suppress_warning.cpp
// compile with /D_CRT_SECURE_NO_DEPRECATE /analyze
#include <string.h>
#include <stdio.h>

int p;

void f()
{
    // char * p hides the global p, but we know this is safe and simply
    // want to suppress the warning.
    #pragma warning (suppress: 6244)
    char* p = new char[10];

    strcpy(p, "xyz");
    printf("%s\n", p);
}

void g()
{
    // the same error here triggers the warning
    char* p = new char[10];

    strcpy(p, "xyz");
    printf("%s\n", p);
}
```

```
int main()
{
    f();
    g();
}
```

Annotating Code for PREfast Checks

In addition to the warnings that are generated simply by turning on the /analyze compiler option, you can achieve further testing with PREfast by annotating your code with specific attributes. For example, you can annotate a function call with an attribute that tells PREfast that the return value of this function must be checked. Then when that function is used, PREfast will report a warning whenever that function is used without checking the return value.

To enable the use of the attributes from C code, simply include the following include directive:

```
#include <CodeAnalysis/SourceAnnotations.h>
```

When compiling C++ code, add the preceding include directive, but also add the following using namespace statement:

```
using namespace vc_attributes;
```

To annotate your code, you add PREfast attributes to parameters and return values. Attributes appear in square brackets and have various properties you can set to signal PREfast to perform a check.

You use two attributes with PREfast:

- The Pre attribute is used with function parameters only and is designed to tell PREfast to check for various conditions whenever parameters are passed to the function whose parameter is attributed.

- The Post attribute is used on the function's return values and on out parameters, such as pointers that are intended to be set or filled in during the function call.

For example, you might use the Pre attribute to enforce that a pointer parameter is a valid non-null pointer. If this attribute is set, then PREfast will check any pointers used when calling this function to ensure that they can be verified to be valid, as demonstrated by the code in Listing 13-5.

Listing 13-5. *Using the Pre Attribute*

```
#include <CodeAnalysis\SourceAnnotations.h>
using namespace vc_attributes;

void f ([Pre(NullTerminated=Yes)] char* str);
```

```
int main ( )
{
    char x[100];
    f(x); // error C6054 - x is not null-terminated
}
```

Listing 13-6 shows an example of using the Post attribute to specify conditions on how the function handles the return value. The attribute contains a tag that specifies that this attribute applies to the return value, not the function as a whole.

Listing 13-6. *Using the Post Attribute*

```
// checkreturn.cpp
#include <stdio.h>
#include <codeanalysis\sourceannotations.h>
using namespace vc_attributes;
[returnvalue:Post(MustCheck=Yes)]
int f()
{
    FILE* fp;
    fopen_s(&fp, "file1.txt", "rw+");
    if (fp == NULL)
        return -1;
    fprintf_s(fp, "add some text");
    fclose(fp);
    return 0;
}

int main()
{
    f();  // triggers an error, C6031 since the return value is not checked
}
```

In this case, the output is as follows:

```
Microsoft (R) 32-bit C/C++ Optimizing Compiler Version 14.00.50727.42 for 80x86
Copyright (C) Microsoft Corporation.  All rights reserved.

checkreturn.cpp
c:\PREfast_code\checkreturn.cpp(19) : warning C6031:
 Return value ignored: 'f'
Microsoft (R) Incremental Linker Version 8.00.50727.42
Copyright (C) Microsoft Corporation.  All rights reserved.

/out:checkreturn.exe
checkreturn.obj
```

Remember that using the /analyze option is not a guarantee that there are no potential problems with the code. It is actually rather easy to fool PREfast, as the example in Listing 13-7 demonstrates.

Listing 13-7. *Missed PREfast Check*

```cpp
// annotated_function.cpp

#include <iostream>
#include <CodeAnalysis/SourceAnnotations.h>
using namespace std;
using namespace vc_attributes;

void f( [Pre(NullTerminated = Yes)] char* str)
{
    cout << str << endl;
}

int main()
{
    // create a string that is not null-terminated
    char test[5] = { 'a', 'b', 'c', 'd' };
    f( test ); // error not flagged

    char* s = (char*) malloc(10 * sizeof (char));
    f(s); // error not flagged

    char s1[10] = "abcdefgh";
    char* s2 =  (char*) malloc(5 * sizeof (char));
    if (s2 != NULL)
        s2 = strncpy(s2, s1, 5);
    f(s2); // error not flagged
}
```

If you run this example with the Visual C++ 2005 compiler with the /analyze option, the use of non-null terminated strings is not detected. The bottom line is that you should run PREfast to catch errors, but you cannot use it as a substitute for any other testing or validation.

Using FxCop

FxCop has been offered as a stand-alone tool since the release of Visual Studio 2002 and .NET Framework version 1.0. It was originally written as a tool to check the work of the Microsoft .NET development teams because it was the only way to ensure consistency in naming conventions, implementation, and overall structure. You will want to use it to perform these checks on your own code.

■Tip FxCop is still offered in a stand-alone format. It is available for download from www.gotdotnet.com.

Enabling FxCop

Up until now, whenever you have done a build, the compiler has gone through and compiled the code, checking for compile errors and nothing else. FxCop is not enabled by default.

To enable FxCop, right-click the project in the Solution Explorer, select Properties, select the Code Analysis node, and check Enable Code Analysis. Alternatively, for a web application, you can select Website ➤ Code Analysis Configuration from the main menu, and then check Enable Code Analysis. After you have enabled code analysis, build the solution. No other steps are necessary to run the code analysis.

■Note Depending on the size of your code base, it can take considerably longer to build a project with FxCop enabled. Rather than enabling FxCop on every build, you should consider running the code analyzer only after you have added a lot of working code that you do not intend to change.

You can also analyze code without performing a build by selecting Build ➤ Run Code Analysis on [*project name*] from the main menu.

Examining FxCop Results

To demonstrate how FxCop works, enable it for the project you created in Chapter 12 (right-click the EffortTrackingServiceTests project in the Solution Explorer, select Properties, select the Code Analysis node, and check Enable Code Analysis), and then build the solution. The results of the build should look those in Figure 13-1.

■Note For the examples in this chapter, you can also use the downloadable code available from the Source Code section of the Apress website (www.apress.com). The code for this chapter contains only methods with no implementation of those methods.

Realize that all of the information reported by the code analysis is reported as a warning; the results are not errors. (Although you can configure them to be errors, as described in the upcoming "Configuring FxCop Rules" section.) Nothing shown here will stop your code from running. Everything is a suggestion based on the code analyzer rules. When running automated builds using Team Foundation Build, these warnings can be logged to the Team Foundation Server, and they can show up in a report later.

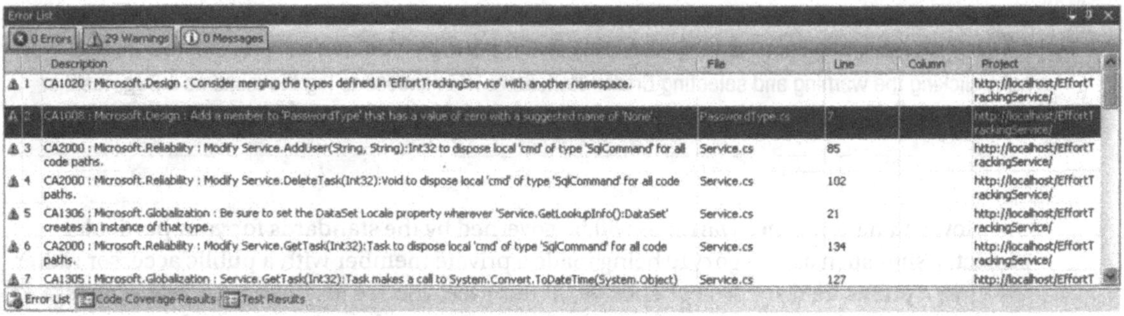

Figure 13-1. *FxCop code analysis warnings*

Tip You can sort the results of an FxCop run, just as can sort any other pieces of information that are displayed in the Error List window. Sorting the list by description will sort the warnings by category.

Let's take a look at the warning highlighted in Figure 13-1:

```
CA1008: Microsoft.Design: Add a member to 'PasswordType' that has a value of zero
with a suggested name of 'None'.
```

The first part of the line, CA1008, is the rule number (also called CheckID). Microsoft.Design is the category under which the warning is classified. The last part of the line is the rule that was broken and a suggested way of fixing it. To get further information about the rule, right-click the rule and select Show Error Help. This opens a web page (for built-in rules, this page is displayed in the online help window) with detailed information about the warning, including why it is a warning and how to fix it. Now, in this case, do you want follow this suggestion? Yes and no. The first value in an enum should always be zero, but the name should not be None. (This particular issue is fixed in the downloadable code for other chapters.)

You'll find that many of the FxCop rules are not applicable to a given circumstance. One of the advantages of FxCop is that it is fully customizable. You can suppress rules and configure rules, as described in the following sections.

Scan through the rest of the list to determine if there are any items that really should be fixed (also, this is a good overview of the types of issues that FxCop can help you catch). The four items that should jump out at you are the naming conventions regarding the term ID. FxCop correctly notifies you that ID is an abbreviation and not an acronym, and therefore it should be correctly cased as Id. Fix each of these four items in the Task structure. Rebuilding the solution will remove each of these warning from the list. In addition, each object in C# should be declared in a namespace, so this is also a valid warning you would want to fix.

Tip If you recognize that a warning is an issue that needs to be fixed, you can also create a work item by right-clicking the warning and selecting Create Work Item. Then choose to log the issue as a Bug, Task, or Quality of Service item. Work items are discussed in Chapter 5.

How you handle other warnings will be governed by the standards for your particular project. Issues such as CategoryID being made a private member with a public accessor rather than just a public field are project-specific. In this case, you are just using the Task structure to serialize your data, so these rules do not apply here. The key benefit is that FxCop provides guidelines, and you can apply them as appropriate.

Suppressing Messages

If you do not want a rule that you see in the results applied in a particular case, say to the PasswordType enum in our example, you can remove it from the list of checked rules by right-clicking it and selecting Suppress Message(s). At this point, the rule is not removed, but is changed to a strike-through font to indicate it is no longer checked. In addition, the SuppressMessage attribute is added to the type, as shown here:

```
[System.Diagnostics.CodeAnalysis.SuppressMessage("Microsoft.Design", "CA1008:
EnumsShouldHaveZeroValue")]
```

This is called an In Source Suppression (ISS). The SuppressMessage attribute has a number of options; this is just the default. The constructor parameters for the SuppressMessage attribute are shown in Table 13-2.

Table 13-2. *SuppressMessage Attribute Constructor Parameters*

Parameter	Description
Category	Category under which the rule is classified
CheckId	The identifier for the rule
Justification	Should be used to indicate why a rule has not been followed (it is often important to note why a developer is not following a particular coding convention)
MessageId	The name of the method to which the suppression applies
Scope	Identifies where the scope of the suppression; valid values are Module, Namespace, Resource, Type, Member, and Parameter
Target	Indicates the full namespace of the target method or namespace.

Messages can be suppressed at various levels of the application. To insert a suppression line at the module level, use the SuppressMessage attribute in the following way:

```
[module: SuppressMessage(. . .)]
```

To unsuppress a message, just delete the attribute from the code file.

Configuring FxCop Rules

To view the list of rules that are available in FxCop (and any custom rules) select Website (or Project if you are creating a Windows Forms application) ➤ Code Analysis Configuration. This will bring up the dialog box shown in Figure 13-2. Notice that this dialog box also contains an Enable Code Analysis check box, which you can check to enable FxCop scanning during the build process.

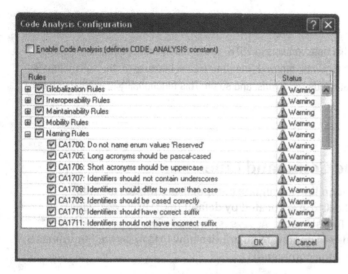

Figure 13-2. *The Code Analysis Configuration dialog box*

The predefined rules are divided into nine categories, as described in Table 13-3.

Table 13-3. *FxCop Rule Categories*

Category	No. of Rules	Description
Design	63	Rules related to the application architecture, such as when to use certain pieces of functionality and rules regarding generics
Globalization	6	Rules regarding the globalization of an application
Interoperability	15	COM and platform invoke rules to help ensure compatibility across systems
Maintainability	3	Rules designed to make application maintenance easier
Naming	25	Rules relating to the naming of methods, parameters, variables, and classes
Performance	20	Rules that can help improve performance such as when boxing becomes an issue
Reliability	7	Rules that help prevent memory leaks
Security	26	Rules to help prevent potential security issues such as SQL injection attacks
Usage	41	Rules to help in proper usage of classes, attributes, parameters, and various other pieces of code

Notice that, by default, all of the rules have a status of Warning. You can change the status to Error simply by double-clicking the status for the rule (and double-click Error to change it back to Warning). This allows you to mark rules as errors, which will prevent your code from running after a build if certain rules are violated. Again, this will depend on the specific requirements of your project or organization.

You can disable rule checking on certain rules or on all rules by unchecking the box next to the specific rules or categories.

Note If you have used the FxCop tool in beta versions of VSTS, you probably noticed that there were checks for correct spelling. This functionality was removed from the release because of the lack of time for building in the management of additional words, acronyms, and so on. This functionality is expected to be included in an upcoming release.

Running FxCop from the Command Line

You can run FxCop from the command line to validate compiled assemblies outside Visual Studio. The executable is `FxCopCmd.exe`, located by default in `C:\Program Files\ Microsoft Visual Studio 8\Team Tools\Static Analysis Tools\FxCop`.

You can use various command-line options to customize how FxCop is run. For information about these rules, run the following command:

```
FxCopCmd /?
```

Creating Custom FxCop Rules

You can extend the capabilities of FxCop by creating your own rules. These rules can be placed in any category or a custom category you create.

Note In VSTS version 1, rules cannot be pulled from a central area. You need to deploy the custom FxCop rules on each machine that has the VSTS client on it in order for everyone to be able to use those rules.

Before you create custom rules, it helps to know where FxCop lives and where you will eventually need to deploy your custom rules. FxCop is located in `C:\Program Files\ Microsoft Visual Studio 8\Team Tools\Static Analysis Tools\FxCop`. The `Engines` folder contains any rules processing engines (in this case, only `IntrospectionAnalysisEngine.dll`). The `Rules` folder contains all of the default rules that ship with VSTS. The `XML` folder contains XSL transformations for use in displaying the output from the FxCop tool.

■**Note** FxCop used to have two different engines to process rules: the Reflection engine and the Introspection engine. The Reflection engine was phased out starting with version 1.30 of FxCop. The version of FxCop that comes with VSTS processes rules exclusively through the Introspection engine. Any rules that you have from the Reflection engine will need to be migrated. See the MSDN documentation for guidelines for migrating rules.

As an example, you will create a rule to check to see that any privately declared fields that have a class scope are prefixed with an underscore (_). While this is not an official naming convention, it has become very common and is an easy way to help differentiate class-scoped private fields.

■**Note** In VB, the common naming convention is to use an m_ or just an m to prefix a module- or class-scoped variable. You are certainly welcome to change the example here to check for that, but the underscore is becoming the standard prefix for these types of fields.

A rule is composed of the rule class that validates a rule and a rule file (XML) that contains details and guidance concerning the rule (displayed to the user if the rule is broken). First, you'll create the project for the custom rule, and then you'll create the rule class and the rule file.

Creating the Custom Rule Project

You can have more than one rule in an assembly, so a good naming practice (and the practice that Microsoft uses) is to create one assembly per category of rule and include all of the rules for that category in the assembly. The naming convention should be something like [Company][Category]Rules.dll, where Company is the company the rules are being created for and Category is the category to which the rules in the assembly belong.

Follow these steps to start a new project for the rule and add a reference to FxCopSdk.dll and Microsoft.Cci.dll.

1. Create a new project called OrgNamingRules.

2. Right-click the References node and select Add Reference.

3. Select the Browse tab and browse to C:\Program Files\Microsoft Visual Studio 8\ Team Tools\Static Analysis Tools\FxCop. Select FxCopSdk.dll and Microsoft.Cci.dll, and then click OK.

■**Caution** The Introspection SDK has not been released. The information contained in this chapter comes largely from the FxCop team and a reverse-engineering of the FxCop SDK and IntrospectionAnalysisEngine assembly. Visit the GotDotNet website (www.gotdotnet.com) to check for a release of the Introspection SDK. Microsoft has said that this will likely be released after VSTS ships. At this point, it is an entirely unsupported feature and is not guaranteed to remain the same for VSTS version 2.

Creating the Rule Class

Microsoft's convention is to create one base rule per rule category, which is what you will do here. This way, the constructor is a little simpler and the type of each rule is clear.

All of your custom rules should inherit from the BaseIntrospectionRule class.

Delete the Class1 class, which is created by default, and create a new class called BaseOrgNamingRule. Import the Microsoft.Tools.FxCop.Sdk.Introspection namespace into this new class file. As shown in Listing 13-8, set the class as abstract and so it inherits from the BaseIntrospectionRule, and then create the two constructors for the class. The default constructor will call the second constructor. The second constructor (the one that takes the name argument) will be used by all of the classes that inherit from the BaseOrgNamingRule class.

Listing 13-8. *OrgNamingRule Base Rule*

```csharp
C#
public abstract class OrgNamingRule:BaseIntrospectionRule
{
    protected BaseOrgNamingRule() : this("BaseOrgNamingRule") { }
    protected BaseOrgNamingRule (string name) :
         base(name, "OrgNamingRules.Rules", typeof(BaseOrgNamingRule).Assembly) { }
}
```

```vbnet
VB
Public MustInherit Class BaseOrgNamingRule : Inherits BaseIntrospectionRule
    Protected Sub New()
        Me.New("BaseOrgNamingRule")
    End Sub
    Protected Sub New(ByVal name As String)
        MyBase.New(name, "OrgNamingRules.Rules",_
        GetType(BaseOrgNamingRule).Assembly)
    End Sub
End Class
```

You now have a custom, base FxCop rule from which all of your other rules can inherit.

To create the actual rule, add a new class to your project called UnderscorePrefixRule. Add the following lines (replace using with Imports in VB):

```csharp
using Microsoft.FxCop.Sdk.Introspection;
using Microsoft.FxCop.Sdk;
```

Set the class to inherit from the BaseOrgNamingRule class and add a constructor and the Check method, as shown in Listing 13-9.

Listing 13-9. *UnderscorePrefixRule FxCop Custom Rule*

C#

```
public class UnderscorePrefixRule:BaseOrgNamingRule
{
    public UnderscorePrefixRule() : base("UnderscorePrefixRule") { }

    public override ProblemCollection Check(Microsoft.Cci.Member member)
    {
        if (member == null || member.IsPublic)
        {
            return null;
        }

        if (member.NodeType == Microsoft.Cci.NodeType.Field)
        {
            if (!member.Name.Name.StartsWith("_"))
            {
                string[] textArray1 =
                    new string[1] { RuleUtilities.Format(member) };
                Resolution resolution1 =
                    this.GetNamedResolution("Member", textArray1);
                Problem problem1 = new Problem(resolution1, "Member");
                base.Problems.Add(problem1);
                return base.Problems;
            }
            else
            {
                return null;
            }
        }
        else
        {
            return null;
        }
    }
}
```

VB

```
Public Class UnderscorePrefixRule : Inherits BaseOrgNamingRule
    Public Sub New()
        MyBase.New("UnderscorePrefixRule")
    End Sub

    Public Overrides Function Check(ByVal member As Microsoft.Cci.Member) As _
        ProblemCollection
```

```
                If member is Nothing OrElse member.IsPublic Then
                    Return Nothing
                End If

        If member.NodeType = Microsoft.Cci.NodeType.Field Then
                If Not member.Name.Name.StartsWith("_") Then
                    Dim textArray1 As String() = _
                        New String(0) {RuleUtilities.Format(member)}
                    Dim resolution1 As Resolution = _
                        Me.GetNamedResolution("Member", textArray1)
                    Dim problem1 As Problem = New Problem(resolution1)
                    Me.Problems.Add(problem1)
                    Return Me.Problems
                Else
                    Return Nothing
                End If
            Else
                Return Nothing
            End If
        End Function
End Class
```

In order to create your own rule, you must override the Check method. This method is overloaded to accept various types as arguments. The member type passes any members of a class—that is, fields, events, delegates, properties, methods, and so on. There are five overloaded methods of Check that can be used to gather information from your project or assembly. The member overload will probably be the most used method.

In the UnderscorePrefixRule, the Check method does the following:

- Check to see if the member being examined is a public member. If it is, the rule is skipped because we want to check only private fields.

- If the type of the member is a field, continue with the check; otherwise, skip the rule.

- If the member name does not start with an underscore, continue with the check; otherwise, skip the rule.

- If the rule was broken, format the member name for display (RuleUtilities is a method in the FxCop SDK for formatting output) and set any values that are needed by the resolution string.

- Get the resolution text from the rule information file and pass it any parameters (in this case, the name of the rule). (Resolutions are discussed in the next section.)

- Create a new Problem object and pass it the resolution of the problem.

- Add the Problem to the Problem collection and exit the method.

This is a fairly straightforward example, but these rules can become extremely complicated and detailed.

Creating the XML Rule File

The rule file contains all of the details regarding the rule that was broken. By default, the rule file is named Rules.xml and is an embedded resource file within the project. Typically, there is one rule file per assembly, and all of the rule information goes in this file. The schema for this file is shown in Listing 13-10.

■**Note** The schema in Listing 13-10 is not complete. Microsoft has yet to release documentation for the Introspection engine. Here, we show the result of research using the Reflection tool from Lutz Roeder (www.aisto.com/roeder/dotnet/). The FxCop team will be releasing detailed documentation of the Introspection engine as soon as possible.

Listing 13-10. *Rule File XML Schema*

```xml
<?xml version="1.0" encoding="utf-8"?>
<xs:schema attributeFormDefault="unqualified" elementFormDefault="qualified"
xmlns:xs="http://www.w3.org/2001/XMLSchema">
  <xs:element name="Rules">
    <xs:complexType>
      <xs:sequence>
        <xs:element name="Rule">
          <xs:complexType>
            <xs:sequence>
              <xs:element name="Name" type="xs:string" />
              <xs:element name="Description" type="xs:string" />
              <xs:element name="LongDescription" type="xs:string" />
              <xs:element name="GroupOwner" type="xs:string" />
              <xs:element name="DevOwner" type="xs:string" />
              <xs:element name="Owner" type="xs:string" />
              <xs:element name="Url" type="xs:string" />
              <xs:element maxOccurs="unbounded" name="Resolution">
                <xs:complexType>
                  <xs:simpleContent>
                    <xs:extension base="xs:string">
                      <xs:attribute name="Name" type="xs:string" use="required" />
                    </xs:extension>
                  </xs:simpleContent>
                </xs:complexType>
              </xs:element>
              <xs:element name="Email" type="xs:string" />
              <xs:element name="MessageLevel">
                <xs:complexType>
                  <xs:simpleContent>
                    <xs:extension base="xs:string">
                      <xs:attribute name="Certainty" type="xs:unsignedByte"
```

```
                        use="required" />
                </xs:extension>
             </xs:simpleContent>
           </xs:complexType>
         </xs:element>
         <xs:element name="FixCategories" type="xs:string" />
       </xs:sequence>
       <xs:attribute name="TypeName" type="xs:string" use="required" />
       <xs:attribute name="Category" type="xs:string" use="required" />
       <xs:attribute name="CheckId" type="xs:string" use="required" />
     </xs:complexType>
    </xs:element>
   </xs:sequence>
   <xs:attribute name="FriendlyName" type="xs:string" use="required" />
  </xs:complexType>
 </xs:element>
</xs:schema>
```

For this example, add an XML file named `Rules.xml` to your project. The complete text of this file is shown in Listing 13-11.

■**Caution** The rule filename must match the fully qualified name of the rule as specified in the base rule constructor (in this case, it is `OrgNamingRules.Rules`, without the xml). While the filename is `Rules`, the root namespace for the project is `OrgNamingRules`, so this must prefix the filename in the constructor.

Listing 13-11. *The Rules.xml File for the UnderscorePrefixRule*

```
<Rules FriendlyName="Organization Naming Rules">
<Rule TypeName="UnderscorePrefixRule" Category="Organization.Naming"
CheckId="OR5555">
   <Name>
     UnderscorePrefixRule: Prefix private class scoped variables (fields)
         with an underscore  "_").
   </Name>
   <Description>
     The [organization name]'s naming standards require an underscore
         to be prefixed to private fields in all cases.
   </Description>
   <LongDescription>
     The underscore is a visual indication that a variable is a private,
         class scoped field and is used for ease of reading and to
         differentiate between class fields and local variables within methods.
   </LongDescription>
   <GroupOwner>
     [organization] Developer Standards Group
```

```
      </GroupOwner>
      <DevOwner>
        John Smith
      </DevOwner>
      <Owner>
        [organization] Developer Standards Group
      </Owner>
      <Url>
        http://localhost/organizationrules/default.aspx
      </Url>
      <Resolution Name="Member">Add an underscore in front of the field {0}.
            </Resolution>
      <Email>
        OrganizationStandards@organization.com
      </Email>
      <MessageLevel Certainty="80">
        Error
      </MessageLevel>
      <FixCategories>
        NonBreaking
      </FixCategories>
    </Rule>
</Rules>
```

Table 13-4 describes each of the nodes in Listing 13-11.

Table 13-4. *Rules.xsd Nodes*

Node Name/Attribute	Description
Rules	Root node. It contains a collection of Rule elements.
FriendlyName	The name displayed in the Code Analysis Configuration dialog box.
Rule	Describes an individual rule.
TypeName	The name of the .NET type that contains the rule.
Category	Displayed when the rule is broken to help categorize the broken rule.
CheckId	Unique identifier for the rule. The ID is two characters followed by four digits.
Name	The name of the rule followed by a very brief description.
Description	A short description of the rule.
LongDescription	A detailed description of the rule.
GroupOwner	The group that developed the rule. In an organization, this would typically be the group in charge of development standards.
DevOwner	The developer who wrote the rule.
Owner	The person or group who owns the rule.
Url	The URL of the web page that contains detailed information about the rule, including code examples and where to go for more information.

Continued

Table 13-4. *Continued*

Node Name/Attribute	Description
Resolution	A series of named resolutions. The resolution names should correspond with the types with which a problem can be associated. For example, a certain type of resolution may exist for members in general, or one resolution may refer to a field problem or another with a property problem for the same rule. There can be multiple named resolutions.
Name	The name of the resolution. This is used to specify which resolution to take to solve a given problem.
Email	The e-mail address where queries regarding the rule can be sent.
MessageLevel	Describes the type of level. This can be Error, Warning, or Information and corresponds with the ability to filter messages in the Error List window.
Certainty	The level of certainty that the rule really has been broken or really is a problem.
FixCategories	This is either Breaking or NonBreaking. A breaking rule indicates that the functionality will not be consistent from one version to the next if this rule is not fixed.

When you have added the Rules.xml file shown in Listing 13-11, you can then compile the project. Copy the resulting assembly to the FxCop Rules folder (C:\Program Files\ Microsoft Visual Studio 8\Team Tools\Static Analysis Tools\FxCop\Rules).

Note If you examine the list of rules, you will note that the new rule you created is listed there, but there is no CheckId. This is a known issue but does not affect how FxCop runs or checks rules.

Close all instances of Visual Studio and then reopen Visual Studio. Create any type of project and add a class field without the underscore in front of the name. Run the code analysis on the project. Your Error List window should show the rule violation, as in Figure 13-3.

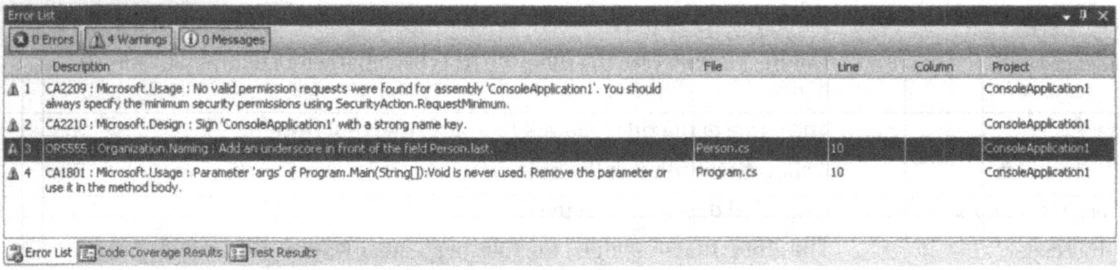

Figure 13-3. *The UnderscorePrefixRule custom FxCop rule implemented*

Pressing F1 on a violated rule will take you to the web page (or the part of the help file) specified by the Url value. Microsoft includes the following on the help pages to aid in fixing the problem:

- *Cause:* Why the rule was broken.

- *Rule Description:* What the rule means.

- *How to Fix Violations:* The changes to make.

- *When to Exclude Warnings:* If it is permissible to exclude this type of warning, this explains when you can exclude it.

- *Example Code:* An example of the incorrect and correct versions of code.

If you open the Code Analysis Configuration dialog box, you'll see your custom rule listed under the Organization Naming Rules node.

Summary

In this chapter, you learned how to perform static code analysis to identify potential problem areas and known defects. Using the PREfast tool, you can eliminate a majority of the problems that may cause your code to have potential security holes and other instabilities. You can suppress messages and ensure that some messages are treated as warnings and others are treated as errors. On the whole, this makes working with C/C++ code much safer.

With the FxCop tool, you can ensure that your code is compliant with the latest Microsoft specifications for writing .NET code. This provides a well-structured, robust code base, which you can expand easily. In addition, as an organization using this tool to enforce coding standards specific to your needs, you can provide custom rules or more advanced rule checking than the defaults provided by FxCop. Combined with the check-in policy feature of VSTS (discussed in Chapter 3), FxCop can ensure that code created with VSTS conforms to your organization's standards.

CHAPTER 14

■■■

Performance Analysis

Testing application performance has always been one of the most difficult things to do. The reasons for this are varied, but mostly it is because performance is just plain difficult to effectively test. For example, how do you know from one test to another which one is accurate? What are you actually performing the test on? Is it the method level or the application level? How do you modify the application to test for performance? Once you are done with the test, how do you interpret the results? How do you know, when you think you are measuring something, that it is all you are measuring (in other words, that you are measuring the subject of the test and not collateral processes)? These and many other questions have, in the past, been very difficult to answer.

Visual Studio Team System aims to help solve these problems and make sense of application performance so you can do the following:

- Assess your application performance before deployment.

- Fix those areas that are performing poorly.

- Verify that the performance quality attributes have been met.

- Monitor production application performance as needed.

In addition, VSTS allows you to understand the results of a performance test. The results of the test are very clearly displayed and easily understood and traced. By traced, we mean that the call stack can be followed to determine the performance of each call made in a chain of calls.

Note The performance tool in VSTS can be used to monitor your applications' performance without logging items to the performance monitor built into Windows. Though this was easier with previous versions of .NET, it was still not "easy" if you wanted to get information that matters to you.

With previous versions of Visual Studio, running performance tests (without the use of very expensive tools) consisted of outputting data to log files or to the Windows Performance Monitor and trying to make sense of these values. In the case of the Performance Monitor, sometimes it is difficult to figure out if you are logging valid information. Performance monitoring in VSTS does away with all of those issues.

This chapter focuses on how to profile an application using the VSTS performance tools, understanding the results of a profile, and identifying performance bottlenecks in an application. In addition, this chapter covers how to profile a production application, which is useful if end users are having performance issues but cannot articulate them well to the development team.

■**Note** Users, when they experience performance problems, are typically unable to provide details on where and when the problems occur in an application. In addition, how do you determine if the problem is your application or another process running on the same system? Because of this, monitoring the performance of a production application is invaluable.

Performance Profiling Terms

Before you get into actually using the performance tools, a few terms need to be explained. This section is intended for those who have not worked with performance profiling and analysis tools before.

■**Note** There is a great deal more to performance profiling and analysis, in an overall sense, than is indicated in this chapter. This chapter focuses on how VSTS performance tools work, rather than on an overall review of how performance analysis is done.

Table 14-1 defines the terms that will help you understand what is presented in this chapter.

Table 14-1. *Performance Terms*

Term	Definition
Sampling	The process of taking periodic "samples" of application processes. This includes incrementing a counter for the currently executing function and recording the call stack leading to this function.
Instrumentation	The process of taking detailed measurements of all aspects of code execution. The code, during compilation, is altered to allow the performance tool to monitor entry and exit times of each and every function in the application.
Application time	A measure of the time the application code is executing. This does not include OS calls or any time spent waiting for threads to execute.
Elapsed time	A total measure of system time spent during a functions time. In other words, the elapsed time is the "clock" time (absolute time) and includes all system and other events.
Exclusive	Information gathered from the executing function, and does not include any subfunctions.

Term	Definition
Inclusive	Information gathered from the executing function and all of the subfunctions.
Exclusive allocations	The allocation of type instances (or memory) that occur only within the given function.
Inclusive allocations	The allocation of type instances (or memory) that occur within the function and in all subfunctions called by the given function.
Instrumenting	The process of inserting probes into the code to record data.
Probes	Code placed within the source code to monitor function start/stop times and other relevant information.
Transition events	Events that occur outside of the application time. The application time + transition events time = elapsed time.
Trace	Another way of saying the application was profiled using instrumentation.
Exclusive bytes allocated	The number of bytes allocated during the execution of a given function, excluding any subfunctions.
Inclusive bytes allocated	The number of bytes allocated during the execution of a given function and any subfunctions.

Instrumentation

As defined previously, *instrumentation* is a process that results in the gathering of comprehensive data relating to the performance of an application. To show you how this works, Listing 14-1 shows a simple console application in C# that writes a line to the console and waits for the user to press a key to end the application.

Listing 14-1. *C# Console Application*

```
static void Main(string[] args)
{
    Console.WriteLine("This is a test.");
    Console.ReadLine();
}
```

Listing 14-2 shows the exact same application after it has been instrumented by the performance tool.

Listing 14-2. *C# Instrumented Console Application*

```
private static void Main(string[] args)
{
    1 _CAP_Enter_Function_Managed((int)    Microsoft.VisualStudio.Instrumentation.
        g_fldMMID_2D71B909-C28E-4fd9-A0E7-ED05264B707A, 0x6000005);
    2 _CAP_StartProfiling_Managed((int) Microsoft.VisualStudio.Instrumentation.
        g_fldMMID_2D71B909-C28E-4fd9-A0E7-ED05264B707A, 0x6000005, 0xa000010);
    3 Console.WriteLine("This is a test.");
```

```
  4 _CAP_StopProfiling_Managed((int) Microsoft.VisualStudio.Instrumentation.
      g_fldMMID_2D71B909-C28E-4fd9-A0E7-ED05264B707A, 0x6000005);
  5 _CAP_StartProfiling_Managed((int) Microsoft.VisualStudio.Instrumentation.
      g_fldMMID_2D71B909-C28E-4fd9-A0E7-ED05264B707A, 0x6000005, 0xa000011);
  6 _CAP_StopProfiling_Managed((int) Microsoft.VisualStudio.Instrumentation.
      g_fldMMID_2D71B909-C28E-4fd9-A0E7-ED05264B707A, 0x6000005);
  7 Console.ReadLine();
  8 _CAP_Exit_Function_Managed((int) Microsoft.VisualStudio.Instrumentation.
      g_fldMMID_2D71B909-C28E-4fd9-A0E7-ED05264B707A, 0x6000005);
}
```

■**Note** The line breaks are for formatting purposes. There are really only eight lines of code here as denoted by the line numbers for clarity.

This illustrates how instrumentation alters the code to gather data. The key thing to note in this example is that instrumentation does add overhead to an application. Is it such a large amount of overhead that you could not do this in production? No. It is not recommended that you instrument a production application—but you can do it. The real issue is that, compared to a noninstrumented application, the performance is slower.

■**Caution** Instrumenting production applications as a matter of course should not be done. It is best done when you know there is a problem with the application and you need to pinpoint it using the performance tools. For day-to-day monitoring of applications, sampling provides better performance and over the longer term will help you narrow down the area of performance problems.

With this implementation, the performance tool can tell how long a function takes to execute, how long subfunctions take to execute, how many times a function is called, and other detailed information. This is the real power of instrumentation: the ability to know everything about an application while it is running. However, there is a drawback to this. Instrumentation uses averages and totals. It does not display information about single calls.

■**Tip** To get information about specific calls, you can instrument an application and run it through one set test at a time; however it can be somewhat tedious.

Sampling

Sampling, as defined in Table 14-1, takes periodic "snapshots" of your application as it is running. It gathers the current function information and the call stack and stores it for later analysis. It does not alter the code output from a build. Instead, the performance tool "interrupts" a running application to gather data at a user-defined interval.

The information provided by sampling is not a complete picture of the application. It does not include information such as the amount of time spent in a function, or the time spent in anything, for that matter. It simply provides information on the number of times a method is invoked, and how many other types are allocated during the invocation. This provides indirect evidence of how an application is performing. A method being called too many times may indicate a problem with how the code is structured.

On the other hand, sampling does not provide information on all the functions in your application. Since it takes only periodic readings, you may not see the allocation information for a method you are curious about. This is one of the drawbacks of using sampling.

Running a Performance Test

Now that you understand the differences between instrumentation and sampling it is time to actually run a performance test and examine the results.

■**Note** For comparison purposes later on, this exact test was run twice: once with instrumentation selected and once with sampling selected.

---

1. Open the sample application.

2. Select Tools ➤ Performance Tools ➤ Performance Wizard.

3. Select the default profile by clicking Next (see Figure 14-1).

4. Select the Instrumentation test and click Next.

5. Click the Finish button.

6. Next, the Performance Explorer will open (see Figure 14-2).

7. Right-click the root node in the Performance Explorer (EffortTrackingWeb.psess) and select Properties.

8. On the General tab of the properties dialog check the "Collect .NET object allocation information" and the "Also collection .NET object lifetime information" options and click OK (this dialog will be covered in detail in the section "Performance Session Options" later in this chapter).

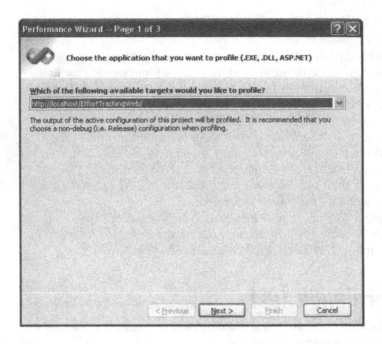

Figure 14-1. *Performance Wizard page 1*

The Performance Explorer window opens with one test that is set to be run on the EffortTrackingWeb and there are no reports. Before running the test, build the application using the Release configuration. To launch the application, click the Launch button on the Performance Tools toolbar and not the regular Run button.

For this first test, keep things simple and perform the following steps:

1. Enter new user login information (username = **PerformanceUser**, password = **password**, Verify Password= **password**) and click New User.

2. Click the Add button.

3. Enter **Chapter 1** for the title, **Read it** for the description.

4. Leave all of the other drop-downs as they are and click Save.

5. After the default screen reloads, select the entry you just added by clicking the Edit link.

6. Change the title to "Test" and click Save.

7. Exit the application.

As you can see, running a performance test is straightforward and simple. There are no additional steps. You just need to remember to launch the test from the Performance Explorer.

■**Tip** When running an instrumented performance test, the probes are inserted during compile, but after the test is run, binaries are reverted. This means that the probes are removed! The code used for a performance test cannot be instrumented for deployment using this process. This is discussed later in the section "Profiling Production Applications."

Understanding the Performance Report

Figure 14-2 shows the results of your first test of the performance analysis tool, and the Performance Explorer (if the report does not show up, double-click the report in the Performance Explorer). In this section you will examine each of the parts of the performance report and learn how to understand the information presented. Each page of the report provides information about your application with a different view into the data. Later you will see how to use the information to improve your application performance.

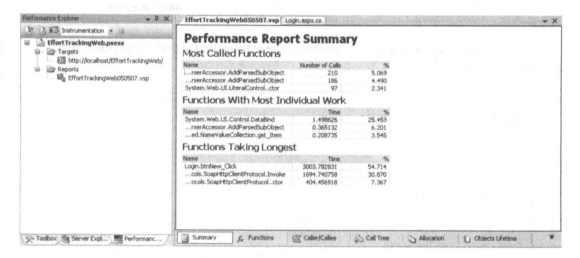

Figure 14-2. *Performance Report Summary (Instrumentation) and Explorer*

Summary Tab

The summary page contains general statistics about your application. Some of the properties (such as the number of most called functions) can be changed via the options dialog, which you will see later in this chapter. Also, each of the tabs displays different information, depending on whether you ran a sampled or instrumented performance test. The differences for each will be discussed in the following sections.

The summary for a performance test using sampling displays other information. The information presented is summarized and described in Table 14-2.

Table 14-2. *Summary Tab Description*

Type	Measurement	Description
Instrumentation	Most Called Functions	List of functions that were called the most.
Instrumentation	Functions With Most Individual Work	List of functions that, exclusively, took the longest time to execute.
Instrumentation	Functions Taking Longest	List of functions that, exclusively, but including application time, took the longest to execute.
Sampling	Functions Allocating Most Memory	List of functions that allocated the most bytes.
Sampling	Types With Most Allocated Memory	List of types and how many bytes were allocated to instances of that type.
Sampling	Types With Most Instances	List of types that were instantiated the most.

For comparison purposes, the summary page of the sampled performance session is shown in Figure 14-3.

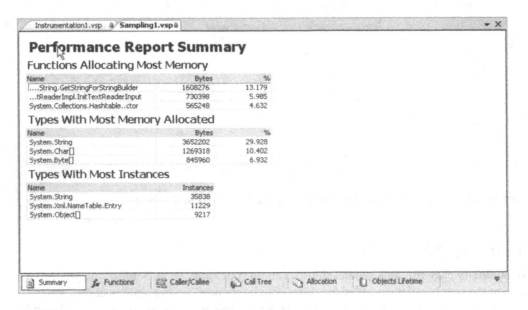

Figure 14-3. *Performance Report Summary (Sampling)*

Double-clicking any item on this page will take you to that item on the Functions view. Optionally you can right-click the item and select one of the following three choices: View Source Code (for non-Framework functions), the Function View for that method, and the Caller/Callee graph for that function (either the functions called by the function or the function that called the functions.

If you look through both reports (included with the downloaded code) you will note that some functions are just not listed in the sampled performance data. Those functions that are listed in both have a lower instance count in the sampled data vs. the instrumented data.

Functions Tab

The function page reports on each individual function (or just the sampled functions) called during the course of the testing run. Figure 14-4 shows one view of the Function tab of the performance report.

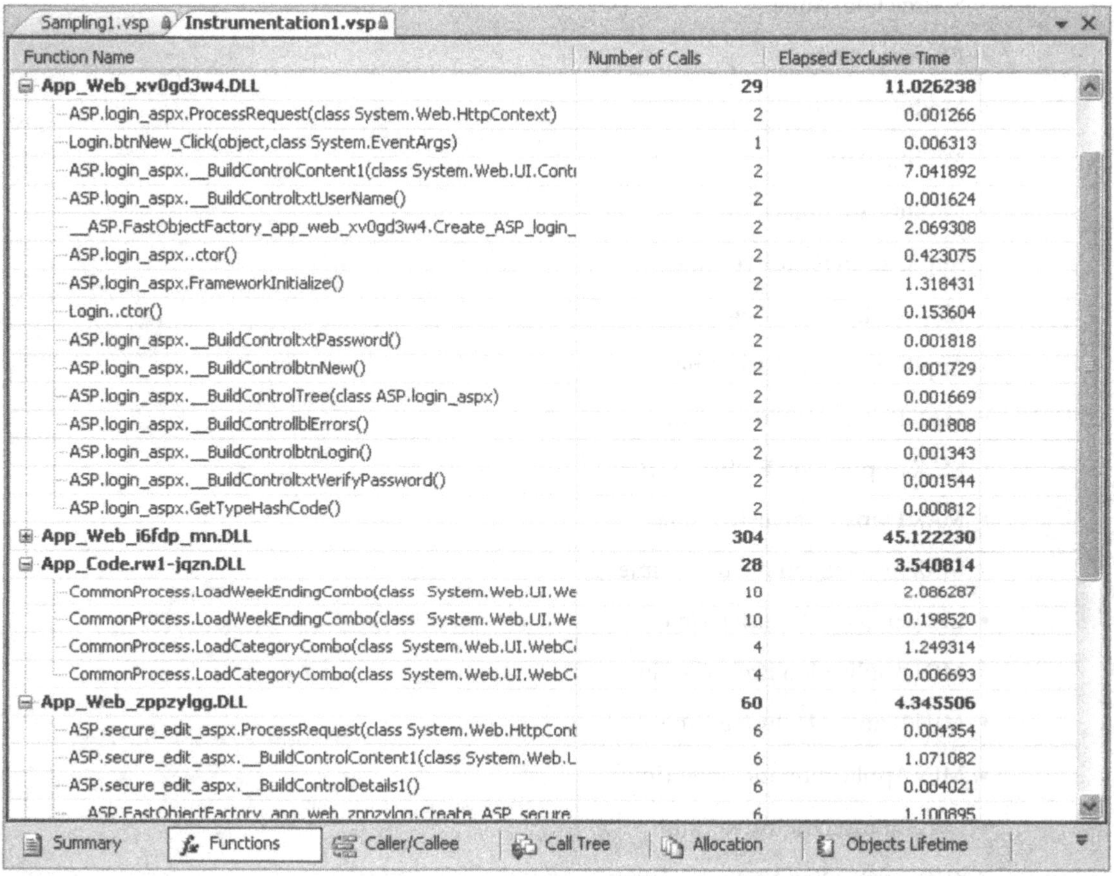

Function Name	Number of Calls	Elapsed Exclusive Time
⊟ App_Web_xv0gd3w4.DLL	29	11.026238
ASP.login_aspx.ProcessRequest(class System.Web.HttpContext)	2	0.001266
Login.btnNew_Click(object,class System.EventArgs)	1	0.006313
ASP.login_aspx.__BuildControlContent1(class System.Web.UI.Conti	2	7.041892
ASP.login_aspx.__BuildControltxtUserName()	2	0.001624
__ASP.FastObjectFactory_app_web_xv0gd3w4.Create_ASP_login_	2	2.069308
ASP.login_aspx..ctor()	2	0.423075
ASP.login_aspx.FrameworkInitialize()	2	1.318431
Login..ctor()	2	0.153604
ASP.login_aspx.__BuildControltxtPassword()	2	0.001818
ASP.login_aspx.__BuildControlbtnNew()	2	0.001729
ASP.login_aspx.__BuildControlTree(class ASP.login_aspx)	2	0.001669
ASP.login_aspx.__BuildControllblErrors()	2	0.001808
ASP.login_aspx.__BuildControlbtnLogin()	2	0.001343
ASP.login_aspx.__BuildControltxtVerifyPassword()	2	0.001544
ASP.login_aspx.GetTypeHashCode()	2	0.000812
⊞ App_Web_i6fdp_mn.DLL	304	45.122230
⊟ App_Code.rw1-jqzn.DLL	28	3.540814
CommonProcess.LoadWeekEndingCombo(class System.Web.UI.We	10	2.086287
CommonProcess.LoadWeekEndingCombo(class System.Web.UI.We	10	0.198520
CommonProcess.LoadCategoryCombo(class System.Web.UI.WebC	4	1.249314
CommonProcess.LoadCategoryCombo(class System.Web.UI.WebC	4	0.006693
⊟ App_Web_zppzylgg.DLL	60	4.345506
ASP.secure_edit_aspx.ProcessRequest(class System.Web.HttpCont	6	0.004354
ASP.secure_edit_aspx.__BuildControlContent1(class System.Web.L	6	1.071082
ASP.secure_edit_aspx.__BuildControlDetails1()	6	0.004021
ASP.FastObjectFactory_app_web_zppzylgg.Create_ASP_secure	6	1.100895

Sampling1.vsp Instrumentation1.vsp

📄 Summary   ƒ✗ Functions   📠 Caller/Callee   🔊 Call Tree   📇 Allocation   📄 Objects Lifetime

Figure 14-4. *Function tab of the Performance Report (Instrumentation)*

The columns on each of the tabs (with the exception of the Summary tab) are customizable. You can add or remove or change the order the columns are displayed in. To do this, right-click anywhere in the report window and select Add/Remove Columns. The list of columns for both types of performance tests is extensive and allows you to see every bit of data collected about each function. The following two lists show the complete data available for the Functions tab. Other windows contain other columns of data specific to those windows.

This list shows the column names for the instrumentation data:

- Function Name
- Number of Calls
- Elapsed Exclusive Time
- Function Address
- Line Number
- Percentage of Calls
- Source File Name
- Process Name
- Module Name
- Module Path
- Module Identifier
- Application Exclusive Time
- Elapsed Inclusive Time
- Application Inclusive Time
- MAX Elapsed Exclusive Time
- MAX Application Exclusive Time
- MAX Elapsed Inclusive Time
- MAX Application Inclusive Time
- MIN Elapsed Exclusive Time
- MIN Application Exclusive Time
- MIN Elapsed Inclusive Time
- MIN Application Inclusive Time
- AVG Elapsed Exclusive Time
- AVG Application Exclusive Time
- AVG Elapsed Inclusive Time
- AVG Application Inclusive Time
- % Elapsed Exclusive Time
- % Application Exclusive Time
- % Elapsed Inclusive Time
- % Application Inclusive Time

- Exclusive Transitions
- Inclusive Transitions
- Process ID
- Unique Process ID
- Unique ID
- Exclusive Transitions Percentage
- Inclusive Transitions Percentage
- Root Node Recursion
- Time Exclusive Probe Overhead
- Time Inclusive Probe Overhead

The following is a list of column names available in the sampling data:

- Function Name
- Exclusive Allocations
- Inclusive Allocations
- Exclusive Bytes Allocated
- Inclusive Bytes Allocated
- Line Number
- Source File Name
- Module Name
- Module Path
- Process Name
- Exclusive Allocations Percent
- Inclusive Allocations Percent
- Exclusive Bytes Percent
- Inclusive Bytes Percent
- Process ID
- Unique Process ID
- Unique ID
- Module Identifier
- Function Address

Note The MSDN documentation on this subject is very complete. Refer to the Functions View in the MSDN documentation to see the definition of each column available for the report.

One thing you may have noticed while looking at the performance results is that it is not at all obvious where the application code is located. This is because with web applications, which use the shadow copy mechanism, the actual website is not instrumented or sampled, the shadow copy is. The way .NET 2.0 works (at least as far as it relates to being able to find code for a website in the performance report) is that the shadow-copied code is prefixed with the folder it resides in for the website. Looking at the report results in Figure 14-4 you can see that App_Web contains code in the root website folder. Code contained in lower branches are prefixed with the folder name. So the edit.aspx page is noted in the App_Web\secure folder and indicated by ASP.secure_edit_aspx. Anything that refers to the actual web page ends with _aspx and any code residing in those pages is noted by the page name, a period, and the method name (for example the Login_aspx.ctor()).

Caller/Callee Tab

This tab displays information about specific calls and the (partially sorted) order in which they are made (explained later on). The function that is being examined is displayed on the Current function line (see Figure 14-5). The function that called that function (the caller) is listed above it and the functions called by it (the callees) are listed below it. The reason the list is only partially ordered is because many different functions can call one function and one function can call many different functions (for example, if you are using many else statements). Therefore, this list of calls is not always accurate.

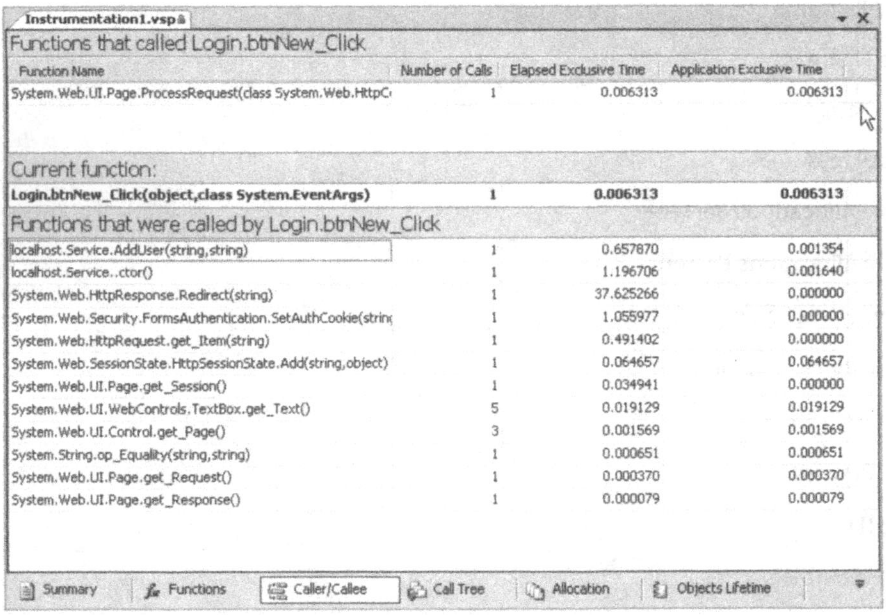

Functions that called Login.btnNew_Click			
Function Name	Number of Calls	Elapsed Exclusive Time	Application Exclusive Time
System.Web.UI.Page.ProcessRequest(class System.Web.HttpC‹	1	0.006313	0.006313

Current function:			
Login.btnNew_Click(object,class System.EventArgs)	**1**	**0.006313**	**0.006313**

Functions that were called by Login.btnNew_Click			
localhost.Service.AddUser(string,string)	1	0.657870	0.001354
localhost.Service..ctor()	1	1.196706	0.001640
System.Web.HttpResponse.Redirect(string)	1	37.625266	0.000000
System.Web.Security.FormsAuthentication.SetAuthCookie(strinç	1	1.055977	0.000000
System.Web.HttpRequest.get_Item(string)	1	0.491402	0.000000
System.Web.SessionState.HttpSessionState.Add(string,object)	1	0.064657	0.064657
System.Web.UI.Page.get_Session()	1	0.034941	0.000000
System.Web.UI.WebControls.TextBox.get_Text()	5	0.019129	0.019129
System.Web.UI.Control.get_Page()	3	0.001569	0.001569
System.String.op_Equality(string,string)	1	0.000651	0.000651
System.Web.UI.Page.get_Request()	1	0.000370	0.000370
System.Web.UI.Page.get_Response()	1	0.000079	0.000079

Summary | Functions | Caller/Callee | Call Tree | Allocation | Objects Lifetime

Figure 14-5. *Caller/Callee tab of the Performance Report (Login.btnNew_Click)*

To understand this information, examine the data in Figure 14-5. This information tells us that the call to the btnNew_Click function triggered a call to the AddUser function of the web service and that the constructor was called next. You might be telling yourself right now that something looks wrong with this. You would be right. This is out of order, as you will see in the next section, "Calltree Tab."

■**Caution** Because in many cases only a partially sorted order of function invocations is listed, it is not always practical or advisable to use this list to determine the order of the call stack at any given time except in a very general sense. Keep this in mind when looking at the following set of points. Being able to view this list and easily understand it only works because the application was run once through a very specific set of steps so it would be easily understandable by the reader.

To help you understand, line by line, this display is telling you

- The New User button was clicked.

- The Service object (web service) was instantiated.

- The AddUser method was called.

- The authorization cookie was set.

- The user was redirected to another page (the default page).

These types of low-level details concerning your applications call stack can be invaluable in solving performance-related issues. One additional piece of very-nice-to-have functionality is that you can double-click any function in the Caller/Callee view and that function will become the Current function.

■**Caution** It is extremely important to note, when looking at the Caller/Callee view, that it is an aggregation of all the calls leading up to and called by a function. This detail is broken down into specific information on the Calltree tab, discussed next.

Calltree Tab

The Calltree tab is used to display all levels of a given call tree, whereas the Caller/Callee tab displays aggregate information and only three levels of the call tree. The Calltree tab gets into the details whereas the Caller/Callee tab really contains the overview information. The call tree helps you trace a call from the beginning to the end of the call sequence and allows you to determine if there are calls that you did not intend to make that may be wasting time unnecessarily.

As was pointed out in the previous section, the call order is incorrect for the invocation of the AddUser function. To see the actual call tree, switch to the Calltree tab. Then expand the Login.btnNew_Click node and all of the other children nodes underneath that node. Your view should look like that in Figure 14-6.

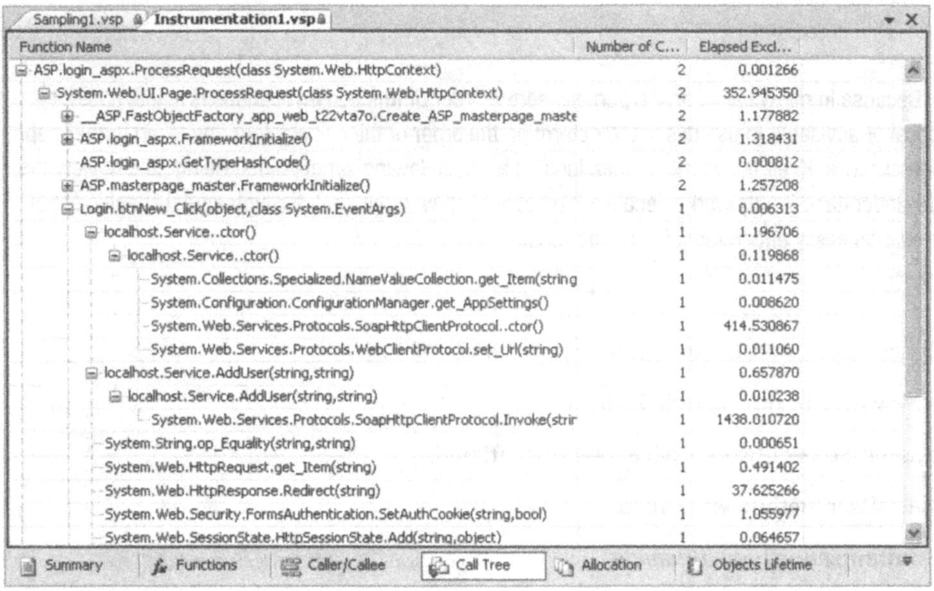
Sampling1.vsp
Instrumentation1.vsp
Function Name
Number of C...
Elapsed Excl...
ASP.login_aspx.ProcessRequest(class System.Web.HttpContext) 2 0.001266
System.Web.UI.Page.ProcessRequest(class System.Web.HttpContext) 2 352.945350
__ASP.FastObjectFactory_app_web_t22vta7o.Create_ASP_masterpage_maste 2 1.177882
ASP.login_aspx.FrameworkInitialize() 2 1.318431
ASP.login_aspx.GetTypeHashCode() 2 0.000812
ASP.masterpage_master.FrameworkInitialize() 2 1.257208
Login.btnNew_Click(object,class System.EventArgs) 1 0.006313
localhost.Service..ctor() 1 1.196706
localhost.Service..ctor() 1 0.119868
System.Collections.Specialized.NameValueCollection.get_Item(string 1 0.011475
System.Configuration.ConfigurationManager.get_AppSettings() 1 0.008620
System.Web.Services.Protocols.SoapHttpClientProtocol..ctor() 1 414.530867
System.Web.Services.Protocols.WebClientProtocol.set_Url(string) 1 0.011060
localhost.Service.AddUser(string,string) 1 0.657870
localhost.Service.AddUser(string,string) 1 0.010238
System.Web.Services.Protocols.SoapHttpClientProtocol.Invoke(strir 1 1438.010720
System.String.op_Equality(string,string) 1 0.000651
System.Web.HttpRequest.get_Item(string) 1 0.491402
System.Web.HttpResponse.Redirect(string) 1 37.625266
System.Web.Security.FormsAuthentication.SetAuthCookie(string,bool) 1 1.055977
System.Web.SessionState.HttpSessionState.Add(string,object) 1 0.064657
Summary
Functions
Caller/Callee
Call Tree
Allocation
Objects Lifetime

Figure 14-6. *The Calltree tab*

The call tree for the AddUser service call involves invoking the service constructor (the service then runs through its startup processes) and then invoking the AddUser function. This is the actual order of calls made for a given set of calls. You can switch to several other views by right-clicking the function in the list and selecting the appropriate view.

Allocation

When you set up the test at the beginning of this chapter, you elected to collect the .NET object allocation information. If you had not selected this option, this tab would be empty. By default, the allocation and lifetime information is not collected as part of a performance session.

This information is extremely useful for determining how much memory objects consumed and how many times they were instantiated (allocated) during the course of an application. This provides a detailed breakdown. Note also that this information can be seen on the Functions tab by selecting the appropriate columns. Figure 14-7 shows the object allocation information (partially) for the performance session.

Expanding the instantiated object type will show you the method that instantiated the object. As you can see in Figure 14-7 the localhost.Service class was instantiated by several different methods, including the LoadCategory method, the LoadRecord method, and the btnNew_Click method.

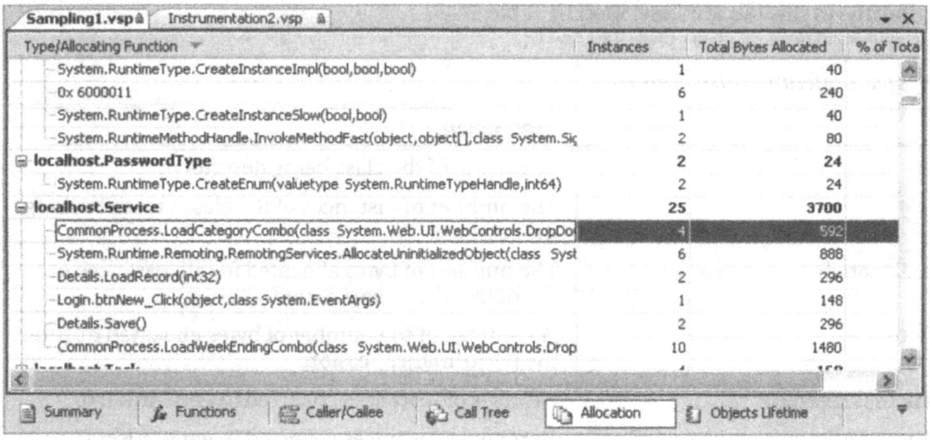

Type/Allocating Function	Instances	Total Bytes Allocated	% of Tota
System.RuntimeType.CreateInstanceImpl(bool,bool,bool)	1	40	
0x 6000011	6	240	
System.RuntimeType.CreateInstanceSlow(bool,bool)	1	40	
System.RuntimeMethodHandle.InvokeMethodFast(object,object[],class System.Sig	2	80	
localhost.PasswordType	**2**	**24**	
System.RuntimeType.CreateEnum(valuetype System.RuntimeTypeHandle,int64)	2	24	
localhost.Service	**25**	**3700**	
CommonProcess.LoadCategoryCombo(class System.Web.UI.WebControls.DropDo	4	592	
System.Runtime.Remoting.RemotingServices.AllocateUninitializedObject(class Syst	6	888	
Details.LoadRecord(int32)	2	296	
Login.btnNew_Click(object,class System.EventArgs)	1	148	
Details.Save()	2	296	
CommonProcess.LoadWeekEndingCombo(class System.Web.UI.WebControls.Drop	10	1480	

Figure 14-7. *Application allocation information*

Objects Lifetime

Object lifetime information is displayed in the last tab of the performance report. This tab gives you details on the garbage collection patterns related to a given object. Figure 14-8 shows the Objects Lifetime tab. However, as a preview of improving performance, this view shows how many objects were collected in Gen2. Objects collected in Gen2 cause performance problems because they require a complete stack walk to collect them. This essentially pauses the application.

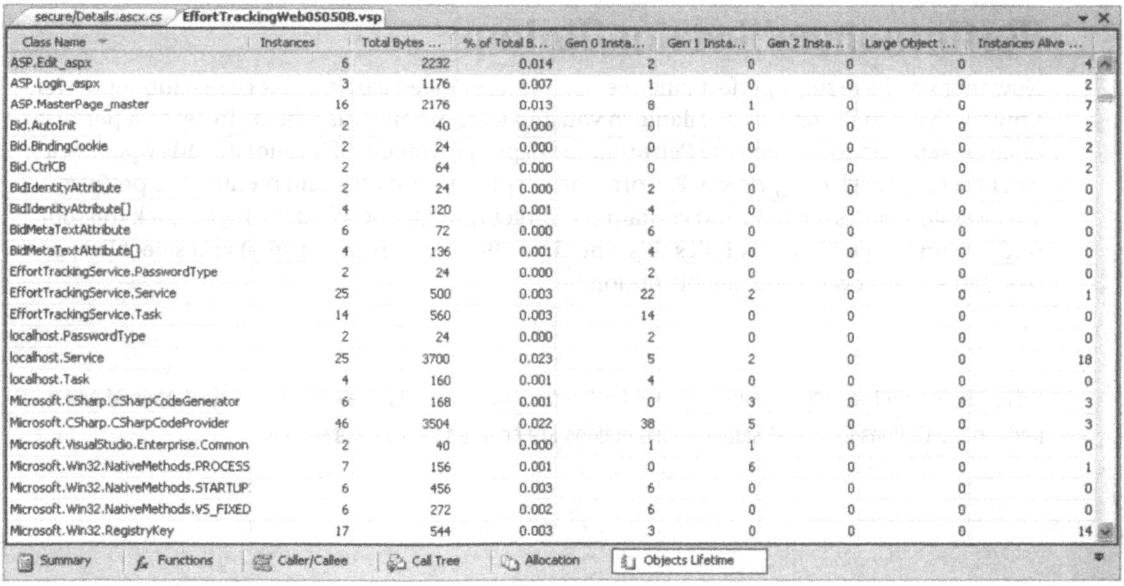

Class Name	Instances	Total Bytes ...	% of Total B...	Gen 0 Insta...	Gen 1 Insta...	Gen 2 Insta...	Large Object ...	Instances Alive ...
ASP.Edit_aspx	6	2232	0.014	2	0	0	0	4
ASP.Login_aspx	3	1176	0.007	1	0	0	0	2
ASP.MasterPage_master	16	2176	0.013	8	1	0	0	7
Bid.AutoInit	2	40	0.000	0	0	0	0	2
Bid.BindingCookie	2	24	0.000	0	0	0	0	2
Bid.CtrlCB	2	64	0.000	0	0	0	0	2
BidIdentityAttribute	2	24	0.000	2	0	0	0	0
BidIdentityAttribute[]	4	120	0.001	4	0	0	0	0
BidMetaTextAttribute	6	72	0.000	6	0	0	0	0
BidMetaTextAttribute[]	4	136	0.001	4	0	0	0	0
EffortTrackingService.PasswordType	2	24	0.000	2	0	0	0	0
EffortTrackingService.Service	25	500	0.003	22	2	0	0	1
EffortTrackingService.Task	14	560	0.003	14	0	0	0	0
localhost.PasswordType	2	24	0.000	2	0	0	0	0
localhost.Service	25	3700	0.023	5	2	0	0	18
localhost.Task	4	160	0.001	4	0	0	0	0
Microsoft.CSharp.CSharpCodeGenerator	6	168	0.001	0	3	0	0	3
Microsoft.CSharp.CSharpCodeProvider	46	3504	0.022	38	5	0	0	3
Microsoft.VisualStudio.Enterprise.Common	2	40	0.000	1	1	0	0	0
Microsoft.Win32.NativeMethods.PROCESS	7	156	0.001	0	6	0	0	1
Microsoft.Win32.NativeMethods.STARTUP	6	456	0.003	6	0	0	0	0
Microsoft.Win32.NativeMethods.VS_FIXED	6	272	0.002	6	0	0	0	0
Microsoft.Win32.RegistryKey	17	544	0.003	3	0	0	0	14

Figure 14-8. *Objects Lifetime tab*

The columns on this tab are described in Table 14-3.

Table 14-3. *Objects Lifetime Tab Columns*

Column	Description
Class Name	The name of the class being described.
Instances	The number of instances of the class created during the session.
Total Bytes Allocated	The number of bytes allocated for all instances of the object that were created.
% of Total Bytes	Percentage of the number of bytes allocated during the performance session.
Gen 0 Instances Collected	Number of instances collected in generation 0.
Gen 1 Instances Collected	Number of instances collected in generation 1.
Gen 2 Instances Collected	Number of instances collected in generation 2.
Large Object Heap Instances Collected	Number of instances collected from the heap.

■**Note** Garbage collection is beyond the scope of this book. For a detailed discussion of garbage collection in .NET, see Jeffrey Richter's excellent MSDN article from December 2000 available on MSDN: http://msdn.microsoft.com/msdnmag/issues/1200/GCI2/default.aspx.

Performance Session Options

Now that you have run a performance session and reviewed a performance session report it is time to dive into the options available to you and learn when to use them. To get to a performance session's options, open the Performance Explorer window (if it is not already open, you can access it by selecting View ➤ Performance Explorer from the main menu). The performance session nodes are bold and contain the Targets and Reports folders. Right-click the root node (from the previous examples this would be EffortTrackingWeb.psess) and select Properties. Table 14-4 covers the available options.

■**Tip** There are two sets of property pages for the performance tools: the one that you just opened and a node in the Options for Visual Studio. Those options are covered later in this section.

Table 14-4. *Performance Session Options*

Tab	Option	Description
General	Profiling collection	Allows you to choose between instrumentation and sampling types of performance monitoring.
	.NET memory profiling collection	Indicates whether the performance session should include statistics about the .NET Framework and its memory usage.
	Report	Allows you to specify the location for the reports, the name, the naming convention, and whether the reports are added to the project.
Launch	Binary selection	Allows you to select the order in which the binaries are launched. The binaries that are identified here are those in the Target folder of the performance session. See the "Target Options" section of this chapter.
Sampling	Sample Event	Allows you to specify what type of event you are sampling. The options are Clock Cycles, Page Faults, System Calls, and Performance Counter.
	Interval	Sets the length of time or number of operations before the data is sampled. This is Sample Event–specific.
	Available performance counters	Shows the performance counters you can choose to sample. This only applies to the Performance Counter sampling event.
Binary	Relocate instrumented binaries	Allows the binaries to be profiled and to be compiled and run from a different location.
Instrumentation	Pre/post instrumentation events	Allows you to specify commands to run either before or after the instrumentation session occurs. These activities can be instrumented or not, depending on your needs.
Advanced	Additional instrumentation options	Allows you to supply command-line arguments to the performance application (discussed in the section "Profiling Production Applications" later in this chapter).
Counters	Collect on-chip counter performance data	Allows you to collect performance information as it relates to the actual CPU. This information is more useful for understanding the processes occurring on the system while your application is being profiled.

Continued

Table 14-4. *Continued*

Tab	Option	Description
Events	Event trace providers	Allows you to specify that you will collect performance trace data from a number of providers. This is information that typically goes directly to the Performance Monitor in Windows.
General*	General settings	Allows you to choose to display the performance information by number of clock cycles or in milliseconds. You can also change the number of functions displayed in the summary view on the first page of the performance report.

* *The General settings are in the Tools ➤ Options ➤ Performance Tools dialog; they are not part of the Other performance options dialog.*

Target Options

Right-clicking the Target folder in the Performance Explorer will allow you to specify the binary, project, or existing website you want to profile. In general, you will be targeting projects you are currently working on, but there will be many instances where you will want to profile an existing application. How many times has a customer come to you and said that the website was acting slow or that certain pages were taking a long time? In such a case, there is no way to go in and diagnose specific problems on the pages except by looking at general server logs and hoping it is the server causing the problems. By using the profiler, you will gain a great deal more information about the application and its performance issues.

■**Note** In order to be able to profile production applications, Visual Studio can be installed on the system where the binaries you want to profile are located. Since the overhead of having Visual Studio installed can have its own effect on the performance of a production application, you can profile applications using the command-line tools, which do not require Visual Studio to be on the target system. This is described in the section "Profiling Production Applications" later in this chapter.

Once you have added a target to the Target folder you can set certain options for just that target (right-clicking the target brings up target-specific options). You may choose to launch a different assembly or website and thereby override the settings of the target you are currently pointing to. Additionally, because multiple targets may be run during a performance session, you can elect to specify code (or command-line applications) to run pre- and post-target activation during the performance session.

Profiling Unit Tests

Yes, exactly what the title says; you can profile a unit test! This allows you to create performance sessions that do not require you to walk through your application each time, and allows you to pinpoint specific functionality for testing. This is an invaluable ability but a little limited in this release.

To profile a unit test (note that this is singular because you can only profile one unit test at a time) you need to run the test first (without profiling it). When the test results are displayed, right-click the test you want to profile and select Create Performance Session.

■**Note** This will not work for Ordered Tests, only for individual tests.

This will bring up the Performance Wizard in which you can select Sampling or Instrumentation for the test. Once you have finished with the wizard, a new Performance Session in the Performance Explorer is displayed. Simply select the correct session and launch the performance test.

■**Tip** Because you can profile only one test, it is a good idea to create a data-driven test to profile—one that will be run many times—in order to get the most valuable results.

When the test is complete, the performance results for the code tested will be displayed. Viewing a performance result in this format is extremely helpful because it does not contain an overwhelming amount of information and you can comfortably digest the information. This will allow you to discover issues in individual methods (or processes, depending on how complicated your unit test is) and fix them easily (well, hopefully).

Profiling Web/Load Tests

After all of this, you have to be asking yourself if it is possible to run performance profiles for existing tests. The answer is yes, you can, but it is not quite an automated process. It is not built into VSTS, per se, but there is a simple workaround for it. To profile a web or load test, do the following:

1. Create a performance test.

2. Create a Web or Load test.

3. Launch the performance session from the Performance Explorer.

4. Minimize the browser (this is the key part here).

5. Run the Web or Load test.

6. Click OK when the message saying the process is already being profiled appears. The test will begin after this.

7. Close the minimized browser window.

■**Caution** You *must* disable code coverage by unselecting all assemblies marked for code coverage in the configuration file used by the Web or Load test.

This will provide you with a set of performance data you can use to consistently compare performance for the same test run again and again. You can either sample or instrument these tests, but we would recommend you instrument them to be able to perform more accurate comparisons between one run and another.

Profiling Production Applications

Now that you have seen how to profile applications in the development environment, it is time to understand how to do it in a production environment. Before you begin profiling a production application you should have a good reason for doing so. Any of the standard answers will work: the application runs slowly; the application is using a huge amount of CPU time or memory; the system the application is running on is starting to slow down; etc. So now that you have your good reason for profiling a production application, you need to know how to profile it.

■**Tip** For non-ASP.NET applications, the best practice is to run a sampled performance profile first in order to help pin down possible problem areas. For ASP.NET applications, however, an instrumented performance profile should be run first. The reason for this is that an instrumented profile will target only the application code. A sampled profile will target not only the application, but the entire ASP.NET/IIS system.

Before you begin profiling a production application you must install the performance tools redistributable on the machine that houses the application you want to profile. You can install Visual Studio on the production box, but it is not recommended because it may cause other problems. When you install the performance tools, you are installing the assemblies you need to run performance tests, and the command-line tools, which allow you to run the tests. These tools are detailed in the next section.

Command-Line Performance Tools

VSTS includes five command-line tools that are available to run performance profiles and report the results. These tools and their purpose are listed in Table 14-5.

Table 14-5. *Command-Line Performance Tools*

Application	Description
VSInstr	Performs the instrumentation of the binaries, which can then be deployed to a production machine.
VSPerfCmd	Starts and stops the performance profiling.
VSPerfMon	Can also be used to start and stop performance profiling, but contains different options than the VSPerfCmd application (discussed briefly below).
VSPerfClrEnv	Sets CLR environment options so the performance tools can be properly loaded.
VSPerfReport	Creates the performance reports (or a subset of those reports that you see in the IDE).

Because the MSDN documentation contains detailed information about each of these applications the information will not be re-presented here.

Tip To find information about these applications in the MSDN documentation, go to its table of contents, navigate to Visual Studio Team System ➤ Team Edition for Developers ➤ Analyzing Application Performance ➤ Command-Line Tools.

The next sections focus on how to profile applications using these tools.

Profiling Windows Applications and Windows Services

By Windows applications, we mean any application deployed to a machine. This can be one part of an application (i.e., the front end of a distributed application, a console application, or a custom server) or the complete application. It does not include Windows services or ASP.NET applications. Windows services are discussed at the end of this section because the steps are only slightly different for a Windows service than for a Windows application. For this example, the application being instrumented is the console application presented in Listing 14-1. It was compiled using the Release configuration. The application name is Performance-InstrumentationExample and it is located in the root of drive C (C:\). To profile this application using instrumentation, take the following steps (sampling is described afterward):

1. Open the Visual Studio Command Prompt.

2. Navigate to the Performance Tools location (the default installation is C:\Program Files\Microsoft Visual Studio 8\Team Tools\Performance Tools).

3. Run the following (use /globalsampleon to run sampling performance tests):

   ```
   vsperfclrenv /globaltraceon
   ```

   This sets up the CLR to enable the loading and running of performance tools.

4. Reboot the machine.

5. Restart the Visual Studio Command Prompt and navigate back to the Performance Tools folder (you can avoid this step by adding the location to your path environment variable—see Windows help for how to do this).

6. Run the following:

```
vsinstr C:\PerformanceInstrumentationExample.exe
```

This instruments the binary and renames the original file to PerformanceInstrumentationExample.exe.orig and creates a symbol file called PerformanceInstrumentationExample.exe.pdb.

7. Run the following (use /sample instead of /trace for a sampled performance test) which starts the profiling:

```
vsperfmon /trace /output:c:\PerformanceInstrumentationResults.vsp
```

8. Launch the application and once the message is displayed press any key to end the PerformanceInstrumentationExample application.

9. Start a new Visual Studio Command Prompt and navigate to the Performance Tools folder. (This is necessary because the first command prompt contains the running VSPerfmon application and nothing else can be entered in that window.)

10. Run the following:

```
vsperfcmd -shutdown
```

11. Run the following:

```
vsperfreport C:\PerformanceInstrumentationResults.vsp /packsymbols
```

This compiles the report with whatever options you choose. Packsymbols stores the symbols so the report can be viewed on another machine.

12. Run the following:

```
vsperfclrenv /globaloff
```

This removes the ability to load profile information and can be a performance issue if not done.

13. Reboot the machine.

The test report can now be viewed in Visual Studio.

■**Tip** If you are running multiple performance tests (i.e., one after another), then do not re-run the vsperfclrenv /globaloff command until after you are done with all of the tests. However, Microsoft notes that not running this once you are done profiling an application can have an adverse effect on the application.

This is the basic process for using the command-line tools to instrument and run performance tests on production applications. This process is essentially the same for ASP.NET applications and for Windows Services applications although there are some differences. These differences are described in the following sections.

■**Tip** Remember that when you are sampling an application you never have to instrument the assemblies; so that step is always skipped. In addition, remember that the options for the CLR environment are /globaltrace (on or off) for instrumentation performance tests, and /globalsample (on or off) for sampling performance tests.

To profile an application using sampling, you would start the application (which in the case of the sample application is not particularly useful since everything occurs on startup) and attach to the process using the vsperfmon /attach [PID]. Then you would use the application; when it is complete you would use the vsperfmon /detach command.

To profile a service, using either sampling or instrumentation, the only changes you would make would be to start the monitor (include the /user parameter option of the vsperfcmd application with the username the service is running under); start the service; attach to the executable the service is running; run the tests; and detach afterward. The setup and shutdown steps are the same as listed above.

Profiling ASP.NET Applications

ASP.NET applications contain their own bit of complexity in that they run under a separate process and can be precompiled or dynamically compiled. On top of this, the process for sampling an ASP.NET application is slightly different than that of instrumenting the same application. ASP.NET applications come in a couple of different flavors with version 2 in .NET. Assemblies in a web application can be precompiled or contain dynamically built assemblies (built at runtime). Precompiled assemblies are those assemblies that are copied to the bin folder of the virtual directory. Everything else is dynamically compiled (this consists of web pages, code behind pages, and code located in the App_Code folder). Either of these can be instrumented.

Instrumenting Precompiled ASP.NET Applications

To instrument precompiled assemblies in ASP.NET, do the following:

1. Open the Visual Studio Command Prompt.

2. Navigate to the Performance Tools location.

3. Run the following:

   vsperfclrenv /globaltraceon

4. Reboot the machine.

5. Restart the Visual Studio Command Prompt and navigate back to the performance tools folder.

6. Run the following:

    ```
    vsinstr [path to assembly]
    ```

7. Run the following:

    ```
    vsperfmon /trace /output:[File Name].vsp /user:"[ASP.NET worker process user]"
    ```

8. Run the tests against the web application.

9. Start a new Visual Studio Command Prompt.

10. Run the following (the iisreset.exe program is located in the %windir%\sytem32 folder):

    ```
    iisreset /stop
    ```

    Note that this will stop IIS, so be aware of everything running under IIS at the time, or just stop the IIS process by using the Services window or the IIS Administrator Console.

11. Run the following:

    ```
    vsperfcmd -shutdown
    ```

12. Run the following:

    ```
    vsperfreport [File Name].vsp /packsymbols
    ```

13. If you are going to perform more testing, run the following (or restart it from the Services window or the IIS Administration Console):

    ```
    iisrestart /start
    ```

14. Run the following:

    ```
    vsperfclrenv /globaloff
    ```

15. Reboot the machine.

Instrumenting Dynamically Built ASP.NET Applications

To instrument dynamically built assemblies in ASP.NET, do the following:

1. Open the Visual Studio Command Prompt.

2. Navigate to the Performance Tools location.

3. Run the following:

    ```
    vsperfclrenv /globaltraceon
    ```

4. Reboot the machine.

5. Back up the application's web.config file.

6. Update (or alter) the web.config file for the website with the information presented in Listing 14-3.

Listing 14-3. *Web.Config Changes for Dynamic Code Instrumentation*

```
<!-- Add or modify the compilation tag -->
<system.web>
<compilation assemblyPostProcessorType=
"Microsoft.VisualStudio.Enterprise.Common.AspPerformanceInstrumenter,
 Microsoft.VisualStudio.Enterprise.ASPNetHelper, Version=8.0.0.0,
 Culture=neutral, PublicKeyToken=b03f5f7f11d50a3a" />
</system.web>


<!-Add or modify the runtime tag
Note there are no spaces in the href - this is a formatting
 consideration for the book. -->
<runtime>
  <assemblyBinding xmlns="urn:schemas-microsoft-com:asm.v1">
    <dependentAssembly>
      <assemblyIdentity name="Microsoft.VisualStudio.Enterprise.ASPNetHelper"
                        publicKeyToken="b03f5f7f11d50a3a" culture="neutral" />
      <codeBase version="8.0.0.0"
          href="file:///C:/Program%20Files/Microsoft%20Visual%20Studio%208
          /Common7/IDE/PrivateAssemblies
          /Microsoft.VisualStudio.Enterprise.ASPNetHelper.DLL" />
    </dependentAssembly>
  </assemblyBinding>
</runtime>


<!-- Add or modify the appSettings tag to include the following two tags
Note, there are no spaces in the value - this is a formatting
 consideration for the book -->
<appSettings>
   <add key="Microsoft.VisualStudio.Enterprise.AspNetHelper.VsInstrLocation"
 value="C:\Program Files\Microsoft Visual Studio 8\Team Tools\Performance
Tools\vsinstr.exe" />
   <add key="Microsoft.VisualStudio.Enterprise.AspNetHelper.VsInstrTools"
 value="C:\Program Files\Microsoft Visual Studio 8\Team Tools\Performance Tools\" />
</appSettings>
```

7. Run the following:

```
vsinstr [path to assembly]
```

8. Run the following:

```
vsperfmon /trace /output:[File Name].vsp /user:"[ASP.NET worker process user]"
```

9. Run the tests against the web application.

10. Start a new Visual Studio Command Prompt.

11. Run the following:

    ```
    iisreset /stop
    ```

    The iisreset.exe program is located in the %windir%\sytem32 folder. (Note that this will stop IIS, so be aware of everything running under IIS at the time, or just stop the IIS process by using the Services window or the IIS Administrator Console.)

12. Run the following:

    ```
    vsperfcmd -shutdown
    ```

13. Run the following:

    ```
    vsperfreport [File Name].vsp /packsymbols
    ```

14. Restore the web.config file (unless you are going to do more testing).

15. Run the following (or restart it from the Services window or the IIS Administration Console):

    ```
    iisrestart /start
    ```

16. Run the following:

    ```
    vsperfclrenv /globaloff
    ```

17. Reboot the machine.

Here are a couple of notes related to what shows up in the changes to the web.config file:

- The public key token for the ASPNetHelper assembly must match the entry here.

- The HREF for the code base must be a file URL and not a path name.

- To determine the username of the ASP.NET worker process, open the Process Manager, display the username and PID columns, and look for either aspnet_wp.exe (usually on Win2k or WinXP machines) or w3wp.exe (on Win2k3).

Sampling an ASP.NET Application

The process for sampling an ASP.NET application is slightly different because the generated code (whether it is the dynamic or precompiled assemblies) is not altered. To sample an ASP.NET application, take the following steps:

1. Open the Visual Studio Command Prompt.

2. Navigate to the Performance Tools location.

3. Run the following:

   ```
   vsperfclrenv /globaltraceon
   ```

4. Reboot the machine.

5. Run the following:

   ```
   vsinstr [path to assembly]
   ```

6. Run the following:

   ```
   vsperfmon /sample /output:[File Name].vsp /user:"[ASP.NET worker process user]"
   ```

7. Run the following:

   ```
   vsperfcmd /attach:[ASP.NET Worker Process PID (Process ID)]
   ```

8. Run the tests against the web application.

9. Start a new Visual Studio Command Prompt.

10. Run the following:

    ```
    vsperfcmd /detach
    ```

11. Run the following:

    ```
    vsperfcmd /shutdown
    ```

12. Run the following:

    ```
    vsperfreport [File Name].vsp /packsymbols
    ```

13. Run the following:

    ```
    vsperfclrenv /globaloff
    ```

14. Reboot the machine.

As you can see, this process is much simpler, since the profiler is only attaching to an existing process.

■**Tip** The VSTS profiling team recommends that you get the CPU running 100% for several minutes during the test to get usable results.

Summary

This chapter has introduced to you what may be a whole set of new concepts regarding performance profiling of an application. You have learned why you need a performance testing/profiling tool and how it can be used by a development team to improve application performance. In addition, you can now read the performance report and understand what the various terms and results mean, and you can put these in perspective to solve a performance problem. This ability will only help developers and development teams write better, more efficient code in the short and long term.

With these tools you can now profile unit tests, web tests, and load tests in order to find problems with an application at various stages in the development life cycle. This allows you to catch problems at an earlier (and less costly) stage. In addition, once you move out of the development phase and into production you also have ways to monitor applications.

Because VSTS allows you to monitor production applications, you can discover why they may not be running correctly. Too often production systems have performance problems that don't occur during testing and become large problems in production. With the ability to monitor production applications, you can quickly and easily diagnose a problem—whether it is in the application itself or in the machine it is running on. This leads to lower maintenance costs, because less time is needed to fix any given problem.

Team Edition for Software Testers

CHAPTER 15

■ ■ ■

Web Testing

Up to this point you have seen various testing tools within Visual Studio Team System. This chapter brings you the one tool that will probably get the most amount of use in today's environment—the web testing tool. Web testing tools allow you to test an application in the same way that a user would actually use your application—that is, by filling in entries on a web page, submitting those entries, navigating web pages, and so forth. This chapter will introduce you to the new (and improved) tools in Visual Studio Team System to help you get the most out of your web applications. You will also learn how to use the web testing tool to test web services by creating SOAP calls.

■**Note** Microsoft has yet to incorporate functional test tools for Windows forms-based applications.

While the next chapter covers load testing, every load test must start with a web test. For this reason, it is almost guaranteed that you will have different versions of various web tests—some that test for specific conditions, to ensure the application responds appropriately, and some that perform a task or a series of tasks correctly every time. The latter tests will be used to test "happy" path functionality, and the former will be used to test happy, alternate, and exception-path functionality. The happy-path functional tests will serve as the basis for running your load tests.

Web testing in previous versions of Visual Studio is accomplished with Application Center Test (ACT). ACT is a decent tool that allows you to script actions and play those scripted actions in order to test functionality. In general, though, ACT is designed as a load-testing tool and does not perform much in the way of functional testing. This lack of functionality is one of the key reasons why the web test tools were created.

Another reason for this flexible and powerful testing tool is the continuing shift toward web-based applications. While web-based applications are not suitable for all applications, there are a large number that can be used in a web environment with little extra work. Web applications also provide the advantage of a simple deployment and maintenance process, since no desktop installations are required. Because many new applications today are web-based, this tool will prove of use to almost anyone writing new applications for the web.

Web tests come in two different flavors—recorded tests and coded tests. Recorded tests, which you launch in a browser, record the session while you run through the functionality in your application. Coded tests are those where you code each step, one at a time. The playback is the same for both except that there is no user interface for a coded test. In general, you will always record a test first and then convert it into code so that you have a good starting point and do not have to do some of the mundane work.

Recording Web Tests

To begin, select Test ➤ New Test from the main menu and then select Web Test. Change the test name to CreateNewUser.webtest and create a new C# or Visual Basic (VB) project to contain the test.

Tip Typically, developers will create unit test projects, and the quality assurance testers will create functional test projects (those projects containing web and load tests).

Call the new project "EffortTrackingWebTests." The first thing that occurs after you create your new test project is that the test recording pane will be displayed in your browser as shown in Figure 15-1.

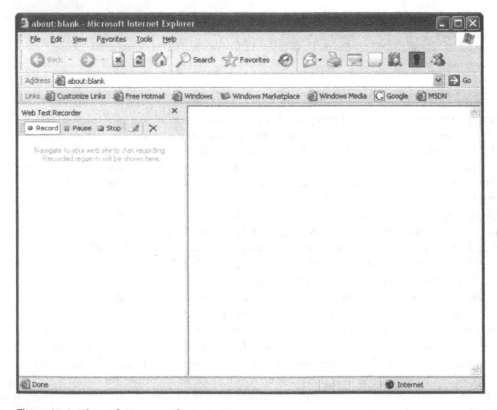

Figure 15-1. *The web test recording pane*

Navigate to the EffortTrackingWeb website (if you used IIS, your website will be at `http://localhost/EffortTrackingWeb/secure/Default.aspx`) to begin recording the web test. This will bring up the Login page. Do the following:

1. In the User Name textbox enter **WebTestUser1**.

2. In the Password textbox enter **password**.

3. In the Verify Password textbox enter **password**.

4. Click Add User.

Once you have done this, the browser window should look like the one in Figure 15-2.

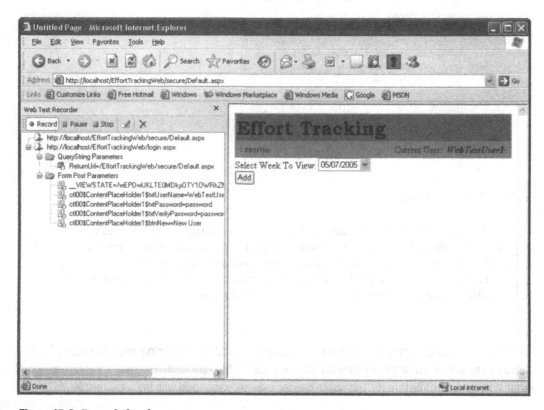

Figure 15-2. *Recorded web test*

Click the Stop button in the Web Test Recorder Pane.

Tip At any point during the test you can pause it in order to take other actions with the browser. An example of this might be when you come to a page that should not have a record on it and you want to delete it before continuing the test. You may pause the test, delete the record, and then continue recording the test.

When you are finished you will see the WebTest1.webtest window in the IDE as shown in Figure 15-3.

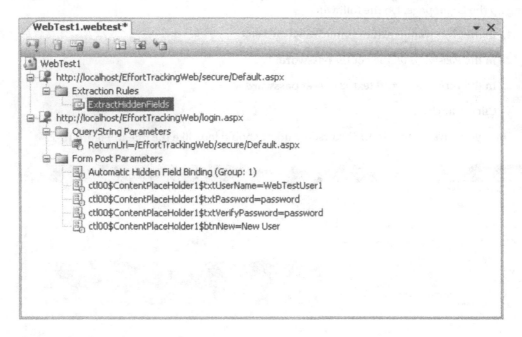

Figure 15-3. *The Web Test window*

You have now recorded your first web test—and it was simple. The first and most obvious thing you will note by looking at this window is that it contains almost the same information as the recording window, in that it records the pages you visit and the order you visit them. It also captures query string content, hidden field content, and form field content. All of this is configurable. There is no more to recording a web test than this.

■**Note** This test as a stand-alone test is not very useful because it can only be run once. The second time it is run an exception will be thrown since the username cannot be duplicated. Therefore, a test preparation script must be run in order to allow this test to be used over and over again with the same results.

To make these demonstrations easier, record a second test that uses the WebTestUser1 user that you just created by doing the following:

1. Select Test ➤ New Test from the main menu.

2. Select Web Test and call it **AddItem** and click OK.

3. When the recording window opens, navigate to http://localhost/EffortTrackingWeb/secure/Default.aspx.

4. On the login page enter the username as **WebTestUser1** and the password as **password** and click Login.

5. Click the Add button.

6. For the Title enter **Test Entry**.

7. For the Description enter **Description of Test Entry**.

8. Click Save.

9. Stop the test.

Now you have a test that can be easily worked with and requires no setup script to run. There are no constraints on the names of the items entered into the effort tracking system, so they can all be identical if you choose (although you will see how to programmatically change this as you progress through the chapter).

Test Steps Explained

The test steps are fairly straightforward, in that they comprise an ordered list of URLs visited during the recording of the test. For each URL, a number of pieces of information are recorded (as explained in the next section "Test Detail Properties") and stored. Since you will be using the AddItem test for the majority of this chapter, it is worthwhile to examine the steps shown. There are four steps listed for this test:

- *Step 1*: This is the initial request for the default page in the secure folder.

- *Step 2*: The user is redirected to the login page where the ReturnUrl parameter notes the page the user is trying to go to so it can redirect the user there after the user has been authenticated. The user enters the username and password and then clicks the btnLogin button.

- *Step 3*: The user is successfully redirected to the default page where they select the week ending with an ID of 1 and click the Add button.

- *Step 4*: The user is directed to the edit page, which received three parameters (id, mode, and we_id). The user then enters various values in the different fields on this page and clicks the btnOK button.

Note that the last page the user is directed to, the default page, is not displayed because the user did not do anything on this page when recording the test (i.e., nothing was tested on this page). All of the information presented in the previous list was taken directly from the request tree, which contains all of the information for a given test.

Test Detail Properties

For a recorded web test, not only does the test itself have properties, but every step in the list of tests also has properties. The list of steps is referred to as the request tree. To begin with, examine the properties for the test itself by right-clicking the AddItem node in the request tree and selecting Properties. The properties for the test are described in Table 15-1.

Table 15-1. *Recorded Web Test Properties*

Property	Description
Description	This describes the test that appears in the Test Manager window.
Name	This is the name of the test.
Password	This is the password required when logging onto a website with Integrated Authentication.
PreAuthenticate	This ensures that the username and password are automatically supplied to websites protected with Integrated Authentication.
Proxy	This notes the server name for connection purposes in case the test has to run through a proxy server. This field can also be bound to a data source.
Request Plug-in	This contains the location of the assembly, which contains the custom request (if you are using one).
User Name	This is the username required when logging onto a website with Integrated Authentication.
Web Test Plug-in	This is the name of the plugin for the entire web test.

■**Note** The Request Plugin and the Web Test Plugin are discussed later in this chapter.

The Password and User Name properties can be bound to a data source. In this case, the web test will use the usernames and passwords from this data source when authenticating against a website protected by Integrated or Basic Authentication. Note that these credentials are used to authenticate you against the web server, not the application you're testing (unless they use the same mechanism).

Next, select the node that reads `http://localhost/EffortTrackingWeb/login.aspx`. The properties for a request node are shown in Table 15-2.

Table 15-2. *Request Node Properties*

Property	Description
Cache Control	Indicates True/False if the request is cached or not.
Follow Redirects	Indicates True/False if a page redirect will be followed when that line of code is run.
Method	Post/Get: Determines how information will be passed to the website.
Parse Dependent Requests	Indicates with True/False whether other URLs within the requested web page are processed (such as images that are loaded from another URL).

Property	Description
Record Results	Indicates True/False if performance data is gathered for use when this test is run as part of a Load Test.
Response Time Goal	Indicates the response time you want to get from a page. It is used as a threshold to mark how many times the page meets or exceeds the set goal.
Think Time (seconds)	Indicates the amount of time that should be used to simulate a think time before moving on to the next step in the request tree. A think time is the amount of time an average user might spend reading a page rather than clicking something on the page.
Timeout (seconds)	Indicates the maximum amount of time to wait before a timeout is declared. This is great for testing what happens when a user session times out, for example, as on an e-commerce site.
URL	Indicates the URL of the requested page. This can be bound to a data source, which allows for dynamic site navigation during a test.
Version	Indicates the HTTP version to use for this request—1.1 is the default, although you can select 1.0.

Each folder beneath the request node contains a different set of properties. Select the first node under the QueryString Parameters node. These properties are shown in Table 15-3.

Table 15-3. *QueryString Parameter Properties*

Property	Description
Name	Indicates the name of the query string parameter
Show Separate Request	Indicates True/False if the specific value should be shown separately in reports, or grouped with the rest of the information about the request
Value	Indicates the value passed for the given query string parameter

The Form Post Parameters have only two properties—name and value of the parameter posted to the form.

Test Options

Once you have recorded a test, you have various options for configuring, altering, or making comments on specific tests or requests. The options range from altering requests and inserting requests to specifying data sources. To access these options, right-click the root test node (AddItem in this example) or any of the request nodes in the request tree. The options are described in Table 15-4.

Table 15-4. *Test/Test Step Options*

Option	Description
Add/Insert Request	Adds a request that was not included in the recorded test.
Add/Insert Web Service Request	Adds a web service request that was not included in the recorded test.
Add/Insert Transaction	Groups a set of web requests into a single transaction. All requests must pass or they all fail.
Add/Insert Comment	Allows the addition of one or more comments associated with the entire test or with single steps.
Add/Insert Recording	Allows additional web test recordings to be made and inserted into the current web test.
Add Data Source	Allows the addition of a data source that is used to bind various parameters to an external set of data.
Add Context Parameter	Holds any value—this can be the result of an extraction, for instance, that can be used as an argument to another call further in the test script.
Add Dependent Request	Is run in parallel (with the other dependent requests) after the current page is finished processing.
Add Header	Allows the addition of custom headers in order to test various scenarios.
Add URL QueryString Parameter	Allows additional parameters.
Add Form Post Parameter	Allows additional parameters.
Add File Upload Parameter	Indicates the path to a file and the context the value should be stored in. This will cause the specified file to be uploaded during the test.
Add Validation Rule	Validates that certain conditions are true on a response page.
Add Extraction Rule	Extracts data from the response page.

Some of these options are available at the root test level and others are only available from a request node.

Running Recorded Web Tests

Now that you have recorded a test, you need to be able to play it back for actual use in a test. There are various ways to replay a test depending on the type of test you are setting up (for example a load test does not work via a user interface so what follows does not apply to this type of playback).

■**Tip** It is a best practice that once you record your test you play it back to ensure that it will work correctly and that nothing unwanted was recorded.

To run a recorded test you can either open the recorded test (the file with the .webtest extension) and click the Run button from the top of the window or select the test from the Test Manager window and click the Run Checked Tests button. Open the recorded test file and click Run to begin this test. This will bring up the Web Test window shown in Figure 15-4.

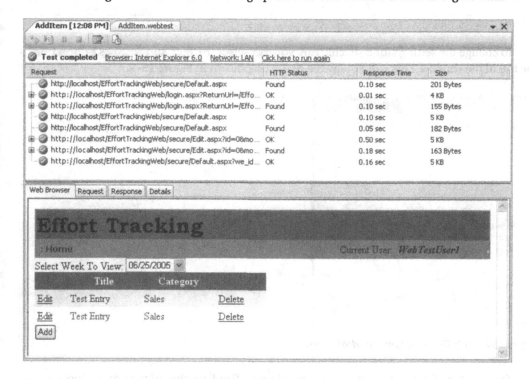

Figure 15-4. *The Web Test window (test completed)*

You have the option of running the test in an automated or interactive fashion in which you can step through each part of the test.

■**Tip** Turn off your firewall for these tests because unless you have previously recognized the program, it will prompt you to allow the application to interact with the web application (if you are using HTTP as opposed to Cassini, the built-in web server).

Clicking the Run button will run through all steps without stopping. You must click the Step button after each step has been completed in order to move to the next step. As you move through the test, the website is displayed in the lower window. Either during the test run (if you are using the Step method) or after the test run you can examine the Request details (header and body), the Response details (header and body), and the test Details (rules, context, and exceptions).

Tip After the test has been run, you will see the test details in the same window as shown in Figure 15-4. You can then click each individual node, which will show the web page as it looked during a particular step of the test.

To change the settings for a specific run, you can select the Edit Run Settings button from the top of the window. This will display the dialog box shown in Figure 15-5.

Figure 15-5. *Web Test Run Settings dialog box*

The number of iterations allows you either to set a fixed number of runs or to bind the count of runs against a data source (you will see this later in this chapter in the section "Data-Driven Web Testing"). The browser type allows you to choose the type of browser that will be "making" and "consuming" the requests and responses. Currently you can choose from five types of browsers but you could also add your own browser types if the one you want to test against is not listed here (for example, Netscape 6.0 is listed, but not Mozilla or Opera). The network type allows you to configure your connection speed. The values range from a 56.6K connection to a T1 line.

Note Customizing these values is discussed in Chapter 16.

The simulated think times allow the automated tests (this doesn't apply to the Step test) to take into account the think times you set for the individual test steps (if any). For a single test run these think times are not very useful, though, so you will most likely find yourself only using these during a load test. You can also turn the think times on and off by selecting the Think Times button on the toolbar in the test window.

Passing or Failing Tests

A test passing or failing is entirely up to whether an error occurs or a specific validation fails. When a web test is first recorded and played back, it is assumed to have passed if no errors occur during the run on the test. However, you can add specific validations to occur at various points of the test, which will throw exceptions if they fail (and fail the test).

To demonstrate how this works, you are going to record a test that validates the Login form via the user interface (this is similar to the initial test recorded previously, but this is explicitly to test a login failure). Start recording a new web test called "LoginFailure" and in the recording window navigate to the EffortTrackingWeb website (if you used IIS your website will be at `http://localhost/EffortTrackingWeb/secure/Default.aspx`) to begin recording the web test. This will bring up the Login page. Do the following:

1. In the User Name textbox enter **Test User 1** (note that this user does not exist).

2. In the Password textbox enter **password**.

3. Click Login.

4. Stop recording the web test.

What should occur is that the login does not succeed and an error message is shown. Now, if this test is run as it is, the test will succeed because no "exceptions" occurred. However, that does not really help you. In many cases you need to ensure that when an expected failure occurs (which is not triggered by throwing an exception), the correct actions are taken. In order to do this you can add a Validation Rule.

To change this test to something more meaningful, the test will check to see if the words "Invalid username or password" (part of the error message if a login fails) are displayed in the resulting web page. Open the `LoginFailure.webtest` file and right-click the Login.aspx node (the last node in the node list) and select Add Validation Rule (validation rules are discussed in more detail later in this chapter in the section "Validation Rules"). Click the Find Test validation rule and enter **Invalid username or password** for the Find Text property and click OK. When it is run, the test will search for this text within the resulting HTML body. If it finds the text, the test will pass; if it does not, it will fail. This ensures that you are checking for a specific type of failure.

Data-Driven Web Testing

Data binding allows a database to provide parameters to the test at various steps instead of having to change multiple tests of the same type by hand. Data binding can be used for individual data-driven web tests or for load testing (discussed in Chapter 16). For data-driven web tests (as with unit tests) the test will cycle through a table in the database and run the test once for each row in the table. Each column can supply a value to various parts of the web test. Because of this, there is no set structure to a table used for data-driven testing.

Tip It is a best practice to add a comment field in the table supplying data to the test so the exact purpose of the provided data can be noted. In other words, let everyone know what is being tested by the data provided—do not make the tests cryptic. This makes it easy for all developers and testers to understand the purpose for a set of test data.

For this example, you will use the previously created AddItem test with data from a SQL Server database to drive the test. To add a data source to the web test you first need to create a table to hold the information to be used for the test. The included testing database (efforttrackingtests) contains a table called save_task_test with the structure shown in Table 15-5.

Table 15-5. *The save_task_test Table Structure*

Column	Description
st_id	Unique identifier
st_wi_title	Title of the item being added
st_wi_description	Description of the item being added
st_cat_id	ID of the category
st_own_id	ID of the owner
st_we_id	ID of the week ending

Once the data source has been created in the database, click the Add Data Source button in the Web Test window (shown in Figure 15-6).

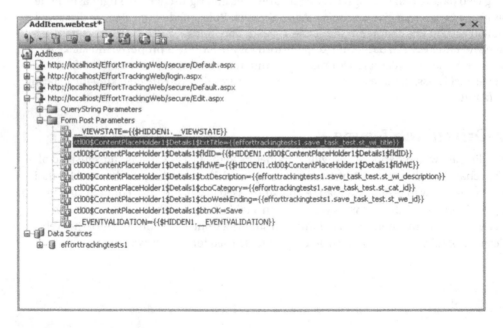

Figure 15-6. *Web Test window*

The data source and the selected table(s) are listed under the Data Sources node in the Web Test window. Now that a data source has been selected, the individual parameters of the form fields can be hooked up to specific columns in the data source. To do this, right-click a form parameter field (the highlighted line in Figure 15-7 is a form parameter field) and select Properties. Select the Value Property and click the drop-down button. Select the data source, table, and column to bind to the parameter field value. In Figure 15-7, the txtTitle field is bound to the `efforttrackingtests1.save_task_test.st_wi_title` column. Do the same for the txtDescription, cboCategory, and cboWeekEnding fields.

■**Tip** Another great feature is the ability to bind to a validation rule or an extraction rule. While not part of this test, in order to do the binding, just select a rule, view the properties for the rule and where you need to bind to a data field, enter the name of the data field in double braces. As an example, if you were to bind a Find Text validation rule to a data source, you would enter `{{efforttrackingtests1.save_task_test.st_wi_title}}` in the Find Text parameter. There is currently no drop-down available for this.

Once the data source has been chosen, the method of access to the database should be chosen (it does not matter what order you take these steps in). To select an access method, right-click a table in the Web Test window (under the Tables node) and select Properties. The Access Method property allows you to choose from three options: Sequential, Random, or Unique. The descriptions are noted in Table 15-6.

Table 15-6. *Data-Driven Access Options*

Option	Description
Sequential	For a load test, this method reads through every row in the table from top to bottom and continues to loop for the duration of the load test.
Random	For a load test, this method reads through every row in the table in a random order and continues to loop for the duration of the load test.
Unique	For a load test, this method reads through every row in the table from top to bottom and runs the test once for each row.

Note that these options only apply to load tests. They have no effect on non–load tests.

The final step before the data-driven test can be run is to change the test configuration settings. As noted in Chapter 12, the `localtestrun` file contains the Web Test configuration settings (shown in Figure 15-7).

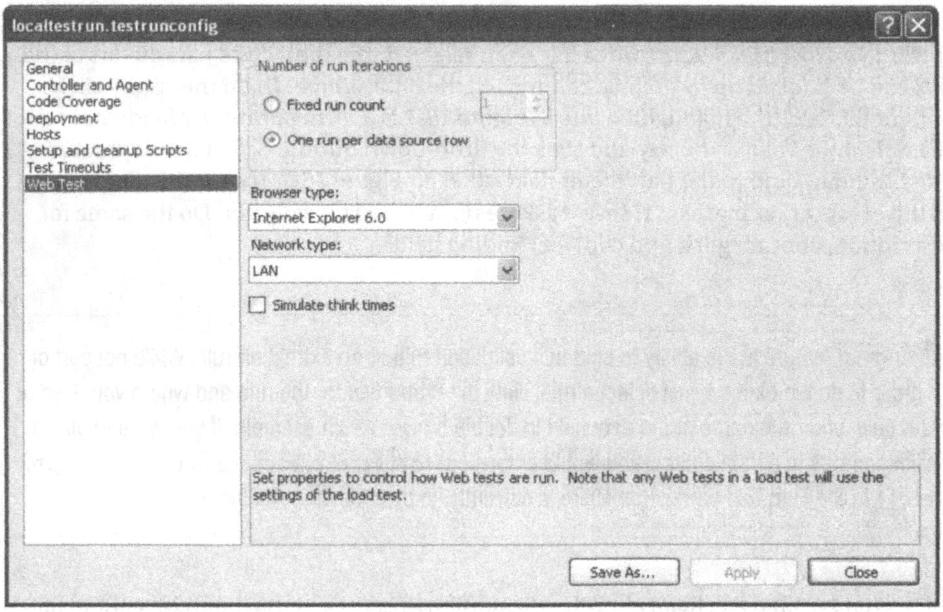

Figure 15-7. *Web Test configuration settings*

The number of run iterations must be switched from "Fixed run count" to "One run per data source row."

Caution If you decide to use the fixed run count instead, it will use the data from the rows in the data source sequentially, looping through them until the test has reached the number of iterations specified.

Apply the changes, switch back to the Web Test window, and run the test. To see the details of the test, double-click the test in the Test Results pane (shown in Figure 15-8).

The most obvious difference between this and the test results in Figure 15-4 is that there is one run for every row in the data source table. You will examine the web test results in more detail in the "Test Results" section of this chapter.

Note The reason the test failed is because there were no checks for invalid values. The test table contained several tests that were designed to fail, but the web test did not reflect that. In the real world, the test should be updated to validate that an error did in fact occur.

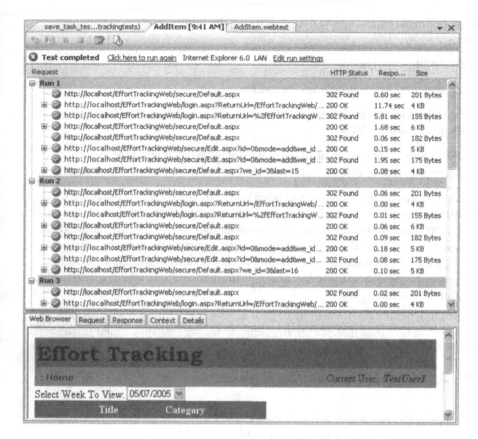

Figure 15-8. *AddItem test results*

Using the web testing tool in a data-driven fashion allows you to create one test and then change the values being tested simply by altering the database. In the past, this would have required a change in the test itself or manually changing parameters. The savings in time from using simple methods like these will be enormous.

Coded Web Tests

Coded web tests are written entirely in code. For the most part, coded web tests are required only when you have to create a loop in the test or dynamically navigate the list of URLs called during the test. Whatever your purpose in creating a coded web test, you will almost always begin from a recorded web test, which will provide the basic outline for your code.

Since the AddItem test has already been created, convert the test into a coded test by following these steps:

1. Open the AddItem request tree by double-clicking the AddItem test in the Solution Explorer.

2. Select the AddItem root node.

3. Click the Generate Code button from the toolbar.

4. Leave the default name of AddItemCoded in the Generate Coded Web Test dialog box that is displayed, and click OK.

5. The AddItemCoded.cs file (or .vb file if you are using VB.NET) is added to the EffortTrackingWebTests project.

These are all the steps required to create a coded web test. The class file contains a single class called AddItemCoded, which inherits from the WebTest class. Within this class there are only two methods (you are free to add as many methods as you like, but you are required to have at least these two methods): the constructor, and the GetRequestEnumerator method, which is part of the IEnumerator interface. The constructor contains information (if there is any) needed to initialize the web test. The IEnumerator implementation, while fairly straight-forward, is helpful to walk through.

The generic implementation of the IEnumerator interface returns a WebTestRequest type. Looking at the method body (partially shown in Listing 15-1) you can see a straightforward list of requests is being returned by the test.

Listing 15-1. *The GetRequestEnumerator/Run Method (partial)*

C#
```
// (GetRequestEnumerator Method)
    WebTestRequest request1 = new WebTestRequest(
    "http://localhost/EffortTrackingWeb/secure/Default.aspx");
    request1.ThinkTime = 5;
    ExtractHiddenFields rule1 = new ExtractHiddenFields();
    rule1.ContextParameterName = "1";
    request1.ExtractValues += new EventHandler<ExtractionEventArgs>(rule1.Extract);
    yield return request1;

    WebTestRequest request2 = new

    . . .

    yield return request2;
```

VB
```
' (Run Method)
  Dim request1 As WebTestRequest = New WebTestRequest( _
  "http://localhost/EffortTrackingWeb/secure/Default.aspx")
  request1.ThinkTime = 10
  Dim rule1 As ExtractHiddenFields = New ExtractHiddenFields
  rule1.ContextParameterName = "1"
  AddHandler request1.ExtractValues, AddressOf rule1.Extract
  MyBase.Send(request1)
```

```
Dim request2 As WebTestRequest = New
   WebTestRequest("http://localhost/EffortTrackingWeb/login.aspx")
. . .
MyBase.Send(request2)
```

Looking at the generated code, you can see that it is pretty simple in terms of what is going on. Each request in the request tree is generated with all of the properties for the previously set request. The extraction rules and any other rules (validation rules, etc.) are also generated. One of the key advantages of coding your own test is that you can respond to specific events. As you can see here, there is an event handler for the ExtractValues event and there are other events (PostRequest, PreRequest, ValidateResponse) you can respond to as well. You can read more about these events in the MSDN documentation.

■**Note** The yield statement (MyBase.Send in VB calls the GetRequestEnumerator in the base class) essentially puts a break in the code and allows the enumerator to iterate over the collection of requests. This is a new statement in C# and VB in the .NET 2.0 Framework. There are differences in how these work which is reflected in the base class that the coded web tests inherit from. C# inherits from WebTest and VB inherits from ThreadedWebTest. For more information, see the MSDN documentation.

Coded web tests can only be run via the Test Manager window, as there is no interface to this type of test.

Coded Data-Driven Tests

The coded data-driven test has a different structure to it. To create this type of test, do the following:

- Record a web test.

- Add a data source.

- Hook up the data source columns to form parameters.

- Select the Generate Coded Test button from the Web Test window for the specific test.

The AddItem test is a good starting point to demonstrate this type of test. Simply generate the coded test from the AddItem test window. A partial view of the coded, data-driven test is shown in Listing 15-2 (please note that the line breaks are due to formatting and do not exist in the generated code). This listing shows the class header and the fourth step of the test so you can see how data binding works in a coded web test.

Listing 15-2. *Coded Data-Driven Web Test*

```
C#
[DataSource("efforttrackingtests1", "Provider=SQLNCLI.1;
Data Source=localhost;Integrated Security=SSPI;
Initial Catalog=efforttrackingtests",
```

```
Microsoft.VisualStudio.TestTools.WebTesting.DataBindingAccessMethod.Sequential,
"save_task_test")]
[DataBinding("efforttrackingtests1", "save_task_test", "st_wi_title",
"efforttrackingtests1.save_task_test.st_wi_title")]
[DataBinding("efforttrackingtests1", "save_task_test", "st_wi_description",
"efforttrackingtests1.save_task_test.st_wi_description")]
[DataBinding("efforttrackingtests1", "save_task_test", "st_cat_id",
"efforttrackingtests1.save_task_test.st_cat_id")]
[DataBinding("efforttrackingtests1", "save_task_test", "st_we_id",
"efforttrackingtests1.save_task_test.st_we_id")]
public class AddItemCoded : WebTest
{
    public AddItemCoded()
    {
        this.PreAuthenticate = true;
    }

    public override IEnumerator<WebTestRequest> GetRequestEnumerator()
    {
        WebTestRequest request1 = new WebTestRequest(
"http://localhost/EffortTrackingWeb/secure/Default.aspx");
        . . .
        . . .
    WebTestRequest request4 = new
        WebTestRequest("http://localhost/EffortTrackingWeb/secure/Edit.aspx");
    request4.Method = "POST";
    request4.QueryStringParameters.Add("id", "0", false, false);
    request4.QueryStringParameters.Add("mode", "add", false, false);
    request4.QueryStringParameters.Add("we_id", "1", false, false);
    FormPostHttpBody request4Body = new FormPostHttpBody();
    request4Body.FormPostParameters.Add("__VIEWSTATE",
      this.Context["$HIDDEN1.__VIEWSTATE"].ToString());
    request4Body.FormPostParameters.Add
        ("ctl00$ContentPlaceHolder1$Details1$txtTitle",
        this.Context["efforttrackingtests1.save_task_test.st_wi_title"]
  .ToString());
    request4Body.FormPostParameters.Add(
        "ctl00$ContentPlaceHolder1$Details1$fldID",
        this.Context["$HIDDEN1.ctl00$ContentPlaceHolder1$Details1$fldID"]
  .ToString());
    request4Body.FormPostParameters.Add(
        "ctl00$ContentPlaceHolder1$Details1$fldWE",
        this.Context["$HIDDEN1.ctl00$ContentPlaceHolder1$Details1$fldWE"]
  .ToString());
    request4Body.FormPostParameters.Add(
        "ctl00$ContentPlaceHolder1$Details1$txtDescription",
        this.Context["efforttrackingtests1.save_task_test.st_wi_description"]
```

```
            .ToString());
                    request4Body.FormPostParameters.Add(
                        "ctl00$ContentPlaceHolder1$Details1$cboCategory",
                        this.Context["efforttrackingtests1.save_task_test.st_cat_id"]
            .ToString());
                    request4Body.FormPostParameters.Add(
                        "ctl00$ContentPlaceHolder1$Details1$cboWeekEnding",
                        this.Context["efforttrackingtests1.save_task_test.st_we_id"].ToString());
                    request4Body.FormPostParameters.Add(
                        "ctl00$ContentPlaceHolder1$Details1$btnOK", "Save");
                    request4Body.FormPostParameters.Add("__EVENTVALIDATION",
                        this.Context["$HIDDEN1.__EVENTVALIDATION"].ToString());
                    request4.Body = request4Body;
                    yield return request4;
    }
```

VB

```
<DataSource("efforttrackingtests1", "Provider=SQLNCLI.1;Data Source=localhost;
Integrated Security=SSPI;Initial Catalog=efforttrackingtests",
Microsoft.VisualStudio.TestTools.WebTesting.DataBindingAccessMethod.Sequential,
"save_task_test"), _
DataBinding("efforttrackingtests1", "save_task_test", "st_wi_title",
"efforttrackingtests1.save_task_test.st_wi_title"), _
DataBinding("efforttrackingtests1", "save_task_test", "st_wi_description",
"efforttrackingtests1.save_task_test.st_wi_description"), _
DataBinding("efforttrackingtests1", "save_task_test", "st_cat_id", _
 "efforttrackingtests1.save_task_test.st_cat_id"), _
DataBinding("efforttrackingtests1", "save_task_test", "st_we_id", _
 "efforttrackingtests1.save_task_test.st_we_id")> _
Public Class AddItemCoded
    Inherits ThreadedWebTest

    Public Sub New()
        MyBase.New()
        Me.PreAuthenticate = True
    End Sub

    Public Overrides Sub Run()
        Dim request1 As WebTestRequest = New
            WebTestRequest("http://localhost/EffortTrackingWeb/secure/Default.aspx")
        . . .
        . . .
        Dim request4 As WebTestRequest = New _
            WebTestRequest("http://localhost/EffortTrackingWeb/secure/Edit.aspx")
        request4.Method = "POST"
        request4.QueryStringParameters.Add("id", "0", False, False)
        request4.QueryStringParameters.Add("mode", "add", False, False)
        request4.QueryStringParameters.Add("we_id", "1", False, False)
```

```
        Dim request4Body As FormPostHttpBody = New FormPostHttpBody
        request4Body.FormPostParameters.Add("__VIEWSTATE", _
            Me.Context("$HIDDEN1.__VIEWSTATE").ToString)
        request4Body.FormPostParameters.Add( _
            "ctl00$ContentPlaceHolder1$Details1$txtTitle", _
            Me.Context("efforttrackingtests1.save_task_test.st_wi_title").ToString)
        request4Body.FormPostParameters.Add( _
            "ctl00$ContentPlaceHolder1$Details1$fldID", _
            Me.Context( _
"$HIDDEN1.ctl00$ContentPlaceHolder1$Details1$fldID").ToString)
        request4Body.FormPostParameters.Add( _
            "ctl00$ContentPlaceHolder1$Details1$fldWE", _
            Me.Context("$HIDDEN1.ctl00$ContentPlaceHolder1$Details1$fldWE").ToString)
        request4Body.FormPostParameters.Add( _
            "ctl00$ContentPlaceHolder1$Details1$txtDescription", _
            Me.Context( _
"efforttrackingtests1.save_task_test.st_wi_description").ToString)
        request4Body.FormPostParameters.Add( _
            "ctl00$ContentPlaceHolder1$Details1$cboCategory", _
            Me.Context("efforttrackingtests1.save_task_test.st_cat_id").ToString)
        request4Body.FormPostParameters.Add( _
            "ctl00$ContentPlaceHolder1$Details1$cboWeekEnding", _
            Me.Context("efforttrackingtests1.save_task_test.st_we_id").ToString)
        request4Body.FormPostParameters.Add( _
            "ctl00$ContentPlaceHolder1$Details1$btnOK", "Save")
        request4Body.FormPostParameters.Add("__EVENTVALIDATION", _
            Me.Context("$HIDDEN1.__EVENTVALIDATION").ToString)
        request4.Body = request4Body
        MyBase.Send(request4)
    End Sub
```

The key to this scenario is the Attributes added to the class (at the top of the code listing). The DataSource attribute specifies the database in which the table to be used for testing is located. There can be as many data sources as necessary to complete a test. The last part of the data source contains the table (or tables) the test is specifically bound to. This controls how many iterations of the test will be performed. The DataBinding attribute maps table columns to form fields and is a simple and straight mapping. To assign the bound fields to the form parameters, use the same syntax as is shown in the Web Test window:

```
request4Body.FormPostParameters.Add("ctl00$ContentPlaceHolder1$Details1$fldID",
    this.Context["$HIDDEN1.ctl00$ContentPlaceHolder1$Details1$fldID"].ToString());
```

Aside from these differences, a data-driven coded web test and a non-data-driven web test are identical.

Now that you have seen how to record, run, and convert a web test into code you can examine how to create plugins and custom extraction and validation rules.

Extraction Rules

Extraction rules are used to extract parts of either the header or the body of a request for whatever purpose you need the extracted information. There are several prebuilt extraction rules that should cover many, it not all, the situations you will run in to. These extraction rules are described in Table 15-7.

Table 15-7. *Built-in Extraction Rules*

Rule	Description
Extract Attribute Value	Extracts the value of a given HTML attribute.
Extract Form Field	Extracts the value of a given form field.
Extract HTTP Header	Extracts the value of a given header.
Extract Regular Expression	Extracts any text that matches the given regular expression.
Extract Text	Extracts any text based on a beginning and ending set of criteria. Regular expressions can be used for this extraction rule also.
Extract Hidden Fields	Extracts all hidden fields from a response.

Based on these rules, there are very few reasons you would want to code a custom extraction rule. One reason is that you have a very complex regular expression and want to code it into an extraction rule or for some other reason such as to encourage reuse when dealing with web tests.

To add an existing extraction rule to a test, right-click a request node and select Add Extraction Rule. This will display the dialog box shown in Figure 15-9.

Figure 15-9. *Add Extraction Rule dialog box*

As with the validation rule demonstrated in the "Data-Driven Web Testing" section of this chapter, any field available here can be bound to a data source.

Each extraction rule has various different properties. One of the properties that you will find most useful is the Required property (if the rule has this property). Setting it to True indicates that the information the rule is trying to extract must exist or else the test will fail.

The Context Parameter Name value is a value available to all extraction rule tests. Providing a value here requires that you have previously created a context parameter.

Tip To create a Context Parameter field, right-click the name of the test in the Web Test window (the root node) or the Context Parameters folder, if it exists, and select Add Context Parameter. This creates a variable you can pass values to and read values from during the test.

Creating Custom Extraction Rules

Custom extraction rules allow you to encapsulate logic and complex extraction processes. Take an example where a regular expression contains recursive groups. This can be a very complex regular expression to write. Or maybe your organization routinely performs a certain type of security test and you want to encapsulate the rules so they do not have to be rewritten for every application. These are good reasons to create a custom extraction rule.

For this example, you will create a simple Extraction Rule that finds all of the telephone numbers, in the North American format (with variations) on a web page. Follow these steps to create the custom extraction rule:

1. Create a new code library called CustomExtractionRules (with either VB or CS appended to it for the example).

2. Add a reference to the Microsoft.VisualStudio.QualityTools.WebTestFramework.dll assembly. This assembly is located in the `C:\Program Files\Microsoft Visual Studio 8\ Common 7\IDE\Public Assemblies` folder.

3. Change the generated class (Class1) to TelephoneExtractionRule (rename the code file as well).

4. Add the following using or Imports statement to the top of the code file: using Microsoft.VisualStudio.TestTools.WebTesting.Rules; or, in VB, Imports Microsoft.VisualStudio.TestTools.WebTesting.Rules.

5. Change the class to inherit from the ExtractRegularExpression Rule class.

6. Implement (override) the RuleName and Extract methods (if needed) (see the code in Listing 15-3).

7. Build the solution.

Listing 15-3. *The Telephone Extraction Rule*

C#

```csharp
using System;
using Microsoft.VisualStudio.TestTools.WebTesting.Rules;

namespace CustomExtractionRulesCS
{
    public class ExtractTelephoneRule : ExtractRegularExpression
    {
        public ExtractTelephoneRule():base()
        {
            this.RegularExpression = @"\(?[0-9]{3}\)?[-. ]?[0-9]{3}[-. ]?[0-9]{4}";
        }

        public override string RuleName
        {
            get { return "Extract Telephone Numbers"; }
        }

        public override string RuleDescription
        {
            get { return "Extracts all telephone numbers which match "
                    + "the North American convention."; }
        }
    }
}
```

VB

```vb
Option Explicit On
Option Strict On

Imports Microsoft.VisualStudio.TestTools.WebTesting.Rules

Public Class ExtractTelephoneRule : Inherits ExtractRegularExpression

    Public Sub New()
        MyBase.New()

        Me.RegularExpression = "\(?[0-9]{3}\)?[-. ]?[0-9]{3}[-. ]?[0-9]{4}"
    End Sub

    Public Overrides ReadOnly Property RuleName() As String
        Get
            Return "Extract Telephone Numbers"
        End Get
    End Property
```

```
    Public Overrides ReadOnly Property RuleDescription() As String
        Get
            Return "Extracts all telephone numbers which match " _
                & "the North American convention."
        End Get
    End Property
End Class
```

As you can see, creating your own custom rule is extremely simple. The regular expression here will return all phone numbers that match the following formats: 1234567890, 123.456.7890, 123-456-7890, 123 456 7890, (123) 456 7890. The rule is also clearly documented by the description. Also note that because the rule simply uses a specific regular expression, the Extract method does not have to be overridden. In other circumstances you may want to override this method (and if you inherit from the base ExtractionRule you have to override this method).

Extract Method

If you were to inherit from the base ExtractionRule you would override the Extract method. This method's signature provides you with the access to both the Request and the Response objects to allow you to not only extract information but to compare the objects to each other. More information on the ExtractEventArgs can be found in the MSDN. It is important to note one particular class exposed by the ExtractEventArgs—the WebTest object. This object provides yet another object—the Context object. The Context object contains information about the running test. With these two objects you can dynamically change a number of values relating to the currently running tests and examine various pieces of information to put the extracted values into a proper context.

As you can see, overriding the Extract method provides a lot of options that are available to you. These same options are available when you create a custom validation rule (see the section below on "Creating Custom Validation Rules").

Implementing Custom Extraction Rules

Once the rule has been created, you need to actually incorporate it into the testing project. In the EffortTrackingWebTests project add a reference to the CustomExtractionRules assembly you just created. Right-click a request node in the Web Test window and select Add Extraction Rule. You should see the same dialog box as shown in Figure 15-10.

There cannot be a whole lot that is simpler than this. What you can do with this, in terms of extracting values, is limited only by what you can dream up. Since this is a standard property dialog you can create enumerations that fill the value lists, connect to databases to grab extraction rules (although this is certainly not recommended), or even provide configuration files that are user changeable to make configurable rules.

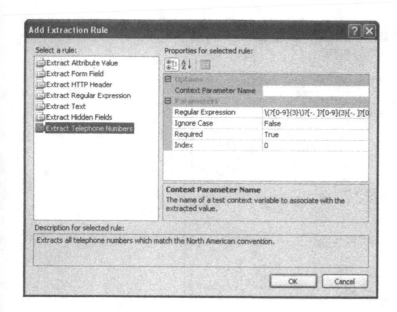

Figure 15-10. *The Extract Telephone Numbers extraction rule implemented*

Tip One possible solution to this problem is to have a variety of regular expressions (a library, as it were) that could be added to a configuration file and read by the rule so they would be easily extensible by the end user.

Validation Rules

Validation rules, as you have previously seen, can be used to test whether certain conditions on a web page are true once a response to a request has been made. In the previous example in the "Data-Driven Web Testing" section, the test validated that the system did return an error notification when a login failed. Likewise, it also validated that no error message was returned when a valid login occurred.

To add a validation rule to a request, right-click the request in the Web Test window and select Insert Validation Rule. This brings up the dialog box shown in Figure 15-11.

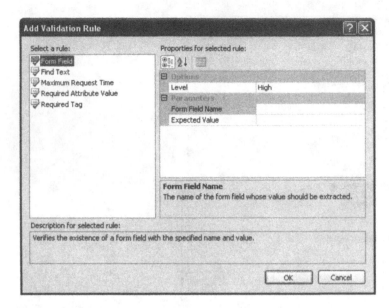

Figure 15-11. *Add Validation Rule dialog box*

The predefined validation rules are described in Table 15-8.

Table 15-8. *Predefined Validation Rules*

Rule	Description
Form Field	Verifies that a field exists on the form and what the value in that field is
Find Text	Verifies that certain text appears somewhere in the response page
Maximum Request Time	Verifies that a request finishes in a given amount of time
Required Attribute Value	Verifies that a specified HTML tag exists in the response and contains an attribute with a given value
Required Tag	Verifies that a specified HTML tag exists in the response

■**Caution** The validation rules operate on the response, not the request, even though they are associated with the request in the Web Test window. They are processed after the response has been returned.

The level option indicates the threshold the validation rule will be tested at during a load test. For example, if the validation rule level is set to Low and the load test validation level is set to Medium or High, then the validation rule will not be checked (this is discussed in a little more detail in Chapter 16).

Creating Custom Validation Rules

Creating a custom validation rule is almost identical to creating a custom extraction rule. To do this, you follow the same steps outlined previously in the "Creating Custom Extraction Rules" section except that instead of inheriting from the base ExtractionRule or one of its derivatives, you inherit from the base ValidationRule class or one of its derivatives. In this case, you would override, in addition to the RuleName property, the Validate method.

Web Test Request Plugins

Request plugins are plugins that allow you to perform external code execution when each request in the web test is executed. This can be used for a variety of reasons, but you will see in the next section that the Web Test Plugin is a more valuable alternative. The problem with the Web Test Request Plugin is that you cannot determine the start and stop of the test.

Web Test Plugins

A web test plugin is an application that can be executed in response to any event that occurs during a web test run. While the Web Test Request Plugin could only respond to individual requests, the Web Test Plugin encompasses all of the functionality of the request plugin plus more. There are various reasons why you might want to create your own test plugin. You may need to log specific details, or log those details in such a way that you can easily compare them from one test to another. Other reasons may include the fact that you need to change aspects of the tests during the test run. This could be something like having to change the URL the test is navigating to based on variables that can't be anticipated in a data-bound test. Whatever the reasons, the ability to dynamically change a test shows just how flexible the web testing tool is in VSTS.

In the example presented in Listing 15-4 you will see how to write a web test plugin that lets you perform custom logging of the test steps. To create a web test plugin, do the following:

1. Create a new project called "WebTestLogger."

2. Add a reference to the Microsoft.VisualStudio.QualityTools.WebTestFramework.dll.

3. Change the generated Class1 file to Logger (.cs or .vb depending on the language) and add the code shown in Listing 15-4.

Listing 15-4. *Logger Web Test Plugin*

```csharp
C#
using System;
using System.Collections.Generic;
using System.Text;
using Microsoft.VisualStudio.TestTools.WebTesting;
using System.IO;
```

```csharp
namespace LoggingRequest
{
    public class Logger: WebTestPlugin
    {
        private FileStream _logStream = null;
        private StreamWriter _logWriter = null;

        public Logger() {  }

        public override void PreWebTest(object sender, PreWebTestEventArgs e)
        {
            _logStream = new FileStream("c:\\logfile.txt", FileMode.Append);
            _logWriter = new StreamWriter(_logStream);
            _logWriter.AutoFlush = true;
            _logWriter.WriteLine("Beginning Test (" +
            DateTime.Now.ToString() + ")");
            e.WebTest.PostRequest += new
                EventHandler<PostRequestEventArgs>(WebTest_PostRequest);
        }

        void WebTest_PostRequest(object sender, PostRequestEventArgs e)
        {
            _logWriter.WriteLine(e.Request.Url.ToString());
        }

        public override void PostWebTest(object sender, PostWebTestEventArgs e)
        {
            _logWriter.WriteLine("Ending Test (" + DateTime.Now.ToString() + ")");
            _logWriter.Close();
            e.WebTest.PostRequest -= new
                EventHandler<PostRequestEventArgs>(WebTest_PostRequest);
        }
    }
}
```

```vbnet
VB
Option Explicit On
Option Strict On

Imports Microsoft.VisualStudio.TestTools.WebTesting
Imports System.IO
```

```
Public Class Logger : Inherits WebTestPlugin
    Private _logStream As FileStream = Nothing
    Private _logWriter As StreamWriter = Nothing
    Private WithEvents _test As WebTest = Nothing

    Public Overrides Sub PreWebTest(ByVal sender As Object, ByVal e As _
        Microsoft.VisualStudio.TestTools.WebTesting.PreWebTestEventArgs)
        _logStream = New FileStream("c:\logfile.txt", FileMode.Append)
        _logWriter = New StreamWriter(_logStream)
        _logWriter.AutoFlush = True
        _logWriter.WriteLine("Beginning Test (" + Now.ToString() + ")")
        _test = e.WebTest
    End Sub

    Public Sub Webtest_PostRequest(ByVal sender As Object, ByVal e As _
        Microsoft.VisualStudio.TestTools.WebTesting.PostRequestEventArgs) Handles _
        _test.PostRequest
        _logWriter.WriteLine(e.Request.Url.ToString())
    End Sub

    Public Overrides Sub PostWebTest(ByVal sender As Object, ByVal e As _
        Microsoft.VisualStudio.TestTools.WebTesting.PostWebTestEventArgs)
        _logWriter.WriteLine("Ending Test (" + Now.ToString() + ")")
        _logWriter.Close()
    End Sub
End Class
```

The Logger class is pretty straightforward. It inherits from the WebTestPlugin class and overrides the PreWebTest and PostWebTest methods. These methods are called at the beginning and end of the test respectively. The additional step taken here is that the PostRequest event of the WebTest is being handled so the URL for each event can be logged to the log file. Aside from that, there are no especially difficult steps for creating your own plugin.

One key thing to note is that the PreWebTest and PostWebTest are called once for *each* data row in a data-driven test. Because of this, the test explicitly closes and opens the file stream for each row in the test. So the constructor should be used for global test initialization and the PreWebTest should be used for individual run initialization.

To implement the plugin, open the EffortTracking Solution. Add a reference to the assembly, which contains the Logger class. Double-click the AddItem web test so it is displayed in the Web Test window. Click the Set Web Test Plugin button at the top of the window. Select the Logger class and click OK.

Note Only one Web Test Plugin and Web Test Request Plugin can be used for each test.

Run the web test as normal. The results will be a log file in the root C drive, which is partially shown in Listing 15-5.

Listing 15-5. *Log File Results*

```
Beginning Test (1/22/2006 2:07:12 PM)
http://localhost/EffortTrackingWeb/secure/Default.aspx
http://localhost/EffortTrackingWeb/login.aspx?
    ReturnUrl=/EffortTrackingWeb/secure/Default.aspx
http://localhost/EffortTrackingWeb/login.aspx
http://localhost/EffortTrackingWeb/secure/Default.aspx
http://localhost/EffortTrackingWeb/secure/Default.aspx
http://localhost/EffortTrackingWeb/secure/Edit.aspx?id=0&mode=add&we_id=1
http://localhost/EffortTrackingWeb/secure/Edit.aspx
http://localhost/EffortTrackingWeb/secure/Default.aspx?we_id=3&last=29
Ending Test (Sunday, January 22, 2006)
Beginning Test (1/22/2006 2:09:52 PM)
http://localhost/EffortTrackingWeb/secure/Default.aspx
http://localhost/EffortTrackingWeb/login.aspx?
    ReturnUrl=/EffortTrackingWeb/secure/Default.aspx
http://localhost/EffortTrackingWeb/login.aspx
http://localhost/EffortTrackingWeb/secure/Default.aspx
http://localhost/EffortTrackingWeb/secure/Default.aspx
http://localhost/EffortTrackingWeb/secure/Edit.aspx?id=0&mode=add&we_id=1
http://localhost/EffortTrackingWeb/secure/Edit.aspx
http://localhost/EffortTrackingWeb/secure/Default.aspx?we_id=3&last=32
Ending Test (Sunday, January 22, 2006)
Beginning Test (1/22/2006 2:10:01 PM)
. . .
```

As you can see from the file, each individual run is recorded separately.

Testing Web Services

Web services are the new "cool" way to implement a service-oriented architecture (SOA). While there are pluses and minuses to this approach, it is fast catching on as the new way to integrate systems. With that in mind, Microsoft built the Web Test tool so that it could also test web services.

Note The main purpose of the Web Test tool is to test websites, not web services. Therefore, while it can be used to test web services, it is not necessarily the best tool, depending on the situation. If you are testing web services that are not very complicated, the Web Test tool is a simple solution. For more complex situations, software from AmberPoint (www.amberpoint.com) may be better suited to your needs.

Since there are some web services in the solution, you will use the EffortTrackingService. To set up the basic test, do the following:

1. Right-click the EffortTrackingWebTests solution in the Solution Explorer and select New Web Test.

2. When the recording window is displayed, click Stop (you do not want to record anything).

3. Rename the webtest1.webtest file to ServiceTest.webtest.

Now you have a blank test you can use to write the web service test. The best way to write these tests is to use the built-in help that ASP.NET provides you when browsing a web service. To begin with, open Internet Explorer and browse to http://localhost/EffortTrackingService/Service.asmx. Select the GetLookupInfo link from the list of available services. This will bring up the page shown in Figure 15-12.

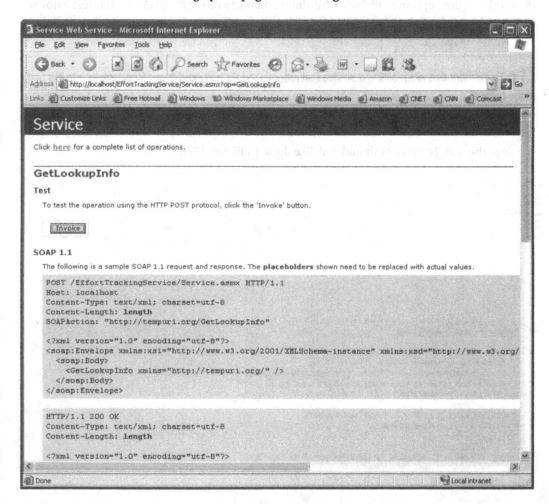

Figure 15-12. *GetLookupInfo service implementation details*

The beauty of this page is that it provides you the text necessary to make the SOAP or HTTP calls. Leaving this alone for the moment, switch back to the IDE browser and right-click the ServiceTest node (the root and only node) in the Web Test window. Select Add Web Service Request. This will add a blank node with a stub URL. Enter the following URL in the URL property of the request node: `http://localhost/EffortTrackingService/Service.asmx/ GetLookupInfo`.

Note The Transport Method at this time is only available as a Post call. The body of the request may be in the format of either a SOAP request or an HTTP request.

Next, click the String Body node beneath the request node. Set the Context Type to text/xml (the only option available at this time) and paste the entire SOAP 1.1 request (shown in Figure 15-12) from the browser into the String Body property.

Tip Remember that when calling a service that requires values you need to put those values into the body of the request.

Run the test. The results should look like those in Figure 15-13.

Figure 15-13. *Web service test result*

As you can see, it is virtually identical to the result of a regular web test except there is no graphical interface, just the service result.

■**Note** In general, the only way to validate the results is to use a regular expression validation rule or a custom validation rule that parses XML looking for specific values.

You can also run data-driven web service tests. To do this, hook up a data source (as described in the "Data-Driven Web Testing" section in this chapter) as usual. However, to place values in the actual SOAP body, use the data field syntax: {{database.table.field}}. Replace any text in the body with this syntax (specific to your data source of course) and the value will be replaced during the test.

Test Results

When viewing the Test Results window (shown in Figure 15-14) you have several options, one of which is exporting the results file to a Test Results XML file (.trx file).

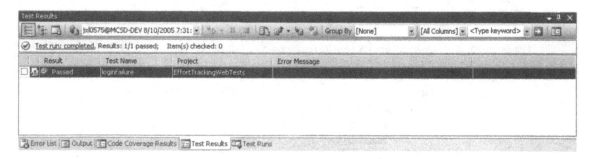

Figure 15-14. *Test Results window*

To export the results, select the Export button from the Test Results window. All of the test results can be exported or just selected test results. The .trx file can be reloaded into the Visual Studio environment at a later date by selecting the Import Test Results button and selecting the .trx file from the browser (this can be from a local computer or a remote computer).

The .trx file is a well-formed XML document you can use in any way you see fit. Transforms can be applied against the XML for either viewing or extracting data.

■**Note** The full description of the XML Schema (XSD) for this file is beyond the scope of this book (it is more than 2,000 lines long). Microsoft is set to release the XML Schemas for most of the documents contained in Visual Studio 2005.

Test Results Schema

The XML Schema, which backs this file, is fairly large so this section only touches on some of the highlights. This schema is very hierarchical in nature with almost every node allowing for an unbounded number of sub-elements. This is because of the nature of the tests it is recording. Take for example the data-driven test run results, which contain four separate tests that went through three or four URL navigations. Representing this data is a fairly complex task, which is why the resulting XSD file is so complex.

Figure 15-15 represents the high-level structure of the XSD file. Figures 15-16 and 15-17 represent the TestRun and the WebTestResults nodes.

■Note The following graphics were taken from the XML development tool Altova XMLSpy 2005. If you work with XML a lot, this is the single best tool available. In addition, if you want to create your own style sheets to view the results in a custom format, use Altova's StyleVision 2005. This is an incredible tool for creating style sheets and transformations with drag-and-drop simplicity.

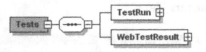

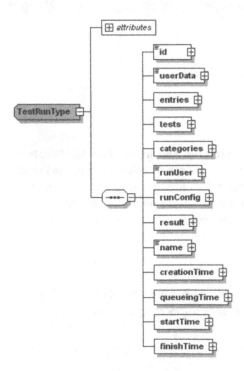

Figure 15-16. *TestRun node of the test results schema*

The TestRun node contains information about each run of the test. It contains information such as who ran a test, what computer a test was run for, when a test started, when it stopped, etc. Specific nodes in the TestRun type are listed in Table 15-9.

Table 15-9. *Notable TestRun Nodes*

Node	Description
Tests	Contains the test name, test file (.webtest) location, associated work item IDs, the project the test is contained in, and various other pieces of information
categories	Contains information related to how the test (or tests) is categorized in the Test Manager
runConfig	Contains all the configuration information from the run configuration associated with the test(s) in general
result	Contains the test result—summed if there was more than one test

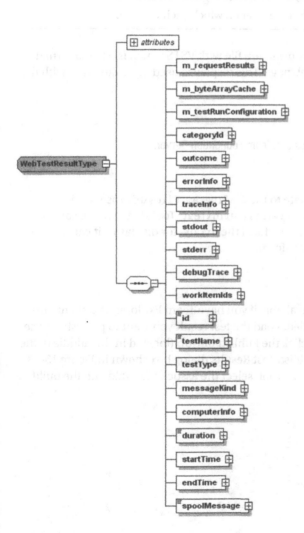

Figure 15-17. *WebTestResult node of the test results schema*

The WebTestResult node contains information specific to each test run. This information includes the request page, the response page, and all the information about each of them and their state for every step of the test (they include the headers but not the body). This is the largest portion of the XSD because of the detailed information contained about each test.

Specific nodes in the WebTestResult type are listed in Table 15-10.

Table 15-10. *WebTestResult Nodes*

Node	Description
m_requestResults	Contains all of the information about specific steps in a test. A simple XSLT applied to a portion of this node can be seen in Figure 15-16.
m_testRunConfiguration	Contains information specific to the configuration as it relates to the specific test run.
errorInfo	Contains any error messages generated by the test step.
computerInfo	Identifies the computer on which each was run.

Microsoft also provides one XML transformation file with VSTS which is used to format the results of the .trx file for display in a web page. This display is used in conjunction with the Builds report.

Tip This file is only available if you have access to a Team Foundation Server.

On the Team Foundation Server, navigate to the `C:\Program Files\Microsoft Visual Studio 2005 Team Foundation Server\Web Services\Build\Test Tools\v1.0\Transforms\testresult.xsl` file. This file can be used to transform the .trx file for display or it can be used as a starting point for creating your own transform.

Publishing Test Results

The option to publish a test result is only available if you have Team Explorer (the client portion of the Team Foundation Server) installed. Load the test result you want to publish (or use the existing one if you just ran a test) and click the Publish button (located in the middle of the Test Results pane). This will display the Publish Test Results dialog box shown in Figure 15-18.

Select the test run(s) you want to publish, then select the associated build and the build flavor and click OK.

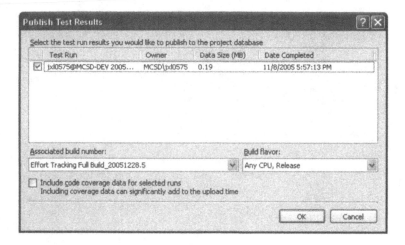

Figure 15-18. *Publish Test Results dialog box*

Note You must do a build with TFSBuild for there to be a build number to associate this test result to. If there are no existing build numbers, then the test result cannot be published. For more information, see Chapter 7.

Multiple test results can be associated with a build/build-flavor combination.

Summary

This chapter has been a whirlwind tour of web testing using Microsoft's new web testing tools. You have seen how to record a web test and dissect all of the steps in order to determine what the test is doing. The various options available to you for the web test have also been covered as well as, more importantly, how to customize the functionality for particular problems you are trying to solve.

You can now convert recorded web tests to coded web tests and implement data binding in either scenario. This gives you a more powerful and controlled way to test different conditions without writing hundreds of individual tests. And, finally, you have seen how to view the test results, publish them, and examine the resulting XML file, so you can create your own transformations to extract the data you feel is the most important.

You have also seen how web services can be tested in a way that exercises the service interface rather than using a unit test. This is especially useful if you are using custom handlers that might inject custom SOAP into the response.

All of this shows the flexibility of the web testing tool. The tool lends itself to being used in almost any situation—from the mundane to the complex. While it is better suited to some tasks than others, as a base testing tool it should cover about 95% of your web testing needs.

CHAPTER 16

■ ■ ■

Load Testing

Up to this point you have seen how to run web tests from a single machine and run performance testing on discrete pieces of code or on the application as a whole. The last step in testing a system is load testing. Load testing can be defined as "the act of determining whether an application will continue to perform at a defined level, given a set number of connections and requests." While this is our definition (and there are many different definitions for load testing), it does give you one important piece of information: It is measurable.

Often the terms scalability testing, stress testing, and performance testing are used interchangeably. And while they are all definitely linked—and in some cases use the exact same type of tests—the goal is different. You have seen that in performance testing the goal is to discover bottlenecks. To do this, the performance tests can use the exact same testing methodology as load tests. In other words, you can instrument your assemblies and run a load test on them. However, you would not look at the load test results when trying to determine if there are bottlenecks in the application—you would examine the performance results at the method or system level. See? Same test but the information you are looking at is completely different. The question now is what would you look at if you were running a load test?

A load test looks at the performance of the application in relationship to the environment that the application is running in. It looks for external causes for application failure. To illustrate, if you navigate to a website and get an internal server error or a "site unavailable" message, does this mean the website (the application) itself failed? Or does it mean that it is taking so many requests (as in a denial of service attack) that it cannot respond to more requests? This is probably not a result of the application failing (although it could be) but of how the environment is handling the requests. Load testing can also be used to determine database connectivity issues under high load as well. It is quite possible that the application can handle 10,000 requests up front but the act of creating 10,000 connections to the database causes it to fail. Why did it fail? It could be the number of allowed users was exceeded or the back-end network failed to meet the demand placed on it. These are all questions that load testing seeks to answer.

Stress testing, which can be a component of load testing, is designed to cause an application to fail. It does this by placing the system under such a high load that it has no choice but to fail. This high load may be because of the number of connections to the application as in a regular stress test or it may be because other variables were introduced into the environment. These variables range from simulating a hard drive failure to a network card failure or a power supply failure. It tells the tester exactly how many things can go wrong with an environment before the application itself no longer performs. Fortunately this chapter does not cover those issues.

■**Note** No application is infinitely scalable or can handle an infinite amount of demand. For one thing, there just is not enough money or need to make that type of system a reality. The types of tests explained here are all determined to help ensure that the application performs as it has been specified to and if it fails the reasons for the failure are known. Then, intelligent decisions can be made concerning how to handle the projected number of users or limitations in the environment.

With the gain in popularity of web services as a sort of "universal" medium through which various applications can communicate, and the increase of web applications, the use of web servers (be it IIS, Apache, or any of a dozen others) is on the rise. This increased usage has ancillary effects on a network environment. If the application is hosted on a machine with other applications, will it negatively affect those applications? Will other applications that happen to use the same network segments as your application be affected? The answers to these questions can help you tune the configuration of both specific machines and the network environment as a whole. And as you will see, Visual Studio Team System provides enough information to allow an organization to make the right decisions.

This chapter will round out your understanding of running tests using VSTS. Many of the previous chapters deferred some of the testing information until this chapter. Load testing is really built on top of web testing. That is, you need to have a web test before you can have a load test. Load testing works by either running the same tests from different machines (using agents) or simulating different machines (through the use of Virtual Machines) even though there may in reality be only one machine.

Controllers and Agents

Before working on actually running a load test, you need to understand how the tests are run (and should be run) and how to deploy the various components of a test. A controller is a service that, conveniently enough, controls a set of agents when performing a specific test. An agent performs the actual work of sending instructions to an application. This set of computers (the controller and all agent computers) is called a rig. For a given load test there can be only one controller, and each agent can belong to only one controller. The physical topography of this setup is shown in Figure 16-1.

Figure 16-1 shows the optimal configuration for a controller/agent deployment, but it is not the only configuration. Essentially any configuration will work provided that a controller and at least one agent are deployed to a machine (this can be the same machine Visual Studio is installed on or the same machine the application is installed on).

■**Note** For the load tests performed in this chapter, the deployment consisted of a laptop with Visual Studio on it and a Win2k3 server with the application, the controller, and one agent installed.

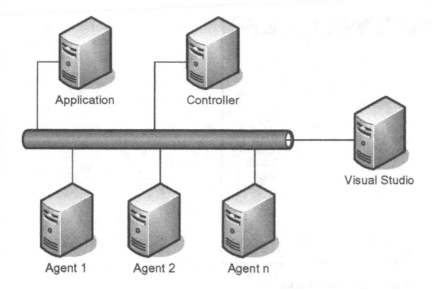

Figure 16-1. *Controller/agent load testing deployment*

Only one agent can be deployed to a given computer, and the controller must be installed first (the controller location information is necessary for the agent installation). Aside from this, there are no limitations on the topography of the test setup.

■**Tip** For this application, a separate controller and agent were installed to perform the load tests. Team Test Load Agent contains the load test agent and controller and needs to be purchased separately. Visual Studio Team System can be used as both the controller and the agent for small load tests (up to about 500 simulated users per processor), but it is best to use a separate controller and agents.

Whenever possible, load testing should be done in an environment that is as close to the real-world environment as possible. This will provide you the most accurate results on which to base decisions.

Once you have the controller and agents set up, you can create and run a load test.

Administering a Controller

Assuming at this point that you have actually set up a controller (or more than one), you can configure it through the Administer Test Controller dialog box shown in Figure 16-2.

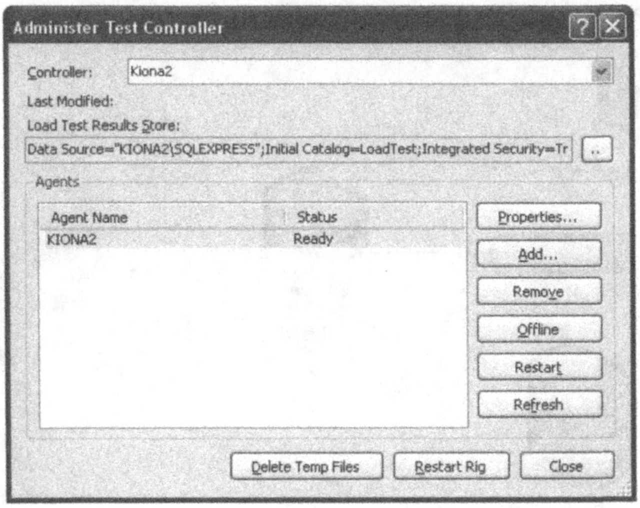

Figure 16-2. *Administer Test Controller dialog box*

Tip SQL Express is installed during the install of the controller.

To add a new controller, you can just type the name of the computer into the controller drop-down. The load test result store holds a copy of the load tests. By default, it is automatically set up on the controller computer.

Caution You can select <local>, which is the machine on which VSTS is installed, as the controller. Agents *cannot* be assigned to the <local> controller (there is a default local agent, but only one when using <local> as the controller).

The agents assigned to each controller are shown in the Agents list. In this case, the controller and the agent are installed on the same machine. Various options are available for each agent and for the controller. An agent can be removed from a particular controller by selecting the Remove button. To re-add the agent, simply select the Add button and enter the name of the agent in the Agent Properties dialog box when it is displayed (shown in Figure 16-3). Specific agents can also be taken offline, in which case it will not be a part of a test run (the status will change to Offline). Restart can be used to bring an offline agent back online, and Refresh will refresh the statuses of the agents.

■ Note The status can also be shown as running (if it is currently running a test) or disconnected if VSTS cannot find the agent on the network.

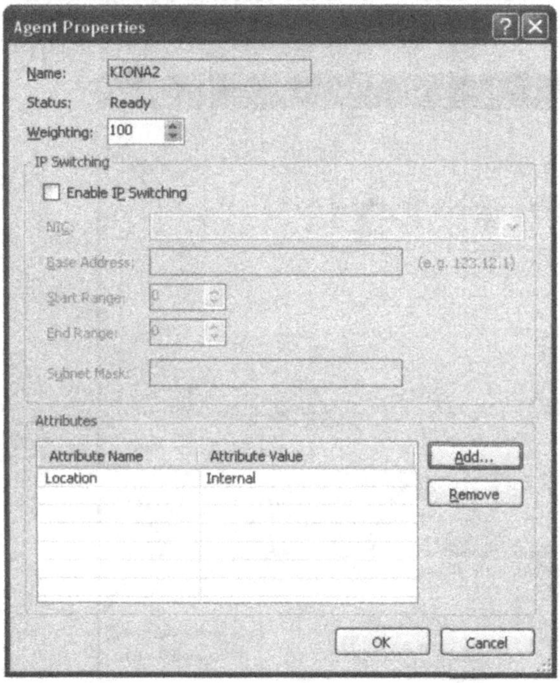

Figure 16-3. *Agent Properties dialog box*

The Delete Temp Files option deletes all files deployed to the agents and controllers. The Restart Rig option restarts the controller and all agents.

■ Note Several of these options are available even if a test is in progress. If there is a test currently running, you will be notified and given the option to cancel the operation.

In the Agent Properties dialog box you can change the weight of the tests run by that agent. This weight number determines the amount of tests sent from the agent to the test system. This number is independent of the other agents (i.e., you can have three agents with a weight of 50%).

Enable IP Switching allows an agent to send requests over a range of IP addresses to the application to be tested, instead of just a single static IP address. You can also specify the network interface card (NIC) that the requests should be sent from, if there is more than one network card installed on the agent machine.

The Attributes section allows you to add a series of name/value pairs that allow you to constrain which agents are used in a given test. This filter is set in the Test Run Configuration dialog box shown in Figure 16-4.

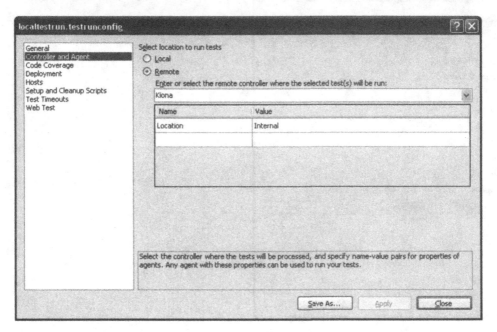

Figure 16-4. *The Controller and Agent configuration tab*

Configuring the Test Run

The solution configuration file has been covered in various chapters (an overview of the entire configuration file was presented in Chapter 12). There is one tab in the configuration file that applies to load testing: the Controller and Agent tab shown in Figure 16-4.

This tab allows you to configure where the tests are run from and allows you to filter the agents used in the run. The tests can be run either from the local machine (if no controller is installed) or from a remote machine (if you have previously installed a controller). When selecting Remote, you have the option of constraining which agents are used as part of the test by specifying the Attribute name you assigned to the agents and the value of that attribute. An example of this may be the network configuration between the agent and the test machine. The situation may be such that several computers are set up as internal to the enterprise and several are external and go through a proxy and a firewall. For this scenario you may add an attribute name to each agent with a value of Location and a value of either Internal or External. Then, when running the test, you can elect to only use some of the agents by entering **Location** in the name and **External** in the value if you want to simulate connections coming in from outside of the firewall.

Tip A best practice is to add the same attribute name to each of the agents. By doing this you are explicitly including an agent with a given value. If you do not add an attribute name and value to a given agent but specify it in the test configuration dialog, the agent without that attribute will not run. By adding the same name to each agent you will not accidentally exclude an agent.

Load Test Wizard

Now that you have seen how to configure the controller and agents, you can create a load test. The easiest way to create a load test is to use the Load Test Wizard. To do this, select Test ➤ New Test from the main menu. Select the Load Test icon and click OK (select the EffortTrackingWebTests as the project in which the test should be located). The first page of the load test is an introduction to the wizard. Click Next on the Introduction screen to move to the Scenario screen (shown in Figure 16-5).

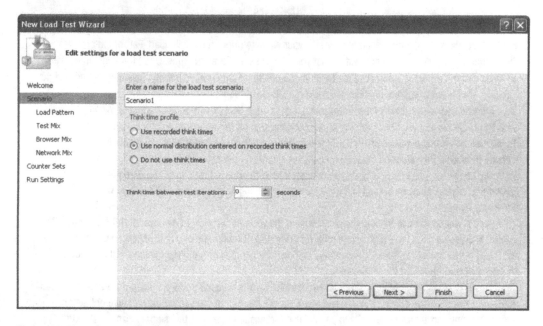

Figure 16-5. *Scenario settings wizard dialog box*

Scenario

This dialog box allows you to set the name for the test and specify think times. The think times control how real the scenario is. The think time is the amount of time a user spends looking at a web page or reading a web page without actually doing anything. A perfect example is a news site. You might browse to a site and read an article. It may take you up to five minutes to read that page, during which time you are not actually hitting the web server at all.

The three think time options are described in Table 16-1. Think times are discussed in more detail in the sidebar.

Table 16-1. *Think Time Options*

Profile	Description
Recorded think times	The test will use the think times you entered for each page of the web test (one of the properties of the Request Node of a web test).
Normal distribution	The test uses a statistical distribution of think times based on the time entered for each page. For example, if you set the think time property of a page to 8 seconds, the test may use times between 5 and 11 seconds as the think time.
No think times	The test executes as fast as it possibly can for the specified number of iterations.

THINK TIMES

Think times allow you to more accurately profile your website under a realistic load. Part of the problem with the testing tool, Application Center Test, is that you cannot simulate think times. Often the think times will give you a much different view of the load that your website can accurately handle. Selecting the normal distribution, which is the default, provides the most realistic load test.

A perfect example of why think times make a difference occurs with a news website. When you visit www.msnbc.com or www.cnn.com you do not click through all the pages as quickly as you can; you read the stories. Often these stories are broken up into multiple pages. Consider how you might design your website to handle this situation. Maybe when a user selects a news story that is three pages long, you automatically cache (or check the cache) on a separate thread to ensure that pages two and three of the story are loaded. You do this because you have a good idea based on logical reasoning that the user will want to read the whole story.

Now if you do not use think times when testing the website, you might discover that the site has a high rate of database access, or a high cache miss rate (the rate at which the cache is accessed but the page is not found in the cache). In reality, the site may be perfectly capable of handling the load, but you would not be aware of that based on the test results.

Similarly, a static set of think times allows the testing of a website under a constant load; but this load is not very realistic. The chance that ten users will access the site at the same time, spend eight seconds on each page, and move through the site in parallel is not realistic either. But by using a normal distribution you can be guaranteed that the page access times will become varied, and it will simulate people accessing the website at various times on each page.

This is not to say that static think times and no think times do not have a place—they do. They allow the testing of a website under a constant but reasonable load and with the worst case scenario. A perfect example of why you would want to test with no think times is a denial of service attack, in which packets requesting pages are constantly sent against one page or many. This provides a great test to see how your website will respond in such a circumstance.

The think time between test iterations allows you to specify how quickly the test will repeat after it has completed.

Load Pattern

The load pattern allows for the specification of how many simulated users will access the website and in what distribution. You can specify a constant load or a step load (shown in Figure 16-6).

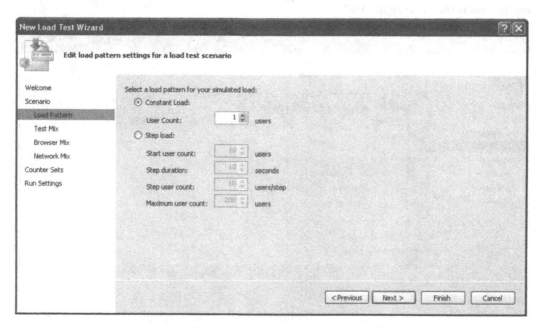

Figure 16-6. *Load Pattern dialog box*

A constant load means that the number of users specified will start accessing the website immediately upon activation of the test. A step load test allows you to specify how the user count will "ramp up" (see Table 16-2).

Table 16-2. *Step Load Values*

Values	Description
Start user count	Number of simulated users who will access the website as soon as the test run is started.
Step duration	Amount of time each step will last.
Step user count	Number of simulated users who will be added to the user count at each step.
Maximum user count	Maximum number of simulated users who will access the website.

It is not necessary to run the step load in order to get an accurate assessment of your website. In the run settings (see the "Run Settings" section later in this chapter) you can specify a warm-up time for the test, which will allow the site time to compile and cache pages before the "real" test starts.

Test Mix

The next part of the wizard is to add the tests you want to load test your site with. The dialog box for this is shown in Figure 16-7.

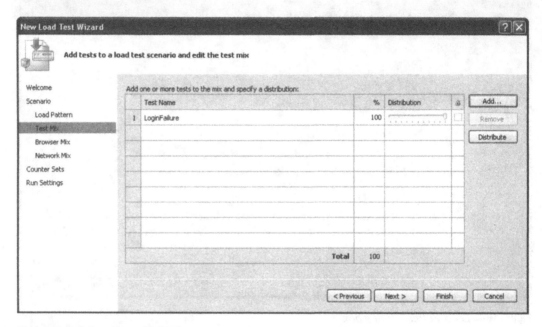

Figure 16-7. *Select Tests dialog box*

To add a test, select the Add button and select each of the tests from the Add Tests dialog box shown in Figure 16-8.

From here you can add any previously created tests.

The distribution value is an indicator of the likelihood of a user actually running through the sequence of events described in the web test. For example, in the effort tracking application there is a higher probability that a user will log on to the application and add a task rather than logging on, selecting a different week, and deleting a task. The distribution must equal 100%.

■**Caution** Nothing prevents you from adding unit tests or manual tests to this list. Do not do this! The load test will run but no usable information will be returned (and it will pause the load test if you specify a manual test).

The check box to the right of the distribution allows you to lock a particular test's distribution so it does not change dynamically as you change the distributions on other tests.

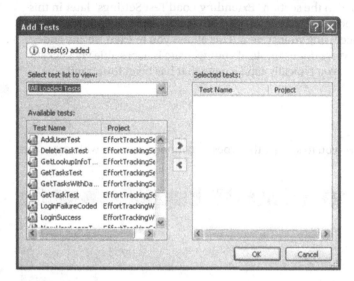

Figure 16-8. *Add Tests dialog box*

Browser Mix

The load test allows you to specify the types of browsers that will be accessing the website and allows you to specify the distribution of those requests (shown in Figure 16-9).

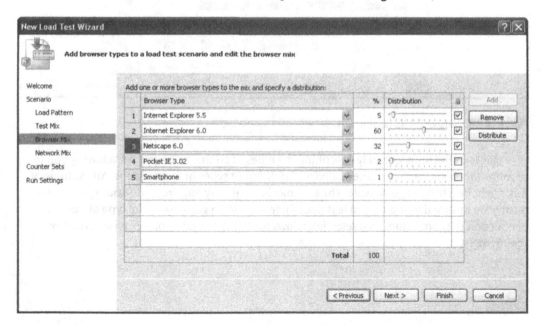

Figure 16-9. *Browser Mix dialog box*

Figure 16-9 shows the list of built-in browsers that are supported by load testing. This list is extensible, although undocumented, so you can create additional browser types such as Opera and Firefox (this is described in the section "Extending Load Test Settings" later in this chapter). The distribution here is identical to that of the tests. It allows you to specify the portion of browsers of a given type accessing your system. This allows you to exercise any code you have that targets specific browsers (for example, if your website is accessible via Pocket Internet Explorer or a Smartphone, you typically send a page that has been formatted differently).

Network Mix

The Network Mix dialog box allows you to specify the types of connections that will access the website (shown in Figure 16-10).

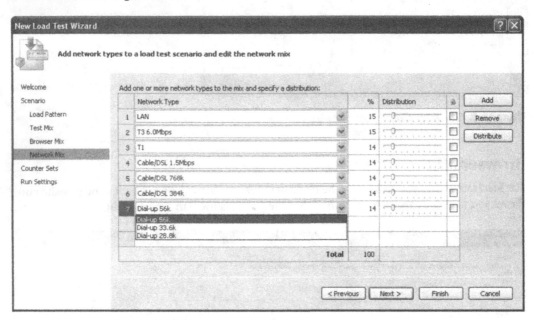

Figure 16-10. *Network Mix dialog box*

This is useful for accurately describing the types of connections and for allowing you to monitor the time it takes to generate pages for different types of connections. An example of this might be a brokerage website. The site may have quality requirements that specify that results are returned to the user in less than three seconds regardless of the type of network connection they are using. This selection allows for the verification of this type of quality requirement.

Counter Sets

Counter sets are literally the set of counters you want to use to monitor information about various computers during the test (shown in Figure 16-11).

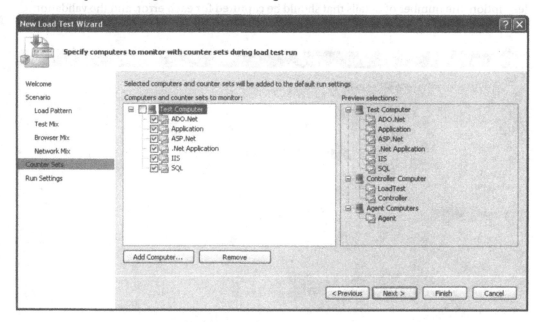

Figure 16-11. *Counter Sets dialog box*

By default, the controller computer and all agent computers are monitored. However, you can elect to monitor additional computers on the network for performance during the testing. A common example of this might be a proxy server. Since some of the requests are going to go through this computer, knowing how it is performing during the test is crucial. Another example would be a load balancing server, a database server, or a failover server. This will tell you if the hardware and network connections on the external systems your application has a dependency on are capable of handling the load.

Note For this chapter, the controller, agent, and website are all located on the same computer, so there is no separate test computer as shown in Figure 16-11. That is an example only.

Run Settings

Run settings allow you to specify the warm-up time (the amount of time the website is "exercised" before the real test begins), the run duration, the frequency of sample collection, a test description, the number of details that should be captured for each error, and the validation level (Figure 16-12).

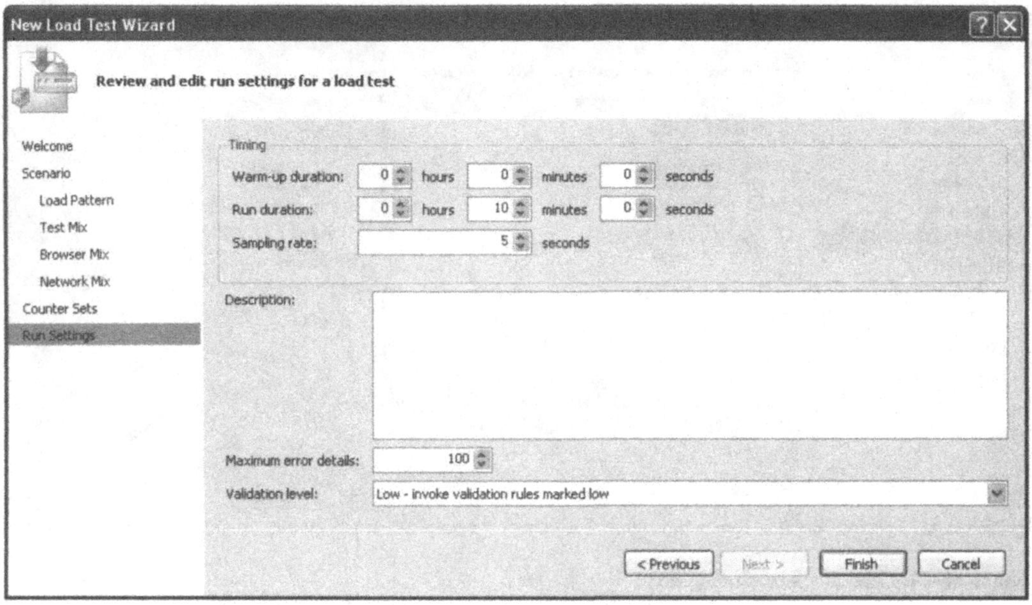

Figure 16-12. *Run Settings dialog box*

The only item that really needs to be described on this dialog box is the validation level; everything else is self-explanatory. The validation level describes what validation rules the load test will ignore or process (see the section "Validation Rules" in Chapter 15 for more details). During a regular web test you most likely want to know when a value violates a rule. During a load test this information is not necessarily important unless you need to know how the site reacts to these violations under load.

Extending Load Test Settings

For a load test you can extend or alter three of the settings for a load test—browser types, network types, and counter sets—using a ridiculously simple feature that is currently undocumented.

Extending the Browsers

The list of browsers included with the out-of-the-box package is pretty small. It does not include such popular browsers as Firefox or Opera and there are numerous other browsers that, while not all that common, are definitely in use by a large number of users (for example, the browsers that work on non-Windows phones). So adding to this list is a fairly logical step. To add a new browser you will create a browser file. The default browser files are located in C:\Program Files\Microsoft Visual Studio 8\Common7\IDE\Templates\LoadTest\Browsers. If you open the IE6.browser file you will see the XML shown in Listing 16-1.

Listing 16-1. *The IE6 Browser File*

```
<Browser Name="Internet Explorer 6.0">
  <Headers>
    <Header Name="User-Agent" Value="Mozilla/4.0 (compatible; MSIE 6.0;
Windows NT 5.1)" />
    <Header Name="Accept" Value="*/*" />
    <Header Name="Accept-Language" Value="{{$IEAcceptLanguage}}" />
    <Header Name="Accept-Encoding" Value="GZIP" />
  </Headers>
</Browser>
```

If you are not familiar with how browsers work, here's a one-sentence introduction (although, hopefully, if you are reading this chapter you know how a browser header works): when the client browser sends a request to the server it includes various pieces of information about itself so the server can take appropriate action. To see this in action, try visiting www.ranks.nl/tools/envtest.html to see what is sent to a server. With this information, understanding what is included here is pretty simple.

Tip More information on header field values can be found at www.w3.org/Protocols/rfc2616/rfc2616-sec14.html (W3C specification).

In Listing 16-1 the User-Agent value indicates the capabilities of the agent (the browser in this case) accessing the server. As you can see, IE is Mozilla 4.0 compliant and compatible with Microsoft Internet Explorer 6 and is running on the Windows NT 5.1 platform (Windows XP).

The Accept header indicates what extensions will be honored in the response. */* indicates that all extensions are acceptable to the client. If, for example, you only want to accept images, you would see image/*, which indicates the type and what subtypes to accept (* indicates all).

The Accept-Language value is the language the browser can understand. The $IEAccept-Language is replaced with the culture in use on the local machine. Some of the actual values (i.e., the values that are actually transmitted) are "en" or "en-us" for English or U.S. English, "hu" for Hungarian, "zh" for Chinese, etc.

Tip More information about the language codes can be found in any book on application globalization or localization. A shorter list can be found here: www.hashemian.com/tools/browser-simulator.htm.

The Accept-Encoding header indicates the type of encoding of the data that can be understood by the browser. In this case, GZIP indicates that IE6 can understand the data transmitted to the client if it is compressed in a gzip format (a compression format that is in standard use by web servers to minimize the size of the data stream sent to the client).

Now that you understand the contents of this file, add a new Opera browser by creating a new browser file called Opera.browser and enter the information contained in Listing 16-2.

Listing 16-2. *The Opera Browser File*

```
<Browser Name="Opera 8.0">
  <Headers>
    <Header Name="User-Agent" Value="Opera/8.00+(Windows+NT+5.1;+U;+en)" />
    <Header Name="Accept" Value="text/html, image/jpeg, image/gif,
      image/x-xbitmap, */*" />
    <Header Name="Accept-Language" Value="en" />
    <Header Name="Accept-Encoding" Value="GZIP" />
  </Headers>
</Browser>
```

Once you save the file, if you edit the Browser Mix you will see Opera 8.0 as an option.

Extending the Network Types

Creating a new network type or altering an existing network type is even easier than adding or changing a browser type. The network types are located in the folder C:\Program Files\Microsoft Visual Studio 8\Common7\IDE\Templates\LoadTest\Networks and have the extension .network. The 56.6 dial-up type is shown in Listing 16-3.

Listing 16-3. *Dial-up 56.6K Network Type*

```
<Network Name="Dial-up 56k" BandwidthInKbps="53.3">
</Network>
```

The bandwidth controller is the BandwidthInKbps attribute. 53.3 represents the number of kilobytes/second. The T1 network is represented by 1544 Kbps. The LAN network is represented by a value of 0, which indicates maximum throughput. To create a new network type just add the code from Listing 16-3 to a file with the extension .network and customize it as you need. This is handy for when more advanced connections are developed or special network needs require nonstandard throughput.

Extending the Counter Sets

The counter sets allow you to preconfigure frequently used counters for performance monitoring. A good use of this might be to create a standard counter configuration file to be used by all of your applications, or a configuration file for any other standards-based testing where you have to ensure that the same counters are captured for different tests. The counter sets are located in C:\Program Files\Microsoft Visual Studio 8\Common7\IDE\Templates\LoadTest\ CounterSets and have the extension .CounterSets. The ADO.NET counter set is shown in Listing 16-4.

Listing 16-4. *The ADO.NET Counter Set*

```
<CounterSet Name="ADO.Net" CounterSetType="ADO.Net">
    <CounterCategories>
        <CounterCategory Name=".NET CLR Data">
            <Counters>
                <Counter Name="SqlClient: Current # connection pools" />
                <Counter Name="SqlClient: Current # pooled and
nonpooled connections" />
                <Counter Name="SqlClient: Current # pooled connections" />
                <Counter Name="SqlClient: Peak # pooled connections" />
                <Counter Name="SqlClient: Total # failed commands" />
                <Counter Name="SqlClient: Total # failed connects" />
            </Counters>
            <Instances>
                <Instance Name="*" />
            </Instances>
        </CounterCategory>
    </CounterCategories>
</CounterSet>
```

The category name is what shows up in the list, and in the list of counters are the names of the specific counters (you can get these values from the Windows Performance Monitor (perfmon). The Instance name specifies the machine from which the counters are to be collected. The star (*) indicates that these counters will be collected from all of the machines involved in the test.

Load Test Window

After the Load Test Wizard has completed, the settings can be viewed in the Load Test window shown in Figure 16-13.

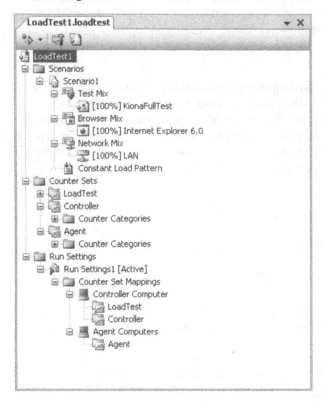

Figure 16-13. *Load Test window*

From the Load Test window you can configure several additional options (shown in Table 16-3) and add additional run settings.

Note While only one run setting can be active at a given time, by being able to configure multiple settings, the same load test can be reused in order to focus given tests on various aspects of the systems under load.

Table 16-3. *Additional Load Test Options*

Option	How To	Description
Add Custom Counters	Right-click the Counter Sets node.	Allows you to add any counters available in the system at a very fine-grained level (Figure 16-14).
Add Threshold Rule	Expand the Counter Sets until you find the counter you want to set a threshold rule for, right-click, and select Add Threshold Rule.	Allows you to add a warning that informs you of when a counter has exceeded a given threshold (Figure 16-15).
Add Run Settings	Right-click the Run Settings node.	Allows you to add additional run settings.

■**Note** When additional run settings are added, make sure you have selected the correct run setting for a test either by right-clicking the settings and selecting Set as Active, or by selecting the load test root node and setting it in the properties dialog box.

Figure 16-14. *Pick Performance Counters dialog box*

In Figure 16-14 the computer Januik (which contains the SQL Server 2005 database) is selected and the SQL Server Statistics counters are displayed. You can select either specific counters or all of the counters from a category.

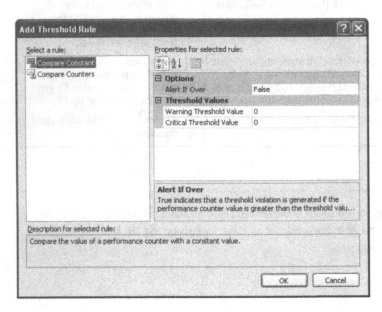

Figure 16-15. *Add Threshold Rule dialog box*

A threshold rule can be set for any counter. It generates either a warning or a critical warning message during the load test run if the counter exceeds a given value. There are two ways of setting a threshold rule: either it can be a constant value or it can be based on the value of another counter. For a constant value you simply enter the values for the warning and critical levels and indicate when an alert should be generated. Do not be fooled by the title "Alert If Over." If this value is set to False, an alert is generated if it is under the stated value. Otherwise it generates an alert if it is over the stated value.

When electing to set threshold rules based on another counter, you select the Compare Counters rule. This rule throws an exception if one counter performs faster than another counter or vice versa. This allows you some degree of dynamic performance monitoring based on the environment.

■**Tip** To see what threshold rules have been set for a test, you need to drill down into the Load Test tree view. Select Counter Sets ➤ [Computer Name] ➤ Counter Categories ➤ [Category] ➤ Counters ➤ [Counter Name] and you will get to the threshold rules. If there is no plus (+) next to the counter name then there is no threshold rule set for that counter.

Once you have set the test run settings and configured the load test you can either run or debug the load test. The reason there is no section called "Running a Load Test" is because it is entirely automatic. You can view various results from the load test while the test is running but once you start the test you can grab a cup of coffee.

Analyzing Load Test Results

There is so much information collected from a load test that you need to be able to understand it effectively in order to be able to use it to improve the performance of your website. Because of this, the various test results are discussed in general terms. There are several hundred counters available to you, which all indicate various things and this book is not about performance counters. Instead, this section discusses what results are found where and the various ways of diving into the data to get answers concerning the load test results.

Figure 16-16 shows the load test results from the FullTest load test.

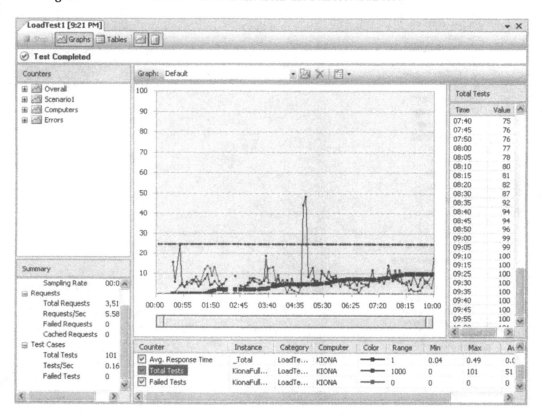

Figure 16-16. *Load test results*

The four panes represented in the load test results window are (clockwise from upper left) Counters, Graphs/Tables, Points, and Summary. Each of the panes is described in the following sections.

Tip You can switch to full-screen mode by selecting View ➤ Full Screen from the main menu or pressing Shift + Alt + Enter (this will also revert the screen to normal mode).

Counters Pane

The Counters pane contains a list of all the counters on all the computers recorded during the test. During the actual test run, only a subset of these counters is shown; but once the test is completed the full set of counters can be found. Figure 16-17 shows a more detailed view of the Counters pane.

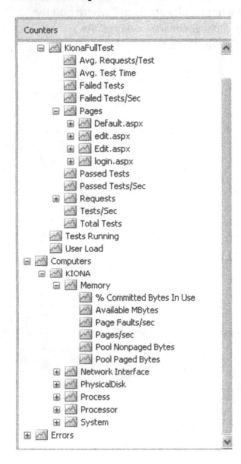

Figure 16-17. *Counters pane*

The first node in the list, Overall, displays (as its name suggests) a list of counters that covers the overall set of counters. These are counters that have been summed and placed into this node.

As you can see in Figure 16-17, the details related to the Scenario (the second node) are shown. One node for each test is displayed here. Drilling into the FullTest (the name of the web test) shows all of the collected data relating to a specific test. Double-clicking on any of the counters in this pane (or dragging and dropping the counter on the graph) will add that item to the graph (and it will be displayed in the legend beneath the graph).

The Computers node shows all of the counters recorded for each computer that you elected to record data from. In this example, data was recorded only from the KIONA computer.

The last node, Errors, records the total number of errors grouped by type.

Graphs/Tables Pane

The pane containing the graphs in Figure 16-16 can be switched to a table view by selecting the Table button from the top of the window. Figure 16-18 shows the table view.

Table: Pages ▼						
Page	Scenario	Test	Total	Page Time	Page Time Goal	% Meeting
Default.aspx	Scenario1	KionaFullTest	707	0.36	-	100
edit.aspx	Scenario1	KionaFullTest	202	0.18	-	100
Edit.aspx	Scenario1	KionaFullTest	404	0.18	-	100
login.aspx	Scenario1	KionaFullTest	202	0.54	-	100

Figure 16-18. *Table view of data*

This view provides access to various tables of data and detail about that data. For example, if there were errors, the Errors table could be selected and you would see details about the types of errors and be able to drill down into the stack trace, depending on the errors.

Note If the web test runs without problems there should not be any errors in the load test caused by the test itself. However, because this is a load test and the system or application may not be able to handle it, you will very likely see errors such as "500 – Internal Server Error."

Caution When you first create a load test, one of the default counters that is set is the Threshold counter. This sets a specified period of time for the page to respond, and if it does not respond in time an exception is thrown. When the exception is thrown, it is recorded, but part of the test ends up being skipped. Because of this, all sorts of weird errors start appearing (though this is partially based on how your test is set up). Our suggestion would be to disable this threshold check if you are running the test on your local machine and manually determine how many pages did not respond in a set period of time (using Excel or some other tool to sort and analyze the data). This will stop the problem of the application throwing unrelated and hard-to-trace exceptions that are not actually occurring.

The graph itself has various options for displaying data. The data displayed on the graph is located below the graph in the legend. To highlight a specific metric, select it from the legend and it will become bolded in the graph.

At the top of the graph there is a drop-down menu containing a list of computers for which counter information was collected, and a Default option. The Default option displays data for all computers. In addition, you can create additional graphs. The purpose of this is to be able to create graphs that display various counters. For example, one graph may show the processor time of all the computers involved in the load test so a comparison can be made (this type of comparison is useful, for example, when your application is deployed to a web farm) and another may show entirely different, unrelated information.

Options for the graph can be set by right-clicking the graph and selecting Graph Options or by selecting the Graph Options button from the top of the graph. The options you can set are the following:

- Select Graph

- Show Legend

- Show Plot Points

- Show Horizontal Grid Lines

- Show Min/Max Lines

- Show Threshold Violations

- Display data for the entire run or recent data only (available while the run is in progress)

Just below the graph but above the legend is a bar (shown in Figure 16-16) which allows you to zoom in on a portion of the graph. You can also zoom in by clicking in the graph and dragging your mouse until the portion you want to zoom in on is highlighted.

Below the graph is the legend. Selecting a counter in the legend will bold it on the graph. A counter can be deleted from the graph by right-clicking it and selecting Delete, or selecting the counter and pressing the Delete key. To temporarily remove the counter from the graph, simply uncheck the box next to the counter. For each counter you can set three options in the Plot Options dialog box shown in Figure 16-19.

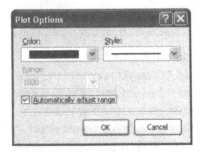

Figure 16-19. *Plot Options dialog box*

As you can see from Figure 16-19, you can change the color of the counter line, the style of the line, and the range of display for the counter. The default is to allow VSTS to automatically control the range, which takes into account other values on the graph.

The columns in the legend give you detailed information on the counter itself: which computer it was recording information from, what counter category it is part of, and the min, max, average, and last values it recorded.

Points Pane

The graph points are actually part of the Graph pane and can be hidden by selecting the Show/Hide Graph Points option of the graph. This pane always displays data in the form of time (in the left column) and the value (in the right column). The time displayed is based on the polling interval selected during the Load Test setup. The value is dependent on the counter selected.

Summary Pane

The Summary pane simply provides a summary of all of the data collected during the test run.

Publishing Test Results

As with web tests, load test results can be published to a Team Foundation Server. For the steps to publish a load test, see the "Publishing Test Results" section in Chapter 15.

Summary

In this chapter you have seen how and why you run a load test and what information you expect to get out of it. Running a load test based on an existing web test (or a set of web tests) in order to validate system performance under high demand is the key focus of this chapter. The setup of the controller and associated agent(s) was covered, which gives you a solid starting place for creating your own load test lab. Setting options for the load test and, finally, being able to view and analyze the load test results was presented.

This chapter used steps from previous chapters, combined with the abilities of the VSTS load testing tool to provide you detailed information about an application's environment. This information will help you build better, more reliable applications by allowing you to configure the environment in which the application runs, with the foreknowledge of how it will perform. While this tool may not solve all of the problems with an environment, it will help you prepare by giving you information about any weaknesses in the environment and allowing you to plan for the future.

Team Edition for Database Professionals

CHAPTER 17

■■■

Database Projects

When Microsoft first released Visual Studio Team System (VSTS), it knew there were some gaps in the offering. After all, Microsoft was releasing a life cycle management tool, but it forgot the database part of applications! But Microsoft didn't. The Database Professionals edition (DBPro) was in the works before the release of VSTS. Microsoft considered it important enough to release out of cycle—and it is. DBPro provides a good first entry with a lot of functionality to not only make the database administrator's (DBA's) life easier but also to make the lives of those who write database applications easier. We would even go a step further and argue that with this release there is no longer any reason to buy separate versions of VSTS—just buy the suite.

■**Tip** If you buy two different editions of VSTS, it becomes cheaper to just purchase the whole suite.

■**Note** As of this writing, the DBPro team has released its first service release (specifically, SR1). The team has also released a set of Power Tools that provide enhanced functionality. These are available as free downloads from Microsoft. You can download SR1 from `http://www.microsoft.com/downloads/details.aspx?familyid=9810808c-9248-41a5-bdc1-d8210a06ed87&displaylang=en`, and you can download the Power Toys from `http://www.microsoft.com/downloads/details.aspx?FamilyID=da3f11ad-bd54-4eda-b08c-4df84df0d641&displaylang=en`.

This chapter covers all the features of DBPro SR1 and the Power Tools.

■**Caution** If you do not have SR1 and the Power Tools installed, some of the items described here will not be available to you.

In this chapter, you will learn about database projects. You'll learn how to create, organize, navigate, and refactor database projects as well as gain an overview of the development life cycle using database projects. You will also get a general overview of how to deploy projects, though we cover this in Chapter 19 in greater detail.

■**Note** As of this writing, the Database Professionals edition works only with SQL Server 2000 and SQL Server 2005. However, the team is addressing extensibility options, so in the future this tool should be usable with multiple database types.

■**Note** For the examples shown in this chapter, we use the Northwind database. We copied the Northwind database to a new database named Northwind_Dev and renamed the original Northwind database to Northwind_Original except where noted.

Why VSTS for Database Professionals?

This question is somewhat more complex than it seems, and it is surprising that it took this long for someone to address it. Typically, a data modeler would create the database structure in a program such as ERwin or Visio or another data-modeling tool. The database would then be generated, and developers would start writing stored procedures, functions, triggers, and so on, against the development environment. These items were never version controlled. Rather, at a certain point in time the developers would say the development environment was good to go, the DBA would copy the structure and functions to the test environment, and away things went.

The "truth" of the database structure was always production. All comparisons were done against what was in production. Developers didn't have access to production. To them, the development database was the "truth." The test environment at any given time could mimic either the production environment or the development environment depending on where you were in the release cycle.

No one knew what code specifically was promoted to production at a given time because no one tracked it. Occasionally the DBA would note the objects that had been added and were to be promoted (sometimes the developers supplied this list). Occasionally the developers would provide the DBA with scripts to run for the new release—these were rarely version controlled either.

The Truth

The database professionals team envisioned one place where you could go that would contain the "truth." It would no longer be in the production, test, or development environments. It wouldn't be on the backup tapes for the database or in random scripts scattered in the application projects. With DBPro and TFS, you can always, always go to a point in time and reconstruct the database. You can know what was promoted to production in a given release.

You can know what scripts were provided to the DBA for a release. This is really the key point of DBPro. This approach also has some incredibly beneficial side effects that Microsoft is taking good advantage of.

Sandbox Development

Because a version-controlled project is the "truth," you can work with that truth in any environment—and it is still the truth. This gives rise to sandbox development. Developers do not have to share a common development environment and worry about breaking each other's code. If one developer writes code that changes another, solve it when you receive a merge conflict at check-in instead of breaking each other's code while you are doing active development. Developers can then deploy their project to the development environment, and the database code will work.

Version Control

The entire database at the object level is placed under version control, as opposed to placing an entire modeling tool under version control where you cannot determine the changes in individual objects. At its most granular level, you have pinpoint control over changes in the schema. This gives rise to the next benefit.

Deployment and Versioning

Because you have intimate knowledge of the changes to the schema, you can script those changes consistently and accurately. Because of this, you will know with certainty what was deployed for every release and who made the changes that were deployed. You will also have a copy of the database at a point in time but be able to have the incremental scripts that were applied for each release.

Unit Testing and Data Generation

Finally, DBPro offers unit testing and data generation. Leveraging the existing unit testing framework, DBPro gives you the ability to test the database independent from any applications that might access the database. In addition, the individual applications can perform their own testing on the database. This also helps when you are dealing with subcontracting work. In the case where the teams working on the database and the application code are different, the database team can ensure that it is providing a solid working system.

The data generation capabilities give unit testing the benefit of being run using consistent data in a repeatable process. The ability to generate data instead of having to use potentially sensitive production data is the key to protecting proprietary, personal, and financial data.

Now that you understand the benefits of DBPro, it's time to start working with it!

Understanding Projects and Databases

With the exception of a couple of pieces of functionality, most of the features of DBPro are available only in the context of a database project. When you installed DBPro, the standard database projects were replaced by four new project types.

These are the SQL Server 2000, SQL Server 2005, SQL Server 2000 Wizard, and SQL Server 2005 Wizard projects. The wizard projects are identical to the nonwizard projects except they automatically implement the reverse-engineering of a database. For this example, select the SQL Server 2005 project, and name it NorthwindDB.

Before looking at the project itself, it is important to understand what a database project actually is and what it is not. When you create a new project, a SQL Server sandbox database is created and is used for validating various aspects of the project.

It is an in-memory database and is reconstituted each time you load your project. Any changes made (by adding objects in the project) are *not* part of your actual database. You will also note that no database is specified in any of the property pages to indicate from *where* you reverse-engineered your schema. Until you actually choose to deploy your updates to a database, nothing you do in a project will affect an actual development, test, or production database.

Database Views

Two views are available to you in a database project—the Solution Explorer and the Schema View. Each is used for a different purpose, and some options are available only depending on the view you are using. Figure 17-1 shows these views; the left pane is the Solution Explorer, and the right pane is the Schema View.

You can toggle between the views by clicking the Schema View button at the top of the Solution Explorer (the last button on the right in Figure 17-1 at the top of the pane).

Solution Explorer

This view is all about the physical structure of the files and folders on disk. It is possible to arrange the files and folders differently *only if* you use one of the project wizards (discussed next). To highlight the differences here, notice the Tables node. Everything about the tables is segregated into different folders. Table definitions are in one folder, keys are in another, and indexes are in another.

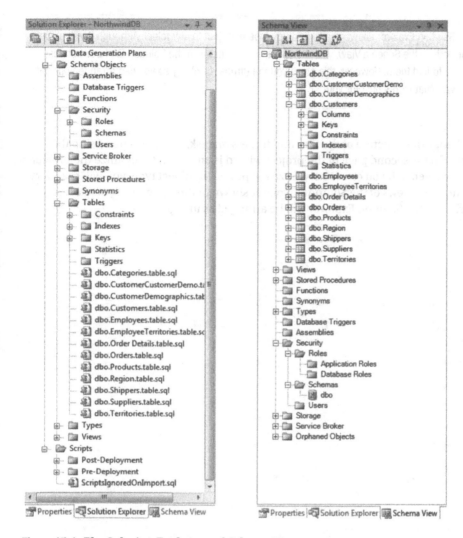

Figure 17-1. *The Solution Explorer and Schema View*

The benefit of this view is it makes it simple to find a specific item related to a problem. For example, if you receive an error message saying there is some problem with a specific index or a key, how do you find the key or index? This is especially problematic if you don't use standard, descriptive names. This view lets you drill straight down into the object type without having to worry about what the object is associated with (with a key you would have to know the exact table or view it is associated with and drill down to it).

Another thing to note about this window is that the last node is unique to the Solution Explorer. The Scripts folder contains user scripts. By default it contains two folders—Post- and Pre-Deployment folders that contain some blank, suggested script titles (such as Logins).

In this view, you can add any type of object to the database project by right-clicking any node and selecting Add and the appropriate object to add.

■**Caution** The Solution Explorer allows you to add any type of object to any folder. Although it will always be organized correctly in the Schema View, you may start "losing" items in the Solution Explorer because you will not be able to find them. However, this gives you the utmost flexibility so you can arrange your database project in a way that works best for you!

You can change the structure of the files and folders on disk, but only when using the project wizards. On the second page of the project wizard is an option to organize the project by object type or schema. If you elect to organize the project by object type, you will see everything as laid out in the views of the Solution Explorer shown in this chapter. If you elect to organize by schema, the Solution Explorer will be arranged as in Figure 17-2.

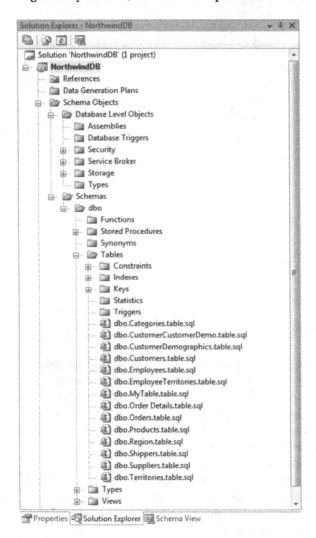

Figure 17-2. *Solution Explorer organized by schema*

Because this is a physical arrangement of files on disk, you cannot change this once a project is started.

Schema View

The Schema View shows objects in a hierarchical view and allows you to see, for example, the columns, keys, and other information associated with a table, view, or other object. This is virtually identical to the view you see in SQL Server Management Studio, so it should be familiar to you. This view is logically organized and is regenerated to reflect recent changes each time you go to this view, so items will always be in the correct place. For example, if you change the schema or user who owns a table by editing the table's Create Table script, the Schema View will reflect this by placing the table under the appropriate owning object.

You can add items to the appropriate sections by right-clicking the root section node (that is, Tables, Views, Stored Procedures, and so on) and selecting Add ➤ [item]. You can add only the item of the type of node you are on. For instance, you can add only a table to the Tables folder. This view also has one unique folder—the Orphaned Objects folder, which is a catchall for any items that cannot be placed in one of the other folders for whatever reason. If, for example, you deleted a table but didn't delete an index to that table (in your project), the index would end up in the Orphaned Objects folder.

Note The Schema View does not have any information regarding source control. You will not see any objects with locks next to them or be able to determine whether an item is checked out. You can see this only in the Solution Explorer. The reason for this is that version control is based on files, and the objects represented in the Schema View can span many files.

Adding Objects to Your Database

You can add objects to your database project in several ways. Some of these ways will be easier or more difficult depending on your skill set. Feel free to use whichever way suits your style—the system is designed with flexibility in mind.

Importing an Existing Schema

This first method of adding objects will almost always be your starting point for working with an existing database. To reverse-engineer a schema, select Data ➤ Import Database Schema (if you do not have the Power Tools installed), select the database you want to import, and select Finish. If you do have the Power Tools installed, right-click the database project name (North-windDB) in the Solution Explorer, and select Import Database Schema.

> **Tip** The databases displayed in the Import Database Wizard are preselected from the database connections in the Server Explorer. Add the database you want to import to the Server Explorer first, or select New Connection when importing a schema.

That's it. Visual Studio will perform the import (the progress of the import is shown on the status bar) and put the database objects into the correct categories in the Solution Explorer and Schema View.

> **Caution** The schema import will *not* import encrypted objects (objects created with the WITH ENCRYPTION statement) or certificates. It is important that the create statements are stored in version control. If you attempt to reverse-engineer these items, what you will get is your original text substituted by a statement such as "-- Text cannot be read," which is probably not what you want to have happen. In general, skip these statements during a reverse-engineer or an import.

For now, import the Northwind_Original database, and leave the options set to their defaults.

Importing a Script

Import a script when you have a script that contains DDL statements and you want to add those objects to the database project. There is really just one caveat here—some items in scripts will not be imported. These items are Alter Table statements, Disable Trigger statements, and Alter Index statements. Because the objects are imported in such a way as to create objects, alter statements will be ignored and moved to the ScriptsIgnoredOnImport file (located in the Scripts folder in the Solution Explorer). To import a script, right-click the project name in the Solution Explorer, and select Import Script.

Adding an Item

Adding an item allows you to add an item (existing or new) from either the Solution Explorer or the Schema View by right-clicking a node and selecting the appropriate item. For a new item, you have the option of adding more than 40 types of SQL Server objects.

> **Tip** The issue with using the Add Item option is that when you select an object type to add, you will be presented with a script window (which makes sense for the majority of objects). However, there are no graphical designers in version 1 of DBPro. If you are comfortable with adding tables by hand and adding indexes and constraints, then by all means use this method. We prefer a graphical designer because it makes adding all the necessary objects to a table far easier and usually provides for greater productivity. Because of this, we recommend the fourth option—but it has some drawbacks.

Note The DBPro team is addressing these concerns in version 2.

Reverse-Engineering Individual Objects

Because SQL Server has a built-in table designer, reverse-engineering makes it easier to import a table and all the related objects (keys, indexes, and constraints). To add a schema object, first perform a schema compare (discussed in "Schema Compare" later in this chapter), select the objects to import, select Export to File from the toolbar, and save it in the Scripts folder of the project. Then right-click the Scripts folder, select Add ➤ Existing Item, and select the script file. Now you can keep it under source code control with the rest of your project.

Note Using this process, you will receive a warning that some SQL statements were not understood. This is because of the transaction and rollback statements placed in the exported script file. You can safely ignore these warnings.

So, having noted this handy way of getting items into the database, what's the drawback? You need a database to place these statements into in the first place. This requires the extra work of generating the database and adding your new table to this database. However, if you are adding multiple tables at once, this is well worth it.

Comparing Schemas

Every DBA or developer at one time or another has said, "What's the difference between this database and that one?" Now you can answer that question using tools built directly into the Visual Studio IDE. A lot of work goes on around keeping schemas in sync between development, test, and production environments. Maybe you are working on a team of developers and you need to gather all the changes to the database from the development environment so you can update the test database without losing all the data. Or perhaps you are getting an error in the test environment that you aren't in the development environment and you need to know whether a schema difference might be causing this. And most critical of all, you might need to deploy updates to the production database. There is no way a DBA would let a developer apply the updates. The DBA would require an update script and then run it on the test database after synchronizing it with the production database to make sure there were no issues. Generating these types of scripts before was difficult and required a lot of work. With the schema comparison functionality, this becomes a simple task.

When you install DBPro, a new menu item is added to the main menu, Data. You do not have to create or open a project to use the schema comparison functionality. Simply select Data ➤ Schema Compare ➤ New Schema Comparison. Figure 17-3 shows the New Schema Comparison dialog box.

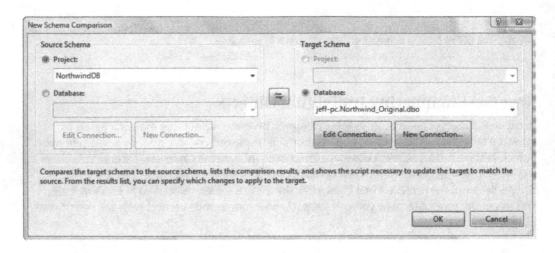

Figure 17-3. *New Schema Comparison dialog box*

Select the Northwind_Original database as the source schema and the Northwind_Dev database as the target schema. The project selections are available if you are working in a database project. You cannot compare one project to another project, but you can compare a project to a database or, as in this example, a database to a database. The button in the middle with the two arrows flips the source and target schema selections. Click OK when you are done.

■**Tip** The difference between source and target is the difference in how the scripts are generated. If the target is different from the source, the update scripts will be generated in such a way as to bring the target schema in-line with the source schema.

The schema comparison will compare the items listed here:

Item	Partition functions	Contracts
Tables	Schemas	Queues
Views	Rules	Services
Stored procedures	Defaults	Routes
Functions	Full-text catalogs	Event notifications
User-defined types	Users	Service bindings
Filegroups	Roles	Certificates
Assemblies	Synonyms	Symmetric keys
Database triggers	XML schema collections	Asymmetric keys
Partition schemes	Message types	

Note that these are for SQL Server 2005; SQL Server 2000 comparisons contain a subset of these items.

Figure 17-4 shows the partial results of the schema comparison.

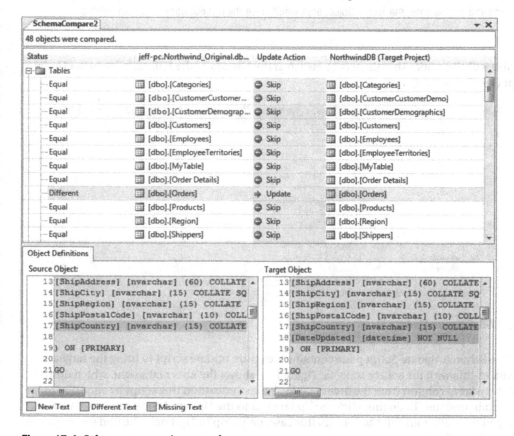

Figure 17-4. *Schema comparison results*

You can clearly see the results of the schema comparison in this dialog box. To give you a rundown, any row that contains an Update Action or Skip means that the rows are equal (as evidenced by the first column that contains one of four values: Different, Missing, New, or Equal). Selecting a given row such as the Orders table in Figure 17-4 displays the source and target *definitions* in the tab below with differences, new, and missing statements highlighted appropriately. As you can see from this figure, the ShipCountry column has changed (scroll to the right to see the change—in this case, it is a change because a comma was added at the end of the column because an additional line of SQL was added in the Target Object area), and the DateUpdated column is missing in the Source Object area (that is, it exists in the target schema but not in the source schema).

Tip If the source and target schemas were flipped, then the DateUpdated column would be highlighted in green in the source script because it would be a new column in the source schema that didn't exist in the target schema. In this case, the Target Object area would have the DateUpdated column deleted.

You will also notice that there is a new tab at the bottom of the IDE called Schema Update Script (see Figure 17-5).

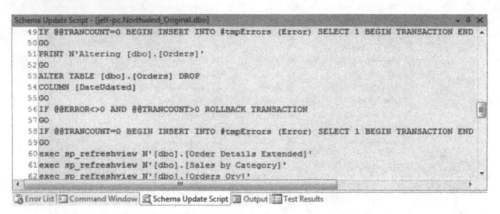

```
Schema Update Script - [jeff-pc.Northwind_Original.dbo]                              ▼ ♯ ✕
49 IF @@TRANCOUNT=0 BEGIN INSERT INTO #tmpErrors (Error) SELECT 1 BEGIN TRANSACTION END ▲
50 GO
51 PRINT N'Altering [dbo].[Orders]'
52 GO
53 ALTER TABLE [dbo].[Orders] DROP
54 COLUMN [DateUdated]
55 GO
56 IF @@ERROR<>0 AND @@TRANCOUNT>0 ROLLBACK TRANSACTION
57 GO
58 IF @@TRANCOUNT=0 BEGIN INSERT INTO #tmpErrors (Error) SELECT 1 BEGIN TRANSACTION END
59 GO
60 exec sp_refreshview N'[dbo].[Order Details Extended]'
61 exec sp_refreshview N'[dbo].[Sales by Category]'
62 exec sp_refreshview N'[dbo].[Orders Qry]'                                           ▼
```

Error List | Command Window | Schema Update Script | Output | Test Results

Figure 17-5. *Schema Update Script pane*

The Schema Update Script pane contains the entire update script to bring the target schema in-line with the source schema. Figure 17-5 shows the alter statement, which drops the DateUpdated column from the Orders table. You can constrain this script by choosing to skip certain updates. To do this, click the Update text in the Update Action column, which will allow you to select from valid actions (in this case, only Skip or Update). The update script will be altered to reflect the new set of updates.

Tip If the Schema Update Script pane isn't visible, you can view it by clicking Show Schema Update Script on the Schema Compare toolbar.

Tip You can also update the Update Action setting for all the rows in a given section at once. Right-click a section folder (such as the Tables section shown in Figure 17-4), and select Update/Create All, Skip All, or Drop All. All objects that can be set to the selected action will be set to the selected action.

Using the Schema Compare toolbar (which is displayed automatically when performing a schema comparison), you can filter the results of the compare to view only new objects, different objects, missing objects, equal objects, or objects that are being skipped and objects that are not being skipped. You can select a different source and target schema, write the updates directly to the target schema (this can either be a database directly or be a database project), export the script to a file or to your favorite editor, refresh the comparison, view the Schema Update Script pane, or stop an in-progress update (which will roll back the changes).

■**Note** All of these options apply to comparing a database to a project as well.

This section showed you how to use the schema comparison feature. In the "Promoting Changes" section later in this chapter and in Chapter 19, you will see how to leverage this tool to help you version and deploy updates to your database.

Comparing Data

As with comparing schemas, there are a lot of reasons for comparing data in different instances of a database. You might want to determine whether data in a test or development environment is stale (or even between schemas), or, better yet, you might want to normalize data across databases. Well, with DBPro, you can! You don't need to be in a database project to compare data between databases either. To compare data, select Data ➤ Compare Data ➤ New Data Comparison from the main menu. This opens the New Data Comparison dialog box shown in Figure 17-6.

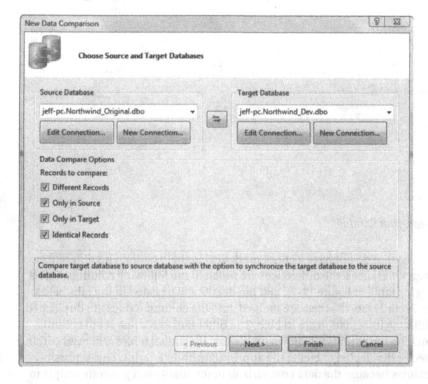

Figure 17-6. *Data Comparison dialog box*

Here again the source database is the database you want to update the target database to match (in terms of data). Select the types of records you want to compare, and click Next. The next page allows you to choose which items you want to compare from the existing tables and views.

Tip To compare tables and views, the schemas must be identical, and there must be a primary key. If you can't compare them, they will not show up in the list of available tables and views.

When you're satisfied with your selection, click Finish. This will open the data comparison window shown in Figure 17-7.

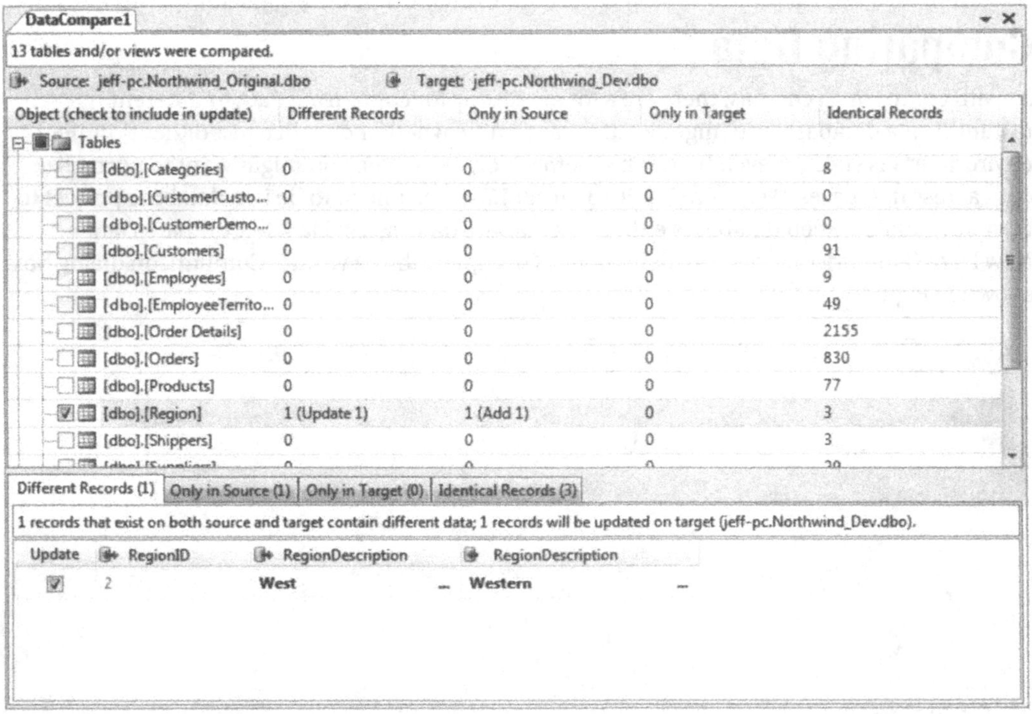

DataCompare1				▾ ✕
13 tables and/or views were compared.				
▮ Source: jeff-pc.Northwind_Original.dbo		▮ Target: jeff-pc.Northwind_Dev.dbo		
Object (check to include in update)	Different Records	Only in Source	Only in Target	Identical Records
⊟ ▣▢ Tables				
─☐▦ [dbo].[Categories]	0	0	0	8
─☐▦ [dbo].[CustomerCusto...	0	0	0	0
─☐▦ [dbo].[CustomerDemo...	0	0	0	0
─☐▦ [dbo].[Customers]	0	0	0	91
─☐▦ [dbo].[Employees]	0	0	0	9
─☐▦ [dbo].[EmployeeTerrito...	0	0	0	49
─☐▦ [dbo].[Order Details]	0	0	0	2155
─☐▦ [dbo].[Orders]	0	0	0	830
─☐▦ [dbo].[Products]	0	0	0	77
─☑▦ [dbo].[Region]	1 (Update 1)	1 (Add 1)	0	3
─☐▦ [dbo].[Shippers]	0	0	0	3
─☐▦ [dbo].[Suppliers]	0	0	0	29

Different Records (1)	Only in Source (1)	Only in Target (0)	Identical Records (3)
1 records that exist on both source and target contain different data; 1 records will be updated on target (jeff-pc.Northwind_Dev.dbo).			

Update	▮ RegionID	▮ RegionDescription	▮ RegionDescription	
☑	2	**West**	... **Western**	...

Figure 17-7. *Data comparison window*

The tables (or views) that do not have a check mark next to them contain no differences. If the tables do contain differences, the differences are noted in the following columns. Select a row (such as the Region table in Figure 17-7), and the details will be listed in the tabs below.

On the Different Records tab, the rows are merged, and the column names are duplicated. The columns with differing information are in bold. The other tabs show one set of columns with the records matching the conditions shown on the tab. Individual tables and rows within a table can be selected or deselected to create the appropriate update script. This is possibly one of the coolest features because the data comparison functionality will generate scripts to normalize data across systems! This makes it easy to update a test environment from production, for example, with a minimal amount of work and without having to delete the test database first. In addition, by performing a data comparison with an empty schema, all your data can be scripted and stored for testing purposes.

As with the schema comparison, you can filter the results, write the updates to a database, export them to an editor, or save them to a file and check them into version control.

Referencing Other Databases

With the addition of SR1, you can now reference other databases and have your SQL statements validated. Before SR1, you would receive a warning in the Error List. You can reference another database in two ways—create another database project in the same solution and add a reference to it or, using the same dialog box, add a reference to a project metadata file.

■**Note** These are really both the same options—when you select a project reference, the project generates a metadata file, and that is the file that is referenced.

The metadata file allows you to reference a completely separate project (you don't even have to have the project, just the file). When you build a database project (assuming you have SR1 installed), one of the outputs in the Sql folder is a file named [*Project Name*].dbmeta. This is a binary representation of your database project that you can provide to someone who is referencing your database, without having to provide them with the project or the details of the project.

The steps to do this are fairly straightforward but not necessarily intuitive. Because you are already working with the Northwind_Original database, right-click the solution, and select Add New Project. Create a SQL Server 2005 Wizard project called Pubs, and import the Pubs database.

■**Note** The SQL script for installing the Pubs database is included with the download for this chapter.

Next, create a new stored procedure in the NorthwindDB project, as shown in Listing 17-1.

Listing 17-1. *usp_get_authors Stored Procedure*

```
CREATE PROCEDURE [dbo].[usp_get_authors]
AS
SELECT  *
FROM    pubs.dbo.authors
```

This will cause a warning because DBPro cannot verify that the table exists since it is outside the database project. To fix this problem, do the following:

1. Right-click References in the Solution Explorer for the NorthwindDB project.

2. Select Add Database Reference, which displays the dialog box in Figure 17-8.

3. Select the Pubs project.

4. Check Define Database Variable, and create the variable named $(Pubs) with the value Pubs.

5. Finally, check Update Schema Objects and Scripts, and click OK.

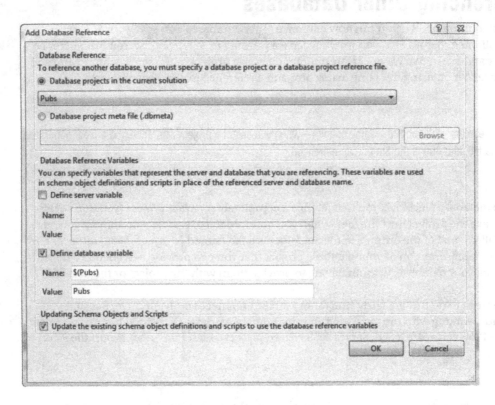

Figure 17-8. *Add Database Reference dialog box*

This will open a Preview Changes dialog box for the Rename Server or Database refactor. In this case, you will note (by selecting the last node in the tree) that pubs.dbo.authors is about to be changed to [$(Pubs)].dbo.authors. Click Apply; the changes will be made, and the warnings will disappear.

Tip The format for variables is the same as that used by SQLCMD, the SQL Server command-line tool, and is designed to be compatible with this tool. The variable format is $(*varname*).

If you switch to the NorthwindDB project properties, you will see this reference on the References tab. Note that no matter what type of reference you created, you will always be referencing the .dbmeta file.

Refactoring Databases

As we have described elsewhere in this book, *refactoring* is the process of changing the structure and implementation of your code while leaving its functionality intact. Often the goals of refactoring are increased efficiency, reduced duplication, and improved maintainability. The process of manually refactoring scripts is frequently a tedious one. It is prone to errors, particularly with languages such as Transact SQL (TSQL) that support runtime binding between objects.

Refactoring is also a key part of the agile development processes. These processes advocate that you do not have to know every little detail before you start writing the first line of code. You start with a general direction and build as you go. With code this is fairly easy, but think back to the last time you had to make a database change—how many layers of code did that change cascade down through? How many pieces of functionality broke instantly? For this reason, many application developers have taken the view that they don't need to know everything about an application before they start building, but they *have* to know everything about the database. The refactoring features in DBPro alleviate many of these concerns.

Note We believe you must understand the relationships between entities before you begin development—not that you need to know every detail of every entity. The refactoring options in DBPro make it fairly easy to rename a column or an object and allow that to trickle down into your code. It will not solve everything, and you will still have some breaking changes the closer you get to the user interface.

Rename Refactoring

Rename refactoring is a feature by which you rename an object in your database and every reference in your database is updated to use the new name. The process itself is relatively simple and lends itself well to the overall development cycle with a minimal amount of pain.

Take, for example, the Order Details table. Common convention suggests you should never have a space in your object name because then you have to add brackets ([ ]), and it becomes a tedious bit of work to reference it everywhere. A more common convention is to use an underscore (_) to separate words in a table name (whereas with C#, for example, you would use camelCase for a type name). So in the Northwind database, you want to change the name of the [Order Details] table to Order_Details.

Typically this involves you hunting through every little procedure, key, trigger, index, assembly, and so on, to find any references to [Order Details]. If you are clever, you might use the sys.sysdepends view to find the dependencies. The only problem with sysdepends is that it is not always accurate (this is another discussion altogether).

To use rename refactoring, first select the object to refactor in the Schema View, and then select Data ➤ Refactor Rename (this is also available by right-clicking the object in the Schema View). Figure 17-9 shows the Rename dialog box.

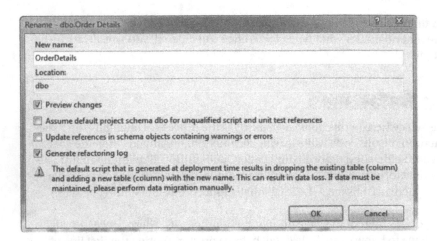

Figure 17-9. *Rename dialog box*

Here you can change the name of the object and set a few options. Note the warning displayed at the bottom. The deployment script drops objects and re-creates them. This means you may need to edit the script.

■**Caution** Rename refactoring does not know the intent of your changes. If you are not going to update an existing production system (in other words, this is a new system and has not been released), then the generated script is fine to use.

The one thing you can be sure of is that all the references will be included in the script. Once you change the name to a new name, the OK button will become enabled.

The Preview Change dialog box will list all the references that will be updated. You can elect to have references updated in your data generation plans and any scripts you may have. When you click Apply, it will change your database project only. To create a script for the database, you perform a schema comparison and use the resulting file.

■**Tip** Because of the warning shown previously, when you are applying a script that contains a rename refactoring (which should, as a best practice, always be done in a separate script), the data should always be scripted from the related tables or the entire database backed up so the appropriate tables can be reloaded after the script has been run.

In addition, a refactor log is created. This log is located in the \Solution Name\Project Name\Refactoring Logs\ folder and is a simple XML file listing what the rename refactor was and all the places the name change was made.

So, how do you apply the results of a rename refactor to your actual database? What steps do you take when attempting to promote this type of change? The answer to this question will be different if you have the Power Tools, so the process described here will be slightly different from the one described in the next section, "Refactor Command Generator":

1. Perform a rename refactor.

2. Perform a schema comparison using the project as the source and the database as the target.

3. Export the resulting script to an editor or to a file for editing.

4. Locate all the table references (or any reference where data loss would occur).

5. Change the drop and create statements to sp_rename statements.

6. Save the script, and use it to deploy updates to the database.

Tip Use the refactoring log to determine which tables have been changed—this will make your search through the generated script a little easier.

Finally, if you have the Power Tools installed, there has been one minor but very much appreciated change. If you happen to use strongly typed datasets in your project and your project is in the same solution as your database project, the rename refactoring feature will now make the appropriate name changes based on a rename operation to the dataset.

Tip Do not keep the files in the Refactoring Logs folder. Each time you run the Refactor Command Generator (described next), it reads all the files in this folder, so you might get the same renames in release scripts over and over again.

Refactor Command Generator

Rename refactoring by itself has one issue in its implementation (as noted earlier). This is not a result of how DBPro is written but rather is a result of how operations are performed.

For example, say a user renames a table from foo to bar. Visual Studio performs a rename refactor on the project. Then, the user performs a schema comparison between the project and a database to generate an update script. The actual script that is created causes the foo table to be dropped and the bar table to be created (this also occurs with column renames). However, this means all the data will be deleted also! This is not a good situation by any stretch of the imagination. Using the Refactor Command Generator provides a solution to this problem. Using the example in the previous section (the refactoring log created by renaming [Order Details] to Order_Details), run the Refactor Command Generator (Data ➤ Refactor ➤ Refactor Command Generator), and you will get the script shown in Listing 17-2.

Listing 17-2. *Refactor Command Generator Results*

```
-- Rename Table [dbo].[Order Details] to Order_Details
IF  EXISTS (SELECT * FROM sysobjects
WHERE id = OBJECT_ID(N'[dbo].[Order Details]') AND type in (N'U'))
EXEC sp_rename @objname=N'[dbo].[Order Details]',
              @newname=N'Order_Details', @objtype=N'OBJECT';
GO
```

This script simply renames the table (or column) instead of dropping and re-creating the table. This script is created by examining the refactor log, which is created when you perform a refactor (you will be prompted for the location of the directory where the log is stored when running the Refactor Command Generator).

■**Note** This really applies only to tables or columns—anywhere there might be a data loss. You would not need to do this for a stored procedure rename.

Now the problem becomes, how do you integrate this change into your build process? You can't simply add this into the predeployment script because if you are dropping and re-creating the database, this change would be lost, and it isn't practical to go in and change the resulting build script (too time-consuming). The best solution (and the only practical solution at this point) is to apply the update statement(s) to the database and then generate a build script (or perform a schema comparison). Because this is a script you are going to apply to the database as part of a release process, you need to do the following:

1. Perform a rename refactor.

2. Use the Refactor Command Generator.

3. Add the resulting script to your solution (and by extension version control).

4. Apply the script to your development database.

5. Perform a comparison between the development environment and the project.

6. Add the resulting script to your solution (and by extension version control).

7. As part of your release process, add the script generated by the Refactor Command Generator to the resulting build file (manually).

This provides, in our opinion, an easier way to deploy changes. Note that the Refactor Command Generator will generate refactor commands based on all the log files found in the folder you point the Refactor Command Generator to, which is why this is easier. You can combine multiple rename refactor updates into a single script using this technique.

Rename Server/Database References

This refactoring option gives you two distinct operations (see Figure 17-10).

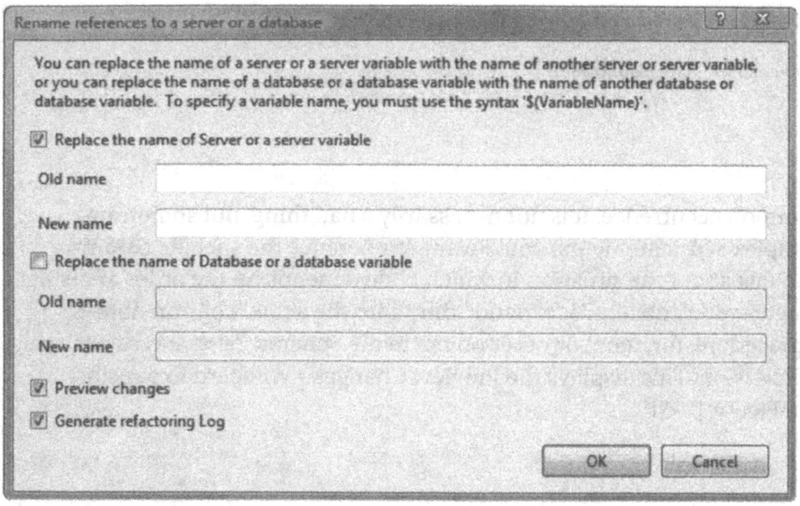

Figure 17-10. *Rename References to a Server or a Database dialog box*

As you can see from Figure 17-10, you can change the name of the server or just change the name of a server variable. You can also perform the same operation on a database or database variable.

Move Schema

This option allows you to move an object from one schema to another and updates all the appropriate references.

■**Note** These are schema as defined in SQL Server 2005 as logical containers holding objects and are themselves objects. This does not mean you can move objects from one database to another!

There are a couple of warnings with this, however. The first is that it performs this operation by dropping an object from one schema and re-creating it in another schema. You can avoid this issue by using the process described in the "Rename Refactor Command" section earlier.

The second item to note is that this will not update security associated with the object (that is, if a login had access to the object in one schema, it may not have access to it in another schema). Because of this, you will have to manually make some changes to the permissions.

Wildcard Expansion

This is one of the cooler new refactor features. Take the example of the stored procedure in Listing 17-3.

Listing 17-3. *usp_get_employees Stored Procedure*

```
CREATE PROCEDURE [dbo].[usp_get_employees]
AS
SELECT  *
FROM    Employees1
```

This is a pretty common occurrence. It is not necessarily a bad thing, but sometimes (especially in more complex SQL statements) you'll want to reference the specific columns (we aren't even going to talk about the situation in which code depends on the order of results, which is a terrible thought—don't do it!). To "expand" the * into the actual column names, right-click the stored procedure, function, or other object in the Schema View, and select Refactor ➤ Wildcard Expansion. This displays the Preview Changes – Wildcard Expansion dialog box, as shown in Figure 17-11.

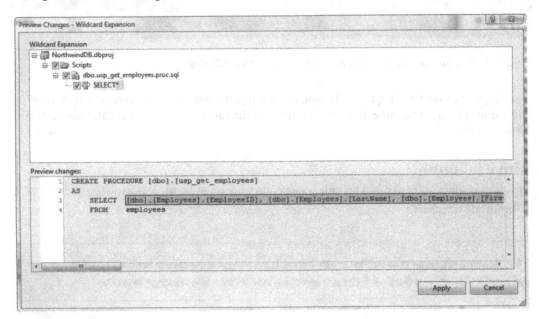

Figure 17-11. *Preview Changes – Wildcard Expansion dialog box*

As you can see, the fully qualified name of every column is inserted in place of the wildcard in your select statement. In addition, it will also use whatever alias you happen to have used in the FROM clause.

Fully Qualify Name

This option fully qualifies the name of any column or table referenced in a select statement. Take the SQL statement in Listing 17-4.

Listing 17-4. *usp_get_employees Stored Procedure*

```
CREATE PROCEDURE [dbo].[usp_get_employees]
AS
    SELECT  EmployeeID,
                LastName,
                FirstName
    FROM    Employees a
```

Right-clicking the stored procedure name in the Schema View and selecting Refactor ➤
Fully Qualify Name displays the dialog box shown in Figure 17-12.

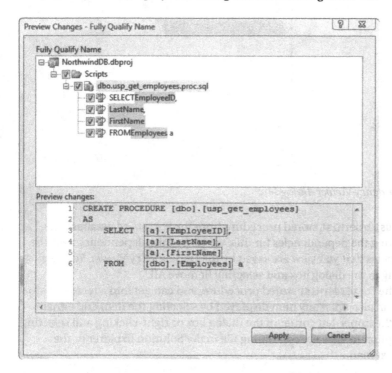

Figure 17-12. *Preview Changes – Fully Qualify Name dialog box*

As you can see, the Employees table in the FROM clause is replaced by [dbo].[Employees],
and the columns are altered to be qualified with the alias for Employees. This is handy for more
complex statements involving multiple tables. Even though SQL Server will not let you create
a statement without knowing explicitly what a column's source table is, this is a handy tool for
qualifying all parts of a select statement.

Viewing Dependencies

The Dependency Viewer is a nice addition (with the Power Tools) that lets you see what
objects reference a selected object and what objects are referenced by a selected object. To
view dependencies, right-click an object in the Schema View, and select View Dependencies.
This displays the dialog box in Figure 17-13.

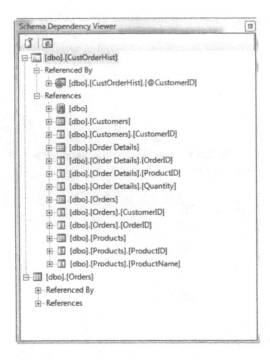

Figure 17-13. *Schema Dependency Viewer dialog box*

In this example, the CustOrderHist stored procedure from the Northwind database has been selected. Before viewing the dependencies for this, we viewed the dependencies for the Order table. The dependencies that you view are saved by the Dependency Viewer. You can clear them by right-clicking in the dialog box and selecting Remove All.

As you can see from the CustOrderHist stored procedure, you can get into a recursive view of your dependency. You can also open any item displayed by selecting the item and either clicking the Open icon in the upper-left corner of the dialog box or right-clicking and selecting Open. You also have the option to view the containing file in the Solution Explorer or the Schema View via the context menu.

Understanding the Database Development Life Cycle

Now that you have seen how to create a database project, navigate the objects, and add new objects, it's time to step back and look at the overall processes associated with databases. As you read the following sections, take into account that this will most likely be a shift in how your organization deals with databases in terms of roles, responsibilities, and processes.

Development Environment

Your development environment should be structured such that there is a "sandbox" database for each developer (provided by DBPro), a development database that the developers have full administrative privileges to, and a test database that is configured with the same permissions as the production database. These best practices assume this type of environment. Different environments can still benefit from these practices, however. An entire discussion of change management configuration is beyond the scope of this book.

■**Note** For a clear and excellent explanation of change management, read *Software Configuration Management Patterns* by Stephen P. Berczuk and Brad Appleton (Addison-Wesley, 2002).

Database Administrators

Database administrators have partial access to TFS by using the MSSCCI Provider (pronounced "miss key") from within SQL Server Management Studio (SSMS). The MSSCCI Provider (available as a free download from Microsoft) gives access to version control and work items in TFS. This means DBAs can have access to the repository containing SQL scripts.

However, this is not enough. DBAs need to have the ability to perform schema comparisons and data comparisons because they are likely the only people with full access to the production and test databases. They should also be given full access to the development database. This means that DBAs will need to have a copy of DBPro. This will be a major change for DBAs who do not ordinarily work within traditional IDEs. In the "Promoting Changes" section, we discuss how DBAs should promote changes without using DBPro.

Database Developers

Developers have responsibility for implementing changes to the database (in their sandboxes), writing unit tests, and creating data generation plans. They are responsible for creating builds and deploying changes to the development database. It is important to note that not every developer should be able to deploy changes to the development database. The development database is not a "development database" in the traditional sense. It is used as a staging/integration area before promoting changes to test and eventually production. It is not a database where day-to-day development work should be taking place. This is a major switch from how most database development is done today.

Promoting Changes

Now you're ready to promote your changes to production. How do you do it? Figure 17-14 shows a process that we believe helps do away with the typical confusion involved in releasing database changes and takes maximum advantage of the DBPro capabilities.

This is a fairly straightforward process but requires the cooperation of the entire team. Walking through Figure 17-14, when all developers have finished making changes for a particular release or feature (how you do releases is beyond the scope of this book, so you may choose to do releases based on some other criteria), a single developer should perform a "get latest" on the database project. The development database should be brought into alignment with the production database through any of several means. The easiest way is to just redeploy the database from the last production release (using DBPro's ability to generate the database—remember that the database project is the "truth").

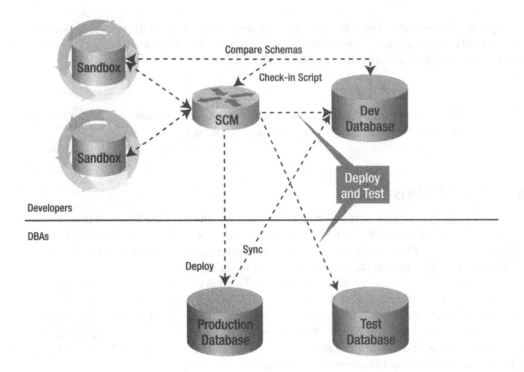

Figure 17-14. *Database release process*

Once the development environment is in the correct state, the developer should perform a build using the development database as the target database. This will generate a change script that, if all goes well with the testing, can be used to promote the changes to the test and production environments. This script should be added to the project and version controlled just as with any other script (see Chapter 19 for more details of this process).

The change script should be applied to the development database, and all database unit tests should be run against the database.

■**Note** As an obvious note, we have not included other parts of the code such as deploying an application and running application unit tests as well as other parts of the release process.

The same process should be performed against the test environment, assuming all went well in the development environment. The DBA will be responsible for updating the change scripts against the test environment if necessary. The DBA will also have to provide an administrative username and password for validating the database unit tests (this can easily be accomplished with command-line parameters). At this point, user acceptance testing can be performed.

> **Tip** At each point in the process, after deploying the change script, the DBA should perform a schema comparison between the project and the environment to ensure that the script ran correctly. Remember that the point of the database project is that it is the "truth."

The script is then labeled as part of the release and promoted into the production environment.

The previous release process will still work, but how things are done will change a little—the intent is still the same. To make this work in as controlled a manner as possible, the DBA must have either Team Explorer or access to Visual Studio Team System Web Access (and the associated Client Access License). Through these options, a DBA will have access to the source files located in TFS. The issue with this is that the DBA will have no easy way to verify deployment script success by performing comparisons.

Summary

In this chapter, you got an overall view of the Database Professionals edition of Visual Studio Team System. You saw what problems it is attempting to solve and how to use various features of DBPro. In addition, you also have some concept of where this edition falls into the overall development life cycle. In the next chapter, you will learn how to perform unit tests and generate data for whatever need you may find. Chapter 19 takes you deeper into the build and deployment processes for databases as well as automated testing. Chapter 20 shows you how to extend DBPro to fit your needs.

CHAPTER 18

■■■

Unit Testing and Data Generation

This chapter deals with testing databases. The ability to generate data *in a repeatable fashion* is integral to being able to perform good unit testing. This chapter walks you through how and why to unit test database and how and when to integrate data generation into the testing process. You will also learn how to write data-driven unit tests and how unit testing works in code so you can make changes to the generated code.

Note For more of a background on unit testing, see Chapter 12.

Data generation is critical to this process because running unit tests on small data samples that are randomly generated may not give you a real enough situation to see whether your code can handle everything. The combination of unit testing and data generation should provide for virtually all your test needs!

Unit Testing a Database

Why do you need to unit test a database? After all, you are (we hope) going to unit test your data access code. And if your data access code passes, all your stored procedures, by default, pass. Right? Yes, absolutely, but what if you aren't the same person who is writing the data access code? What if those guys are on the other side of the planet? If they do find a mistake and it is with your code, they are *not* going to be happy. We guarantee it.

How about the situation where you are accessing a database that is shared between multiple applications? Organizations today are finding more and better ways to integrate their data, which means more applications are being written to show only a facet of the accumulated data. Jason Clark, an architect at Microsoft, stated it best this way: "The app-tier's relationship to the data-tier is not so different from Word's relationship to Windows. One is the platform, and the other is the application. Both deserve tests in their own right."

Basically, the need to unit test your database separately comes down to several issues: being able to consistently ensure that the database code is free of defects and being able to easily regression test a change to your database. The fact that you may have code that also

527

exercises your stored procedures again is perfectly acceptable, especially when many aspects of applications are being reused in other applications or different teams work on different layers of an application.

Creating a Unit Test

Database unit testing is done slightly differently than the unit testing in the Developers Edition. To see how it works, open the NorthwindDB database project you created earlier, switch to the Schema View, and expand the Stored Procedures node. Right-click the CustOrderHist stored procedure, and select Create Unit Tests.

■**Note** Alternatively, you could select Test ➤ New Test and select Database Unit Test; however, Visual Studio will not generate any stub code for you for the selected stored procedures.

You can also unit test functions, triggers, and any SQL statement you might use to access a table or view (in other words, you can unit test SQL statements that you are planning to use in-line with code in your data access tier).

This will open the Create Unit Tests dialog box, as shown in Figure 18-1.

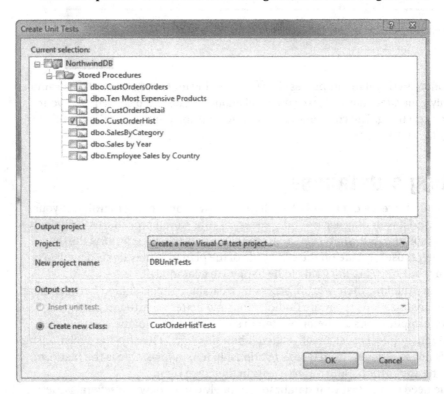

Figure 18-1. *Create Unit Tests dialog box for database unit tests*

Change the project name to DBUnitTests, change the name of the class to
CustOrderHistTests, and click OK. When you create a database unit test for the first time,
you are asked to configure the unit testing options (Figure 18-2).

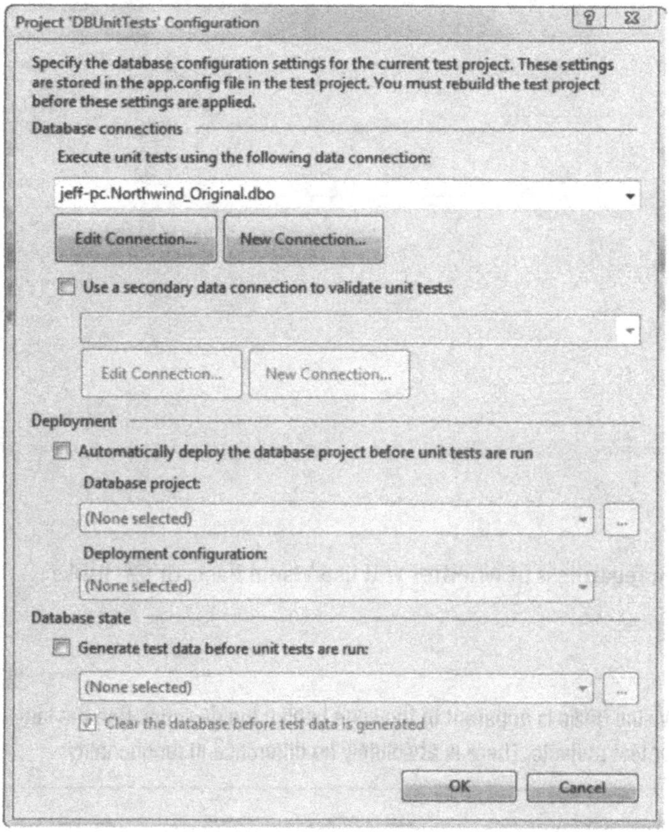

Figure 18-2. *Database unit test configuration dialog box*

We discuss these options in more detail in the "Configuration Options" section later in
this chapter. For now, select the database you are going to run the tests against (in this case,
Northwind_Original), and click OK. This will open the CustOrderHistTests window, as shown
in Figure 18-3.

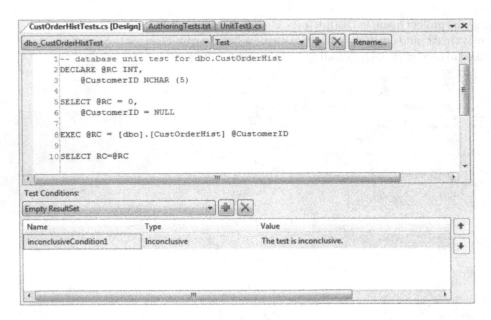

Figure 18-3. *A database unit test*

The database unit test window, regardless of whether you use Visual Basic or C#, looks the same.

Tip The difference between C# and Visual Basic is apparent in the code behind the designer. Use the language you are most comfortable with for test projects. There is absolutely no difference in functionality!

In the upper-left corner is a drop-down list to allow you to select a specific test (that is, it lists all your database unit tests) or a common script. A *common script* is either a test initialize or a test cleanup script that runs before and after each and every test. The next drop-down list contains the scripts for the individual test selected in the first drop-down list. There are always three options: Pre-Test, Test, and Post-Test. The order of script execution for a test is pretty straightforward: Test Initialize, Pre-Test, Test, Post-Test, and Test Cleanup.

The green plus sign and the red *X* allow you to add and delete database tests, and the Rename button allows you to rename a test and takes care of renaming the underlying class. The script window contains straight SQL statements—no code.

The Test Conditions window on the bottom is where you validate your test results. Table 18-1 lists the included test conditions.

Table 18-1. *Test Conditions*

Condition	Description
Empty ResultSet	This checks to see whether a result set has any rows. If it does not, the test passes.
Execution Time	The test must complete within a set period of time, or the test fails.
Inconclusive	This is the default test condition and simply indicates that the test did not pass or fail, just that no one changed the default setting, so the test is invalid.
Not Empty ResultSet	This checks to see whether a result set has any rows. If it does, the test passes.
Row Count	This allows you to verify that a given result set contains a specific amount of rows.
Scalar Value	This spot-checks the results; it will verify the value at a given intersection (column name and row number) against an expected value. If the values match, the test passes.

> **Tip** Chapter 20 shows you how to create your own test conditions.

To set a test condition, just select a condition from the drop-down list, click the green plus sign, and then set the properties for the condition in the Properties window.

You also have the option of disabling a given test. We recommend you do *not* do this. The goal of a unit test is to ensure that code passes a set of criteria. The unit test is the developer's understanding of a given requirement. If a unit test does not pass, disabling it does not make the code work right—it just skips the problem! You should not be checking in code that does not pass a unit test that has been validated as accurate. We think that disabling a unit test avoids the root cause of the issue.

Change the @CustomerID variable to be equal to ALFKI (instead of null, which is the default for any variables in a generated script). Add a Row Count test condition, set the count to 11 rows using the Properties window, and delete the Inconclusive condition (select the condition and click the red *X*). Switch to the Test Manager (or Test View) window, select dbo_CustOrderHistTests, and run the test. And the test should pass (using the default installation of Northwind).

> **Tip** It is often advisable to rename a test condition to reflect what you are really testing. In the case of RowCountTestCondition, you'll never have more than one of these conditions for a given unit test.

As with all the unit tests in Visual Studio Team System, database unit tests run the same way using the same infrastructure. Everything you can do in other types of unit tests you can do in database unit tests. This includes data-driven testing, which you will see shortly.

■**Tip** You can also cause tests to *not* affect your database environment at all by wrapping the test in a transaction. In the example shown in Figure 18-3, you would add the following lines before and after the block of code shown: `Begin Transaction`/`End Transaction`. This allows you to get the correct test results but then revert the database to the prior state.

Configuration Options

Table 18-2 shows the configuration options and their descriptions.

Table 18-2. *Unit Test Configuration Options*

Option	Description
Database Connection	The database against which the unit tests will be executed.*
Secondary Connection	The login used to validate a successful test.
Deployment	The database project to physically deploy to a database server prior to running the test.
Deployment Configuration	The build configuration to release (this makes a difference when deploying assemblies).
Generate Test Data	The ability to optionally generate test data prior to running the unit tests. You can select a single deployment plan.

* It's important to remember that unit tests are conducted against the physical database and have nothing to do with the database project or the sandbox database.

Most of these items are pretty simple and do not require further explanation. One of these items requires a little bit of explanation, though. The Secondary Connection option allows you to specify a different connection string for the same database (or a different database altogether, which does not usually make sense). This allows you to perform an operation logged on as a user, for example, but validate the results as a database owner (especially if all your data access is through stored procedures and you want to validate the data in a table—see the "Data Security" sidebar).

■**Note** The settings noted here are stored in the `app.config` file for the test project. Please remember to avoid storing database credentials in this file because it is in plain text, unless you have previously performed some type of security review.

■**Tip** If you elect to use a SQL Server login and provide a username and password, do not check the Save Password box. Your password is *still saved!* However, it is saved in an encrypted state in the registry using the Data Protection API (DPAPI). If another developer gets the project, it is best that they use the same username and password. They will be prompted for the password the first time, and it will be saved for each subsequent call.

DATA SECURITY

Data security in today's world is a critical issue. It should have always been an important issue, but in recent years as the number of security breaches has increased and as the attack vectors have increased, it has become even more critical. There are two camps on how to access data—do everything through stored procedures for added security or access tables directly with in-line SQL to avoid database vendor lock-in.

The latter argument just doesn't make sense in light of so many threats. The purpose of avoiding being tied to one database presupposes that it is cheaper to move to another database than to rewrite stored procedures. How expensive is it to have a database security breach? The cost is too high to even have this argument anymore. Use stored procedures to stay safe.

Now, having said that, how does this apply to database unit testing? Well, because you followed this advice, all that your users have access to are the stored procedures and nothing else. When you run unit tests, you should always do it under an ID that has the same permissions as the user, not as the database owner. This means in order to validate any test that performs an insert, update, or delete, you have to access the table(s) directly in order to verify the success or failure of a test.

Take the example of running unit tests against a test environment. In theory (and in practice), the test environment should mimic the production environment, including valid logins. So if you wrote your unit tests and used integrated authentication, well, it was a development environment, and you are a database owner. The tests would run fine on any development member's machine but fail in the test environment because the results could not be validated. Worse yet, maybe the user didn't have access to a specific object—the test would run fine for you but fail in the test environment. As with development in general, get into the habit of writing unit tests using the security of an actual user and validating the test results as a database owner.

Static Code Analysis

With the Power Tools, static code analysis has been added to database unit tests. It works in the same way as the static code analysis in the Developers Edition. This means you can easily scan your database code (stored procedures, functions, triggers, and so on) for common issues. Currently there are three categories of rules—design, naming, and performance. Although this static code analysis sits on the same static code analysis that is available as part of the Developers Edition, it is not extensible at this time.

To run or configure the static code analysis, select Data ➤ Static Code Analysis, and select either Run or Configure. The static code analysis settings are located in the project properties, so you can also access them via the project properties. The results of a static code analysis run will be displayed in the Errors List.

Creating Data-Driven Database Unit Tests

Data-driven testing works much like it does in the unit testing functionality of the Developers Edition. To take the most advantage of these tests, you'll need to start by creating a test database. Now that you have the Database Professionals edition, you can easily keep it under version control as well as a central test database. The format of a test table is essentially the same as the format we laid out in Chapter 12. There are a couple of minor differences, though, because of how a database unit test runs.

Your test table should have a primary key column simply so each row is uniquely identifiable. Your table should also have one column per parameter for the stored procedure or function you are testing and the expected result. Before you get into the problems with this overly simplistic view, we will show you how to create a simple data-driven database unit test (referred to as a DUT after this point). For this example, you will use the unit test you created earlier. Before altering the DUT, you need to create a test database. For this example, create a new database called NorthwindTestDB. Create a table called CustOrderHistTests with the column layout in Table 18-3.

Table 18-3. *CustOrderHistTests Table Schema*

Column Name	Type	Description
CustOrderHistTestID	identity(1,1)	Primary key
CustomerID	nvarchar(5)	Argument to pass for the CustomerID parameter
ExpectedRowCount	int	Number of rows the stored procedure should return

Insert the following two records: CustomerID = 'ALFKI', ExpectedRowCount = 11 and CustomerID = 'GODOS', ExpectedRowCount = 21.

To make a DUT data driven, you need to add a data source. You can do this manually by adding DataSourceAttribute to the test method, or you can open the Test Manager or Test View window and select the properties for the DUT. In the properties, set the data connection string to point to your SQL Server (or Oracle or whatever database you use—why aren't you using SQL Server?). Set the data table name to CustOrderHistTests, and set the data access method to Sequential.

Tip Unlike the standard unit tests and web tests, the data access method does affect data-driven DUTs. Aside from DUTs, the data access method takes effect only when running load tests.

Next, switch to code view, and make the changes shown in Listing 18-1.

Listing 18-1. *Data-Driven Database Unit Test Code*

```
[C#]
[TestMethod(),
 DataSource("System.Data.SqlClient", "Server=.;Integrated Security=True;Initial "
    + "Catalog=NorthwindTestDB", "CustOrderHistTests", DataAccessMethod.Random)]
public void dbo_CustOrderHistTest()
{
   DatabaseTestActions testActions = this.dbo_CustOrderHistTestData;
   // Execute the pre-test script
   System.Diagnostics.Trace.WriteLineIf((testActions.PretestAction != null),
      "Executing pre-test script...");
   ExecutionResult[] pretestResults = TestService.Execute(this.PrivilegedContext,
      this.PrivilegedContext, testActions.PretestAction);
```

```
// Execute the test script
// Add code starting here
//Set the rowcount condition with the database value
    RowCountCondition cond1 =
    (RowCountCondition)testActions.TestAction.Conditions[0];
cond1.RowCount =
    Convert.ToInt32(TestContext.DataRow["ExpectedRowCount"].ToString());
//Set the customer parameter
DbParameter p = this.ExecutionContext.Provider.CreateParameter();
p.Direction = ParameterDirection.Input;
p.ParameterName = "@CustomerID";
p.Value = TestContext.DataRow["CustomerID"];
// End new code
System.Diagnostics.Trace.WriteLineIf((testActions.TestAction != null),
        "Executing test script...");
ExecutionResult[] testResults = TestService.Execute(this.ExecutionContext,
        this.PrivilegedContext,
    testActions.TestAction, p);
// Execute the post-test script
System.Diagnostics.Trace.WriteLineIf((testActions.PosttestAction != null),
    "Executing post-test script...");
ExecutionResult[] posttestResults = TestService.Execute(this.PrivilegedContext,
    this.PrivilegedContext, testActions.PosttestAction);
}
```

[VB]
```
<DataSource("System.Data.SqlClient", _
    "Data Source=.;Initial Catalog=NorthwindTestDB;Integrated Security=True", _
    "CustOrderHistTests", DataAccessMethod.Sequential)> <TestMethod()> _
Public Sub dbo_CustOrderHistTest()
    Dim testActions As DatabaseTestActions = Me.dbo_CustOrderHistTestData
    'Execute the pre-test script
    System.Diagnostics.Trace.WriteLineIf((Not (testActions.PretestAction) _
        Is Nothing),"Executing pre-test script...")
    Dim pretestResults() As ExecutionResult = _
        TestService.Execute(Me.PrivilegedContext, _
        Me.PrivilegedContext, testActions.PretestAction)
    'Execute the test script
    'Set the rowcount condition with the database value
    Dim cond1 As RowCountCondition = CType(testActions.TestAction.Conditions(0), _
        RowCountCondition)
    cond1.RowCount = Convert.ToInt32(TestContext.DataRow("ExpectedRowCount"))
    'Set the customer parameter
    Dim p As DBParameter = Me.ExecutionContext.Provider.CreateParameter()
    p.Direction = Data.ParameterDirection.Input
    p.ParameterName = "@CustomerID"
    p.Value = TestContext.DataRow("CustomerID")
```

```
    System.Diagnostics.Trace.WriteLineIf((Not (testActions.TestAction) _
        Is Nothing), "Executing test script...")
    Dim testResults() As ExecutionResult = _
        TestService.Execute(Me.ExecutionContext, _
        Me.PrivilegedContext, testActions.TestAction, p)
    'Execute the post-test script
    System.Diagnostics.Trace.WriteLineIf((Not (testActions.PosttestAction) _
Is Nothing), _"Executing post-test script...")
    Dim posttestResults() As ExecutionResult = _
        TestService.Execute(Me.PrivilegedContext, _
        Me.PrivilegedContext, testActions.PosttestAction)
End Sub
```

This simply sets the value of RowCountCondition (and overwrites whatever you may have entered in the designer) using the TestContext.DataRow value (for more information on this, refer to Chapter 11). The next section sets the value of the @CustomerID parameter. This step is pretty straightforward; you create a parameter by calling CreateParameter (ExecutionContext is discussed in the "Database Unit Tests Behind the Scenes" section later in this chapter), set the direction to Input (in this case), assign the parameter name (taken from the designer), and set the value equal to the CustomerID column of the current row.

Here is the critical part: delete the variable declaration from the designer, or this will not work (but do not delete the variable being passed to the stored procedure)!

If you fail to do this, your test will fail with a message stating that the variable is declared twice. The last step is to update the TestService.Execute statement and append the parameter to the end of the call. (You can actually pass an array of parameters if there is more than one, but you do not have to declare a single parameter as a array of one length.)

Tip Although it is not necessary to "hard-code" a test condition (you can add a test condition at runtime), it makes data-driven testing more difficult. The reason for this is that you cannot be sure of the table structure for your test data. In the case of RowCountCondition, you know there needs to be a column to hold the expected row count. You cannot do this if you are dynamically creating test conditions at the time of the test.

Once this is done, you can run the test, which should note three out of three passed—one for each row in the database (that's two) and one for the overall test. It's as simple as that to build data-driven tests when using the designer.

Database Unit Tests Behind the Scenes

Now that you have seen how to run a unit test and create a data-driven unit test, it is time to see what is really happening behind the scenes and how to make modifications. For the moment, you will work with the CustOrderHistTests class you created earlier. Open the Solution Explorer, select the CustOrderHistTests.cs (or .vb) file, and switch to code view. Listing 18-2 contains a partial listing of the CustOrderHistTests class.

Listing 18-2. *CustOrderHistTests Class*

```C#
[C#]
[TestClass()]
public class CustOrderHistTests : DatabaseTestClass
{
    public CustOrderHistTests()
    {
        InitializeComponent();
    }

     [TestInitialize()]
    public void TestInitialize()
    {
        base.InitializeTest();
    }
     [TestCleanup()]
    public void TestCleanup()
    {
        base.CleanupTest();
    }

    //Designer Support Code goes here but is excluded

    #region Additional test attributes
    // [ClassInitialize()]
    // public static void MyClassInitialize(TestContext testContext) { }

    // [ClassCleanup()]
    // public static void MyClassCleanup() { }
    #endregion

     [TestMethod()]
    public void dbo_CustOrderHistTest()
    {
        DatabaseTestActions testActions = this.dbo_CustOrderHistTestData;
        // Execute the pre-test script
        System.Diagnostics.Trace.WriteLineIf((testActions.PretestAction != null),
            "Executing pre-test script...");
        ExecutionResult[] pretestResults =
            TestService.Execute(this.PrivilegedContext,
             this.PrivilegedContext, testActions.PretestAction);
        // Execute the test script
        System.Diagnostics.Trace.WriteLineIf((testActions.TestAction != null),
            "Executing test script...");
        ExecutionResult[] testResults = TestService.Execute(this.ExecutionContext,
            this.PrivilegedContext, testActions.TestAction);
        // Execute the post-test script
```

```
            System.Diagnostics.Trace.WriteLineIf((testActions.PosttestAction != null),
                "Executing post-test script...");
            ExecutionResult[] posttestResults =
                TestService.Execute(this.PrivilegedContext,
                  this.PrivilegedContext, testActions.PosttestAction);
      }
    private DatabaseTestActions dbo_CustOrderHistTestData;
}

[VB]
<TestClass()> _
Public Class CustOrderHistTest
    Inherits DatabaseTestClass

    Sub New()
        InitializeComponent()
    End Sub

    <TestInitialize()> _
    Public Sub TestInitialize()
        InitializeTest()
    End Sub

    <TestCleanup()> _
    Public Sub TestCleanup()
        CleanupTest()
    End Sub

    ' <ClassInitialize()> Public Shared Sub MyClassInitialize(ByVal testContext As _
    'TestContext)
    ' End Sub

    ' <ClassCleanup()> Public Shared Sub MyClassCleanup()
    ' End Sub

<TestMethod()> _
    Public Sub dbo_CustOrderHistTest()
        Dim testActions As DatabaseTestActions = Me.dbo_CustOrderHistTestData
        'Execute the pre-test script
        System.Diagnostics.Trace.WriteLineIf((Not (testActions.PretestAction) _
                Is Nothing), "Executing pre-test script...")
        Dim pretestResults() As ExecutionResult = _
                TestService.Execute(Me.PrivilegedContext, _
                Me.PrivilegedContext, testActions.PretestAction)
        'Execute the test script
```

```
    System.Diagnostics.Trace.WriteLineIf((Not (testActions.TestAction)  -
            Is Nothing), "Executing test script...")
    Dim testResults() As ExecutionResult = _
            TestService.Execute(Me.ExecutionContext, _
            Me.PrivilegedContext, testActions.TestAction)
    'Execute the post-test script
    System.Diagnostics.Trace.WriteLineIf((Not (testActions.PosttestAction) _
            Is Nothing), "Executing post-test script...")
    Dim posttestResults() As ExecutionResult = _
            TestService.Execute(Me.PrivilegedContext, _
            Me.PrivilegedContext, testActions.PosttestAction)
End Sub
Private dbo_CustOrderHistTestData As DatabaseTestActions
```

As you can see at a quick glance, this is virtually identical to a standard unit test. Although the class inherits from DatabaseTestClass, the class must be decorated with the TestClass attribute and supports the TestInitialize, TestCleanup, ClassInitialize, and ClassCleanup attributes. The actual tests must be decorated with the TestMethod attribute. Of these methods, only the methods decorated with the ClassInitialize and ClassCleanup attributes are not available from the designer.

■**Note** The "Designer Support Code" section of code is not included in the listing. There is no reason to change this code because it is dynamically regenerated based on selections made in the test design window.

Test Method

Now, what looks wildly different from the standard unit test code is the test method. You will immediately see that the SQL for the test (or any other SQL) or any of the conditions that you are testing against is listed here. The "Designer Support Code" section contains the test conditions against which you are testing. You are more than welcome to look at them. However, you will not find the SQL there either. The SQL statements shown in the designer are stored in the resource file located below the test class in the Solution Explorer (in this case, the file is CustOrderHistTest.resx). If you open this, you will see your SQL statement.

So, how does the test execution actually occur? The execution is actually incredibly simple, but you have to know what two of the classes are for—the DatabaseTestActions class and the DatabaseTestAction class. The DatabaseTestActions class contains the pre- and post-test scripts and also the actual test as a DatabaseTestAction instance. The DatabaseTestAction class contains the SQL statements that are your actual test and the list of conditions associated with the test. Now that you know what the classes are, you can take a look at the test execution. The class that actually executes the test is the DatabaseTestService class. In practice, you will not need to deal with the DatabaseTestService class other than to call the Execute method if you choose to manually write your DUTs.

ConnectionContext Class

One class you may find lots of uses for is the ConnectionContext class. Through this class you can dynamically create your SQL statements, connect to data sources, create parameters, wrap items in transactions, and create data adapters, among other things. You can access the ConnectionContext class through the ExecutionContext of the DatabaseTestClass (in other words, calling [Code]this.ExecutionContext). The Provider property of the ConnectionContext class returns a DBProviderFactory that you have already seen. You will get the most use from this class when you do not want to use the designer at all (in other words, just leave it as a blank window and create your SQL and conditions in code).

Doing this provides some benefits but has one drawback—readability. The benefit is that if you use data-driven testing, you do not have to remember to remove declarations, and you do not have to have row conditions in the designer and in code—you can keep them together and set values just once. In addition, setting items in code means that whatever is in the designer window is generally wrong, which can make readability difficult.

Tip We recommend you use the designer window for all tests except when performing data-driven unit tests. In this case, it makes more sense to include everything as code, and you can use the designer simply to generate the SQL and variables. When not performing data-driven tests, you should use the designer and not write custom code.

Data Generation

Being able to generate data for your database was, in the past, frequently not a big deal. You would simply copy over production data, and off you went. If you needed to have a consistent set of data, you might write a clever select statement that would create inserts for you for all your data so you could perform consistent tests. However, if your database schema was in flux, maintaining referential integrity could be incredibly difficult because you would have to hand edit your insert statements.

Now, data generation is becoming more important because of data privacy issues. Say you are working on a project that is subcontracted to outside developers. And take it a step further to say that you had Social Security numbers or credit card numbers stored in your database. These are two of the biggest gotcha areas in data theft today. So, naturally you want to give the developers dummy data. That is all well and good except up to this point you've generally gone the route of setting pricing data to $1.00, Social Security numbers to 111-11-1111, and credit card numbers to a fixed number of the right format depending on the type of credit card you were dealing with. Basically, what you generated was data that looked right but was totally inappropriate for testing (none of these generation schemes deals with min/max values, normal distribution, or being able to tell what row generated an error because all of the rows looked the same—as well as other issues)!

The data generation tool in the Database Professionals edition is just flat-out cool, and it's extensible. You can use data from an existing data source if you want or generate your own data. Let's look at a basic data generation scenario using the Northwind_Original database.

To add a data generation plan, right-click the Data Generation Plans node in the Solution Explorer, and select Add ➤ Data Generation Plan. When the New Item dialog box is displayed, name it CustomersDGP, and click OK. Figure 18-4 shows the data generation plan views.

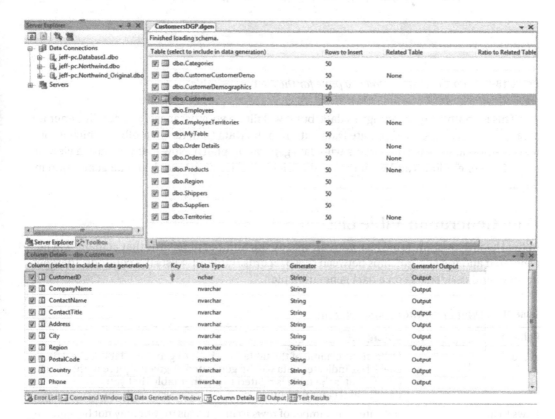

Figure 18-4. *Data generation plan views*

The top pane shows all the tables in the schema. By default they are all checked for population. The bottom pane is the Details pane and shows how each column of the selected table will be generated. The third pane, the Data Generation Preview pane, will show you a preview of the data generated for the selected table. If you switch to the Data Generation Preview pane right now, you will see a bunch of randomly generated Unicode values of varying length that do not exceed the columns' maximum lengths (Figure 18-5).

Figure 18-5. *Data Generation Preview pane for the* Customers *table*

This is completely meaningless data, but it will fill up your database! To actually generate data, you simply click the Generate Data button in the Data Generation toolbar (which is displayed automatically when working with data generation plans). Now that you have a view of what data generation is and what the windows look like, it's time to look at data generation in detail.

Data Generation Table List

In the Data Generation Table List, you can specify the number of records that actually will be generated and the relationships between those records. Table 18-4 lists the columns, their definitions, and their effects on a data generation plan.

Table 18-4. *Data Generation Plan Columns*

Column	Description
Table	Indicates the name of the table for which to generate data. A check in the check box indicates data will be generated. A green square in the check box indicates the table is related to another table that you are generating data for and cannot be unselected.
Rows to Insert	Indicates the number of rows to insert. This may or may not be editable depending on whether there is a related table. If there is, then Ratio to Related Table controls the number of generated records.
Related Table	Allows you to select a parent table to which records in the child are related. If None does not appear, by default it indicates the table is a parent table or has no relationships with other tables.
Ratio to Related Table	Indicates the ratio of generated rows compared to the parent table. For example, if you selected Customers as the related table for Orders and entered **10:1** in the Ratio column, the number of rows to insert for the Orders table increases to 500 since you have requested 10 orders for everyone 1 customer.
Status	Indicates the status of the data generation while the plan is executing.

Details Window

In the Details window you can specify which columns to generate data for, specify what type of generator to use, or hook up your data generation to a database and several other things. Table 18-5 shows the options for the Details window.

Table 18-5. *Detail Columns*

Column	Description
Column	Indicates for which columns to generate data. Note that for columns not selected, the column must be nullable. If it is not, a message box will be displayed saying the column is not nullable.
Key	Indicates whether the column is a primary key column (gold key) or a foreign key column (gray key).
Data Type	Specifies the SQL Server data type of the column.
Generator	Specifies the type of generator used for the column. By default this is the generator of the same type as the data type (in other words, a String generator for any type of string column—char, nchar, nvarchar, and so on).
Generator Result	Indicates which result set, if you're hooked to a data bound generator or a custom generator, will be used to fill the column. Otherwise, the default is Result and cannot be changed.

Generators

A *generator*, as its name implies, generates data. The Database Professionals edition comes with several built-in generators:

- Data Bound (explained in a moment)
- Sequential Data Bound (available with the Power Tools)
- Float
- Integer
- Real
- Regular Expression
- SmallInt
- String
- TinyInt
- DateTime
- SQL Computed Value (If these generators are listed, they cannot be changed. These are system-generated values.)

- Foreign Key (If these generators are listed, they cannot be changed. These are system-generated values.)

- Money

- BigInt

- Bit

- Image

- Binary

Not all of these values will be available in the Generator list. Only generators with outputs coercible to the column type without data loss will be listed for a given data type. For example, if a column is of type smallint, only SmallInt and TinyInt will be available options (and the Data Bound generator, which is always available as an option).

■**Tip** You can set the default generators for a given column type by selecting Tools ➤ Options ➤ Database Tools ➤ Data Generator ➤ Default Generators.

By default, each of the prebuilt generators will generate random, valid data. (For example, a DateTime generator will never generate an invalid date, and a string generator will never generate a string longer than the maximum length of the column.)

■**Note** The exceptions to this rule are the Data Bound generator and the Foreign Key generator. The Data Bound generator selects random data from a nonrandom data source.

But you can also set properties for each type of generator, which can help control certain aspects of the data generation.

Before we talk about the properties for each generator, we must explain one issue that will help you in your data generation endeavors: the data that is generated is random *but repeatable*. OK, the first question you'll ask is probably, how is a random process repeatable? Well, each generator is assigned a *seed* value (this property is available in all generators except the system generated values noted in Table 18-5). By default, the value is 5. This is used to randomize the data generation pattern. However, if the same value is entered as the seed each time, then the same *random* results will also be generated. The reason for this is straightforward—since you can use this tool to generate test data, you want the data to be identical from one run to the next, or otherwise you cannot test your application correctly!

Now that we have that out of the way, we can cover the properties for each generator. Table 18-6 lists the properties common across all generators.

Table 18-6. *Data Generator Common Properties*

Property	Description
Allow Nulls	[From schema] Indicates whether nulls are allowed
Check Constraints	[From schema] Any user-defined constraints against the column
Default Value	[From schema] Default column value
Foreign Key	[From schema] Indicates whether this column is constrained by a foreign key
Percentage Null	The percentage of values during generation that should be null
Primary Key	[From schema] Indicates whether this is a primary key column
Seed	Value for randomization (explained previously)
Size	[From data type] The maximum size on disk of a generated value
Unique	[From schema] Indicates whether the column contains unique values*
Unique	Generates unique values for the column

* This does not apply to the Regular Expression data generator because that is not based on a column type.

In addition to the common properties shared by all data generators, a few properties are specific to some of the data generators, as listed in Table 18-7.

Table 18-7. *Properties Unique to a Generator*

Generator	Property	Description
String	Locale	Specifies the code page used as the source for string values
String, Regular Expression, Binary	Maximum Length	Constrains the maximum length of the generated value
String	Minimum Length	Constrains the minimum length of the generated value
Numeric*	Distribution	Controls the statistical distribution of values
Image	Height	Specifies the height of a generated image**
Image	Width	Specifies the width of a generated image**
Regular Expression	Expression	Specifies the regular expression used to generate the result

* This includes all numeric generators except the Bit generator.
** The binary data generated for the image is garbage data (that is, it isn't actually an image), but these values constrain how much data is generated.

Of the items listed here, the only two that require a little bit more information are the Regular Expression generator and the Distribution property of the numeric generators. We'll cover those two in the next section with an example.

Generating Data

To demonstrate some data generation capabilities, create a new SQL Server database called testdb. Create a single table called employees with the schema shown in Figure 18-6.

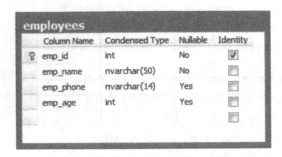

Figure 18-6. *The* employees *table*

Now create a new SQL Server 2005 database project called TestGeneration in Visual Studio. Import the database schema from the testdb database. Then add a data generation plan (leave the default name). In the Details window, select the emp_phone column from the employees table, and change the generator from String to Regular Expression. The default regular expression is [a-zA-Z0-9]*, which will create a random string of alphanumeric characters only. No nonalphanumeric characters will be included (such as the @, $, and so on). Change this to the following regular expression: \([0-9]{3}\) [0-9]{3}-[0-9]{4}. In a regular expression, this matches the following pattern of data: (555) 555-5555. If you have the Power Tools installed, select Phone2 from the regular expressions list (see "Regular Expression Builder" later in the chapter for more information about this dialog box).

■**Note** This is absolutely not a book on regular expressions. For more information, see the excellent reference *Mastering Regular Expressions* by Jeffrey Friedl. It isn't specific to the .NET Framework but is just a good overall book on expressions. Alternatively, check out the tool RegexBuddy, which is our personal favorite. It's available from www.regexbuddy.com.

For the data generator, it specifies the pattern to which the data conforms. Once you enter this value, switch to the Data Generation Preview pane. You should see the results in Figure 18-7.

emp_id ⓘ	emp_name	emp_phone	emp_age	
Identity	ebÒxøPúÒMánHH...	(422) 649-1951	726643700	
Identity	azH60UòY1øLDõg...	(930) 141-9082	610783965	
Identity	mCzIVGúìĖáSØBÙ...	(508) 817-2791	564707973	
Identity	ÇôjOI	(173) 239-1717	1342984399	
Identity	OÙ4IZÒ4RvavBãW...	(419) 851-0568	995276750	
Identity	ÙwKõLMñèÁEfRÓ...	(992) 512-4447	1993667614	
Identity	U6HErGùÒ	(730) 502-0965	314199522	
Identity	ÀÚô4QTzÉaåDÍÀÈ...	(918) 193-0929	2041397713	
Identity	jfôìvÉnWBóÑØÁÍÙ...	(761) 110-5891	1280186417	
Identity	akZáeál dñzbãz3èú...	(563) 519-0473	252243313	

Error List   Command ...   Data Gener...   Column De...   Output   Test Results

Figure 18-7. *Regular Expression generator results*

Pretty cool is the only way to describe it.

■**Tip** And no, before you ask, Microsoft is not including a credit card number generator!

But, we obviously have some other issues here. Let's start with the emp_age column. If you have employees that old, please contact Guinness! So, the age needs a little fixing. First you have to put it in a valid range. Select the properties for the emp_age column in the Details window and set the minimum to 20 and the maximum to 70 (after all, people are working longer into their lives now). Next, you can be pretty sure that a certain aged employee will come work for your company—say between the ages of 20 to 25 and older than 55 because this is a retail store. To get this type of distribution, which is statistically easy to generate, set the distribution to NormalInverse, and expand the Distribution option (you can expand this property depending on the type of distribution you select).

■**Note** Nope, this isn't a book about statistics either, and quite honestly neither of us is any type of expert with statistics. We know just enough to get by.

The default deviation is set to .15. Generate the data (note that for this example, we generated 500 rows to give a more accurate statistical view), or preview it.

■**Tip** You can set how many rows are generated as part of the Preview window by selecting Tools ➤ Options ➤ Database Tools ➤ Data Generator and setting the Preview row count to the desired value. You'll see several other useful options here as well.

If you generate the data, you will note that you are prompted for the database to connect to, and you will be prompted that all of the existing data in the table is going to be deleted. Because of the potential relationships between tables, the Visual Studio Team System team for version 1 did not want to tackle the idea of single column or selected column data generation. This can be a tricky and difficult situation in complex databases.

Note If you do want to do single-column generation, you could generate a single column's worth of data (if you uncheck all columns but one, nulls will be generated in the unchecked columns), paste it into Excel, and manipulate it to perform updates on a full table's worth of data. This is time-consuming and difficult, but it may be necessary in some cases.

When you generate the data, you will find that it looks pretty close to what is shown in Figure 18-8.

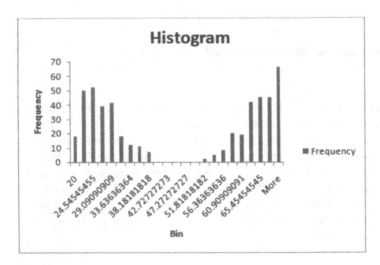

Figure 18-8. *Histogram of age distribution (inverse)*

You'll note that this is almost an exact inverse of a bell curve, which is what an inverse normal distribution is—the opposite of a normal distribution. This allows you to uniformly distribute data via various statistical functions.

Data Bound Generator

Finally, the Data Bound generator really falls into a class all by itself. The beauty of this generator is that it is simple to use. To continue with the TestGeneration project, we'll show how to update the employees table to use real employee names for the emp_name column. To do this, select emp_name in the Details window, and set the generator to a Data Bound generator. View the properties for the emp_name column, and select the Connection Information property. A drop-down with a list of database connections (from the Server Explorer) will be displayed.

Select the Northwind database (or Northwind_Original). Then set the Select Query property to the following:

```
Select FirstName + ' ' + LastName From Employees
```

Notice that the Generator Result column in the Details window is now set to [ResultTable1].[Column1].

■Note If you have the Power Tools installed and you use the dialog box to enter the select statement, it will require you to alias the column (see "Sequential Data Bound Generator" later in this chapter).

Changing the select statement to the following:

```
Select FirstName + ' ' + LastName As FullName From Employees
```

will change the Generator Result column to [ResultTable1].[FullName]. Switching to the Data Generation Preview pane, you should see something similar to the view in Figure 18-9.

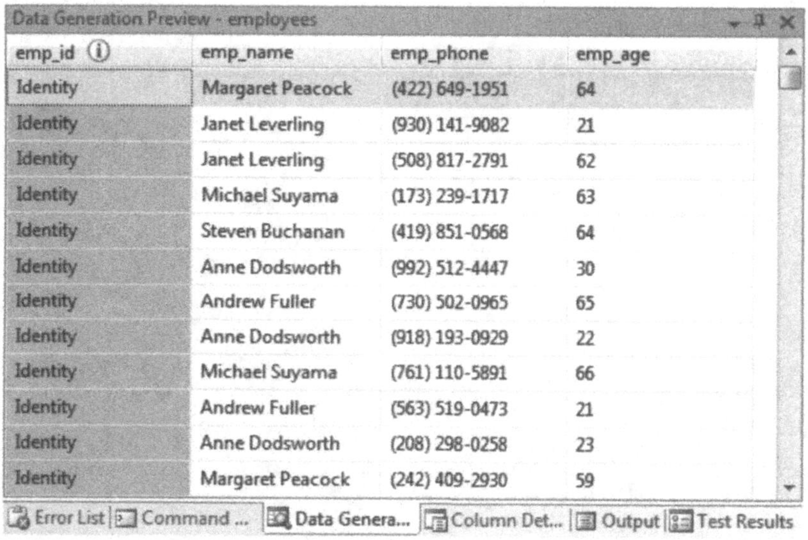

emp_id ⓘ	emp_name	emp_phone	emp_age
Identity	Margaret Peacock	(422) 649-1951	64
Identity	Janet Leverling	(930) 141-9082	21
Identity	Janet Leverling	(508) 817-2791	62
Identity	Michael Suyama	(173) 239-1717	63
Identity	Steven Buchanan	(419) 851-0568	64
Identity	Anne Dodsworth	(992) 512-4447	30
Identity	Andrew Fuller	(730) 502-0965	65
Identity	Anne Dodsworth	(918) 193-0929	22
Identity	Michael Suyama	(761) 110-5891	66
Identity	Andrew Fuller	(563) 519-0473	21
Identity	Anne Dodsworth	(208) 298-0258	23
Identity	Margaret Peacock	(242) 409-2930	59

Data Generation Preview - employees

Error List | Command ... | Data Genera... | Column Det... | Output | Test Results

Figure 18-9. *Data Generation Preview pane*

You can select any column from any result set returned from the select query.

Nulls and the Seed Value

The Percentage Null property noted earlier allows you to specify a given percentage of values for a column that will be null during a data generation. In the earlier example, set the emp_phone column Percentage Null property to 50, and switch to the Data Generation Preview pane. This shows you what you expect to see—a number of rows in the emp_phone column are null. Now, change the emp_age column so the Percentage Null property is also 50, and then switch back to the preview. You will note that the same rows of each column are null. This is because both the Seed property and the Percentage Null property are identical between each column.

Tip To vary your null values, change the seed and or null values to be different between columns.

Regular Expression Builder

The Power Tools includes a new Regular Expression Builder to help you create common regular expressions. This provides more flexibility for entering data (see Figure 18-10).

Note At this time, it is not possible to extend the ability to create entry screens. The DBPro team is working on this for a future release, however.

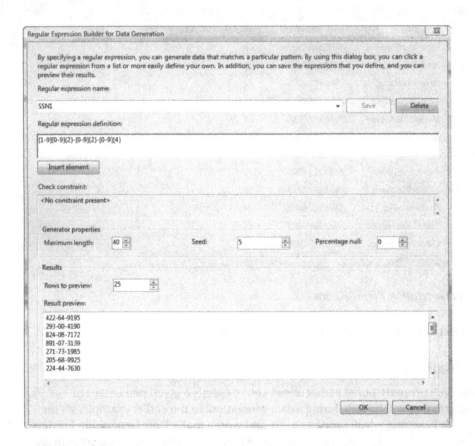

Figure 18-10. *Regular Expression Builder for Data Generation dialog box*

Create a new data generation plan, and select a table. View the column details for a string column, and select Regular Expression from the Generator column. Next, click the ellipsis button that appears to the right of the Output column (note that you can still set the regular expression in the Properties window). This will display the dialog box shown earlier in Figure 18-8. Included with the Power Tools are several prebuilt regular expressions, from telephone numbers to Social Security numbers.

In addition to this, you can add your own regular expressions to this list. To add a new regular expression, select Add New Expression from the Regular Expression Name list, and enter a new regular expression in the Regular Expression Definition box. The Insert Element button provides access to some standard regular expression syntax help to make building the expression easier. When you are finished, click Save. Table 18-8 shows the supported regular expression operators and their output.

Table 18-8. *Supported Regular Expression Operators*

Operator	Output
.	Any character.
\	Escape character—the next character is read as a literal; for example, \(is used to output a left brace for the telephone number shown in Figure 18-10.
()	Group operator—outputs the items in the braces as a single output.
{n}	Generates n number of whatever expression this follows. In the telephone example in Figure 18-10, [0-9]{3} outputs three numbers that range from 0 to 9 such as 492.
{n,m}	Generates at least n but no more than m instances of an expression. For example, a{2,4} can generate aa, aaa, or aaaa.
{n,}	Generates n or more instances of the previous expression. For example, a{2,} generates aa, aaa, or aaaa, so on.
*	Generates 0 or more instances of the previous expression.
+	Generates 1 or more instances of the previous expression.
?	Generates 0 or 1 instance of the previous expression.
|	This is the Or operator and generates an item on one side or the other of this operator. For example, a|b can generate either an a or a b.
[]	Generates any character in the brackets. These can be used several ways.
[abc]	As a discrete list, this will generate any single item in the bracket. The result of this expression can be a, b, or c.
[0-9]	As a ranged list, this will generate any single item that falls within the range of 0–9 (including 0 and 9).
[^abc]	As an exclusion list this will generate any valid character *not* contained within this list. In other words, anything but a, b, or c will be generated.

Additions to the regular expression list are stored in the RegexHelperConfig.xml file, which is located in the AppData\Roaming folder under your username in documents and settings or Users depending on your operating system. This file has three sections, which are fairly self-explanatory but which we will list here for reference. The "Record" section contains regular expressions that are provided with the Power Tools. The "SyntaxMenu" section contains prebuilt constructs with descriptions that are displayed when you click the Insert Element button. At the bottom of the file is another section containing record values that contains custom regular expression values you added through the Add New Expression option in the dialog box. The only difference is that these values use a GUID as the key. You can edit this file manually and also redistribute it to other developers so they can use any regular expressions you may have created.

Sequential Data Bound Generator

Additionally, the Power Tools includes a new data bound generator, the Sequential Data Bound generator. Along with this, the DBPro team has provided a new window to set properties in instead of relying on the Properties window. Select the Sequential Data Bound Generator for a string column, and click the ellipsis button next to the Output column. This displays the Data Generator Wizard dialog box shown in Figure 18-11.

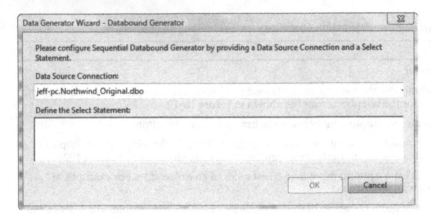

Figure 18-11. *Data Generator Wizard dialog box*

This is also the same dialog box (minus a few options) that is displayed for the Data Bound generator. Once you enter the select statement and click OK, you will be able to select an output column in the Column Details window.

Using Data Generation with Unit Testing

So far you have seen how to write unit tests, and you have seen how to generate data independently of a unit test. This section shows you how to combine the two to provide the ability for repeatable, automated testing of your database.

To begin with, switch back to the NorthwindDB solution (which should have the NorthwindDB project and the DBUnitTests project). Delete the CustomersDGP data generation plan, and create a new data generation plan called AllTables. Leave all the default settings as they are. At this point, you have one unit test called CustOrderHistTests (note that for this example you are not using the data-driven version of this test, so you may want to delete it and re-create it).

At the beginning of this chapter, when you generated the CustOrderHistTests test, you created a new test project and left the default settings alone. You need to change those settings in order to be able to generate the database and the data before the test is run. Unfortunately, there is no dialog box to go back to in order to edit these settings—you have to edit the test project's app.config file. Listing 18-3 shows the app.config file that was initially created, and Listing 18-4 shows the configuration required to deploy and load data before a test (line breaks are for formatting purposes only).

Listing 18-3. *Original Testing app.config File (Line Breaks for Formatting Only)*

```xml
<?xml version="1.0" encoding="utf-8" ?>
<configuration>
    <configSections>
        <section name="DatabaseUnitTesting"
            type="Microsoft.VisualStudio.TeamSystem.Data.UnitTesting.Configuration.
            DatabaseUnitTestingSection,
            Microsoft.VisualStudio.TeamSystem.Data.UnitTesting,
            Version=2.0.0.0, Culture=neutral, PublicKeyToken=b03f5f7f11d50a3a" />
    </configSections>
    <DatabaseUnitTesting>
        <DataGeneration ClearDatabase="true" />
        <ExecutionContext Provider="System.Data.SqlClient" ConnectionString=
        "Data Source=.;Initial Catalog=Northwind_Original;
          Integrated Security=True;Pooling=False" />
        <PrivilegedContext Provider="System.Data.SqlClient" ConnectionString=
          "Data Source=.;Initial Catalog=Northwind_Original;
            Integrated Security=True;Pooling=False" />
    </DatabaseUnitTesting>
</configuration>
```

Listing 18-4. *app.config file for Deployment and Data Loading*

```xml
<?xml version="1.0" encoding="utf-8" ?>
<configuration>

    <configSections>
        <section name="DatabaseUnitTesting"
            type="Microsoft.VisualStudio.TeamSystem.Data.UnitTesting.Configuration.
    DatabaseUnitTestingSection, Microsoft.VisualStudio.TeamSystem.Data.UnitTesting,
            Version=2.0.0.0, Culture=neutral, PublicKeyToken=b03f5f7f11d50a3a" />
    </configSections>
    <DatabaseUnitTesting>
        <DatabaseDeployment DatabaseProjectFileName=
            "..\..\..\NorthwindDB\NorthwindDB.dbproj"
            Configuration="Default" />
        <DataGeneration DataGenerationFileName="..\..\..\NorthwindDB\Data Generation
            Plans\AllTables.dgen"
            ClearDatabase="true" />
        <ExecutionContext Provider="System.Data.SqlClient" ConnectionString=
          "Data Source=.;Initial Catalog=Northwind_Original;
            Integrated Security=True;Pooling=False" />
```

```
        <PrivilegedContext Provider="System.Data.SqlClient" ConnectionString=
          "Data Source=.;Initial Catalog=Northwind_Original;
            Integrated Security=True;Pooling=False" />
      </DatabaseUnitTesting>
</configuration>
```

The new app.config file in Listing 18-4 contains the following additional items:

- A DatabaseDeployment element that lists the relative path to the database project (from the unit testing project).

- A DataGeneration element that provides the relative path to the data generation plan (from the unit testing project). This element originally provided only a ClearDatabase attribute.

It is important to note that only one data generation plan can be run per unit test project.

When you first run this test, it will fail. Because the data is generated for you and is random, the customer ALFKI will not be in the database. The easiest way to handle this is to run the tests once and let them fail. Then examine the generated data and pick a customer (in this case use ADAAA) and count the number of orders that customer has. Then update RowCountCondition so it has the appropriate number of rows to indicate the test has passed (the correct number of rows is 1).

As you have seen by this, it is critically important you create your data generation plan that will be used for testing before you start creating your first tests. If you do not, you'll have to come back and change the parameter names and the test conditions to match the generated data.

Best Practices

There are several ways to go about setting up your development database in order to ensure a smooth unit testing experience. Some of these practices will not be useful to you, but others will be depending on the environment you work in.

Lookup Tables

A *lookup table* is a table that contains relatively static data designed for combo boxes or other options from which a user may choose. For example, if you are working on an automobile application where a user can select the model type, you may have a model_type table containing Compact, Mid-size, SUV, Luxury, and so on. Where possible, use real data for these tables. That means you have several choices to load data into these types of tables:

- You can store the data in a text file and load the data from that for each data generation.

- You can run a post-deployment script that executes a series of inserts to add the static data.

- You can create a test data database from which you use the Data Bound generator to load data (we recommend the Sequential Data Bound generator for this).

General Items

For generated data, remember that the data should be part of your project because you will need it for testing and in some cases your actual deployment. But realize that any developer will have access to the data. Because of these two conditions, you should consider these tips:

- Do not use sensitive data such as personally identifiable information (PII) or financial data.

- Version control your data generation plans and *all* the supporting files such as static data stored in text files or in test databases.

- If you create a test data database, create that as a DBPro project as well and version control it. The same goes if you are performing data-driven tests—version control that database as well!

- Do not place usernames or passwords into plain-text files such as the `app.config` file. These can be supplied as parameters from the command line.

- Create your data generation plan *before* you start writing unit tests.

- Try to use data as realistic as possible. Since you'll want to run these tests against your test environment, it means users will also be looking at this data.

Summary

This chapter showed you how to create and run unit tests and customize the test using the code behind the designers. You learned how to create data-driven unit tests and dynamically provide parameters to a test. You can now generate data using the data generation tools and provide a variety of realistic data that looks the way users expect it to look. And you can generate the same data consistently or vary the output as necessary. Finally, you can combine data generation and unit testing to provide a repeatable testing process at the heart of quality software! The next chapter will show you how to extend the Database Professionals edition by creating your own test conditions and data generators and will allow you to go far beyond what has been hinted at in this chapter.

■ ■ ■

CHAPTER 19

Building and Deploying Databases

This chapter will walk you through the process of building and deploying projects on a build server and on your local machine and will show how to best deploy projects. You will also use the new command-line tool sqlspp.exe, which you can use to run scripts created with DBPro. We'll cover the process for deploying your database project and running automated build verification tests (or unit tests) in detail.

Note As explained in the Chapter 15, a build verification test is simply a test to determine whether the build worked correctly. This may be a simple test such as a NotEmptyResult set to determine whether data was loaded or an EmptyResult set to make sure a stored procedure ran correctly. It does not attempt to test detailed functionality.

Building Database Projects

For the purpose of this chapter, you will create a new database project and perform several operations on it. If you want to follow along with the examples, you'll need to create this project. This first section covers the various options and outcomes of building your projects.

Setting Up the Project

Create a new SQL Server 2005 database project called NorthwindCustom, and import the Northwind_Original database.

Note If you've made changes to the Northwind_Original database, rerun the instnwndoriginal.sql script to re-create it.

Follow these steps to create the data generation and unit test:

1. Right-click NorthwindCustom, and select the Data Generation Plans folder in the Solution Explorer.

2. Select Add ➤ Data Generation Plan, and name it Categories.

3. Include only the Categories table, and set the number of rows to 10 (leave the default generators as is).

4. Next, select Test ➤ New Test from the main menu, and select Database Unit Test.

5. Call the test CategoryTests and the project NorthwindCustomTests, and click OK.

6. When the options are displayed for the new test project, select Northwind_Original for the database, check Deployment, and select the NorthwindCustom.dbproj project and the Default configuration. Select Generate Test Data, select the Categories data generation plan, and click OK.

7. In the CategoryTests designer, add the following SQL statement:

   ```
   Select * From Categories
   ```

8. Remove the inconclusive condition, and add a row count condition with the number of rows set to 10.

9. Run the test to make sure it works.

10. Next, open the Test Manager window, and create a new test list called BVT.

11. Add DatabaseTest1 to the BVT list.

This is the example used for the rest of this chapter. In addition, we have added the project to a team project in order to demonstrate some of the benefits of version control during this process. You do not have to add the project to version control until the "TFS Build" section later in this chapter. We are using the MSF for Agile template.

Full and Incremental Builds

Before you build the project and in order to illustrate one of the differences in the build option, add the stored procedure (you have added this before, but in another project) in Listing 19-1.

Listing 19-1. *usp_get_employees Stored Procedure*

```
CREATE PROCEDURE [dbo].[usp_get_employees]
AS
SELECT  *
FROM    Employees
```

You have just introduced a change. So, what behavior would you expect when you build the project? You would expect it to build a script that contained just the addition of the stored procedure. Select Build ➤ Build Solution from the main menu. Once the build has succeeded, navigate to the NorthwindCustom\sql folder, and examine the `NorthwindCustom.sql` file. You will note that it has scripted the entire database project. Why? The reason is the name of the database to which you are deploying. Because DBPro uses the project name by default (which is different from the name of the database where the schema originated), it doesn't find a database on the server to perform a schema compare against, so it assumes the database doesn't exist.

There may come a time when this is exactly the behavior you want because you want to script the entire database at a point in time. However, this is rarely the result you will want if you are performing an incremental update against an existing database. To fix this situation, view the database project properties. Right-click the NorthwindCustom project, and select Properties. Select the Build tab. These settings are of considerable importance when building, and eventually deploying, database projects. Of the options here, the ones that will cause the most variation are the target connection and target database name. The target connection is pretty straightforward; it's the connection string to the server where your database will be deployed. By default it is blank. Click the Edit button, create a connection string to your local SQL Server 2005 server, and point it to `Northwind_Original`, not `NorthwindCustom` (which is the default because that is the project name). It's this setting that caused the earlier problem. Now that you've made this change, rebuild your project, and examine the `NorthwindCustom.sql` output file. In addition to all the start-up and teardown scripts, there is only one statement—the `create` procedure statement for the earlier stored procedure.

Select Show All Files from the top of the Solution Explorer, right-click the `Northwind Custom.sql` file, and select Include in Project. Check in your changes. Subsequent builds will *not* cause this file to be checked out, so be careful when performing a build for deployment. If you're going to version control builds, make sure as part of your checklist you do a Check Out for Edit operation on this file before you do a build.

Command-Line Builds

Earlier you saw how to perform builds from within Visual Studio, but you can also perform builds from the command line. If you are going to use the Visual Studio settings, then you can perform a build using the following syntax:

```
Msbuild NorthwindCustom.dbproj /t:Build
```

The /t indicates which target to build—in this case the Build target. If you open the `NorthwindCustom.dbproj` file in Notepad, you will notice that the first line reads (partially) as follows:

```
<Project DefaultTargets="Build" ...>
```

You can, since Build is the default target, also omit /t:Build, and the build will still work. However, it's always better to specify a target to build rather than take the chance that the default target will change!

You can also overwrite specific settings at the command line using the following syntax (depending on the changes you want to make):

```
Msbuild NorthwindCustom.dbproj /t:Build /p:targetdatabase="NorthwindDemo"
```

Essentially, any property noted in the .dbproj file is fair game for being overwritten from the command line. One good reason to use this method is if, for example, you wanted to provide a connection string that contained a username and password at the time of the build rather than storing them.

Script Files

Chapter 17 notes that the Solution Explorer contains Scripts\Pre-Deployment and Scripts\Post-Deployment folders. These folders contain straight SQL script files or files that point to script files. As noted earlier, the Script.PostDeployment and Script.PreDeployment files are the key files here. These are the files that are read to insert SQL statements into the final build script.

Tip You can change the Script.PostDeployment and Script.PreDeployment scripts by right-clicking a file and selecting Properties. Then change Build Action to either PreDeploy or PostDeploy. Only one file can be marked as PreDeploy, and one file can be marked as PostDeploy.

Listing 19-2 shows the default Script.PreDeployment script.

Listing 19-2. *Default Script.PreDeployment Script*

```
:r .\Logins.sql
:r .\LinkedServers.sql
:r .\CustomErrors.sql
:r .\EncryptionKeysAndCertificates.sql
```

The :r syntax is used by SQLCMD (and SQLSPP, which wraps SQLCMD) to read the contents of the file pointed to. So in this case, the Scripts.PreDeployment.sql file will cause all four of these files to have their SQL statements entered into the final build script. Similarly, Scripts.PostDeployment.sql points to all the files in the Post-Deployment folder. With the exception of these two script files, all other files are empty by default.

You can find valid commands that you can execute in these script files by looking up the Help for the SQLCMD command-line tool in Books Online.

Note sqlspp.exe resides in the C:\Program Files\Microsoft Visual Studio 8\DBPro folder. It accepts four input values: InputFile, OutputFile, Property, and a response file (sqlspp stands for SQL script preprocessor). Its purpose is to expand all of the includes and variable definitions (that is, replace them with the appropriate values).

MSBuild

The Database Professionals edition adds five new MSBuild tasks. These are SqlBuildTask, SqlDeployTask, SqlSchemaCompareTask, SqlDataCompareTask, and DataGeneratorTask. You can use these options in conjunction with MSBuild to perform builds, deploy the database project, and generate data into the new database. However, without using these MSBuild tasks directly, you can create builds by way of the project and test project properties.

Note This is not a primer on MSBuild, so it omits much of the detailed information relating to MSBuild and focuses on the tasks listed earlier. For a more complete reference, pick up a copy of *Deploying .NET Applications: Learning MSBuild and ClickOnce* (Apress, 2006) by Sayed Y. Hashimi and Sayed Ibrahim Hashimi.

Database Professionals uses a "targets" file to replace items in the .dbproj and .dbproj. user files. By default, in your .dbproj file you will see this line (line breaks for formatting purposes):

```
<Import
Project=
"$(MSBuildExtensionsPath)\Microsoft\VisualStudio\v8.0\TeamData\Microsoft.
VisualStudio.TeamSystem.Data.Tasks.targets" />
```

This referenced file is the targets file. The file is commented to explain each of the items contained within it. For the purposes of the build, the order files are imported into other files is important because each successive layer overwrites the properties in the previous layers. For example:

- The .dbproj file is the first file executed.

- It imports the .targets file, which can overwrite any of the settings of the .dbproj file.

- The .targets file imports the common targets file and the .user file.

- Lastly there are the command-line parameters that can overwrite any property in the earlier mentioned files.

Using the DataGenerator Task

In general, you probably will not need to use any of these MSBuild tasks directly. But, the DBPro team thought there were enough reasons you might want to use the tasks, so let's look at how to use each of them. Create a new text file, populate it with the text in Listing 19-3, and name it dgenbuildfile.txt.

Listing 19-3. *Data Generation MSBuild File*

```
<Project
DefaultTargets="DataGen" xmlns="http://schemas.microsoft.com/developer/
msbuild/2003">
  <!--Import the settings-->
  <Import Project=
"$(MSBuildExtensionsPath)\Microsoft\VisualStudio\v8.0\TeamData\Microsoft.
VisualStudio.TeamSystem.Data.Tasks.targets" />

  <Target Name="DataGen">
  <DataGeneratorTask
  ConnectionString=
"Data Source=.;Integrated Security=True;Pooling=False;Initial Catalog=$(MyCatalog)"
  SourceFile="Categories.dgen"
  PurgeTablesBeforePopulate="true"
  />
  </Target>
</Project>
```

This MSBuild file does the following—it imports the `.targets` file and kicks off a data generation task as defined in the named `.dgen` file. In addition, note the property `$(MyCatalog)`—this is a custom property, so you can specify the name of the database. To try this, either use an existing data generation plan that you created earlier in this section or just create a new data generation plan in Visual Studio. Copy this text file into the Data Generation folder, and run the following from the Visual Studio command prompt (it is easier to be in the Data Generation folder; otherwise, you have to supply full file paths):

```
Msbuild dgenbuildfile.txt /p:MyCatalog="NorthwindCustom"
```

You should see the results shown in Figure 19-1.

Figure 19-1. *A custom MSBuild file result*

Using the SqlSchemaCompare Task

This task could prove valuable for running a schema comparison before deploying to verify what will be changed. This example uses the Northwind_Dev and Northwind_Original databases. Create a text file as shown in Listing 19-4, and save it in the root of drive C as schemacompare.txt.

Listing 19-4. *Schema Compare MSBuild File (Line Breaks Are for Formatting Only)*

```
<Project DefaultTargets="SchemaCompare"
 xmlns="http://schemas.microsoft.com/developer/msbuild/2003">
  <!--Import the settings-->
  <Import Project=
"$(MSBuildExtensionsPath)\Microsoft\VisualStudio\v8.0\TeamData\
Microsoft.VisualStudio.TeamSystem.Data.PowerTools.Tasks.targets"/>
  <Target Name ="SchemaCompare">
    <SqlSchemaCompareTask
 SourceConnectionString="Data Source=(local);Integrated Security=True;Pooling=False"
      SourceDatabaseName="Northwind_Dev"
 TargetConnectionString="Data Source=(local);Integrated Security=True;Pooling=False"
      TargetDatabaseName="Northwind_Original"
      OutputPath = "C:\"
      OutputFileName = "NorthwindSchemaCompare.sql"/>
  </Target>
</Project>
```

This is a straightforward task. You provide a source and a target database, an output location, and an output filename. To run it, open the Visual Studio 2005 command prompt, navigate to C:\, and execute the following line:

```
Msbuild schemacompare.txt
```

This will execute a schema compare and output the script containing the necessary SQL to bring the target in-line with the source. You can provide other values to the MSBuild task, but these are the required values. See the file Microsoft.VisualStudio.TeamSystem.Data. PowerTools.Tasks.xsd located at C:\Program Files\Microsoft Visual Studio 8\Xml\Schemas\ 1033\MSBuild (where 1033 is your locale identifier) for a list of all the commands available to you.

You can use the same types of files to execute any of the new tasks. The community itself has created an enormous number of custom tasks. Some are available on CodePlex; others are available from http://msbuildtasks.tigris.org.

TFS Build

Setting up TFS Build with Database Professionals is somewhat painful. However, once it's set up, it's a breeze. The steps for creating a build with TFS Build are described here in detail. Each step is explained, and if you miss a step, the build will fail. Before beginning this process, place the entire solution into version control—if you don't have a team project created, create one and then add the solution.

Creating the Team Build

In Team Explorer, right-click the Team Builds node, and select New Team Build Type. Name it Test Build, and click Next. On the Selections screen, select NorthwindCustom. On the Configurations screen, select Release from the configuration column, and overwrite it with Default (note that this is not in the drop-down selection). For the location, set the appropriate location for your build system. For the purposes of this example, the build system is called VS2005, the Build folder is C:\Builds, and the drop share is \\VS2005\Drops. On the Options screen, check the Run Tests check box, and then select the BVT test list. Click Next and then Finish, and the Test Build build type will be created.

Creating an Alternate Test app.config File

This seems like a strange title for a section. Why should you have to create another app.config file? What's wrong with the one you have? The answer is that the file paths coded into the app.config file that currently exists for the test project don't work for the build because the paths are different. When you finished creating the NorthwindCustomTests project earlier, the app.config file looked like (roughly) Listing 19-5.

Listing 19-5. *The Original app.config File*

```
<?xml version="1.0" encoding="utf-8" ?>
<configuration>
    <configSections>
        <section name="DatabaseUnitTesting"
        type="Microsoft.VisualStudio.TeamSystem.Data.UnitTesting.Configuration.
        DatabaseUnitTestingSection, Microsoft.VisualStudio.TeamSystem.Data.
        UnitTesting,Version=2.0.0.0, Culture=neutral,
        PublicKeyToken=b03f5f7f11d50a3a" />
    </configSections>
    <DatabaseUnitTesting>
        <DatabaseDeployment
        DatabaseProjectFileName="..\..\..\NorthwindCustom\NorthwindCustom.dbproj"
            Configuration="Default" />
        <DataGeneration
            DataGenerationFileName=
            "..\..\..\NorthwindCustom\Data Generation Plans\Categories.dgen"
            ClearDatabase="true" />
        <ExecutionContext Provider="System.Data.SqlClient" ConnectionString=
    "Data Source=.;Initial Catalog=Northwind;Integrated Security=True;
     Pooling=False" />
        <PrivilegedContext Provider="System.Data.SqlClient" ConnectionString=
    "Data Source=.;Initial Catalog=Northwind;Integrated Security=True;
     Pooling=False" />
    </DatabaseUnitTesting>
</configuration>
```

Copy the app.config file to another file called TeamBuild.app.config, and make the following changes to this file:

- Change DatabaseProjectFileName to ..\..\..\Sources\NorthwindCustom\ NorthwindCustom.dbproj.

- Change DataGenerationFileName to ..\..\..\Sources\NorthwindCustom\ Data Generation Plans\Categories.dgen.

Save this file, and ensure it is part of the NorthwindCustomTests project.

Editing the Database Project File

The problem here is that the target connection string and target database values (entered when you created the initial NorthwindCustom project) are *not* stored in the database project file. They are stored in the dbproj.user file. This file is virtually never version controlled (and it shouldn't be), so you need to update a couple of values in the .dbproj file. Copy the target connectionstring and targetdatabase elements from the .user file, and overwrite those same values in the database project file (both files are stored in the same folder—NorthwindCustom).

■**Caution** Remember that you will have to check out the .dbproj file from the Source Control Explorer, edit it in Notepad (or some other editor), and check it back in from the Source Control Explorer. The solution needs to be closed while you are doing this.

Editing the TFSBuild File

This is the last step but in many ways the most confusing. To begin with, go into Source Control Explorer, and navigate to the Server\Team Project Name\Team Build Types\Test Build\ folder. Right-click the TFSBuild.proj file, and select Get Latest Version. Right-click the TFSBuild.proj file again, select Check Out For Edit, and click the Checkout button in the following dialog box. Then, right-click the TFSBuild.proj file again, and select View, which will open the file for editing in Visual Studio.

The first thing to check on is the ConfigurationToBuild node (shown in Listing 19-6).

Listing 19-6. *ConfigurationToBuild Node*

```
<ConfigurationToBuild Include="Default|Any CPU">
    <FlavorToBuild>Default</FlavorToBuild>
    <PlatformToBuild>Any CPU</PlatformToBuild>
</ConfigurationToBuild>
```

Ensure that the configuration is Default. This should be shown on the first and second lines, as shown in Listing 19-6. Next, add the code in Listing 19-7 to the configuration file after the first property group but before the first item group.

■**Note** It is important that you not add these items in the property group or in another item group, or the file will be invalid according to its schema.

Listing 19-7. *TFSBuild Lines to Add*

```
<Target Name="AfterDropBuild">
    <MSBuild
    Projects=
"$(SolutionRoot)\NorthwindCustom\NorthwindCustom\NorthwindCustom.dbproj"
    Properties="Configuration=Default;OutDir=$(SolutionRoot)\..\binaries\Default\"
    Targets="Deploy" />
  </Target>
  <ItemGroup>
    <TestProjectConfigFile Include=
"$(SolutionRoot)\NorthwindCustomTests\TeamBuild.app.config" />
  </ItemGroup>
  <Target Name="AfterCompile">
    <Copy
    SourceFiles="@(TestProjectConfigFile)"
    DestinationFiles="@(TestProjectConfigFile->
    '$(SolutionRoot)\..\Binaries\Default\NorthwindCustomTests.dll.config')" />
  </Target>
```

Note the frequent use of $(SolutionRoot). This variable, during the build, points to C:\Builds\Team Project Name\Team Build Type\Sources. For use in a real application, replace NorthwindCustom with the appropriate values. Note also that where you see NorthwindCustom twice in a row, it refers to SolutionName\ProjectName.

Now for some explanations. Target AfterDropBuild indicates that this section will execute after the build has been placed into the drop location. The MSBuild element indicates that the project is to be deployed according to the settings in the database project file (Northwind Custom.dbproj).

The next element, ItemGroup, creates a variable called TestProjectConfigFile that points to the TeamBuild.app.config file. Target AfterCompile is executed after the compile has completed. It copies the TeamBuild.app.config file from the source folder (in the Builds folder) and overwrites the existing app.config file (which is renamed to NorthwindCustomTests.dll.config during the build process) so that the new paths you entered earlier will be used.

Check in the TFSBuild.proj file.

Running the Build

Once you have completed these steps, right-click Test Build in Team Explorer, and select Build Team Project. At this point, the build should run, and the tests should execute. If there is a problem and the build fails, check the build log. The most common cause of errors in this process is getting the paths to the files wrong. Double-check the previous steps, and retry the build.

Deploying a Database Project

In the previous section, you saw how to perform a build and run tests as part of a build. This section discusses the actual process of deploying a database project through the various environments and the steps to take at each point. This is a detailed set of steps that assumes you have sandbox, development, test, and production environments. The steps also assume that you, as a developer, have full control over the sandbox and development environment and *no* access to the test and production environments. These also assume that a DBA is on your team who works closely with you and has full administrative access to the test and production environments.

In Chapter 17 you were presented with a high-level overview of the process for deploying a database to production. Table 19-1 presents you with a step-by-step process for deploying changes to each of the environments and the role that should perform those tasks.

Table 19-1. *Deployment Steps*

Step	Role	Action
1	DBA	Sync development schema with production.
2	Dev lead*	Perform a "get latest" from TFS.
3	Dev lead	Perform a build against the development database.
4	Dev lead	Take the resulting script, and add it to the solution with the appropriate name (that is, Release 2.0).
5	Dev lead	Execute the release script against the development environment.
6	Dev lead	Execute all unit tests against the development environment.
7	DBA	Perform a "get latest" on the release script using either Team Explorer (from the Source Control Explorer) or VSTS Web Access.
8	DBA	Perform a schema compare between the production and development environments.
9	Dev lead	Check the release script and solution back into TFS.
10	DBA	Execute the release script against the test environment.
11	DBA	Perform a schema compare between production and test.
12	DBA	Execute test scripts against the test environment (if all is good, at this point testers can test).
13	DBA	Execute the release script against the production environment.

* This can also be done by the build master if you have one. The key point here is that only one person performs these steps.

As you can see, this process is fairly straightforward and results in verifications at each step in the process. For the final step you could perform another verification by comparing the production environment to the test environment that has already been approved as correct.

The actual steps you take will vary based on a couple of other items—was a rename refactoring performed? If so, remember to follow the steps in Chapter 17 (in the "Refactor Command Generator" section). Insert the steps noted there between steps 1 and 2 in Table 19-1. Another issue is data: did a change you make result in data that has to be stored and reloaded (or simply inserted) as part of the process? For inserting data, you can insert the SQL statements directly into the build script. You can approach storing and reloading data in several different ways. Most notably, do *not* load production data into the development environment.

■**Caution** Obviously this will depend on your environment and certain pieces of data you can feel free to use—lookup information in particular. Just remember that no sensitive information should be used from the production environment.

Whatever steps you do take will have to be performed by the DBA.

Build Configurations

Do not use the build configuration to target different servers or databases. The reason for this is that if you select a different target name for the default, development, test, or production configurations (or whatever other configurations you may create), Visual Studio will try to script the differences between your project and that target database. The problem is that the deployment is a progression using the *same* script—not a different script per environment. This introduces too many variables into the process of deploying a script.

It is recommended that you use different build configurations to store variables and file group arrangements. This functionality is available only with SR1 installed. Variables and file groups are specific to the build type. Remember to leave the database target alone (this target should almost always be the database on the development server—refer to Chapter 17, specifically, Figure 17-14).

Adding Build Scripts to the Solution

As noted in step 4 in Table 19-1, once you perform a build, you need to add the resulting script to the solution and version control it. The easiest way to do this is to switch to the Solution Explorer and toggle the Show All Files button from the top of the Solution Explorer. This will display a folder called Sql (by default it is displayed at the bottom of the Solution Explorer because this view displays items alphabetically). In this folder you will find your build script (by default it is called *projectname*.sql). Simply right-click the file, and select Include in Project. However, before adding it to the project, rename it to something appropriate. Visual Studio will overwrite this file on each build if you do not rename it.

■**Caution** If you have an output file called foo.sql and you add it to version control and check it the next time you perform a build, this file will be updated in place. It will not be checked out, and there will be no indication to you that it has changed. For this reason, before you perform a build, do a checkout. Also, remember that builds are not additive to this file—Visual Studio will completely re-create this file each time. The only way to maintain a history of changes is to version control each script.

Summary

After reading this chapter, you have the ability to perform builds on your local machines and builds using TFS. You can also update the appropriate files in order to execute unit tests in an automated manner using TFSBuild. You also learned how to use the pre- and post-deployment scripts and edit them as necessary. Finally, you learned the steps for correctly deploying a project to production in a controlled manner. The next chapter shows you how to extend the DBPro edition to customize the data generation and unit testing conditions.

■ ■ ■

Extending the Database Professionals Edition

In the previous chapters, you saw how to generate data and to some extent customize how the data is generated. You also saw how to write unit tests for your database objects. This chapter will expand your knowledge and give you the ability to write your own data generators and your own unit test conditions to suit your development needs. You will learn how to extend DBPro and deploy your custom generators and test conditions so the rest of the development team can benefit from them. At the end of this chapter, you will learn how to customize the object templates, which are the generic structure presented when you add a new item to the database project.

Extending the Data Generator

The built-in data generators are extremely useful and will fulfill a lot of needs right out of the box. With a Data Bound generator or a Regular Expression generator, you can generate meaningful, patterned data that you can use to help test your applications. An organization can even create a central repository of test data that all developers can use with the Data Bound generator. However, often you will want to customize the type of data that is generated or the source of the data that is generated. For example, what if you wanted to pull test data from a web service? Or a web page? Or an XML file? Or even to eliminate the randomness provided by the default generators? And so on. The list of what you might want to do is endless, and over the years we have seen some very creative methods of building test data.

We will use two examples—a simple generator and the last case mentioned earlier, which is eliminating the randomness of the default Data Bound generator.

Before you start building the generators, it's important to understand all the classes involved and how they relate to each other. In addition, you'll see the easy way to make this work, and we'll talk about the hard way to make this work.

Classes Involved in the Custom Generators

Table 20-1 lists the classes involved in creating a custom generator.

Table 20-1. *Custom Generator Classes*

Class	Description
GeneratorStylesAttribute	This class controls how your generator is displayed in the IDE in the selection list. Earlier we mentioned that only certain generators were available depending on the data type of the column—this is the reason why.
GeneratorAttribute	This attribute indicates that a class is a generator and allows you to specify the designer for the class (discussed in detail later).
InputAttribute	This notes which properties are inputs into the generator. This allows the property to show up in the property grid in the IDE and also causes an event to be fired, noting that a property of the generator has changed.
OutputAttribute	This notes which property is the output of the generator (this is optional, as you'll see with the Data Bound generator).
IGenerator	This is the generator interface from which everything starts. In terms of extensibility, this is the lowest you can go—but we don't recommend it (discussed later).
Generator	This is the base generator class from which all generators inherit (inherit from this class for your custom generators).
DefaultGeneratorDesigner	This is the base designer that allows outputs to be selected. This is an attribute on the Generator class. This automatically sets the property in the Generator Output column of the Column Details view.

You will see a couple of other classes before this chapter is over, but these are the key classes. The best way to understand how these classes work together is to create your own generator. The first example is a simple generator that opens a text file, reads in the values, and outputs them in the data generation. The prerequisite for this is that the text file can contain only a single column of data—one piece of information per line.

Building Your First Data Generator

Start a new Visual Studio Class Library project (in either C# or Visual Basic), and call it CustomDataGenerators. Add a reference to the Microsoft.VisualStudio.TeamSystem.Data assembly (located in C:\Program Files\Microsoft Visual Studio 8\DBPro but available on the .NET tab of the Add Reference dialog box).

Rename the initial Class1 to FileSourceGenerator. Add the following Using or Imports statement to the class file:

```
Using Microsoft.VisualStudio.TeamSystem.Data.DataGenerator;
```

or

```
Imports Microsoft.VisualStudio.TeamSystem.Data.DataGenerator
```

Add the code shown in Listing 20-1, which we'll explain after the listing.

Listing 20-1. *Basic FileSourceGenerator Code*

```csharp
[C#]
namespace CustomDataGenerators
{
    public class FileSourceGenerator: Generator
    {
        private string _path;
        private int _currentRecord;
        private List<string> _values;

        [Input(Name="File Path",
        Description="Path to the file which contains the input values.")]
        public string FilePath
        {
            get
            {
                return _path;
            }
            set
            {
                _path = value;
            }
        }

        protected override void OnInitialize(GeneratorInit initInfo)
        {
            _values = new List<string>();

            FileStream fs = new FileStream(_path, FileMode.Open, FileAccess.Read);
            StreamReader sr = new StreamReader(fs);

            while (!sr.EndOfStream)
            {
                _values.Add(sr.ReadLine());
            }

            sr.Close();
        }

        [Output(Name="Result")]
        public string Result
        {
            get
            {
                if (_currentRecord >= _values.Count)
                    _currentRecord = 0;
```

```
                return _values[_currentRecord];
            }
        }

        protected override void OnGenerateNextValues()
        {
            _currentRecord++;
        }

        protected override void OnValidateInputs()
        {
            if (!File.Exists(_path))
                throw new InputValidationException
                        ("The specified file does not exist.");
        }
    }
}
```

```
[VB]
Public Class FileSourceGenerator : Inherits Generator
    Private _path As String
    Private _currentRecord As Integer
    Private _values As List(Of String)

    <Input(Name:="File Path", _
     Description:="Path to the file which contains the input values.")>
    Public Property FilePath() As String
        Get
            Return _path
        End Get
        Set(ByVal value As String)
            _path = value
        End Set
    End Property

    Protected Overrides Sub OnInitialize(ByVal initInfo As GeneratorInit)
        _values = New List(Of String)()

        Dim fs As FileStream = New FileStream(_path, FileMode.Open, FileAccess.Read)
        Dim sr As StreamReader = New StreamReader(fs)

        While (Not sr.EndOfStream)
            _values.Add(sr.ReadLine())
        End While

        sr.Close()
    End Sub
```

```vb
    <Output(Name:="Result")> _
    Public ReadOnly Property Result() As String
        Get
            If (_currentRecord >= _values.Count) Then
                _currentRecord = 0
            End If
            Return _values(_currentRecord)
        End Get
    End Property

    Protected Overrides Sub OnGenerateNextValues()
        _currentRecord += 1
    End Sub

    Protected Overrides Sub OnValidateInputs()
        If (Not File.Exists(_path)) Then
            Throw New InputValidationException("The specified file does not exist.")
        End If
    End Sub
End Class
```

This code is fairly straightforward, so we'll just walk you through it from the top down. The FilePath property is decorated with the Input attribute so a user can enter the path to the file they want to use as the data source. The OnInitialize method is executed before data is generated (in other words, when you select the Data Generation Preview tab in the IDE). Here the list is initialized, the file is opened and read, and the values are added to the list. The Result property is read-only and returns a single value. This is called for every row of data that needs to be generated. Here you have to check to see whether you are beyond the end of the list, and if so, you're just resetting it to the beginning of the list. OnGenerateNextValues is called *before* the property is decorated with the Output attribute, which is why the pointer to the current record is incremented here. Finally, OnValidateInputs is called before each data execution. Any exceptions thrown here will be displayed in the Error List. That's it for the code—there's not much to it.

Deploying a Custom Data Generator

Before actually deploying the data generator, you have to sign the data generator and create a configuration file for it. Start by signing the assembly. In Visual Studio 2005 the easiest way to do this is to right-click the CustomDataGenerators project and select Properties. Go to the Signing tab, and check Sign the Assembly. For the key file, you can use an existing one, or you select the drop-down, choose <New...>, and enter a filename (the password is optional). This file will be added to the project as well. Rebuild the solution. Now that the project is signed, you need to get the public token. The easiest way to do this is to select View ➤ Other Windows ➤ Command Window from the Visual Studio main menu. Enter the following in the Command window:

```
? System.Reflection.Assembly.LoadFrom([Path to file here]).FullName
```

> ■**Note** If you're using C#, remember to either escape the directory slashes or add an at (@) symbol before the path to the file. Also, remember to enclose the path in quotes if the path contains spaces.

The Command window will return the following line (with a different public key token):

```
"CustomDataGenerators, Version=1.0.0.0, Culture=neutral,
        PublicKeyToken=41431f8bc8ff31b6"
```

> ■**Tip** In addition to this, you can also deploy the custom generator to the global assembly cache (GAC). When you do this, you can navigate to the C:\Windows\Assembly folder, right-click the assembly, and select Properties. The Public Key token will be listed here.

Now that you have this, you can create the configuration file. Add a new XML file to the solution, and call it CustomDataGenerators.Extensions.xml (note that the name must be the same as the assembly name and end with Extensions.xml). Enter the items in Listing 20-2.

Listing 20-2. *CustomDataGenerators.Extensions.xml Configuration File*

```
<?xml version="1.0" encoding="utf-8" ?>
<extensions assembly="CustomDataGenerators, Version=1.0.0.0, Culture=neutral,
    PublicKeyToken=41431f8bc8ff31b6" version="1"
    xmlns="urn:Microsoft.VisualStudio.TeamSystem.Data.Extensions"
    xmlns:xsi="http://www.w3.org/2001/XMLSchema-instance"
    xsi:schemaLocation="urn:Microsoft.VisualStudio.TeamSystem.Data.Extensions
    Microsoft.VisualStudio.TeamSystem.Data.Extensions.xsd">
    <extension type="CustomDataGenerators.FileSourceGenerator" enabled="true" />
</extensions>
```

Finally, you need to copy the files to the correct locations. For version 1 of the DB Professionals edition, you must copy the CustomDataGenerators.dll file to the C:\Program Files\ Microsoft Visual Studio 8\DBPro\Extensions folder *and* the C:\Program Files\Microsoft Visual Studio 8\Common7\IDE\PrivateAssemblies folder (or you can add it to the GAC). The configuration file must be copied to the C:\Program Files\Microsoft Visual Studio 8\DBPro folder (you'll also see that the included data generators are listed in a similar configuration file).

Now, start a Visual Studio instance, and create (or open an existing one) a database project. Hook this up to any database, and reverse-engineer the schema. Create a data generation plan, select a table, and view the column details for the table. Find a string data type column, and select the Generator drop-down list. You should see the FileSourceGenerator option. Select this, and view the properties for the data generator. For the File Path property, name it c:\names.txt. Obviously at this point you do not have a text file at this location. Now switch to the Data Generation Preview tab. You should have an exception in the selected column. Switch to the Error List, and you will see the specified file does not exist. To fix this, create a file with a list of names, call it names.txt, and place it in C:\. Now switch back to the Data Generation Preview pane. You should see the values that you provided in the text file in the column to which you attached the custom data generator.

Congratulations, you've just created your first data generator! Now, you could probably add some error handling to the OnInitialize method to deal with issues such as the file not opening correctly and other issues surrounding files—but this is an example, so we didn't go over the top on error handling. There are two things we want to elaborate on—the Seed property and the File Path property. On the Seed property, you cannot override the property, and you cannot hide it or ignore it. If you want to implement the IGenerator interface to get rid of it, that is entirely up to you, but we do not think it is necessary if you clearly document your generator. The other item is the File Path property, which we discuss in the "Editors" sidebar.

EDITORS

In the Visual Studio environment you are used to seeing a property in the property grid, say for choosing a color, and having a color dialog box be accessible to you. This functionality is fully available when creating your own generators, with some exceptions. To implement FileNameEditor for your generator, change the Input attribute of the File Path property and add the following:

```
[C#]
[Input(EditorType=typeof(FileNameEditor), TypeConverter=typeof(StringConverter),
Name="xxx",
Description="xxx")]
[VB]
<Input(EditorType=typeof(FileNameEditor), _
TypeConverter=typeof(StringConverter), Name="xxx", Description="xxx")>
```

You will need to add a reference to the System.Windows.Forms and System.Drawing assemblies. FileNameEditor actually resides in the System.Windows.Forms.Design namespace.

Other editors are available to you as well for various other uses. You can find out more about these editors by looking up UITypeEditor in the MSDN Help and clicking the Derived Classes link at the bottom of the Help topic. Virtually everything there is available for your use.

The exception to this is that the editors that come with the DB Professionals edition are sealed, and you do not have access to them—you'll see why this can be a pain in terms of consistency in the next example.

Building a Custom Data Bound Generator

Building a Data Bound generator, needless to say, is a lot more complicated that what you have already built. The reason for this is simple—you do not know the output ahead of time. This means in addition to creating the generator, you also have to create a generator designer. In this case, a designer is what shows up in the Output column of the Column Details window. Remember that in the previous example, you were outputting a single known value; now you want to (as with the existing Data Bound generator) give the users the ability to select a column from a list of columns. You are also dealing with the added complexity of pulling back a schema from the database and presenting the column names to the user. However, even this, once you know the trick, is remarkably simple because the base Generator class handles much of the heavy lifting for you.

Note As you may have noticed, if you install the Power Tools, there is a new Sequential Data Bound generator (as noted in Chapter 17). This section was written before the Power Tools were released, and although it will not prove as useful a tool as we had hoped, it does demonstrate the appropriate concepts for building a Data Bound generator, which is the point!

The generator you are going to create is similar to the Data Bound generator except in one key area—it will read, sequentially, the values from a select statement. We hit upon this example because we had an issue when we were using the Database Professionals edition to build a database and insert data into it for testing purposes. Without using the generator you are about to build, you would have to (as described previously) add a script file with the insert statements to the Post-Deployment folder and have that run after you deployed the database. However, this required making changes to a text file, and if you had a lot of data, it could be not only annoying but also difficult to do and keep in sync.

Note This in no way has the full functionality of the built-in Data Bound generator. It will not allow you to have multiple select statements, and it does not perform all of the error checking. However, aside from that, it is a fully functional piece of code that you can use or extend however you want.

Ever since the introduction of data-bound unit and web testing, we have been storing test data in databases. Now these are stored as Database Professionals projects because they are our test data databases, but adding values to tests is much easier and allows you to play with the values without checking items out from version control just for fun. Using a Sequential Data Bound generator to load your tables, you have a well-defined load of data (or you can combine data from multiple tables), and you will know the exact order and amount of records that will be retrieved. You still have to perform tasks such as setting the number of rows to be generated (otherwise the generation will start over again, as you will see), but that's a minor issue compared to the ease of use.

To begin, add a new class to the CustomDataGenerators project, and call it SequentialGeneratorDesigner. This new class will inherit from DefaultGeneratorDesigner, which provides by default two useful methods that can be overridden—OnInputValueChanged and GetOutputs. So, what does the designer actually need? It needs to store the connection string and the select statement, which will be passed to it by way of the generator. It would also be a good idea to cache the output in case the user accidentally changes a value (although this is not necessary). Aside from this, nothing else is needed except to override the previously mentioned methods. Listing 20-3 contains the entire SequentialGeneratorDesigner class.

Listing 20-3. *SequentialGeneratorDesigner Class*

```csharp
[C#]
using System;
using System.Collections.Generic;
using System.Text;
using Microsoft.VisualStudio.TeamSystem.Data.DataGenerator;
using System.Data;
using System.Data.SqlClient;

namespace CustomDataGenerators
{
    public class SequentialGeneratorDesigner: DefaultGeneratorDesigner
    {
        private string _cn;
        private string _select;
        private OutputDescriptor[] _cache;

        public override string Name
        {
            get
            {
                return "Sequential Databound Generator";
            }
        }

        public override void OnInputValueChanged(object sender,
            InputChangedEventArgs eventArgs)
        {
            if (eventArgs.Input.Key == "ConnectionInfo")
            {
                _cn = eventArgs.Input.Value as string;
            }

            if (eventArgs.Input.Key == "SelectStatement")
            {
                _select = eventArgs.Input.Value as string;
            }
        }

        public override OutputDescriptor[] GetOutputs()
        {
            if (_cn != null && _select != null)
            {
                DataTable dt = new DataTable();
                SqlConnection cn = new SqlConnection(_cn);
                SqlCommand cmd = new SqlCommand(_select, cn);
                SqlDataReader dr;
```

```
              cn.Open();
              cmd.CommandType = CommandType.Text;
              dr = cmd.ExecuteReader(CommandBehavior.SchemaOnly);
              dt = dr.GetSchemaTable();
              cn.Close();

              List<OutputDescriptor> od = new List<OutputDescriptor>();
              for (int i = 0; i < dt.Rows.Count; i++)
              {
                  if (dt.Rows[i].Table.Columns.Contains("ColumnName"))
                  {
                      OutputDescriptor desc = new OutputDescriptor("[" +
                          dt.Rows[i]["ColumnName"].ToString() + "]",
                          (Type)dt.Rows[i]["DataType"]);
                      od.Add(desc);
                  }
              }
              _cache = od.ToArray();
          }
          return _cache;
      }
  }
}


[VB]
Imports System.Collections.Generic
Imports Microsoft.VisualStudio.TeamSystem.Data.DataGenerator
Imports System.Data
Imports System.Data.SqlClient

Public Class SequentialGeneratorDesigner : Inherits DefaultGeneratorDesigner
    Private _cn As String
    Private _select As String
    Private _cache As OutputDescriptor()

    Public Overrides ReadOnly Property Name() As String
        Get
            Return "Sequential Databound Generator"
        End Get
    End Property

    Public Overrides Sub OnInputValueChanged(ByVal sender As Object, _
        ByVal eventArgs As InputChangedEventArgs)
        If eventArgs.Input.Key = "ConnectionInfo" Then
            _cn = eventArgs.Input.Value.ToString()
        End If
```

```
        If eventArgs.Input.Key = "SelectStatement" Then
            _select = eventArgs.Input.Value.ToString()
        End If
    End Sub

    Public Overrides Function GetOutputs() As _
        Microsoft.VisualStudio.TeamSystem.Data.DataGenerator.OutputDescriptor()
        If (Not _cn Is Nothing) AndAlso (Not _select Is Nothing) Then
            Dim dt As DataTable = New DataTable()
            Dim cn As SqlConnection = New SqlConnection(_cn)
            Dim cmd As SqlCommand = New SqlCommand(_select, cn)
            Dim dr As SqlDataReader

            cn.Open()
            cmd.CommandType = CommandType.Text
            dr = cmd.ExecuteReader(CommandBehavior.SchemaOnly)
            dt = dr.GetSchemaTable()
            cn.Close()

            Dim od As List(Of OutputDescriptor) = New List(Of OutputDescriptor)()
            For i As Integer = 0 To dt.Rows.Count
                If dt.Rows(i).Table.Columns.Contains("ColumnName") Then
                    Dim desc As OutputDescriptor = New OutputDescriptor("[" _
                    & dt.Rows(i)("ColumnName").ToString() & "]", _
                    CType(dt.Rows(i)("DataType"), Type))
                    od.Add(desc)
                End If
            Next

            _cache = od.ToArray()
        End If

        Return _cache
    End Function
End Class
```

Some of this may look familiar to you because you have written code of this type before, but we'll step through the code so you can understand how everything works. As we mentioned earlier, the OnInputValueChanged method is called every time a change is made to any property that is decorated with InputAttribute in the generator. In the OnInputValueChanged method, the key of the input item is checked (the key is just the name of the property), and the property value is assigned to the correct variable for internal storage.

The GetOutputs method is where the real fun is. The OutputDescriptor class returns the list of columns displayed when you select the Output column of the Column Details window. The OutputDescriptor class contains four properties: Description, Key, Name, and Type. For our purposes, the Key and Type values are the most important, but you can use the others as needed (discussed in a moment). The first part of the GetOutputs method simply connects to the database and executes the select statement using the CommandBehavior.SchemaOnly argument. This returns the schema information for all the columns contained in the query. Next, a new generic list is instantiated to hold the list of OutputDescriptor because it is far easier and faster than redimming an array while you determine exactly how many values you have. Then the code reads the results one line at a time and looks to ensure that the ColumnName attribute exists for the given row (this check is not strictly necessary in this simple scenario, but in more complex scenarios it will save you grief—trust us). Then the OutputDescriptor class is created which, in this overload, accepts the Key value and data type.

The Key value of the OutputDescriptor class appears in the drop-down list of the Output column *if* you do not provide a name value. To make life easier, you can use a Key value and come up with any name you want. However, following the Data Bound generator's naming convention, the code here just wraps the key in brackets. The description is displayed when the user mouses over the selected column in the Output column.

Tip The data type of the column is critical. It is a coercible output—that is, the list of values a user can select from in the Output column will be tailored based on the data type of the column and the data type of the selected Output column. This prevents you from putting a string value in a datetime field, for example. You will see an example of this shortly.

The other aspect of the designer to note is the cache. In case the user deletes the select string or deletes the connection, you still want something to show up there. This is just here because it follows the conventions of the data-bound designer. Finally, the Name property of the *designer* is what shows up in the list of generators—there is no Name property associated with the actual generator. If you do not override this property, the name in the designer will show up as the name of the generator (SequentialDataBoundGenerator). Now, onto the actual data generator!

Listing 20-4 contains the entire class for SequentialDataBoundGenerator, which we explain after the listing.

Listing 20-4. *SequentialDataBoundGenerator Class*

```
using System;
using System.Collections.Generic;
using System.Text;
using Microsoft.VisualStudio.TeamSystem.Data.DataGenerator;
using System.Data;
using System.Data.SqlClient;
using System.ComponentModel;

namespace CustomDataGenerators
{
    [GeneratorStyles(DesignerStyles = GeneratorDesignerStyles.None),
     Generator(typeof(SequentialGeneratorDesigner))]
    public class SequentialDataBoundGenerator : Generator
    {
```

```csharp
#region Private Members
private string _connectionInfo = "";
private string _selectStatement = "";
private DataSet _ds;
private int _currentRecord = 0;
#endregion

#region Inputs
[Input(Name = "Select Statement")]
public string SelectStatement
{
    get { return _selectStatement; }
    set { _selectStatement = value; }
}

[Input(EditorType=typeof(System.Web.UI.Design.ConnectionStringEditor),
TypeConverter=typeof(StringConverter),Name = "Connection Info")]
public string ConnectionInfo
{
    get { return _connectionInfo; }
    set { _connectionInfo = value; }
}
#endregion

protected override void OnGenerateNextValues()
{
    _currentRecord++;
    if (_currentRecord >= _ds.Tables[0].Rows.Count)
        _currentRecord = 0;
}

protected override object OnGetOutputValue()
{
    return
    _ds.Tables[0].Rows[_currentRecord][StripBrackets(base.OutputKey)];
}

protected override void OnInitialize(GeneratorInit initInfo)
{
    SqlConnection cn = new SqlConnection(_connectionInfo);
    SqlCommand cmd = new SqlCommand(_selectStatement, cn);
    SqlDataAdapter da = new SqlDataAdapter(cmd);
    _ds = new DataSet();
    da.Fill(_ds);
}
```

```csharp
        protected override void OnValidateInputs()
        {
            if (_connectionInfo.Length == 0)
                throw new
                InputValidationException("Connection Info must be supplied.");
            if (_selectStatement.Length == 0)
                throw new
                 InputValidationException("Select statement must be supplied.");
        }

        private string StripBrackets(string column)
        {
            return column.Substring(1, column.Length - 2);
        }
    }
}
```

```vbnet
[VB]
Imports System
Imports System.Colit)
        Dim cn As Sq System.Text
Imports Microsoft.VisualStudio.TeamSystem.Data.DataGenerator
Imports System.Data
Imports System.Data.SqlClient
Imports System.ComponentModel

<GeneratorStyles(DesignerStyles:=GeneratorDesignerStyles.None), _
Generator(GetType(SequentialGeneratorDesigner))> _
Public Class SequentialDataBoundGenerator : Inherits Generator

#Region "Private Members"
    Private _connectionInfo As String = ""
    Private _selectStatement As String = ""
    Private _ds As DataSet
    Private _currentRecord As Integer = 0
#End Region

#Region "Inputs"
    <Input(Name:="Select Statement")> _
    Public Property SelectStatement() As String
        Get
            Return _selectStatement
        End Get
        Set(ByVal value As String)
            _selectStatement = value
        End Set
    End Property
```

```vb
    <Input(EditorType:=GetType(System.Web.UI.Design.ConnectionStringEditor), _
      TypeConverter:=GetType(StringConverter), Name:="Connection Info")> _
    Public Property ConnectionInfo() As String
        Get
            Return _connectionInfo
        End Get
        Set(ByVal value As String)
            _connectionInfo = value
        End Set
    End Property
#End Region

    Protected Overrides Sub OnGenerateNextValues()
        _currentRecord += 1
    End Sub

    Protected Overrides Function OnGetOutputValue() As Object
        Return _ds.Tables(0).Rows(_currentRecord)(StripBrackets(MyBase.OutputKey))
    End Function

    Protected Overrides Sub OnInitialize(ByVal initInfo As GeneratorInit)
        Dim cn As SqlConnection = New SqlConnection(_connectionInfo)
        Dim cmd As SqlCommand = New SqlCommand(_selectStatement, cn)
        Dim da As SqlDataAdapter = New SqlDataAdapter(cmd)
        _ds = New DataSet()
        da.Fill(_ds)
    End Sub

    Protected Overrides Sub OnValidateInputs()
        If _connectionInfo.Length = 0 Then
            Throw New InputValidationException("Connection Info must be supplied.")
        End If
        If _selectStatement.Length = 0 Then
            Throw New InputValidationException("Select statement must be supplied.")
        End If
    End Sub

    Private Function StripBrackets(ByVal column As String) As String
        Return column.Substring(1, column.Length - 2)
    End Function
End Class
```

The first place to start with this code is GeneratorStylesAttribute and GeneratorAttribute. The GeneratorStylesAttribute attribute allows you to tell Visual Studio not to restrict what columns the SequentialDataBoundGenerator can be applied to—this is especially important since you have no default output type! The GeneratorAttribute attribute allows you to specify a custom designer, and this is what links the designer to the generator.

By default, the Generator class is decorated with the DefaultGeneratorDesigner and is of consequence only when an output type is not defined. The class, as before, inherits from the Generator class.

The SelectStatement property holds the SQL select statement and is decorated with the InputAttribute attribute to allow it to show up in the property grid. The ConnectionInfo property holds the connection string information for the database. Note that we have decorated it with the ConnectionStringEditor editor type. When you see it, you'll see that it is not as convenient as the ConnectionInfo editor provided with the default Data Bound generator, but you do not have access to that one.

As with the previous generator, the OnInitialize method loads the data to use in the generation, and the OnGenerateNextValues method increments the pointer you use to pull a value. You are still validating the inputs in the OnValidateInputs method, but there is a new method you are overriding here—OnGetOutputValue. In this method, you are returning the value of the select statement in the specified row and the column noted in the OutputKey property of the base (Generator) class. This is the value the user selects in the Output column of the Column Details window. The StripBrackets method simply removes the brackets because there is no column named [columnName]. It would simply be columnName. Again, if you use the Name value to provide a formatted name, you do not have to do this.

That is all there is to it. Before building and deploying your new generator, edit the CustomDataGenerators.Extensions.xml file by adding the following line:

```
<extension type="CustomDataGenerators.SequentialDataBoundGenerator"
    enabled="true" />
```

Recopy this file to the DBPro folder, and redeploy the CustomDataGenerators.dll assembly. You are good to go.

■**Tip** This particular data generator, SequentialDataBoundGenerator, is particularly useful when you are trying to generate data that conforms to specific business rules. By preloading data into a "test data database" and simply reading from it, you don't have the overhead of trying to validate that the data saved in the database conforms to all of your business rules. On the other hand, if you have already created your middle-tier logic and you can save records to your database, you may want to generate your own custom generator to save rows via your middle tier. The drawback to this is that it is far more intensive and requires a painful amount of work for very little gain.

As a side note, when Microsoft released the Power Tools, it included a Sequential Data Bound generator!

Extending Database Unit Testing

In this section, you will explore how to create custom database unit test conditions. For this example you will create a test condition that will check to see whether every value in every column in a given row matches a set of values you provide.

■**Note** The built-in test condition that checks for a Scalar value could be used by simply adding multiple instances of the test condition. However, this provides an easier, more compact approach to checking all the values in a row. It also provides some added benefits, as you will see.

To begin, create a new Class Library project called CustomConditions. Add a reference to Microsoft.VisualStudio.QualityTools.UnitTestFramework and Microsoft.VisualStudio. TeamSystem.Data.UnitTesting. Delete the Class1 file that is created automatically.

■**Caution** If you are writing a custom unit test in Visual Basic, you must add an extra reference to the Microsoft.VisualStudio.QualityTools.Resources assembly that is located in the GAC. You must manually browse to this in the Add Resources dialog box. This is required depending on what type of objects you are using in the UnitTesting namespace. For this example in particular, it is required in order to be able to throw an AssertFailedException exception.

Add a new class called ColumnData to hold a single column's worth of data against which to validate. This class must be marked as Serializable because of how you will use the class. Listing 20-5 shows the definition of the ColumnData class.

Listing 20-5. *The ColumnData Class*

```
[C#]
using System;
using System.Collections.Generic;
using System.Text;
using System.ComponentModel;

namespace CustomConditions
{
    [Serializable()]
    public class ColumnData
    {
        private string _colName = "";
        private string _colValue = "";

        [DisplayName("Column Name")]
        public string ColumnName
        {
            get { return _colName; }
            set { _colName = value; }
        }
```

```
            [DisplayName("Value")]
            public string ColumnValue
            {
                get { return _colValue; }
                set { _colValue = value; }
            }
        }
}
```

```
[VB]
Imports System.ComponentModel

<Serializable()> _
Public Class ColumnData
    Private _colName As String = ""
    Private _colValue As String = ""

    <DisplayName("Column Name")> _
    Public Property ColumnName() As String
        Get
            Return _colName
        End Get
        Set(ByVal value As String)
            _colName = value
        End Set
    End Property


    <DisplayName("Value")> _
    Public Property ColumnValue() As String
        Get
            Return _colValue
        End Get
        Set(ByVal value As String)
            _colValue = value
        End Set
    End Property

End Class
```

TestCondition Class

The real work of the unit test extension takes place in the `ValidateRowTestCondition` class.
Add this class to your project. Listing 20-6 shows the code for this class. We describe the code
in detail after the listing.

CHAPTER 20 ■ EXTENDING THE DATABASE PROFESSIONALS EDITION

Listing 20-6. *ValidateRowTestCondition Class*

```csharp
[C#]
using System;
using System.Collections.Generic;
using System.Text;
using Microsoft.VisualStudio.TeamSystem.Data.UnitTesting.Conditions;
using System.ComponentModel;
using System.Data;

namespace CustomConditions
{
    [DisplayName("Validate Row Data")]
    public class ValidateRowTestCondition : TestCondition
    {
        private ColumnData[] _rowData;
        private int _rowNumber = 0;
        private bool _errorOnColumns = false;
        private int _resultSet = 1;

        public override void Assert(System.Data.Common.DbConnection
            validationConnection,
            Microsoft.VisualStudio.TeamSystem.Data.UnitTesting.ExecutionResult[]
          results)
        {
            //Store the data table to check against
            DataTable resultData = results[0].DataSet.Tables[_resultSet - 1];

            //If the user wants to fail a test because of invalid columns in
            //the result set
            if (_errorOnColumns)
            {
                //First check the number of columns returned against the number set.
                if (resultData.Columns.Count != _rowData.Length)
                    throw new
                Microsoft.VisualStudio.TestTools.UnitTesting.AssertFailedException(
                    "The actual column count in the result set does not match the "
                    + "expected column count.");
            }

            //Validate the data
            //Check to see if the column names and values all match
            for (int i = 0; i < _rowData.Length; i++)
            {
                try
                {
                    //Get the value of the column
                    string value =
```

```
                resultData.Rows[_rowNumber - 1][_rowData[i].ColumnName].ToString();
                    if (_rowData[i].ColumnValue != value)
                        throw new
                Microsoft.VisualStudio.TestTools.UnitTesting.AssertFailedException(
                "Actual value (" + value + ") does not match expected value ("
                            + _rowData[i].ColumnValue + ") for column " +
                                _rowData[i].ColumnName + ".");
                }
                catch (ArgumentException ex)
                //This will catch the result of a column not being valid
                {
                    //Error will be caught if the column is not a valid column
                    //If the user doesn't care about this exception, ignore it
                    //and continue with the loop
                    if (_errorOnColumns)
                        throw new
                Microsoft.VisualStudio.TestTools.UnitTesting.AssertFailedException(
                        "Actual columns do not match the expected columns. (" +
                        _rowData[i].ColumnName
                        + ")");
                }
            }
        }
    }


    [EditorAttribute(typeof(System.ComponentModel.Design.ArrayEditor),
        typeof(System.Drawing.Design.UITypeEditor)),
     DisplayName("Row Data"),
     Description("Row data to validate against the result set.")]
    public ColumnData[] RowData
    {
        get { return _rowData; }
        set { _rowData = value; }
    }


    [DisplayName("Row Number"),
     Description("The row number of the result set to validate against.")]
    public int RowNumber
    {
        get { return _rowNumber; }
        set { _rowNumber = value; }
    }


    [DisplayName("Error On Column Mismatch"),
     Description("Condition fails if the number of columns do not match " +
     "the expected number ""of columns, there are extra columns or " +
     "missing columns.")]
    public bool ErrorOnColumns
```

```
    {
        get { return _errorOnColumns; }
        set { _errorOnColumns = value; }
    }

    [DisplayName("Result Set"),
     Description("The result set number returned by the select statement.")]
    public int ResultSet
    {
        get { return _resultSet; }
        set { _resultSet = value; }
    }
}
}
```

```
[VB]
Imports Microsoft.VisualStudio.TeamSystem.Data.UnitTesting.Conditions
Imports Microsoft.VisualStudio.TestTools.UnitTesting
Imports System.ComponentModel
Imports System.Data

<DisplayName("Validate Row Data")> _
    Public Class ValidateRowTestCondition : Inherits TestCondition
    Private _rowData As ColumnData()
    Private _rowNumber As Integer = 0
    Private _errorOnColumns As Boolean = False
    Private _resultSet As Integer = 1

    Public Overrides Sub Assert( _
      ByVal validationConnection As System.Data.Common.DbConnection, _
      ByVal results() As _
      Microsoft.VisualStudio.TeamSystem.Data.UnitTesting.ExecutionResult)
        'Store the data table to check against
        Dim resultData As DataTable = results(0).DataSet.Tables(_resultSet - 1)

        'If the user wants to fail a test because of invalid
        'columns in the result set
        If _errorOnColumns Then
            'First check the number of columns returned against
            'the number set.
            If Not resultData.Columns.Count = _rowData.Length Then
                Throw New AssertFailedException( _
                "The actual column count in the result set does not match "
              & "the expected column count.")
            End If
        End If
```

```vbnet
        'Validate the data
        'Check to see if the column names all match
        For i As Integer = 0 To _rowData.Length - 1
            Try
                'Get the value of the column
                Dim value As String = resultData.Rows( _
                 _rowNumber - 1)(_rowData(i).ColumnName).ToString()
                If Not _rowData(i).ColumnValue = value Then
                    Throw New AssertFailedException( _
                    "Actual value (" & value & ") does not match expected value ("
                    & _rowData(i).ColumnValue & ") for column " _
                    & _rowData(i).ColumnName & ".")
                End If
            Catch ex As Exception
                'Error will be caught if the column is not a valid column
                'If the user doesn't care about this exception, ignore it and
                'continue with the loop
                If _errorOnColumns Then
                    Throw New AssertFailedException( _
                     "Actual columns do not match the expected columns. (" _
                     & _rowData(i).ColumnName & ")")
                End If
            End Try
        Next
    End Sub

    <EditorAttribute(GetType(System.ComponentModel.Design.ArrayEditor), _
    GetType(System.Drawing.Design.UITypeEditor)), _
     DisplayName("Row Data"), _
     System.ComponentModel.Description("Row data to validate " _
    & "against the result set.")> _
    Public Property RowData() As ColumnData()
        Get
            Return _rowData
        End Get
        Set(ByVal value As ColumnData())
            _rowData = value
        End Set
    End Property

    <DisplayName("Row Number"), _
     System.ComponentModel.Description("The row number of the result " _
    & "set to validate against.")> _
    Public Property RowNumber() As Integer
        Get
            Return _rowNumber
        End Get
```

```
        Set(ByVal value As Integer)
            _rowNumber = value
        End Set
    End Property

    <DisplayName("Error On Column Mismatch"), _
     System.ComponentModel.Description("Condition fails if the number of columns "
     & "do not match the expected number of columns, there are " _
     & "extra columns or missing columns.")> _
    Public Property ErrorOnColumns() As Boolean
        Get
            Return _errorOnColumns
        End Get
        Set(ByVal value As Boolean)
            _errorOnColumns = value
        End Set
    End Property

    <DisplayName("Result Set"), _
     System.ComponentModel.Description("The result set number returned " _
     & "by the select" _
     & "statement.")> _
    Public Property ResultSet() As Integer
        Get
            Return _resultSet
        End Get
        Set(ByVal value As Integer)
            _resultSet = value
        End Set
    End Property
End Class
```

The first item to note is that you must inherit from the TestCondition base class. This is the class from which all test conditions inherit. The RowData property stores all the data for a given row in the ColumnData array. Note the use of the ArrayEditor, which provides Visual Studio support for adding multiple items to a property.

Each property has a DisplayName attribute and a Description attribute, which allow you to provide information to the user in the Properties window in Visual Studio.

■**Tip** Both the ComponentModel and UnitTesting namespaces have a DescriptionAttribute attribute. Do not confuse them! UnitTesting.DescriptionAttribute is used for applying custom description information to a unit test. ComponentModel.DescriptionAttribute is used for providing descriptions of items in the Properties window. For this reason, it is usually a good idea to import only one of the namespaces!

The `Assert` method is where the real work happens. The `ExecutionResult` array that is returned contains all the results of given SQL batch statement. In this case, you are interested in the first item of the array and in particular the first DataTable of the DataSet containing the result set returned by the SQL statement.

The other interesting and important part of the `Assert` method is `AssertFailedException`. This is the exception you should throw from the `Assert` method to indicate that the test failed. You can also simply call `Assert.Fail` to fail a test. The rest of the `Assert` method provides the rules and checks for the test condition.

Deploying a Custom Test Condition

Deploying a unit test condition is the same as with the custom data generator. See the earlier section called "Deploying a Custom Data Generator" for more information.

Tip Name the XML file used to deploy custom conditions and data generators appropriately. In this case, consider using `CustomConditions.extensions.xml` for conditions and `CustomGenerators.extensions.xml` for data generators.

Tip Only one assembly's worth of custom conditions or generators can be noted in a given file. There is no limit on the number of extension XML files you can have.

Modifying Item Templates

Many organizations have various requirements for object headers or a certain type of structure they want their objects to follow. As with other templates in Visual Studio, these are all customizable. Because the item templates are all plain-text files, this is easy to accomplish. Listing 20-7 shows the default template for a stored procedure.

Listing 20-7. *Default Stored Procedure Template*

```
CREATE PROCEDURE $SchemaQualifiedObjectName$
          @param1 int = 0,
          @param2 int
AS
          SELECT @param1, @param2
RETURN 0;
```

What if your organization likes developers to put comments at the top of the stored procedure indicating what the stored procedure does? You may want to modify this so that when a developer adds a new stored procedure, they get the code shown in Listing 20-8.

Listing 20-8. *Modified Default Stored Procedure Template*

```
/*
            Author:
            Description:
            Date:
*/
CREATE PROCEDURE $SchemaQualifiedObjectName$
            @param1 int = 0,
            @param2 int
AS
            SELECT @param1, @param2
RETURN 0;
```

The item templates are stored in the C:\Program Files\Microsoft Visual Studio 8\DBPro\Items folder. You can edit any of the files ending with .sql and save those changes. The next time you create an item, the contents you created will be displayed in Visual Studio. Don't forget to distribute these items to other team members.

Summary

This chapter gave you the tools to create a truly robust data generator. Using what you have learned here, you can extend data generation to grab data from the Web, from an XML file, or from virtually any other location you can think of. You can order the data as needed and control the output of the data. With this in hand, you should be able to generate usable testing data for any situation.

You have also learned how to create custom test conditions, which will go a long way to easing the database unit testing process. Using this you can spot-check test results according to your needs or even extend what you have already created to check every single value of a given result set!

In addition, you can now customize item templates to display the format required by your organization or to insert standard text, which should save a large amount of time and increase your productivity.

APPENDIX

■ ■ ■

Command-Line Tools Reference

Various command-line tools are available for performing Visual Studio Team System operations. In many cases, the functionality provided by these tools is also available from the IDE. When possible, it is best to use the functionality presented by the IDE because of the complexity of the command-line tools. For example, the TFSSecurity server command-line tool allows you to control security, but the command-line options can be overwhelming and difficult to use. It's much more straightforward to use the IDE tools for controlling security, as described in Chapter 2 of this book.

Also be aware that the use of the command-line tools is not recommended by Microsoft in most cases. This is especially true of the server tools. Certain tools can cause a lot of problems when used incorrectly (for example, accidentally deleting items, erasing all permissions, ruining existing assemblies, and so on). These tools should be used with caution, and you should test their usage in a nonproduction environment first, so you understand all of their nuances. While many of these tools are well documented, some are not.

That said, this appendix presents brief lists of the server and client command-line tools. More information about each tool can be found in the MSDN documentation, and some are discussed in more detail in this book.

Server Command-Line Tools

Table A-1 describes each of the server command-line tools. All of the server tools are located in C:\Program Files\Microsoft Visual Studio 2005 Team Foundation Server\Tools.

Table A-1. *Server Command-Line Tools*

Tool	Description
CreateDS	Used to create a data source for reporting services.
InstanceInfo	Used to return a GUID for the specified Team Foundation Server (TFS) database(s). It works for most TFS databases, but not the data warehouse.
ProcessTemplateManager	Used to upload a new process template.

Continued

Table A-1. *Continued*

Tool	Description
SetupWarehouse	TFS Server Warehouse Setup tool, used to set up a new instance of the TFS data warehouse. It can also be used to repopulate an existing data warehouse.
TFRSConfig	TFS Reporting Server Configuration tool.
TFSAdminUtil	TFS Administration Utility, used to change passwords, accounts, machine locations, and connections between the application tier and the data tier.
TFSReg	TFS Registration tool.
TFSSecurity	TFS Server Security tool, used to control security of projects, users, and groups (Windows and TFS groups). It can also be used to report on that information.

Client Command-Line Tools

The client command-line tools that you have available depend on the version of Visual Studio Team System that is installed. The majority of these tools are available from within the IDE. Table A-2 describes these tools and notes their location.

Table A-2. *Client Command-Line Tools*

Tool	Description	Location
VSInstr	Used to perform the instrumentation of binaries, which can then be deployed to a production machine.	C:\Program Files\ Microsoft Visual Studio 8\ Team Tools\ Performance Tools
VSPerfCmd	Used to start and stop performance profiling.	C:\Program Files\ Microsoft Visual Studio 8\ Team Tools\Performance Tools
VSPerfMon	Used to start and stop performance profiling, but contains different options than the VSPerfCmd application.	C:\Program Files\ Microsoft Visual Studio 8\ Team Tools\ Performance Tools
VSPerfClrEnv	Used to set Common Language Runtime (CLR) environment options so the performance tools can be properly loaded.	C:\Program Files\ Microsoft Visual Studio 8\ Team Tools\ Performance Tools
VSPerfReport	Used to create performance reports (or a subset of those reports that you see in the IDE).	C:\Program Files\ Microsoft Visual Studio 8\ Team Tools\ Performance Tools
FxCopCmd	Used to run managed static code analysis.	C:\Program Files\ Microsoft Visual Studio 8\ Team Tools\Static Analysis Tools\FxCop

Tool	Description	Location
WitExport	Used to export work items from TFS.	C:\Program Files\ Microsoft Visual Studio 8\ Common7\IDE
TFSBuild	Used to perform command-line builds, with the results published to TFS.	C:\Program Files\ Microsoft Visual Studio 8\ Common7\IDE
TFSDeleteProject	Used to delete a project from TFS. This can be done only via the command line.	C:\Program Files\ Microsoft Visual Studio 8\ Common7\IDE
TFSFieldMapping	Used to change the mappings from the server fields to local fields and to add or remove mappings for Microsoft Project and Excel integration.	C:\Program Files\ Microsoft Visual Studio 8\ Common7\IDE
MSTest	Used to run tests from the command line. It can publish the test results to TFS, if TFS is installed.	C:\Program Files\ Microsoft Visual Studio 8\ Common7\IDE
MSBuild	Used to build a solution and optionally run tests associated with the solution.	C:\%winnt%\Microsoft.NET\ Framework\v2.0.50727

Index

You Need the Companion eBook